SOLIDWORKS 2020
A Power Guide for Beginners and Intermediate Users

CADArtifex

The premium provider of learning products and solutions
www.cadartifex.com

SOLIDWORKS 2020: A Power Guide for Beginners and Intermediate Users

Published by
CADArtifex
www.cadartifex.com

Copyright © 2019 CADArtifex

NOTICE TO THE READER

The publisher and the author make no representations or warranties with respect to the accuracy or completeness of the contents of this work and specifically disclaim all warranties, including without limitation warranties of fitness for a particular purpose. Publisher does not guarantee any of the products described in the text or perform any independent analysis in connection with any of the product information contained in the text. No warranty may be created or extended by sales or promotional materials. This work is sold with the understanding that the publisher is not engaged in rendering legal, accounting, or other professional services. Neither the publisher nor the author shall be liable for damages arising herefrom. Further, readers should be aware that Internet Websites listed in this work may have changed or disappeared between when this work was written and when it is read.

Examination Copies

Textbooks received as examination copies in any form such as paperback and eBook are for review only and may not be made available for the use of the student. These files may not be transferred to any other party. Resale of examination copies is prohibited.

Electronic Files

The electronic file/eBook in any form of this textbook is licensed to the original user only and may not be transferred to any other party.

Disclaimer

The author has made sincere efforts to ensure the accuracy of the material described herein, however the author makes no warranty, expressed or implied, with respect to the quality, correctness, accuracy, or freedom from error of this document or the products it describes.

www.cadartifex.com

Dedication

First and foremost, I would like to thank my parents for being a great support throughout my career and while writing this book.

Heartfelt thanks goes to my wife and my sisters for their patience and support in taking this challenge, and letting me spare time for it.

I would also like to acknowledge the efforts of the employees at CADArtifex for their dedication in editing the content of this textbook.

Contents at a Glance

Part 1. Introduction to SOLIDWORKS and Drawing Sketches

Chapter 1. Introduction to SOLIDWORKS .... 19 - 38

Chapter 2. Drawing Sketches with SOLIDWORKS .... 39 - 106

Chapter 3. Editing and Modifying Sketches .... 107 - 156

Chapter 4. Applying Geometric Relations and Dimensions .... 157 - 204

Part 2. Creating 3D Models/Components

Chapter 5. Creating First/Base Feature of Solid Models .... 205 - 240

Chapter 6. Creating Reference Geometries .... 241 - 276

Chapter 7. Advanced Modeling - I .... 277 - 340

Chapter 8. Advanced Modeling - II .... 341 - 430

Chapter 9. Patterning and Mirroring .... 431 - 480

Chapter 10. Advanced Modeling - III .... 481 - 558

Chapter 11. Working with Configurations .... 559 - 578

Part 3. Working with Assemblies

Chapter 12. Working with Assemblies - I .... 579 - 660

Chapter 13. Working with Assemblies - II .... 661 - 722

Part 4. Creating Drawings

Chapter 14. Working with Drawings .... 723 - 792

Index .... 793 - 800

Table of Contents

Dedication **3**

Preface **15**

Part 1. Introduction to SOLIDWORKS and Drawing Sketches

    Chapter 1. Introduction to SOLIDWORKS .... **19 - 38**

      Installing SOLIDWORKS 20

      Getting Started with SOLIDWORKS 20

      Invoking a New SOLIDWORKS Documents 22

      Invoking the Part Modeling Environment 22

          Standard Toolbar 23

          SOLIDWORKS Menus 24

          SOLIDWORKS Search 24

          CommandManager 24

          FeatureManager Design Tree 28

          View (Heads-Up) Toolbar 29

          Status Bar 29

          Task Pane 29

      Invoking the Assembly Environment 30

          Assembly CommandManager 31

      Invoking the Drawing Environment 31

          Drawing CommandManager 32

          Annotation CommandManager 33

      Identifying SOLIDWORKS Documents 34

      Invoking a Shortcut Menu 34

      Customizing the Context Toolbar 34

      Customizing the CommandManager 36

      Working with Mouse Gestures 37

      Saving Documents 38

      Opening Existing Documents 38

      Summary 38

      Questions 38

    Chapter 2. Drawing Sketches with SOLIDWORKS .... **39 - 106**

      Invoking the Part Modeling Environment 41

      Invoking the Sketching Environment 42

      Working with the Selection of Planes 44

      Specifying Units 45

      Specifying Grids and Snap Settings 47

      Drawing a Line Entity 48

          Procedure for Drawing a Line 50

      Tutorial 1 51

6 Table of Contents

Hands-on Test Drive 1 55
Drawing an Arc by using the Line Tool 55
    Procedure for Drawing an Arc by using the Line Tool 55
Tutorial 2 56
Hands-on Test Drive 2 62
Drawing a Centerline 62
Drawing a Midpoint Line 63
    Procedure for Drawing a Midpoint Line 63
Drawing a Rectangle 64
    Corner Rectangle Tool 64
    Center Rectangle Tool 66
    3 Point Corner Rectangle Tool 66
    3 Point Center Rectangle Tool 67
    Parallelogram Tool 68
Drawing a Circle 69
    Circle Tool 69
    Perimeter Circle Tool 70
Drawing an Arc 71
    Centerpoint Arc Tool 71
    3 Point Arc Tool 72
    Tangent Arc Tool 72
Drawing a Polygon 74
    Procedure for Drawing a Polygon 75
Drawing a Slot 76
    Straight Slot Tool 76
    Centerpoint Straight Slot Tool 78
    3 Point Arc Slot Tool 78
    Centerpoint Arc Slot Tool 79
Drawing an Ellipse 80
    Procedure for Drawing an Ellipse 80
Drawing an Elliptical Arc 81
    Procedure for Drawing an Elliptical Arc 81
Drawing a Parabola 82
    Procedure for Drawing a Parabola 82
Drawing Conic Curves 83
    Procedure for Drawing Conic Curves 83
Drawing a Spline 84
    Spline Tool 84
    Equation Driven Curve Tool 85
    Style Spline Tool 88
    Fit Spline Tool 89
Editing a Spline 91
Modifying the Tangency Direction of Arc/Spline 92
Tutorial 3 93
Tutorial 4 99
Hands-on Test Drive 3 105
Hands-on Test Drive 4 105

Summary 105
Questions 106

Chapter 3. Editing and Modifying Sketches .... 107 - 156

Trimming Sketch Entities 108
    Procedure for Trimming Entities by using the Trim Entities Tool 111
Extending Sketch Entities 111
    Procedure for Extending Entities by using the Extend Entities Tool 112
Offsetting Sketch Entities 112
    Procedure for Offsetting Entities 115
Mirroring Sketch Entities 115
    Mirroring Entities by using the Mirror Entities Tool 115
    Mirroring Entities by using the Dynamic Mirror Tool 117
Patterning Sketch Entities 117
    Linear Sketch Pattern 117
    Circular Sketch Pattern 121
Creating a Sketch Fillet 125
Creating a Sketch Chamfer 126
Adding Text 128
Moving a Sketch Entity 129
    Procedure for Moving Sketch Entities 130
Creating a Copy of Sketch Entities 130
    Procedure for Creating a Copy of Sketch Entities 131
Rotating an Entity 131
    Procedure for Rotating Sketch Entities 132
Scaling Sketch Entities 132
    Procedure for Scaling Sketch Entities 134
Stretching an Entity 134
    Procedure for Stretching Sketch Entities 135
Tutorial 1 135
Tutorial 2 143
Tutorial 3 150
Hands-on Test Drive 1 155
Hands-on Test Drive 2 155
Summary 155
Questions 156

Chapter 4. Applying Geometric Relations and Dimensions .... 157 - 204

Working with Geometric Relations 157
Applying Geometric Relations 160
    Applying Geometric Relation by using the Add Relation Tool 160
    Applying Geometric Relation by using the Pop-up Toolbar 162
Controlling the Display of Geometric Relations 162
Applying Dimensions 163
    Working with Smart Dimension Tool 163
    Working with Horizontal Dimension and Vertical Dimension Tools 169

Working with Baseline Dimension Tool 170
Working with Chain Dimension Tool 171
Working with Ordinate Dimension Tool 171
Working with Path Length Dimension Tool 173
Working with Auto Insert Dimension Tool 174
Modifying/Editing Dimensions 174
Working with Different States of a Sketch 174
Under Defined Sketch 175
Fully Defined Sketch 175
Over Defined Sketch 175
Tutorial 1 177
Tutorial 2 186
Tutorial 3 195
Hands-on Test Drive 1 202
Hands-on Test Drive 2 203
Hands-on Test Drive 3 203
Summary 203
Questions 204

Part 2. Creating 3D Models/Components

Chapter 5. Creating First/Base Feature of Solid Models .... 205 - 240
Creating an Extruded Feature 207
Creating a Revolved Feature 215
Navigating a 3D Model in Graphics Area 220
Zoom In/Out 220
Zoom To Fit 221
Zoom to Area 221
Zoom to Selection 221
Pan 221
Rotate 221
Manipulating View Orientation of a Model 222
Manipulating View Orientation by using the View Orientation Flyout 222
Manipulating View Orientation by using the Orientation Dialog box 224
Manipulating View Orientation by using the View Selector Cube 225
Manipulating View Orientation by using the Reference Triad 226
Changing the Display Style of a Model 226
Shaded With Edges 226
Shaded 226
Hidden Lines Removed 227
Hidden Lines Visible 227
Wireframe 227
Changing the View of a Model 228
Shadows In Shaded Mode 228
Perspective 228
Ambient Occlusion 228
Cartoon 228

Tutorial 1 229
Tutorial 2 231
Tutorial 3 234
Hands-on Test Drive 1 238
Hands-on Test Drive 2 238
Hands-on Test Drive 3 239
Summary 239
Questions 239

Chapter 6. Creating Reference Geometries .... **241 - 276**

Creating Reference Planes 242
   Creating a Plane at an Offset Distance 245
   Creating a Parallel Plane 246
   Creating a Plane at an Angle 246
   Creating a Plane passing through Three Points/Vertices 246
   Creating a Plane Normal to a Curve 247
   Creating a Plane at the middle of two Faces/Planes 247
   Creating a Plane Tangent to a Cylindrical Face 248
   Creating a Plane Parallel to the Screen 248
   Creating a Projected Plane onto a Non-Planar Face 249
Creating a Reference Axis 250
Creating a Reference Coordinate System 252
   Procedure for Creating a Reference Coordinate System 253
Creating a Reference Point 254
Creating a Bounding Box 257
   Procedure for Creating a Bounding Box 257
Tutorial 1 258
Tutorial 2 264
Tutorial 3 271
Hands-on Test Drive 1 275
Hands-on Test Drive 2 275
Summary 276
Questions 276

Chapter 7. Advanced Modeling - I .... **277 - 340**

Using Advanced Options of the Extruded Boss/Base Tool 277
Using Advanced Options of the Revolved Boss/Base Tool 281
Creating Cut Features 282
   Creating Extruded Cut Features 282
   Creating Revolved Cut Features 283
Working with Different Types of Sketches 285
   Closed Sketches 285
   Open Sketches 285
   Nested Sketches 285
   Intersecting Sketches 287
Working with Contours of a Sketch 287

Procedure for Extruding Contours by using the Selected Contours Rollout 288
Procedure for Extruding Contours by using the Contour Select Tool 289
Displaying Shaded Sketch Contours 291
Projecting Edges onto the Sketching Plane 292
Projecting Edges of Existing Features 292
Projecting Edges of a Body 294
Projecting Intersecting Geometries of Existing Features 295
Editing a Feature and its Sketch 295
Procedure for Editing a Feature 295
Procedure for Editing the Sketch of a Feature 296
Importing 2D DXF or DWG Files 296
Displaying Earlier State of a Model 297
Reordering Features of a Model 297
Measuring the Distance between Entities 298
Assigning an Appearance/Texture 302
Assigning a Predefined Appearance/Texture 302
Assigning a Customized Appearance 304
Applying a Material 307
Procedure for Applying a Standard Material 307
Procedure for Applying Customized Material Properties 308
Calculating Mass Properties 310
Tutorial 1 314
Tutorial 2 322
Tutorial 3 332
Hands-on Test Drive 1 339
Hands-on Test Drive 2 339
Summary 340
Questions 340

Chapter 8. Advanced Modeling - II .... 341 - 430

Creating a Sweep Feature 341
Procedure for Creating a Sweep Feature with Sketch Profile 356
Procedure for Creating a Sweep Feature with Circular Profile 357
Procedure for Creating a Sweep Feature with One Guide Curve 357
Procedure for Creating a Sweep Feature with Two Guide Curves 357
Procedure for Creating a Sweep Feature with Twist 357
Creating a Sweep Cut Feature 358
Creating a Lofted feature 360
Procedure for Creating a Lofted Feature 370
Procedure for Creating a Lofted Feature by using Guide Curves 370
Procedure for Creating a Lofted Feature by using Centerline 370
Creating a Lofted Cut Feature 370
Creating a Boundary Feature 371
Procedure for Creating a Boundary Feature 375
Creating a Boundary Cut Feature 375

Creating Curves 375
    Creating Projected Curves 376
    Creating Helical and Spiral Curves 379
    Creating Curves by Specifying XYZ Points 383
    Creating Curves by Selecting Reference Points 384
    Creating a Composite Curve 385
Splitting Faces of a Model 386
Creating 3D Sketches 390
    Using the Line Tool in the 3D Sketching Environment 390
    Using the Spline Tool in the 3D Sketching Environment 392
Tutorial 1 395
Tutorial 2 403
Tutorial 3 414
Tutorial 4 420
Hands-on Test Drive 1 428
Hands-on Test Drive 2 429
Summary 429
Questions 430

Chapter 9. Patterning and Mirroring .... **431 - 480**

Patterning Features/Faces/Bodies 431
    Creating a Linear Pattern 432
    Creating a Circular Pattern 442
    Creating a Curve Driven Pattern 445
    Creating a Sketch Driven Pattern 449
    Creating a Table Driven Pattern 451
    Creating a Fill Pattern 453
    Creating a Variable Pattern 456
Mirroring Features/Faces/Bodies 460
Tutorial 1 462
Tutorial 2 470
Hands-on Test Drive 1 477
Hands-on Test Drive 2 478
Hands-on Test Drive 3 479
Summary 479
Questions 480

Chapter 10. Advanced Modeling - III .... **481 - 558**

Working with the Hole Wizard 481
    Procedure for Creating a Hole by using the Hole Wizard Tool 489
Creating Advanced Holes 489
Adding Cosmetic Threads 494
    Procedure for Adding a Cosmetic Thread 498
Creating Threads 498
    Procedure for Creating a Thread 502

Creating Fillets 503
    Creating a Constant Radius Fillet 503
    Creating a Variable Radius Fillet 512
    Creating a Face Fillet 515
    Creating a Full Round Fillet 517
Creating Chamfers 519
    Procedure for Creating a Chamfer 524
Creating Rib Features 525
    Procedure for Creating a Rib Feature 527
Creating Shell Features 527
    Procedure for Creating a Shell Feature with Uniform Thickness 530
    Procedure for Creating a Shell Feature with Multi-Thickness 530
Creating Wrap Features 530
Tutorial 1 533
Tutorial 2 547
Hands-on Test Drive 1 556
Hands-on Test Drive 2 557
Summary 558
Questions 558

Chapter 11. Working with Configurations .... **559 - 578**

Creating Configurations by using the Manual Method 559
    Procedure for Creating Configurations by using the Manual Method 564
Creating Configurations by using the Design Table 564
    Procedure for Creating Configurations by using the Design Table 569
Saving Configurations as a Separate File 569
Suppressing and Unsuppressing Features 570
Tutorial 1 571
Hands-on Test Drive 1 577
Hands-on Test Drive 2 577
Summary 578
Questions 578

Part 3. Working with Assemblies

Chapter 12. Working with Assemblies - I .... **579 - 660**

Working with Bottom-up Assembly Approach 580
Working with Top-down Assembly Approach 580
Creating an Assembly by using Bottom-up Approach 580
    Inserting Components in the Assembly Environment 582
    Inserting Components by using the Insert Components Tool 584
Working with Degrees of Freedom 586
Applying Relations or Mates 586
    Working with Standard Mates 588
    Working with Advanced Mates 593
    Working with Mechanical Mates 601
Hiding Faces while Applying a Mate 608

Moving and Rotating Individual Components 608
    Moving a Component by using the Move Component Tool 609
    Rotating a Component by using the Rotate Component Tool 612
Working with SmartMates 613
Tutorial 1 614
Tutorial 2 624
Hands-on Test Drive 1 646
Hands-on Test Drive 2 652
Summary 659
Questions 660

Chapter 13. Working with Assemblies - II .... 661 - 722
Creating an Assembly by using the Top-down Approach 662
Creating Flexible Components 669
Editing Assembly Components 670
    Editing Assembly Components within the Assembly Environment 670
    Editing Assembly Components in the Part Modeling Environment 671
Editing Mates 672
Patterning Assembly Components 673
    Creating a Linear Component Pattern 673
    Creating a Circular Component Pattern 676
    Creating a Pattern Driven Component Pattern 677
    Creating a Chain Component Pattern 681
Mirroring Components of an Assembly 686
    Procedure for Mirroring Components of an Assembly 688
Creating Assembly Features 688
Suppressing or Unsuppressing Components 689
Inserting Parts having Multiple Configurations 689
Creating and Dissolving Sub-Assemblies 690
Publishing Envelopes 691
Creating an Exploded View 694
    Procedure for Creating a Regular Exploded View 700
    Procedure for Creating a Radial Exploded View 700
Collapsing an Exploded View 701
Animating an Exploded View 701
Editing an Exploded View 702
Adding Explode Lines 703
    Creating Exploded Lines by using Explode Line Sketch 703
    Creating Exploded Lines by using Insert/Edit Smart Explode Lines 704
Detecting Interference in an Assembly 705
Creating Bill of Material (BOM) of an Assembly 707
Tutorial 1 707
Hands-on Test Drive 1 719
Hands-on Test Drive 2 719
Summary 722
Questions 722

Part 4. Creating Drawings

Chapter 14. Working with Drawings .... 723 - 792

Invoking the Drawing Environment 724
Creating the Base View of a Model 727
Invoking Drawing Environment from the Part or the Assembly Environment 731
Creating a Model View 732
    Procedure for Creating a Model/Base View 733
Creating Projected Views 733
    Procedure for Creating Projected Views 734
Creating 3 Standard Views 735
Working with Angle of Projection 735
Defining the Angle of Projection 737
Editing the Sheet Format 738
Creating other Drawing Views 739
    Creating a Section View 739
    Creating an Auxiliary View 746
    Creating a Detail View 746
    Creating a Removed Section View 748
    Creating a Broken-out Section View 749
    Creating a Break View 750
    Creating a Crop View 751
    Creating an Alternate Position View 752
Applying Dimensions 753
    Applying Reference Dimensions 753
    Applying Driving Dimensions 754
Modifying the Driving Dimension 756
Modifying Dimension Properties 756
Controlling the Default Dimension/Arrow Style 769
Adding Notes 769
Adding a Surface Finish Symbol 770
Adding a Weld Symbol 771
Adding a Hole Callout 772
Adding Center Marks 773
Adding Centerlines 775
Creating the Bill of Material (BOM) 775
Adding Balloons 778
    Adding Balloons Automatically 779
    Adding Balloons Manually 781
Detailing Mode 781
Tutorial 1 782
Hands-on Test Drive 1 791
Summary 792
Questions 792

Index .... 793 - 800

Preface

SOLIDWORKS, developed by Dassault Systèmes SOLIDWORKS Corp., world leader in engineering software, offers complete 3D software tools that let you create, simulate, publish, and manage your data. By providing advanced solid modeling techniques, SOLIDWORKS helps engineers to optimize performance while designing with capabilities, that cut down on costly prototypes, eliminate rework and delays, thereby saving time as well as development costs.

SOLIDWORKS is a feature-based, parametric solid-modeling mechanical design and automation software which allows you to convert 2D sketches into solid models by using simple but highly effective modeling tools. The 3D components and assemblies created in SOLIDWORKS can be converted into 2D drawings within few mouse clicks. In addition, you can validate your designs by simulating their real-world conditions and assessing the environmental impact of products.

SOLIDWORKS 2020: A Power Guide for Beginners and Intermediate Users textbook has been designed for instructor-led courses as well as self-paced learning. It is intended to help engineers and designers interested in learning SOLIDWORKS for creating 3D mechanical design. This textbook is a great help for new SOLIDWORKS users and a great teaching aid in classroom training. This textbook consists of 14 chapters, total 800 pages covering the major environments of SOLIDWORKS such as Sketching environment, Part modeling environment, Assembly environment, and Drawing environment. This textbook teaches users to use SOLIDWORKS mechanical design software for creating parametric 3D solid components, assemblies, and 2D drawings. This textbook also includes a chapter on creating multiple configurations of a design.

This textbook not only focuses on the usage of the tools and commands of SOLIDWORKS but also on the concept of design. Every chapter in this textbook contains tutorials that provide users with step-by-step instructions for creating mechanical designs and drawings with ease. Moreover, every chapter ends with hands-on test drives which allow users to experience the user friendly and technical capabilities of SOLIDWORKS.

Who Should Read This Book

This book is written with a wide range of SOLIDWORKS users in mind, varying from beginners to advanced users as well as SOLIDWORKS instructors. The easy-to-follow chapters of this book allow you to clearly understand different design techniques, SOLIDWORKS tools, and design principles.

What Is Covered in This Textbook

SOLIDWORKS 2020: A Power Guide for Beginners and Intermediate Users textbook is designed to help you understand everything you need to know to start using SOLIDWORKS 2020 with clear step-by-step tutorials. This textbook covers the following:

Chapter 1, "*Introduction to SOLIDWORKS*," introduces SOLIDWORKS interface, different SOLIDWORKS environments, various components SOLIDWORKS, invoking and customizing the shortcut menu, saving documents, and opening documents in SOLIDWORKS.

Chapter 2, "***Drawing Sketches with SOLIDWORKS***," discusses how to invoke Sketching environment, specify unit system, grids and snaps settings. Also, it introduces you to various sketching tools such as Line, Arc, Circle, Rectangle, and Spline for creating sketches.

Chapter 3, "***Editing and Modifying Sketches***," introduces various editing and modifying operations such as trimming unwanted sketched entities, extending sketch entities, mirroring, patterning, moving, and rotating sketch entities by using various editing/modifying tools of the Sketching environment.

Chapter 4, "***Applying Geometric Relations and Dimensions***," introduces the concept of fully defined sketches, and to create fully defined sketches by applying geometric relations and dimensions. Also, it introduces different methods of applying geometric relations and dimensions. You can modify the already applied dimensions and dimension properties such as dimension style, tolerance, and precision. This chapter also introduces you to different sketch states.

Chapter 5, "***Creating First/Base Feature of Solid Models***," discusses how to create extruded and revolved base features by using the Extruded Boss/Base and Revolved Boss/Base tools. This chapter also introduces you to various navigating tools such as Zoom In/Out and Zoom To Fit. Moreover, it explains how to manipulate the orientation of a model. Additionally, this chapter also elaborates changing the display style and view of the model.

Chapter 6, "***Creating Reference Geometries***," introduces three default planes: Front, Top, and Right. As these may not be enough for creating models having multiple features therefore, the chapter discusses how to create additional reference planes. Additionally, this chapter also elaborates creating reference axes, coordinates systems, and points.

Chapter 7, "***Advanced Modeling - I***," introduces advanced options for creating extruded and revolved features. In addition, this chapter discusses how to create cut features and, how to work with different types of sketches, along with creating multiple features by using a single sketch having multiple contours, projecting edges of the features, editing individual features of a model, importing 2D DXF and DWG files into current file as reference sketches. Moreover, this chapter also elaborates measuring distance and angle between lines, points, faces, planes, and so on by using the Measure tool, as well as assigning appearance and material properties to a model. Additionally, calculation of the mass properties of a model is also discussed.

Chapter 8, "***Advanced Modeling - II***," discusses how to create sweep features, sweep cut features, lofted features, lofted cut features, boundary features, boundary cut features, curves, split faces, and 3D Sketches.

Chapter 9, "***Patterning and Mirroring***," introduces various patterning and mirroring tools. After successfully completing this chapter, you can create different type of patterns such as linear pattern, circular pattern, and curve driven pattern. Also, you can mirror features, faces, or bodies.

Chapter 10, "***Advanced Modeling - III***," discusses how to create standard and customized holes such as counterbore and countersink. You will learn about creating cosmetic threads. In addition, you will learn about creating real threads on holes, fasteners, and cylindrical features. Additionally, this chapter explains how to create constant and variable radius fillets. Also, how to create chamfer, rib features, and shell features.

Chapter 11, *"Working with Configurations,"* discusses how to create multiple variations of a model within a single file by using the configurations. You will learn about creating configurations by using the Manual method and the Design Table method. This chapter also teaches how to save configurations as a separate file and how to suppress and unsuppress features of a model.

Chapter 12, *"Working with Assemblies - I,"* discusses how to create assemblies by using the bottom-up assembly approach and how to work with standard, advanced, and mechanical mates. This chapter also explains how to move and rotate the individual component within the Assembly environment, detect collisions between the components of an assembly, and working with SmartMates.

Chapter 13, *"Working with Assemblies - II,"* discusses how to create assemblies by using the top-down assembly approach and creating flexible components. You can also edit the individual components of an assembly within the Assembly environment or in the Part environment. This chapter also teaches you to edit the existing mates applied between the components and create different types of patterns such as linear component pattern and pattern driven component pattern. Also, it introduces you to mirroring components in the Assembly environment, creating assembly features, suppressing or unsuppressing the components of an assembly, and inserting components in the Assembly environment having multiple configurations. You can also create and dissolve sub-assemblies, and include components as envelopes into sub-assemblies. This chapter also discusses creating, editing, or collapsing the exploded view of an assembly. Animating the exploded/collapse view, adding exploded lines in an exploded view, detecting interference and creating BOM is also explained.

Chapter 14, *"Working with Drawings,"* discusses how to create 2D drawings from parts and assemblies. This chapter introduces the concept of angle of projections, defining the angle of projection, and editing sheet format. In addition, this chapter discusses the application of reference and driving dimensions, adding notes, surface finish symbol, weld symbols, hole callouts, and so on in drawing views. In this chapter, adding Bill of Material (BOM) and balloons have also been introduced.

Icons/Terms used in this Textbook

The following icons and terms are used in this textbook:

Note

Note: Notes highlight information requiring special attention.

Tip

Tip: Tips provide additional advice, which increases the efficiency of the users.

New

New New icons highlight new features of this release.

Update

Updated Updated icons highlight updated features of this release.

Flyout

A Flyout is a list in which a set of tools are grouped together, see Figure 1.

Drop-down List

A drop-down list is a list in which a set of options is grouped together, see Figure 2.

Rollout

A rollout is an area in which drop-down list, fields, buttons, check boxes are available to specify various parameters, see Figure 2. A rollout can either be in expanded or in collapsed form. You can expand/collapse a rollout by clicking on the arrow available on the right of its title bar.

Field

A Field allows you to enter new value, or modify existing/default value, as per your requirement, see Figure 2. Also, a field allows you to select entities from the graphics area.

Check box

A Check box allows you to turn on or off the functions of a particular option, see Figure 2.

Button

A Button appears as a 3D icon and is used to turn on or off the functions of a particular option.

How to Contact the Author

We value your feedback and suggestions. Please email us at *info@cadartifex.com*. You can also login to our website *www.cadartifex.com* and write your feedback regarding the textbook as well as download the free learning resources.

Thank you very much for purchasing SOLIDWORKS 2020: A Power Guide for Beginners and Intermediate Users textbook, we hope that the information and concepts introduced in this textbook help you to accomplish your professional goals.

Introduction to SOLIDWORKS

This chapter discusses the following topics:

- Installing SOLIDWORKS
- Getting Started with SOLIDWORKS
- Invoking a New SOLIDWORKS Documents
- Invoking the Part Modeling Environment
- Invoking the Assembly Environment
- Invoking the Drawing Environment
- Identifying SOLIDWORKS Documents
- Invoking a Shortcut Menu
- Customizing the Context Toolbar
- Customizing the CommandManager
- Working with Mouse Gestures
- Saving Documents
- Opening Existing Documents

Welcome to the world of Computer Aided Design (CAD) with SOLIDWORKS. SOLIDWORKS, a product of Dassault Systèmes SOLIDWORKS Corp., world leader in engineering software, offers complete 3D software tools that let you create, simulate, publish, and manage your data. By providing advanced solid modeling techniques, SOLIDWORKS helps engineers to optimize performance while designing with capabilities, that cut down on costly prototypes and eliminate rework and delays, thereby saving time as well as development costs.

SOLIDWORKS is a feature-based, parametric solid-modeling mechanical design and automation software which allows you to convert 2D sketches into solid models by using simple but highly effective modeling tools. SOLIDWORKS provides a wide range of tools that allow you to create real-world components and assemblies. These real-world components and assemblies can then be converted into 2D engineering drawings for production. In addition, you can validate your designs by simulating their real-world conditions and assessing the environmental impact of products.

SOLIDWORKS utilizes a parametric feature-based approach for creating models. With SOLIDWORKS you can share your designs with your partners, subcontractors and colleagues in smart new ways, which improves knowledge transfer and shortens the design cycle.

Installing SOLIDWORKS

If you do not have SOLIDWORKS installed on your system, you first need to get it installed. However, before you start installing SOLIDWORKS, you need to evaluate the system requirements and make sure that you have a system capable of running SOLIDWORKS adequately. Below are the system requirements for installing SOLIDWORKS 2020.

1.   Operating Systems: Windows 10 or Windows 7 SP1 - 64-bit
2.   RAM: 8 GB or more (16 GB or more recommended)
3.   Disk Space: 10 GB or more
4.   Processor: 3.3 GHz or higher
5.   Graphics Card: SOLIDWORKS certified graphics card drivers

For more information about the system requirements for SOLIDWORKS, visit the SOLIDWORKS website at *https://www.solidworks.com/sw/support/SystemRequirements.html*

Once the system is ready, install SOLIDWORKS by using the SOLIDWORKS DVD or by using the downloaded SOLIDWORKS setup files.

Getting Started with SOLIDWORKS

Once SOLIDWORKS 2020 is installed on your system, start SOLIDWORKS 2020 by double-clicking on the **SOLIDWORKS 2020** icon on the desktop of your system. As soon as you double-click on the SOLIDWORKS 2020 icon, the system prepares for starting SOLIDWORKS by loading all required files. Once all the required files have been loaded, the startup user interface of SOLIDWORKS 2020 appears along with the **Welcome** dialog box, see Figure 1.1. If you are starting SOLIDWORKS for the first time after installing the software, the **SOLIDWORKS License Agreement** window appears, see Figure 1.2. Click on the **Accept** button in the **SOLIDWORKS License Agreement** window to accept the license agreement and start SOLIDWORKS 2020.

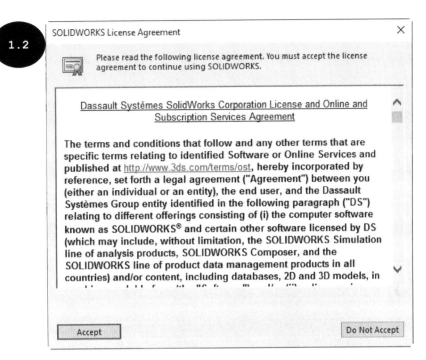

In SOLIDWORKS, the **Welcome** dialog box appears every time you start SOLIDWORKS and provides a convenient way to invoke new SOLIDWORKS documents, open existing documents, view recent documents and folders, access SOLIDWORKS resources, and stay updated on SOLIDWORKS news.

The **Welcome** dialog box has four tabs: **Home, Recent, Learn,** and **Alerts.** The options in the **Home** tab are used for invoking new SOLIDWORKS documents, opening existing documents, viewing recent documents and folder, and accessing SOLIDWORKS resources. The **Recent** tab displays a list of recent documents and folders. The **Learn** tab is used for accessing instructional resources such as tutorials, sample models, access to 3D Content Center, certification program, and so on to help you learn more about SOLIDWORKS. The **Alerts** tab is used for updating you with SOLIDWORKS news and provides different types of alerts in different sections including **Troubleshooting** and **Technical Alerts.**

Tip: If the **Welcome** dialog box does not appear on the screen, then you can invoke it by clicking on the **Welcome to SOLIDWORKS** tool 🏠 in the **Standard** toolbar or by pressing the CTRL + F2 keys. Alternatively, you can click on **Help > Welcome to SOLIDWORKS** in the SOLIDWORKS Menus or the **Welcome to SOLIDWORKS** option in the **SOLIDWORKS Resources Task Pane** to invoke the **Welcome** dialog box. You will learn more about **Standard** toolbar, SOLIDWORKS Menus, and **SOLIDWORKS Resources Task Pane** later in this chapter.

Invoking a New SOLIDWORKS Documents

New SOLIDWORKS documents such as Part modeling environment, Assembly environment, and Drawing environment can be invoked by using the **Part**, **Assembly**, and **Drawing** buttons of the **Welcome** dialog box, respectively. Alternatively, you can invoke new SOLIDWORKS documents by using the **New SOLIDWORKS Document** dialog box. This dialog box can be invoked by clicking on the **New** tool in the **Standard** toolbar. You can also invoke the **New SOLIDWORKS Document** dialog box by clicking on **File** > **New** in the SOLIDWORKS Menus.

Invoking the Part Modeling Environment

To invoke the Part modeling environment, click on the **Part** button in the **Welcome** dialog box. The Part modeling environment gets invoked and the startup user interface of the Part modeling environment appears, as shown in Figure 1.3. Alternatively, to invoke the Part modeling environment, click on the **New** tool 🗋 in the **Standard** toolbar. The **New SOLIDWORKS Document** dialog box appears, see Figure 1.4. In this dialog box, make sure that the **Part** button is activated and then click on the **OK** button.

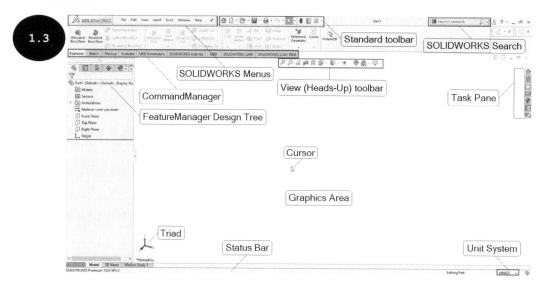

Note: If you are invoking the Part modeling environment for the first time after installing the software, the **Units and Dimension Standard** dialog box appears, see Figure 1.5. You can specify the unit system as the default unit system for SOLIDWORKS by using this dialog box. In this textbook, the metric unit system and ANSI standard have been used as the default unit system.

It is evident from the startup user interface of the Part modeling environment that SOLIDWORKS is very user-friendly. Some of the components of the startup user interface are discussed next.

Standard Toolbar

The **Standard** toolbar contains a set of the most frequently used tools such as **New**, **Open**, and **Save**, see Figure 1.6.

SOLIDWORKS Menus

The SOLIDWORKS Menus contains different menus such as **File**, **View**, and **Tools** for accessing different tools of SOLIDWORKS, see Figure 1.7.

Note that the SOLIDWORKS Menus appears when you move the cursor on the SOLIDWORKS logo, which is available at the top left corner of the screen. You can keep the SOLIDWORKS Menus visible all the time by clicking on the push-pin button ↗ available at the end of the SOLIDWORKS Menus. Note that the tools in the different menus are dependent upon the type of environment invoked.

SOLIDWORKS Search

The SOLIDWORKS Search is a search tool for searching commands/tools, knowledge base (help topic), community forum, files, models, and so on, see Figure 1.8.

CommandManager

CommandManager is available at the top of the graphics area. It provides access to different SOLIDWORKS tools. There are various CommandManagers such as **Features CommandManager**, **Sketch CommandManager**, **Evaluate CommandManager**, and so on are available in the Part modeling environment. When the **Features** tab is activated in the CommandManager (see Figure 1.9), the **Features CommandManager** appears, which provides access to different tools for creating 3D solid models. On clicking on the **Sketch** tab, the **Sketch CommandManager** appears, which provides access to different tools for creating sketches.

Note: The different environments (Part, Assembly, and Drawing) of SOLIDWORKS are provided with different sets of CommandManagers.

Some of the CommandManagers of the Part modeling environment are discussed next.

Features CommandManager

The **Features CommandManager** is provided with different sets of tools that are used for creating 3D models. To invoke the tools of the **Features CommandManager**, click on the **Features** tab in the CommandManager. Note that initially, most of the tools of the **Features CommandManager** are not activated. These tools are activated as soon as you create a base or a first feature of a model. Figure 1.9 shows the **Features CommandManager** and Figure 1.10 shows a 3D model for your reference only.

Sketch CommandManager

The **Sketch CommandManager** is provided with different sets of tools that are used for creating 2D and 3D sketches. To invoke the tools of the **Sketch CommandManager**, click on the **Sketch** tab in the CommandManager. Figure 1.11 shows the **Sketch CommandManager** and Figure 1.12 shows a 2D sketch for your reference only.

Evaluate CommandManager

The tools in the **Evaluate CommandManager** are used for evaluating a model by measuring entities, calculating mass properties, checking the tangent or curvature continuity, performing draft analysis, calculating section properties, performing geometry analysis, and so on. To invoke the tools of the **Evaluate CommandManager**, click on the **Evaluate** tab in the CommandManager, see Figure 1.13.

Note: The Surface modeling environment as well as the Sheet Metal environment of SOLIDWORKS can also be invoked within the Part modeling environment.

Surfaces CommandManager

The **Surfaces CommandManager** is provided with different sets of tools that are used for creating surface models. To invoke the tools of the **Surfaces CommandManager**, click on the **Surfaces** tab in the CommandManager, see Figure 1.14. Note that if the **Surfaces** tab is not available in the CommandManager then right-click on any of the CommandManager tab. A shortcut menu appears. In this shortcut menu, click on the **Tabs > Surfaces** option. The **Surfaces** tab becomes available in the CommandManager. Figure 1.14 shows the **Surfaces CommandManager** and Figure 1.15 shows a surface model for your reference only. Note that initially, most of the tools of the **Surfaces CommandManager** are not activated. These tools get activated as soon as you create a base or first surface feature of a surface model.

Note: In addition to the default CommandManagers such as **Features CommandManager** and **Sketch CommandManager**, you can also add additional CommandManagers that are not available by default. To add a CommandManager, right-click on any of the available CommandManager tab. A shortcut menu appears. In this shortcut menu, move the cursor over the **Tabs** option. A cascading menu appears, see Figure 1.16. This cascading menu displays a list of the available CommandManagers. Also, a tick-mark in front of the CommandManager indicates that the respective CommandManager is already added. Click on the required CommandManager in the shortcut menu. The respective CommandManager tab is added in the CommandManager.

Sheet Metal CommandManager

The **Sheet Metal CommandManager** is provided with different sets of tools for creating sheet metal components. If the **Sheet Metal** tab is not available in the CommandManager then right-click on a CommandManager tab to display a shortcut menu. Next, click on the **Tabs > Sheet Metal** option in the shortcut menu. Figure 1.17 shows the **Sheet Metal CommandManager** and Figure 1.18 shows a sheet metal component for your reference only.

Weldments CommandManager

The **Weldments CommandManager** is provided with different sets of tools for creating weldments structures. Figure 1.19 shows the **Weldments CommandManager** and Figure 1.20 shows a weldments component for your reference only.

FeatureManager Design Tree

FeatureManager Design Tree appears on the left of the graphics area and keeps a record of all operations or features used for creating a model, see Figure 1.21. Note that the first created feature appears at the top and the next created features appear one after the other in the FeatureManager Design Tree. Also, in the FeatureManager Design Tree, three default planes and an origin appear, by default.

Tip: The features are logical operations that are performed to create a component. In other words, a component can be designed by creating a number of features such as extrude, sweep, hole, fillet, draft, and so on.

View (Heads-Up) Toolbar

The View (Heads-Up) toolbar is available at the top center of the graphics area, see Figure 1.22. It is provided with different sets of tools that are used for manipulating the view and display of a model available in the graphics area.

Status Bar

The Status Bar is available at the bottom of the graphics area and provides information about the action to be taken based on the currently active tool. It also displays the current state of the sketch being created, coordinate system, and so on.

Task Pane

Task Pane appears on the right side of the screen with various tabs such as **SOLIDWORKS Resources, Design Library, File Explorer, Appearances, Scenes, and Decals,** and **Custom Properties** for accessing various online resources of SOLIDWORKS, several applications, subscription services, library, and so on, see Figure 1.23. Some of the tabs of the Task Pane are discussed next.

SOLIDWORKS Resources

The **SOLIDWORKS Resources Task Pane** is provided with tools to invoke the **Welcome** dialog box and links to access various SOLIDWORKS applications, Online Resources, and Subscription Services.

To display the **SOLIDWORKS Resources Task Pane**, click on the **SOLIDWORKS Resources** tab in the Task Pane, refer to Figure 1.23. Some of the options of the **SOLIDWORKS Resources Task Pane** are discussed next.

Welcome to SOLIDWORKS
The **Welcome to SOLIDWORKS** tool of the **SOLIDWORKS Resources Task Pane** is used for invoking the **Welcome** dialog box to start a new document or open an existing document of SOLIDWORKS.

SOLIDWORKS Tools
The **SOLIDWORKS Tools** rollout is used for accessing several applications such as **Property Tab Builder, SOLIDWORKS Rx, Performance Benchmark Test**, and so on.

Online Resources
The **Online Resources** rollout is used for accessing SOLIDWORKS partner solutions and 3D experience marketplace network.

Design Library
The **Design Library Task Pane** is used for accessing SOLIDWORKS design library, toolbox components, 3D Content Central, and SOLIDWORKS Content.

Appearances, Scenes, and Decals
The **Appearances, Scenes, and Decals Task Pane** is used for changing or modifying the appearance of the model and the graphics display area.

Invoking the Assembly Environment
To invoke the Assembly environment, click on the **Assembly** button in the **Welcome** dialog box. The Assembly environment is invoked with the display of the **Open** dialog box along with the **Begin Assembly PropertyManager**, see Figure 1.24.

Alternatively, to invoke the Assembly environment, click on the **New** tool ⬚ in the **Standard** toolbar. The **New SOLIDWORKS Document** dialog box appears. In this dialog box, click on the **Assembly** button and then click on the **OK** button.

The **Open** dialog box is used for inserting a component in the Assembly environment and appears automatically on invoking the Assembly environment, if no components are opened in the current session of SOLIDWORKS. You will learn about inserting components in the Assembly environment and different methods of creating assemblies in later chapters.

Some of the components of the Assembly environment are same as the Part modeling environment. The **Assembly CommandManager** of the Assembly environment is discussed next.

Assembly CommandManager

The **Assembly CommandManager** is provided with different sets of tools that are used for inserting components in the assembly environment, applying mates between the inserted components, creating exploded views, patterns, and so on. Figure 1.25 shows the **Assembly CommandManager** and Figure 1.26 shows an assembly for your reference only.

Invoking the Drawing Environment

To invoke the Drawing environment, click on the **New** tool in the **Standard** toolbar. The **New SOLIDWORKS Document** dialog box appears. In this dialog box, click on the **Drawing** button and then click on the **OK** button. The **Sheet Format/Size** dialog box appears, see Figure 1.27. The options in this dialog box are used for selecting sheet size/format to be used for creating drawings. You can also invoke the **Sheet Format/Size** dialog box by clicking on the **Drawing** button in the **Welcome** dialog box. Once you have defined the sheet size and format in the **Sheet Format/Size** dialog box, click on the **OK** button. The startup user interface of the Drawing environment appears with the display of the **Model View PropertyManager** on the left of the drawing sheet, see Figure 1.28. The **Model View PropertyManager** is used for inserting a component or an assembly in the Drawing environment for creating its drawing views. You will learn about creating drawing views of a component or an assembly in later chapters.

Most of the components of the Drawing environment are same as the Part modeling environment. The **Drawing CommandManager** and **Annotation CommandManager** of the Drawing environment are discussed next.

Drawing CommandManager

The **Drawing CommandManager** is provided with different sets of tools that are used for creating different drawing views such as orthogonal views, section views, and detail views. Figure 1.29 shows the **Drawing CommandManager** and Figure 1.30 shows different drawing views of a component.

1.30

Annotation CommandManager

The **Annotation CommandManager** is provided with different sets of tools that are used for applying dimensions, note, surface/welding symbols, creating BOM, and so on. Figure 1.31 shows the **Annotation CommandManager** of the Drawing environment and Figure 1.32 shows a drawing with dimensions for your reference only.

1.31

1.32

Identifying SOLIDWORKS Documents

The documents created in different environments (Part, Assembly, and Drawing) of SOLIDWORKS have different file extensions, see the table given below:

Environments	File Extension
Part Modeling Environment	*.sldprt
Assembly Modeling Environment	*.sldasm
Drawing Modeling Environment	*.slddrw

Invoking a Shortcut Menu

A shortcut menu is invoked when you right-click in the graphics area. It provides quick access to the most frequently used tools such as **Zoom to Fit**, **Zoom In/Out**, and **Pan**, see Figure 1.33. A shortcut menu also contains the **Context** toolbar, see Figure 1.33. Note that the availability of the tools in the **Context** toolbar and the shortcut menu depends on the entity selected to invoke the shortcut menu. Figure 1.33 shows a shortcut menu, which appears on right-clicking in the empty area of the Part modeling environment and Figure 1.34 shows a shortcut menu, which appears after selecting a face of a model in the Part modeling environment.

You can also customize the **Context** toolbar of a shortcut menu to add frequently used tools, as required. The method for customizing the **Context** toolbar is discussed next.

Customizing the Context Toolbar

In addition to the display of default tools in the **Context** toolbar of a shortcut menu, you can also customize it to add frequently used tools. To customize the **Context** toolbar, move the cursor over the **Context** toolbar in the shortcut menu and then right-click. The **Customize** option appears, see Figure 1.35. Next, click on the **Customize** option. The **Customize** dialog box appears along with the **Graphics Area** toolbar, see Figure 1.36.

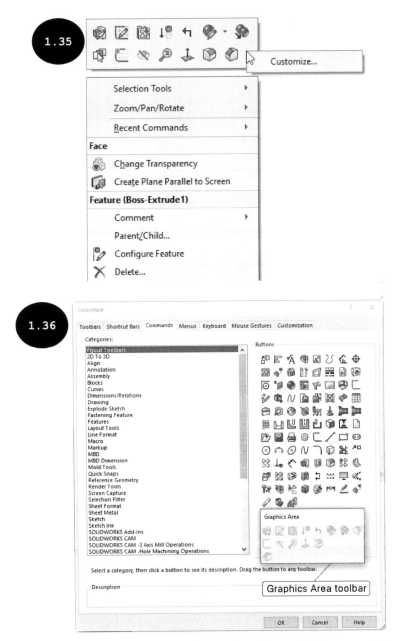

In the **Categories** area of the **Customize** dialog box, select the required category. The tools of the selected category appear on the right side of the dialog box in the **Buttons** area. You can drag and drop the tools from the **Buttons** area of the dialog box to the **Graphics Area** toolbar. Note that the tools added to the **Graphics Area** toolbar appear in the **Context** toolbar of the shortcut menu. Once you have added the required tools in the **Graphics Area** toolbar, click on the **OK** button in the dialog box.

Customizing the CommandManager

In addition to the default set of tools in a CommandManager, you can customize to add more tools, as required. To customize a CommandManager, right-click on a tool of the CommandManager to be customized. A shortcut menu appears, see Figure 1.37. Next, click on the **Customize** tool in the shortcut menu. The **Customize** dialog box appears, see Figure 1.38. Next, click on the **Commands** tab in the **Customize** dialog box, see Figure 1.38.

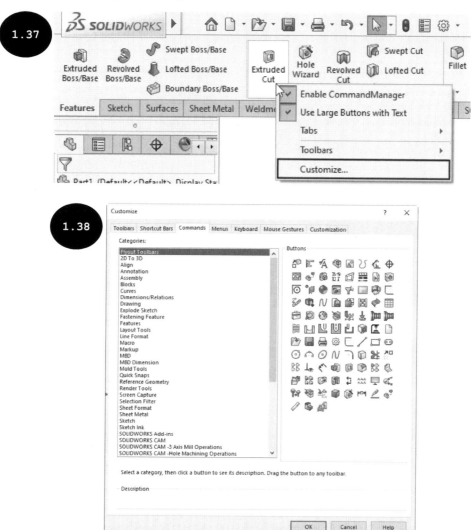

Next, select the required category of tools in the **Categories** area of the dialog box. The tools in the selected category appear on the right side of the dialog box in the **Buttons** area. Now, you can drag and drop the tools from the **Buttons** area of the dialog box to the CommandManager. You can also drag and drop the tools back to the **Buttons** area of the dialog box from the CommandManager. Once you have added the required tools in the CommandManager, click on the **OK** button in the dialog box.

Working with Mouse Gestures

Mouse Gestures act as a shortcut to quickly access the frequently used tools, see Figure 1.39. To display the Mouse Gestures, press and hold the right mouse button in the graphics area and then drag the cursor to a small distance. Note that the availability of default tools in the Mouse Gestures depends upon the currently opened environment of SOLIDWORKS. Also, by default, four tools are displayed in the Mouse Gestures. You can display 2, 3, 4, 8, or 12 tools (gestures) in the Mouse Gestures. For doing so, click on the **Tools > Customize** in the SOLIDWORKS Menus. The **Customize** dialog box appears. In this dialog box, click on the **Mouse Gestures** tab and then select the required option: **2 Gestures (Vertical)**, **2 Gestures (Horizontal)**, **3 Gestures**, **4 Gestures**, **8 Gestures**, or **12 Gestures** in the **Mouse Gestures** drop-down list of the dialog box, see Figure 1.40. Note that the preview of the Mouse Gestures with default available tools for different environments of SOLIDWORKS appears on the right of the **Customize** dialog box.

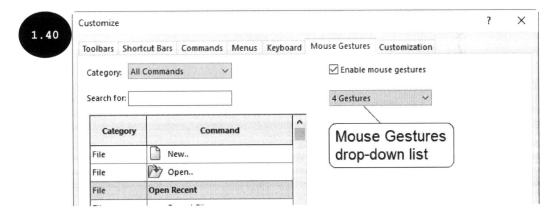

You can also customize the tools of the Mouse Gestures for different environments of SOLIDWORKS by using the tools available in the **Mouse Gestures** tab of the **Customize** dialog box. For doing so, drag the required tool from the list of tools in the **Mouse Gestures** tab of the dialog box and drop in the required Mouse Gestures that appears on the right of the dialog box. After customizing the Mouse Gestures, close the **Customize** dialog box.

Saving Documents

To save a document created in any of the environments of SOLIDWORKS, click on the **Save** tool in the **Standard** toolbar or click on **File** > **Save** in the SOLIDWORKS Menus. The **Save As** dialog box appears. Enter the name of the document in the **File name** field of the dialog box and then browse to the location where you want to save the document. Next, click on the **Save** button.

Opening Existing Documents

To open an existing SOLIDWORKS Document, click on the **Open** button in the **Welcome** dialog box. Alternatively, click on the **Open** tool in the **Standard** toolbar or click on **File** > **Open** in the SOLIDWORKS Menus. The **Open** dialog box appears. In this dialog box, select the **SOLIDWORKS Files (*.sldprt; *.sldasm; *.slddrw)** file extension in the **File Type** drop-down list. Note that you can select the file extension depending upon the type of document to be opened. After selecting the required file extension, browse to the location where the SOLIDWORKS document is saved and then click on the document to be opened. Next, click on the **Open** button in the dialog box. The selected document gets opened.

Similar to opening existing SOLIDWORKS documents, you can also open/import documents created in other CAD applications. SOLIDWORKS allows you to open documents created in CATIA V5, ProE/Creo, Unigraphics/NX, Inventor, Solid Edge, CADKEY, Rhino, DWG, and so on by selecting the respective file extension in the **File Type** drop-down list of the **Open** dialog box. In addition to this, you can also open documents saved in universal CAD formats such as IGES, STEP, SLT, and Parasolid.

Summary

In this chapter, you have learned about system requirements for installing SOLIDWORKS. You have also learned how to invoke different SOLIDWORKS environments, identifying SOLIDWORKS documents, various components of the startup user interface of SOLIDWORKS, invoking and customizing the shortcut menu, saving documents, and opening documents in SOLIDWORKS.

Questions

- The surface modeling environment and the Sheet Metal environment of SOLIDWORKS can be invoked within the _____ environment.

- The file extension of the documents created in the Part modeling environment is _____, the Assembly environment is _____, and the Drawing environment is _____.

- The **Features CommandManager** is provided with different sets of tools that are used for creating _____ .

- In SOLIDWORKS, you can open IGES and STEP files. (True/False)

- The FeatureManager Design Tree is used for keeping a record of all operations/features in an order. (True/False)

Drawing Sketches with SOLIDWORKS

This chapter discusses the following topics:

- Invoking the Part Modeling Environment
- Invoking the Sketching Environment
- Working with the Selection of Planes
- Specifying Units
- Specifying Grids and Snap Settings
- Drawing a Line Entity
- Drawing an Arc by using the Line tool
- Drawing a Centerline
- Drawing a Midpoint Line
- Drawing a Rectangle
- Drawing a Circle
- Drawing an Arc
- Drawing a Polygon
- Drawing a Slot
- Drawing an Ellipse
- Drawing an Elliptical Arc
- Drawing a Parabola
- Drawing Conic Curves
- Drawing a Spline
- Editing a Spline
- Modifying the Tangency Direction of Arc/Spline

SOLIDWORKS is a feature-based, parametric, solid modeling mechanical design and automation software. Before you start creating solid 3D components in SOLIDWORKS, you need to understand the same. To design a component in this software, you need to create all its features one by one, see Figures 2.1 and 2.2. Note that the features are divided into two main categories: sketch based features and placed features. A feature created by using a sketch is known as a sketch based feature, whereas a feature created on an existing feature without using a sketch is known as a placed feature. Of the two categories, the sketch based feature is the first feature to be designed for any real world component. Therefore, it is important to first learn drawing a sketch.

Figure 2.1 shows a component consisting of an extruded feature, cut feature, chamfer, and fillet. Of all these features, extruded and cut features are created by using a sketch, see Figure 2.2. Therefore, these features are known as sketch based features. On the other hand, the fillet and the chamfer are known as placed features because no sketch is used for creating these features.

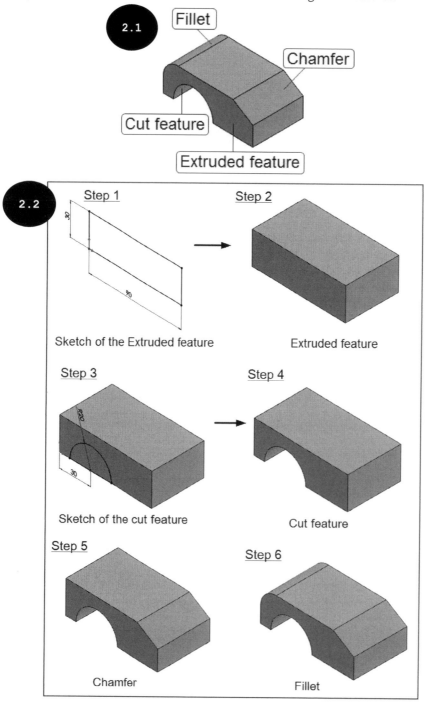

As the first feature of any component is a sketch based feature, first you need to learn how to create sketches in the Sketching environment. In SOLIDWORKS, the Sketching environment can be invoked within the Part modeling environment.

Invoking the Part Modeling Environment

Start SOLIDWORKS by double-clicking on the SOLIDWORKS 2020 icon on your desktop. After loading all the required files, the startup user interface of SOLIDWORKS appears along with the **Welcome** dialog box, see Figure 2.3. The **Welcome** dialog box appears every time you start SOLIDWORKS and is used for starting a new SOLIDWORKS document, opening an existing document, accessing SOLIDWORKS resources, and so on. In the **Welcome** dialog box, click on the **Part** button. The startup user interface of the Part modeling environment of SOLIDWORKS appears, see Figure 2.4. Various components of the Part modeling environment have been discussed in Chapter 1. Once the Part modeling environment is invoked, you can invoke the Sketching environment for creating the sketch of the first feature of a model.

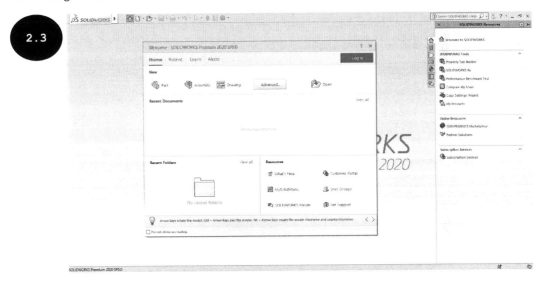

Note: If you are invoking the Part modeling environment for the first time after installing the software, the **Units and Dimension Standard** dialog box appears. You can specify the unit system as the default unit system for SOLIDWORKS by using this dialog box. In this textbook, the metric unit system and ANSI standard have been used as the default unit system. You will learn about specifying units later in this chapter.

Invoking the Sketching Environment

After invoking the Part modeling environment, you need to invoke the Sketching environment for creating the sketch of the first feature of a model. For doing so, click on the **Sketch** tab in the CommandManager. The tools of the **Sketch CommandManager** appear, see Figure 2.5.

In the **Sketch CommandManager**, click on the **Sketch** tool, see Figure 2.5. The three default planes: Front, Top, and Right, which are mutually perpendicular to each other appear in the graphics area, see Figure 2.6. Also, the **Edit Sketch PropertyManager** appears to the left of the graphics area. Now, you can select any of the three default planes as the sketching plane for creating the sketch. To select a plane, move the cursor over the plane to be selected. Next, click the left mouse button when the boundary of the plane gets highlighted in the graphics area. As soon as you select a plane, the Sketching environment gets invoked with a Confirmation corner at the top right corner in the graphics area, see Figure 2.7. Also, the selected plane becomes the sketching plane for drawing the sketch and it is oriented normal to the viewing direction, so that you can create the sketch easily. Note that the Confirmation corner consists of two icons: **Exit Sketch** and **Cancel Sketch**. The **Exit Sketch** icon is used for confirming the creation of the sketch successfully and exiting the Sketching environment, whereas, the **Cancel Sketch** icon is used for discarding the sketch created.

The Sketching environment also displays a red colored point with two perpendicular arrows at the center of the graphics area. The red colored point represents the origin (0,0) of the Sketching environment and the perpendicular arrows represent the X axis and Y axis of the sketching plane. If the red colored point does not appear by default in the graphics area, you can turn on its appearance by clicking on **Hide/Show Items > View Origins** in the **View (Heads-Up)** toolbar, see Figure 2.8. The **View Origins** tool of the **View (Heads-Up)** toolbar is a toggle button.

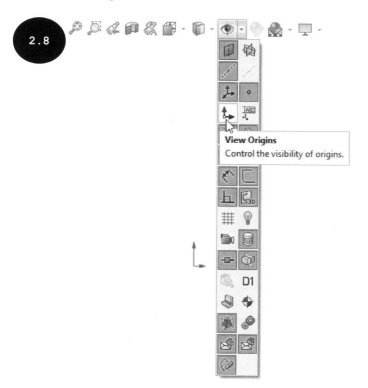

Working with the Selection of Planes

As discussed earlier, to invoke the Sketching environment, you need to select a plane as the sketching plane. Selection of an appropriate plane is very important for defining the right orientation of a model. Figure 2.9 shows the isometric view of a model having length 200 mm, width 100 mm, and height 40 mm. To create this model with the same orientation, you can select the Top plane as the sketching plane and then draw a rectangular sketch of 200 mm X 100 mm. However, if you select the Front plane as the sketching plane for creating this model, then you need to draw a rectangular sketch of 200 mm X 40 mm. Likewise, if you select the Right plane as the sketching plane, then you need to draw a rectangular sketch of 100 mm X 40 mm.

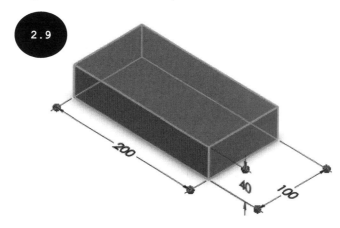

Once the Sketching environment has been invoked, you can start drawing the sketch by using different sketching tools in the **Sketch CommandManager**. However, before you start drawing the sketch, it is important to understand the procedure for setting the units of measurement and grids.

Specifying Units

When you invoke the SOLIDWORKS software for the first time after the installation, the **Units and Dimension Standard** dialog box appears. This dialog box allows you to specify units and measurement standard as the default settings. Note that the units and measurement settings specified in the **Units and Dimension Standard** dialog box become the default units for all new documents to be opened. However, SOLIDWORKS allows you to modify the default unit settings at any point of your design for any particular document.

To modify the default unit settings, click on the **Options** tool in the **Standard** toolbar, see Figure 2.10. The **System Options** dialog box appears, see Figure 2.11.

The **System Options** dialog box contains two tabs: **System Options** and **Document Properties**. By default, the **System Options** tab is activated. Click on the **Document Properties** tab in the dialog box. The name of the dialog box changes to **Document Properties** and the options for setting document properties appear in the dialog box. Next, click on the **Units** option in the left panel of the dialog box. The options for setting the units appear on the right panel of the dialog box, see Figure 2.12.

The **Unit system** area of the dialog box displays a list of predefined standard unit systems. In this area, you can select the required predefined unit system for the currently opened document. For example, to set the metric unit system for the currently opened document, click on the **MMGS (millimeter, gram, second)** radio button. Note that in the metric unit system, length is measured in millimeters, mass is calculated in grams, and time is represented in seconds.

You can also specify a unit system other than the default predefined standard unit systems by using the **Custom** radio button. For doing so, click on the **Custom** radio button, the fields of the table available at the bottom of the dialog box get enabled. Now, you can change the unit of length measurement, angle measurement, mass calculation, and time as per your requirement other than the standard combination. For example, to change the unit of length measurement, click on the field corresponding to the **Unit** column and the **Length** row in the table. An arrow facing downward appears. Click on this arrow. A drop-down list appears with a list of different units for length measurement. Now, you can select the required unit from this drop-down list. Similarly, you can change units for other measurements in this table. You can also specify decimal places for the measurement as per the requirement by using this table. Once you have set all the required units of measurements for the currently opened document, click on the **OK** button to accept the changes made in the dialog box.

Specifying Grids and Snap Settings

Grids help you specify points in the drawing area for creating sketch entities and act as reference lines. By default, the display of grids is turned off in the drawing area. You can turn on the display of grids in the drawing area and specify snap settings to restrict the movement of the cursor at specified intervals.

To turn on the display of grids and specify snap settings, click on the **Options** tool in the Standard toolbar. The **System Options - General** dialog box appears. In this dialog box, click on the **Document Properties** tab. The options related to document properties appear and the name of the dialog box changes to **Document Properties - Drafting Standard**. Next, click on the **Grid/Snap** option in the left panel of the dialog box. The options related to grids and snap settings appear on the right panel of the dialog box. Also, the name of the dialog box changes to **Document Properties - Grid/Snap**, see Figure 2.13.

In the **Major grid spacing** field of the **Grid** area in the dialog box, specify the distance between two major grid lines. In the **Minor-lines per major** field of the dialog box, specify the number of minor lines between two major grid lines. Note that the value entered in the **Minor-lines per major** field defines the number of division between two major grid lines. For example, if you enter 5 in the **Minor-lines per major** field, then two major grid lines will be divided into 5 smaller sections horizontally and vertically. In the **Snap points per minor** field, you can specify the number of snap points for the cursor between two minor grid lines.

You can turn on the display of grids in the drawing area by selecting the **Display grid** check box in the **Grid** area of the dialog box. Similarly, you can turn the snap mode on for snapping the cursor to the specified snap settings. For doing so, click on the **Go To System Snaps** button in the dialog box. The name of the dialog box changes to **System Options - Relations/Snaps**. In this dialog box, you can select the **Grid** check box for turning the snap mode on. If you select the **Snap only when grid is displayed** check box of this dialog box, then the cursor snaps only when the grids are displayed in the drawing area. Note that snapping the cursor at specific intervals is useful for defining exact points in the drawing area for creating sketch entities. Once you have specified the grid and snap settings in the dialog box, click on the **OK** button to accept the changes made in the dialog box. Figure 2.14 shows the drawing area with the display of grids turned on.

Note: In this textbook, the background color of the graphics area has been changed to white for clarity. To change the background color, click on the **Option** tool ⚙ in the **Standard** toolbar and then click on the **Colors** option in the left panel of the **System Options - General** dialog box that appears. The options for specifying color scheme settings appear on the right panel of the dialog box. Select the **Plain (Viewport Background color above)** radio button in the **Background appearance** area of the dialog box. Next, make sure that the **Viewport Background** option is selected in the **Color scheme settings** area of the dialog box. Next, click on the **Edit** button available in the right of the **Color scheme settings** area. The **Color** window appears. In this window, select the white color and then click on the **OK** button. Next, click on the **OK** button in the **System Options - General** dialog box. The background color of the drawing area is changed to white.

Drawing a Line Entity

A line is defined as the shortest distance between two points. To draw a line, click on the **Line** tool in the **Sketch CommandManager**. The **Insert Line PropertyManager** appears on the left of the drawing area, see Figure 2.15. Also, the appearance of the cursor changes to line cursor ✎. The line cursor appears with the symbol of a pencil and a line. You can click in the drawing area to specify a start point and then an endpoint for drawing a line. Note that you can draw a chain of continuous lines by clicking the left mouse button repeatedly in the drawing area. To end the creation of the continuous chain of lines, press the ESC key. Alternatively, right-click in the drawing area and then click on the **Select** option in the shortcut menu that appears. The options in the

Insert Line PropertyManager are used for controlling the settings for drawing lines. The options are discussed next.

Message

The **Message** rollout of the **Insert Line PropertyManager** displays appropriate information about the required action to be performed for creating a line entity.

Orientation

The **Orientation** rollout is used for controlling the orientation of a line. The options in the **Orientation** rollout are discussed next.

As sketched

By default, the **As sketched** radio button is activated in the **Orientation** rollout. As a result, you can draw a line of required orientation by clicking the left mouse button in the drawing area. In this case, the orientation of the line depends upon the points you specify in the drawing area by clicking the left mouse button.

Horizontal

On selecting the **Horizontal** radio button in the **Orientation** rollout, you can draw horizontal lines by clicking the left mouse button in the drawing area. Notice that when you select this radio button, the **Parameters** rollout appears below the **Options** rollout in the PropertyManager, see Figure 2.16. In this rollout, the **Length** field is activated, by default. You can specify a required length value for the horizontal line in this field. By default, the value **0** is entered in this field. As a result, you can draw a horizontal line of any length by specifying two points in the drawing area.

Vertical

Similar to drawing horizontal lines by selecting the **Horizontal** radio button, you can draw vertical lines by selecting the **Vertical** radio button in the **Orientation** rollout of the PropertyManager.

Angle

The **Angle** radio button is used for drawing a line at an angle. As soon as you select this radio button, the **Parameters** rollout appears in the PropertyManager with the **Length** and **Angle** fields. You can specify the required length and angle values for the line in the respective fields of this rollout. By default, the value **0** is entered in both the fields. As a result, you can draw a line of any length and angle by specifying the points in the drawing area.

Note: The angle value of a line, entered in the **Angle** field of the **Parameters** rollout, is measured from the X axis.

Options

The options in the **Options** rollout of the **PropertyManager** are discussed next.

For construction

The **For construction** check box of the **Options** rollout is used for drawing a construction or reference line.

Infinite length

The **Infinite length** check box is used for drawing a line of infinite length. On selecting the **Infinite length** check box, you can draw a line of infinite length by specifying two points in the drawing area.

Midpoint line

The **Midpoint line** check box is used for drawing a line that is symmetric about a point. On selecting the **Midpoint line** check box, you need to first specify the midpoint of the line and then an endpoint by clicking the left mouse button in the drawing area. A line symmetric about the midpoint is drawn.

Procedure for Drawing a Line

1. Click on the **Line** tool in the **Sketch CommandManager**. The **Line** tool gets activated.
2. Click to specify the start point of the line in the drawing area.
3. Move the line cursor away from the start point. A rubber band line appears with one of its ends fixed at the start point and the other end attached to the cursor. Notice that as you move the cursor, the length of the rubber band line changes and appears near the cursor, see Figure 2.17.

Note: If you move the cursor horizontally or vertically after specifying the start point of the line, a symbol of horizontal ▬ or vertical ▮ relation appears near the cursor. The symbol of relation indicates that if you click the left mouse button to specify the second point of the line, the corresponding relation will be applied. You will learn more about relations in later chapters.

4. Click the left mouse button to specify the second point of the line. A line between the specified points is drawn. Also, notice that the rubber band line is still displayed with one of its ends fixed to the last specified point and the other end attached to the cursor. This indicates that a chain of continuous lines can be drawn by clicking the left mouse button in the drawing area.

Tip: As SOLIDWORKS is a parametric, 3D solid modeling software, you can draw a sketch by specifying points arbitrarily in the drawing area. Once the sketch has been drawn, you need to apply dimensions. You will learn about dimensioning sketch entities in later chapters.

5. Once all the line entities have been drawn, right-click in the drawing area and then click on the **Select** option in the shortcut menu that appears to exit the **Line** tool.

Tutorial 1

Draw a sketch of the model shown in Figure 2.18. The dimensions and the 3D model shown in the figure are for your reference only. You will learn about applying dimensions and creating 3D models in later chapters. All dimensions are in mm.

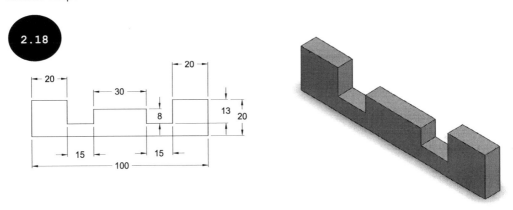

2.18

Section 1: Starting SOLIDWORKS

1. Start SOLIDWORKS by double-clicking on the SOLIDWORKS icon on your desktop. The startup user interface of SOLIDWORKS appears along with the **Welcome** dialog box, see Figure 2.19.

2.19

Note: If SOLIDWORKS is already open and the **Welcome** dialog box does not appear on the screen, then you can invoke the **Welcome** dialog box by clicking on the **Welcome to SOLIDWORKS** tool 🏠 in the **Standard** toolbar or by pressing the CTRL + F2 keys.

Section 2: Invoking the Sketching Environment

1.   Click on the **Part** button in the **Welcome** dialog box. The Part modeling environment is invoked.

2.   Click on the **Sketch** tab in the CommandManager, see Figure 2.20. The tools of the **Sketch CommandManager** appear.

3.   Click on the **Sketch** tool in the **Sketch CommandManager**, see Figure 2.20. Three default planes mutually perpendicular to each other appear in the graphics area.

4.   Move the cursor over the Front plane and then click the left mouse button, when the boundary of the plane is highlighted. The Sketching environment is invoked. Also, the Front plane is orientated normal to the viewing direction and the Confirmation corner appears at the upper right corner of the drawing area, see Figure 2.21.

Note: In Figure 2.21, the display of grids and snap settings is turned off.

Section 3: Drawing the Sketch

1. Click on the **Line** tool in the **Sketch CommandManager**. The **Line** tool gets activated and the **Insert Line PropertyManager** appears on the left of the drawing area. Also, the appearance of the cursor changes to line cursor ⟍.

2. Move the cursor to the origin and then click to specify the start point of the line when the cursor snaps to the origin.

3. Move the cursor horizontally toward right and then click to specify the endpoint of the line when the length of the line appears close to 100 mm near the cursor, see Figure 2.22.

4. Move the cursor vertically upward and then click the left mouse button when the length of the line appears close to 20 mm near the cursor, see Figure 2.23.

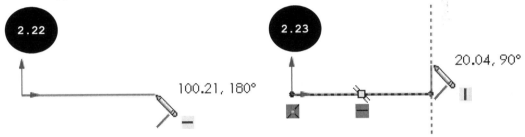

5. Move the cursor horizontally toward left and then click when the length of the line appears close to 20 mm.

6. Move the cursor vertically downward and then click when the length of the line appears close to 13 mm near the cursor, see Figure 2.24.

7. Move the cursor horizontally toward left and then click when the length of the line appears close to 15 mm.

8. Move the cursor vertically upward and then click when the length of the line appears close to 8 mm, see Figure 2.25.

9. Move the cursor horizontally toward left and then click when the length of the line appears close to 30 mm.

10. Move the cursor vertically downward and then click when the length of the line appears close to 8 mm, see Figure 2.26.

2.26

11. Similarly, draw the remaining sketch entities. Figure 2.27 shows the sketch after all the sketch entities have been drawn.

12. Right-click in the drawing area. A shortcut menu appears. In this shortcut menu, click on the **Select** option to exit the **Line** tool.

Tip: In the Figure 2.27, the display of automatically applied relations such as horizontal and vertical is turned off. To turn on or off the display of relations in the drawing area, click on **Hide/Show Items** > **View Sketch Relations** in the **View (Heads-Up)** toolbar, see Figure 2.28.

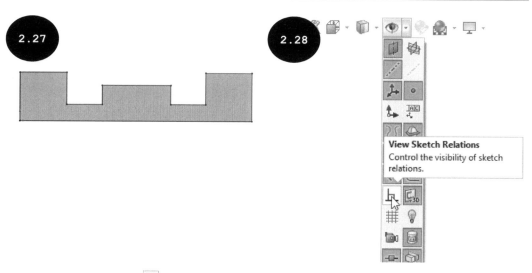

2.27

2.28

View Sketch Relations
Control the visibility of sketch relations.

13. Click on the **Save** tool in the **Standard** toolbar. The **Save As** dialog box appears. Next, browse to the local drive of your system and create a folder with the name **SOLIDWORKS**. Next, create another folder with the name **Chapter 2** in the SOLIDWORKS folder.

14. Enter **Tutorial 1** in the **File name** field of the dialog box and then click on the **Save** button. The sketch is saved in the specified location.

Hands-on Test Drive 1

Draw a sketch of the model shown in Figure 2.29. The dimensions and the 3D model shown in the figure are for your reference only. You will learn about applying dimensions and creating 3D models in later chapters. All dimensions are in mm.

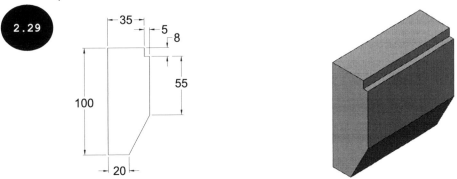

Drawing an Arc by using the Line Tool

SOLIDWORKS is provided with a set of tools for drawing arcs: **Centerpoint Arc**, **3 Point Arc**, and **Tangent Arc**. The tools for drawing arcs are discussed later in this chapter. In addition to drawing arcs by using these tools, you can also draw a tangent arc by using the **Line** tool. In order to do this, at least one line or arc entity has to be drawn in the drawing area. The procedure for drawing a tangent arc by using the **Line** tool is discussed next.

Procedure for Drawing an Arc by using the Line Tool

1. Invoke the Sketching environment.
2. Invoke the **Line** tool and then draw a line by specifying two points in the drawing area. Once the line is drawn, do not exit the **Line** tool.
3. Move the cursor to a distance and then move it back to the last specified point. An orange colored dot appears in the drawing area, see Figure 2.30.
4. Move the cursor away from the point. The arc mode is activated and the preview of a tangent arc appears in the drawing area, see Figure 2.31.

Note: The tangency of arc depends upon how you move the cursor from the last specified point in the drawing area. Figure 2.32 shows the possible movements of the cursor and the creation of arcs in the respective movements.

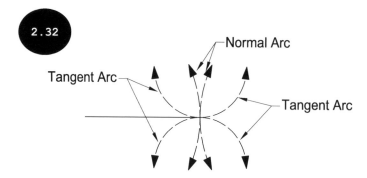

5.   Click the left mouse button to specify the endpoint of the arc when the angle and radius values appear close to the required values. An arc is drawn and the line mode is activated again. You can continue with the creation of line entities or move the cursor back to the last specified point to invoke the arc mode for drawing an arc.
6.   Once you have created all entities, right-click in the drawing area and then click on the **Select** option in the shortcut menu that appears to exit the **Line** tool.

Tutorial 2

Draw a sketch of the model shown in Figure 2.33 by using the **Line** tool. The dimensions and the 3D model shown in this figure are for your reference only. All dimensions are in mm. You will learn about applying dimensions and creating 3D models in later chapters.

Section 1: Starting SOLIDWORKS

1.   Start SOLIDWORKS by double-clicking on the SOLIDWORKS icon on your desktop, if not started already. The startup user interface of SOLIDWORKS appears along with the **Welcome** dialog box, see Figure 2.34.

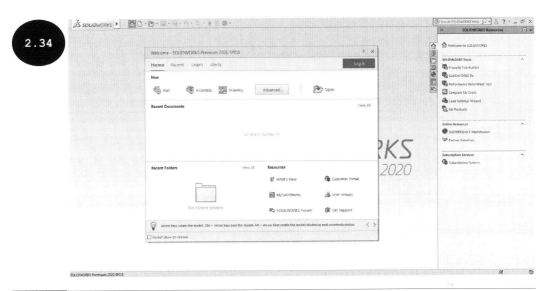

Note: If SOLIDWORKS is already open and the **Welcome** dialog box does not appear on the screen, then you can invoke the **Welcome** dialog box by clicking on the **Welcome to SOLIDWORKS** tool ⌂ in the **Standard** toolbar or by pressing the CTRL + F2 keys.

Section 2: Invoking the Sketching Environment

1. Click on the **Part** button in the **Welcome** dialog box. The Part modeling environment is invoked.

2. Click on the **Sketch** tab in the CommandManager, see Figure 2.35. The tools of the **Sketch CommandManager** appear.

3. Click on the **Sketch** tool in the **Sketch CommandManager**, see Figure 2.35. Three default planes that are mutually perpendicular to each other appear in the graphics area.

4. Move the cursor over the Front plane and then click when the boundary of the plane is highlighted. The Sketching environment is invoked and the Front plane is orientated normal to the viewing direction, see Figure 2.36.

Note: It is evident from Figure 2.33 that all the sketch entities are multiples of 5 mm. Therefore, you can set the snap settings such that the cursor snaps to an increment of 5 mm only.

Section 3: Specifying Units, Grids, and Snap Settings

1. Click on the **Options** tool ⚙ in the **Standard** toolbar. The **System Options - General** dialog box appears.

2. Click on the **Document Properties** tab in the dialog box. The name of the dialog box changes to **Document Properties - Drafting Standard**.

3. Click on the **Units** option in the left panel of the dialog box. The options for specifying the unit system appear on the right panel of the dialog box.

4. Select the **MMGS (millimeter, gram, second)** radio button in the **Unit system** area of the dialog box, if not selected by default.

    Now, you need to specify the grids and snap settings such that the cursor snaps to an increment of 5 mm.

5. Click on the **Grid/Snap** option in the left panel of the dialog box. The options for grids and snap settings appear on the right panel of the dialog box. Also, the name of the dialog box changes to **Document Properties - Grid/Snap**.

6. Enter **20** in the **Major grid spacing** field, **4** in the **Minor -lines per major** field, and **1** in the **Snap points per minor** field of the **Grid** area in the dialog box.

7. Select the **Display grid** check box in the **Grid** area of the dialog box to turn on the display of grids in the drawing area based on the grid settings specified in the above step.

8. Click on the **Go To System Snaps** button in the **Document Properties - Grid/Snap** dialog box. The name of the dialog box changes to **System Options - Relations/Snaps**.

9. Select the **Grid** check box in the **Sketch snaps** area of the dialog box to turn on the snap mode.

10. Click on the **OK** button in the dialog box. The grids and snap settings have been specified and the dialog box is closed. Also, the drawing area appears similar to the one shown in Figure 2.37.

Once the units, grids, and snap settings have been specified, you can start creating the sketch by using the **Line** tool.

Section 4: Drawing the Sketch

1. Click on the **Line** tool in the **Sketch CommandManager**. The **Line** tool gets activated and the **Insert Line PropertyManager** appears on the left of the drawing area. Also, the appearance of the cursor changes to the line cursor.

2. Move the cursor to the origin and click to specify the start point of the line when the cursor snaps to the origin.

3. Move the cursor horizontally toward left and then click to specify the second point of the line when the length of the line appears 100 mm near the cursor, see Figure 2.38. Notice that when you move the cursor in the drawing area, it snaps gradually to an incremental distance of 5 mm.

4. Move the cursor to a distance and then move it back to the last specified point. An orange colored dot appears in the drawing area, see Figure 2.39.

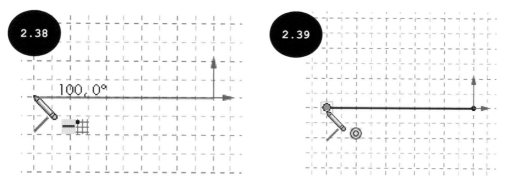

5. Move the cursor horizontally toward left to a distance and then move it vertically upward. The arc mode is activated and the preview of the tangent arc appears in the drawing area, see Figure 2.40.

6. Click to specify the endpoint of the tangent arc when the angle and radius values of the arc appear 180 degrees and 40 mm, respectively near the cursor, see Figure 2.41. The tangent arc is created and the preview of a line appears attached to the cursor.

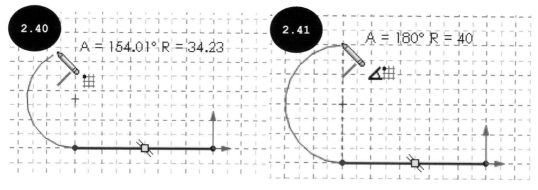

7. Move the cursor horizontally toward right and click when the length of the line appears 100 mm near the cursor.

8. Move the cursor vertically downward and click when the length of the line appears 15 mm.

9. Move the cursor horizontally toward left and click when the length of the line appears 100 mm.

10. Move the cursor to a distance and then move it back to the last specified point. An orange colored dot appears in the drawing area, see Figure 2.42.

11. Move the cursor horizontally toward left to a distance and then move it vertically downward. The arc mode is activated and the preview of the tangent arc appears in the drawing area, see Figure 2.43.

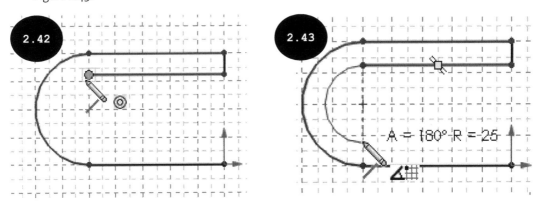

12. Click to specify the endpoint of the tangent arc when the angle and radius values of the arc appear 180 degrees and 25 mm, respectively, refer to Figure 2.43. The tangent arc is created and the line mode is activated.

13. Move the cursor horizontally toward right and then click when the length of the line appears 100 mm near the cursor.

14. Move the cursor vertically downward and then click when the cursor snaps to the start point of the first sketch entity.

15. Right-click in the drawing area and then click on the **Select** option in the shortcut menu that appears to exit the **Line** tool. The final sketch is drawn, see Figure 2.44.

16. Click on the **Save** tool ▦ in the **Standard** toolbar. The **Save As** dialog box appears. Next, browse to the Chapter 2 folder of the SOLIDWORKS folder. You need to create these folders in the local drive of your system, if not created earlier.

17. Enter **Tutorial 2** in the **File name** field of the dialog box and then click on the **Save** button. The sketch is saved in the specified location.

Hands-on Test Drive 2

Draw a sketch of the model shown in Figure 2.45. The dimensions and the 3D model shown in the figure are for your reference only. Draw all entities of the sketch by using the **Line** tool. As all the dimensions of the sketch are multiples of 5 mm, you can set the snap settings such that the cursor snaps to an increment of 5 mm only. All dimensions are in mm.

Drawing a Centerline

Centerlines are defined as reference or construction lines, which are drawn for the aid of sketches. In SOLIDWORKS, you can draw a centerline by using the **Centerline** tool. To draw a centerline, click on the down arrow next to the **Line** tool in the **Sketch CommandManager**. The **Line** flyout appears, see Figure 2.46. In this flyout, click on the **Centerline** tool. The **Centerline** tool gets activated and the **Insert Line PropertyManager** appears to the left of the drawing area, see Figure 2.47. In this PropertyManager, the **For construction** check box is selected, by default. You can therefore create construction lines by specifying points in the drawing area. The options in this PropertyManager are same as those discussed earlier while drawing line entities. Also, the procedure for drawing centerlines is the same as that of drawing lines. Figure 2.48 shows a horizontal centerline drawn by specifying two points in the drawing area.

Drawing a Midpoint Line

A midpoint line is created symmetrically about its midpoint. In SOLIDWORKS, you can draw midpoint lines by using the **Midpoint Line** tool. To activate the **Midpoint Line** tool, click on the arrow next to the **Line** tool in the **Sketch CommandManager**. The **Line** flyout appears, refer to Figure 2.46. In this flyout, click on the **Midpoint Line** tool. The **Midpoint Line** tool gets activated and the **Insert Line PropertyManager** appears to the left of the drawing area, see Figure 2.49. In this PropertyManager, the **Midpoint Line** check box is selected, by default. You can therefore create a midpoint line by specifying points in the drawing area. The options in this PropertyManager are the same as those discussed earlier while drawing line entities. The procedure for drawing a midpoint line is discussed next.

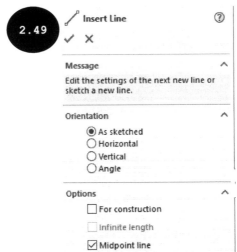

Procedure for Drawing a Midpoint Line

1. Invoke the **Line** flyout and then click on the **Midpoint Line** tool.
2. Click to specify the midpoint of the line in the drawing area, see Figure 2.50.
3. Move the cursor to the required location for defining the endpoint of the line. Note that as you move the cursor, a preview of a line symmetry about the midpoint appears, see Figure 2.50.
4. Click to specify the endpoint of the line. A line symmetrical about the midpoint is created.

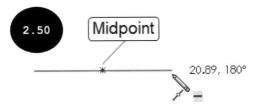

Drawing a Rectangle

In SOLIDWORKS, you can draw a rectangle by different methods using the tools in the **Rectangle** flyout of the **Sketch CommandManager**, see Figure 2.51. To invoke the **Rectangle** flyout, click on the arrow next to the active rectangle tool in the **Sketch CommandManager**, see Figure 2.51. The tools for drawing a rectangle are discussed next.

Corner Rectangle Tool

The **Corner Rectangle** tool is used for drawing a rectangle by specifying its two diagonally opposite corners. The first corner defines the position of the rectangle and the second corner defines the length and width of the rectangle, see Figure 2.52.

To create a rectangle by using the **Corner Rectangle** tool, invoke the **Rectangle** flyout, refer to Figure 2.51, and then click on the **Corner Rectangle** tool. The **Corner Rectangle** tool gets activated and the **Rectangle PropertyManager** appears to the left of the drawing area, see Figure 2.53. The options in the **Rectangle PropertyManager** are discussed next.

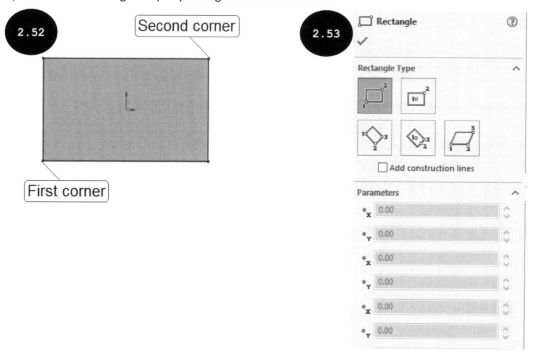

Rectangle Type

The **Rectangle Type** rollout of the PropertyManager is used for switching between different methods of drawing the rectangle. By default, depending upon the rectangle tool invoked, the respective button is activated in this rollout.

The **Add construction lines** check box of the **Rectangle Type** rollout is used for adding construction lines in the rectangle. On selecting this check box, the **From Corners** and **From Midpoints** radio buttons become available, see Figure 2.54. On selecting the **From Corners** radio button, the construction lines connecting the diagonally opposite corners are added in the rectangle, see Figure 2.55. On selecting the **From Midpoints** radio button, the construction lines connecting the midpoints of the line segments are added in the rectangle, see Figure 2.56.

Parameters

The options in the **Parameters** rollout of the **Rectangle PropertyManager** are used for displaying or controlling parameters of the rectangle. Note that all options of this rollout get enabled once the rectangle is drawn and is selected in the drawing area.

Procedure for Drawing a Rectangle by using the Corner Rectangle Tool

1. Invoke the **Rectangle** flyout and then click on the **Corner Rectangle** tool.
2. Click to specify the first corner of the rectangle in the drawing area.
3. Move the cursor away from the first specified corner to specify the diagonally opposite corner of the rectangle, see Figure 2.57.
4. Click to specify the second corner of the rectangle in the drawing area. The rectangle is drawn.

x = 100.21, y = 54.09

Center Rectangle Tool

The **Center Rectangle** tool is used for drawing a rectangle by specifying its center point and a corner point, see Figure 2.58.

Procedure for Drawing a Rectangle by using the Center Rectangle Tool

1. Invoke the **Rectangle** flyout and then click on the **Center Rectangle** tool.
2. Click to specify the center point of the rectangle in the drawing area.
3. Move the cursor to a distance. The preview of the rectangle appears, see Figure 2.59.
4. Click to specify the corner of the rectangle in the drawing area. The rectangle is drawn.

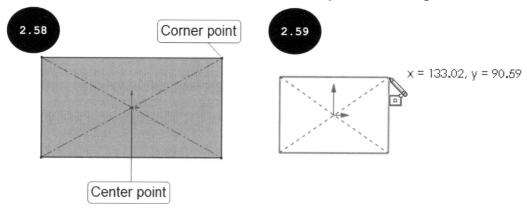

Corner point

Center point

x = 133.02, y = 90.59

3 Point Corner Rectangle Tool

The **3 Point Corner Rectangle** tool is used for drawing a rectangle by specifying three corners. The first two corners define the width and orientation of the rectangle and the third corner defines the length of the rectangle, see Figure 2.60.

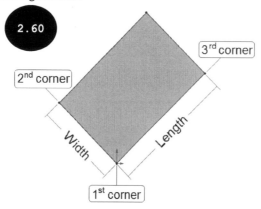

3rd corner

2nd corner

Width

Length

1st corner

Procedure for Drawing a Rectangle by using the 3 Point Corner Rectangle Tool
1. Invoke the **Rectangle** flyout and then click on the **3 Point Corner Rectangle** tool.
2. Click to specify the first corner of the rectangle in the drawing area.
3. Move the cursor to a distance in the drawing area. An inference line appears attached to the cursor, see Figure 2.61.
4. Click to specify the second corner of the rectangle in the drawing area.
5. Move the cursor to a distance in the drawing area. The preview of the rectangle appears, see Figure 2.62.
6. Click to specify the third corner of the rectangle. The rectangle is drawn.

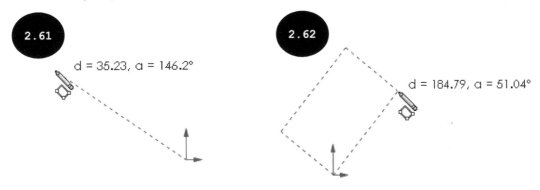

d = 35.23, a = 146.2°

d = 184.79, a = 51.04°

3 Point Center Rectangle Tool
The **3 Point Center Rectangle** tool is used for drawing a rectangle by specifying three points. The first point defines the center of the rectangle, the second point defines the width and orientation of the rectangle, and the third point defines the length of the rectangle, see Figure 2.63.

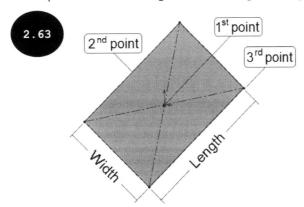

Procedure for Drawing a Rectangle by using the 3 Point Center Rectangle Tool
1. Invoke the **Rectangle** flyout and then click on the **3 Point Center Rectangle** tool.
2. Click to specify a point (first point) as the center point of the rectangle.
3. Move the cursor to a distance in the drawing area. An inference line appears attached to the cursor, see Figure 2.64.
4. Click to specify the second point of the rectangle.

5. Move the cursor to a distance in the drawing area. The preview of the rectangle appears in the drawing area, see Figure 2.65.
6. Click to specify the third point of the rectangle in the drawing area. The rectangle is drawn.

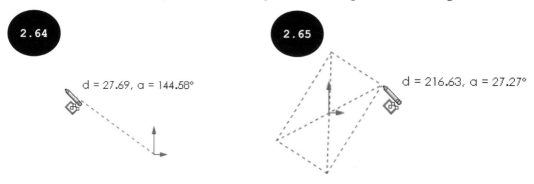

Parallelogram Tool

The **Parallelogram** tool is used for drawing a parallelogram, whose sides are not perpendicular to each other. You can draw a parallelogram by specifying three points. The first two points define the width and orientation of the parallelogram and the third point defines the length and the angle between the parallelogram sides, see Figure 2.66.

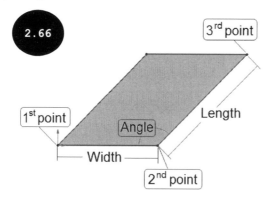

Procedure for Drawing a Parallelogram

1. Invoke the **Rectangle** flyout and then click on the **Parallelogram** tool.
2. Click to specify the first point of the parallelogram, refer to Figure 2.66.
3. Move the cursor away from the first specified point in the drawing area. An inference line appears attached to the cursor.
4. Click to specify the second point of the parallelogram in the drawing area, refer to Figure 2.66.
5. Move the cursor away from the second specified point in the drawing area. The preview of the parallelogram appears.
6. Click to specify the third point of the parallelogram. The parallelogram is drawn.

Drawing a Circle

In SOLIDWORKS, you can draw a circle by using the **Circle** and **Perimeter Circle** tools available in the **Circle** flyout of the **Sketch CommandManager**, see Figure 2.67. To invoke the **Circle** flyout, click on the arrow next to an active circle tool in the **Sketch CommandManager**, see Figure 2.67. The tools for drawing a circle are discussed next.

Circle Tool

The **Circle** tool is used for drawing a circle by specifying its center point and a point on its circumference, see Figure 2.68.

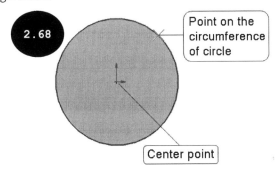

Procedure for Drawing a Circle by using the Circle Tool

1. Click on the **Circle** tool in the **Sketch CommandManager**. The **Circle PropertyManager** appears, see Figure 2.69.
2. Click to specify the center point of the circle in the drawing area.
3. Move the cursor to a distance in the drawing area. The preview of the circle appears, see Figure 2.70.
4. Click to specify a point in the drawing area. The circle is drawn.

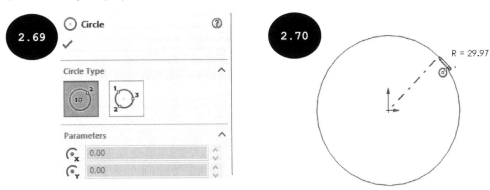

Perimeter Circle Tool

The **Perimeter Circle** tool is used for drawing a circle by specifying three points on its circumference, see Figure 2.71.

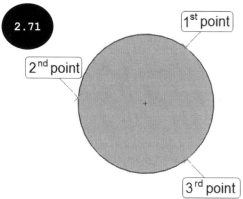

Procedure for Drawing a Circle by using the Perimeter Circle Tool

1. Invoke the **Circle** flyout and then click on the **Perimeter Circle** tool. The **Circle PropertyManager** appears to the left of the drawing area.
2. Click to specify the first point in the drawing area, see Figure 2.72.
3. Move the cursor away from the first specified point. The preview of the circle appears.
4. Click to specify the second point in the drawing area, see Figure 2.72.
5. Click to specify the third point. The circle is drawn by defining three points on its circumference.

Tip: You can also convert a circle into a construction circle. For doing so, select the circle in the drawing area. The **Circle PropertyManager** and a Pop-up toolbar appear. Select the **For construction** check box in the **Options** rollout of the **Circle PropertyManager**. The selected circle converts into a construction circle. Alternatively, click on the **Construction Geometry** tool in the Pop-up toolbar to convert the circle into a construction circle.

Drawing an Arc

In SOLIDWORKS, you can draw an arc by different methods using the tools in the **Arc** flyout of the **Sketch CommandManager**, see Figure 2.73. To invoke the **Arc** flyout, click on the arrow next to the active arc tool in the **Sketch CommandManager**, see Figure 2.73. The tools for drawing an arc are discussed next.

Centerpoint Arc Tool

The **Centerpoint Arc** tool is used for drawing an arc by defining its center point, start point, and endpoint, see Figure 2.74.

Procedure for Drawing an Arc by using the Centerpoint Arc Tool

1. Click on the **Centerpoint Arc** tool. The **Arc PropertyManager** appears, see Figure 2.75.
2. Click to specify the center point of the arc in the drawing area.
3. Move the cursor to a distance. A construction circle appears attached to the cursor.
4. Click in the drawing area to define the start point of the arc.
5. Move the cursor clockwise or anti-clockwise. The preview of the arc appears in the drawing area.
6. Click to specify the endpoint of the arc in the drawing area. The arc is drawn.

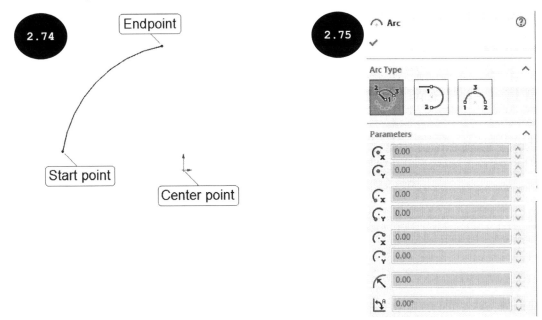

3 Point Arc Tool

The 3 Point Arc tool is used for drawing an arc by defining three points on its arc length, see Figure 2.76.

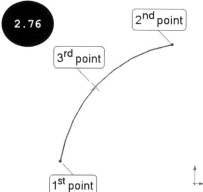

Procedure for Drawing an Arc by using the 3 Point Arc Tool

1. Invoke the **Arc** flyout and then click on the 3 **Point Arc** tool.
2. Click to specify the first point of the arc in the drawing area, see Figure 2.77.
3. Move the cursor away from the first specified point and then click to specify the second point of the arc in the drawing area, see Figure 2.77.
4. Move the cursor to a distance. The preview of the arc appears in the drawing area, see Figure 2.77. Next, click to specify a point on the arc length. The arc is drawn.

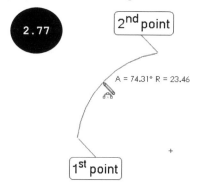

Tangent Arc Tool

The **Tangent Arc** tool is used for drawing an arc tangent to an existing entity, see Figure 2.78. You can draw an arc tangent to a line, an arc, or a spline entity by using this tool.

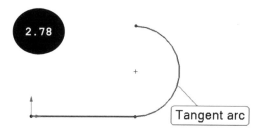

Procedure for Drawing a Tangent Arc by using the Tangent Arc Tool

1. Click on the **Tangent Arc** tool in the **Arc** flyout.
2. Move the cursor to the endpoint of an existing entity (line, arc, or spline) in the drawing area and then click to specify the start point of the tangent arc when the cursor snaps to the endpoint.
3. Move the cursor to a distance. The preview of the tangent arc appears in the drawing area such that its endpoint is attached to the cursor.

Note: The tangency of arc depends upon how you move the cursor from the specified point in the drawing area. Figure 2.79 shows the possible movements of the cursor and the creation of arcs in the respective movements.

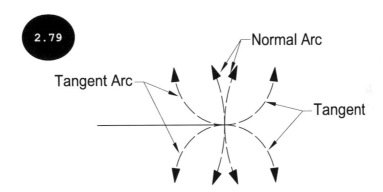

4. Click to specify the endpoint of the tangent arc in the drawing area, see Figure 2.80. The tangent arc is drawn. Note that the **Tangent Arc** tool remains activated. As a result, the preview of another tangent arc appears in the drawing area. This indicates that you can continue creating tangent arcs, one after another by clicking the left mouse button.
5. Once you have finished drawing tangent arcs, right-click in the drawing area and then click on the **Select** option in the shortcut menu that appears to exit the **Tangent Arc** tool.

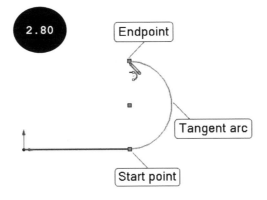

Drawing a Polygon

A polygon is a multi-sided geometry having all sides of equal length and equal angle, see Figure 2.81. In SOLIDWORKS, you can draw a polygon of sides ranging from 3 to 40.

To draw a polygon, click on the **Polygon** tool ⬡ in the **Sketch CommandManager**. The **Polygon PropertyManager** appears, see Figure 2.82. The options in the **Polygon PropertyManager** are discussed next.

Options

By default, the **For construction** check box is cleared in the **Options** rollout of the PropertyManager, refer to Figure 2.82. Therefore, the resultant polygon has solid sketch entities, see Figure 2.83. If you select the **For construction** check box, the resultant polygon has construction entities, see Figure 2.84.

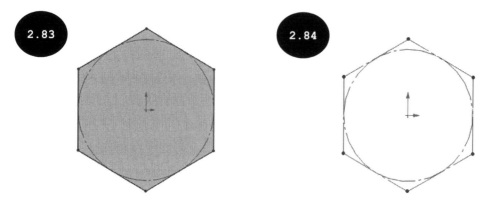

Parameters

The options in the **Parameters** rollout are used for specifying parameters for creating a polygon. The options are discussed next.

Number of Sides

The **Number of Sides** field is used for specifying the number of sides for the polygon. You can specify the number of sides for the polygon in the range between 3 to 40.

Inscribed circle

The **Inscribed circle** radio button is used for drawing a polygon by drawing an imaginary construction circle inside the polygon. In this case, the midpoints of all sides of the polygon touch the imaginary construction circle, see Figure 2.85.

Circumscribed circle

The **Circumscribed circle** radio button is used for drawing a polygon by drawing an imaginary construction circle outside the polygon. In this case, all vertices of the polygon touch the imaginary construction circle, see Figure 2.86.

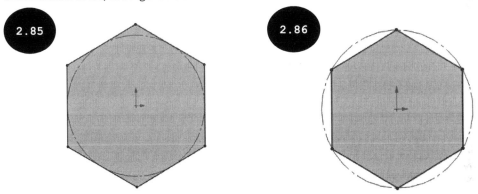

New Polygon

The **New Polygon** button is used for drawing a new polygon.

Procedure for Drawing a Polygon

1. Click on the **Polygon** tool. The **Polygon PropertyManager** appears.
2. Enter the number of sides of the polygon in the **Number of Sides** field of the PropertyManager.
3. Select the **Inscribed circle** or **Circumscribed circle** radio button, as required.
4. Click to specify the center point of the polygon in the drawing area.
5. Move the cursor to a distance in the drawing area. The preview of the polygon appears in the drawing area.
6. Click to specify a point in the drawing area. The polygon is drawn and the **Polygon** tool is still activated.

> **Note:** After creating a polygon, it is selected in the drawing area. Also, the current parameters of the polygon appear in the respective fields of the PropertyManager. You can modify the current parameters such as X and Y coordinate values of the center of the polygon, diameter of the imaginary construction circle, and the angle of rotation of the polygon by using the **Center X Coordinate**, **Center Y Coordinate**, **Circle Diameter**, and **Angle** fields of the PropertyManager, respectively.

7.　Press the **ESC** key to exit the tool.

Drawing a Slot

In SOLIDWORKS, you can draw straight and arc slots by using the tools in the **Slot** flyout, see Figure 2.87. To invoke the **Slot** flyout, click on the arrow next to the active slot tool in the **Sketch CommandManager**, see Figure 2.87. The tools for drawing slots are discussed next.

Straight Slot Tool

The **Straight Slot** tool is used for drawing a straight slot by specifying its start point, endpoint, and a point to define its width, see Figure 2.88. To draw a straight slot, click on the **Straight Slot** tool in the **Slot** flyout. The **Slot PropertyManager** appears, see Figure 2.89. The options in the **Slot PropertyManager** are discussed next.

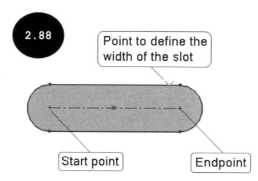

Slot Types

The **Slot Types** rollout is used for switching between different methods of drawing a slot. By default, depending upon the slot tool invoked, the respective button is activated in this rollout.

The **Add dimensions** check box in the **Slot Types** rollout is cleared, by default. As a result, no dimensions are applied to the resultant slot. On selecting this check box, the dimensions get automatically applied to the resultant slot in the drawing area, see Figure 2.90.

The **Center to Center** button of the **Slot Type** rollout is activated, by default. As a result, the straight slot measures the length from center to center of the slot. On choosing the **Overall Length** button, the straight slot measures the overall (end to end) length of the slot.

Parameters

The options in the **Parameters** rollout of the PropertyManager are used for displaying or controlling the parameters of the slot. Note that the options of this rollout get enabled once the slot is drawn and is selected in the drawing area. You can modify the X and Y coordinate values of the center point of the slot, the width of the slot, and the length of the slot by using the respective fields of this rollout.

Procedure for Drawing a Slot by using the Straight Slot Tool

1. Click on the **Straight Slot** tool. The **Slot PropertyManager** appears.
2. Click to specify the start point of the slot.
3. Move the cursor to a distance in the drawing area. A straight rubber band construction line with its one end attached to the cursor appears.
4. Click the left mouse button in the drawing area to define the endpoint of the slot.
5. Move the cursor to a distance in the drawing area. The preview of the slot appears.
6. Click to specify a point in the drawing area to define the width of the slot. The straight slot is drawn.

Centerpoint Straight Slot Tool

The **Centerpoint Straight Slot** tool is used for drawing a straight slot by specifying its center point, endpoint, and a point to define its width, see Figure 2.91.

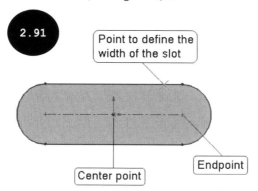

Procedure for Drawing a Slot by using the Centerpoint Straight Slot Tool

1. Click on the **Centerpoint Straight Slot** tool in the **Slot** flyout.
2. Click to specify the center point of slot, see Figure 2.92.
3. Move the cursor to a distance in the drawing area. A straight rubber band construction line with its one end attached to the cursor appears.
4. Click to define the endpoint of the slot, see Figure 2.92.
5. Move the cursor to a distance. The preview of the slot appears, see Figure 2.92.
6. Click to specify a point in the drawing area to define the width of the slot. The straight slot is drawn.

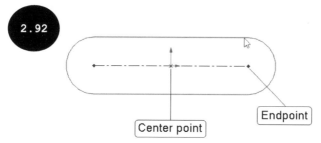

3 Point Arc Slot Tool

The **3 Point Arc Slot** tool is used for drawing an arc slot by specifying three points on its arc length, see Figure 2.93.

Procedure for Drawing an Arc Slot by using the 3 Point Arc Slot Tool

1. Click on the 3 Point Arc Slot tool in the Slot flyout.
2. Click to specify the first (start point) point of the arc slot, see Figure 2.94.
3. Move the cursor to a distance. A construction arc appears in the drawing area.
4. Click to specify the second (endpoint) point of the arc slot, see Figure 2.94.
5. Move the cursor to a distance and then click to specify the third point of the slot, see Figure 2.94.
6. Move the cursor to a distance. The preview of the arc slot appears, see Figure 2.94.
7. Click to specify a point in the drawing area to define the width of the slot. The arc slot is drawn.

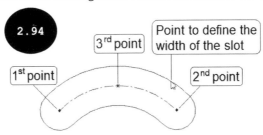

Centerpoint Arc Slot Tool

The Centerpoint Arc Slot tool is used for drawing an arc slot by specifying its center point, start point, and endpoint, see Figure 2.95.

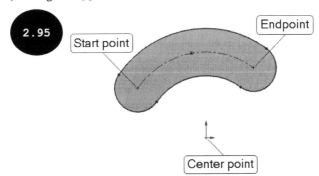

Procedure for Drawing an Arc Slot by using the Centerpoint Arc Slot Tool

1. Click on the Centerpoint Arc Slot tool in the Slot flyout.
2. Click to specify the center point of the arc slot, see Figure 2.96.
3. Move the cursor to a distance in the drawing area. A rubber band construction circle appears.
4. Click to specify the start point of the arc slot, see Figure 2.96.
5. Move the cursor clockwise or counterclockwise in the drawing area. A construction arc appears.
6. Click to specify the endpoint of the arc slot, see Figure 2.96.
7. Move the cursor to a distance in the drawing area. The preview of the arc slot appears, see Figure 2.96.
8. Click to specify a point in the drawing area to define the width of the arc slot. The arc slot is drawn.

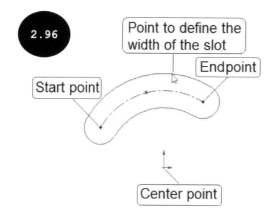

Drawing an Ellipse

An ellipse is drawn by defining its major axis and minor axis, see Figure 2.97. You can draw an ellipse by using the **Ellipse** tool of the **Sketch CommandManager**.

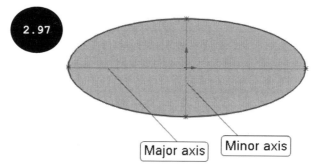

Procedure for Drawing an Ellipse

1.   Click on the **Ellipse** tool ⊘ in the **Sketch CommandManager**. The **Ellipse** tool gets activated.
2.   Click to specify the center point of the ellipse, see Figure 2.98.
3.   Move the cursor to a distance in the drawing area. A construction circle appears.
4.   Click to define the major axis of the ellipse, see Figure 2.98.
5.   Move the cursor to a distance. The preview of the ellipse appears, see Figure 2.98.
6.   Click to specify the minor axis of the ellipse. The ellipse is drawn.
7.   Right-click in the drawing area and then click on the **Select** option in the shortcut menu that appears to exit the **Ellipse** tool.

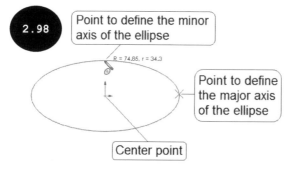

Drawing an Elliptical Arc

You can draw an elliptical arc by using the **Partial Ellipse** tool of the **Ellipse** flyout, see Figure 2.99. To invoke the **Ellipse** flyout, click on the arrow next to the **Ellipse** tool in the **Sketch CommandManager**, see Figure 2.99. Figure 2.100 shows an elliptical arc.

Procedure for Drawing an Elliptical Arc

1. Invoke the **Ellipse** flyout and then click on the **Partial Ellipse** tool, refer to Figure 2.99.
2. Click to specify the center point of the elliptical arc in the drawing area.
3. Move the cursor to a distance in the drawing area. A reference circle appears.
4. Click to define the major axis of the elliptical arc in the drawing area and then move the cursor to a distance. The preview of an imaginary ellipse appears, see Figure 2.101.
5. Click to specify the start point of the elliptical arc in the drawing area, see Figure 2.102.
6. Move the cursor to a distance in the drawing area. The preview of the elliptical arc appears, see Figure 2.102.
7. Click to specify the endpoint of the elliptical arc. The elliptical arc is created, see Figure 2.103.
8. Right-click in the drawing area and then click on the **Select** option in the shortcut menu that appears to exit the **Partial Ellipse** tool.

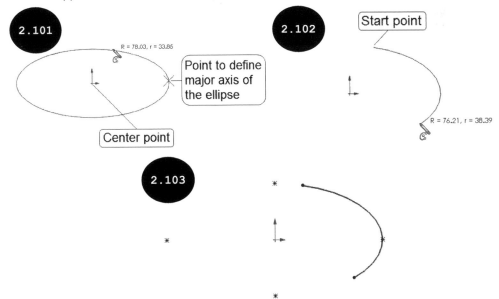

Drawing a Parabola

A Parabola is a symmetrical plane curve formed by the intersection of a cone and a plane parallel to its side. You can draw a parabola by defining its focus point, apex point, and two points (start point and endpoint) on the parabolic curve, see Figure 2.104. You can draw a parabola by using the **Parabola** tool of the **Ellipse** flyout.

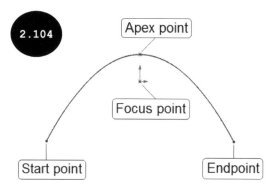

Procedure for Drawing a Parabola

1.   Invoke the **Ellipse** flyout and then click on the **Parabola** tool. The **Parabola** tool gets activated.
2.   Click to specify the focus point of the parabola in the drawing area, see Figure 2.105.
3.   Move the cursor to a distance. A construction parabola appears and the cursor is attached at its apex, see Figure 2.105.
4.   Click to specify the apex of the parabola. The preview of an imaginary parabola appears.
5.   Move the cursor over the imaginary parabola and then click to specify the start point of the parabola, see Figure 2.106.
6.   Move the cursor clockwise or counterclockwise. The preview of the parabolic arc appears in the drawing area, depending upon the movement of the cursor.
7.   Click to specify the endpoint of the parabola. The parabola is drawn, see Figure 2.106.
8.   Right-click in the drawing area and then click on the **Select** option in the shortcut menu that appears to exit the tool.

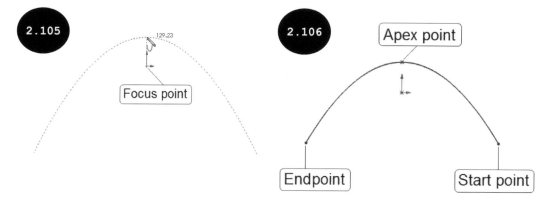

Drawing Conic Curves

SOLIDWORKS allows you to draw conic curves by specifying the start point, endpoint, top vertex, and Rho value, see Figure 2.107. You can draw conic curves by using the **Conic** tool in the **Ellipse** flyout.

Procedure for Drawing Conic Curves

1. Click on the **Conic** tool in the **Ellipse** flyout. The **Conic** tool gets activated.
2. Click to specify the start point of the curve in the drawing area, see Figure 2.108.
3. Move the cursor to a distance in the drawing area. A construction line appears.
4. Click to specify the endpoint of the curve, see Figure 2.108.
5. Move the cursor to a distance in the drawing area. The preview of the conic curve appears, see Figure 2.108.
6. Click to specify the top vertex of the conic curve, see Figure 2.109.
7. Move the cursor upward or downward to a distance. The preview of the conic curve appears in the drawing area. Also, the current Rho value of the curve appears near the cursor, see Figure 2.109.

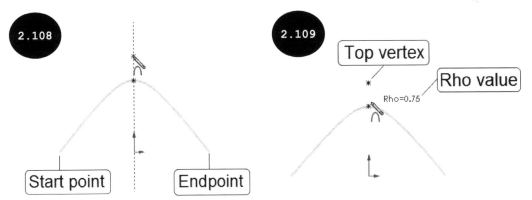

8. Move the cursor at the location where the Rho value appears closer to the required one and then click to specify the apex of the conic curve, see Figure 2.110.

Note: The Rho value of the conic curve defines the type of curve. If the Rho value is less than 0.5 then the conic curve will be an ellipse. If the Rho value is equal to 0.5 then the conic curve will be a parabola. If the Rho value is greater than 0.5 then the conic curve will be a hyperbola.

9. Right-click in the drawing area and then click on the **Select** option in the shortcut menu that appears to exit the **Conic** tool.

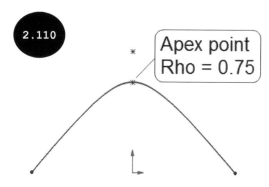

Drawing a Spline

A Spline is defined as a curve having high degree of smoothness and is used for creating free form features. You can draw a spline by specifying two or more than two control points in the drawing area. In SOLIDWORKS, you can also draw a spline by defining mathematical equations. The different tools for drawing splines are discussed next.

Spline Tool

The **Spline** tool is used for creating a spline by defining two or more than two control points in the drawing area, see Figure 2.111. Note that the spline is created such that it passes through the specified control points.

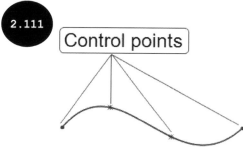

Procedure for Drawing a Spline by using the Spline Tool

1. Click on the **Spline** tool in the **Sketch CommandManager**. The **Spline** tool gets activated and the cursor changes to spline cursor ⟩.
2. Click to specify the first control point of the spline in the drawing area.
3. Move the cursor to a distance. A reference curve appears in the drawing area with one end fixed at the specified point and the other end attached to the cursor.
4. Click to specify the second control point of the spline and then move the cursor to a distance. The preview of the spline curve appears in the drawing area such that it passes through the specified control points, see Figure 2.112.
5. Click to specify the third control point of the spline. The preview of the curve, passing through the three control points, appears in the drawing area. You can continue specifying control points for drawing the spline in a similar manner.
6. Once all control points have been specified for drawing the spline, right-click and then click on the **Select** option in the shortcut menu that appears to exit the tool. Figure 2.113 shows a spline drawn by specifying five control points in the drawing area.

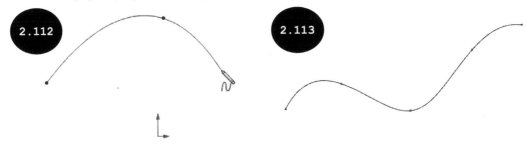

Equation Driven Curve Tool

The **Equation Driven Curve** tool is used for creating an equation driven spline. For doing so, click on the arrow next to the **Spline** tool in the **Sketch CommandManager**. The **Spline** flyout appears, see Figure 2.114. Next, click on the **Equation Driven Curve** tool in the **Spline** flyout. The **Equation Driven Curve PropertyManager** appears on the left of the drawing area, see Figure 2.115. The options in this PropertyManager are discussed next.

Message

The **Message** rollout of the PropertyManager displays appropriate information about the action to be taken for drawing the equation driven spline.

Equation Type

The **Equation Type** rollout is used for selecting the type of equation for drawing a spline. The options in this rollout are discussed next.

Explicit

The **Explicit** radio button is used for creating a spline by defining an equation for calculating the 'Y' values of the control points as the function of 'X'. You can define the equation in the **Parameters** rollout of the PropertyManager. The procedure for creating a spline by selecting this radio button is discussed later in this section.

Parametric

The **Parametric** radio button is used for creating a spline by defining two equations. The first equation calculates the 'X' values and the second equation calculates the 'Y' values of the control points as the function of 't'. You can define the equations in the **Parameters** rollout of the PropertyManager. The procedure to create a spline by selecting this radio button is discussed later in this section.

Parameters

The **Parameters** rollout is used for defining driving equations, and the start and end function values. The availability of options in this rollout depends on the type of radio button (**Explicit** or **Parametric**) selected in the **Equation Type** rollout of the PropertyManager, see Figures 2.116 and 2.117.

When the **Explicit** radio button is selected, you can define an equation for 'Y' as the function of 'X' in the **Yx** field of the **Equation** area in the rollout. Also, you can define the start and end values for the function 'X' in the **X1** and **X2** fields of the rollout.

When the **Parametric** radio button is selected, you can define equations for 'X' and 'Y' as the functions of 't' in the **Xt** and **Yt** fields of the **Parameters** rollout. Also, you can define the start and end values for the function 't' in the **t1** and **t2** fields. The procedures for drawing equation driven spline by using the explicit and parameter equation types are discussed next.

Procedure for Drawing an Explicit Equation Spline

1. Click on the **Equation Driven Curve** tool in the **Spline** flyout. The **Equation Driven Curve** PropertyManager appears.
2. Make sure that the **Explicit** radio button is selected in the **Equation Type** rollout.
3. Enter the equation for 'Y' as the function of 'X' in the **Yx** field of the **Parameters** rollout. For example, enter the equation '2* sin(x)^12' in the **Yx** field.
4. Enter start and end values of the function 'X' in the x1 and x2 fields. For example, enter 'o' in the X1 field and '38' in the X2 field as the start and end function values, respectively.
5. Press ENTER. The preview of the equation driven spline appears in the drawing area.
6. Click on the green tick-mark ✓ button in the PropertyManager. The equation driven spline is drawn, see Figure 2.118.

2.118

Procedure for Drawing a Parametric Equation Spline

1. Click on the **Equation Driven Curve** tool in the **Spline** flyout. The **Equation Driven Curve** PropertyManager appears.
2. Select the **Parametric** radio button in the **Equation Type** rollout.
3. Enter equations for 'X' and 'Y' as the functions of 't' in the **Xt** and **Yt** fields of the **Parameters** rollout, respectively. For example, enter '(t + sin(t)^2)' in the **Xt** field and '2* sin(t)' in the **Yt** field of the PropertyManager.
4. Enter start and end values of the function 't' in the t1 and t2 fields of the **Parameters** area. For example, enter 'o' in the t1 field and '38' in the t2 field as the start and end values, respectively.
5. Press ENTER. The preview of the equation driven spline appears in the drawing area.
6. Click on the green tick-mark ✓ button in the PropertyManager to accept the creation of spline and to exit the PropertyManager. Figure 2.119 shows a spline drawn by selecting the **Parametric** radio button.

2.119

Style Spline Tool

The **Style Spline** tool is used for creating bezier splines of 3 degrees, 5 degrees, and 7 degrees by defining control points in the drawing area, see Figure 2.120. A bezier spline is created such that it passes near the control points specified in the drawing area and is used for creating smooth and complex shaped features. Note that minimum number of control points required to create bezier splines of 3 degrees, 5 degrees, and 7 degrees are 4, 6, and 8, respectively.

2.120

3 degrees bezier spline   5 degrees bezier spline   7 degrees bezier spline

Procedure for Drawing a Style/Bezier Spline

1. Click on the **Style Spline** tool in the **Spline** flyout. The **Insert Style Spline PropertyManager** appears, see Figure 2.121.
2. Select the **Bezier, B-Spline: Degree 3, B-Spline: Degree 5,** or **B-Spline: Degree 7** radio button in the PropertyManager, see Figure 2.121.
3. Click to specify the first control point of the spline in the drawing area.
4. Move the cursor to a distance and then click to specify the second control point of the spline.
5. Click to specify the third control point of the spline. The preview of the spline appears in the drawing area such that it passes near the specified control points, see Figure 2.122. You can continue specifying control points for drawing the spline in the drawing area in a similar manner.

2.121

2.122

6. Once all control points have been specified for drawing the spline, right-click and then click on the **Select** option in the shortcut menu that appears to exit the tool.

Fit Spline Tool

The **Fit Spline** tool is used for converting multiple sketch entities into a single spline curve. To convert the sketch entities into a spline, click on the **Tools > Spline Tools > Fit Spline** in the SOLIDWORKS Menus. The **Fit Spline PropertyManager** appears, see Figure 2.123. The options in the **Fit Spline PropertyManager** are discussed next.

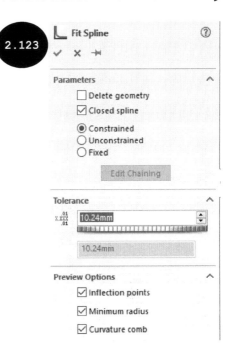

Parameters

The options in the **Parameters** rollout of the PropertyManager are used for specifying different parameters for converting sketch entities into a spline curve. The options are discussed next.

Delete geometry
On selecting the **Delete geometry** check box, the original/parent selected entities will be deleted from the drawing area and the resultant spline will be created.

Constrained
By default, the **Constrained** radio button is selected. As a result, the parametric links are applied between the original sketch entities and the resultant spline curve. Therefore, a change made in the original entities will also reflect in the spline and vice-versa.

Unconstrained
On selecting the **Unconstrained** radio button, the parametric links between the original sketch entities and the resultant spline curve will be broken. As a result, a change made in the original entities will not reflect in the spline and vice-versa.

Fixed
On selecting the **Fixed** radio button, the fixed relation will be applied to the resultant spline. As a result, changes such as position, dimensions, and so on cannot be made to the resultant spline. However, the original entities will be free to change, which is unconstrained with the resultant spline curve.

Closed spline
By default, the **Closed spline** check box is selected. As a result, a closed spline will be created by closing the open ends of the selected entities. Figures 2.124 and 2.125 show the preview of a resultant spline with the **Closed spline** check box cleared and checked, respectively.

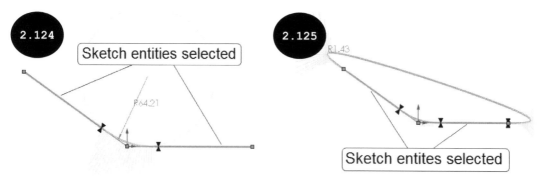

Edit Chaining

The **Edit Chaining** button is used for altering the creation of a chain of contiguous splines. Note that this button is activated only on selecting non-contiguous entities. Figure 2.126 shows non-contiguous entities (entities that are not in contact with each other). Figure 2.127 shows the preview of the default resultant contiguous spline and Figure 2.128 shows the preview of the resulting contiguous spline that appears on clicking the **Edit Chaining** button.

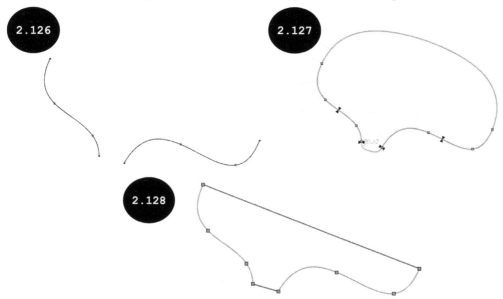

Tolerance

The **Tolerance** rollout is used for specifying the maximum deviation allowed for the original sketch entities. You can enter tolerance value in the **Tolerance** field of this rollout. You can also drag the thumbwheel on the bottom of the **Tolerance** field to set the tolerance value.

Preview Options
The options in this rollout are used for controlling the preview of the resultant spline and are discussed next.

Inflection points
By default, the **Inflection points** check box is selected. As a result, the preview of the spline appears with inflection points where the concavity of the spline changes. You can click on an inflection point to check for an alternative solution.

Minimum radius
By default, the **Minimum radius** check box is selected. As a result, the preview of the spline appears with minimum radius measurement on the spline.

Curvature comb
By default, the **Curvature comb** check box is selected. As a result, the visual enhancement of the slope as well as the curvature appears in the drawing area.

Procedure for Drawing a Fit Spline
1. Click on the **Tools > Spline Tools > Fit Spline** in the SOLIDWORKS Menus. The **Fit Spline PropertyManager** appears.
2. Select sketch entities to be converted into a spline, see Figure 2.129. The preview of the fit spline appears in the drawing area.
3. Specify parameters for creating fit spline, as required by using the options in the **Fit Spline PropertyManager**.
4. Click on the green tick-mark ✓ button in the PropertyManager. The fit spline is created. Figure 2.130 shows an open fit spline created with its original sketched entities deleted.

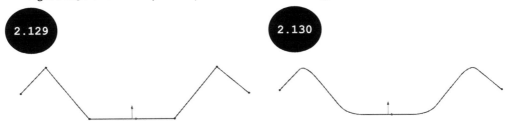

Editing a Spline
Editing a spline is important in order to achieve the complex shape and maintain the high degree of smoothness and curvature. You can edit a spline by using its control points and spline handle. Control points are the points which are specified in the drawing area for drawing the spline. To modify or edit a spline by using control points, click on the control point of the spline to be modified. The selected control point gets highlighted and appears with spline handles in the drawing area, see Figure 2.131. Also, the **Point PropertyManager** appears to the left of the drawing area. You can drag the selected control point by pressing and holding the left mouse button to change its location in the drawing area. Alternatively, enter the new X and Y coordinate values of the selected control point in the respective fields of the **Control Vertex Parameters** rollout of the **Point PropertyManager**.

You can use the spline handle to edit the curvature of a spline. Figure 2.132 shows the spline handle components. The different components of a spline handle are discussed next.

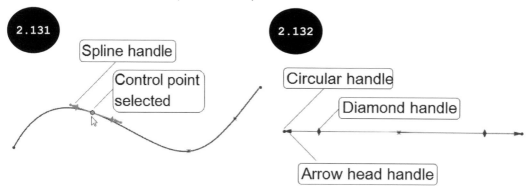

Circular handle

The circular handles of a spline handle are used for controlling the tangency, curvature, and angle of inclination of the spline, asymmetrically about the control point by dragging the spline handle. If you drag a circular handle by pressing the ALT key, the tangency, curvature, and the angle of inclination of the spline are controlled, symmetrically about the control point.

Arrow head handle

The arrow head handles of a spline handle are used for controlling the tangency of the spline, asymmetrically about the control point by dragging it. If you drag the arrow head handle by pressing the ALT key, the tangency is controlled, symmetrically about the control point.

Diamond handle

The diamond handles of a spline handle are used for controlling the tangent vector or the tangency angle of the spline by dragging it.

Modifying the Tangency Direction of Arc/Spline

In SOLIDWORKS, you can reverse/flip the tangency direction of an arc or a spline, see Figure 2.133. For doing so, right-click on the tangent arc/spline whose tangency direction is to be flipped and then click on the **Reverse Endpoint Tangent** tool in the shortcut menu that appears.

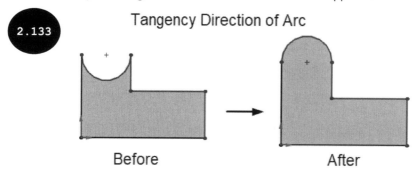

Tutorial 3

Draw a sketch of the model shown in Figure 2.134. The dimensions and the 3D model shown in the figure are for your reference only. All dimensions are in mm. You will learn about applying dimensions and creating the 3D model in later chapters.

Section 1: Starting SOLIDWORKS

1. Start SOLIDWORKS by double-clicking on the SOLIDWORKS icon on your desktop. The startup user interface of SOLIDWORKS appears along with the **Welcome** dialog box, see Figure 2.135.

Note: If SOLIDWORKS is already open and the **Welcome** dialog box does not appear on the screen, then you can invoke the **Welcome** dialog box by clicking on the **Welcome to SOLIDWORKS** tool 🏠 in the **Standard** toolbar or by pressing the CTRL + F2 keys.

Section 2: Invoking the Sketching Environment

1.   Click on the **Part** button in the **Welcome** dialog box. The Part modeling environment is invoked.

2.   Click on the **Sketch** tab in the CommandManager, see Figure 2.136. The tools of the **Sketch CommandManager** appear.

3.   Click on the **Sketch** tool in the **Sketch CommandManager**, see Figure 2.136. Three default planes mutually perpendicular to each other appear in the graphics area.

4.   Move the cursor over the Front plane and then click the left mouse button when the boundary of the plane gets highlighted. The Sketching environment is invoked. Also, the Front plane is orientated normal to the viewing direction.

As all the sketch entities are multiples of 5 mm, you need to set the snap settings such that the cursor snaps to an increment of 5 mm only.

Section 3: Specifying Units, Grids, and Snap Settings

1.   Click on the **Options** tool ⚙ in the **Standard** toolbar. The **System Options - General** dialog box appears.

2.   Click on the **Document Properties** tab in the **System Options - General** dialog box. The name of the dialog box changes to **Document Properties - Drafting Standard**.

3.   Click on the **Units** option in the left panel of the dialog box. The options for specifying the unit system appear on the right panel of the dialog box.

4.   Make sure that the **MMGS (millimeter, gram, second)** radio button is selected in the **Unit system** area of the dialog box.

Now, you need to specify the grids and snap settings such that the cursor snaps to an increment of 5 mm.

5.   Click on the **Grid/Snap** option in the left panel of the dialog box. The options for specifying the grids and snap settings appear on the right panel of the dialog box. Also, the name of the dialog box changes to **Document Properties - Grid/Snap**.

6. Enter **20** in the **Major grid spacing** field, **4** in the **Minor-lines per major** field, and **1** in the **Snap points per minor** field of the **Grid** area in the dialog box.

7. Select the **Display grid** check box in the **Grid** area of the dialog box to turn on the display of grids in the drawing area.

8. Click on the **Go To System Snaps** button in the **Document Properties - Grid/Snap** dialog box. The name of the dialog box changes to **System Options - Relations/Snaps**.

9. Make sure that the **Grid** check box and the **Angle** check box are selected in the **Sketch snaps** area of the dialog box.

10. Make sure that the snap angle value is specified as 45 degrees in the **Snap angle** field of the dialog box.

11. Click on the **OK** button in the dialog box. The grids and snap settings are specified and the dialog box is closed. Also, grids appear in the drawing area, see Figure 2.137.

2.137

Section 4: Drawing the Sketch

Once the units, grids, and snap settings have been specified, you need to start drawing the sketch.

1. Click on the **Circle** tool in the **Sketch CommandManager**. The **Circle** tool gets activated and the **Circle PropertyManager** appears on the left of the drawing area. Also, the appearance of the cursor changes to circle cursor .

2. Move the cursor to the origin and then click to specify the center point of the circle when the cursor snaps to the origin.

3. Move the cursor horizontally toward right and then click to specify a point when the radius of the circle appears 25 mm near the cursor, see Figure 2.138. A circle of radius 25 mm is drawn. Next, press the **ESC** key to exit the **Circle** tool.

4. Invoke the **Arc** flyout by clicking on the arrow next to the active arc tool in the **Sketch CommandManager**, see Figure 2.139.

5. Click on the **Centerpoint Arc** tool in the **Arc** flyout. The **Centerpoint Arc** tool gets activated and the **Arc PropertyManager** appears on the left of the drawing area.

6. Move the cursor to the origin and then click to specify the center point of the arc when the cursor snaps to the origin.

7. Move the cursor horizontally toward right. The preview of an imaginary circle appears in the drawing area, see Figure 2.140. Next, click to specify the start point of the arc when the radius of the imaginary circle appears 35 mm near the cursor, see Figure 2.140.

8. Move the cursor in the clockwise direction. The preview of an arc appears in the drawing area. Next, click to specify the endpoint of the arc when the angle value appears 180 degrees near the cursor, see Figure 2.141. The arc is drawn. Next, press the ESC key to exit the tool.

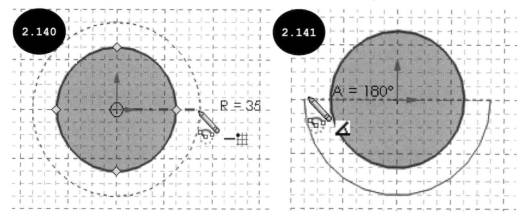

9. Click on the **Line** tool in the **Sketch CommandManager**. The **Line** tool gets activated.

10. Move the cursor to the start point of the previously drawn arc and then click the left mouse button when the cursor snaps to it, see Figure 2.142.

11. Move the cursor vertically upward and click when the length of the line appears 20 mm near the cursor. A line of length 20 mm is drawn.

12. Move the cursor horizontally toward left and click when the length of the line appears 5 mm.

13. Move the cursor vertically upward and click when the length of the line appears 60 mm, see Figure 2.143.

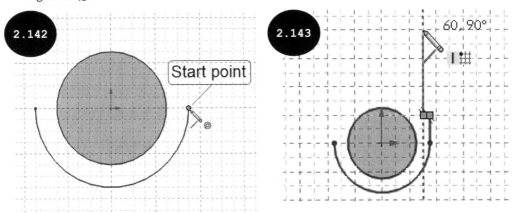

14. Move the cursor horizontally toward left and click when the length of the line appears 10 mm.

15. Move the cursor vertically downward and click when the length of the line appears 5 mm.

16. Move the cursor horizontally toward left and click when the length of the line appears 40 mm.

17. Move the cursor vertically upward and click when the length of the line appears 5 mm.

18. Move the cursor horizontally toward left and click when the length of the line appears 10 mm.

19. Move the cursor vertically downward and click when the length of the line appears 60 mm.

20. Move the cursor horizontally toward left and click when the length of the line appears 5 mm.

21. Move the cursor vertically downward and click when the cursor snaps to the endpoint of the arc. The sketch appears similar to the one shown in Figure 2.144. Next, press the **ESC** key to exit the **Line** tool.

22. Invoke the **Rectangle** flyout, see Figure 2.145 and then click on the **Corner Rectangle** tool.

23. Move the cursor in the drawing area and then click the left mouse button when the coordinates (X, Y, Z) appear "**20, 65, 0**" respectively in the Status Bar, which is available at the bottom of the screen, see Figure 2.146.

24. Move the cursor toward the left and click to specify the second corner point of the rectangle when "**X = 40**" and "**Y = 10**" values appear near the cursor, see Figure 2.147. Next, press the **ESC** key to exit the tool. Figure 2.148 shows the final sketch of Tutorial 3.

Section 5: Saving the Sketch

1. Click on the **Save** tool 🖫 in the **Standard** toolbar. The **Save As** dialog box appears.

2. Browse to **SOLIDWORKS > Chapter 2** folder in the local drive of your system. Note that you need to create these folders, if not created earlier.

3. Enter **Tutorial 3** in the **File name** field of the dialog box.

4. Click on the **Save** button in the dialog box. The sketch is saved with the name Tutorial 3.

Tutorial 4

Draw a sketch of the model shown in Figure 2.149. The dimensions and the model shown in the figure are for your reference only. All dimensions are in mm. You will learn about applying dimensions and creating the 3D model in later chapters.

2.149

Section 1: Starting SOLIDWORKS

1. Start SOLIDWORKS by double-clicking on the SOLIDWORKS icon on your desktop. The startup user interface of SOLIDWORKS appears along with the **Welcome** dialog box.

> **Note:** If SOLIDWORKS is already open and the **Welcome** dialog box does not appear on the screen, then you can invoke the **Welcome** dialog box by clicking on the **Welcome to SOLIDWORKS** tool 🏠 in the **Standard** toolbar or by pressing the CTRL + F2 keys.

Section 2: Invoking the Sketching Environment

1. Click on the **Part** button in the **Welcome** dialog box. The Part modeling environment is invoked.

> **Tip:** You can also invoke the Part modeling environment by using the **New SOLIDWORKS Document** dialog box. For doing so, click on the **New** tool in the **Standard** toolbar. The **New SOLIDWORKS Document** dialog box appears. In this dialog box, make sure that the **Part** button is selected and then click on the **OK** button.

2. Click on the **Sketch** tab in the CommandManager, see Figure 2.150. The tools of the **Sketch CommandManager** appear.

2.150

3.   Click on the **Sketch** tool in the **Sketch CommandManager**. Three default planes mutually perpendicular to each other, appear in the graphics area.

4.   Move the cursor over the Front plane and then click the left mouse button when the boundary of the plane gets highlighted. The Sketching environment is invoked. Also, the Front plane is orientated normal to the viewing direction.

As all the sketch entities are multiples of 5 mm, you need to set the snap settings such that the cursor snaps to an increment of 5 mm. Also, specify the metric unit system for the measurement.

Section 3: Specifying Unit, Grid, and Snap Settings

1.   Click on the **Options** tool ⚙ in the **Standard** toolbar. The **System Options - General** dialog box appears.

2.   Click on the **Document Properties** tab in the **System Options - General** dialog box. The name of the dialog box changes to **Document Properties - Drafting Standard**.

3.   Click on the **Units** option in the left panel of the dialog box. The options for specifying the unit system appear on the right panel of the dialog box.

4.   Make sure that the **MMGS (millimeter, gram, second)** radio button is selected in the **Unit system** area of the dialog box.

Now, you need to specify the grids and snap settings.

5.   Click on the **Grid/Snap** option in the left panel of the dialog box. The options for specifying the grids and snap settings appear on the right panel of the dialog box.

6.   Enter **20** in the **Major grid spacing** field, **4** in the **Minor-lines per major** field, and **1** in the **Snap points per minor** field of the **Grid** area in the dialog box.

7.   Select the **Display grid** check box in the **Grid** area of the dialog box to turn on the display of grids in the drawing area.

8.   Click on the **Go To System Snaps** button in the dialog box.

9.   Make sure that the **Grid** check box and the **Angle** check box are selected in the **Sketch snaps** area of the dialog box.

10. Make sure that the snap angle value is specified as 45 degrees in the **Snap angle** field of the dialog box.

11. Click on the **OK** button in the dialog box. The grids and snap settings are specified and the dialog box is closed. Also, grids appear in the drawing area.

Once the units, grids, and snap settings have been specified, you can start drawing the sketch. First, you need to draw the outer loop of the sketch and then the inner slot and the circle of the sketch.

Section 4: Drawing the Outer Loop of the Sketch

1. Invoke the **Arc** flyout in the **Sketch CommandManager**, see Figure 2.151.

2. Click on the **Centerpoint Arc** tool in the **Arc** flyout. The **Centerpoint Arc** tool gets activated.

3. Move the cursor to the origin and then click when the cursor snaps to the origin.

4. Move the cursor horizontally toward right. The preview of an imaginary circle appears in the drawing area. Next, click the left mouse button when the radius of the imaginary circle appears 25 mm near the cursor.

5. Move the cursor in the anti-clockwise direction. The preview of the arc appears in the drawing area. Next, click the left mouse button when the angle value appears 180 degrees near the cursor, see Figure 2.152. Next, press the ESC key to exit the **Centerpoint Arc** tool.

6. Click on the **Line** tool in the **Sketch CommandManager**. The **Line** tool gets activated.

7. Move the cursor to the start point of the previously drawn arc and then click the left mouse button when the cursor snaps to it, see Figure 2.153.

8. Move the cursor horizontally toward right and click when the length of the line appears 35 mm near the cursor, see Figure 2.154.

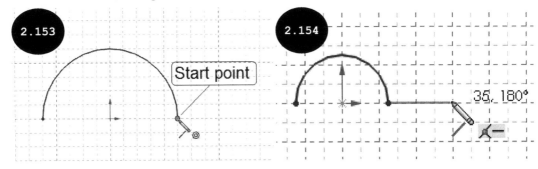

9.   Move the cursor vertically upward and click when the length of the line appears 10 mm.

10. Move the cursor horizontally toward right and click when the length of the line appears 25 mm.

11. Move the cursor vertically upward and click when the length of the line appears 10 mm.

12. Move the cursor horizontally toward left and click when the length of the line appears 10 mm.

13. Move the cursor vertically upward and click when the length of the line appears 105 mm.

14. Move the cursor to a distance and then move it back to the last specified point. An orange colored dot appears in the drawing area, see Figure 2.155.

15. Move the cursor vertically upward to a distance and then move it horizontally toward left. The arc mode is activated and the preview of the tangent arc appears, see Figure 2.156.

16. Click to specify the endpoint of the arc when the angle and radius values of the arc appear 180 degrees and 55 mm, respectively near the cursor, see Figure 2.156.

17. Move the cursor vertically downward and click when the length of the line appears 125 mm.

18. Move the cursor horizontally toward right and click when the cursor snaps to the endpoint of the arc. The outer loop of the sketch is drawn, see Figure 2.157. Next, press the ESC key.

Section 5: Drawing the Slot and the Circle of the Sketch

1.   Click on the **Circle** tool in the **Sketch CommandManager**. The **Circle** tool gets activated and the **Circle PropertyManager** appears on the left of the drawing area.

2.   Move the cursor in the drawing area and then click the left mouse button when the coordinates (X, Y, Z) appear "**0, 120, 0**" respectively in the Status Bar, which is available at the bottom of the screen, see Figure 2.158.

3.   Move the cursor horizontally toward right and click when the radius of the circle appears 20 mm, see Figure 2.159. The circle of radius 20 mm is drawn. Next, press the ESC key to exit the **Circle** tool.

After creating the circle, you need to create the slot.

4.   Invoke the **Slot** flyout in the **Sketch CommandManager** and then click on the **Centerpoint Arc Slot** tool, see Figure 2.160. The **Centerpoint Arc slot** tool gets activated.

5.   Move the cursor to the center point of the previously drawn circle and then click the left mouse button when the cursor snaps to it.

6.   Move the cursor at the location where the coordinates "-10, 70, and 0" appear in the Status Bar and then click the left mouse button at that location in the drawing area.

7.   Move the cursor to a distance in the anti-clockwise direction. The preview of the arc appears. Next, click the left mouse button when coordinates "50, 110, 0" appear in the Status Bar.

8.   Move the cursor to a distance in the drawing area. The preview of the slot arc appears in the drawing area. Next, click the left mouse button when the width of the slot appears close to 20 mm in the **Slot Width** field of the **Slot PropertyManager**.

9.   Enter **20** in the **Slot Width** field of the **Slot PropertyManager**, see Figure 2.161. The slot of width 20 mm is drawn, see Figure 2.162.

10. Click on the green tick-mark ✓ button in the PropertyManager. The final sketch of Tutorial 4 is shown in Figure 2.162.

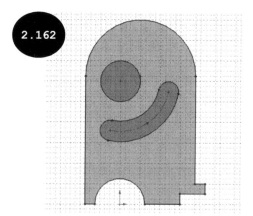

Section 6: Saving the Sketch

After creating the sketch, you need to save it.

1.   Click on the **Save** tool 💾 in the **Standard** toolbar. The **Save As** dialog box appears.

2.   Browse to the Chapter 2 folder of the SOLIDWORKS folder. You need to create these folders, if not created earlier in the local drive of your system.

3.   Enter **Tutorial 4** in the **File name** field of the dialog box and then click on the **Save** button. The sketch is saved with the name Tutorial 4.

Hands-on Test Drive 3

Draw a sketch of the model shown in Figure 2.163. The dimensions and the 3D model shown in the figure are for your reference only. All dimensions are in mm.

Hands-on Test Drive 4

Draw a sketch of the model shown in Figure 2.164. The dimensions and the 3D model shown in the figure are for your reference only. All dimensions are in mm.

Summary

In this chapter, you have learned that the Sketching environment is invoked within the Part modeling environment. To invoke the Sketching environment, you need to select a plane as the sketching plane. Once the Sketching environment has been invoked, you can specify the unit system as per your requirement by using the **Document Properties - Units** dialog box as well as specify the grids and snaps settings. This chapter discusses the drawing of sketches using different sketching tools such as **Line**, **Arc**, **Circle**, **Rectangle**, and **Spline** in addition to editing a spline and flipping the tangency direction of an arc or a spline.

Questions

- Features are divided into two main categories: _____ and _____ .

- The _____ feature of any real world component is a sketch based feature.

- A polygon has number of sides ranging from _____ to _____.

- To draw an ellipse, you need to define its _____ axis and _____ axis.

- If the Rho value of a conic curve is less than 0.5 then the conic is an _____.

- A parabola is a symmetrical plane curve which is formed by the intersection of a cone with a plane parallel to its side. (True/False)

- You cannot draw a tangent arc by using the **Line** tool. (True/False)

- A fillet feature is known as placed feature. (True/False)

Editing and Modifying Sketches

This chapter discusses the following topics:

- Trimming Sketch Entities
- Extending Sketch Entities
- Offsetting Sketch Entities
- Mirroring Sketch Entities
- Patterning Sketch Entities
- Creating a Sketch Fillet
- Creating a Sketch Chamfer
- Adding Text
- Moving a Sketch Entity
- Creating a Copy of Sketch Entities
- Rotating an Entity
- Scaling Sketch Entities
- Stretching an Entity

Editing and modifying a sketch is very important to give the sketch a desired shape. In SOLIDWORKS, various editing operations such as trimming unwanted sketched entities, extending sketch entities, mirroring, patterning, moving, and rotating sketch entities can be performed in the Sketching environment. The various editing operations are discussed next.

Trimming Sketch Entities

You can trim the unwanted sketch entities by using the **Trim Entities** tool of the **Sketch CommandManager**. Besides using this tool for trimming unwanted sketch entities, you can also use this tool to extend sketch entities up to the next intersection. However, in SOLIDWORKS, a separate tool named as **Extend Entities** is also available for extending sketch entities, which is discussed later in this chapter.

To trim sketch entities, click on the **Trim Entities** tool in the **Sketch CommandManager**. The **Trim PropertyManager** appears, see Figure 3.1. The options in this PropertyManager are discussed next.

Message

The **Message** rollout of the PropertyManager displays the information about the action to be taken. The display of information in the **Message** rollout depends on the options selected in the **Options** rollout of the PropertyManager.

Options

The **Options** rollout is provided with various options for trimming sketch entities. The options are discussed next.

Power trim

The **Power trim** button of the **Options** rollout is used for trimming sketch entities by dragging the cursor across the entities to be trimmed. Notice, that when you hold the left mouse button and drag the cursor after activating this button, a light colored tracing line following the cursor appears and the sketch entities coming across the tracing line get trimmed from their nearest intersection. Figure 3.2 shows a sketch before trimming the sketch entities and Figure 3.3 shows the same sketch after trimming the entities coming across the tracing line.

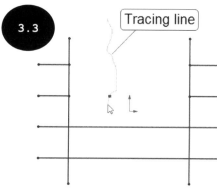

Tracing line

In addition to trimming sketch entities by using the **Power trim** button, you can also extend sketch entities up to their nearest intersection. To extend sketch entities, activate the **Power trim** button. Next, drag the cursor by pressing and holding the **SHIFT** key and the left mouse button. A light colored tracing line following the cursor appears and the entities coming across the tracing line get extended up to their nearest intersection. Figure 3.4 shows a sketch before extending a sketch entity and Figure 3.5 shows the same sketch after extending the entity that comes across the tracing line.

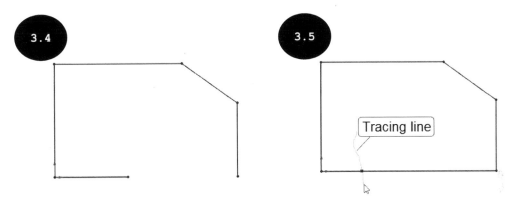

Tip: You can also extend a sketch entity up to a particular distance by using the **Power trim** button. To extend an entity up to a distance, activate the **Power trim** button. Next, click on the entity to be extended in the drawing area and then move the cursor in the required direction. The preview of the extended sketch entity appears. Next, click the left mouse button to specify the endpoint. The selected entity is extended to the specified point.

Corner

The **Corner** button is used for creating a corner between two entities by trimming or extending them. For doing so, click on the **Corner** button in the **Trim PropertyManager** and then select two sketch entities one by one. A corner is created between the selected entities either by trimming or extending them, see Figures 3.6 and 3.7.

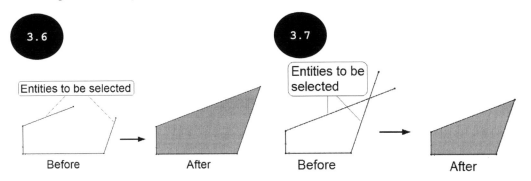

Trim away inside

The **Trim away inside** button is used for trimming entities that lie inside a defined boundary. For doing so, click on the **Trim away inside** button and then select two entities as the boundary entities one by one. Next, select the entities to be trimmed. The portion of the entities lying inside the boundary gets trimmed. Figure 3.8 shows the boundary entities and the entities to be trimmed. Figure 3.9 shows the resultant sketch after trimming the portion of the entities that lies inside the boundary.

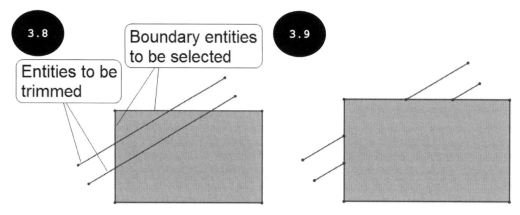

Trim away outside

The **Trim away outside** button is used for trimming the entities that lie outside a defined boundary. For doing so, click on the **Trim away outside** button and then select two entities as the boundary entities one by one. Next, select the entities to be trimmed. The portion of the entities that lies outside the boundary gets trimmed. Figure 3.10 shows the boundary entities and the entities to be trimmed. Figure 3.11 shows the resultant sketch after trimming the portion of the entities that lies outside the boundary.

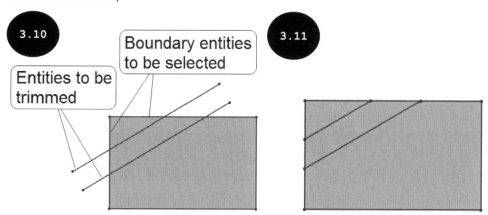

Trim to closest

The **Trim to closest** button is used for trimming sketch entities from their nearest intersection by clicking the left mouse button. For doing so, click on the **Trim to closest** button and then click on the entity to be trimmed. The selected entity is trimmed from its nearest intersection, see Figures 3.12 and 3.13.

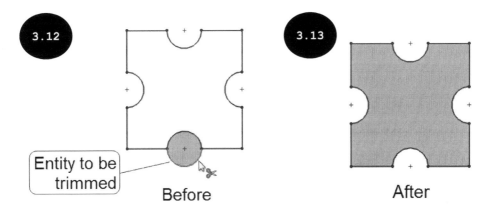

Before

After

Keep trimmed entities as construction geometry
In SOLIDWORKS, you can convert the trimmed entities into a construction geometry by selecting the **Keep trimmed entities as construction geometry** check box of the PropertyManager.

Ignore trimming of construction geometry
In SOLIDWORKS, you can ignore the construction geometries of the sketch while trimming the entities by selecting the **Ignore trimming of construction geometry** check box of the PropertyManager.

Procedure for Trimming Entities by using the Trim Entities Tool
1. Click on the **Trim Entities** tool. The **Trim PropertyManager** appears.
2. Select the required method for trimming entities by activating the respective button in the **Options** rollout of the PropertyManager.
3. Depending upon the button selected in the **Options** rollout, you can trim the sketch entities.

Extending Sketch Entities
You can extend sketch entities up to their nearest intersection by using the **Extend Entities** tool. This tool is available in the **Trim** flyout of the **Sketch CommandManager**, see Figure 3.14. Figure 3.15 shows a sketch entity to be extended and Figure 3.16 shows the resultant sketch after extending the entity. The procedure for extending entities is discussed next.

Entity to be extended

Procedure for Extending Entities by using the Extend Entities Tool

1. Click on the arrow at the bottom of the **Trim Entities** tool in the **Sketch CommandManager**. The **Trim** flyout appears, refer to Figure 3.14. Next, click on the **Extend Entities** tool.
2. Move the cursor over the entity to be extended. The preview of the extended line appears up to their next intersection in the drawing area, see Figure 3.17.

3. Click the left mouse button when the preview of the extended line appears. The selected entity is extended up to the next intersection.
4. Similarly, you can extend other sketch entities. Once you have extended all the sketch entities, press the ESC key to exit the **Extend Entities** tool.

Note: The direction of the extended entity depends upon the position of the cursor over the entity. The endpoint of the entity, which is closer to the position of the cursor will be extended. To change the direction of extension, move the cursor to the other side of the sketch entity.

Offsetting Sketch Entities

You can offset sketch entities or edges at a specified offset distance by using the **Offset Entities** tool. For doing so, click on the **Offset Entities** tool in the **Sketch CommandManager**. The **Offset Entities PropertyManager** appears, see Figure 3.18.

Offset Entities

Once the **Offset Entities PropertyManager** has been invoked, select the entity to be offset in the drawing area. The preview of the offset entity appears with default parameters. You can modify the default parameters by using the options of the PropertyManager. The options of the PropertyManager are discussed next.

Offset Distance

The **Offset Distance** field of the **Parameters** rollout is used for specifying the offset distance.

Tip: Besides controlling the offset distance by using the **Offset Distance** field, you can also dynamically control the offset distance. For doing so, press and hold the left mouse button in the drawing area and then drag the cursor. Note that as you drag the cursor, the offset distance gets modified dynamically in the drawing area. Once the required offset distance has been achieved, release the left mouse button. The offset entity is created at the specified offset distance.

Add dimensions

On selecting the **Add dimensions** check box, the offset dimension is applied to the resultant sketch, see Figure 3.19.

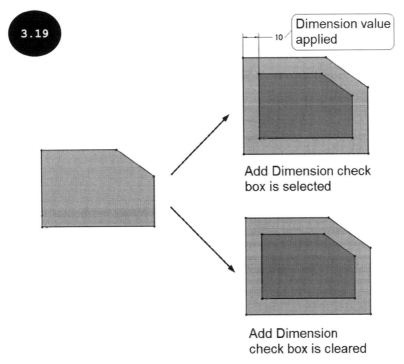

3.19

Dimension value applied

10

Add Dimension check box is selected

Add Dimension check box is cleared

Reverse

On selecting the **Reverse** check box, the direction of offset entities gets reversed.

Select chain

On selecting the **Select chain** check box, all the contiguous entities of the selected entity get selected, automatically in the drawing area.

Bi-directional

On selecting the **Bi-directional** check box, entities get offset on both sides, see Figure 3.20.

Cap ends

On selecting the **Cap ends** check box, the open ends of the offset entities get capped with lines or arcs, see Figures 3.21 and 3.22.

On selecting the **Cap ends** check box, the **Arcs** and **Lines** radio buttons get enabled in the PropertyManager. On selecting the **Arcs** radio button, the offset entities get capped with arcs, see Figure 3.21. If you select the **Lines** radio button, the offset entities get capped with lines, see Figure 3.22.

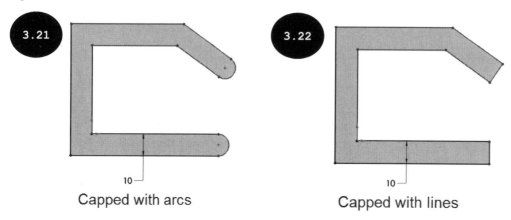

Capped with arcs   Capped with lines

Construction geometry

On selecting the **Base geometry** check box in the **Construction geometry** area, the original/base sketch entities get converted into construction entities, see Figure 3.23 (a). If you select the **Offset geometry** check box, then the resultant offset entities are created as construction entities, see Figure 3.23 (b).

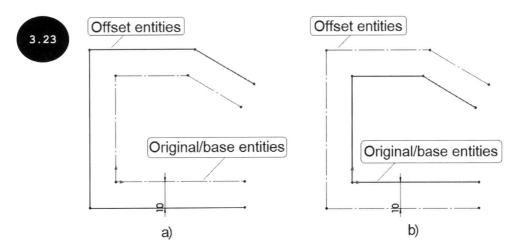

a)   b)

Procedure for Offsetting Entities

1. Invoke the **Offset PropertyManager** by clicking on the **Offset Entities** tool.
2. Select the sketch entities to be offset. The preview of the offset entities appears.
3. Enter the required offset distance value in the **Offset distance** field.
4. Select the **Reverse** check box to reverse the direction of offset, if required.
5. Specify the other parameters for offsetting the entities in the PropertyManager.
6. Click on the green tick-mark ✓ button in the PropertyManager. The offset entities are created.

Mirroring Sketch Entities

In SOLIDWORKS, you can mirror sketch entities about a mirroring line by using the **Mirror Entities** and **Dynamic Mirror** tools. You can select a line, a centerline, a linear edge, a reference plane, or a planar face as the mirroring line. The tools for mirroring sketch entities are discussed next.

Mirroring Entities by using the Mirror Entities Tool

To mirror the sketch entities about a mirroring line by using the **Mirror Entities** tool, click on the **Mirror Entities** tool in the **Sketch CommandManager**. The **Mirror PropertyManager** appears, see Figure 3.24. The options in this PropertyManager are discussed next.

Entities to mirror

The **Entities to mirror** field of the PropertyManager is used for selecting entities to be mirrored. By default, this field is activated. As a result, you can select entities by clicking the left mouse button or by dragging the cursor over the entities to be mirrored. Note that as soon as you select entities, the names of the selected entities appear in this field. You can select entities to be mirrored before or after invoking the PropertyManager.

Copy

By default, the **Copy** check box is selected. As a result, the original/parent sketch entities are retained and the mirror image of the selected entities is created. If you clear this check box, then the original sketch entities are removed in the sketch.

Mirror about

The **Mirror about** field is used for selecting a mirroring line about which the selected entities get mirrored. Click on the **Mirror about** field in the PropertyManager and then select a line, a centerline, a linear edge, a reference plane, or a planar face as the mirroring line. The preview of the mirror image appears in the drawing area. Next, click on the green tick-mark ✓ button in the PropertyManager. The mirror image of the selected entities is created. Figure 3.25 shows entities to be mirrored and a mirroring line. Figure 3.26 shows the resultant sketch after mirroring the entities about the mirroring line.

> **Note:** When you mirror entities, a symmetric relation is applied between the original entities and the mirrored entities with respect to the mirroring line. As a result, on modifying the original entities, the mirrored entities get automatically modified and vice-versa. You will learn more about relations in later chapters.

Procedure for Mirroring Entities by using the Mirror Entities Tool

1. Click on the **Mirror Entities** tool. The **Mirror PropertyManager** appears. ⬚ Mirror Entities
2. Select the entities to be mirrored in the drawing area.
3. Make sure that the **Copy** check box is selected in the PropertyManager.
4. Click on the **Mirror about** field and then select a mirroring line. The preview of the mirror image appears.
5. Click on the green tick-mark ✓ button in the PropertyManager. The mirror image of the selected entities is created.

Mirroring Entities by using the Dynamic Mirror Tool

The **Dynamic Mirror** tool is used for mirroring entities about a mirroring line similar to mirroring entities using the **Mirror Entities** tool with the only difference that this tool dynamically mirrors entities while drawing them.

Procedure for Mirroring Entities by using the Dynamic Mirror Tool

1. Click on **Tools > Sketch Tools > Dynamic Mirror** in the SOLIDWORKS Menus. The **Dynamic Mirror** tool gets activated and the **Mirror PropertyManager** appears.
2. Select a mirroring line. The symbol of dynamic mirror appears on both ends of the selected mirroring line, see Figure 3.27. This symbol indicates that if you draw a sketch entity on either side of the mirroring line, the respective mirror image will automatically be created on the other side of the mirroring line.
3. Draw entities on one side of the mirroring line by using the sketching tools such as **Line** and **Circle**. The respective mirror images of the entities are created dynamically on the other side of the mirroring line, see Figure 3.28.
4. Once you have created the sketch, click on **Tools > Sketch Tools > Dynamic Mirror** in the SOLIDWORKS Menus to exit the **Dynamic Mirror** tool.

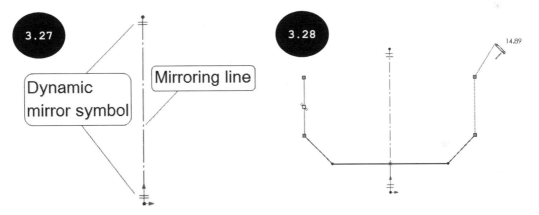

Patterning Sketch Entities

In SOLIDWORKS, you can create linear and circular patterns of sketch entities by using the **Linear Sketch Pattern** and **Circular Sketch Pattern** tools, respectively. Both the tools are discussed next.

Linear Sketch Pattern

The **Linear Sketch Pattern** tool is used for creating multiple instances of a sketch entity in linear directions. For doing so, click on the **Linear Sketch Pattern** tool in the **Sketch CommandManager**. The **Linear Pattern PropertyManager** appears, refer to Figure 3.29.

Once the **Linear Pattern PropertyManager** has been invoked, select a sketch entity or entities to be patterned in the drawing area. The preview of the linear pattern with default parameters appears in the drawing area. You can select the sketch entity to be patterned before or after invoking the PropertyManager. The options in the **Linear Pattern PropertyManager** are used for defining the parameters for creating the linear sketch pattern and are discussed next.

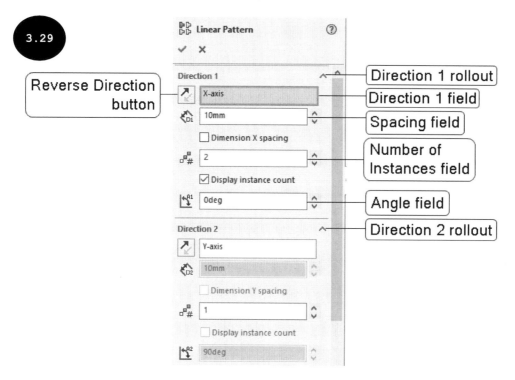

Direction 1

The options in the **Direction 1** rollout of the PropertyManager are used to specify the parameters for patterning sketch entities in direction 1. The options of this rollout are discussed next.

Direction 1

By default, the **X-axis** is selected in the **Direction 1** field of the **Direction 1** rollout. As a result, the selected entities get patterned along the X axis. You can also select a linear edge or a linear sketch entity as direction 1 of the pattern.

Reverse Direction

The **Reverse Direction** button is used for reversing the direction 1 of the pattern.

Spacing

The **Spacing** field is used for specifying the spacing between two pattern instances.

Number of Instances

The **Number of Instances** field is used for specifying number of instances to be created in direction 1.

Note: The number of pattern instances specified in the **Number of Instances** field is counted along with the parent or original instance. For example, if 6 is specified in the **Number of Instances** field, then the 6 pattern instances will be created including the parent instance.

Angle

The **Angle** field is used for specifying an angle for direction 1 with respect to the X axis. By default, a 0 degree angle is specified in this field. As a result, a linear pattern is created along direction 1 at a 0 degree angle, see Figure 3.30. Figure 3.31 shows the preview of the linear pattern along direction 1 (X axis) at a 12 degrees angle.

Note: In the preview of the linear pattern, an arrow appears with a dot at its tip, refer to Figures 3.30 and 3.31. You can also change the orientation or the angle of the pattern direction by dragging this dot in the drawing area.

Dimension X spacing

On selecting the **Dimension X spacing** check box, the distance specified between two pattern instances is applied in the resulting pattern sketch, see Figure 3.32.

Display Instance count

On selecting the **Display instance count** check box, the number of pattern instances specified in direction 1 are displayed in the resultant pattern sketch, see Figure 3.32.

Direction 2

The options in the **Direction 2** rollout are the same as the options in the **Direction 1** rollout with the only difference that the options of the **Direction 2** rollout are used for specifying parameters for the linear pattern in the second direction (direction 2), which is Y axis, by default, see Figure 3.33.

Note: By default, none of the options of the **Direction 2** rollout are enabled except the **Number of Instances** field. This is because 1 is specified in the **Number of Instances** field of the **Direction 2** rollout as the number of pattern instances. On specifying the number of pattern instances as two or more than two, the other options of the **Direction 2** rollout get enabled.

Entities to Pattern

The **Entities to Pattern** field of the **Entities to Pattern** rollout displays the list of entities that are selected for patterning. You can select entities to be patterned before or after invoking the PropertyManager.

Instances to Skip

The **Instances to Skip** rollout of the PropertyManager is used for skipping or removing the unwanted instances of the pattern. To skip instances of the pattern, expand the **Instances to Skip** rollout by clicking on the arrow available in its title bar. Next, click on the field in the expanded **Instances to Skip** rollout to activate it. Pink dots appear in all the instances of the pattern in the drawing area, see Figure 3.34. Next, move the cursor over the pink dot, of the instance to be skipped and then click the left mouse button. The preview of the selected instance gets disabled and is no longer a part of the resultant pattern, see Figure 3.35. Also, the skipped instance appears in the field of the **Instances to Skip** rollout. You can similarly skip multiple instances of the pattern by clicking the left mouse button on the pink dots of instances to be skipped.

Note: To recall the skipped instances of the pattern, click on the dots of the skipped instances that appear in the preview of the pattern. Alternatively, you can select an instance in the field of the **Instances to Skip** rollout and then right-click to display a shortcut menu. Next, click on the **Delete** option in the shortcut menu to remove the selected instance from the list of skipped instances and to recall it.

After defining parameters for patterning the sketch entities in the **Linear Pattern PropertyManager**, click on the green tick-mark button in the PropertyManager. The linear pattern is created.

Procedure for Creating a Linear Pattern

1. Click on the **Linear Sketch Pattern** tool. The **Linear Pattern** PropertyManager appears.

2. Select the entities to be patterned in the drawing area. The preview of the linear pattern along the X axis appears with the default parameters.

3. Reverse the direction of the pattern if required, by clicking on the **Reverse Direction** button.

4. Specify the distance between pattern instances in the **Spacing** field of the **Direction 1** rollout.

5. Specify the number of pattern instances to be created along the X axis in the **Number of Instances** field of the **Direction 1** rollout.

6. Specify the number of pattern instances to be created along the Y axis in the **Number of Instances** field of the **Direction 2** rollout.

7. Specify other parameters such as distance between instances and the number of instances for direction 2 in the respective fields of the **Direction 2** rollout.

8. After specifying all the parameters for creating a linear pattern in direction 1 and direction 2, click on the green tick-mark ☑ button in the PropertyManager. The linear pattern is created.

Circular Sketch Pattern

The **Circular Sketch Pattern** tool is used for creating multiple instances of a sketch entity in a circular manner about a center point. For doing so, invoke the **Pattern** flyout by clicking on the arrow next to the **Linear Sketch Pattern** tool in the **Sketch CommandManager**, see Figure 3.36. Next, click on the **Circular Sketch Pattern** tool. The **Circular Pattern PropertyManager** appears, see Figure 3.37.

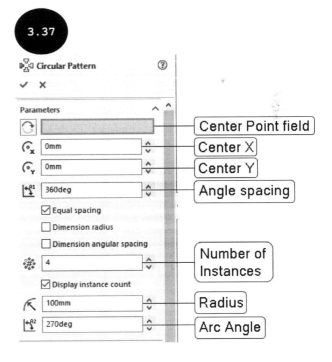

Once the **Circular Pattern PropertyManager** has been invoked, select one or more sketch entities to be patterned in the drawing area. The preview of the circular pattern with default parameters appears, see Figure 3.38. Also, the names of the selected entities appear in the **Entities to Pattern** field of the PropertyManager. You can select entities to be patterned before or after invoking the PropertyManager. The options in the **Circular Pattern PropertyManager** are used for defining parameters for creating the circular sketch pattern. The options are discussed next.

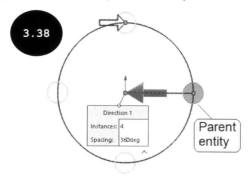

Parameters

The options in the **Parameters** rollout are used for specifying parameters for patterning sketch entities in a circular manner. The options of this rollout are discussed next.

Center Point

The **Center Point** field is used for specifying a center point for patterning the instances, circularly. Note, that as soon as you select entities to be patterned, the origin point (0,0) is selected as the center point of the circular pattern, see Figure 3.38. You can also select any sketch point as the center point of the circular pattern by activating this field.

Center X / Center Y

The **Center X** and **Center Y** fields are used for specifying the X and Y coordinates of the center point, respectively.

Tip: You can also define the center point of the pattern by dragging the dot that appears at the tip of the arrow in the preview of the circular pattern. As you change the location of the dot by dragging it, the coordinates of the center point update accordingly in the **Center X** and **Center Y** fields.

Angle spacing

The **Angle spacing** field is used for specifying the total angle value of the pattern. By default, the value entered in this field is 360 degrees. As a result, a circular pattern is created such that it covers 360 degrees in the pattern and the number of pattern instances are adjusted within the total 360 degrees, equally. This is because the **Equal spacing** check box is selected by default in this rollout.

Equal spacing

By default, the **Equal spacing** check box is selected. As a result, all the pattern instances are adjusted within the total angle value specified in the **Angle spacing** field, equally. However, on clearing this check box, the angle value entered in the **Angle spacing** field is used as the angle between two instances of the pattern.

Dimension radius
On selecting the **Dimension radius** check box, the radius dimension of the circular pattern is applied in the resultant pattern, see Figure 3.39.

Dimension angular spacing
On selecting the **Dimension angular spacing** check box, the angular spacing between two instances is applied in the resultant pattern, see Figure 3.39.

Number of Instances
The **Number of Instances** field is used for specifying the total number of instances in the pattern. Note that the number of instances specified in this field are counted along with the parent instance. In SOLIDWORKS, you can specify number of instances without any limit.

Display instance count
On selecting the **Display instance count** check box, the pattern instances count appears in the resultant pattern, see Figure 3.39.

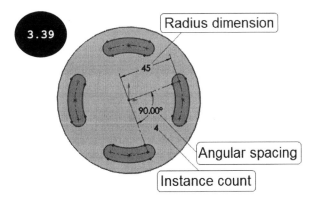

Radius
The **Radius** field is used for specifying the pattern radius. By default, the **Radius** field displays the pattern radius by keeping the origin as the center point. You can change the default radius value by entering a new radius value in this field.

Arc Angle
The **Arc Angle** field is used for specifying the angle value from the center of the selected entities to the center point of the pattern.

Instances to Skip
The **Instances to Skip** rollout of the PropertyManager is used for skipping pattern instances of the circular pattern. For doing so, expand the **Instances to Skip** rollout by clicking on the arrow available in its title bar. Next, click on the field in the expanded **Instances to Skip** rollout. Pink dots appear in all the instances of the pattern in the drawing area, see Figure 3.40. Next, move the cursor over the pink dot of the instance to be skipped and then click the left mouse button.

The preview of the selected instance is disabled and it is no longer a part of the resultant pattern, see Figure 3.41. Also, the pink dot changes to an orange dot and the respective instance number is displayed in the field of the **Instances to Skip** rollout.

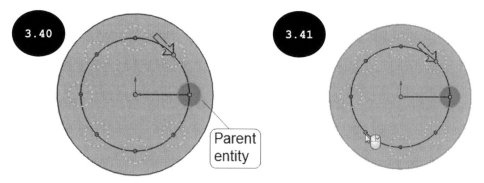

Parent entity

Note: To recall the skipped instances of the pattern, click on the dots of the skipped instances that appear in the preview of the pattern. Alternatively, you can select an instance in the field of the **Instances to Skip** rollout and then right-click to display a shortcut menu. Next, click on the **Delete** option in the shortcut menu to remove the selected instance from the list of skipped instances and to recall it.

After defining the required parameters for patterning the sketch entities in the **Circular Pattern PropertyManager**, click on the green tick-mark ✔ button. The circular pattern is created.

Procedure for Creating the Circular Pattern

1. Click on the **Circular Sketch Pattern** tool in the **Pattern** flyout. The **Circular Pattern PropertyManager** appears.
2. Select the entities to be patterned. The preview of the circular pattern appears such that the origin is selected as the center point of the pattern.
3. Click on the **Reverse Direction** button to reverse the direction of the pattern, if needed.
4. Change the center point of the pattern by dragging the dot that appears at the arrow tip in the preview or by specifying coordinates of the center point in the **Center X** and **Center Y** fields of the PropertyManager, if needed.
5. Specify the total angle value of the pattern or the angle between two instances in the **Angle spacing** field.

Tip: If the **Equal spacing** check box is selected, the angle specified in the **Angle spacing** field measures the total angle between which all the pattern instances are arranged, equally. However, if the **Equal spacing** check box is cleared, the angle specified in the **Angle spacing** field measures the angle between two pattern instances.

6. Specify the number of pattern instances to be created in the **Number of Instances** field.
7. After specifying all the parameters, click on the green tick-mark ✔ button. The circular pattern is created.

Creating a Sketch Fillet

A sketch fillet is used for removing the corner at the intersection of two sketch entities by creating a tangent arc of constant radii, see Figure 3.42. In the Sketching environment, you can create sketch fillets by using the **Sketch Fillet** tool.

Before   After

To create sketch fillets, click on the **Sketch Fillet** tool in the **Sketch CommandManager**, see Figure 3.43. The **Sketch Fillet PropertyManager** appears, see Figure 3.44. Next, enter the fillet radius in the **Fillet Radius** field of the **Fillet Parameters** rollout in the PropertyManager. By default, the **Keep constrained corners** check box is selected in the **Fillet Parameters** rollout. As a result, if the corner/vertex to be filleted has dimensions, then a virtual intersection point is created at the corner to maintain dimensions, whereas if the corner/vertex has relations, then the SOLIDWORKS message window appears which informs that if the fillet is created, the applied relation will be deleted. The **Dimension each fillet** check box of the PropertyManager is used for applying radius dimension to all the fillets created in the drawing area.

After specifying the fillet radius, move the cursor over the corner/vertex of the sketch to be filleted. The preview of fillet appears in the drawing area, see Figure 3.45. Next, click the left mouse button to accept the fillet preview. Similarly, click on the other corners of the sketch to create fillets of specified radius, see Figure 3.46. Next, click on the green tick-mark button ✔ in the PropertyManager. The fillets of specified radius are created at the selected corners of the sketch, see Figure 3.47. By default, the fillet radius is applied to one of the fillets and an equal relation is applied among all the fillets. However, if the **Dimension each fillet** check box is selected in the **Fillet Parameters** rollout of the PropertyManager, then the fillet radius is applied to all the fillets created in the drawing area.

Tip: Instead of selecting a corner to create the fillet, you can also select two intersecting sketch entities for creating the fillet of specified radius at their intersection.

Creating a Sketch Chamfer

A chamfer is a bevel edge that is non-perpendicular to its adjacent sketch entities. You can create a sketch chamfer to the adjacent entities of the sketch by using the **Sketch Chamfer** tool, see Figure 3.48.

To create a sketch chamfer, click on the arrow next to the **Sketch Fillet** tool in the **Sketch CommandManager**. A flyout appears, see Figure 3.49. In this flyout, click on the **Sketch Chamfer** tool. The **Sketch Chamfer PropertyManager** appears, see Figure 3.50.

The **Distance-distance** radio button of the PropertyManager is used for creating a chamfer by specifying distance values from both the adjacent sketch entities in the **Distance 1** and **Distance 2** fields of the PropertyManager, see Figure 3.51. Note that if the **Equal distance** check box is selected in the PropertyManager then the **Distance 2** field is not available in the PropertyManager and the distance value specified in the **Distance 1** field is applied on both sides of the sketch entities, see Figure 3.52.

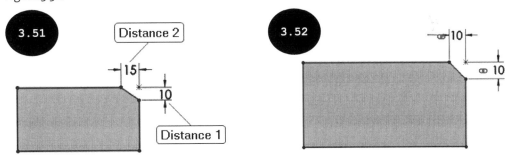

The **Angle-distance** radio button of the PropertyManager is used for creating a chamfer by specifying the angle and distance values in the **Direction 1 Angle** and **Distance 1** fields of the PropertyManager, respectively, see Figure 3.53. After selecting the required radio button (**Distance-distance** or **Angle-distance**) and specifying the required parameters in the PropertyManager, select the adjacent entities of the sketch one by one. The chamfer is created between the selected entities. Note that instead of selecting adjacent entities of the sketch, you can also select a vertex that is created at the intersection of two sketch entities for creating the chamfer. After creating the chamfer, press the ESC key to exit the **Sketch Chamfer** tool.

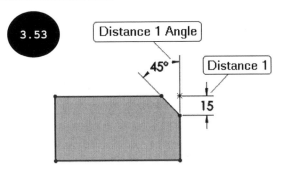

Adding Text

To add text in the sketching environment, click on the Text tool 🄰 in the **Sketch CommandManager**. The **Sketch Text PropertyManager** appears, see Figure 3.54. The options in this PropertyManager are discussed next.

Curves

By default, the **Curves** field is activated in the **Curves** rollout. As a result, you can select edges, curves, sketches, and sketch segments along which the text is to be added. You can select a single or multiple connected sketch entities one by one by clicking the left mouse button.

Text

In the **Text** field of the **Text** rollout, you can enter the required text. Note that as you enter the text, it appears in the drawing area along the selected curve. If a curve is not selected in the **Curves** field of the PropertyManager, then the entered text appears horizontally starting from the origin.

You can use the default document font for the text by selecting the **Use document font** check box. You can also define a font other than the default document font. For doing so, clear the **Use document font** check box and then click on the **Font** button. The **Choose Font** dialog box appears. In this dialog box, select the required font, font style, font height, and so on.

You can also define the width of each text character and the spacing between two text characters by using the **Width Factor** and **Spacing** fields respectively, see Figure 3.55. Note that these fields are enabled when the **Use document font** check box is cleared.

The other options in the **Sketch Text PropertyManager** are used for specifying the text style, text alignment, and for flipping the text horizontally or vertically. Note that some of these options are activated only if an entity is selected in the **Curves** field. After writing the required text and specifying the required settings, click on the green tick-mark in the PropertyManager. The text gets added in the drawing area.

Moving a Sketch Entity

You can move a sketch entity from one position to another in the drawing area by using the **Move Entities** tool. For doing so, click on the **Move Entities** tool in the **Sketch CommandManager**. The **Move PropertyManager** appears, see Figure 3.56. The options in this PropertyManager are discussed next.

Entities to Move

The options in the **Entities to Move** rollout are used for selecting entities to be moved. These options are discussed next.

Sketch items or annotations

The **Sketch items or annotations** field of the **Entities to Move** rollout is used for selecting entities to be moved. By default, this field is activated. As a result, you can select entities to be moved in the drawing area. You can select entities to be moved before or after invoking the PropertyManager. The names of the selected entities are displayed in this field.

Keep relations

The **Keep relations** check box is used for maintaining existing relations between the entities. If the **Keep relations** check box is selected, the existing relations between the sketch entities to be moved and the other entities of the sketch are maintained. However, on clearing this check box, the relations between the sketch entities to be moved and the other entities of the sketch will be broken.

Parameters

The options in the **Parameters** rollout are used for selecting parameters for moving the entities and are discussed next.

From/To

By default, the **From/To** radio button is selected in the **Parameters** rollout. As a result, you can move the selected entities from one location to the other with respect to a base point. To move entities, when this radio button is selected, click on the **Start point** field and then specify a point in the drawing area as the base point for moving the selected entities. As soon as you specify a base point, the selected entities get attached to the cursor and as you move the cursor, the entities move dynamically in the drawing area. Next, click to specify a new position for the selected entities in the drawing area.

X/Y

The X/Y radio button is used for moving sketch entities by specifying translation distances along the X and Y axes from the original location of the entities. When you select the X/Y radio button, the △X and △Y fields get enabled in the rollout. In these fields, you can specify the translation distance along the X and Y axes. Note that the distance specified in the △X and △Y fields is measured from the center point of the original location of the sketch entities.

Repeat

The **Repeat** button is used for moving sketch entities with an incremental distance specified in the △X and △Y fields. Note that every time you click on the **Repeat** button, the selected entities move to the incremental distance that is specified in the △X and △Y fields.

Procedure for Moving Sketch Entities

1. Click on the **Move Entities** tool. The **Move PropertyManager** appears.   ⟦ Move Entities ⟧
2. Select the entities to be moved.
3. Select the **From/To** or X/Y radio button for moving the entities. By default, the **From/To** radio button is selected. As a result, you can move the sketch entities with respect to a base point.
4. Depending upon the radio button selected in Step 3, specify a new position for the sketch entities in the drawing area.

Creating a Copy of Sketch Entities

You can create a copy of a set of sketch entities by using the **Copy Entities** tool. To copy sketch entities, click on the arrow next to the **Move Entities** tool. A flyout appears, see Figure 3.57. In this flyout, click on the **Copy Entities** tool. The **Copy PropertyManager** appears, see Figure 3.58. The options in this PropertyManager are the same as of the **Move PropertyManager** with the only difference that the options in this PropertyManager are used for copying selected entities in the new location.

Procedure for Creating a Copy of Sketch Entities

1. Click on the arrow next to the **Move Entities** tool and then click on the **Copy Entities** tool in the flyout that appears. The **Copy PropertyManager** appears.
2. Select the sketch entities to be copied.
3. Select the **From/To** or **X/Y** radio button in the **Parameters** rollout, as required.
4. Depending upon the radio button selected in Step 3, specify a new location for the entities in the drawing area. The copy of selected entities is created at the specified location.

Rotating an Entity

You can rotate one or more sketch entities at an angle by using the **Rotate Entities** tool. For doing so, click on the arrow next to the **Move Entities** tool. A flyout appears, refer to Figure 3.57. In the flyout, click on the **Rotate Entities** tool. The **Rotate PropertyManager** appears, see Figure 3.59. The options in this PropertyManager are discussed next.

Entities to Rotate

The options of the **Entities to Rotate** rollout are used for selecting entities to be rotated. The options are discussed next.

Sketch items or annotations

The **Sketch items or annotations** field is used for selecting entities to be rotated. By default, this field is activated. As a result, you can select entities to be rotated in the drawing area. You can select entities to be rotated before or after invoking the PropertyManager. The names of the selected entities are displayed in this field.

Keep relations

The **Keep relations** check box is used for maintaining existing relations between sketch entities. If this check box is selected, the existing relations between sketch entities to be rotated and the other entities of the sketch are maintained. However, on clearing this check box, the relations between the sketch entities to be rotated and the other entities of the sketch will be broken.

Parameters

The **Parameters** rollout of the PropertyManager is used for specifying parameters for rotating sketch entities. The options in this rollout are discussed next.

Center of rotation

The **Center of rotation** field is used for specifying a base point or a center point of rotation. For doing so, click on the **Center of rotation** field and then specify a point in the drawing area by clicking the left mouse button. A triad appears in the drawing area, see Figure 3.60. Also, the **Angle** field gets activated below this field in the PropertyManager. Now, you can specify the angle of rotation in the **Angle** field and then press ENTER. The preview of the rotated sketch entities appears in the drawing area. You can also use the spinner arrows ‡ in the **Angle** field to specify the angle of rotation. Next, click on the green tick-mark button ✔ in the PropertyManager. The selected entities get rotated at the specified angle of rotation. Figure 3.60 shows a sketch before or after rotating its slot at an angle of 30 degrees around its center point.

Tip: When you specify a positive angle value, the direction of rotation will be anti-clockwise, whereas, on specifying a negative angle value, the direction of rotation will be clockwise.

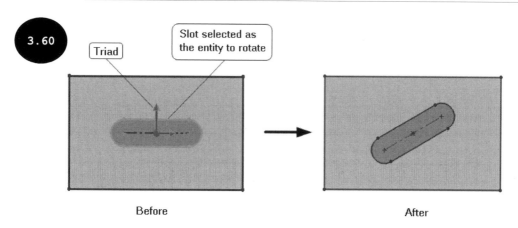

Before   After

Procedure for Rotating Sketch Entities

1.   Click on the arrow next to the **Move Entities** tool and then click on the **Rotate Entities** tool in the flyout that appears. The **Rotate PropertyManager** appears.
2.   Select the sketch entities to be rotated.
3.   Click on the **Center of rotation** field in the PropertyManager and then specify a center point of rotation.
4.   Specify the angle of rotation in the **Angle** field of the PropertyManager.
5.   Click on the green tick-mark ✔ button in the PropertyManager. The selected entities are rotated at the specified angle.

Scaling Sketch Entities

You can increase or decrease the scale of sketch entities by using the **Scale Entities** tool. For doing so, click on the arrow next to the **Move Entities** tool and then click on the **Scale Entities** tool in the flyout that appears. The **Scale PropertyManager** appears, see Figure 3.61. The options in this PropertyManager are discussed next.

Entities to Scale

The **Sketch items or annotations** field of the **Entities to Scale** rollout is used for selecting entities to be scaled. You can select entities before or after invoking the PropertyManager.

Parameters

The options in the **Parameters** rollout are used for specifying parameters for scaling the selected sketch entities. The options are discussed next.

Base point / Scale Factor

The **Base point** field of the **Parameters** rollout is used for specifying a base point or a center point for scaling the selected entities. For doing so, click on the **Base point** field and then click in the drawing area to specify a base point. A dot filled with yellow color appears in the drawing area, which represents the base point for scaling the entities, see Figure 3.62. Next, specify the scale factor in the **Scale Factor** field. You can also use the spinner arrows ↕ of the **Scale Factor** field to specify the scale factor. The preview of the scaled sketch of specified scale factor appears in the drawing area, see Figure 3.62. Next, click on the green tick-mark ✓ button in the PropertyManager. The selected entities are scaled.

Copy

By default, the **Copy** check box is cleared in the PropertyManager. As a result, the selected entities are scaled to the new scaled factor without retaining a copy of the original entities in the drawing area. However, if you select the **Copy** check box, the original entities are retained and a copy of scaled entities is created in the drawing area. Note that on selecting the **Copy** check box, the **Number of**

Copies field gets enabled in the rollout. In this field, you can specify the number of copies of the scaled entities to be created.

Note: The original set of sketch entities is excluded or not counted in the number of copies specified in the **Number of Copies** field. For example, if you specify 2 in this field, then two copies of the scaled entities are created, in addition to the original sketch entities. Also, note that every copy will be created with the incremental scale factor.

Procedure for Scaling Sketch Entities

1. Click on the arrow next to the **Move Entities** tool and then click on the **Scale Entities** tool in the flyout that appears. The **Scale PropertyManager** appears.
2. Select the entities to be scaled.
3. Click on the **Base point** field to activate it.
4. Select a base point for scaling the sketch entities.
5. Enter the scale factor in the **Scale Factor** field for scaling the entities.
6. Click on the green tick-mark ✓ button in the PropertyManager. The selected entities are scaled.

Stretching an Entity

You can stretch entities of a sketch by using the **Stretch Entities** tool. For doing so, click on the arrow next to the **Move Entities** tool. A flyout appears. In this flyout, click on the **Stretch Entities** tool. The **Stretch PropertyManager** appears, see Figure 3.63. The options in this PropertyManager are discussed next.

Entities to Stretch

The **Sketch items or annotations** field of the **Entities to Stretch** rollout is used for selecting entities to be stretched. By default, this field is activated. As a result, you can select entities to be stretched.

Tip: It is recommended to select entities by drawing a cross window such that it partially encloses the entities to be stretched. You can draw a cross window by dragging the cursor from the right to left, diagonally.

Parameters

The options in the **Parameters** rollout are used for specifying parameters for stretching the entities. The options are discussed next.

From/To

The **From/To** radio button is used for stretching entities from a base point. On selecting this radio button, the **Base point** field gets enabled in the **Parameters** rollout. Click on this field to activate it and then select a base point for stretching the entities. After specifying a base point, move the cursor. The preview of the stretched entities appears in the drawing area. Next, click to specify a new position for the stretched entities in the drawing area.

X/Y
The X/Y radio button is used for stretching entities by specifying a translation distance along the X and Y axes from the original location of the entities. When you select the X/Y radio button, the $\triangle$X and $\triangle$Y fields get enabled in the **Parameters** rollout. In these fields, you can specify translation distances along the X and Y axes.

Repeat
The **Repeat** button is used for stretching entities to an incremental distance specified in the $\triangle$X and $\triangle$Y fields.

Procedure for Stretching Sketch Entities
1. Click on the arrow next to the **Move Entities** tool and then click on the **Stretch Entities** tool in the flyout that appears. The **Stretch PropertyManager** appears.
2. Select the entities to be stretched by drawing a cross window around them such that the entities to be stretched are partially enclosed in the window.
3. Select the **From/To** or **X/Y** radio button from the **Parameters** rollout.
4. Depending upon the radio button selected in the Step 3, specify a new position for the stretched entities in the drawing area.

Tutorial 1

Draw a sketch of the model, as shown in Figure 3.64. The dimensions and the 3D model shown in this figure are for your reference only. You will learn about applying dimensions and creating the 3D model in later chapters. All dimensions are in mm.

Section 1: Starting SOLIDWORKS
1. Start SOLIDWORKS by double-clicking on the SOLIDWORKS icon on your desktop. The startup user interface of SOLIDWORKS appears along with the **Welcome** dialog box.

> **Note:** If SOLIDWORKS is already open and the **Welcome** dialog box does not appear on the screen, then you can invoke the **Welcome** dialog box by clicking on the **Welcome to SOLIDWORKS** tool 🏠 in the **Standard** toolbar or by pressing the CTRL + F2 keys.

Section 2: Invoking the Sketching Environment

1. Click on the **Part** button in the **Welcome** dialog box. The Part modeling environment is invoked.

> **Tip:** You can also invoke the Part modeling environment by using the **New SOLIDWORKS Document** dialog box. For doing so, click on the **New** tool in the **Standard** toolbar. The **New SOLIDWORKS Document** dialog box appears. In this dialog box, make sure that the **Part** button is selected and then click on the **OK** button.

2. Click on the **Sketch** tab in the CommandManager. The tools of the **Sketch CommandManager** appears.

3. Click on the **Sketch** tool in the **Sketch CommandManager**. Three default planes mutually perpendicular to each other appear in the graphics area.

4. Move the cursor over the Front plane and click when the boundary of the plane gets highlighted. The Sketching environment is invoked. Also, the Front plane is orientated normal to the viewing direction and the Confirmation corner appears at the upper right corner of the drawing area.

Section 3: Specifying the Units and Snap Settings

Once the Sketching environment has been invoked, you need to set the snap settings such that the cursor snaps to an increment of 5 mm. Also, specify the metric unit system.

1. Click on the **Options** tool ⚙ in the **Standard** toolbar. The **System Options - General** dialog box appears.

2. In this dialog box, click on the **Document Properties** tab. The name of the dialog box changes to **Document Properties - Drafting Standard**.

3. Click on the **Units** option in the left panel of the dialog box. The options for specifying the unit system are displayed on the right panel of the dialog box.

4. Make sure that the **MMGS (millimeter, gram, second)** radio button is selected in the **Unit system** area of the dialog box. Do not exit the dialog box.

    Now, you need to specify snap settings such that the cursor snaps to an increment of 5 mm.

5. Click on the **Grid/Snap** option in the left panel of the dialog box. The options for specifying the grids and snap settings are displayed on the right panel of the dialog box.

6. Enter **20** in the **Major grid spacing** field, **4** in the **Minor-lines per major** field, and **1** in the **Snap points per minor** field of the **Grid** area in the dialog box.

7. Make sure that the **Display grid** check box of the **Grid** area in the dialog box is cleared to turn off the display of grids in the drawing area.

8. Click on the **Go To System Snaps** button in the dialog box. The name of the dialog box changes to **System Options - Relations/Snaps**.

9. Make sure that the **Grid** and **Angle** check boxes are selected in the **Sketch snaps** area of the dialog box to turn on the snap mode.

10. Make sure that the **Snap only when grid is displayed** check box, available below the **Grid** check box is cleared.

11. Click on the **OK** button in the dialog box. The snap settings are specified and the dialog box is closed.

Section 4: Drawing Sketch Entities

Once the units and snap settings have been specified, you need to start drawing the sketch.

1. Click on the **Circle tool** ⊙ in the **Sketch CommandManager**. The **Circle** tool gets activated and the **Circle PropertyManager** appears on the left of the drawing area.

2. Move the cursor to the origin and then click to specify the center point of the circle when the cursor snaps to the origin.

3. Move the cursor horizontally toward right to a distance. A preview of the circle attached to the cursor appears. Also, the radius of the circle is displayed near the cursor tip.

4. Click to specify a point in the drawing area when the radius of the circle appears 60 mm near the cursor, see Figure 3.65. A circle of radius 60 mm is created. Note that the **Circle** tool is still active.

5. Move the cursor to the origin and then click to specify the center point of the another circle when the cursor snaps to the origin.

6. Move the cursor horizontally to the right and click when the radius of the circle appears 30 mm, see Figure 3.66.

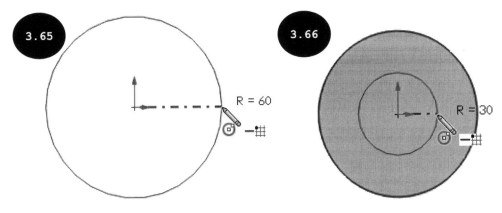

R = 60

R = 30

After creating circles of radii 60 mm and 30 mm, you need to create a construction circle of radius 45 mm that will define the PCD of holes.

7. Create a circle of radius 45 mm whose center point is at the origin, refer to Figure 3.67. After creating a circle of radius 45 mm, right-click in the drawing area and click on the **Select** option in the shortcut menu to terminate the creation of the circle and to exit the **Circle** tool.

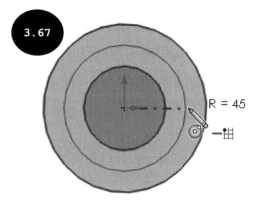

Once you have created a circle of radius 45 mm, you need to convert it into a construction circle.

8. Click on the circle of radius 45 mm in the drawing area. The **Circle PropertyManager** appears on the left of the drawing area. Also, a Pop-up toolbar appears near the cursor, see Figure 3.68.

9. Click on the **Construction Geometry** tool in the Pop-up toolbar, see Figure 3.68. The selected circle of radius 45 mm is converted into a construction circle, see Figure 3.69. Alternatively, select the **For construction** check box in the **Options** rollout of the PropertyManager to convert the circle into a construction circle.

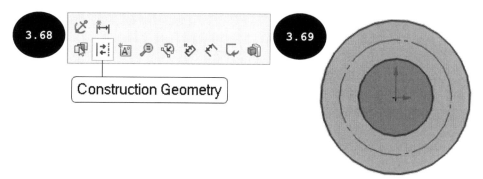

10. Click on the **Line** tool in the **Sketch CommandManager**. The **Insert Line PropertyManager** appears.

11. Specify the start point of the line at the origin and then move the cursor horizontally toward left.

12. Click to specify the endpoint of the line when the length of the line appears as 60 mm and the cursor snaps to the outer circle, see Figure 3.70.

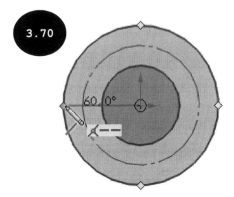

3.70

13. Right-click in the drawing area and then click on the **End chain (double-click)** option in the shortcut menu to terminate the creation of the continuous chain of lines. However, the **Line** tool is still active for creating other line entities.

Tip: To exit the **Line** tool, click on the **Select** option in the shortcut menu, which appears on right-clicking in the drawing area. If you select the **End chain (double-click)** option in the shortcut menu, the creation of continuous chain of lines gets terminated but the **Line** tool remains active.

14. Move the cursor to the origin and click to specify the start point of the line when cursor snaps to the origin.

15. Move the cursor vertically downward and click to specify the endpoint of the line when the length of the line appears as 60 mm and the cursor snaps to the outer circle, see Figure 3.71.

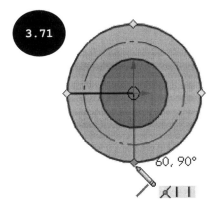

3.71

16. Right-click in the drawing area and then click on the **Select** option in the shortcut menu that appears to exit the **Line** tool.

Now, you need to create a circle of diameter 10 mm. It is evident from Figure 3.64 that the circles of diameter 10 mm are 10 in count. As the diameter of all the circles is same and the circles are on the same PCD (Pitch Circle Diameter), you can create one circle and then create a circular pattern to create the remaining circles.

17. Click on the **Circle** tool ⊙ in the **Sketch CommandManager**. The **Circle PropertyManager** appears.

18. Click to specify the center point of the circle when the coordinates (X, Y, Z) appear "**-45, 10, 0**" in the Status Bar, see Figure 3.72 and the construction circle gets highlighted, see Figure 3.73.

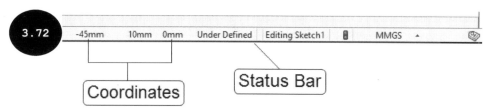

19. Move the cursor horizontally toward right and then click when the radius of the circle appears close to 5 mm near the cursor, see Figure 3.74. A circle of radius close to 5 mm is created and is selected in the drawing area. Also, the options in the **Circle PropertyManager** are enabled to control the parameters of the selected circle.

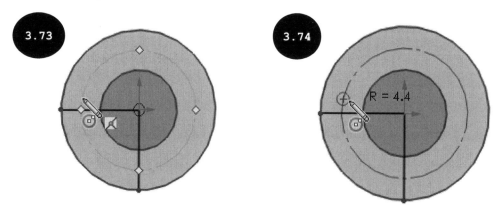

20. Enter **5** as the radius of the selected circle in the **Radius** field of the **Parameters** rollout in the PropertyManager. Next, press ENTER. The radius of the circle is modified to 5 mm.

21. Right-click in the drawing area and then click on the **Select** option in the shortcut menu that appears to exit the **Circle** tool.

Section 5: Trimming Sketch Entities

Now, you need to trim the unwanted sketch entities of the sketch.

1. Click on the **Trim Entities** tool in the **Sketch CommandManager**. The **Trim PropertyManager** appears on the left of the drawing area.

2. Click on the **Trim to closest** button in the **Options** rollout of the PropertyManager.

3. Make sure that the **Keep trimmed entities as construction geometry** and **Ignore trimming of construction geometry** check boxes are cleared in the PropertyManager.

4. Move the cursor over the portion of the entity to be trimmed, see Figure 3.75 and then click the left mouse button when it is highlighted in the drawing area. The selected portion of the entity is trimmed, see Figure 3.76.

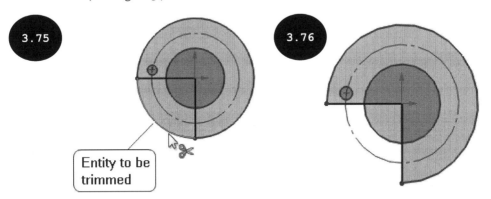

5. Similarly, trim the other unwanted portions of the entities of the sketch. Figure 3.77 shows entities to be trimmed and Figure 3.78 shows the sketch after trimming all the unwanted entities.

6. Click on the green tick-mark ✔ in the PropertyManager to exit the **Trim Entities** tool.

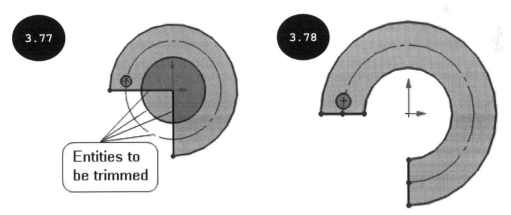

Section 6: Creating the Circular Pattern

Now, you need to create a circular pattern.

1. Select the previously created circle of radius 5 mm in the drawing area.

2. Click on the arrow next to the **Linear Sketch Pattern** tool. The **Pattern** flyout appears, see Figure 3.79.

3. Click on the **Circular Sketch Pattern** tool in the **Pattern** flyout. The preview of the circular pattern appears in the drawing area. Also, the **Circular Pattern PropertyManager** appears on the left of the drawing area.

4. Clear the **Equal spacing** check box in the **Parameters** rollout of the PropertyManager.

5. Enter **27** in the **Angle spacing** field of the **Parameter** rollout as the angle between two instances.

6. Enter **10** in the **Number of Instances** field as the number of pattern instances to be created.

7. Click on the green tick-mark ✔ in the PropertyManager. The circular pattern is created, see Figure 3.80.

> **Note:**   The circular pattern shown in Figure 3.80 has been created with the **Dimension angular spacing** and **Display instance count** check boxes selected in the PropertyManager.

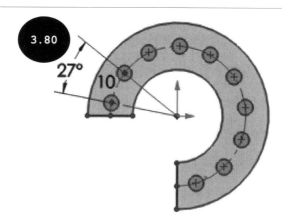

Section 7: Saving the Sketch

1. Click on the **Save** tool in the **Standard** toolbar. The **Save As** dialog box appears.

2. Browse to the SOLIDWORKS folder and then create a folder with the name **Chapter 3** in the SOLIDWORKS folder.

3. Enter **Tutorial 1** in the **File name** field of the dialog box. Next, click on the **Save** button. The sketch is saved with the name Tutorial 1.

Tutorial 2

Draw a sketch of the model, as shown in Figure 3.81. The dimensions and the 3D model shown in the figure are for your reference only. You will learn about applying dimensions and creating the 3D model in later chapters. All dimensions are in mm.

Section 1: Starting SOLIDWORKS

1. Start SOLIDWORKS by double-clicking on the SOLIDWORKS icon on your desktop. The startup user interface of SOLIDWORKS appears along with the **Welcome** dialog box.

Note: If SOLIDWORKS is already open and the **Welcome** dialog box does not appear on the screen, then you can invoke the **Welcome** dialog box by clicking on the **Welcome to SOLIDWORKS** tool 🏠 in the **Standard** toolbar or by pressing the CTRL + F2 keys.

Section 2: Invoking the Sketching Environment

1. Click on the **Part** button in the **Welcome** dialog box. The Part modeling environment is invoked.

Tip: You can also invoke the Part modeling environment by using the **New SOLIDWORKS Document** dialog box. For doing so, click on the **New** tool in the **Standard** toolbar. The **New SOLIDWORKS Document** dialog box appears. In this dialog box, make sure that the **Part** button is selected and then click on the **OK** button.

2. Click on the **Sketch** tab in the CommandManager. The tools of the **Sketch CommandManager** appear.

3. Click on the **Sketch** tool in the **Sketch CommandManager**. Three default planes mutually perpendicular to each other appear in the graphics area.

4. Move the cursor over the Top plane and then click the left mouse button when the boundary of the plane gets highlighted. The Sketching environment is invoked. Also, the Top plane is orientated normal to the viewing direction.

Section 3: Specifying the Unit and Snap Settings

Once the Sketching environment has been invoked, you can set the snap settings such that the cursor snaps to an increment of 2 mm, since all dimensions of the sketch are multiples of 2 mm. Also, specify the metric unit system for measurement.

1. Click on the **Options** tool ⚙ in the **Standard** toolbar. The **System Options - General** dialog box appears.

2. Click on the **Document Properties** tab in this dialog box. The name of the dialog box changes to **Document Properties - Drafting Standard**.

3. Click on the **Units** option in the left panel of the dialog box. The options for specifying the unit system are displayed on the right panel of the dialog box.

4. Make sure that the **MMGS (millimeter, gram, second)** radio button is selected in the **Unit system** area of the dialog box.

    Now, you need to specify the snap settings such that the cursor snaps to an increment of 2 mm.

5. Click on the **Grid/Snap** option in the left panel of the dialog box. The options for specifying the grids and snap settings are displayed on the right panel of the dialog box.

6. Enter 10 in the **Major grid spacing** field, 5 in the **Minor-lines per major** field, and 1 in the **Snap points per minor** field of the **Grid** area in the dialog box.

7. Make sure that the **Display grid** check box is cleared in the **Grid** area of the dialog box to turn off the display of grids in the drawing area.

8. Click on the **Go To System Snaps** button in the dialog box. The name of the dialog box changes to **System Options - Relations/Snaps**.

9. Select the **Grid** and **Angle** check boxes in the **Sketch snaps** area of the dialog box in order to turn on the snap mode. Also, make sure that the **Snap only when grid is displayed** check box, below the **Grid** check box is cleared in the dialog box.

10. Click on the **OK** button. The snap settings have been specified and the dialog box is closed.

Section 4: Drawing the Sketch

It is evident from the Figure 3.81 that the sketch is symmetric about its center line, therefore, you can draw the right half of the outer loop of the sketch and then mirror it to create its left half.

1. Click on the **Line** tool in the **Sketch CommandManager**. The **Line** tool gets invoked.

2. Move the cursor to the origin and then click to specify the start point of the line when the cursor snaps to the origin.

3. Move the cursor horizontally toward right and then click to specify the endpoint of the first line when the length of the line appears 60 mm near the cursor, see Figure 3.82.

4. Move the cursor vertically upward and then click to specify the endpoint of the second line entity when the length of the line appears 20 mm, see Figure 3.83.

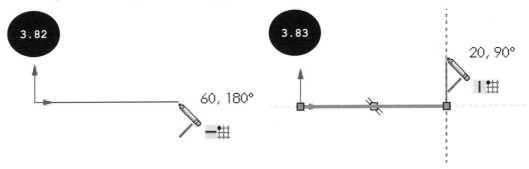

5. Move the cursor horizontally toward right and click to specify the endpoint of the line when the length of the line appears as 24 mm, see Figure 3.84.

    Now, you need to create an arc of radius 16 mm. To create an arc, you can use the arc tools. However in this tutorial, you will create arcs by using the **Line** tool.

6. Move the cursor to a distance and then move it back to the last specified endpoint. An orange colored dot appears, see Figure 3.85.

7. Move the cursor horizontally toward right to a distance and then vertically upward. The arc mode is invoked and the preview of an arc appears in the drawing area, see Figure 3.86.

8. Click to specify the endpoint of the arc when the radius and angle values of the arc appear as 16 mm and 180 degrees, respectively, near the cursor, see Figure 3.86. The arc is created and the line mode is invoked again.

9. Move the cursor horizontally toward left and click when the length of line appears as 24 mm, see Figure 3.87.

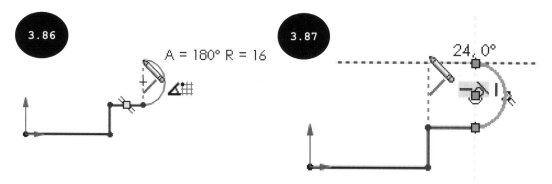

10. Move the cursor vertically upward and click when the length of the line appears as 80 mm.

11. Move the cursor horizontally toward right and then click when the length of the line appears as 24 mm.

   Now, you need to create an arc of radius 16 mm.

12. Move the cursor to a distance and then move it back to the last specified endpoint. An orange colored dot appears, see Figure 3.88.

13. Move the cursor horizontally toward right to a distance and then vertically upward. The arc mode is invoked and the preview of an arc appears in the drawing area, see Figure 3.89.

14. Click to specify the endpoint of the arc when the radius and angle values of the arc appear as 16 mm and 180 degrees, respectively, see Figure 3.89. The arc is created and the line mode is invoked again.

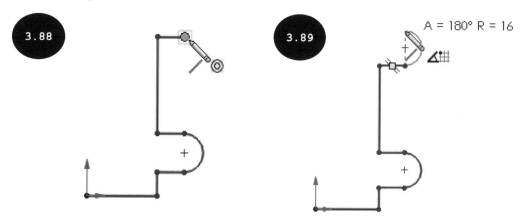

15. Move the cursor horizontally toward left and click when the length of the line appears as 24 mm.

16. Move the cursor vertically upward and click when the length of the line appears as 18 mm.

17. Move the cursor horizontally toward left and then click when the length of the line appears as 60 mm. The outer right half of the sketch is created, see Figure 3.90. Next, right-click in the drawing area and then click on the **Select** option in the shortcut menu that appears, to exit the **Line** tool.

3.90

Section 5: Drawing the Centerline

After creating the right half of the sketch, you can mirror it about a centerline to create the left half of the sketch.

1. Click on the arrow next to the **Line** tool. The **Line** flyout appears, see Figure 3.91.

2. Click on the **Centerline** tool in the **Line** flyout. The **Insert Line PropertyManager** appears with the **For construction** check box selected in it.

3. Move the cursor to the origin and then click to specify the start point of the centerline when the cursor snaps to the origin.

4. Move the cursor vertically upward and then click to specify the endpoint of the vertical centerline of any length, see Figure 3.92. Next, right-click and then click on the **Select** option in the shortcut menu that appears to exit the **Centerline** tool.

3.91

3.92

Section 6: Mirroring Sketch Entities

After creating the centerline, you need to mirror the sketch about the centerline.

1. Click on the **Mirror Entities** tool in the **Sketch CommandManager**. The Mirror **PropertyManager** appears.

2. Select all the sketch entities except the centerline. The names of the selected entities appear in the **Entities to mirror** field of the PropertyManager.

3. Click on the **Mirror about** field in the PropertyManager to activate it.

4. Click on the centerline as the mirroring line in the drawing area. The preview of the mirror entities appears.

5. Make sure that the **Copy** check box is selected in the PropertyManager.

6. Click on the green tick-mark ✓ in the PropertyManager. The selected entities get mirrored about the centerline, see Figure 3.93.

3.93

Section 7: Creating the Circle

Now, you need to create a circle of diameter 16 mm and then its linear pattern along the X and Y axes to create the remaining circles.

1. Click on the **Circle** tool ⊙ in the **Sketch CommandManager**. The **Circle PropertyManager** appears.

2. Click to specify the center point of the circle in the drawing area when the coordinates (X, Y, Z) appear "**-26, 16, 0**" in the Status Bar, see Figure 3.94.

3.94   -26mm   16mm   0mm   Under Defined   Editing Sketch1   🔒   MMGS   ▲

X, Y, Z Coordinates

3. Move the cursor horizontally toward right and then click when the radius of the circle appears as 8 mm, see Figure 3.95. The circle of radius 8 mm is created.

4. Right-click in the drawing area and then click on the **Select** option in the shortcut menu that appears to exit the **Circle** tool.

Section 8: Creating the Linear Pattern

Now, you need to create the linear pattern of the circle to create remaining circles of the sketch.

1. Make sure that the previously created circle of radius 8 mm is selected in the drawing area.

2. Click on the **Linear Sketch Pattern** tool in the **Sketch CommandManager**.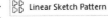
The **Linear Pattern PropertyManager** appears. Also, the preview of the linear pattern along the X axis appears with the default parameters.

3. Enter **2** in the **Number of Instances** field of the **Direction 1** rollout in the PropertyManager.

4. Enter **52** in the **Spacing** field of the **Direction 1** rollout as the distance between two instances.

5. Enter **7** in the **Number of Instances** field of the **Direction 2** rollout as the number of instances to be created along the Y axis. Next, click anywhere in the drawing area. The preview of the linear pattern appears along the Y axis.

6. Enter **24** in the **Spacing** field of the **Direction 2** rollout as the distance between two instances along the Y axis.

7. Click on the green tick-mark ✔ in the PropertyManager. The linear pattern is created, see Figure 3.96.

3.96

Note: Figure 3.96 shows the display of instance counts (7 and 2) in direction 1 and direction 2 of the linear pattern, respectively, as the **Display instance count** check box was selected in the **Direction 1** and **Direction 2** rollouts of the **Linear Pattern PropertyManager** while creating the linear pattern.

Section 9: Saving the Sketch

1.   Click on the **Save** tool in the **Standard** toolbar. The **Save As** dialog box appears.

2.   Browse to the Chapter 3 folder in the SOLIDWORKS folder.

3.   Enter **Tutorial 2** in the **File name** field of the dialog box. Next, click on the **Save** button. The sketch is saved with the name Tutorial 2.

Tutorial 3

Draw a sketch of the model, as shown in Figure 3.97. The dimensions and the 3D model shown in the figure are for your reference only. You will learn about applying dimensions and creating the 3D model in later chapters. All dimensions are in mm.

3.97

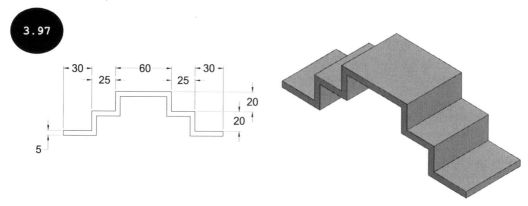

Section 1: Starting SOLIDWORKS

1. Start SOLIDWORKS by double-clicking on the SOLIDWORKS icon on your desktop. The startup user interface of SOLIDWORKS appears along with the **Welcome** dialog box.

Note: If SOLIDWORKS is already open and the **Welcome** dialog box does not appear on the screen, then you can invoke the **Welcome** dialog box by clicking on the **Welcome to SOLIDWORKS** tool ⌂ in the **Standard** toolbar or by pressing the CTRL + F2 keys.

Section 2: Invoking the Sketching Environment

1. Click on the **Part** button in the **Welcome** dialog box. The Part modeling environment is invoked.

Tip: You can also invoke the Part modeling environment by using the **New SOLIDWORKS Document** dialog box. For doing so, click on the **New** tool in the **Standard** toolbar. The **New SOLIDWORKS Document** dialog box appears. In this dialog box, make sure that the **Part** button is selected and then click on the **OK** button.

2. Click on the **Sketch** tab in the CommandManager. The tools of the **Sketch CommandManager** appear.

3. Click on the **Sketch** tool in the **Sketch CommandManager**. Three default planes mutually perpendicular to each other appear in the graphics area.

4. Select the Front plane as the sketching plane. The Sketching environment is invoked and the Front plane gets orientated normal to the viewing direction.

Section 3: Specifying the Unit and Snap Settings

Once the Sketching environment has been invoked, you need to set the snap settings such that the cursor snaps to an increment of 5 mm, as the dimensions of all the sketch entities are multiples of 5 mm. Also, specify the metric unit system for measurement.

1. Click on the **Options** tool ⚙ in the **Standard** toolbar. The **System Options - General** dialog box appears.

2. Click on the **Document Properties** tab in this dialog box. The name of the dialog box changes to **Document Properties - Drafting Standard**.

3. Click on the **Units** option in the left panel of the dialog box.

4. Make sure that the **MMGS (millimeter, gram, second)** radio button is selected in the **Unit system** area of the dialog box.

5. Click on the **Grid/Snap** option in the left panel of the dialog box.

6. Enter 50 in the **Major grid spacing** field, 10 in the **Minor-lines per major** field, and 1 in the **Snap points per minor** field in the **Grid** area of the dialog box.

7. Make sure that the **Display grid** check box is cleared in the **Grid** area of the dialog box to turn off the display of grids in the drawing area.

8. Click on the **Go To System Snaps** button in the dialog box.

9. Select the **Grid** and **Angle** check boxes in the **Sketch snaps** area of the dialog box to turn on the snap mode. Also, make sure that the **Snap only when grid is displayed** check box, below the **Grid** check box is cleared.

10. Click on the **OK** button in the dialog box. The snap settings are specified and the dialog box is closed.

Section 4: Drawing the Sketch

In this tutorial, you will create the left half of the upper sketch entities and mirror it dynamically about the center line to create the right half of the upper entities of the sketch.

1. Click on the arrow next to the **Line** tool. The **Line** flyout appears, see Figure 3.98.

2. Click on the **Centerline** tool in the flyout. The **Insert Line PropertyManager** appears with the **For construction** check box selected.

3. Move the cursor to the origin and then click to specify the start point of the centerline when the cursor snaps to the origin.

4. Move the cursor vertically upward and then click to specify the endpoint of the vertical centerline of any length in the drawing area. Next, press ESC key.

    After creating a vertical centerline, you need to invoke the **Dynamic Mirror** tool so that while creating entities on one side of the centerline, the respective mirror entities are created dynamically on the other side of the centerline.

5. Click on **Tools > Sketch Tools > Dynamic Mirror** in the SOLIDWORKS Menus. The **Mirror PropertyManager** appears.

6. Move the cursor over the centerline in the drawing area and then click on it. The symbol of dynamic mirror, which is represented by two small horizontal lines appears on both sides of the centerline, see Figure 3.99.

7. Click on the **Line** tool in the **Sketch CommandManager**. The **Insert Line PropertyManager** appears.

8. Move the cursor in the drawing area, where the coordinates (X, Y, Z) appear "-85, 0, 0" respectively, in the Status Bar and then click the left mouse button at that location to specify the start point of the line.

9. Move the cursor horizontally toward right and then click to specify the endpoint of the first line when the length of the line appears 30 mm near the cursor. A horizontal line of length 30 mm is created. Also, its mirror image is created on the other side of the centerline, automatically, see Figure 3.100.

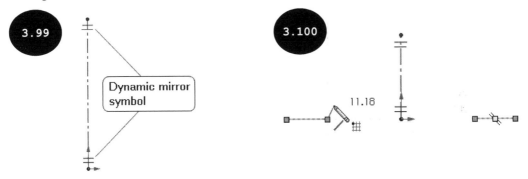

10. Move the cursor vertically upward and then click to create a line of length 20 mm. A line of length 20 mm is also created on the other side of the centerline, see Figure 3.101. Note that as you are creating entities on the left of the centerline, the respective mirror images are being created on the right of the centerline since the **Dynamic Mirror** tool is invoked.

11. Move the cursor horizontally toward right and then click to create a line of length 25 mm.

12. Move the cursor vertically upward and then click to create a line of length 20 mm.

13. Move the cursor horizontally toward right and click when the cursor snaps to the centerline. The upper loop of the sketch is created, see Figure 3.102.

14. Right-click in the drawing area and then click on the **Select** option in the shortcut menu that appears to exit the **Line** tool.

Now, you need to exit the **Dynamic Mirror** tool.

15. Click on **Tools** > **Sketch Tools** > **Dynamic Mirror** in the SOLIDWORKS Menus to exit the **Dynamic Mirror** tool.

Section 5: Offsetting the Sketch Entities

After creating the upper loop of the sketch, you need to offset it to a distance of 5 mm.

1. Click on the **Offset Entities** tool. The **Offset Entities PropertyManager** appears.

Offset
Entities

2. Make sure that the **Select chain** check box is selected in the PropertyManager.

3. Select an entity of the upper loop of the sketch. All contiguous entities of the selected entity get selected and the preview of offset entities appear in the drawing area, see Figure 3.103.

4. Make sure that the direction of offset entities is on the lower side of the sketch, see Figure 3.103. If not, click on the **Reverse** check box to reverse the direction of offset entities to downward.

5. Enter 5 in the **Offset Distance** field of the PropertyManager and then press ENTER.

6. Select the **Cap ends** check box. The **Arcs** and **Lines** radio buttons get enabled.

7. Select the **Lines** radio button in order to cap the open ends of offset entities with lines.

8. Make sure that the **Base geometry** and **Offset geometry** check boxes are cleared.

9. Click on the green tick-mark ✔ button. The sketch is created, see Figure 3.104.

3.103   3.104

Section 6: Saving the Sketch

1. Click on the **Save** tool in the **Standard** toolbar. The **Save As** dialog box appears.

2. Browse to the Chapter 3 folder in the SOLIDWORKS folder.

3. Enter **Tutorial 3** in the **File name** field of the dialog box. Next, click on the **Save** button. The model is saved with the name Tutorial 3.

Hands-on Test Drive 1

Draw the sketch of the model, as shown in Figure 3.105. The dimensions and the 3D model are for your reference only. All dimensions are in mm.

3.105

Hands-on Test Drive 2

Draw the sketch of the model, as shown in Figure 3.106. The dimensions and the 3D model are for your reference only. All dimensions are in mm.

3.106

Summary

In this chapter, you have learned about editing and modifying sketch entities by using various editing tools such as **Trim Entities**, **Extend Entities**, **Offset Entities**, **Mirror Entities**, and **Linear Sketch Pattern**. The pattern tools discussed in this chapter allow you to create linear and circular patterns. The mirror tools allow you to create a mirror image of the selected entities about a mirroring line. You can also dynamically mirror sketch entities while drawing them by using the **Dynamic Mirror** tool. Besides, the chapter discusses how to move sketch entities from one position to the other, copy sketch entities, rotate sketch entities, scale, and stretch sketch entities by using the respective tools.

Questions

- The _____ tool is used for offsetting sketch entities at a specified offset distance.

- You can rotate sketch entities at an angle by using the _____ tool.

- You can stretch the sketch entities of a sketch by using the _____ tool.

- To rotate sketch entities anti-clockwise, you need to define a _____ angle value.

- While offsetting sketch entities, if you select the _____ check box, all the contiguous entities of the selected entity get selected.

- The number of pattern instances specified in the **Number of Instances** field include the parent or original instance selected to pattern. (True/False)

- You cannot recall the skipped pattern instances. (True/False)

- In addition to trimming sketch entities, you can extend sketch entities by using the **Trim Entities** tool. (True/False)

Applying Geometric Relations and Dimensions

This chapter discusses the following topics:

- Working with Geometric Relations
- Applying Geometric Relations
- Controlling the Display of Geometric Relations
- Applying Dimensions
- Modifying/Editing Dimensions
- Modifying Dimension Properties
- Working with Different States of a Sketch

Once you are done with creating a sketch by using sketching tools, you need to make your sketch fully defined by applying proper geometric relations and dimensions. A fully defined sketch is a sketch, in which all degrees of freedom are fixed and its shape and position cannot be changed by simply dragging its entities. You will learn more about fully defined sketches later in this chapter. Before that, you need to understand geometric relations and dimensions.

Working with Geometric Relations

Geometric relations are used for restricting some degrees of freedom of a sketch. You can apply geometric relations on a sketch entity, between sketch entities, and between sketch entities and planes, axes, edges, or vertices. Some geometric relations such as horizontal, vertical, and coincident are applied automatically while drawing sketch entities. For example, while drawing a line, if you move the cursor horizontally toward left or right, a symbol of horizontal relation appears near the cursor, see Figure 4.1. This indicates that if you specify the endpoint of the line, the horizontal relation will be applied to the line. Likewise, if you move the cursor vertically upward or downward, a symbol of vertical relation appears near the cursor, see Figure 4.1. This indicates that if you specify the endpoint of the line, the vertical relation will be applied to it. Various geometric relations are discussed next.

Horizontal Relation

Horizontal relation is used for changing the orientation of an entity to horizontal. This relation can be applied to a line, centerline, or between two points or vertices.

Vertical Relation

Vertical relation is used for changing the orientation of an entity to vertical. This relation can be applied to a line, centerline, or between two points or vertices.

Coincident Relation

Coincident constraint is used for coinciding two points or vertices. You can apply this relation between a point and a line/arc/ellipse. Besides, you can also apply a coincident relation between a sketch point and the origin.

Collinear Relation

Collinear relation is used for making two or more than two lines collinear with each other. You can also make line entities collinear to a linear edge or a reference plane.

Perpendicular Relation   ⊥

Perpendicular relation is used for making two line entities perpendicular to each other. You can also make a line perpendicular to a linear edge or a plane.

Parallel Relation   ⟍

Parallel relation is used for making two or more than two line entities parallel to each other. You can also make line entities parallel to a linear edge or a plane.

Tangent Relation   ∂

Tangent relation is used for making two sketch entities such as a circle and a line tangent to each other. You can also make two circles, two arcs, two ellipses, two splines, and a combination of these entities tangent to each other. Besides, you can also make sketch entities tangent to a linear or a circular edge of a model.

Concentric Relation

Concentric relation is used for making two or more than two arcs or circles, a point and an arc, or a point and a circle concentric to each other. In a concentric relation, the selected entities share the same center point. You can also make sketch entities such as arcs or circles concentric to a vertex or cylindrical edge of a model.

Coradial Relation

Coradial relation is used for making two or more than two arcs/circles coradial to each other. In a coradial relation, the selected entities share the same center point as well as radius. You can also make sketch entities such as arcs/circles coradial to a circular edge of a model.

Equal Relation

Equal relation is used for making two or more than two arcs/circles/lines equal to each other. In an equal relation, the length of line entities and radii of arc entities become equal.

Equal Curve Length Relation

Equal Curve Length relation is used for making curved segments equal to each other. This relation can be applied between a circle and an arc, two circles, two arcs, a line and a circle, a circle and a spline, or a spline and a line.

Midpoint Relation

Midpoint relation is used for making a point coincident at the middle of a line entity. You can apply this relation between a sketch point and a line, a vertex and a line, or a sketch point and a linear edge.

Symmetric Relation

Symmetric relation is used for making two points, two lines, two arcs, two circles, or two ellipses symmetric about a centerline.

Merge Relation

Merge relation is used for merging two points together such that they share a single point. You can merge endpoints of two lines by applying this relation.

Pierce Relation

Pierce relation is used for coinciding a sketch point to an axis, an edge, or a curve of another sketch.

Fix Relation

Fix relation is used for fixing the current position and size of a sketch entity. However, in case of a fixed line or arc entity, their endpoints are free to move without changing the position of the entity.

Torsion Continuity Relation New

Torsion continuity relation is used for creating smooth continuity with equal curvature between a spline and another sketch entity (a line, an arc, or a spline) that share a common endpoint, see Figure 4.2. You can also apply this relation between a spline and an edge of a model sharing a common endpoint.

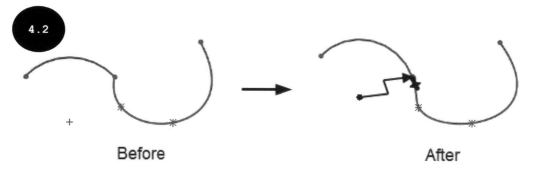

4.2

Before   After

Applying Geometric Relations

In SOLIDWORKS, you can apply geometric relations either by using the **Add Relation** tool or by using the Pop-up toolbar. Both the methods of applying geometric relations are discussed next.

Applying Geometric Relation by using the Add Relation Tool

To apply a geometric relation by using the **Add Relation** tool, click on the arrow at the bottom of the **Display/Delete Relations** tool in the **Sketch CommandManager**. A flyout appears, see Figure 4.3. In this flyout, click on the **Add Relation** tool. The **Add Relations PropertyManager** appears, see Figure 4.4. The **Selected Entities** rollout of the PropertyManager is used for selecting entities for applying relation in the drawing area.

After selecting the entities for applying a relation in the drawing area, the **Add Relations PropertyManager** gets modified and the names of selected entities appear in the **Selected Entities** rollout. Figure 4.5 shows the modified PropertyManager after selecting two circles. The options in the modified PropertyManager are discussed next.

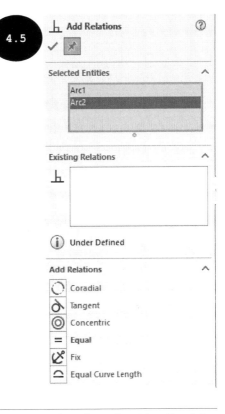

Selected Entities

The **Selected Entities** rollout displays the list of entities selected for applying a relation. You can select entities by clicking the left mouse button in the drawing area. You can also remove an entity from the selection list. For doing so, select the entity in the **Selected Entities** field and then right-click. A shortcut menu appears. In this shortcut menu, click on the **Delete** option. The selected entity gets removed from the selection list. If you click on the **Clear Selections** option in the shortcut menu that appears, all the selected entities get removed from the selection list.

Existing Relations

The **Existing Relations** rollout displays a list of already applied relations between the selected entities.

Tip: You can delete relations that are already applied between the selected entities. For doing so, select the relations in the **Existing Relations** field of the rollout and then right-click. A shortcut menu appears. In this shortcut menu, click on the **Delete** option. The selected relations get deleted and removed from the list. If you click on the **Delete All** option in the shortcut menu that appears, all the existing relations that were applied between the selected entities get deleted.

Add Relations

The **Add Relations** rollout displays a list of all the possible relations that can be applied between the selected entities. Also, the most suitable relation gets highlighted in the rollout by default, refer to Figure 4.5.

Procedure for Applying Relations by using the Add Relation Tool

1. Click on the arrow at the bottom of the **Display/Delete Relations** tool in the **Sketch CommandManager**. A flyout appears, refer to Figure 4.3.
2. Click on the **Add Relation** tool in the flyout. The **Add Relations PropertyManager** appears.
3. Select sketch entities by clicking the left mouse button in the drawing area.
4. Click on the relation to be applied between the selected entities in the **Add Relations** rollout. The selected relation is applied.
5. Click on the green tick-mark ✔ button in the PropertyManager.

Applying Geometric Relation by using the Pop-up Toolbar

In addition to applying geometric relations by using the **Add Relations PropertyManager**, you can apply relations by using the Pop-up toolbar, which is a time saving method. For doing so, select entities in the drawing area by pressing the CTRL key without invoking any tool. Next, release the CTRL key and do not move the cursor. A Pop-up toolbar appears near the tip of the cursor, see Figure 4.6. Click on the required relation in the Pop-up toolbar. The selected relation is applied between the selected entities.

Note: The availability of relations in the Pop-up toolbar depends upon the type of entities selected for applying the relation. Figure 4.6 shows the Pop-up toolbar that appears on selecting two circles.

Procedure for Applying Relations by using the Pop-up Toolbar

1.   Select sketch entities in the drawing area by pressing the CTRL key.
2.   Release the CTRL key and do not move the cursor. A Pop-up toolbar appears.
3.   Click on the required relation in the Pop-up toolbar. The selected relation is applied.

Controlling the Display of Geometric Relations

You can control the display or visibility of the applied geometric relations in the drawing area by using the **View Sketch Relations** tool of the **View (Heads-Up)** toolbar. To turn on or off the display of the applied geometric relations, click on the **Hide/Show Items** arrow in the **View (Heads-Up)** toolbar. A flyout appears, see Figure 4.7. In this flyout, click on the **View Sketch Relations** tool. The display of all the applied geometric relations is either turned on or off. Note that this is a toggle tool.

Tip: You can also delete an already applied relation by selecting it in the drawing area and then pressing the DELETE key.

Applying Dimensions

Once a sketch has been drawn and required geometric relations have been applied, you need to apply dimensions by using the dimension tools. As SOLIDWORKS is a parametric software, the parameters of sketch entities such as length and angle are controlled or driven by dimension values. On modifying a dimension value, the respective sketch entity also gets modified, accordingly. The tools used for applying dimensions are grouped together in the **Dimensions** flyout. To invoke this flyout, click on the arrow at the bottom of the **Smart Dimension** tool in the **Sketch CommandManager**, see Figure 4.8. The dimension tools are discussed next.

Working with Smart Dimension Tool

The **Smart Dimension** tool is used for applying a dimension, depending upon the type of entity selected. For example, if you select a circle, the diameter dimension is applied and if you select a line entity, the linear dimension is applied. To apply dimensions by using the **Smart Dimension** tool, click on the **Smart Dimension** tool in the **Sketch CommandManager**. The cursor changes to dimension cursor and you are prompted to select the entity to be dimensioned. Select an entity in the drawing area. A dimension with the current dimension value is attached to the cursor depending upon the type of entity selected, see Figure 4.9. In Figure 4.9 (a), a diameter dimension is attached to the cursor on selecting a circle. In Figure 4.9 (b), a radius dimension is attached to the cursor on selecting an arc. In Figure 4.9 (c), a linear dimension is attached to the cursor on selecting a line. After selecting the entity, move the cursor to a location where you want to place the dimension in the drawing area and then click the left mouse button. The **Modify** dialog box appears, see Figure 4.10. By default, the **Modify** dialog box displays the current dimension value of the sketch entity. Enter the required dimension value and then click on its green tick-mark button. The dimension is applied to the selected entity. Figure 4.10 shows various components of the **Modify** dialog box. These components are discussed next.

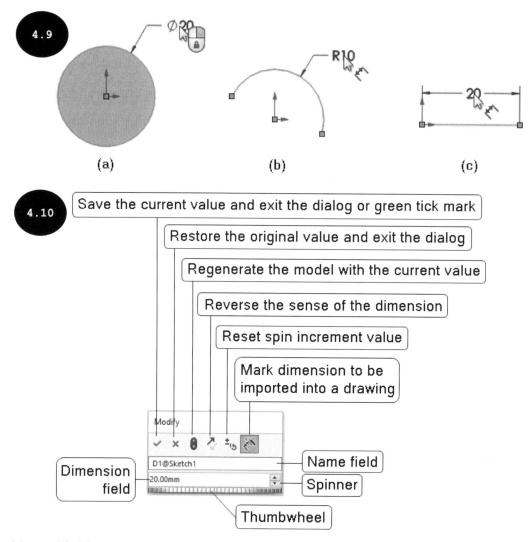

(a)   (b)   (c)

Name Field

The **Name** field of the **Modify** dialog box displays the name of the dimension. By default, the name of a dimension is assigned as D1, D2, D3 ..., or Dn. You can specify a required name other than the default one in this field.

Dimension field

The **Dimension** field is used for specifying the dimension value for the sketch entity. By default, this field displays the current dimension value of the sketch entity. You can enter a new dimension value in this field.

Spinner

You can also set or control the dimension value by using the Spinner. On clicking the up arrow of the Spinner, the dimension value increases. Similarly, on clicking the down arrow of the Spinner, the dimension value decreases. Note that the increment or decrement of the dimension value is based on the predefined spin increment value set. You can control the predefined spin increment value by using the **Reset spin increment value** button of the dialog box, which is discussed next.

Reset spin increment value

The **Reset spin increment value** button is used for setting the spin increment value for dimension. For doing so, click on the **Reset spin increment value** button in the **Modify** dialog box. The **Increment** window appears with the default spin increment value. Enter the required spin increment value in the field of this window and then press the **ENTER** key. The newly entered value is set as the current spin increment value for the dimension and the window is closed.

Note: On selecting the **Make Default** check box in the **Increment** window, the specified spin increment value is set as default for other dimensions as well.

You can also set the spin increment value by using the **System Options - Spin Box Increments** dialog box. For doing so, click on the **Options** tool in the **Standard** toolbar. The **System Options - General** dialog box appears. Select the **Spin Box Increments** option in the left panel of the dialog box. The name of the dialog box changes to **System Options - Spin Box Increments** and the options for setting the spin increment value appear on the right panel of the dialog box. Next, set the required spin increment value for linear dimensions by using the **English units** and the **Metric units** fields of the **Length increments** area of the dialog box. You can specify the spin increment value for angle and time measurements by using the **Angle increments** and **Time increments** fields of the dialog box, respectively.

Thumbwheel

You can also set or control the dimension value by sliding the thumbwheel of the **Modify** dialog box.

Regenerate the model with the current value

The **Regenerate the model with the current value** button is used for regenerating or refreshing the drawing with the current dimension value that is entered in the **Dimension** field. You can regenerate or refresh your drawing, if the change in the dimension value is not reflected in the drawing area.

Reverse the sense of the dimension

The **Reverse the sense of the dimension** button is used for flipping or reversing the dimension value from a positive dimension value to negative dimension value and vice versa. Note that this button is enabled only when the selected dimension is a linear dimension.

Save the current value and exit the dialog

The **Save the current value and exit the dialog** button (green tick-mark) of the dialog box is used for accepting the change made in the dimension value in the **Dimension** field and to exit the dialog box.

Restore the original value and exit the dialog ☒

The **Restore the original value and exit the dialog** button (red cross mark) is used for discarding the changes made in the dimension value. On clicking this button, the original dimension value is restored and the **Modify** dialog box is closed.

As discussed earlier, the **Smart Dimension** tool is used for applying dimensions depending upon the type of sketch entity or entities selected. You can apply horizontal, vertical, aligned, angular, diameter, radius, and linear diameter dimensions by using this tool. The methods of applying various types of dimensions by using the **Smart Dimension** tool are discussed next.

Applying Horizontal Dimension by using the Smart Dimension Tool

To apply horizontal dimension by using the **Smart Dimension** tool, click on the **Smart Dimension** tool and then select the required sketch entity or entities. You can select a horizontal sketch entity, an inclined sketch entity, two points, or two vertical sketch entities for applying the horizontal dimension, see Figure 4.11. After selecting an entity or entities, the current dimension value of the selected entity or entities is attached to the cursor. Next, move the cursor vertically up or down and then click the left mouse button in the drawing area to specify the placement point for the horizontal dimension. The **Modify** dialog box appears. Next, enter the required dimension value in the **Dimension** field of the **Modify** dialog box and then click on the green tick-mark button. The horizontal dimension is applied, see Figure 4.11.

> **Tip:** After selecting an inclined entity or two sketch points, if you move the cursor in a direction other than vertically up or down, then the vertical or aligned dimension gets attached to the cursor.

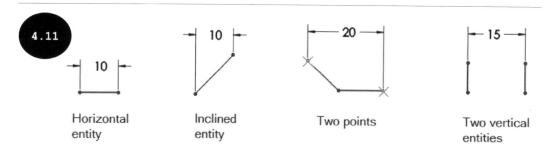

| Horizontal entity | Inclined entity | Two points | Two vertical entities |

Applying Vertical Dimension by using the Smart Dimension Tool

Similar to applying horizontal dimension by using the **Smart Dimension** tool, you can apply vertical dimension to a vertical sketch entity, an inclined sketch entity, between two points, or between two horizontal sketch entities, see Figure 4.12. Note that to apply a vertical dimension, you need to move the cursor horizontally toward right or left after selecting the desired entity.

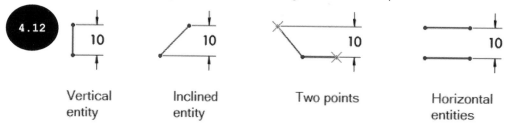

| Vertical entity | Inclined entity | Two points | Horizontal entities |

Applying Aligned Dimension by using the Smart Dimension Tool

Similar to applying horizontal and vertical dimensions by using the **Smart Dimension** tool, you can apply aligned dimension to an inclined sketch entity or between two points, see Figure 4.13. The aligned dimension is generally used for measuring the aligned length of an inclined line. Note that after selecting an entity or entities for applying aligned dimension, you need to move the cursor in a direction perpendicular to the selected entity for specifying the placement point.

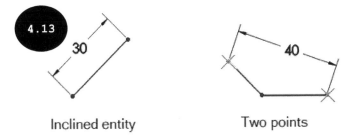

Inclined entity   Two points

Applying Angular Dimension by using the Smart Dimension Tool

You can apply angular dimension between two non-parallel line entities or three points by using the **Smart Dimension** tool. For doing so, invoke the **Smart Dimension** tool and then select two non-parallel line entities in the drawing area. The angular dimension between the selected entities gets attached to the cursor, see Figure 4.14. Next, move the cursor to a location where you want to place the dimension and then click to specify the placement point. The **Modify** dialog box appears. Enter the required angular value in this dialog box and then press ENTER or click on the green tick-mark button. The angular dimension is applied between the two selected line entities. Note that the angular dimension gets applied between the selected entities depending upon the location of the placement point in the drawing area, see Figure 4.14.

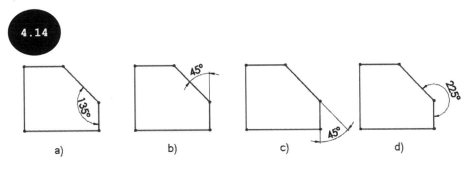

To apply angular dimension between three points, invoke the **Smart Dimension** tool and then select three points in the drawing area, see Figure 4.15. An angular dimension between the selected points is attached to the cursor. Next, move the cursor to a location where you want to place the attached angular dimension and then click to specify the placement point. The **Modify** dialog box appears. Enter the required angular value in this dialog box and then press ENTER. The angular dimension is applied between the three selected points, see Figure 4.15.

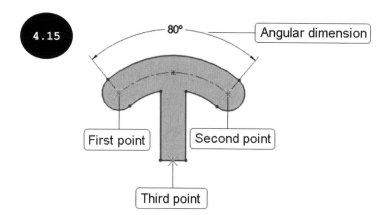

Applying Diameter Dimension by using the Smart Dimension Tool

The diameter dimension can be applied to a circle by using the **Smart Dimension** tool. For doing so, click on the **Smart Dimension** tool and then select a circle. The diameter dimension gets attached to the cursor. Next, move the cursor to the required location and then click to specify a placement point in the drawing area. The **Modify** dialog box appears. Enter the diameter value in this dialog box and then press ENTER. The diameter dimension is applied, see Figure 4.16.

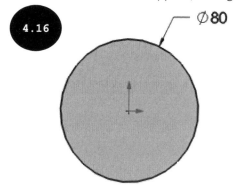

Note: You can also apply radius dimension to a circle. For doing so, first apply the diameter dimension to the circle, as discussed above. Next, right-click on the applied diameter dimension and then click on **Display Options > Display As Radius** in the shortcut menu that appears. The selected diameter dimension is converted to the radius dimension. Note that if the **Smart Dimension** tool is activated when you right-click on a diameter dimension, then you can directly select the **Display As Radius** option in the shortcut menu that appears.

Applying Radius Dimension by using the Smart Dimension Tool

The radius dimension can be applied to an arc by using the **Smart Dimension** tool. For doing so, click on the **Smart Dimension** tool and then select an arc. The radius dimension gets attached to the cursor. Move the cursor to the required location and click to specify a placement point in the drawing area. The **Modify** dialog box appears. Enter the radius value in this dialog box and then press ENTER. The radius dimension is applied, see Figure 4.17.

4.17 R40

> **Note:** You can also apply diameter dimension to an arc. For doing do, first apply the radius dimension to an arc and then right-click on the applied radius dimension. A shortcut menu appears. In this shortcut menu, click on **Display Options > Display As Diameter**. The selected radius dimension is converted to the diameter dimension. Note that if the **Smart Dimension** tool is activated when you right-click on a radius dimension, then you can directly select the **Display As Diameter** option in the shortcut menu that appears.

Applying Linear Diameter Dimension by using the Smart Dimension Tool

The Linear diameter dimension can be applied to a sketch of a revolved feature, see Figure 4.18. To apply a linear diameter dimension, click on the **Smart Dimension** tool and then select a linear sketch entity of the sketch. The linear dimension gets attached to the cursor. Next, select a centerline or revolving axis of the sketch. The linear dimension between the selected line and the centerline gets attached to the cursor. Move the cursor to the other side of the centerline or the revolving axis. The linear diameter dimension appears. Next, click to specify a placement point in the drawing area. The **Modify** dialog box appears. Enter the linear diameter value in the dialog box and then press ENTER. The linear diameter dimension is applied.

4.18 Linear diameter dimension · Centerline · 95 · 54 · 50 · 10 · 2 · 20 · 5 · 20 · 10 · 65 · 80

Working with Horizontal Dimension and Vertical Dimension Tools

In addition to applying horizontal and vertical dimensions by using the **Smart Dimension** tool, you can also apply these dimensions by using the **Horizontal Dimension** and **Vertical Dimension** tools in the **Dimension** flyout, see Figure 4.19.

To apply horizontal dimension by using the Horizontal Dimension tool, click on the arrow below the Smart Dimension tool. The Dimension flyout appears, see Figure 4.19. Next, click on the Horizontal Dimension tool and then click on the sketch entity to be dimensioned. The horizontal dimension gets attached to the cursor. Move the cursor to a location where you want to place the dimension and then click to specify a placement point in the drawing area. The Modify dialog box appears. Enter the required dimension value in the Modify dialog box and then press ENTER. The horizontal dimension is applied.

Similarly, you can apply vertical dimension by using the Vertical Dimension tool.

Working with Baseline Dimension Tool   New

The Baseline Dimension tool is used for applying baseline dimensions to a sketch. Baseline dimensions are a series of parallel linear dimensions that measured from the same base entity, see Figure 4.20. The baseline dimensions are used for eliminating cumulative errors that can occur due to the rounded dimension values between consecutive adjacent dimensions or due to the upper and lower dimension limits.

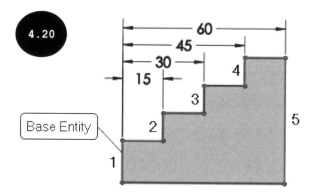

To apply baseline dimensions, click on the arrow below the Smart Dimension tool and then click on the Baseline Dimension tool in the Dimension flyout that appears. You are prompted to select a base entity. Click to select a linear sketch entity (1) as the base entity, refer to Figure 4.20. You can select a line or a vertex as the base entity. Next, click to select the second entity (2) to be dimensioned from the base entity. A dimension gets applied between the base entity (1) and the second entity (2). Next, select the third entity. A linear dimension is applied between the base entity and the third entity, refer to Figure 4.20. Similarly, you can select other entities one by one for applying baseline dimensions measuring from the base entity, refer to Figure 4.20.

Working with Chain Dimension Tool

The **Chain Dimension** tool is used for applying chain dimensions to a sketch. Chain dimensions are a chain of linear dimensions which are placed end to end such that the second extension line of the first linear dimension is used as the first extension line for the next linear dimension, see Figure 4.21.

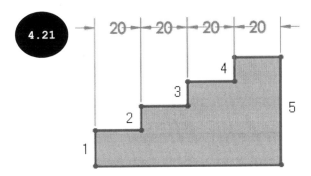

To apply chain dimensions, invoke the **Dimension** flyout and then click on the **Chain Dimension** tool. You are prompted to select a line entity or a vertex. Click to select the first line entity (1) and then the second line entity (2) in the drawing area. A linear dimension gets applied between the selected entities, refer to Figure 4.21. Next, select the third line entity (3). A linear dimension gets applied between the second and the third line entities. Similarly, you can select other line entities one by one in the drawing area to continue applying chain dimensions, refer to Figure 4.21. Note that the chain dimensions are driven dimensions and cannot be edited.

Working with Ordinate Dimension Tool

The **Ordinate Dimension** tool is used for applying ordinate dimensions to a sketch. Ordinate dimensions are measured from a base entity. The base entity is defined as the starting point from where all other entities are measured, see Figure 4.22. Generally, ordinate dimensions are used for the components created by using CNC machines. Figure 4.23 shows a component and Figure 4.24 shows a sketch used for creating this model. Notice that in Figure 4.24, the horizontal dimensions applied to the sketch have a symmetric tolerance value of 0.1. This means that the maximum accepted length of entities measuring 100 mm, 30 mm, and 40 mm are 100.1 mm, 30.1 mm, and 40.1 mm, respectively. If you sum up the maximum accepted length of these entities (2, 4, and 6), you will get 100.3 mm (30.1+40.1+30.1). However, the actual maximum accepted horizontal length of the component is 100.1 mm, see Figure 4.24. There is a difference of 0.2 mm, therefore you need to apply ordinate dimensions to overcome this problem. Figure 4.22 shows a sketch with ordinate dimensions applied and shows 100.1 mm as the maximum accepted horizontal length of the component.

You can apply horizontal and vertical ordinate dimensions by using the **Ordinate Dimension** tool. The methods for applying horizontal and vertical ordinate dimensions are discussed next.

Applying Horizontal Ordinate Dimensions

To apply horizontal ordinate dimension, click on the arrow below the **Smart Dimension** tool. The **Dimension** flyout appears. In the **Dimension** flyout, click on the **Ordinate Dimension** tool. You are prompted to select an entity as the base entity to measure all dimensions. Click on a vertical entity (1) as the base entity, see Figure 4.25. The 0 (zero) dimension value gets attached to the cursor. Next, click to specify a placement point in the drawing area and then select the second vertical entity (2), see Figure 4.25. The horizontal distance measuring from the 0 (zero) dimension value is applied. Similarly, select other vertical entities of the sketch to be measured from the 0 (zero) dimension value, see Figure 4.25.

Applying Vertical Ordinate Dimensions

Similar to applying horizontal ordinate dimension, you can apply vertical ordinate dimension by using the **Ordinate Dimension** tool. For doing so, invoke the **Ordinate Dimension** tool and then select a horizontal entity as the base entity. The 0 (zero) dimension value gets attached to the cursor. Next, click to specify a placement point for the attached 0 (zero) dimension value, see Figure 4.26. Next, select the second horizontal entity. The vertical distance measuring from the 0 (zero) dimension value is applied. Similarly, select other entities of the sketch to be measured from the 0 (zero) dimension value, see Figure 4.26.

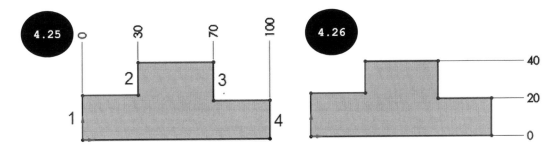

Similar to applying horizontal and vertical ordinate dimensions by using the **Ordinate Dimension** tool, you can apply horizontal and vertical ordinate dimensions by using the **Horizontal Ordinate Dimension** and **Vertical Ordinate Dimension** tools, respectively.

Working with Path Length Dimension Tool

The **Path Length Dimension** tool is used for applying path length dimensions to a series of end to end connected sketch entities forming a chain, see Figure 4.27. Note that the path length dimensions are driving dimensions. As a result, on modifying or editing the path length dimension value, the sketch entities of the path get modified or driven accordingly in the drawing area.

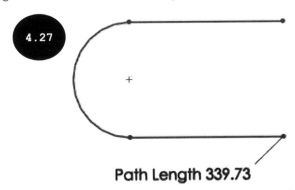

Path Length 339.73

To apply a path length dimension, invoke the **Dimension** flyout and then click on the **Path Length Dimension** tool. The **Path Length PropertyManager** appears and you are prompted to select entities that are connected end to end and form a chain of entities. Select two or more sketch entities in the drawing area. All the selected entities get listed in the **Selected Entities** field of the PropertyManager. Next, click on the green tick-mark ☑ button in the PropertyManager or press ENTER. The selected entities become a single chain of entities and the path length dimension gets applied, refer to Figure 4.27.

Tip: You can also remove an entity from the selection list in the **Selected Entities** field of the **Path Length PropertyManager**. For doing so, select the entity in the **Selected Entities** field and then right-click. A shortcut menu appears. In this shortcut menu, click on the **Delete** option. The selected entity gets removed from the selection list. If you click on the **Clear Selections** option in the shortcut menu that appears, all the selected entities get removed from the selection list.

Working with Auto Insert Dimension Tool

In SOLIDWORKS, you can apply the most appropriate dimension to the selected sketch entity or entities, automatically by using the **Auto Insert Dimension** tool. You can access this tool in the Pop-up toolbar, which appears on selecting one or more sketch entities in the drawing area, see Figure 4.28.

To apply a dimension by using the **Auto Insert Dimension** tool, select a sketch entity: line, arc, or circle in the drawing area. You can also select two sketch entities: two lines at an angle, two parallel lines, two arcs, two circles, an arc and a line, a circle and a line, a point and a line, an arc and a point, a circle and a point, or an arc and a circle by pressing the CTRL key. On selecting one or more entities, the Pop-up toolbar appears in the drawing area, refer to Figure 4.28. In this toolbar, click on the **Auto Insert Dimension** tool. The **Modify** toolbar appears. In this toolbar, enter the required dimension value and then click on the green tick-mark button in the dialog box. The most appropriate dimension depending upon the entity/entities selected is applied in the drawing area. For example, the linear dimension is applied to a line, radial dimension is applied to an arc, diameter dimension is applied to a circle, and angular dimension is applied between two non-parallel lines.

Modifying/Editing Dimensions

After applying dimensions, you may need to modify them due to changes or revisions in the design. To modify an already applied dimension, click on the dimension value to be modified. The **Dimension Input Value** box appears with the display of current dimension value in the drawing area, see Figure 4.29. Enter the new dimension value in this box and then press ENTER. The selected dimension value gets modified. Alternatively, double-click on a dimension value in the drawing area. The **Modify** dialog box appears. In this dialog box, enter the new dimension value and then press ENTER or click on the green tick-mark button in the dialog box.

Dimension Input Value box

Note: The **Dimension Input Value** box appears on clicking a dimension value, only if the Instant2D tool is activated in the **Sketch CommandManager**.

Working with Different States of a Sketch

In SOLIDWORKS, a sketch can be either Under defined, Fully defined, or Over defined. All these states of the sketch are discussed next.

Under Defined Sketch

An under defined sketch is a sketch, in which all degrees of freedom are not fixed, which means that the entities of the sketch can change their shape, size, and position on being dragged. Figure 4.30 shows a rectangular sketch in which the length of the rectangle is defined as 50 mm. However, the width and position of the rectangle with respect to the origin are not defined. This means that the width and position of the rectangle can be changed by dragging the respective entities of the rectangle. Note that the current status of the sketch appears on the right in the Status Bar, which is available on the lower side of the drawing area. By default, the entities of an under defined sketch appear in blue color in the drawing area.

Fully Defined Sketch

A fully defined sketch is a sketch, in which all degrees of freedom are fixed. This means the entities of the sketch cannot change their shape, size, and position by being dragged. Figure 4.31 shows a rectangular sketch in which the length, width, and position of the sketch is defined. Note that the entities of a fully defined sketch appear in black color.

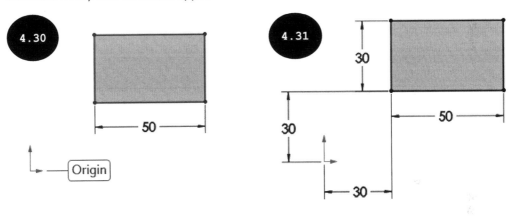

Tip: The sketch shown in Figure 4.31 is a fully defined sketch as all its entities are dimensioned and the required geometrical relations have been applied, that is horizontal relations applied to the horizontal entities and vertical relations applied to the vertical entities. Note that horizontal and vertical relations are applied automatically to the entities while they are being drawn.

Over Defined Sketch

An over defined sketch is a sketch that is over defined by dimensions or geometric relations. Figure 4.32 shows an over defined rectangular sketch in which applying dimension to both sides of the rectangle makes it over defined. Note that the entities of an over defined sketch appear in yellow color.

Note that when you apply an over defined dimension to an entity, the **Make Dimension Driven?** dialog box appears, see Figure 4.33. In this dialog box, if you select the **Make this dimension driven** radio button and click on the **OK** button, then the newly applied dimension becomes a driven dimension and acts as a reference dimension only. As a result, the sketch cannot become an over defined sketch. However, if you select the **Leave this dimension driving** radio button and click on the **OK** button, then the newly applied dimension becomes a driving dimension. As a result, the sketch becomes over defined.

Note: In SOLIDWORKS, when you apply a dimension, it is applied with default properties. You can modify default dimension properties such as dimension style, tolerance, and precision by using the **Dimension PropertyManager** that appears when a dimension is selected in the drawing area. You will learn about modifying dimension properties in Chapter 14, while creating 2D drawings in the Drawing environment. The options for modifying dimension properties of a dimension in the Sketching environment are same as in the Drawing environment.

Tutorial 1

Draw the sketch shown in Figure 4.34 and make it fully defined by applying all dimensions and relations. The 3D model shown in this figure is for your reference only. You will learn about creating the 3D model in the later chapters. All dimensions are in mm.

Section 1: Starting SOLIDWORKS

1. Start SOLIDWORKS by double-clicking on the SOLIDWORKS icon on your desktop. The startup user interface of SOLIDWORKS appears along with the **Welcome** dialog box.

> **Note:** If SOLIDWORKS is already open and the **Welcome** dialog box does not appear on the screen, then you can invoke the same by clicking on the **Welcome to SOLIDWORKS** tool 🏠 in the **Standard** toolbar or by pressing the CTRL + F2 keys.

Section 2: Invoking the Sketching Environment

1. Click on the **Part** button in the **Welcome** dialog box. The Part modeling environment is invoked.

> **Tip:** You can also invoke the Part modeling environment by using the **New SOLIDWORKS Document** dialog box. For doing so, click on the **New** tool in the **Standard** toolbar. The **New SOLIDWORKS Document** dialog box appears. In this dialog box, make sure that the **Part** button is selected and then click on the **OK** button.

2. Click on the **Sketch** tab in the CommandManager. The tools of the **Sketch CommandManager** appear, see Figure 4.35.

3. Click on the **Sketch** tool in the **Sketch CommandManager**. Three default planes mutually perpendicular to each other appear in the graphics area.

4. Move the cursor over the Top plane and then click on it when the boundary of the plane highlights. The Sketching environment is invoked. Also, the Top plane is orientated normal to the viewing direction.

Section 3: Specifying Unit Settings

Once the Sketching environment has been invoked, you need to specify the metric unit system for measurement.

1. Click on the **Options** tool ⚙ in the **Standard** toolbar. The **System Options - General** dialog box appears.

2. Click on the **Document Properties** tab in the dialog box. The name of the dialog box changes to **Document Properties - Drafting Standard**.

3. Click on the **Units** option in the left panel of the dialog box. The options for specifying the unit system appear on the right panel of the dialog box.

4. Make sure that the **MMGS (millimeter, gram, second)** radio button is selected in the **Unit system** area of the dialog box.

    Now, you need to make sure that the snap mode is turned off. As SOLIDWORKS is a parametric software, you can turn off the snap mode and create the sketch entities by specifying points arbitrarily in the drawing area and then apply required dimensions.

5. Click on the **Grid/Snap** option in the left panel of the dialog box. The options related to grid and snap settings appear.

6. Make sure the **Display grid** check box is cleared in the **Grid** area.

7. Click on the **Go To System Snaps** button in the dialog box. The name of the dialog box changes to **System Options - Relations/Snaps**.

8. Make sure the **Grid** check box in the **Sketch snaps** area of the dialog box is cleared.

9. Click on the **OK** button to accept the changes made and close the dialog box.

Section 4: Creating the Sketch

Now, you need to create the sketch by using the sketching tools.

1. Click on the **Circle** tool ⊙ in the **Sketch CommandManager**. The **Circle** tool is invoked and the **Circle PropertyManager** appears.

2. Move the cursor to the origin and then click to specify the center point of the circle when the cursor snaps to the origin.

3. Move the cursor horizontally toward right and click when the radius of the circle appears close to 60 mm near the cursor, see Figure 4.36. A circle of radius close to 60 mm is created and the **Circle** tool is still active.

4. Move the cursor to the origin again and click to specify the center point of another circle when the cursor snaps to it.

5. Move the cursor horizontally toward right and click when the radius of the circle appears close to 140 mm near the cursor, see Figure 4.37. A circle of radius close to 140 mm is created and the **Circle** tool is still active.

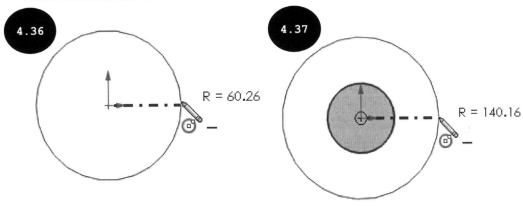

Tip: While drawing sketch entities, you may need to zoom in or zoom out of the drawing display area. For doing so, scroll the middle mouse button. Alternatively, you can click on the **View > Modify > Zoom In/Out** in the SOLIDWORKS Menus and then drag the cursor upward or downward. Next, to exit the tool, press the ESC key.

6. Right-click in the drawing area and then click on the **Select** option in the shortcut menu that appears to exit the **Circle** tool.

7. Invoke the **Slot** flyout, see Figure 4.38 and then click on the **Centerpoint Straight Slot** tool.

8. Move the cursor to the origin and then click to specify the center point of the slot when the cursor snaps to the origin.

9. Move the cursor horizontally toward right and click when the half length of the slot appears close to 260 mm (520/2 = 260) near the cursor, see Figure 4.39. Next, move the cursor to a distance in the drawing area. A preview of the slot appears.

10. Click the left mouse button when the width of the slot appears close to 200 mm in the **Parameters** rollout of the **Slot PropertyManager**, see Figure 4.40. The slot is created, see Figure 4.41. Next, press the ESC key to exit the **Centerpoint Straight Slot** tool.

11. Click on the **Zoom to Fit** tool 🔍 in the **View (Heads-Up)** toolbar to fit the sketch completely inside the screen.

12. Click on the **Circle** tool ⊙ in the **Sketch CommandManager** and then move the cursor toward the midpoint of the right slot arc, see Figure 4.42.

13. Click to specify the center point of the circle when the circle snaps to the midpoint of slot arc, see Figure 4.42.

14. Move the cursor horizontally toward right and click when the radius of the circle appears close to 18 mm near the cursor, see Figure 4.43. A circle of radius close to 18 mm is created and the **Circle** tool is still active.

15. Move the cursor to the center point of the previously created circle of radius close to 18 mm and then click to specify the center point of another circle when the cursor snaps to it.

16. Move the cursor horizontally toward right and click when the radius of the circle appears close to 38 mm near the cursor, see Figure 4.44. The circle is created.

17. Similarly, create two circles of same diameters on the left side of the slot, see Figure 4.45. Next, press the ESC key to exit the **Circle** tool.

18. Click on the arrow next to the **Line** tool. The **Line** flyout appears, see Figure 4.46.

19. Click on the **Centerline** tool in the **Line** flyout and then create a vertical centerline of any length starting from the origin, see Figure 4.47. Next, press the ESC key to exit the **Centerline** tool.

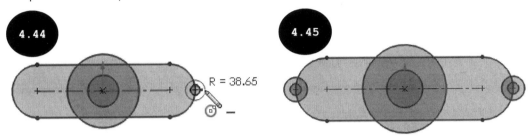

Section 5: Trimming Sketch Entities

Now, you need to trim the unwanted entities of the sketch.

1. Click on the **Trim Entities** tool in the **Sketch CommandManager**. The **Trim PropertyManager** appears on the left of the drawing area.

2. Click on the **Trim to closest** button in the **Options** rollout of the PropertyManager. The appearance of the cursor changes to trim cursor ꝗ×.

3. Make sure that the **Keep trimmed entities as construction geometry** and **Ignore trimming of construction geometry** check boxes are cleared in the PropertyManager.

4. Move the cursor over the portion of the lower horizontal slot entity that lies inside the circle, see Figure 4.48. Next, click the left mouse button when it gets highlighted. The **SOLIDWORKS** message window appears informing you that the trim operation will destroy the slot entity.

5. Click on the **OK** button in the **SOLIDWORKS** message window. The selected portion of the entity is trimmed, see Figure 4.49. Also, the **Trim Entities** tool is still active.

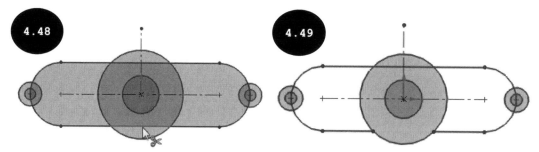

6. Similarly, click on the other unwanted entities of the sketch one by one to trim them. Figure 4.50 shows the sketch after trimming all the unwanted entities. Note that while trimming the sketch entities, if the **SOLIDWORKS** message window appears, then click on the **Yes** button in the **SOLIDWORKS** message window to continue the process of trimming sketch entities.

Tip: While drawing sketch entities, you may need to zoom in or zoom out of the drawing display area. For doing so, scroll the middle mouse button. Alternatively, you can click on the **View > Modify > Zoom In/Out** in the SOLIDWORKS Menus and then drag the cursor upward or downward. Next, to exit the tool, press the ESC key.

7. Once you have completed the trimming operation, press the ESC key to exit the tool.

Section 6: Applying Relations

After creating the sketch, you need to make it fully defined by applying proper relations and dimensions to the sketch entities.

1. Select two smaller circles of diameter 36 mm (radius 18 mm) by pressing the CTRL key to apply equal relation between them, see Figure 4.51. Next, release the CTRL key and do not move the cursor. The Pop-up toolbar appears, see Figure 4.52. Also, the **Properties PropertyManager** appears on the left of the drawing area.

2. Click on the **Make Equal** tool in the Pop-up toolbar, see Figure 4.52. An equal relation is applied between the selected circles.

Circles of diameter 36 mm

3. Similarly, select arcs of radius 38 mm by pressing the CTRL key and then apply an equal relation between them, see Figure 4.53.

Arcs of radius 38 mm

4. Select the center points of slot arcs and the vertical centerline by pressing the CTRL key, see Figure 4.54. Next, release the CTRL key. The Pop-up toolbar appears.

5. Click on the **Make Symmetric** tool in the Pop-up toolbar. A symmetric relation is applied between center points of slot arcs and the vertical centerline.

6. Similarly, select the center points of two circles of diameter 36 mm and the vertical centerline by pressing the CTRL key, see Figure 4.55 and then apply a symmetric relation between them.

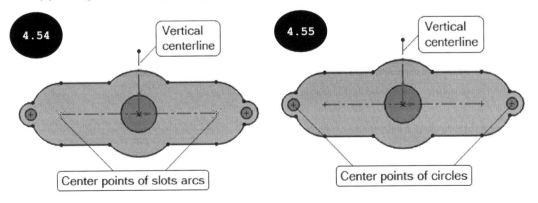

Vertical centerline

Center points of slots arcs

Vertical centerline

Center points of circles

7. Similarly, apply tangent relations between four sets of tangent line and arc entities one by one, see Figure 4.56.

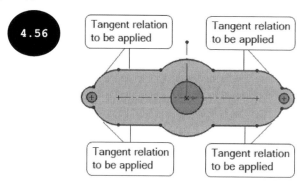

4.56

Tangent relation to be applied

Tangent relation to be applied

Tangent relation to be applied

Tangent relation to be applied

8. Select the horizontal centerline and the origin by pressing the CTRL key, see Figure 4.57 and then release the CTRL key. The Pop-up toolbar appears.

4.57

Origin

Horizontal centerline

9. Click on the **Make Coincident** tool in the Pop-up toolbar. A coincident relation is applied between the horizontal centerline and the origin.

10. Similarly, apply horizontal relation — to all horizontal lines (four) of the sketch one by one.

11. Select the center points of two circles of diameter 36 mm and the origin by pressing the CTRL key, see Figure 4.58 and then release the CTRL key. The Pop-up toolbar appears. In this Pop-up toolbar, click on the **Make Horizontal** tool to apply the horizontal relation between them.

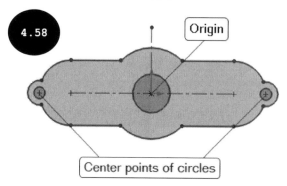

4.58

Origin

Center points of circles

Note: You can turn on or off the display of the applied relations in the drawing area by clicking on the **View Sketch Relations** tool in the **Hide/Show Items** flyout of the **View (Heads-Up)** toolbar, see Figure 4.59.

4.59

Section 7: Applying Dimensions

After applying the required relations, you need to apply dimensions to make the sketch fully defined.

1. Click on the **Smart Dimension** tool in the **Sketch CommandManager**.

2. Select a circle whose center point is at the origin. The diameter dimension of the selected circle gets attached to the cursor, see Figure 4.60.

3. Move the cursor to the location where you want to place the dimension in the drawing area and then click to specify the placement point. The **Modify** dialog box appears, see Figure 4.61.

4.60

4.61

4. Enter **120** in the **Modify** dialog box and then click on the green tick-mark ☑ button. The diameter of the circle is modified to 120 mm and the diameter dimension is applied, see Figure 4.62.

5. Similarly, apply the remaining dimensions to the sketch. Figure 4.63 shows the fully defined sketch after applying all dimensions.

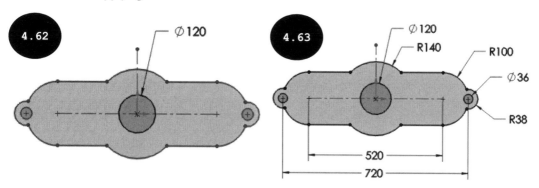

Section 8: Saving the Sketch

1. Click on the **Save** tool 💾 in the **Standard** toolbar. The **Save As** dialog box appears.

2. Browse to the SOLIDWORKS folder and then create a folder with the name **Chapter 4** in the SOLIDWORKS folder. Next, save the sketch with the name Tutorial 1 in the Chapter 4 folder.

Tutorial 2

Draw the sketch shown in Figure 4.64 and make it fully defined by applying all the required dimensions and relations. The 3D model shown in the figure is for your reference only. You will learn about creating the 3D model in the later chapters. All dimensions are in mm.

Section 1: Starting SOLIDWORKS

1. Start SOLIDWORKS by double-clicking on the SOLIDWORKS icon on your desktop. The startup user interface of SOLIDWORKS appears along with the **Welcome** dialog box.

Note: If SOLIDWORKS is already open and the **Welcome** dialog box does not appear on the screen, then you can invoke the same by clicking on the **Welcome to SOLIDWORKS** tool 🏠 in the **Standard** toolbar or by pressing the CTRL + F2 keys.

Section 2: Invoking the Sketching Environment

1. Click on the **Part** button in the **Welcome** dialog box. The Part modeling environment is invoked.

Tip: You can also invoke the Part modeling environment by using the **New SOLIDWORKS Document** dialog box. For doing so, click on the **New** tool in the **Standard** toolbar. The **New SOLIDWORKS Document** dialog box appears. In this dialog box, make sure that the **Part** button is selected and then click on the **OK** button.

2. Click on the **Sketch** tab in the CommandManager. The tools of the **Sketch CommandManager** appears, see Figure 4.65.

3. Click on the **Sketch** tool in the **Sketch CommandManager**. Three default planes mutually perpendicular to each other appear in the graphics area.

4. Move the cursor over the Front plane and then click on it when the boundary of the plane gets highlighted. The Sketching environment is invoked and the Front plane is orientated normal to the viewing direction.

Section 3: Specifying Unit Settings

Once the Sketching environment has been invoked, you need to specify the metric unit system for measurement.

1. Click on the **Options** tool ⚙ in the **Standard** toolbar. The **System Options - General** dialog box appears.

2. Click on the **Document Properties** tab in the dialog box. The name of the dialog box changes to **Document Properties - Drafting Standard**.

3. Click on the **Units** option in the left panel of the dialog box. The options for specifying the unit system appear on the right panel of the dialog box.

4. Make sure that the **MMGS (millimeter, gram, second)** radio button is selected in the **Unit system** area of the dialog box.

    Now, you need to make sure that the snap mode is turned off. As SOLIDWORKS is a parametric software, you can turn off the snap mode and create a sketch by specifying points arbitrarily in the drawing area and then applying the required dimensions.

5. Click on the **Grid/Snap** option in the left panel of the dialog box and then make sure that the **Display grid** check box in the **Grid** area is cleared.

6. Click on the **Go To System Snaps** button and then make sure that the **Grid** check box in the **Sketch snaps** area of the dialog box is cleared.

7. Click on the **OK** button to accept the changes and close the dialog box.

Section 4: Drawing the Upper Half of the Sketch

In this section, you need to draw the upper half of the sketch.

1. Click on the arrow next to the **Line** tool. The **Line** flyout appears, see Figure 4.66.

2. Click on the **Centerline** tool in the flyout. The **Centerline** tool is invoked.

3. Create vertical and horizontal centerlines of any length starting from the origin one by one, see Figure 4.67. Next, exit the **Centerline** tool.

4. Press and hold the right mouse button and then drag the cursor toward left. The **Mouse Gestures** appears in the drawing area, see Figure 4.68.

5. Drag the cursor over the **Line** tool in the **Mouse Gestures** by pressing and holding the right mouse button, see Figure 4.68. The **Line** tool gets activated and the **Mouse Gestures** is disabled. Also, the **Insert Line PropertyManager** appears on the left of the drawing area. Next, release the right mouse button.

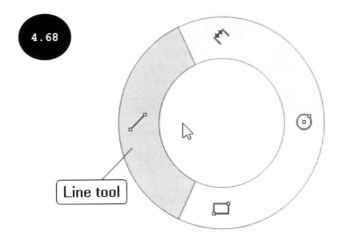

4.68

6. Move the cursor over the horizontal centerline in the drawing area, see Figure 4.69 and then click to specify the start point of the line when the coordinates (X, Y, Z) appear close to "15, 0, 0" in the Status Bar, see Figure 4.70.

4.69

4.70

| 15.09mm | 0.62mm | 0mm | Fully Defined | Editing Sketch1 | | MMGS | ▲ | |

X, Y, Z coordinates

7. Move the cursor vertically upward and then click to specify the endpoint of the line when the length of the line appears close to 22.5 mm near the cursor, see Figure 4.71. A vertical line of length close to 22.5 mm is created.

4.71

22.62, 90°

8. Move the cursor horizontally toward right and click to specify the endpoint of the second line when the length of the line appears close to 7.5 mm. A horizontal line of length close to 7.5 mm is created.

9. Move the cursor vertically upward and click to specify the endpoint of the line when the length of the line appears close to 10 mm. A vertical line of the length close to 10 mm is created.

10. Move the cursor horizontally toward right and click when the length of the line appears close to 6.5 mm. A horizontal line of the length close to 6.5 mm is created.

11. Move the cursor vertically downward and click when the length of the line appears close to 25 mm.

12. Move the cursor horizontally toward right and click when the length of the line appears close to 6 mm.

13. Move the cursor vertically downward and click when the length of the line appears close to 4 mm.

14. Move the cursor toward right at an angle, see Figure 4.72 and then click to specify the endpoint of the inclined line when a line appears similar to the one shown in Figure 4.72.

15. Move the cursor vertically upward and click when the length of the line appears close to 4 mm, see Figure 4.73.

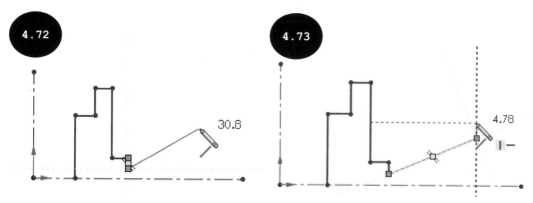

16. Move the cursor horizontally toward right and click when the length of the line appears close to 5 mm.

17. Move the cursor vertically downward and click when the length of the line appears close to 8 mm.

18. Move the cursor parallel to the inclined line toward the left, see Figure 4.74 and then click the left mouse button just above the horizontal centerline, see Figure 4.74.

4.74

19. Move the cursor vertically downward and then click the left mouse button when the cursor snaps to the horizontal centerline. Next, press the ESC key to exit the **Line** tool. Figure 4.75 shows the sketch after creating the upper half.

4.75

Section 5: Mirroring Sketch Entities

After creating the upper half of the sketch, you need to mirror it to create the lower half of the sketch.

1. Click on the **Mirror Entities** tool in the **Sketch CommandManager**. The Mirror **PropertyManager** appears on the left of the drawing area.

2. Select all the sketch entities except the vertical and horizontal centerlines as the entities to be mirrored.

3. Click on the **Mirror about** field in the PropertyManager and then click on the horizontal centerline as the mirroring line in the drawing area. The preview of the lower half of the sketch appears.

4. Make sure that the **Copy** check box is selected in the PropertyManager. Next, click on the green tick-mark ✓ button in the PropertyManager. The lower half of the sketch is created, see Figure 4.76.

Section 6: Applying Dimensions

Now, you need to apply dimensions to make the sketch fully defined.

1. Press and hold the right mouse button and then drag the cursor vertically upward to a distance. The **Mouse Gestures** appears in the drawing area, see Figure 4.77.

2. Drag the cursor over the **Smart Dimension** tool in the **Mouse Gestures** by pressing and holding the right mouse button, see Figure 4.77. The **Smart Dimension** tool gets activated and you are prompted to select the entities to be dimensioned. Now, release the right mouse button.

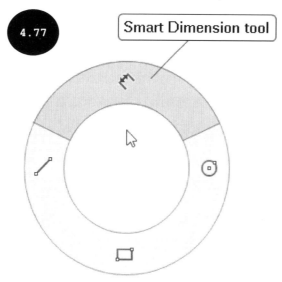

Smart Dimension tool

3. Click the left mouse button on the left most vertical line of the sketch, see Figure 4.78. The linear dimension of the selected line gets attached to the cursor.

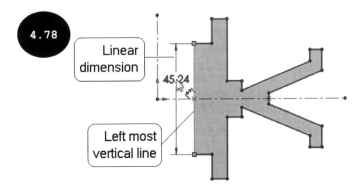

4. Move the cursor toward the left to a distance and then click to specify the placement point. The **Modify** dialog box appears, see Figure 4.79.

5. Enter **45** in the **Modify** dialog box and then click on the green tick-mark ✓. The length of the line is modified to 45 mm and the linear dimension is applied, see Figure 4.80.

6. Similarly, apply the remaining linear dimensions, see Figure 4.81.

Now, you need to apply linear diameter dimensions to the sketch.

7. Make sure that the **Smart Dimension** tool is activated, and then select the left most vertical line of length 45 mm. The linear dimension gets attached to the cursor. Next, select the vertical centerline and then move the cursor to the left of the vertical centerline. The linear diameter dimension is attached to the cursor, see Figure 4.82.

8. Click the left mouse button to specify the placement point for the linear diameter dimension. The **Modify** dialog box appears.

9. Enter **30** in the **Modify** dialog box and then click on the green tick-mark ✓. The linear diameter dimension is applied, see Figure 4.83.

10. Select the vertical line of length 10 mm, see Figure 4.84 and then move the cursor above the previously applied dimension. The linear diameter dimension gets attached to the cursor, see Figure 4.84.

11. Click to specify the placement point for the linear diameter dimension. The **Modify** dialog box appears.

12. Enter **45** in the **Modify** dialog box and then click on the green tick-mark ✓. The linear diameter dimension gets applied, see Figure 4.85.

13. Similarly, apply the remaining linear diameter dimensions to the sketch, see Figure 4.86.

14. Press the ESC key to exit the **Smart Dimensions** tool. Figure 4.86 shows the fully defined sketch.

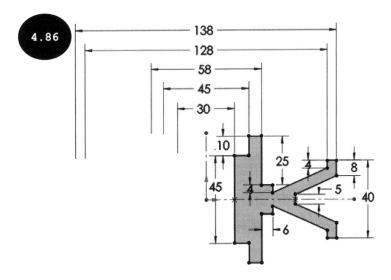

Section 7: Saving the Sketch

After creating the sketch, you need to save it.

1. Click on the **Save** tool of the **Standard** toolbar. The **Save As** window appears.

2. Browse to the Chapter 4 folder and then save the sketch with the name Tutorial 2. If the folder is not created, create a folder with name **Chapter 4** in the SOLIDWORKS folder.

Tutorial 3

Draw the sketch shown in Figure 4.87 and make it fully defined by applying all the required dimensions and relations. The 3D model shown in the figure is for your reference only. You will learn about creating the 3D model in later chapters. All dimensions are in mm.

Section 1: Starting SOLIDWORKS

1. Start SOLIDWORKS by double-clicking on the SOLIDWORKS icon on your desktop. The startup user interface of SOLIDWORKS appears along with the **Welcome** dialog box.

Note: If SOLIDWORKS is already open and the **Welcome** dialog box does not appear on the screen, then you can invoke the same by clicking on the **Welcome to SOLIDWORKS** tool 🏠 in the **Standard** toolbar or by pressing the CTRL + F2 keys.

Section 2: Invoking the Sketching Environment

1. Click on the **Part** button in the **Welcome** dialog box. The Part modeling environment is invoked.

Tip: You can also invoke the Part modeling environment by using the **New SOLIDWORKS Document** dialog box. For doing so, click on the **New** tool in the **Standard** toolbar. The **New SOLIDWORKS Document** dialog box appears. In this dialog box, make sure that the **Part** button is selected and then click on the **OK** button.

2. Click on the **Sketch** tab in the CommandManager. The tools of the **Sketch CommandManager** appear.

3. Click on the **Sketch** tool in the **Sketch CommandManager**. Three default planes mutually perpendicular to each other appear in the graphics area.

4. Move the cursor over the Front plane and then click the left mouse button when the boundary of Front plane gets highlighted. The Sketching environment is invoked and the Front plane is orientated normal to the viewing direction.

Section 3: Specifying Unit Settings

Once the Sketching environment has been invoked, specify the metric unit system for measurement.

1. Click on the **Options** tool ⚙ in the **Standard** toolbar. The **System Options - General** dialog box appears.

2. Click on the **Document Properties** tab in this dialog box.

3. Click on the **Units** option in the left panel of the dialog box.

4. Make sure that the **MMGS (millimeter, gram, second)** radio button is selected in the **Unit system** area of the dialog box. Also, make sure that the snap mode is turned off.

5. Click on the **OK** button to accept the changes and close the dialog box.

Section 4: Drawing Sketch Entities

Now, you need to create the sketch by using the sketching tools.

1. Press and hold the right mouse button and then drag the cursor toward left. The **Mouse Gestures** appear in the drawing area, see Figure 4.88.

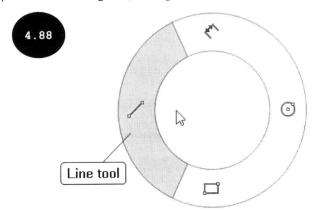

2. Drag the cursor over the **Line** tool in the **Mouse Gestures** by pressing and holding the right mouse button. The **Line** tool gets activated and the **Mouse Gestures** is disabled. Next, release the right mouse button.

3. Move the cursor to the origin and then click to specify the start point of the line when the cursor snaps to the origin and the coincident symbol appears, see Figure 4.89.

Note: If you specify a point when a relation symbol appears such as coincident, horizontal, or vertical near the cursor, the respective relation will be applied between entities.

4. Move the cursor horizontally toward right and click to specify the endpoint of the line when a length close to 210 mm and the symbol of horizontal relation appear near the cursor, see Figure 4.90. A horizontal line of length close to 210 mm is created. Also, the horizontal relation is applied to the line.

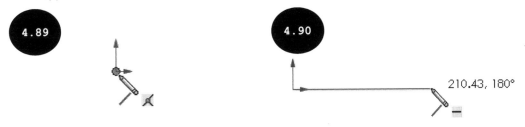

Tip: While drawing sketch entities, you may need to increase or decrease the drawing display area. You can Zoom in or Zoom out the drawing display area by scrolling the middle mouse button. Alternatively, click on the **View > Modify > Zoom In/Out** in the SOLIDWORKS Menus and then drag the cursor upward or downward by pressing the left mouse button.

5. Move the cursor vertically upward and create a vertical line of length close to 80 mm.

    Now, you need to create a tangent arc.

6. Move the cursor to a distance and then move it back to the last specified point. An orange colored dot appears, see Figure 4.91.

7. Move the cursor vertically upward to a distance and then move it horizontally toward left. The arc mode is activated and the preview of a tangent arc appears, see Figure 4.92.

8. Click to specify the endpoint of the tangent arc when the angle and radius of the arc appear close to 180 degrees and 25 mm, respectively, see Figure 4.92. A tangent arc of radius close to 25 mm is created and the line mode is activated again.

9. Move the cursor vertically downward and create a vertical line of length close to 20 mm.

10. Move the cursor horizontally toward left and create a horizontal line close to 90 mm.

11. Move the cursor vertically upward and create a vertical line of length close to 40 mm.

12. Create a tangent arc of radius close to 35 mm and angle close to 180 degrees, see Figure 4.93. Also, make sure that the endpoint of the tangent arc is aligned to the start point of the first line entity, see Figure 4.93.

13. Move the cursor vertically downward and click to specify the endpoint of the line when the cursor snaps to the start point of the first line entity, see Figure 4.94.

14. Press the ESC key to exit the **Line** tool.

    Now, you need to create circles of the sketch.

15. Press and hold the right mouse button and then drag the cursor toward right. The **Mouse Gestures** appears in the drawing area, see Figure 4.95.

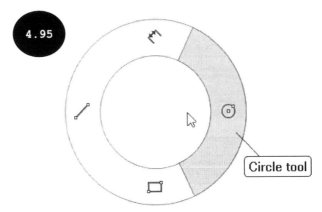

Circle tool

16. Drag the cursor over the **Circle** tool in the **Mouse Gestures**. The **Circle** tool gets activated and the **Mouse Gestures** is disabled. Next, release the right mouse button.

17. Create two circles of diameter close to 50 mm and 30 mm, respectively, see Figure 4.96. Next, exit the **Circle** tool.

Diameter 50 mm

Diameter 30 mm

18. Invoke the **Slot** flyout, see Figure 4.97, and then click on the **Straight Slot** tool in the flyout.

19. Create a straight slot similar to the one shown in Figure 4.98 and then exit the tool. You can create a slot with any parameters, because later in this tutorial, you will be required to apply dimensions in order to make the sketch fully defined.

Now, you need to create fillets in the sketch.

20. Click on the **Sketch Fillet** tool in the **Sketch CommandManager**. The **Sketch Fillet PropertyManager** appears.

21. Enter **10** in the **Fillet Radius** field of the **Fillet Parameters** rollout in the PropertyManager.

22. Move the cursor over the upper right vertex of the sketch, see Figure 4.99. The preview of the fillet appears. Next, click the left mouse button to accept the fillet preview.

23. Similarly, move the cursor over the upper left vertex of the sketch, see Figure 4.100. The preview of the fillet appears. Next, click the left mouse button to accept the fillet preview.

Upper right vertex

Upper left vertex

24. After selecting the vertices to create fillets, click on the green tick-mark button ☑ twice in the PropertyManager. Fillets of radius 10 mm are created, see Figure 4.101. Also, the radius dimension is applied to one of the fillets and equal relation is applied between both the fillets.

Section 5: Applying Dimensions

After creating the sketch, you need to apply the required relations and dimensions to make the sketch fully defined. In this sketch, all the required relations have been applied automatically while creating the entities. Therefore, you need to apply dimensions only.

1. Click on the **Smart Dimension** tool in the **Sketch CommandManager**.

2. Click on the lower horizontal line of the sketch and then move the cursor downward. The linear dimension gets attached to the cursor, see Figure 4.102.

3. Click to specify the placement point for the attached linear dimension in the drawing area. The **Modify** dialog box appears, see Figure 4.103.

4. Enter **210** in the **Modify** dialog box and then click on the green tick mark button ☑. The length of the line is modified to 210 mm and the linear dimension is applied.

5. Similarly, apply the remaining dimensions to the sketch by using the **Smart Dimension** tool, see Figure 4.104. Next, press the ESC key to exit the tool. Figure 4.104 shows the final sketch.

> **Tip:** After placing a dimension in the required location, you may need to further change its location in order to place other dimensions. To change the location of an existing dimension, press and hold the left mouse button over the dimension and then drag it to a new location. Next, release the left mouse button.

Section 6: Saving the Sketch

1. Click on the **Save** tool in the **Standard** toolbar. The **Save As** dialog box appears.

2. Browse to the Chapter 4 folder and then save the sketch with the name Tutorial 3.

Hands-on Test Drive 1

Draw a sketch of the model shown in Figure 4.105 and apply dimensions to make it fully defined. The 3D model shown in the figure is for your reference only. You will learn about creating the 3D model in later chapters. All dimensions are in mm.

Hands-on Test Drive 2

Draw a sketch of the model shown in Figure 4.106 and apply dimensions to make it fully defined. The 3D model shown in the figure is for your reference only. You will learn about creating the 3D model in later chapters. All dimensions are in mm.

Hands-on Test Drive 3

Draw a sketch of the model shown in Figure 4.107 and apply dimensions to make it fully defined. The 3D model shown in the figure is for your reference only. You will learn about creating the 3D model in later chapters. All dimensions are in mm.

Summary

In this chapter, you have learned about creating fully defined sketches by applying geometric relations and dimensions. Geometric relations can be applied by using the **Add Relation** tool and the Pop-up toolbar. Once the sketch has been drawn and the required geometric relations have been applied, dimensions need to be applied by using various dimension tools. The already applied dimensions and dimension properties such as dimension style, tolerance, and precision can also be modified. This chapter also discusses different sketch states such as under defined, fully defined, and over defined.

Questions

- The _____ relation is used for coinciding a sketch point on to a line, an arc, or an elliptical entity.

- You can control the display or visibility of the applied geometric relations by using the _____ tool.

- The _____ dimension is applied to a sketch representing revolve features.

- The _____ dimensions are measured from a base entity.

- All degrees of freedom of a _____ sketch are fixed.

- The availability of the suggested relations in the Pop-up toolbar depends upon the type of entities selected. (True/False)

- You cannot modify dimensions once they have been applied. (True/False)

- You cannot delete relations that have already been applied between the selected entities. (True/False)

- Geometric relations are used for restricting some degrees of freedom of a sketch. (True/False)

Creating First/Base Feature of Solid Models

This chapter discusses the following topics:

- Creating an Extruded Feature
- Creating a Revolved Feature
- Navigating a 3D Model in Graphics Area
- Manipulating View Orientation of a Model
- Changing the Display Style of a Model
- Changing the View of a Model

Once a sketch has been created and fully defined, you can convert it into a solid feature by using the feature modeling tools, see Figure 5.1.

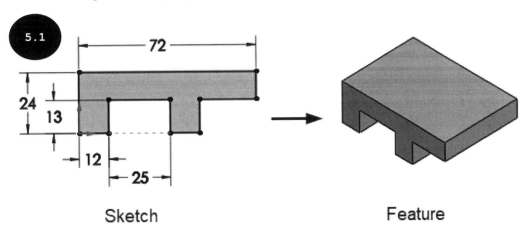

Sketch   Feature

All the feature modeling tools are available in the **Features CommandManager** in the Part modeling environment, see Figure 5.2. To create a 3D solid model, you need to create all its feature one by one using the feature modeling tools, see Figure 5.3. The first created feature of a model is known as the base feature or the parent feature of the model.

Note that most of the tools in the **Features CommandManager** are not activated, initially. These tools get activated after creating the base feature of a model. In SOLIDWORKS, you can create the base feature of a model by using the **Extruded Boss/Base, Revolved Boss/Base, Swept Boss/Base, Lofted Boss/Base,** or **Boundary Boss/Base** tool. Note that the **Swept Boss/Base, Lofted Boss/Base,** and **Boundary Boss/Base** tools are not activated in the **Features CommandManager**, initially. These tools get activated after creating the profiles or sketches required for creating features by using these tools. You will learn more about these tools in the later chapters. In this chapter, you will learn about creating a base feature by using the **Extruded Boss/Base** and **Revolved Boss/Base** tools.

Creating an Extruded Feature

An extruded feature is created by adding material normal or at an angle to the sketching plane. In SOLIDWORKS, you can create an extruded feature by using the **Extruded Boss/Base** tool. Note that the sketch of the extruded feature defines its geometry. Figure 5.4 shows different extruded features created from the respective sketches.

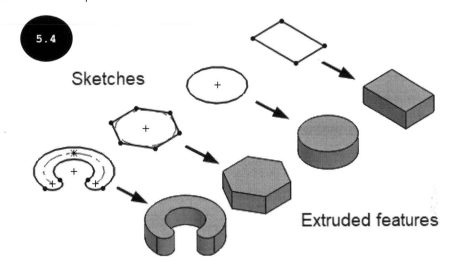

After drawing the sketch by using the sketching tools, do not exit the Sketching environment. Click on the **Features** tab in the CommandManager. The tools of the **Features CommandManager** appear. Next, click on the **Extruded Boss/Base** tool in the **Features CommandManager**. The preview of the extruded feature appears in the graphics area with the default extrusion parameters. Also, the orientation of the model is changed to trimetric orientation and the **Boss-Extrude PropertyManager** appears on the left of the graphics area, see Figure 5.5.

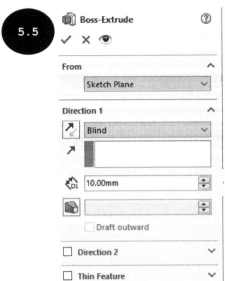

Figure 5.6 shows a rectangular sketch created on the Top Plane in the Sketching environment and Figure 5.7 shows a preview of the resultant extruded feature in Trimetric orientation.

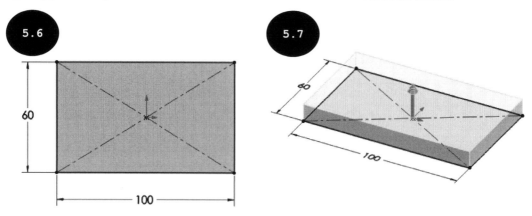

Note: If you exit the Sketching environment after creating the sketch and the sketch is not selected in the graphics area, then on invoking the **Extruded Boss/Base** tool, the **Extrude PropertyManager** appears similar to the one shown in Figure 5.8. Also, you are prompted to select either a sketch to be extruded or a sketching plane for creating the sketch. Select the sketch to be extruded in the graphics area. The preview of the extruded feature appears with default parameters and the **Boss-Extrude PropertyManager** appears on the left of the graphics area. Note that if the sketch to be extruded is not created then you can select the sketching plane for creating the sketch in the Sketching environment. Once the sketch has been created, exit the Sketching environment.

You can exit the Sketching environment by clicking on the **Exit Sketch** tool in the **Sketch CommandManager**. You can also click on the **Exit Sketch** icon ⎣↵ in the Confirmation corner, which is available at the top right corner in the graphics area to exit the Sketching environment.

The options in the **Boss-Extrude PropertyManager** are used for specifying parameters for the extruded feature. Some of the options of this PropertyManager are discussed next.

From

The options in the **Start Condition** drop-down list of the **From** rollout are used for specifying the start condition for the extruded feature, see Figure 5.9. The options of this drop-down list are discussed next.

Sketch Plane

By default, the **Sketch Plane** option is selected in the **Start Condition** drop-down list of the **From** rollout. As a result, extrusion starts exactly from the sketching plane of the sketch. Figure 5.10 shows the preview of the extruded feature from its front view when the **Sketch Plane** option is selected.

Offset

The **Offset** option is used for creating an extruded feature at an offset distance from the sketching plane. On selecting this option, the **Enter Offset Value** field and the **Reverse Direction** button appear in the **From** rollout, see Figure 5.11. By default, the **0** value is entered in the **Enter Offset Value** field. You can enter the required offset value in this field. You can also use the up and down arrows of the Spinner ⬍ available to the right of this field to set the offset value. Figure 5.12 shows the preview of the extruded feature from its front view after specifying an offset distance. To reverse the offset direction, click on the **Reverse Direction** button in the **From** rollout.

Note: The **Surface/Face/Plane** and **Vertex** options of the **Start Condition** drop-down list are used while creating the second and further features of the model and are discussed in later chapters.

Direction 1

The options in the **Direction 1** rollout of the PropertyManager are used for specifying the end condition for the extruded feature in direction 1. The options are discussed next.

End Condition

The options in the **End Condition** drop-down list are used for defining the end condition for the extruded feature, see Figure 5.13. The options of this drop-down list are discussed next.

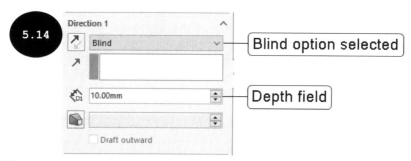

Blind

The **Blind** option of the **End Condition** drop-down list is used for specifying the end condition of the extrusion by specifying the depth value in the **Depth** field of the **Direction 1** rollout, see Figure 5.14.

Mid Plane

The **Mid Plane** option of the **End Condition** drop-down list is used for extruding the feature symmetrically about the sketching plane, see Figure 5.15. After selecting this option, you can enter the depth value of extrusion in the **Depth** field of the rollout. The depth value specified in this field is divided equally on both sides of the sketching plane and creates a symmetrically extruded feature. For example, if the depth value specified in the **Depth** field is 100 mm then the resultant feature is created by adding 50 mm of material to each side of the sketching plane.

Note: The other options such as **Up To Vertex, Up To Surface,** and **Offset From Surface** of the **End Condition** drop-down list are used while creating the second and further features of the model and are discussed in later chapters.

Reverse Direction

The **Reverse Direction** button of the **Direction 1** rollout is used for reversing the direction of extrusion from one side of the sketching plane to the other.

Depth

The **Depth** field of the **Direction 1** rollout is used for specifying the depth of extrusion. You can enter a value for the depth of extrusion in this field or use the up and down arrows ⬍ of the Spinner that is available to the right of this field to set the depth value. Note that on clicking the down arrow of the Spinner, the depth value decreases, whereas on clicking the up arrow of the Spinner, the depth value increases. Also, note that the **Depth** field appears only when the **Blind** or **Mid Plane** option is selected in the **End Condition** drop-down list.

Direction of Extrusion

The **Direction of Extrusion** field is used for defining the direction of extrusion for the extruded feature other than the direction normal to the sketching plane. Note that, by default, the direction of extrusion is normal to the sketching plane. To specify the direction of extrusion other than the direction normal to the sketching plane, click on the **Direction of Extrusion** field and then select a linear sketch entity, a linear edge, or an axis as the direction of extrusion. Figure 5.16 shows a sketch to be extruded and a linear sketch line as the direction of extrusion. Figure 5.17 shows the preview of the resultant extruded feature.

Tip: In Figure 5.16, the sketch to be extruded has been created on the Top plane and the sketch to be used as the direction of extrusion is created on the Front plane at an angle of 60 degrees from the X axis.

Draft On/Off

The **Draft On/Off** button is used for adding tapering to the extruded feature. By default, the **Draft On/Off** button is not activated. As a result, the resultant extruded feature is created without having any tapering in it. To add tapering to an extruded feature, click on the **Draft On/Off** button. The preview of the feature with default draft angle appears in the graphics area. Also, the **Draft Angle** field and the **Draft outward** check box get enabled in the rollout of the PropertyManager.

You can enter a draft angle in the **Draft Angle** field. By default, the **Draft outward** check box is cleared in the rollout. As a result, the draft is added in the inward direction of the sketch, see Figure 5.18. If you select this check box, the draft will be added in the outward direction of the sketch, see Figure 5.19.

Direction 2

The options in the **Direction 2** rollout are same as those in the **Direction 1** rollout of the PropertyManager with the only difference that the options of the **Direction 2** rollout are used for specifying the end condition in the second direction of the sketching plane. Note that by default, this rollout is collapsed. As a result, extrusion takes place only in one direction of the sketching plane. To add material in the second direction of the sketching plane, expand this rollout by selecting the check box in its title bar, see Figure 5.20. Figure 5.21 shows the preview of a feature, extruded on both sides of the sketching plane with different extrusion depths. Note that the **Direction 2** rollout will not be available if the **Mid Plane** option is selected in the **End Condition** drop-down list of the **Direction 1** rollout.

Thin Feature

The options in the **Thin Feature** rollout of the PropertyManager are used for creating a thin solid feature of specified wall thickness, see Figure 5.22. By default, this rollout is collapsed. To expand the **Thin Feature** rollout, select the check box in the title bar of this rollout, see Figure 5.23. As soon as this rollout is expanded, the preview of the thin feature with the default wall thickness appears in the graphics area. The options in this rollout are discussed next.

Type

The options in the **Type** drop-down list of the **Thin Feature** rollout are used for selecting a method to add thickness and are discussed next.

One-Direction

By default, the **One-Direction** option is selected in the **Type** drop-down list, see Figure 5.23. As a result, the thickness is added in one direction of the sketch. You can enter thickness value for the thin feature in the **Thickness** field of this rollout. To reverse the direction of thickness to the other side of the sketch, click on the **Reverse Direction** button of this rollout. Figures 5.24 and 5.25 show the previews of a thin feature with material added in outward and inward directions of the sketch, respectively.

Mid-Plane

The **Mid-Plane** option of the **Type** drop-down list is used for adding thickness, symmetrically on both sides of the sketch. You can enter thickness value in the **Thickness** field of the rollout. Note that the thickness value entered in the **Thickness** field is divided equally on both sides of the sketch and creates a thin feature.

Two-Direction

The **Two-Direction** option is used for adding different thickness to both sides of the sketch. As soon as you select this option, the **Direction 1 Thickness** and **Direction 2 Thickness** fields become available in the rollout. You can enter different thickness values in direction 1 and direction 2 of the sketch in the respective fields.

> **Note:** You can create a thin feature from a closed or an open sketch. Figure 5.26 shows the preview of a thin feature by using an open sketch. Note that if the sketch is an open sketch, then the **Thin Feature** rollout of the PropertyManager expands automatically for creating the thin extruded feature.

Cap ends

The **Cap ends** check box is used for closing the thin feature by adding caps on both its open ends. On selecting this check box, the open ends of the thin feature are capped and a hollow thin feature is created. You can also specify the required thickness for cap ends of the hollow thin feature in the **Cap Thickness** field. Note that the **Cap ends** check box is available only when you create a thin feature by using a closed sketch.

Selected Contours

The **Selected Contours** rollout of the PropertyManager is used for selecting contours or closed regions of a sketch for extrusion. Figure 5.27 shows a sketch with multiple contours/ closed regions (3 contours). Note that by default, when you extrude a sketch having multiple contours, the most suitable contour gets extruded, see Figure 5.28. In this figure, the contour 1 of the sketch shown in Figure 5.27 has been extruded by default and the remaining contours are left unextruded.

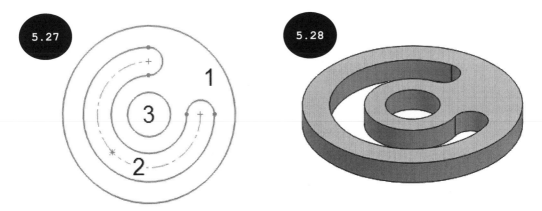

In addition to the default extrusion of the most suitable closed region of a multi-contour sketch, SOLIDWORKS allows you to select a required contour of a sketch to be extruded by using the **Selected Contours** rollout. For doing so, expand the **Selected Contours** rollout of the PropertyManager and then move the cursor over a closed contour of the sketch to be extruded in the graphics area and then click the left mouse button when it gets highlighted, see Figure 5.29. As soon as you select a contour, the preview of the extruded feature appears such that the material is added to the selected closed contour of the sketch. Similarly, you can select multiple contours of a sketch to be extruded.

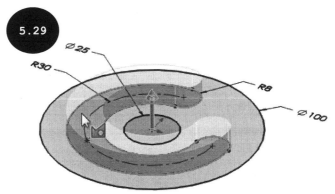

After specifying the required parameters for extruding the sketch, click on the green tick-mark ✓ button in the **Boss-Extrude PropertyManager** to accept the defined parameters and create the extruded feature.

Creating a Revolved Feature

A revolved feature is a feature created such that material is added by revolving the sketch around an axis of revolution. Note that the sketch to be revolved should be on one of the sides of the axis of revolution. You can create a revolved feature by using the **Revolved Boss/Base** tool. Figure 5.30 shows sketches and the resultant revolved features that are created by revolving the sketches around the respective axes of revolution.

5.30

Sketches

Revolved features

After drawing the sketch and a centerline as the axis of revolution of a revolved feature in the Sketching environment, do not exit the Sketching environment. Click on the **Features** tab in the CommandManager and then click on the **Revolved Boss/Base** tool. A preview of the revolved feature appears in the graphics area with default parameters. Also, the **Revolve PropertyManager** appears on the left of the graphics area, see Figure 5.31. If the preview does not appear in the graphics area, select a centerline as the axis of revolution. Figure 5.32 shows a sketch with a centerline created on the Front plane and Figure 5.33 shows the preview of the resultant revolved feature.

5.31

Note: If the sketch to be revolved has only one centerline, then the centerline drawn will automatically be selected as the axis of revolution and the preview of the resultant revolved feature appears in the graphics area. However, if the sketch has two or more than two centerlines or does not have any centerline, then on invoking the **Revolved Boss/Base** tool, the preview of the revolved feature does not appear and you are prompted to select a centerline as the axis of revolution. As soon as you select a centerline, the preview of the revolved feature appears in the graphics area. You can select a linear sketch entity, a centerline, an axis, or an edge as the axis of revolution.

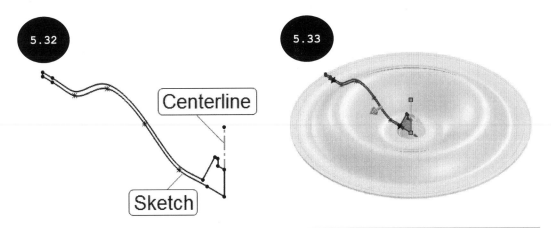

Note: If you exit the Sketching environment after creating the sketch of the revolved feature and the sketch is not selected in the graphics area, then on clicking the **Revolved Boss/Base** tool, the **Revolve PropertyManager** appears similar to the one shown in Figure 5.34. Also, you are prompted to select either the sketch to be revolved or a sketching plane for creating the sketch. Select the sketch to be revolved. The preview of the revolved feature appears in the graphics area. Also, the **Revolve PropertyManager** gets modified and appears as shown in Figure 5.31. Note that if the sketch to be revolved is not created then you can select the sketching plane for creating the sketch of the revolved feature.

The options in the **Revolve PropertyManager** are used for specifying parameters for creating the revolved feature. Some of the options of the **Revolve PropertyManager** are discussed next.

Axis of Revolution

The **Axis of Revolution** field of the **Axis of Revolution** rollout in the PropertyManager is used for selecting the axis of revolution of the revolved feature. You can select a linear sketch entity, a centerline, an axis, or a linear edge as the axis of revolution. Note that if the sketch has only one centerline, then it is automatically selected as the axis of revolution on invoking the **Revolve PropertyManager.** However, if the sketch is having two or more than two centerlines then you are prompted to select the axis of revolution.

Direction 1

The options in the **Direction 1** rollout of the PropertyManager are used for defining the end condition of the revolved feature in one side of the Sketching plane. The options are discussed next.

Revolve Type

The **Revolve Type** drop-down list of the **Direction 1** rollout is used for selecting a method for revolving the sketch, see Figure 5.35. The options of this drop-down list are discussed next.

Blind

The **Blind** option of the **Revolve Type** drop-down list is used for defining the end condition or termination of the revolved feature by specifying the angle of revolution. By default, this option is selected in this drop-down list. As a result, the **Direction 1 Angle** field is available in the **Direction 1** rollout. You can enter a required angle value in this field.

Mid Plane

The **Mid Plane** option is used for revolving a sketch about a centerline, symmetrically on both sides of the sketching plane, see Figure 5.36. After selecting this option, you can enter the angle of revolution in the **Direction 1 Angle** field of the rollout. Depending upon the angle value entered in this field, material is added symmetrically on both sides of the sketching plane by revolving the sketch about the axis of revolution.

Note: The **Up To Vertex**, **Up To Surface**, and **Offset From Surface** options of the **Revolve Type** drop-down list are used while creating the second and further features of the model and are discussed in the later chapters.

Reverse Direction

The **Reverse Direction** button of the rollout is used for reversing the direction of revolution from one side of the sketching plane to the other side. This option is not available if the **Mid Plane** option is selected in the **Revolve Type** drop-down list of the PropertyManager.

Direction 2

The options in the **Direction 2** rollout are the same as those in the **Direction 1** rollout of the PropertyManager with the only difference that the options of the **Direction 2** rollout are used for specifying the end condition of the revolved feature in the second direction of the sketching plane. Note that by default, this rollout is collapsed. As a result, the material is added only in one direction of the sketching plane by revolving the sketch. To add material in the second direction of the sketching plane, expand this rollout by selecting the check box in its title bar, see Figure 5.37. Figure 5.38 shows the preview of a revolved feature with different revolving angles in direction 1 and direction 2 of the sketching plane. Note that the **Direction 2** rollout is not available in the PropertyManager, if the **Mid Plane** option is selected in the **Revolve Type** drop-down list of the **Direction 1** rollout.

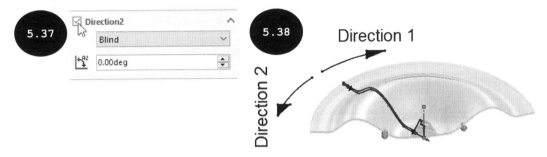

Thin Feature

The options in the **Thin Feature** rollout are used for creating a thin revolved feature with a uniform wall thickness, see Figure 5.39. By default, this rollout is collapsed and the options in this rollout are not activated. To expand the **Thin Feature** rollout, click on the check box in its title bar. As soon as the **Thin Feature** rollout expands, the preview of the thin feature with default parameters appears in the graphics area. The options in this rollout are same as discussed earlier, while creating the thin extruded feature.

Selected Contours

The **Selected Contours** rollout is used for selecting contours or closed regions of a multi-contour sketch. To revolve a contour of a multi-contour sketch, expand the **Selected Contours** rollout of the PropertyManager and then move the cursor over a closed contour of the sketch to be revolved. Next, click on the closed contour when it gets highlighted in the graphics area. The preview of the revolved feature appears such that material has been added by revolving the selected contour about the centerline.

After specifying the required parameters for revolving the sketch, click on the green tick-mark ✓ button in the **Revolve PropertyManager** to accept the defined parameters and create the revolved feature.

Navigating a 3D Model in Graphics Area

In SOLIDWORKS, you can navigate a model by using the mouse buttons and the navigating tools. You can access the navigating tools in the **View (Heads-Up)** toolbar, see Figure 5.40. Alternatively, you can also access the navigating tools in the SOLIDWORKS Menus or in the shortcut menu that appears on right-clicking in the graphics area. The different navigating tools are discussed next.

Zoom In/Out

You can zoom in or out of the graphics area, dynamically by using the **Zoom In/Out** tool. In other words, you can enlarge or reduce the view of the model, dynamically by using the **Zoom In/Out** tool.

To zoom in or out a model in the graphics area by using the **Zoom In/Out** tool, click on **View > Modify > Zoom In/Out** in the SOLIDWORKS Menus, see Figure 5.41. The **Zoom In/Out** tool gets activated. Next, drag the cursor upward or downward in the graphics area by pressing and holding the left mouse button. On dragging the cursor upward, the view gets enlarged, whereas on dragging the cursor downward, the view gets reduced. Note that in the process of zooming in or zooming out the view, the scale of the model remains the same. However, the viewing distance gets modified in order to enlarge or reduce the view of the model.

Alternatively, you can invoke the **Zoom In/Out** tool from the shortcut menu. For doing so, right-click in the graphics area and then click on the **Zoom In/Out** tool in the shortcut menu that appears, see Figure 5.42. Next, drag the cursor upward or downward in the graphics area.

You can also zoom in or zoom out the graphics area by scrolling up or down the middle mouse button. Besides, you can press and hold the SHIFT key plus the middle mouse button and then drag the cursor in the graphics area upward or downward to zoom in or zoom out, respectively.

Zoom To Fit
The **Zoom To Fit** tool is used for fitting a model completely inside the graphics area. For doing so, click on the **Zoom To Fit** tool in the **View (Heads-Up)** toolbar. Alternatively, click on **View > Modify > Zoom to Fit** in the SOLIDWORKS Menus. You can also invoke this tool from the shortcut menu that appears on right-clicking in the graphics area. Besides, you can also press the F key to fit the model completely inside the graphics area.

Zoom to Area
The **Zoom to Area** tool is used for zooming a particular portion or an area of a model by defining a boundary box. For doing so, click on the **Zoom to Area** tool in the **View (Heads-Up)** toolbar and then define a boundary box by dragging the cursor around the portion of a model to be zoomed. The area inside the boundary box gets enlarged. You can also access the **Zoom to Area** tool from the SOLIDWORKS Menus or from the shortcut menu.

Zoom to Selection
The **Zoom to Selection** tool is used for fitting a selected object or geometry completely in the graphics area. To fit a selected object or geometry in the graphics area, invoke the **Zoom to Selection** tool by clicking on **View > Modify > Zoom to Selection** in the SOLIDWORKS Menus. Note that this tool gets enabled only if the object to be fit is selected in the graphics area.

Pan
The **Pan** tool is used for panning or moving a model in the graphics area. You can invoke this tool from the SOLIDWORKS Menus or from the shortcut menu. Once the **Pan** tool is invoked, you can pan the model in the graphics area by dragging the cursor while pressing and holding the left mouse button. Alternatively, you can also pan the model by dragging the cursor while pressing the CTRL key and the middle mouse button.

Rotate
The **Rotate** tool is used for rotating a model freely in the graphics area. To rotate a model, invoke the **Rotate** tool by clicking on **View > Modify > Rotate** in the SOLIDWORKS Menus. You can also

invoke this tool from the shortcut menu that appears on right-clicking in the graphics area. After invoking the **Rotate** tool, press and hold the left mouse button and then drag the cursor to rotate the model freely in the graphics area. Alternatively, you can drag the cursor by pressing the middle mouse button to rotate the model.

Manipulating View Orientation of a Model

Manipulating the view orientation of a 3D model is very important in order to review it from different views and angles. In SOLIDWORKS, you can manipulate the orientation of a 3D model to predefined standard views such as front, back, top, right, left, bottom, and isometric by using the **View Orientation** flyout, **Orientation** dialog box, **Reference Triad**, or **View Selector Cube**, see Figure 5.43. In addition to the predefined standard views, you can also create custom views. Various methods for manipulating the orientation of a model are discussed next.

View Orientation flyout   Orientation dialog box   Reference Triad   View Selector Cube

Manipulating View Orientation by using the View Orientation Flyout

To manipulate the orientation of a model by using the **View Orientation** flyout, click on the arrow next to the **View Orientation** tool in the **View (Heads-Up)** toolbar. The **View Orientation** flyout appears, see Figure 5.44. By using the tools of the **View Orientation** flyout, you can manipulate the orientation of a model. The tools are discussed next.

Top, Front, Right, Left, Bottom, Back, Isometric Tools

The **Top**, **Front**, **Right**, **Left**, **Bottom**, **Back**, and **Isometric** tools of the **View Orientation** flyout are used for displaying predefined standard views such as front, top, right, and isometric, of a model in the graphics area.

Normal To Tool

The **Normal To** tool of the **View Orientation** flyout is used for displaying a selected face of a model normal to the viewing direction. If you are in the Sketching environment, then you can use this tool to make the current sketching plane normal to the viewing direction.

View Drop-down List

The tools in the **View** drop-down list of the **View Orientation** flyout are used for displaying the isometric, dimetric, or trimetric views of a model. Figure 5.45 shows the **View** drop-down list of the **View Orientation** flyout. By default, the **Trimetric** tool is activated in this drop-down list. As a result, on invoking the **View Orientation** flyout, the trimetric view of the model is displayed in the graphics area. You can activate the required tool to display the respective view of the model.

View Selector Tool

The **View Selector** tool of the **View Orientation** flyout is used for displaying the **View Selector Cube** around the 3D model available in the graphics area, see Figure 5.46. By default, this tool is activated. As a result, on invoking the **View Orientation** flyout, the **View Selector Cube** appears in the graphics area around the model. Note that the orientation of the model inside the **View Selector Cube** depends upon the tool activated in the **View** drop-down list of the flyout.

You can also use the faces of the **View Selector Cube** to manipulate the orientation of the model which is discussed later in this chapter.

New View

The **New View** tool is used for creating a custom or user defined view of a model. For doing so, first set the orientation of the model, as required by using different navigating tools. Next, click on the **New View** tool. The **Named View** dialog box appears. In the **View name** field of this dialog box, enter the name of the custom view and then click on the **OK** button. The view is created and the name of the view created is added in the **View Orientation** flyout. You can display the model as per the custom view at any time by clicking on its name in the **View Orientation** flyout. Similarly, you can create multiple custom views of a model.

`Updated`

Manipulating View Orientation by using the Orientation Dialog box

To manipulate the view orientation of a model by using the **Orientation** dialog box, press the SPACEBAR key. The **Orientation** dialog box appears in the graphics area with the **View Selector** tool activated by default. As a result, the **View Selector Cube** appears around the 3D model available in the graphics area, refer to Figure 5.46. Most of the tools available in the **Orientation** dialog box are the same as discussed earlier and the remaining tools are discussed next.

Pin/Unpin the dialog

The **Pin/Unpin the dialog** tool is used for pinning the dialog box in the graphics area. By default, this tool is not activated. As a result, when you invoke a view such as front, top, or right of a model by clicking on the respective tool in the **Orientation** dialog box, the view of the model is invoked and the dialog box gets disappeared or closed. If you do not want to exit the dialog box, click to activate the **Pin/Unpin the dialog** tool in the dialog box.

Previous View

The **Previous View** tool is used for orientating a model to its previous orientation. Note that you can undo the last ten views of the model by using this tool.

Update Standard Views Tool

The **Update Standard Views** tool is used for updating or changing the predefined standard views such as top, front, and right of a model, as required. For doing so, first orient the 3D model in the graphics area according to your requirement and then click on the **Update Standard Views** tool. Next, click on the required standard tool such as **Top** or **Front** in the **Orientation** dialog box. The SOLIDWORKS message window appears. The message window informs that changing the standard view will change the orientation of the standard orthogonal views of this model. Click on the **Yes** button to make this change. The selected standard view gets updated to the current display of the model in the graphics area.

Reset Standard Views Tool

The **Reset Standard Views** tool is used for resetting all the standard views back to the default settings. If you have updated any of the standard views as per your requirement and you want to restore the default standard orientations, click on the **Reset Standard Views** tool. The SOLIDWORKS message window appears. The message window asks you whether you want to reset all the standard views to the default settings. Click on the **Yes** button to reset all the views to the default settings.

Up Axis Flyout

By default, the **Apply Y-up views** option is selected in the **Up Axis Flyout** of the **Orientation** dialog box. As a result, the Y-axis is set as the default up axis for the orientation of all the standard orthogonal, named, and child views in the graphics area. On selecting the **Apply Z-up views** option in the flyout, the Z-axis becomes the default up axis for the orientation of all views. Note that when you select the **Apply Z-up views** option, the SOLIDWORKS message window appears which informs you that switching to Z-up views will change the orientation of all standard orthogonal, named, and child views. Click on the **Yes** button in this message window if you wish to make this change. Figure 5.47 shows the isometric view of a model when **Apply Y-up views** option is selected and Figure 5.48 shows the isometric view of a model when **Apply Z-up views** option is selected.

Manipulating View Orientation by using the View Selector Cube

You can also manipulate the view orientation of a model by using the **View Selector Cube**. It is one of the easiest ways to achieve different views such as right, left, front, back, top, bottom, or isometric of a 3D model. By default, on invoking the **View Orientation** flyout and the **Orientation** dialog box, the **View Selector Cube** appears around the 3D model because the **View Selection** tool is activated in the **View Orientation** flyout as well as in the **Orientation** dialog box, by default.

To manipulate the orientation of a 3D model by using the **View Selector Cube**, move the cursor over a face of the **View Selector Cube**. The face gets highlighted and the **Preview** window appears at the upper right corner of the graphics area. Next, click on the face, see Figure 5.49. The orientation of the model depends upon the face of the **View Selector Cube** selected.

Note: The default orientation of a model inside the **View Selector Cube** depends upon the tool activated in the **View** drop-down list of the **View Orientation** flyout as well as in the **Orientation** dialog box.

Manipulating View Orientation by using the Reference Triad

 The reference triad appears at the lower left corner of the graphics area and guides you while changing the view orientation of a model. You can also use the reference triad to manipulate the view orientation of a model normal to the screen, 180 degrees, or 90 degrees about an axis.

To orient the model normal to the screen, click on an axis of the triad. The model gets oriented normal to the screen with respect to the selected axis of the triad. Note that the direction of axis selected becomes normal to the screen. To orient the model by 180 degrees, click on the axis that is normal to the screen. To orient the model by 90 degrees about an axis, press the SHIFT key and then click on an axis as the axis of rotation.

You can also rotate the model at a predefined angle that is specified in the **System Options - View** dialog box. For doing so, press the ALT key and then click on an axis of the triad. To specify the predefined angle, click on the **Options** tool in the **Standard** toolbar. The **System Options - General** dialog box appears. In this dialog box, click on the **View** option in the left panel of the dialog box. The name of the dialog box changes to **System Options - View**. By using the **Arrow keys** field of this dialog box, you can specify the predefined angle for rotation by using the triad.

Changing the Display Style of a Model

You can change the display style of a 3D model to wireframe, hidden lines visible, hidden lines removed, shaded, and shaded with edges display styles. The tools used for changing the display style of the model are available in the **Display Style** flyout of the **View (Heads-Up)** toolbar, see Figure 5.50. The tools are discussed next.

Shaded With Edges

The **Shaded With Edges** tool is used for displaying a model in 'shaded with edges' display style. In this style, the model is displayed in shaded mode with the display of outer edges turned on, see Figure 5.51. This tool is activated by default. As a result, the model is displayed in 'shaded with edges' display style in the graphics area, by default.

Shaded

The **Shaded** tool is used for displaying a model in 'shaded' display style. In this style, the model is displayed in shaded mode with the display of edges turned off, see Figure 5.52.

Hidden Lines Removed

The **Hidden Lines Removed** tool is used for displaying a model in 'hidden lines removed' display style. In this style, the hidden lines of the model are not visible in the display of the model, see Figure 5.53.

Hidden Lines Visible

The **Hidden Lines Visible** tool is used for displaying a model in 'hidden lines visible' display style. In this style, the visibility of the hidden lines of the model is turned on and hidden lines appear as dotted lines, see Figure 5.54.

Wireframe

The **Wireframe** tool is used for displaying a model in 'wireframe' display style. In this style, the hidden lines of the model are displayed as solid lines , see Figure 5.55.

Changing the View of a Model

In SOLIDWORKS, you can change the view of a model to perspective, shadows, ambient occlusion, and cartoon effect by using the tools in the **View Settings** flyout of the **View (Heads-Up)** toolbar, see Figure 5.56. The tools are discussed next.

Shadows In Shaded Mode

The **Shadows In Shaded Mode** tool is used for displaying a model with its shadow, see Figure 5.57. In this view of the model, the shadow appears at the bottom of the model as the light appears from the top. Note that the shadow of the model rotates in accordance with the rotation of the model.

Perspective

The **Perspective** tool is used for displaying the perspective view of a model, see Figure 5.58. A perspective view appears as it is viewed normally from the eyes. Note that the perspective view depends upon the size of the model and the distance between the model and the viewer.

Ambient Occlusion

The **Ambient Occlusion** tool is used for displaying the ambient view of a model. The ambient view is displayed due to the attenuation of the ambient light.

Cartoon

The **Cartoon** tool is used for displaying the cartoon rendering view of a model. The cartoon rendering view is displayed by adding a non-photorealistic cartoon effect to a model.

Tutorial 1

Open the sketch created in Tutorial 1 of Chapter 4, see Figure 5.59, and then create the 3D model by extruding it to a depth of 40 mm, see Figure 5.60. All dimensions are in mm.

Section 1: Starting SOLIDWORKS

1. Start SOLIDWORKS by double-clicking on the SOLIDWORKS icon on your desktop. The startup user interface of SOLIDWORKS appears along with the **Welcome** dialog box.

Note: If SOLIDWORKS is already open and the **Welcome** dialog box does not appear on the screen, then you can invoke the **Welcome** dialog box by clicking on the **Welcome to SOLIDWORKS** tool 🏠 in the **Standard** toolbar or by pressing the CTRL + F2 keys.

Section 2: Opening the Sketch of Tutorial 1, Chapter 4

Now, you need to open the sketch of Tutorial 1 that is created in Chapter 4.

1. Click on the **Open** button in the **Welcome** dialog box. The **Open** dialog box appears.

Tip: You can also invoke the **Open** dialog box by clicking on the **Open** tool in the **Standard** toolbar.

2. Browse to the Chapter 4 folder of the SOLIDWORKS folder and then select the **Tutorial 1** file.

3. Click on the **Open** button in the dialog box. The sketch of Tutorial 1 created in Chapter 4 is opened in the current session of SOLIDWORKS, see Figure 5.61.

Section 3: Saving the Sketch

Now, you need to save the sketch with the name "Tutorial 1" in *Chapter 5* folder.

1. Click on **File** > **Save As** in the SOLIDWORKS Menus. The **Save As** dialog box appears.

2. Browse to the SOLIDWORKS folder and then create a folder with the name **Chapter 5** in it with the name Tutorial 1.

3. Click on the **Save** button to save the sketch in the Chapter 5 folder.

Note: It is important to save the sketch in different locations or different names before making any modification, so that the original file does not get modified.

Section 4: Extruding the Sketch

Now, you can extrude the sketch and convert it into a feature.

1. Click on the **Features** tab in the CommandManager. The tools of the **Features CommandManager** appears, see Figure 5.62.

2. Click on the **Extruded Boss/Base** tool in the **Features Command Manager**. The **Boss-Extrude PropertyManager** and the preview of the extruded feature appear, see Figure 5.63. Also, the orientation of the model changes to Trimetric.

Note: If you exit the Sketching environment after creating the sketch, then you need to select the sketch to be extruded before or after invoking the **Extruded Boss/Base** tool.

3. Enter **40** in the **Depth** field of the **Direction 1** rollout in the PropertyManager and then press ENTER. The default depth of the extruded feature changes to 40 mm.

4. Click on the green tick-mark ☑ in the PropertyManager. The extruded feature is created, see Figure 5.64.

Section 5: Saving the Model

Now, you need to save the model.

1. Click on the **Save** tool in the **Standard** toolbar. The model is saved with the name **Tutorial 1** in the Chapter 5 folder.

Tutorial 2

Open the sketch created in Tutorial 2 of Chapter 4, see Figure 5.65, and then revolve it around the vertical centerline at an angle of 270 degrees, see Figure 5.66. Also, change the display style of the model to the 'hidden lines removed' display style. All dimensions are in mm.

Section 1: Starting SOLIDWORKS

1. Start SOLIDWORKS by double-clicking on the SOLIDWORKS icon on your desktop. The startup user interface of SOLIDWORKS appears along with the **Welcome** dialog box.

Note: If SOLIDWORKS is already open and the **Welcome** dialog box does not appear on the screen, then you can invoke the same by clicking on the **Welcome to SOLIDWORKS** tool 🏠 in the **Standard** toolbar or by pressing the CTRL + F2 keys.

Section 2: Opening the Sketch of Tutorial 2, Chapter 4

Now, you need to open the sketch of Tutorial 2 that is created in Chapter 4.

1. Click on the **Open** button in the **Welcome** dialog box. The **Open** dialog box appears.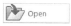

Tip: You can also invoke the **Open** dialog box by clicking on the **Open** tool in the **Standard** toolbar.

---

2. Browse to the Chapter 4 folder of the SOLIDWORKS folder and then select the **Tutorial 2** file.

3. Click on the **Open** button in the dialog box. The sketch of Tutorial 2 created in Chapter 4 is opened in the current session of SOLIDWORKS, see Figure 5.67.

Section 3: Saving the Sketch

Now, you need to save the sketch with the name "Tutorial 2" in Chapter 5 folder.

1. Click on **File > Save As** in the SOLIDWORKS Menus. The **Save As** dialog box appears.

2. Browse to the Chapter 5 folder of the SOLIDWORKS folder and then save the sketch in it with the name Tutorial 2. If the Chapter 5 folder is not created then you need to first create this folder inside the SOLIDWORKS folder.

Section 4: Revolving the Sketch

1. Click on the **Features** tab in the CommandManager. The tools of the **Features** CommandManager appear, see Figure 5.68.

2. Click on the **Revolved Boss/Base** tool in the **Features Command Manager**. The **Revolve PropertyManager** appears and the orientation of the sketch changes to Trimetric. Also, you are prompted to select a centerline as the axis of revolution.

Tip: If the sketch to be revolved has only one centerline, then the centerline drawn will automatically be selected as the axis of revolution and the preview of the resultant revolved feature appears in the graphics area. However, if the sketch has two or more than two centerlines then on invoking the **Revolved Boss/Base** tool, you are prompted to select a centerline as the axis of revolution.

3. Select the vertical centerline of the sketch as the axis of revolution. The preview of the revolved feature appears in the graphics area, see Figure 5.69.

4. Enter **270** degrees in the **Direction 1 Angle** field of the **Direction 1** rollout in the PropertyManager and then press the ENTER key.

5. Click on the green tick-mark ☑ in the PropertyManager. The revolved feature is created, see Figure 5.70.

Section 5: Changing the Display Style

As mentioned in the tutorial description, you need to change the display style of the model to the 'hidden lines removed' display style.

1. Invoke the **Display Style** flyout of the **View (Heads-Up)** toolbar, see Figure 5.71.

2. Click on the **Hidden Lines Removed** tool in the **Display Style** flyout. The display style of the model is changed to 'hidden lines removed' display style, see Figure 5.72.

Section 6: Saving the Model

Now, you need to save the model.

1.   Click on the **Save** tool in the **Standard** toolbar. The model is saved with the name **Tutorial 2** in the Chapter 5 folder.

Tutorial 3

Open the sketch created in Tutorial 3 of Chapter 4, see Figure 5.73, and then extrude it to a depth of 60 mm, symmetrically about the sketching plane, see Figure 5.74. Also, change the view orientation of the model to isometric and navigate the model in the graphics area. All dimensions are in mm.

Section 1: Starting SOLIDWORKS

1.   Start SOLIDWORKS by double-clicking on the SOLIDWORKS icon on your desktop. The initial screen of SOLIDWORKS appears along with the **Welcome** dialog box.

Note: If SOLIDWORKS is already open and the **Welcome** dialog box does not appear on the screen, then you can invoke the same by clicking on the **Welcome to SOLIDWORKS** tool 🏠 in the **Standard** toolbar or by pressing the CTRL + F2 keys.

Section 2: Opening the Sketch of Tutorial 3, Chapter 4

Now, you need to open the sketch of Tutorial 3 that is created in Chapter 4.

1. Click on the **Open** button in the **Welcome** dialog box. The **Open** dialog box appears.

Tip: You can also invoke the **Open** dialog box by clicking on the **Open** tool in the **Standard** toolbar.

---

2. Browse to the Chapter 4 folder of the SOLIDWORKS folder and then select the **Tutorial 3** file.

3. Click on the **Open** button in the dialog box. The sketch of Tutorial 3 created in Chapter 4 is opened in the current session of SOLIDWORKS, see Figure 5.75.

Section 3: Saving the Sketch

Now, you need to save the sketch as Tutorial 3 of Chapter 5.

1. Click on **File > Save As** in the SOLIDWORKS Menus. The **Save As** dialog box appears.

2. Browse to the Chapter 5 folder of the SOLIDWORKS folder and then save the sketch in it with the name **Tutorial 3**.

Section 4: Extruding the Sketch

Now, you can extrude the sketch and convert it into an extruded feature.

1. Click on the **Features** tab in the CommandManager to display the tools of the **Features** CommandManager.

2. Click on the **Extruded Boss/Base** tool in the **Features Command Manager**. The **Boss-Extrude PropertyManager** and the preview of the extruded feature appear, see Figure 5.76.

3. Enter **60** in the **Depth** field of the **Direction 1** rollout and then press the ENTER key. The depth of the extruded feature is modified to 60 mm.

4. Invoke the **End Condition** drop-down list of the **Direction 1** rollout, see Figure 5.77.

5. Click on the **Mid Plane** option in the **End Condition** drop-down list. The depth of the extrusion gets added symmetrically on both sides of the sketching plane, see Figure 5.78.

6. Click on the green tick-mark ☑ in the PropertyManager. The extruded feature is created symmetrically about the Sketching plane, see Figure 5.79.

Section 5: Changing the Orientation to Isometric

1. Invoke the **View Orientation** flyout in the **View (Heads-Up)** toolbar, see Figure 5.80. The **View Selector Cube** appears around the model in the graphics area, see Figure 5.81.

Tip: You can change the view orientation of the model by using the tools of the **View Orientation** flyout or by using the **View Selector Cube**.

2. Invoke the **View** drop-down list in the **View Orientation** flyout, see Figure 5.82. Next, click on the **Isometric** tool. The view orientation of the model changes to isometric.

Section 6: Navigating the Model

Now, you need to navigate the model.

1. Right-click in the graphics area and then click on the **Zoom In/Out** tool in the shortcut menu that appears, see Figure 5.83.

2. Press and hold the left mouse button and then drag the cursor upward or downward in the graphics area to enlarge or reduce the view of the model, respectively. Next, press the ESC key to exit the tool.

3. Similarly, you can invoke the remaining navigating tools such as **Rotate View** and **Pan** to navigate the model.

Section 7: Saving the Model

Now, you need to save the model.

1. Click on the **Save** button in the **Standard** toolbar. The model is saved with the name **Tutorial 3** in the Chapter 5 folder.

Hands-on Test Drive 1

Create the revolved model, as shown in Figure 5.84. All dimensions are in mm. Note that, to create a revolved feature, you need to create its sketch on either side of the axis of revolution.

5.84

Hands-on Test Drive 2

Create the extruded model, as shown in Figure 5.85. All dimensions are in mm. The depth of extrusion is 2 mm.

5.85

Hands-on Test Drive 3

Create the revolve model as shown in Figure 5.86. All dimensions are in mm. The angle of revolution is 360-degrees.

Summary

In this chapter, you have learned about creating the extruded and revolved base features by using the **Extruded Boss/Base** and **Revolved Boss/Base** tools, respectively. An extruded feature is created by adding material normal or at an angle to the sketching plane, whereas a revolved feature is created by revolving a sketch around an axis of revolution. The chapter describes how to navigate a model by using the mouse buttons and the navigating tools such as **Zoom In/Out** and **Zoom To Fit**, and manipulate the view orientation of the model to the predefined standard views such as front, top, right, left, and custom views, in addition to changing the display style and view of the model.

Questions

- The _____ tool is used for creating a feature by adding material normal to the sketching plane.

- The _____ tool is used for creating a feature by revolving the sketch around a centerline as the axis of revolution.

- The _____ tool is used for fitting a model completely inside the graphics area.

- The _____ tool of the **View Orientation** flyout is used for displaying the **View Selector Cube** around the 3D model available in the graphics area.

- The _____ button of the **Boss-Extrude PropertyManager** is used for tapering the extrude feature.

- The _____ option is used for extruding a feature symmetrically about the sketching plane.

- You can only create a thin feature from an open sketch. (True/False)

- In SOLIDWORKS, manipulating the view orientation of a model by using the **View Selector Cube** is one of the easiest ways to achieve different views such as right, left, and isometric. (True/False)

- In SOLIDWORKS, you cannot navigate a model by using the mouse buttons. (True/False)

- While creating a revolved feature, if the sketch to be revolved has only one centerline, then the drawn centerline is automatically selected as the axis of revolution. (True/False)

Creating Reference Geometries

This chapter discusses the following topics:

- Creating Reference Planes
- Creating a Reference Axis
- Creating a Reference Coordinate System
- Creating a Reference Point
- Creating a Bounding Box

In SOLIDWORKS, the three default reference planes Front, Top, and Right are available, by default. You can use these reference planes to create the base feature of a model by extruding or revolving the sketch, as discussed in earlier chapters. However, to create a real world model having multiple features, you may need additional reference planes. In other words, the three default reference planes may not be enough for creating all features of a real world model and you may need to create additional reference planes. SOLIDWORKS allows you to create additional reference planes for creating real world models, as required. You can create additional reference planes by using the **Plane** tool, which is available in the **Reference Geometry** flyout of the **Features CommandManager**, see Figure 6.1.

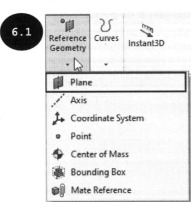

Figure 6.2 shows a multiple-feature model, which is created by creating all its features one by one. This model has six features. Its first feature is an extruded feature created on the Top plane. The second feature is an extruded feature created on the top planar face of the first feature. The third feature is a cut feature created on the top planar face of the second feature. The fourth feature is a user-defined reference plane created by using the **Plane** tool. The fifth feature is an extruded feature created on the user-defined reference plane and the sixth feature is a circular pattern of the fifth feature.

6.2

6th feature (pattern)

5th feature (extruded)

4th feature (reference plane)

3rd feature (cut)

2nd feature (extruded)

1st feature (extruded)

Note: It is clear from the above figure that additional reference planes may be required for creating features of a model.

Creating Reference Planes

6.3

In SOLIDWORKS, you can create reference planes at an offset distance from an existing plane or planar face, parallel to an existing plane or planar face, at an angle to an existing plane or planar face, normal to a curve, and so on, by using the **Plane** tool.

To create a reference plane, click on the arrow at the bottom of the **Reference Geometry** tool in the **Features CommandManager**. The **Reference Geometry** flyout appears, refer to Figure 6.1. In this flyout, click on the **Plane** tool. The **Plane PropertyManager** appears, see Figure 6.3. The options in this PropertyManager are used for creating different types of reference planes and are discussed next.

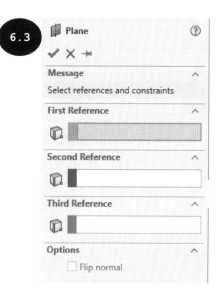

Message

The **Message** rollout of the PropertyManager displays appropriate information about the action to be taken for creating a reference plane as well as displays the current status of the reference plane. If the current status of the plane is displayed as fully defined, then it means that all the required references for creating the plane have been defined. Note that the background color of the rollout changes to green as soon as the status of the plane becomes fully defined. Also, note that for creating a fully defined reference plane, maximum three references are required.

First Reference

The **First Reference** rollout is used for defining the first reference for a plane. You can select a face, a plane, a vertex, a point, an edge, or a curve as the first reference for creating a plane. Note that the selection of a reference depends upon the type of plane to be created. For example, to create a plane at an offset distance from a planar face of a model, you need to select the planar face of the model as the first reference. As soon as you select the first reference, the **First Reference** rollout expands with the display of all possible relations and options that can be applied between the selected reference and the plane, see Figure 6.4. Also, the most suitable relation is selected by default in the expanded rollout. Figure 6.4 shows the expanded **First Reference** rollout when a planar face is selected as the first reference. If you select a planar face or a plane as the first reference, then the **Offset distance** button gets selected, by default in the rollout, which allows you to specify the offset distance between the selected planar face and the plane. The different relations and options of the expanded **First Reference** rollout are discussed next.

Coincident

The **Coincident** button is used for creating a reference plane that passes through a selected reference (a planar face, a plane, a vertex, or a point). Note that on selecting the **Coincident** button, the coincident relation is applied between the selected reference and the plane.

Parallel

The **Parallel** button is used for creating a plane parallel to a selected reference (a planar face or a plane). On selecting the **Parallel** button, the parallel relation is applied between the selected reference and the plane. Note that for creating a plane parallel to a planar face or a plane, you also need to select a second reference. You will learn more about creating parallel planes later in this chapter.

Perpendicular

The **Perpendicular** button is used for creating a plane perpendicular to a selected reference (a planar face or a plane). On selecting the **Perpendicular** button, the perpendicular relation is applied between the selected reference and the plane. Note that for creating a plane perpendicular to a planar face or a plane, you also need to select a second reference. You will learn more about creating perpendicular planes later in this chapter.

Tangent

The **Tangent** button is used for creating a plane tangent to a selected reference (a cylindrical, a conical, a non-cylindrical, or a non-planar face). On selecting the **Tangent** button, the tangent relation is applied between the selected reference and the plane. Note that for creating a plane tangent to a cylindrical, a conical, a non-cylindrical, or a non-planar face, you also need to select a second reference (an edge, an axis, or a sketch line). You will learn more about creating tangent planes later in this chapter.

At angle

The **At angle** button is used for creating a plane at an angle to a selected reference (a planar face, a cylindrical face, or a plane). Note that for creating a plane at an angle to a cylindrical face, a planar face, or a plane, you also need to select a second reference (an edge, an axis, or a sketch line). You will learn more about creating planes at an angle later in this chapter.

Mid Plane

The **Mid Plane** button is used for creating a plane at the middle of two planar faces. Note that for creating a mid plane, you need to select two planar faces as the first and second references. You will learn more about creating a plane at the middle of two planar faces later in this chapter.

Project

The **Project** button is used for creating a plane by projecting a point, a vertex, an origin, or a coordinate system into a non-planar face. You will learn more about creating a projected plane onto a non-planar face later in this chapter.

Offset distance

The **Offset distance** button is used for creating a plane at an offset distance from the selected reference. You will learn more about creating a plane at an offset distance later in this chapter.

Parallel to screen

The **Parallel to screen** button is used for creating a plane normal to the viewing direction and passing through a vertex. Note that this button is enabled in the PropertyManager when you select a vertex or a point as the first reference. You will learn more about creating a plane parallel to the screen later in this chapter.

Number of planes to create

You can specify the number of planes to be created in the **Number of planes to create** field of the PropertyManager. By default, 1 is entered in this field. As a result, only one reference plane is created with the specified parameters. Note that this field is enabled only when the **At angle** or **Offset distance** button is selected in the PropertyManager.

Second Reference

The **Second Reference** rollout is used for defining the second reference for creating a reference plane. The options in this rollout are the same as those discussed in the **First Reference** rollout. You need to define the second reference while creating planes such as plane at an angle, plane tangent to a cylindrical face, plane perpendicular to a planar face, and so on. You will learn more about creating different types of planes by specifying second reference later in this chapter.

Third Reference

The **Third Reference** rollout is used for defining the third reference for creating a reference plane. The options in this rollout are the same as those discussed in the **First Reference** rollout. You need to define the third reference while creating a reference plane, which passes through three points or vertices.

In SOLIDWORKS, you need to focus more on creating reference planes rather than selecting options in the **Plane PropertyManager**. This is because when you select a reference geometry for creating a plane, the most suitable option gets automatically selected in the PropertyManager. Also, the preview of the respective reference plane appears in the graphics area. The procedures for creating different types of reference planes are discussed next.

Creating a Plane at an Offset Distance

1. Click on the arrow at the bottom of the **Reference Geometry** tool in the **Features CommandManager**. The **Reference Geometry** flyout appears.
2. Click on the **Plane** tool in the **Reference Geometry** flyout. The **Plane PropertyManager** appears.
3. Click on a planar face or a plane in the graphics area as the first reference. A preview of the offset plane appears, see Figure 6.5.
4. Enter the required offset distance value in the **Distance** field, which is available in front of the **Offset distance** button.
5. Flip the direction of the plane by selecting the **Flip offset** check box, see Figure 6.6, if needed.
6. Click on the green tick-mark ✔ in the PropertyManager. A reference plane at the specified offset distance is created.

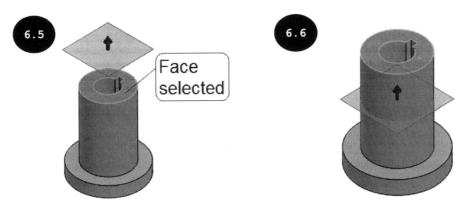

Creating a Parallel Plane

1. Invoke the **Reference Geometry** flyout and then click on the **Plane** tool.
2. Select a planar face or a plane as the first reference in the graphics area.

Note: As soon as you select a planar face or a plane, the preview of an offset plane appears in the graphics area with the default offset value. Also, the **Offset distance** button gets selected automatically in the **First Reference** rollout of the PropertyManager.

3. Select a point, a vertex, or a linear edge as the second reference in the graphics area. A preview of the reference plane parallel to the selected face and passing through the selected vertex/point appears in the graphics area, see Figure 6.7.
4. Click on the green tick-mark ✅ in the PropertyManager. A parallel plane is created.

Note: On selecting a linear edge as the second reference, you need to click on the **Parallel** button in the **First Reference** rollout of the PropertyManager to create a parallel plane.

Creating a Plane at an Angle

1. Invoke the **Plane PropertyManager**.
2. Select a planar face or a plane as the first reference in the graphics area. Next, click on the **At angle** button in the **First Reference** rollout of the PropertyManager.
3. Enter the required angle value in the **Angle** field that appears in front of the **At angle** button.
4. Select an edge (linear), an axis, or a sketch line as the second reference. A preview of the reference plane appears, see Figure 6.8.
5. Flip the direction of the angle by selecting the **Flip offset** check box, if needed.
6. Click on the green tick-mark ✅ in the PropertyManager. A reference plane at the specified angle is created.

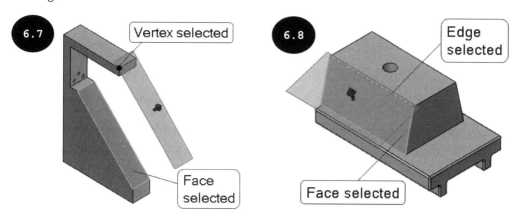

Creating a Plane passing through Three Points/Vertices

1. Invoke the **Plane PropertyManager**.
2. Select a point or a vertex as the first reference in the graphics area.
3. Select the second point or vertex as the second reference.

4. Select the third point or vertex as the third reference. A preview of the reference plane passing through three points/vertices appears in the graphics area, see Figure 6.9.
5. Click on the green tick-mark ✅ in the PropertyManager. A reference plane passing through three specified points/vertices is created.

Creating a Plane Normal to a Curve

1. Invoke the **Plane PropertyManager**.
2. Select a curve as the first reference in the graphics area, see Figure 6.10.
3. Select a point of the curve as the second reference, see Figure 6.10. A preview of the reference plane normal to the curve and passing through the selected point appears, see Figure 6.11.
4. Click on the green tick-mark ✅ in the PropertyManager. A reference plane normal to the curve and passing through the point is created.

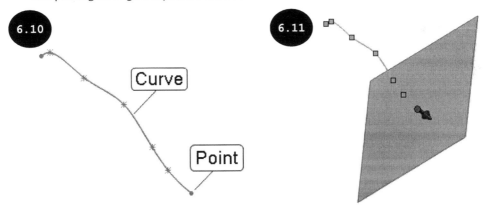

Creating a Plane at the middle of two Faces/Planes

1. Invoke the **Plane PropertyManager**.
2. Select a planar face of the model as the first reference, see Figure 6.12.
3. Select the second planar face of the model as the second reference, see Figure 6.12. A preview of the plane passing through the middle of the two selected faces appears in the graphics area, see Figure 6.12.
4. Click on the green tick-mark ✅ in the PropertyManager. A reference plane at the middle of the two selected faces is created.

Creating a Plane Tangent to a Cylindrical Face

1.   Invoke the **Plane PropertyManager**.
2.   Select a cylindrical face of the model as the first reference, see Figure 6.13. A preview of the plane tangent to the selected cylindrical face appears in the graphics area.
3.   Select a planar face or a plane as the second reference, see Figure 6.13. A preview of the plane tangent to the cylindrical face and perpendicular to the planar face appears, see Figure 6.14.

Note: As soon as you specify the second reference (a planar face), the **Perpendicular** button gets activated automatically in the **Second Reference** rollout. As a result, the preview of the reference plane appears tangent to the cylindrical face and perpendicular to the selected planar face. If you click on the **Parallel** button in the **Second Reference** rollout, the preview of the tangent plane gets modified and appears as tangent to the cylindrical face and parallel to the selected planar face. You can also flip the direction of the plane by selecting the **Flip offset** check box in the **First Reference** rollout.

4.   Click on the green tick-mark ✔ in the PropertyManager. A reference plane tangent to the selected cylindrical face and perpendicular/parallel to the planar face is created.

Creating a Plane Parallel to the Screen

1.   Invoke the **Plane PropertyManager**.
2.   Select a vertex as the first reference, see Figure 6.15.

3. Click on the **Parallel to screen** button ⬚ in the **First Reference** rollout. A preview of the plane normal to the viewing direction and passing through the vertex appears, see Figure 6.16.
4. Enter the offset distance in the **Offset distance** field of the PropertyManager, if needed.

Note: If the value entered in the **Offset distance** field is 0 (zero) then the plane will be created normal to the viewing direction and passing through the selected vertex. To create a plane at an offset distance from the vertex and normal to the viewing direction, you need to enter the offset distance value in the **Offset distance** field of the PropertyManager.

---

5. Click on the green tick-mark ✔ in the PropertyManager. A reference plane normal to the viewing direction (parallel to the screen) and passing through the vertex is created.

Note: Alternatively, you can create a reference plane parallel to the screen without invoking the **Plane PropertyManager**. For doing so, right-click on a face or an edge of a model in the graphics area and then click on the **Create Plane Parallel to Screen** option in the shortcut menu that appears. A 3D point is created where you right-clicked on the model and a reference plane parallel to the screen is created at that point.

Creating a Projected Plane onto a Non-Planar Face

1. Invoke the **Plane PropertyManager**.
2. Select a point to be projected onto a non-planar face as the first reference, see Figure 6.17.
3. Select the non planar face of the model to create a projected plane, see Figure 6.17. A preview of the projected plane appears in the graphics area, see Figure 6.18.

Note: By default, the preview of the projected plane appears by projecting the selected point to the nearest location on the non-planar face, see Figure 6.18. This is because the **Nearest location on surface** radio button is selected by default in the **First Reference** rollout. On selecting the **Along sketch normal** radio button, the preview of the plane appears by projecting the selected point normal to the non-planar face, see Figure 6.19. You can also flip the projection direction of the plane by selecting the **Flip offset** check box. Note that the **Flip offset** check box is enabled only when the **Along sketch normal** radio button is selected in the PropertyManager.

4.   Select the required radio button in the **First Reference** rollout (**Nearest location on surface** or **Along sketch normal**). The preview of the projected plane appears.
5.   Click on the green tick-mark ✔ in the PropertyManager. The projected plane is created.

Creating a Reference Axis

Similar to creating a reference plane, you can create a reference axis. Reference axis is used as the axis of revolution for creating features such as revolved and circular pattern. To create a reference axis, click on the **Axis** tool in the **Reference Geometry** flyout, see Figure 6.20. The **Axis PropertyManager** appears, see Figure 6.21. The options in the **Axis PropertyManager** are used for creating different types of axes and are discussed next.

One Line/Edge/Axis

The **One Line/Edge/Axis** button of the PropertyManager is used for creating an axis along an existing line, linear edge, or axis. For doing so, click on the **One Line/Edge/Axis** button in the PropertyManager and then select a line, a linear edge, or an axis in the graphics area. The preview of the axis along the selected entity appears in the graphics area. Next, click on the green tick-mark ✔ in the PropertyManager. The reference axis is created. Figure 6.22 shows a reference axis created along the edge of a model.

Two Planes

The **Two Planes** button is used for creating an axis at the intersection of two planar faces or planes. For doing so, click on the **Two Planes** button of the PropertyManager and then select two planar faces or planes. The preview of the axis at the intersection of the selected entities appears in the graphics area. Next, click on the green tick-mark ✔ in the PropertyManager. The reference axis is created. Note that the planes or the planar faces selected need to be non-parallel to each other. Figure 6.23 shows a reference axis created at the intersection of two selected faces.

Two Points/Vertices

The **Two Points/Vertices** button is used for creating an axis that passes through two points or vertices. For doing so, click on the **Two Points/Vertices** button and then select two points or vertices. A preview of the resultant axis appears in the graphics area, see Figure 6.24. Next, click on the green tick-mark ✔ in the PropertyManager. The reference axis is created such that it passes through the selected vertices.

Cylindrical/Conical Face

The **Cylindrical/Conical Face** button is used for creating an axis along the axis of a cylindrical/conical face. For doing so, click on the **Cylindrical/Conical Face** button and then select a cylindrical or a conical face. A preview of the resultant axis appears in the graphics area, see Figures 6.25 and 6.26. Next, click on the green tick-mark ✔ in the PropertyManager. A reference axis is created.

Point and Face/Plane

The **Point and Face/Plane** button is used for creating an axis normal to a face or a plane and passing through a point or a vertex. For doing so, click on the **Point and Face/Plane** button and then select a planar face or a plane and a point or a vertex, see Figure 6.27. A preview of an axis normal to the selected face and passing through the selected point appears in the graphics area, see Figure 6.28. Next, click on the green tick-mark ✔ in the PropertyManager. A reference axis is created.

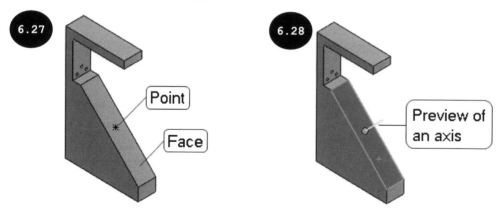

Creating a Reference Coordinate System

In addition to creating a reference plane and an axis, you can also create a reference coordinate system by using the **Coordinate System** tool of the **Reference Geometry** flyout, see Figure 6.29. The coordinate system is mainly used for machining or analyzing a model by positioning the origin of the model relative to its features. You can also use a reference coordinate system for applying relations, calculating mass properties, measurements, and so on.

Procedure for Creating a Reference Coordinate System

1. Invoke the **Reference Geometry** flyout and then click on the **Coordinate System** tool, see Figure 6.29. The **Coordinate System PropertyManager** appears, see Figure 6.30. Also, a preview of the coordinate system appears at the origin of the graphics area.

2. Select a point or a vertex as the origin of the coordinate system. Next, you need to define the direction of its axes.

3. Click on the **X Axis Direction Reference** field in the PropertyManager and then select a linear edge of the model. The X axis of the coordinate system is aligned along with the selected linear edge. You can also reverse the direction of axis by clicking on the **Reverse X Axis Direction** button on the left of the **X Axis Direction Reference** field.

4. Similarly, specify the direction of the Y axis and the Z axis of the coordinate system by using the **Y Axis Direction Reference** and the **Z Axis Direction Reference** fields of the PropertyManager, respectively.

5. Click on the green tick-mark ☑ in the PropertyManager. The resultant coordinate system is created, see Figure 6.31.

6.31 Edge selected to define X axis

Coordinate System2

Edge selected to define Y axis

Creating a Reference Point

A reference point can be created anywhere in a 3D model or space and is used as a reference for measuring distance, creating planes, and so on. To create a reference point, invoke the **Reference Geometry** flyout and then click on the **Point** tool. The **Point PropertyManager** appears, see Figure 6.32. The options in this PropertyManager are discussed next.

Reference Entities

The **Reference Entities** field is used for selecting reference entities for creating a point.

Arc Center

The **Arc Center** button is used for creating a point at the center of a circular or semi-circular edge, see Figure 6.33. As soon as you select a circular edge or a semi-circular edge, the preview of the reference point at its center appears and the **Arc Center** button gets activated in the PropertyManager.

Center of Face

The **Center of Face** button is used for creating a point at the center of a planar or a non-planar face, see Figure 6.34. As soon as you select a planar or a non-planar face, the preview of the reference point at the center of the selected face appears and the **Center of Face** button gets activated in the PropertyManager.

Intersection ✕

The **Intersection** button is used for creating a point at the intersection of two entities. You can select edges, curves, sketch segments, or a combination of these with a face or with each other as the entities to create a point. As soon as you select entities, the preview of a reference point appears at the intersection of the selected entities. Also, the **Intersection** button gets activated in the PropertyManager. Figure 6.35 shows the preview of a reference point at the intersection of two edges.

Projection

The **Projection** button is used for creating a point by projecting one entity onto another entity of a model. You can select sketch points, end points of curves, or vertices as the entities to be projected and a planar or a non-planar face as the entity onto which you want to project the selected point/vertex. Figure 6.36 shows the preview of a reference point after projecting a vertex onto a planar face.

On point ✎

The **On point** button is used for creating a reference point onto a point of a sketch. On selecting a point of a sketch, the **On point** button gets activated in the PropertyManager and the preview of the resultant reference point appears in the graphics area. Figure 6.37 shows a sketch point and Figure 6.38 shows the preview of the resultant reference point that appears on the selected point of the sketch.

Along curve distance or multiple reference point

The **Along curve distance or multiple reference point** button is used for creating a reference point on an edge, a curve, or a sketch entity. As soon as you select an edge, a curve, or a sketch entity, this button gets activated and the preview of a reference point appears in the graphics area with default settings, see Figure 6.39. Also, three radio buttons: **Distance**, **Percentage**, and **Evenly Distribute** appear in the PropertyManager, see Figure 6.40. These radio buttons are discussed next.

Distance

This radio button is used for specifying the position of a reference point by specifying a distance value in the **Distance/Percentage** field of the PropertyManager.

Percentage

This radio button is used for specifying the position of a reference point by specifying a percentage value in the **Distance/Percentage** field. Note that the percentage value is calculated in terms of the total length of the selected entity.

Evenly Distribute
This radio button is used for evenly distributing the number of reference points on the entity.

Number of reference points
This field is used for specifying the number of reference points to be created on a selected entity. By default, 1 is displayed in this field. As a result, only one reference point is created on the selected entity. You can create multiple reference points on the selected entity by specifying the required number in this field.

Once the preview of the reference point appears in the graphics area, click on the green tick-mark ✔ in the PropertyManager. The respective reference point is created.

Creating a Bounding Box
Bounding Box is a box that completely encloses a model (multibody, single body, or sheet metal) within a minimum volume, see Figure 6.41. It is used for determining the overall size and space of the model which is required to pack and ship the product. You can create a bounding box by using the **Bounding Box** tool. The procedure for creating a bounding box is discussed next.

Procedure for Creating a Bounding Box
1. Invoke the **Reference Geometry** flyout and then click on the **Bounding Box** tool. You can also click on **Insert > Reference Geometry > Bounding Box** in the SOLIDWORKS Menus. The **Bounding Box PropertyManager** appears, see Figure 6.42. Also, a preview of the bounding box appears around the model in the graphics area.

2. Make sure that the **Best Fit** radio button is selected in the PropertyManager to define the orientation of the bounding box based on the X-Y plane. Alternatively, you can select a reference plane to define its orientation by using the **Custom Plane** radio button.

Note: You can also include the hidden bodies and surfaces of the model in the bounding box by selecting the **Include hidden bodies** and **Include surfaces** check boxes.

3. Click on the green tick-mark ☑ in the PropertyManager. The bounding box is created around the model in the graphics area. Also, it is added in the **FeatureManager Design Tree** after the origin.

Note: The bounding box updates automatically on adding or removing features in the model. Also, you can hide/show or suppress/unsuppress the bounding box. For doing so, right-click on **Bounding Box** in the FeatureManager Design Tree and then click on the Hide ◈ /Show ◉ or Suppress ↓▣ /Unsuppress ↑▣ in the Pop-up menu.

In SOLIDWORKS, when you suppress or hide the bounding box feature, it does not rebuild, which improves the overall performance of the system.

Now, you can view the properties of the bounding box.

4. Click on **File** > **Properties** in the SOLIDWORKS Menus. The **Summary Information** window appears. In this window, click on the **Configuration Specific** tab to view the properties such as length, width, and volume of the bounding box.

Tutorial 1

Create a multi-feature model, as shown in Figure 6.43. You need to create the model by creating all its features one by one. All dimensions are in mm.

6.43

SECTION A-A

Section 1: Starting SOLIDWORKS

1. Start SOLIDWORKS by double-clicking on the SOLIDWORKS icon on your desktop. The startup user interface of SOLIDWORKS appears along with the **Welcome** dialog box.

Note: If SOLIDWORKS is already open and the **Welcome** dialog box does not appear on the screen, then you can invoke the same by clicking on the **Welcome to SOLIDWORKS** tool in the **Standard** toolbar or by pressing the CTRL + F2 keys.

Section 2: Invoking the Part Modeling Environment

1. Click on the **Part** button in the **Welcome** dialog box. The Part modeling environment is invoked.

Tip: You can also invoke the Part modeling environment by using the **New SOLIDWORKS Document** dialog box. For doing so, click on the **New** tool in the **Standard** toolbar. The **New SOLIDWORKS Document** dialog box appears. In this dialog box, make sure that the **Part** button is selected and then click on the **OK** button.

Now, you can set the unit system and create the base/first feature of the model.

Section 3: Specifying Unit Settings

1. Move the cursor toward the lower right corner of the screen over the Status Bar and then click on the **Unit System** area, see Figure 6.44. The **Unit System** flyout appears.

2. Make sure that the **MMGS (millimeter, gram, second)** option is tick-marked in the flyout.

Tip: A tick-mark in front of any unit system in the **Unit System** flyout indicates that it is selected as the unit system for the current document of SOLIDWORKS. You can also open the **Document Properties - Units** dialog box to specify the unit system for the current document by clicking on the **Edit Document Units** option in the flyout.

Section 4: Creating the Base/First Feature

1. Invoke the Sketching environment by selecting the Top plane as the sketching plane and then create two circles of diameters 9 mm and 16 mm as the sketch of the base feature, see Figure 6.45. Make sure that the center points of the circles are at the origin.

2.   Click on the **Features** tab in the CommandManager, see Figure 6.46. The tools of the **Features CommandManager** appear.

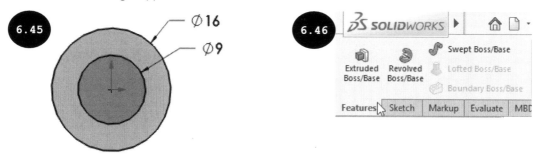

3.   Click on the **Extruded Boss/Base** tool in the **Features CommandManager**. The **Boss-Extrude PropertyManager** and the preview of the extruded feature appear, see Figure 6.47.

4.   Enter **10** in the **Depth** field of the **Direction 1** rollout and then press ENTER. Next, click on the green tick-mark ✔ in the PropertyManager. The base feature is created, see Figure 6.48.

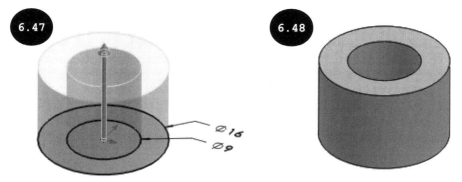

Section 5: Creating Second Feature

1.   Click on the **Sketch** tab to invoke the **Sketch CommandManager**, see Figure 6.49 and then click on the **Sketch** tool. The **Edit Sketch PropertyManager** appears and you are prompted to select a sketching plane for creating the sketch of the second feature.

2.   Click on the top planar face of the base feature as the sketching plane, see Figure 6.50. The Sketching environment is invoked.

3. Invoke the **View Orientation** flyout by clicking on the **View Orientation** tool in the **View (Heads-Up)** toolbar, see Figure 6.51. Next, click on the **Normal To** tool in the flyout to change the orientation of the model as normal to the viewing direction.

4. Create a polygon of 6 sides and a circle of diameter 9 mm by using the **Polygon** and **Circle** tools as the sketch of the second feature, see Figure 6.52. Also, apply required dimensions and relations to make the sketch fully defined.

Tip: In addition to the required dimensions, you need to apply a vertical relation to a vertical line of the polygon to make the sketch fully defined.

5. Click on the **Features** tab in the CommandManager to display the tools of the **Features** CommandManager.

6. Click on the **Extruded Boss/Base** tool in the **Features CommandManager**. The **Boss-Extrude PropertyManager** and a preview of the extruded feature appear. Next, change the orientation of the model to isometric, see Figure 6.53. For doing so, invoke the **View Orientation** flyout of the **View (Heads-Up)** toolbar and then click on the **Isometric** tool.

Extruded
Boss/Base

7. Enter **8** in the **Depth** field of the **Direction 1** rollout and then press ENTER.

8. Click on the green tick-mark ✔ in the PropertyManager. The extruded feature is created, see Figure 6.54.

6.54

Section 6: Creating the Third Feature

1. Invoke the Sketching environment by selecting the top planar face of the second feature as the sketching plane.

2. Change the orientation of the model as normal to the viewing direction. For doing so, click on the **View Orientation** tool in the **View (Heads-Up)** toolbar and then click on the **Normal To** tool in the **View Orientation** flyout that appears, see Figure 6.55.

3. Create the sketch of the third feature by creating two circles of diameter 9 mm and 16 mm by using the **Circle** tool and then apply dimensions, see Figure 6.56.

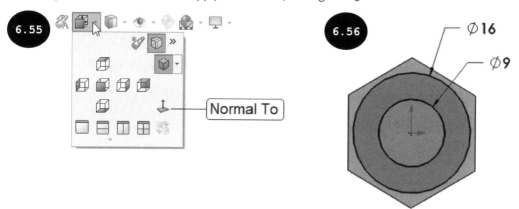

6.55   Normal To

6.56   Ø16   Ø9

4. Click on the **Features** tab in the CommandManager to display the tools of the **Features** CommandManager.

5. Click on the **Extruded Boss/Base** tool in the **Features Command Manager**. The preview of the extruded feature appears. Next, change the orientation of the model to isometric, see Figure 6.57.

    Extruded Boss/Base

6. Enter 5 in the **Depth** field in the **Direction 1** rollout and then press ENTER.

7. Click on the green tick-mark ✔ in the PropertyManager. The extruded feature is created, see Figure 6.58.

Section 7: Creating the Fourth Feature

1. Invoke the Sketching environment by selecting the top planar face of the third feature as the sketching plane, see Figure 6.59 and then change the orientation of the model as normal to the viewing direction by using the **Normal To** tool.

2. Create the sketch of the fourth feature by creating two circles of diameter 9 mm and 11 mm by using the **Circle** tool and then apply dimensions, see Figure 6.60.

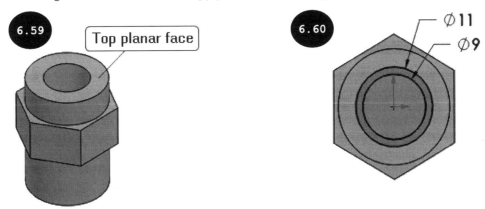

3. Click on the **Features** tab in the CommandManager to display the tools of the **Features** CommandManager.

4. Click on the **Extruded Boss/Base** tool in the **Features CommandManager**. The **Boss-Extrude PropertyManager** and the preview of the extruded feature appear. Next, change the orientation of the model to isometric, see Figure 6.61.

5. Enter 14 in the **Depth** field of the **Direction 1** rollout and then press ENTER.

6. Click on the green tick-mark ☑ in the PropertyManager. The extruded feature is created. Figure 6.62 shows the model after creating all its features.

Section 8: Saving the Sketch

1.   Click on the **Save** tool in the **Standard** toolbar. The **Save As** dialog box appears.

2.   Browse to the SOLIDWORKS folder and then create a folder with the name Chapter 6.

3.   Enter **Tutorial 1** in the **File name** field as the name of the file and then click on the **Save** button. The model is saved with the name Tutorial 1 in the Chapter 6 folder.

Tutorial 2

Create a model, as shown in Figure 6.63. All dimensions are in mm.

Section 1: Starting SOLIDWORKS

1. Start SOLIDWORKS by double-clicking on the SOLIDWORKS icon on your desktop. The startup user interface of SOLIDWORKS appears along with the **Welcome** dialog box.

> **Note:** If SOLIDWORKS is already open and the **Welcome** dialog box does not appear on the screen, then you can invoke the same by clicking on the **Welcome to SOLIDWORKS** tool 🏠 in the **Standard** toolbar or by pressing the CTRL + F2 keys.

Section 2: Invoking the Part Modeling Environment

1. Click on the **Part** button in the **Welcome** dialog box. The Part modeling environment is invoked.

Section 3: Specifying Unit Settings

1. Move the cursor toward the lower right corner of the screen over the Status Bar and then click on the **Unit System** area. The **Unit System** flyout appears, see Figure 6.64.

2. Make sure that the **MMGS (millimeter, gram, second)** option is tick-marked in the flyout.

Section 4: Creating the Base/First Feature

1. Invoke the Sketching environment by selecting the Right plane as the sketching plane.

2. Create the sketch of the base feature and then apply the required relations and dimensions to the sketch, see Figure 6.65.

Tip: To make the sketch fully defined, you need to apply the tangent relation between line 2 and arc 3, arc 3 and arc 4 of the sketch, refer to Figure 6.66. Also, apply the concentric relation between arc 4 and arc 6, refer to Figure 6.66. The sketch shown in the Figure 6.66 has been numbered for your reference only. The relations such as horizontal and vertical are applied automatically while drawing the horizontal and vertical lines of the sketch.

3. Click on the **Features** tab in the CommandManager and then click on the **Extruded Boss/Base** tool. The **Boss-Extrude PropertyManager** and a preview of the extruded feature appear, see Figure 6.67.

4. Invoke the **End Condition** drop-down list in the **Direction 1** rollout of the PropertyManager, see Figure 6.68.

5. Click on the **Mid Plane** option in the **End Condition** drop-down list.

6. Enter **60** in the **Depth** field of the **Direction 1** rollout and then press ENTER. The depth of extrusion is added symmetrically to both sides of the sketching plane, see Figure 6.69.

7. Click on the green tick-mark ✅ in the PropertyManager. The extruded feature is created symmetrically about the sketching plane.

Section 5: Creating the Second Feature

To create the second feature of the model, you first need to create a reference plane at an offset distance of 10 mm from the right planar face of the base feature.

1. Invoke the **Reference Geometry** flyout in the **Features CommandManager**, see Figure 6.70.

2. Click on the **Plane** tool of this flyout. The **Plane PropertyManager** appears.

3. Select the right planar face of the base feature as the first reference. The preview of an offset reference plane appears in the graphics area, see Figure 6.71.

4. Enter **10** in the **Distance** field of the **First Reference** rollout in the PropertyManager and then select the **Flip offset** check box to flip the direction of the plane.

5. Click on the green tick-mark ✅ in the PropertyManager. The offset reference plane is created, see Figure 6.72.

After creating the reference plane, create the second feature of the model.

6. Invoke the Sketching environment by selecting the newly created reference plane as the sketching plane.

7. Change the orientation of the model as normal to the viewing direction by clicking on the **Normal To** tool ⬇ in the **View Orientation** flyout.

8. Create the sketch of the second feature and then apply the required dimensions to the sketch, see Figure 6.73.

6.73

9. Click on the **Features** tab in the CommandManager to display the tools of the **Features** CommandManager.

10. Click on the **Extruded Boss/Base** tool in the **Features CommandManager**. The **Boss-Extrude PropertyManager** and the preview of the extruded feature appear. Next, change the orientation of the model to isometric.

Extruded Boss/Base

11. Click on the **Reverse Direction** button ⬆ in the **Direction 1** rollout to reverse the direction of extrusion similar to the one shown in Figure 6.74.

12. Enter **50** in the **Depth** field of the **Direction 1** rollout and then press ENTER. Next, click on the green tick-mark ✔ in the PropertyManager. The extruded feature is created, see Figure 6.75.

6.74

6.75

Section 6: Creating the Third Feature

To create the third feature of the model, you need to create a reference plane at the middle of the second feature.

1. Invoke the **Reference Geometry** flyout in the **Features CommandManager**, see Figure 6.76.

2. Click on the **Plane** tool in this flyout. The **Plane PropertyManager** appears.

3. Select the right planar face of the second feature as the first reference. The preview of an offset reference plane appears in the graphics area, see Figure 6.77.

4. Rotate the model such that the left planar face of the second feature can be viewed in the graphics area, see Figure 6.78. To rotate the model, right-click in the graphics area and then click on **Zoom/Pan/Rotate > Rotate View** in the shortcut menu that appears. Next, drag the cursor in the graphics area by pressing and holding the left mouse button. Once the required view of the model has been achieved, exit the **Rotate View** tool by pressing the ESC key. Alternatively, you can rotate the model by dragging the cursor while pressing the middle mouse button.

5. Click on the left planar face of the second feature as the second reference for creating the plane. A preview of the reference plane at the middle of the two selected faces appears in the graphics area, see Figure 6.79.

6. Change the view orientation of the model to isometric.

7. Click on the green-tick mark ☑ in the PropertyManager. The reference plane at the middle of two selected faces is created.

    After creating the reference plane, you can create the third feature of the model. This feature can be created easily by using the **Rib** tool. You will learn about the **Rib** tool in later chapters. In this tutorial, you will create the feature by using the **Extruded Boss/Base** tool.

8. Invoke the Sketching environment by selecting the newly created reference plane as the sketching plane.

9. Change the orientation of the model as normal to the viewing direction by clicking on the **Normal To** tool ⬇ in the **View Orientation** flyout.

10. Create the closed sketch of the third feature (three line entities), see Figure 6.80. The entities of the sketch shown in Figure 6.80 have been created by taking reference of the vertices of the existing features of the model.

6.80

11. Click on the **Features** tab in the CommandManager to display the tools of the **Features** CommandManager.

12. Click on the **Extruded Boss/Base** tool in the **Features** CommandManager. The Boss-Extrude PropertyManager and a preview of the extruded feature appear. Next, change the orientation of the model to isometric.

Extruded Boss/Base

13. Invoke the **End Condition** drop-down list in the **Direction 1** rollout, see Figure 6.81 and then click on the **Mid Plane** option.

6.81

14. Enter 8 in the **Depth** field of the **Direction 1** rollout and then press ENTER. The depth of extrusion is added symmetrically to both sides of the sketching plane, see Figure 6.82.

15. Click on the green tick-mark ☑ in the PropertyManager. The extruded feature is created. Figure 6.83 shows the final model after creating all its features.

Section 7: Saving the Sketch

1. Click on the **Save** tool of the **Standard** toolbar, the **Save As** dialog box appears.

2. Browse to the Chapter 6 folder of the SOLIDWORKS and then save the model with the name Tutorial 2. You need to create the Chapter 6 folder inside the SOLIDWORKS folder, if not created earlier.

Tutorial 3

Create a model, as shown in Figure 6.84. All dimensions are in mm.

Section 1: Starting SOLIDWORKS

1. Start SOLIDWORKS by double-clicking on the SOLIDWORKS icon on your desktop. The initial screen of SOLIDWORKS appears along with the **Welcome** dialog box.

Note: If SOLIDWORKS is already open and the **Welcome** dialog box does not appear on the screen, then you can invoke the **Welcome** dialog box by clicking on the **Welcome to SOLIDWORKS** tool 🏠 in the **Standard** toolbar or by pressing the CTRL + F2 keys.

Section 2: Invoking the Part Modeling Environment

1. Click on the **Part** button in the **Welcome** dialog box. The Part modeling environment is invoked.

2. Make sure that the metric unit system is selected as the unit system for this document.

Section 3: Creating the Base/First Feature

1. Invoke the Sketching environment by selecting the Right plane as the sketching plane.

2. Create a circle and apply the diameter dimension, see Figure 6.85. Make sure that the center point of the circle is at the origin.

3. Click on the **Features** tab in the CommandManager and then click on the **Extruded Boss/Base** tool. The preview of the extruded feature appears in the graphics area.

4. Enter **20** in the **Depth** field of the **Direction 1** rollout and then press ENTER.

5. Click on the green tick-mark ✔ in the PropertyManager. The extruded feature is created, see Figure 6.86.

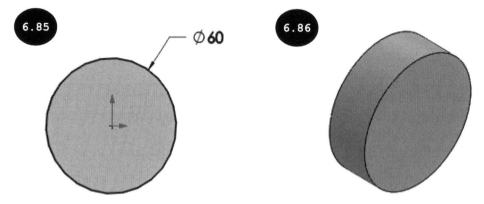

Section 4: Creating the Second Feature

1. Invoke the Sketching environment by selecting the right planar face of the base feature as the sketching plane, see Figure 6.87.

2. Press CTRL + 8 to change the orientation of the model as normal to the viewing direction.

3. Create the sketch of the second feature and then apply required relations and dimensions, see Figure 6.88.

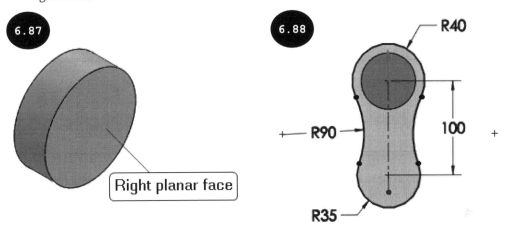

4. Click on the **Features** tab and then click on the **Extruded Boss/Base** tool. The **Boss-Extrude PropertyManager** and the preview of the extruded feature appear. Next, change the orientation of the model to isometric, see Figure 6.89.

5. Enter **20** in the **Depth** field of the **Direction 1** rollout and then press ENTER.

6. Click on the green tick-mark ✔ in the PropertyManager. The extruded feature is created, see Figure 6.90.

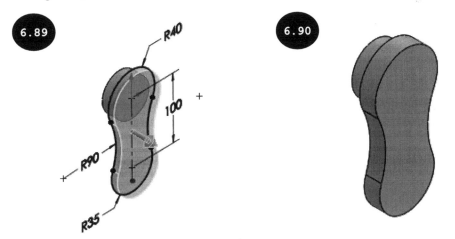

Section 5: Creating the Third Feature

1. Invoke the Sketching environment by selecting the right planar face of the second feature as the sketching plane.

2. Press CTRL + 8 to change the orientation of the model as normal to the viewing direction.

3. Create a circle and apply diameter dimension, see Figure 6.91. Make sure that a concentric relation is applied between the circle and the bottom semi-circular edge of the second feature.

4. Click on the **Features** tab and then click on the **Extruded Boss/Base** tool. The **Boss-Extrude PropertyManager** and the preview of the extruded feature appear. Next, change the orientation of the model to isometric.

5. Enter **50** in the **Depth** field of the **Direction 1** rollout and then press ENTER.

6. Click on the green tick-mark ✔ in the PropertyManager. The extruded feature is created. Figure 6.92 shows the final model after creating all its features.

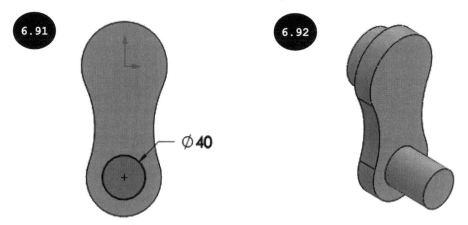

Section 6: Saving the Sketch

1. Click on the **Save** tool in the **Standard** toolbar. The **Save As** dialog box appears.

2. Browse to the Chapter 6 folder of the SOLIDWORKS folder and then save the model with the name Tutorial 3.

Hands-on Test Drive 1

Create the model, as shown in Figure 6.93. All dimensions are in mm.

6.93

Hands-on Test Drive 2

Create the model, as shown in Figure 6.94. All dimensions are in mm.

6.94

Summary

In this chapter, you have learned that the three default planes may not be enough for creating models having multiple features. Therefore, you need to create additional reference planes, the method for which has been described. The chapter also describes methods for creating a reference axis, reference coordinates system and a reference point by using the respective tools, in addition to method for creating a bounding box to determine the overall size and space of the model which is required to pack and ship the product.

Questions

• You can create reference planes by using the _____ tool.

• To create a reference plane parallel to a planar face of a model, you need to define two references: first reference can be a planar face and second reference can be a _____, _____, or _____ .

• To create a reference plane at an angle to a planar face/plane, you need to define two references: first reference can be a planar face/plane and second reference can be a _____, _____, or _____ .

• The _____ tool is used for creating reference axis.

• The _____ tool is used for creating coordinate systems.

• The _____ tool is used for creating a bounding box that completely encloses a model within a minimum volume.

• In SOLIDWORKS, you can create a reference point at the intersection of two entities. (True/False)

• You cannot select a planar face of existing features as the sketching plane for creating a feature. (True/False)

Advanced Modeling - I

This chapter discusses the following topics:

- Using Advanced Options of the Extruded Boss/Base Tool
- Using Advanced Options of the Revolved Boss/Base Tool
- Creating Cut Features
- Working with Different Types of Sketches
- Working with Contours of a Sketch
- Displaying Shaded Sketch Contours
- Projecting Edges onto the Sketching Plane
- Editing a Feature and its Sketch
- Importing 2D DXF or DWG Files
- Displaying Earlier State of a Model
- Reordering Features of a Model
- Measuring the Distance between Entities
- Assigning an Appearance/Texture
- Applying a Material
- Calculating Mass Properties

In the previous chapters, you have learned how to create features by using the **Extruded Boss/Base** and **Revolved Boss/Base** tools. In this chapter, you will learn how to use the advanced options of the **Extruded Boss/Base** and **Revolved Boss/Base** tools for creating features. You will also learn about creating cut features by using the **Extruded Cut** and **Revolved Cut** tools. Besides, you will learn how to work with different types of sketches, measure the distance between entities of a model, assign appearance to a model, apply material properties, calculate mass properties of a model, and so on.

Using Advanced Options of the Extruded Boss/Base Tool

As discussed earlier, while extruding a sketch by using the **Extruded Boss/Base** tool, the **Boss-Extrude PropertyManager** appears to the left of the graphics area, see Figure 7.1. Some of the options of this PropertyManager have been discussed earlier while creating the base feature of a model. The remaining options of this PropertyManager are discussed next.

Start Condition Drop-down List

The options in the **Start Condition** drop-down list of the **From** rollout are used for defining the start condition of extrusion, see Figure 7.2. The **Sketch Plane** and **offset** options of this drop-down list have been discussed earlier while creating base features and the remaining options are discussed next.

Surface/Face/Plane

The **Surface/Face/Plane** option of the **Start Condition** drop-down list is used for selecting a surface, a face, or a plane as the start condition of the extrusion. On selecting this option, the **Select A Surface/Face/Plane** field appears below the **Start Condition** drop-down list and is activated by default. As a result, you can select a surface, a face, or a plane as the start condition of the extrusion. Figure 7.3 shows a sketch to be extruded and a face to be selected as the start condition of extrusion. Figure 7.4 shows the preview of the resultant extruded feature after selecting the face as the start condition.

Note: You can select a surface, a face, or a plane as the start condition of extrusion, even if the selected surface, face, or plane does not encapsulate the entire sketch.

Vertex

The **Vertex** option is used for selecting a vertex of a model as the start condition of the extrusion. On selecting this option, the **Select A Vertex** field appears below the **Start Condition** drop-down list and is activated by default. As a result, you can select a vertex as the start condition of the extrusion, see Figure 7.5.

End Condition Drop-down List

The **End Condition** drop-down list of the **Direction 1** rollout is used for defining the end condition of the extrusion, see Figure 7.6. The **Blind** and **Mid Plane** options of this drop-down list have been discussed earlier while creating base features and the remaining options are discussed next.

Up To Vertex

The **Up To Vertex** option is used for defining the end condition or termination of the extrusion by selecting a vertex. On selecting this option, the **Vertex** field becomes available in the rollout and is activated, by default. As a result, you can select a vertex of the model up to which you want to extrude the feature. Figure 7.7 shows a preview of a feature whose end condition is defined by selecting a vertex of the model.

Up To Surface

The **Up To Surface** option is used for defining the end condition or termination of the extrusion up to a surface. When you select the **Up To Surface** option, the **Face/Plane** field becomes available in the **Direction 1** rollout and is activated, by default. As a result, you can select a surface, a face, or a plane up to which you want to extrude the feature. Figure 7.8 shows the preview of a feature whose end condition is defined by selecting a face of the model.

Offset From Surface

The **Offset From Surface** option is used for defining the end condition or termination of the extrusion at an offset distance from a surface, see Figure 7.9. When you select the **Offset From Surface** option, the **Face/Plane** and **Offset Distance** fields become available in the **Direction 1** rollout. Select an existing surface, a face, or a plane of the model as the end condition of extrusion and enter the offset distance value in the **Offset Distance** field. Once you enter the offset distance value, the resultant feature is terminated at an offset distance from the selected face. Figure 7.9 shows the preview of a feature whose end condition is defined at an offset distance from a face of the model.

Up To Body

The **Up To Body** option is used for defining the end condition or termination of extrusion up to a body. When you select this option, the **Solid/Surface Body** field becomes available in the **Direction 1** rollout of the PropertyManager and is activated, by default. As a result, you can select a solid body or a surface body up to which you want to extrude the feature. Note that this option can be used when multiple bodies are available in the graphics area. You can create bodies in the Part environment by clearing the **Merge result** check box of the PropertyManager, which is discussed next.

Merge result

The **Merge result** check box of the **Direction 1** rollout is used for merging a feature with the existing features of the model. By default, this check box is selected. As a result, the feature of the model being created merges with the existing features of the model. If you clear this check box, the feature being created does not merge with the existing features and a separate body will be created. Note that this check box is not available while creating the base/first feature of a model.

Note: The options in the **Direction 2** rollout of the **Boss-Extrude PropertyManager** are same as those of the **Direction 1** rollout with the only difference that the options of the **Direction 2** rollout are used for specifying the end condition of extrusion in the second direction of the sketching plane.

Using Advanced Options of the Revolved Boss/Base Tool

As discussed earlier, while revolving a sketch by using the **Revolved Boss/Base** tool, the **Revolve PropertyManager** appears to the left of the graphics area, see Figure 7.10. Some of the options in the **Revolve Type** drop-down list of the PropertyManager have been discussed earlier while creating the base revolved feature of a model. The remaining options such as **Up To Vertex** and **Up To Surface** of this drop-down list are the same as discussed earlier with the only difference that these options are used for creating a revolved feature. Figure 7.10 shows the **Revolve PropertyManager** with the expanded **Revolve Type** drop-down list.

Creating Cut Features

Similar to adding material by extruding and revolving a sketch, you can remove material from a model by using the **Extruded Cut** and **Revolved Cut** tools. By using these tools, you can create an extruded cut feature and a revolved cut feature. Both the features are discussed next.

Creating Extruded Cut Features

You can create an extruded cut feature by using the **Extruded Cut** tool of the **Features CommandManager**. An extruded cut feature is created by removing material from a model. Note that the geometry of the material removed is defined by the sketch of the cut feature. Figure 7.11 shows a sketch, which is created on the top planar face of the model and the resultant extruded cut feature.

To create an extruded cut feature, click on the **Extruded Cut** tool in the **Features CommandManager**. The **Extrude PropertyManager** appears. Next, select the sketch in the graphics area. The preview of the extruded cut feature appears in the graphics area with default parameters. Also, the **Cut-Extrude PropertyManager** appears on the left of the graphics area, see Figure 7.12. Note that you can select the sketch before or after invoking the **Extruded Cut** tool. The options in the **Cut-Extrude PropertyManager** are used for defining parameters of the extruded cut feature. These options are same as those discussed earlier while creating the extruded feature, with the only difference that these options are used for removing material from the model. You can also flip the side of the material to be removed by using the **Flip side to cut** check box of the PropertyManager, see Figure 7.13. After specifying parameters for creating the extruded cut feature, click on the green tick-mark ✔ in the PropertyManager. The extruded cut feature is created.

7.13 Sketch of the extruded cut feature

Flip side to cut check box is cleared

Flip side to cut check box is selected

Procedure for Creating an Extruded Cut Feature

1. Create a sketch by using the sketching tools in the Sketching environment. After creating the sketch, do not exit the Sketching environment.
2. Click on the **Features** tab in the CommandManager and then click on the **Extruded Cut** tool. The preview of the cut feature appears in the graphics area. Also, the **Cut-Extrude PropertyManager** appears to the left of the graphics area.

Tip: If you exit the Sketching environment after creating the sketch and the sketch is not selected in the graphics area, then on clicking the **Extruded Cut** tool, the **Extrude PropertyManager** appears and you are prompted to select a sketch or create a sketch. Select the sketch in the graphics area. A preview of the extruded cut feature and the **Cut-Extrude PropertyManager** appear.

3. Specify parameters required for removing the material in the PropertyManager.
4. Click on the green tick-mark ✓ in the PropertyManager. The extruded cut feature is created.

Creating Revolved Cut Features

You can create a revolved cut feature by using the **Revolved Cut** tool. A revolved cut feature is created by removing material from a model by revolving a sketch around an axis of revolution. Note that the sketch to be revolved should be on either side of the axis of revolution. Figure 7.14 shows a sketch to be revolved and Figure 7.15 shows the resultant revolved cut feature.

Revolved Cut

7.14 Axis of revolution / Sketch to be revolved

7.15

Procedure for Creating a Revolved Cut Feature

1. Create a sketch of the revolved cut feature with a centerline as the axis of revolution. After creating the sketch, do not exit the Sketching environment.
2. Click on the **Features** tab in the CommandManager and then click on the **Revolved Cut** tool. The preview of the revolved cut feature appears in the graphics area. Also, the **Cut-Revolve PropertyManager** appears to the left of the graphics area, see Figure 7.16.

Note: If the sketch has two or more than two centerlines then on invoking the **Revolved Cut** tool, you are prompted to select a centerline as the axis of revolution. After selecting a centerline, a preview of the revolved cut feature appears. You can select a centerline, a linear sketch entity, a linear edge, or an axis as the axis of revolution.

Tip: If you exit the Sketching environment after creating the sketch and the sketch is not selected in the graphics area, then on clicking the **Revolved Cut** tool, the **Revolve PropertyManager** appears. Also, you are prompted to select a sketch to be revolved or a sketching plane to create a sketch of the revolved cut feature. Select a centerline of the sketch as the axis of revolution, a preview of the revolved cut feature appears in the graphics area. Also, the **Cut-Revolve PropertyManager** appears on the left of the graphics area.

3. Specify the required parameters of revolved cut feature in the PropertyManager. The options in the **Cut-Revolve PropertyManager** are same as those discussed earlier.
4. Click on the green tick-mark ✓ in the PropertyManager. The revolved cut feature is created.

Working with Different Types of Sketches

It is important to understand different types of sketches and their performance, some of the important types being Closed sketches, Open sketches, Nested sketches, and Intersecting sketches. All these sketches have been discussed next.

Closed Sketches

Closed sketches are those in which all entities are connected end to end with each other without any gaps. On extruding a closed sketch, a solid extruded feature is created. Figure 7.17 shows a closed sketch having one closed contour and its resultant extruded feature.

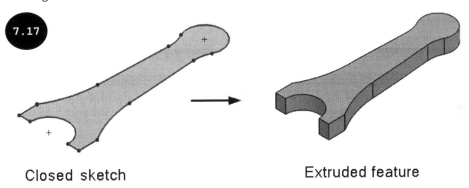

Closed sketch   Extruded feature

Open Sketches

Open Sketches are those that are open from one or more ends. On extruding an open sketch, a thin feature is created. Figure 7.18 shows an open sketch and its resultant thin extruded feature.

Open sketch   Thin extruded feature

Nested Sketches

Nested sketches are similar to closed sketches with the only difference that the nested sketches have more than one closed contour. On extruding a nested sketch having multiple closed contours, a solid feature is created by adding the material to the most suitable closed contour of the sketch. Figure 7.19 shows a nested sketch having two closed contours and its resultant extruded feature. Figure 7.20 shows a nested sketch having three closed contours and its resultant extruded feature.

7.19

Contour 2

Contour 1

Nested sketch

Extruded feature

7.20

Contour 3

Contour 2

Contour 1

Nested sketch

Extruded feature

However, on extruding a nested sketch similar to the one shown in Figure 7.21, you will be prompted to select a contour of the sketch to be extruded. You can select the required closed contour of the sketch by using the **Selected Contours** rollout of the PropertyManager, as discussed in earlier chapters. Figure 7.22 shows the preview of an extruded feature by selecting a contour of a nested sketch. You will learn more about extruding different contours or closed regions of a nested sketch later in this chapter.

7.21

Contour 1

Contour 2

Contour 3

7.22

Intersecting Sketches

Intersecting sketches have intersection among the entities of the sketch, see Figure 7.23. On extruding an intersecting sketch, automatic selection of a closed contour to add material does not take place and you are prompted to select a closed contour of the intersecting sketch to be extruded. You can select the required contour by using the **Selected Contours** rollout of the PropertyManager. Figure 7.23 shows an intersecting sketch and Figure 7.24 shows the preview of an extruded feature by extruding a closed contour of the intersecting sketch. You will learn more about extruding closed contours of a sketch later in this chapter.

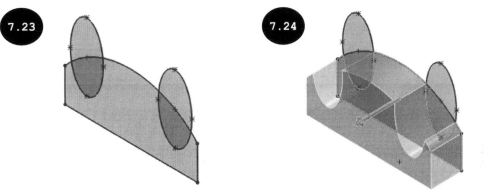

Note: Working with different types of sketches such as closed sketches, open sketches, nested sketches, and intersecting sketches is the same for all tools such as **Extruded Base/Boss** and **Revolved Base/Boss** tools.

Working with Contours of a Sketch

In SOLIDWORKS, you can also create multiple features by using a single sketch that has multiple contours. Figure 7.25 shows a sketch having multiple contours and Figure 7.26 shows the resultant multi-feature model created by using this sketch.

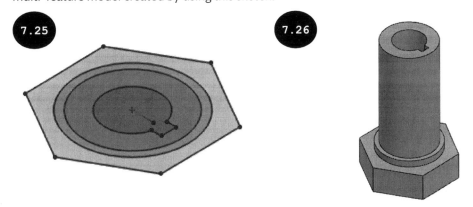

To extrude contours of a sketch, you can use the **Selected Contours** rollout of the PropertyManager or the **Contour Select Tool**. The procedures for creating features by extruding contours of a sketch are discussed next.

Procedure for Extruding Contours by using the Selected Contours Rollout

1. Create a sketch that has multiple contours in the Sketching environment, refer to Figure 7.27. Next, exit the Sketching environment.
2. Make sure that the sketch is selected in the graphics area. If not selected, click on the sketch name in the FeatureManager Design Tree to select it.
3. Invoke the **Extruded Boss/Base** or **Revolved Boss/Base** tool, as required. Depending upon the tool invoked, the PropertyManager of the respective tool appears with the expanded **Selected Contours** rollout. Also, the cursor changes to contour cursor ◔.
4. Move the cursor ◔ over the contour of the sketch to be selected and then click when it gets highlighted in the graphics area. A preview of the feature appears, see Figure 7.28.

5. Specify parameters for creating the feature in the PropertyManager.
6. Click on the green tick-mark ✓ in the PropertyManager. The feature is created and its name is added in the FeatureManager Design Tree. Also, the sketch disappears from the graphics area.
7. In the FeatureManager Design Tree, expand the node of the previously created feature by clicking on the arrow in front of it, see Figure 7.29.
8. Click on the sketch of the previously created feature in the FeatureManager Design Tree. A Pop-up toolbar appears, click on the **Show** tool in it, see Figure 7.29.

Show tool

9. Repeat steps 2 to 6 for creating the remaining features by using different contours of the same sketch. Figure 7.30 shows a model created by extruding multi-contours of a sketch.

Note: In Figure 7.30, the sketch has been hidden. To hide the sketch, click on the sketch in the graphics area. A Pop-up toolbar appears. Next, click on the **Hide** tool.

Procedure for Extruding Contours by using the Contour Select Tool

1. Create a sketch that has multiple contours in the Sketching environment and then do not exit the Sketching environment.
2. Change the orientation of the model to isometric.
3. Press and hold the ALT key in the graphics area. The **Contour Select Tool** gets activated and the cursor changes to the contour cursor.
4. Move the cursor over the contour to be extruded and then click the left mouse button when the contour gets highlighted in the graphics area. The **Extruded Boss/Base** tool appears near the cursor, see Figure 7.31.

5. Click on the **Extruded Boss/Base** tool that appears near the cursor in the graphics area. The preview of the feature appears to the graphics area with default parameters, see Figure 7.32. Also, the **Boss-Extrude PropertyManager** appears on the left of the graphics area.

6. Specify parameters for creating the feature in the PropertyManager.
7. Click on the green tick-mark ✓ in the PropertyManager. The feature is created and its name is added in the FeatureManager Design Tree. Also, the sketch disappears from the graphics area.

Note: Alternatively, to invoke the **Contour Select Tool**, right-click in the graphics area. A shortcut menu appears. Expand the shortcut menu by clicking on the double arrows available at its bottom. Next, click on **Contour Select Tool** in the expanded shortcut menu. You can invoke the **Contour Select Tool** from the shortcut menu in the Sketching environment as well as in the Part modeling environment.

---

8. In the FeatureManager Design Tree, expand the node of the previously created feature. Next, click on the sketch of the feature and then click on the **Show** tool in the Pop-up toolbar that appears, see Figure 7.33. The display of the sketch gets turned on in the graphics area.

9. Right-click in the graphics area. A shortcut menu appears.
10. Expand the shortcut menu by clicking on the double arrows available below it.
11. Click on **Contour Select Tool** in the expanded shortcut menu, see Figure 7.34. The **Contour Select Tool** gets activated and the cursor is changed to contour cursor ⬚. Also, you are prompted to select a sketch, whose contour is to be extruded.
12. Move the cursor toward the sketch and then click on it.
13. Move the cursor over the required contour of the sketch and then click on it when it gets highlighted in the graphics area.
14. Click on the **Extruded Boss/Base** tool in the **Features CommandManager**. The preview of the feature appears in the graphics area.
15. Specify parameters for creating the feature in the PropertyManager.
16. Click on the green tick-mark ✓ in the PropertyManager. The feature is created and its name is added in the FeatureManager Design Tree.
17. Repeat steps 9 to 16 for creating the remaining features by using different contours of the same sketch. Figure 7.35 shows a model created by using multi-contours of a sketch.

> **Note:** In Figure 7.35, the sketch has been hidden. To hide the sketch, click on the sketch in the graphics area. A Pop-up toolbar appears. Next, click on the **Hide** tool in the toolbar.

Displaying Shaded Sketch Contours

In SOLIDWORKS, the closed contours of a sketch are displayed in different blue shades (lightest to darkest blue shades), see Figure 7.36. In this figure, the outermost circle has the lightest blue shade and the innermost circle has the darkest blue shade. It helps to easily identify whether the geometry is fully closed or not. Note that if the geometry is not fully closed then it will not be displayed in blue shade. You can turn on or off the display of shaded sketch contours in the Sketching environment by using the **Shaded Sketch Contours** tool. By default, the **Shaded Sketch Contours** tool is activated in the **Sketch CommandManager**. As a result, the display of shaded sketch contours is turned on. To turn off the display of shaded sketch contours, click on the **Shaded Sketch Contours** tool in the **Sketch CommandManager**, see Figure 7.37.

Projecting Edges onto the Sketching Plane

In SOLIDWORKS, while sketching, you can project edges of the existing features onto the current sketching plane by using the **Convert Entities** tool, see Figure 7.38. In SOLIDWORKS 2020, you can also project the edges of a body or a component onto the current sketching plane by using the **Silhouette Entities** tool. Besides, you can project the geometries of the existing features that intersect with the currently active sketching plane by using the **Intersection Curve** tool. All these tools are discussed next.

Projecting Edges of Existing Features

To project the edges of the existing features onto the current sketching plane, click on the **Convert Entities** tool in the **Sketch CommandManager**. The **Convert Entities** PropertyManager appears, see Figure 7.39. The options in the PropertyManager are discussed next.

Entities to Convert

The **Entities to Convert** field is used for selecting edges, faces, or sketch entities to be projected onto the current sketching plane. By default, this field is activated. As a result, you can select edges, faces, or sketch entities by clicking the left mouse button.

> **Note:** On selecting a face, you can project all its outer or inner loops onto the current sketching plane. By default, the edges of the outer loop of the face will be projected onto the current sketching plane. To project the edges of the inner loops of the face, you need to click on the **Select all inner loops** button in the PropertyManager.

Select chain

The **Select chain** check box is used for selecting all contiguous entities of a selected entity.

Inner loops one by one

The **Inner loops one by one** check box allows you to select inner loops of the face one by one.

Select all inner loops

The **Select all inner loops** button is used for selecting all inner loops of the selected face. Note that this button is enabled only after selecting a face of a model. As soon as you click on the **Select all inner loops** button, the edges of all inner loops of the face get selected for projection.

After selecting edges, faces, or sketch entities to be projected, click on the green tick-mark ✓ in the PropertyManager. The selected edges are projected onto the current sketching plane as sketch entities. Now, you can convert the sketch into a feature by using the feature modeling tools such as **Extruded Boss/Base** and **Revolved Boss/Base**.

> **Note:** You can select edges, faces, or sketch entities of the existing features of a model before or after invoking the **Convert Entities** tool. However, if you select a face to be projected before invoking the **Convert Entities** tool, then only the edges of the outer loop of the selected face get projected onto the current sketching plane.

Projecting Edges of a Body

You can project the edges of an existing body onto the current sketching plane by using the **Silhouette Entities** tool. For doing so, click on the arrow below the **Convert Entities** tool to invoke a flyout, see Figure 7.40. Next, click on the **Silhouette Entities** tool. The **Silhouette Entities PropertyManager** appears, see Figure 7.41. The options in the PropertyManager are discussed next.

Entities to Silhouette

The **Entities to Silhouette** field is used for selecting bodies for projecting their edges onto the current sketching plane. By default, this field is activated. As a result, you can select bodies by clicking the left mouse button.

External Silhouette

When the **External Silhouette** check box is selected, then only the outer boundaries of the selected bodies get projected onto the current sketching plane as sketch entities. However, when this check box is cleared, then the inner loops of the bodies get projected as well.

After selecting the bodies, click on the green tick-mark ☑ in the PropertyManager. The edges of the selected body or bodies get projected as sketch entities onto the current sketching plane.

Projecting Intersecting Geometries of Existing Features

In SOLIDWORKS, you can project the geometries of the existing features that intersect with the currently active sketching plane by using the **Intersection Curve** tool, see Figure 7.42. For doing so, click on the arrow below the **Convert Entities** tool and then click on the **Intersection Curve** tool in the flyout that appears. The **Intersection Curves PropertyManager** appears and you are prompted to select intersecting geometries of the features to be projected. Select all the intersecting geometries of the model in the graphics area one by one and then click on the green tick-mark ☑ in the PropertyManager. The sketch curve is created at the intersection of the selected geometries and the sketching plane, see Figure 7.42.

7.42

Editing a Feature and its Sketch

SOLIDWORKS allows you to edit features of a model as per the design change. As mentioned earlier, the FeatureManager Design Tree displays a list of all features created for a model, see Figure 7.43. In SOLIDWORKS, you can edit individual features and their sketches. The procedures for editing a feature and its sketch are discussed next.

Procedure for Editing a Feature

1. Click on the feature to be edited in the FeatureManager Design Tree. A Pop-up toolbar appears, see Figure 7.43.
2. Click on the **Edit Feature** tool in the Pop-up toolbar, see Figure 7.44. The respective PropertyManager appears to the left of the graphics area.
3. Change the parameters as per your requirement by entering the new values in the PropertyManager.
4. After editing the feature parameters, click on the green tick-mark ☑ in the PropertyManager.

Procedure for Editing the Sketch of a Feature

1. Click on a feature in the FeatureManager Design Tree. A Pop-up toolbar appears.
2. Click on the **Edit Sketch** tool in the Pop-up toolbar, see Figure 7.45. The Sketching environment is invoked.

3. By using the sketching tools in the Sketching environment, you can modify the sketch of the feature as per your requirement.
4. After modifying the sketch of the feature, exit the Sketching environment.

Note: You can also select a sketch to be edited in the FeatureManager Design Tree and then click on the **Edit Sketch** tool in the Pop-up toolbar to invoke the Sketching environment for editing it.

Importing 2D DXF or DWG Files

In SOLIDWORKS 2020, you can import an existing 2D DXF or DWG file as a reference sketch. For doing so, click on the **Open** button in the **Welcome** dialog box. Alternatively, click on the **Open** tool in the **Standard** toolbar or click on **File > Open** in the SOLIDWORKS Menus. The **Open** dialog box appears. In this dialog box, select the **Autodesk AutoCAD Files** (*.dwg; *.dxf) file extension in the **File Type** drop-down list. Next, browse to the location where the required document (.*dxf* or .*dwg*) is saved and then click on the document to be opened. Next, click on the **Open** button in the dialog box. The **DXF/DWG Import** dialog box appears. In this dialog box, select the **Import to a new part as** radio button. Next, select the **Import as reference** check box under **2D sketch** radio button and then click on the **Finish** button. The selected file is opened as a reference sketch.

By default, the imported reference sketch cannot be edited. To make the reference sketch editable, right-click on its name in the FeatureManager Design Tree and then select the **Make Edit Sketch** option in the shortcut menu that appears. The imported reference sketch becomes an editable sketch. Now, you can edit it similar to editing a sketch of a feature.

Displaying Earlier State of a Model

In SOLIDWORKS, you can display the earlier state of a model by using the Rollback Bar. By default, the Rollback Bar is displayed at the end of the last feature of the model in the FeatureManager Design Tree, see Figure 7.46. You can drag the Rollback Bar up in the FeatureManager Design Tree and place it above the features to be rolled back, see Figure 7.47. The earlier state of the model appears in the graphics area such that all the features that are below the Rollback Bar are not displayed in the model. Also, the names of the features that are below the Rollback Bar appear in grey in the FeatureManager Design Tree. You can add new features or edit existing features while the model is in the rolled-back state. You can also drag the Rollback Bar down in the FeatureManager Design Tree.

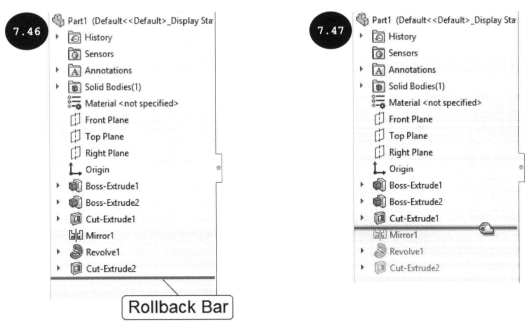

Reordering Features of a Model

By default, all the features of a model appear in a sequential order in FeatureManager Design Tree. The first created feature appears at the top and the next created features appear one after another in FeatureManager Design Tree. In SOLIDWORKS, you can also change the order of a feature by dragging it to a new location in the FeatureManager Design Tree. Note that you cannot place a child feature above its parent feature in the FeatureManager Design Tree.

Measuring the Distance between Entities

In SOLIDWORKS, you can measure the distance and angle between lines, points, faces, planes, and so on by using the **Measure** tool in the **Evaluate CommandManager**, see Figure 7.48. Also, you can measure the radius and other parameters of different geometrical entities.

To measure the distance between entities, click on the **Evaluate** tab and then click on the **Measure** tool in the **Evaluate CommandManager**, see Figure 7.48. The **Measure** window appears, see Figure 7.49. You can expand the **Measure** window to display the Input box and Display area by clicking on the arrow available on its right, see Figure 7.50. Some of the options of this window are discussed next.

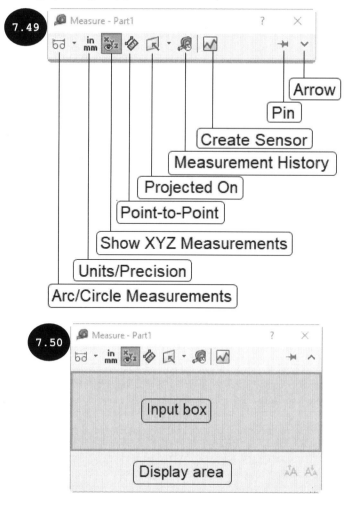

Arc/Circle Measurements

The options in the **Arc/Circle Measurements** drop-down list are used for specifying the method of measuring distance between circular or semi-circular entities, see Figure 7.51. To invoke this drop-down list, click on the arrow next to the **Arc/Circle Measurements** button in the window. The options in the **Arc/Circle Measurements** drop-down list are discussed next.

Center to Center

This option of the **Arc/Circle Measurements** drop-down list is used for measuring the center to center distance between two arc entities, circular entities, or cylindrical faces. On selecting this option, the center to center distance between the selected entities is measured and appears in the graphics area as well as in the Display area of the expanded **Measure** window, see Figure 7.52.

> **Note:** You can increase or decrease the Display area of the **Measure** window by dragging its border.

Minimum Distance

This option is used for measuring the minimum distance between two selected arcs or circular entities, see Figure 7.53.

Maximum Distance

This option is used for measuring the maximum distance between two selected arcs or circular entities, see Figure 7.54.

Custom Distance

The Custom Distance option is used for measuring the distance between entities, as per a user-defined arrangement. When you move the cursor over the Custom Distance option in the drop-down list, a cascading menu appears, see Figure 7.55. By using this cascading menu, you can specify the start and end conditions of the measurement. Depending upon the start and end conditions specified, the respective distance between the selected entities is measured and appears in the graphics area as well as in the Display area of the Measure window.

Note: As discussed, the results of measurement appear in the graphics area as well as in the Display area of the **Measure** window. You can copy a numerical value of the measurement results to the clipboard. For doing so, move the cursor over a numerical value in the **Display** area of the **Measure** window, the value gets highlighted and the **Copy** button appears near the cursor, see Figure 7.56. Click on this **Copy** button to copy the value to the clipboard. Now, you can paste the copied value at a required location in any file.

You can increase or decrease the font size of the text that appears in the Display area of the **Measure** dialog box by using the **Increase Font Size** AA or **Decrease Font Size** AA buttons, respectively. These buttons appear in the Display area of the window. Note that you cannot decrease the font size below the default size.

In SOLIDWORKS 2020, you can invoke the **Measure** tool for measuring distance between entities even if any other tool is active. You can also use this tool while working with a sketch, a part, an assembly, or a drawing file.

Units/Precision in mm

This button is used for specifying units and precision of measurement. When you click on this button, the **Measure Units/Precision** dialog box appears, see Figure 7.57. By default, the **Use document settings** radio button is selected in this dialog box. As a result, the units and precision specified in the current document of SOLIDWORKS are used for measurement. By selecting the **Use custom settings** radio button, you can customize the units and precision values for measurement.

7.56

7.57

Show XYZ Measurements

This button is used for measuring the dX, dY, and dZ measurements between the selected entities, see Figure 7.58.

Point-to-Point

This button is used for measuring the distance between two points or vertices.

Measurement History

This button is used for displaying the history of all measurements made in the current session of SOLIDWORKS. When you click on this button, the **Measurement History** dialog box appears with the details of measurement made so far in the current session, see Figure 7.59.

Assigning an Appearance/Texture

In SOLIDWORKS, you can change the default appearance or texture of a model by assigning a predefined or customized appearance to the model, its features and faces. The methods for assigning a predefined and customized appearance are discussed next.

Assigning a Predefined Appearance/Texture

You can assign a predefined appearance or texture to a model by using the **Appearances, Scenes, and Decals Task Pane**, see Figure 7.60. The method for the same is discussed next.

1.   Click on the **Appearances, Scenes, and Decals** tab in the Task Pane, see Figure 7.60. The **Appearances, Scenes, and Decals Task Pane** appears.

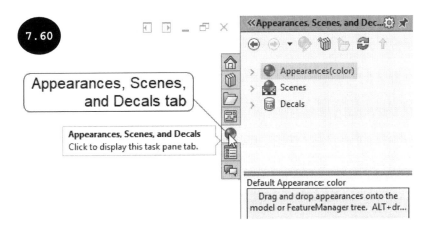

2. Expand the **Appearances(color)** node by clicking on the arrow in front of it. The predefined appearance categories appear.

3. Expand the required predefined category such as **Plastic**, **Metal**, or **Glass**. The sub-categories of the selected category appear.

4. Select the required sub-category, see Figure 7.61. The thumbnails of the predefined appearances available in the selected sub-category appear in the lower half of the Task Pane, see Figure 7.61. In this figure, the **Steel** sub-category of the **Metal** category is selected.

5. Drag and drop the required predefined appearance (thumbnail) from the lower half of the Task Pane over a face of the model by pressing and holding the left mouse button. A Pop-up toolbar appears, see Figure 7.62.

Note: The options in the Pop-up toolbar allow you to choose the required target for assigning the appearance. You can assign the appearance to a face, a feature, a body, or a part by clicking on the respective tool in the Pop-up toolbar.

6. Click on the required tool in the Pop-up toolbar. The appearance is assigned to the model depending upon the tool selected in the Pop-up toolbar.

Note: If you drag and drop the appearance thumbnail in the empty area, the appearance will be assigned to the entire model.

Assigning a Customized Appearance

In addition to assigning a predefined appearance to faces, features, or bodies, you can also customize the appearance properties as required and then assign it. For doing so, click on the **Edit Appearance** tool in the **View (Heads-up)** toolbar, see Figure 7.63. The **color PropertyManager** appears to the left side of the graphics area, see Figure 7.64. The **Appearances, Scenes, and Decals Task Pane** also appears to the right of the graphics area. The options in the **color PropertyManager** are used for assigning colors, material appearances, and transparency to faces, features, or bodies.

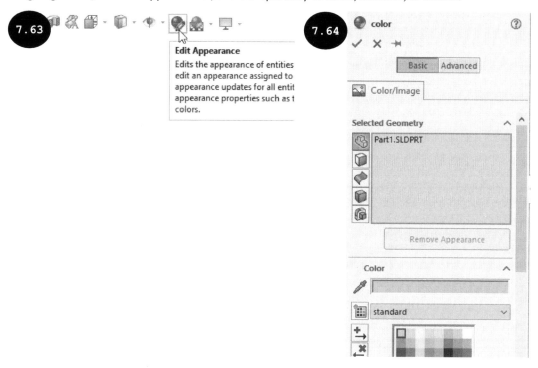

> **Note:** If the model already has an appearance or texture assigned, then on clicking the **Edit Appearance** tool in the **View (Heads-up)** toolbar, the respective PropertyManager appears, which allows you to edit properties of the assigned appearance or texture.

You can also invoke the **color PropertyManager** by clicking on **Edit > Appearance > Appearance** in the SOLIDWORKS Menus. Alternatively, select a face of the model. A Pop-up toolbar appears, see Figure 7.65. In this Pop-up toolbar, click on the arrow next to the **Appearances** tool and then click on the *face name, feature name, body name,* or *part name* in the flyout that appears to display the **color PropertyManager**.

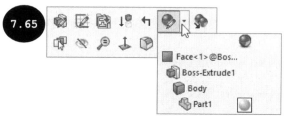

The options in the **color PropertyManager** are divided into two categories: Basic and Advanced. By default, on invoking the **color PropertyManager**, the **Basic** tab gets activated. As a result, the PropertyManager displays the basic and important options for customizing or editing the appearance properties. To access the advanced options, you need to activate the **Advanced** tab of the PropertyManager. Some of the options of these tabs are discussed next.

Basic Tab

The **Basic** tab of the **color PropertyManager** displays options for assigning appearance to faces, features, or bodies. Some of the options are discussed next.

Selected Geometry

The **Selected Geometry** rollout is used for selecting geometries for applying appearances. You can select a part, faces, surfaces, bodies, or features as geometries by clicking on the respective button (**Select Part**, **Select Faces**, **Select Surfaces**, **Select Bodies**, or **Select Features**) available to the left of this rollout, see Figure 7.66. For example, to assign a color on the faces of a model, click on the **Select Faces** button and then select faces of the model in the graphics area. The name of the selected faces appears in the **Selected Entities** field of this rollout.

Note: To remove the already selected geometries from the **Selected Entities** field, right-click on the **Selected Entities** field in the **Selected Geometry** rollout and then select the **Clear Selection** option from the shortcut menu that appears. All the selected geometries get removed from the selection. You can also remove individual geometries. For doing so, select a geometry in the **Selected Entities** field of the rollout and then right-click. A shortcut menu appears. In this shortcut menu, click on the **Delete** option. The selected geometry gets removed from the selection.

Color

The **Color** rollout is used for selecting the required color to be assigned to the selected geometry or geometries, see Figure 7.67.

Advanced Tab

The **Advanced** tab of the **color PropertyManager** displays additional and advanced options for assigning appearance to the selected faces, features, or bodies, see Figure 7.68. Some of the options of the **Advanced** tab are discussed next.

Color/Image

By default, the **Color/Image** button is activated in the **Advance** tab of the PropertyManager. As a result, the additional and advanced options for assigning an appearance (color or image file) appear in the PropertyManager, see Figure 7.68. Some of these options are same as those discussed earlier and the remaining options are discussed next.

Appearance: This rollout is used for selecting an image file as the appearance for the selected geometries. By default, the **color.p2m** file is selected. You can also select any other file such as JPG and TIFF as the image file to be assigned. For doing so, click on the **Browse** button of this rollout. The **Open** dialog box appears. Select the required file type in the **File Type** drop-down list of the dialog box and then browse to the location where the image file has been saved. Next, select it and then click on the **Open** button in the dialog box. The **Save As** dialog box appears. Click on the **Save** button to save the file as *.p2m* for future use. The selected image file is assigned to the model. You can also save the current appearance file for future use by using the **Save Appearance** button of the rollout.

Illumination

On clicking the **Illumination** button in the **Advanced** tab, the options used for specifying lighting properties for the selected appearance are displayed.

Mapping

On clicking the **Mapping** button in the **Advanced** tab, the options used for mapping the selected image file on the selected geometry are displayed. By using these options, you can control the size, orientation, and location of the image file. Note that these options become available only when an image file or a predefined appearance has been applied to the geometry.

Surface Finish

On clicking the **Surface Finish** button in the **Advanced** tab, the options that are used to specify the surface finishing for the appearance such as knurled, dimpled, or sandblasted are displayed.

After customizing or editing the appearance properties and assigning them to a model or its geometries, exit the PropertyManager.

Applying a Material

In SOLIDWORKS, you can apply standard material properties such as density, elastic modulus, tensile strength to a model. Note that assigning standard material properties to a model is important in order to calculate its mass properties as well as to perform static and dynamic analysis. SOLIDWORKS contains almost all standard materials in its material library. You can directly apply the required standard material to a model from the material library. In addition to applying standard material, you can also customize the material properties and apply to a model. The procedures for applying a standard material and a custom material are discussed next.

Procedure for Applying a Standard Material

1. Right-click on the **Material <not specified>** option in the FeatureManager Design Tree. A shortcut menu appears, see Figure 7.69.

2. Click on the **Edit Material** option in the shortcut menu. The **Material** dialog box appears, refer to Figure 7.70.
3. Expand the **SOLIDWORKS Materials** node, if not expanded by default. The different material categories such as Steel, Iron, and Aluminium Alloys appear in the dialog box.
4. Expand the required material category. The materials available in the expanded material category appear, see Figure 7.70.
5. Select the required material from the list of available materials. The properties of the selected material appear on the right half of the dialog box, see Figure 7.70.

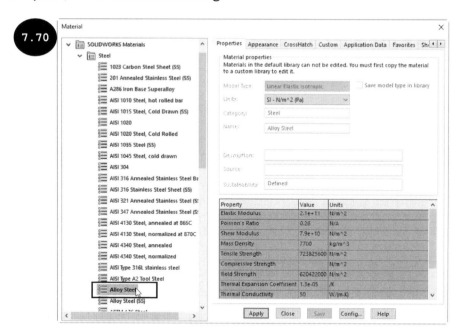

6. Click on the **Apply** button in the dialog box. The material properties of the selected material get applied to the model. Next, click on the **Close** button to exit the dialog box.

Procedure for Applying Customized Material Properties

1. Invoke the **Material** dialog box and then right-click on the **Custom Materials** node in the dialog box. A shortcut menu appears, see Figure 7.71.

2. Click on the **New Category** option in the shortcut menu, see Figure 7.71. A new category is added. Also, its default name **New Category** appears in an edit field.

3. Enter a new name for the newly added category in the edit field and then click anywhere in the dialog box.
4. Right-click on the newly added category in the dialog box to display a shortcut menu.
5. Click on the **New Material** option in the shortcut menu. A new material is added under the selected category. Also, its default name **Default** appears in an edit field.
6. Enter a new name for the newly added material in the edit field and then click anywhere in the drawing area.
7. Click on the newly added material. The default properties of the selected newly added material appear on the right half of the dialog box, see Figure 7.72. In this figure, **SW CAD** material category and the **SW 1001** material are added in the **Custom Material** node.
8. Specify new material properties such as Poisson's ratio, Density, and Yield Strength as required in the respective fields of the dialog box. Next, click on the **Save** button to save the specified properties.
9. Click on the **Apply** button to apply the custom material to the model.
10. Click on the **Close** button to exit the dialog box.

Note: You can also copy material properties of a standard material and then edit them. For doing so, select a standard material and then right-click to display a shortcut menu. Next, click on the **Copy** option in the shortcut menu. After copying a standard material, select a custom material category in the **Custom Material** node of the dialog box and then right-click to display a shortcut menu. In the shortcut menu, click on the **Paste** option. The copied standard material is added in the selected custom material category. Now, you can edit the material properties of the standard material as required and then click on the **Apply** button in the dialog box.

Calculating Mass Properties

In SOLIDWORKS, after assigning material properties to a model, you can calculate its mass properties such as mass and volume by using the **Mass Properties** tool of the **Evaluate CommandManager**, see Figure 7.73. To calculate the mass properties of a model, click on the **Mass Properties** tool. The **Mass Properties** dialog box appears and displays the mass properties of the model, see Figure 7.74. The options of the dialog box are discussed next.

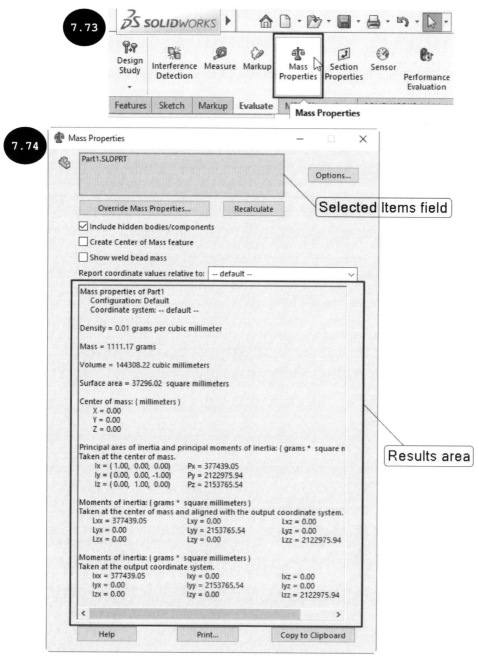

Selected Items

This field of the dialog box is used for selecting a model for calculating its mass properties. By default, on invoking the **Mass Properties** tool, the model available in the graphics area gets automatically selected and its name appears in this field, see Figure 7.74. Also, the properties such as mass, volume, and center of mass of the selected model appear in the **Result** area of the dialog box, see Figure 7.74.

Options

This button is used for specifying unit settings for calculating the mass properties. When you click on the **Options** button, the **Mass/Section Property Options** dialog box appears. By default, the **Use document settings** radio button is selected in this dialog box. As a result, the units and precision values specified for the current document of SOLIDWORKS are used for calculating mass properties. To specify the custom unit settings for calculating the mass properties, select the **Use custom settings** radio button, see Figure 7.75. All the edit fields of the dialog box get activated which allow you to specify custom unit settings, see Figure 7.75. After customizing the unit settings, click on the **OK** button.

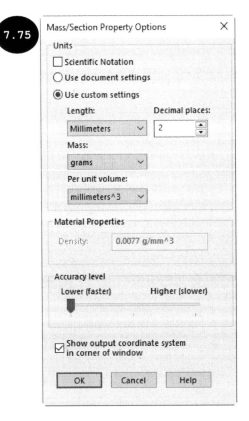

Recalculate

This button is used for recalculating the mass properties of the model in case you have made changes in the model or added/deleted any item in the selection set.

Override Mass Properties

This button is used for overriding the calculated mass properties of a model. On clicking this button, the **Override Mass Properties** dialog box appears. This dialog box is used for overriding the default calculated mass properties such as mass and center of mass of the model. Note that the edit fields of this dialog box are not enabled, by default. To enable these edit fields, you need to select the respective check boxes: **Override mass**, **Override center of mass**, and **Override moments of inertia** of the dialog box, see Figure 7.76. In this figure, the **Override mass**, **Override center of mass**, and **Override moments of inertia** check boxes of the dialog box are selected. As a result, all the respective edit fields of the dialog box are enabled. In these edit fields, you can specify override values for mass, center of mass, and moments of inertia. After defining the override mass properties, click on the **OK** button in the dialog box.

Note: The override properties specified for a model are not the actual properties of the model.

Include hidden bodies/components

By default, the **Include hidden bodies/components** check box of the **Mass Properties** dialog box is selected. As a result, all hidden bodies or components of the selected model are included while calculating the mass properties. However, on clearing this check box, the hidden bodies/components are not included in the calculation.

Create Center of Mass feature

On selecting the **Create Center of Mass feature** check box, the center of mass of the model appears in the graphics area and its symbol is added in the FeatureManager Design Tree as soon as you exit the **Mass Properties** dialog box.

Note: The center of mass of the model appears in the graphics area either when it is selected in the FeatureManager Design Tree or its visibility is turned on in the graphics area. To turn on the visibility of the center of mass, invoke the **Hide/Show Items** flyout of the **View (Heads-Up)** toolbar and then click on the **View Center of Mass** tool, see Figure 7.77.

Report coordinate values relative to

This drop-down list of the **Mass Properties** dialog box is used for selecting a coordinate system with respect to which the mass properties are to be calculated. By default, the **default** option is selected in this drop-down list. As a result, the default coordinate system is used for calculating mass properties of the model.

Note: The **Report coordinate values relative to** drop-down list displays coordinate systems that are created in the current document of SOLIDWORKS. In case you have not created any coordinate system, then only the **default** option is available in this drop-down list.

Result

This area of the dialog box is used for displaying the calculated results of the model.

Print

This button is used for printing the calculated results.

Copy to Clipboard

This button is used for copying the results to the clipboard.

After reviewing the results of the mass properties of the model in the **Mass Properties** dialog box, exit the dialog box.

Tutorial 1

Create a model, as shown in Figure 7.78. You need to create the model by creating all its features one by one. All dimensions are in mm.

Section 1: Starting SOLIDWORKS

1. Start SOLIDWORKS by double-clicking on the SOLIDWORKS icon on your desktop. The initial screen of SOLIDWORKS appears along with the **Welcome** dialog box.

Section 2: Invoking the Part Modeling Environment

1. Click on the **Part** button in the **Welcome** dialog box. The Part modeling environment is invoked.

Tip: You can also invoke the Part modeling environment by using the **New SOLIDWORKS Document** dialog box. For doing so, click on the **New** tool in the **Standard** toolbar. The **New SOLIDWORKS Document** dialog box appears. In this dialog box, make sure that the **Part** button is selected and then click on the **OK** button.

Now, you can set the unit system and create the base/first feature of the model.

Section 3: Specifying Unit Settings

1. Move the cursor toward the lower right corner of the screen over the Status Bar and then click on the **Unit System** area. The **Unit System** flyout appears, see Figure 7.79.

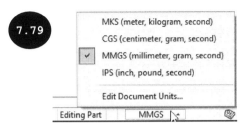

2. Make sure that the **MMGS (millimeter, gram, second)** option is tick-marked in this flyout.

Tip: The tick-mark in front of a unit system indicates that it has been selected as the unit system for the current document of SOLIDWORKS. You can also open the **Document Properties - Units** dialog box to specify unit system by selecting the **Edit Document Units** option of the **Unit System** flyout.

Section 4: Creating the Base/First Feature - Revolved Feature

1. Invoke the Sketching environment by selecting the Top plane as the sketching plane and then create the sketch of the base feature, see Figure 7.80. The base feature of the model is a revolved feature.

Tip: To make the sketch of the base feature fully defined as shown in Figure 7.80, you need to make sure that the centerpoint of the circle has coincident relation with the horizontal centerline. The vertical centerline in the figure will be used as the axis of revolution for creating the revolved feature.

2. Click on the **Features** tab in the CommandManager to display the tools of the **Features CommandManager**, see Figure 7.81.

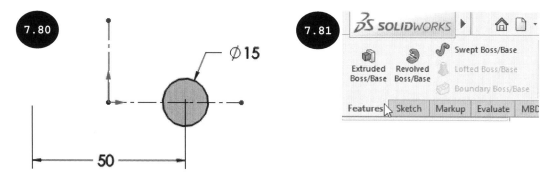

3. Click on the **Revolved Boss/Base** tool in the **Features CommandManager**. The **Revolve PropertyManager** appears. Also, the orientation of the sketch changes to trimetric orientation, see Figure 7.82.

Note: If the sketch to be revolved has only one centerline, then on invoking the **Revolved Boss/Base** tool, the available centerline will automatically be selected as the axis of revolution and the preview of the revolved feature appears in the graphics area.

4. Click on the vertical centerline of the sketch as the axis of revolution. A preview of the revolved feature appears in the graphics area, see Figure 7.83.

5. Make sure that the 360-degree angle is specified in the **Direction 1 Angle** field of the PropertyManager.

6. Click on the green tick-mark ✓ in the PropertyManager. The base/first revolved feature is created, see Figure 7.84.

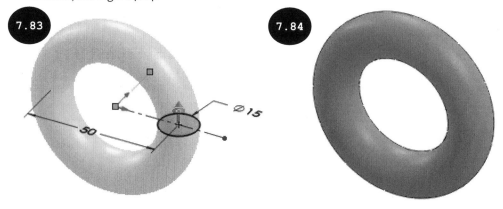

Section 5: Creating the Second Feature - Extruded Feature

To create the second feature of the model, you first need to create a reference plane at an offset distance of 40 mm from the Top plane.

1. Invoke the **Reference Geometry** flyout in the **Features CommandManager**, see Figure 7.85.

2. Click on the **Plane** tool in this flyout. The **Plane PropertyManager** appears.

3. Expand the FeatureManager Design Tree, which is now available at the top left corner of the graphics area by clicking on the arrow in its front, see Figure 7.86.

4. Click on the **Top Plane** in the FeatureManager Design Tree as the first reference. The preview of an offset plane appears in the graphics area, see Figure 7.87.

5. Select the **Flip offset** check box in the **First Reference** rollout of the PropertyManager to flip the direction of plane downward.

6. Enter **40** in the **Distance** field in the **First Reference** rollout of the PropertyManager.

7. Click on the green tick-mark ✅ in the PropertyManager. The offset reference plane is created, see Figure 7.88.

Now, you need to create the second feature of the model by selecting the newly created plane as the sketching plane.

8. Invoke the Sketching environment by selecting the newly created plane as the sketching plane.

9. Press CTRL + 8 to change the orientation of the model as normal to the viewing direction.

10. Create the sketch of the second feature (a circle of diameter 15 mm) and then apply the diameter dimension, see Figure 7.89.

11. Click on the **Features** tab in the CommandManager to display the tools of the **Features** **CommandManager**.

12. Click on the **Extruded Boss/Base** tool. The **Boss-Extrude PropertyManager** and the preview of the extruded feature appear. Next, change the orientation of the model to isometric, see Figure 7.90.

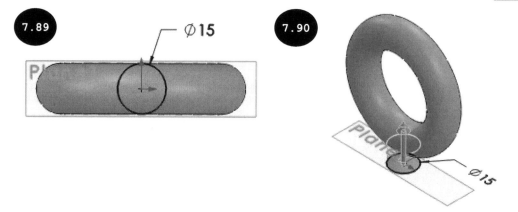

13. Invoke the **End Condition** drop-down list in the **Direction 1** rollout, see Figure 7.91.

14. Click on the **Up To Next** option in the **End Condition** drop-down list. The preview of the feature gets modified in the graphics area such that it gets terminated at its next intersection, see Figure 7.92.

15. Click on the green tick-mark ✓ in the PropertyManager. The extruded feature is created, see Figure 7.93.

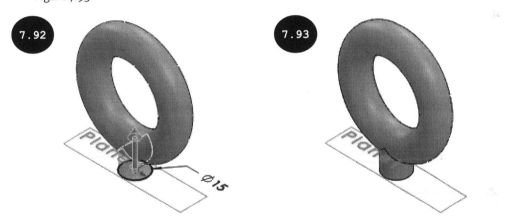

Section 6: Hiding the Reference Plane

1. Click on the reference plane in the graphics area. A Pop-up toolbar appears, see Figure 7.94.

2. Click on the **Hide** tool in the Pop-up toolbar, see Figure 7.94. The selected reference plane no longer appears in the graphics area.

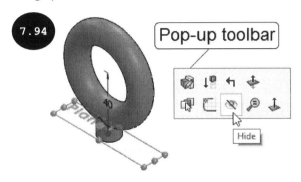

Section 7: Creating the Third Feature - Extruded Feature

1. Rotate the model such that the bottom planar face of the second feature can be viewed, see Figure 7.95.

7.95

Bottom face

2. Invoke the Sketching environment by selecting the bottom planar face of the second feature as the sketching plane.

3. Press CTRL + 8 to change the orientation of the model as normal to the viewing direction.

4. Create the sketch of the third feature (a circle of diameter 32 mm), see Figure 7.96.

5. Click on the **Features** tab and then click on the **Extruded Boss/Base** tool. The **Boss-Extrude PropertyManager** and the preview of the extruded feature appear. Next, change the orientation of the model to isometric.

Extruded Boss/Base

6. Enter **5** in the **Depth** field of the **Direction 1** rollout and then press ENTER.

7. Click on the green tick-mark ☑ in the PropertyManager. The extruded feature is created, see Figure 7.97.

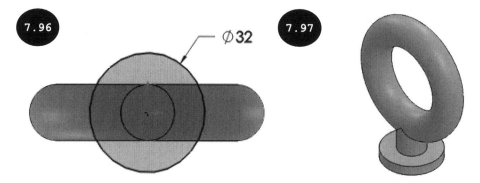

7.96   Ø**32**

7.97

Section 8: Creating the Fourth Feature - Extruded Feature

1. Rotate the model such that the bottom planar face of the third feature can be viewed. Next, invoke the Sketching environment by selecting the bottom planar face of the third feature as the sketching plane.

2. Press CTRL + 8 to change the orientation of the model as normal to the viewing direction.

3. Create the sketch of the fourth feature (a circle of diameter 18 mm), see Figure 7.98.

4. Click on the **Extruded Boss/Base** tool in the **Features CommandManager**. The **Boss-Extrude PropertyManager** and the preview of the extruded feature appear. Next, change the orientation of the model to isometric.

5. Enter **32** in the **Depth** field of the **Direction 1** rollout and then press ENTER.

6. Click on the green tick-mark ☑ in the PropertyManager. The extruded feature is created, see Figure 7.99.

Section 9: Saving the Model

1. Click on the **Save** tool in the **Standard** toolbar. The **Save As** window appears.

2. Browse to the SOLIDWORKS folder and then create a folder with the name **Chapter 7**.

3. Enter **Tutorial 1** in the **File name** field of the dialog box as the name of the file and then click on the **Save** button. The model is saved as Tutorial 1 in the Chapter 7 folder.

Tutorial 2

Create a model, as shown in Figure 7.100. After creating the model, assign the Alloy Steel material and calculate the mass properties of the model. All dimensions are in mm.

Section 1: Invoking the Part Modeling Environment
1. Start SOLIDWORKS and then invoke the Part modeling environment.

Section 2: Specifying Unit Settings
1. Click on the **Unit System** area in the Status Bar. The **Unit System** flyout appears, see Figure 7.101.

2. Make sure that the **MMGS (millimeter, gram, second)** option is tick-marked in this flyout.

Section 3: Creating the Base/First Feature - Revolved Feature

1. Invoke the Sketching environment by selecting the Front plane as the sketching plane and then create the sketch of the base feature, see Figure 7.102. Do not exit the Sketching environment. Note that the base feature of the model is a revolved feature.

> **Tip:** The sketch of the base feature shown in Figure 7.102 is symmetric about the vertical centerline. As a result, you need to apply symmetric relations to the sketch entities with respect to the vertical centerline. Also, you need to apply equal relations between the entities of equal length and collinear relations between the aligned entities of the sketch. You can also create line entities on one side of the vertical centerline and then mirror them to create entities on the other side of the vertical centerline.

2. Click on the **Features** tab in the CommandManager and then click on the **Revolved Boss/Base** tool. The **Revolve PropertyManager** appears. Also, the orientation of the sketch changes to trimetric, see Figure 7.103.

> **Note:** If the sketch to be revolved has only one centerline, then on invoking the **Revolved Boss/Base** tool, the available centerline will automatically be selected as the axis of revolution and the preview of the revolved feature appears in the graphics area.

3.   Click on the horizontal centerline of the sketch as the axis of revolution. A preview of the revolved feature appears in the graphics area.

4.   Make sure that the 360 degrees angle is specified in the **Direction 1 Angle** field of the PropertyManager.

5.   Click on the green tick-mark ✔ in the PropertyManager. The base/first revolved feature is created, see Figure 7.104.

Section 4: Creating the Second Feature - Extruded Feature

To create the second feature of the model, you first need to create a reference plane at the offset distance of 70 mm from the Top plane.

1.   Invoke the **Reference Geometry** flyout of the **Features CommandManager**, see Figure 7.105.

2.   Click on the **Plane** tool of the **Reference Geometry** flyout. The **Plane PropertyManager** appears.

3.   Expand the FeatureManager Design Tree, which is now available at the top left corner of the graphics area by clicking on the arrow in front of it.

4.   Click on the **Top Plane** in the FeatureManager Design Tree as the first reference. The preview of an offset reference plane appears in the graphics area.

5.   Enter **70** in the **Distance** field of the **First Reference** rollout in the PropertyManager.

6.   Click on the green tick-mark ✔ in the PropertyManager. The reference plane at an offset distance of 70 mm is created, see Figure 7.106.

Now, you can create the second feature of the model by using the newly created plane.

7. Invoke the Sketching environment by selecting the newly created reference plane as the sketching plane.

8. Press CTRL + 8 to change the orientation of the model as normal to the viewing direction. Alternatively, click on the **Normal To** tool in the **View Orientation** flyout.

9. Create the sketch of the second feature (a circle of diameter 48 mm), see Figure 7.107. Do not exit the Sketching environment.

10. Click on the **Features** tab to display the tools of the **Features CommandManager**.

11. Click on the **Extruded Boss/Base** tool in the **Features CommandManager**. The **Boss-Extrude PropertyManager** and the preview of the extruded feature appear. Next, change the orientation of the model to isometric, see Figure 7.108.

Extruded Boss/Base

12. Click on the **Reverse Direction** button in the **Direction 1** rollout of the PropertyManager to reverse the direction of extrusion to downward.

13. Invoke the **End Condition** drop-down list in the **Direction 1** rollout, see Figure 7.109.

14. Click on the **Up To Next** option in the **End Condition** drop-down list. The preview of the feature gets modified in the graphics area such that it has been terminated at its next intersection.

15. Click on the green tick-mark ☑ in the PropertyManager. The extruded feature is created, see Figure 7.110.

Section 5: Hiding the Reference Plane

1. Click on the reference plane in the graphics area. A Pop-up toolbar appears, see Figure 7.111.

2. Click on the **Hide** tool in the Pop-up toolbar, see Figure 7.111. The selected reference plane gets hidden in the graphics area.

Section 6: Creating the Third Feature - Extruded Feature

1. Invoke the Sketching environment by selecting the top planar face of the second feature as the sketching plane.

2. Press CTRL + 8 to change the orientation of the model as normal to the viewing direction.

3. Create the sketch of the third feature (a circle of diameter 90 mm), see Figure 7.112.

Ø**90**

4. Click on the **Features** tab to display the tools of the **Features CommandManager**.

5. Click on the **Extruded Boss/Base** tool. The **Boss-Extrude PropertyManager** and the preview of the extruded feature appear. Next, change the orientation of the model to isometric.

6. Enter **10** in the **Depth** field in the **Direction 1** rollout and then press ENTER.

7. Click on the green tick-mark ☑ in the PropertyManager. The extruded feature is created, see Figure 7.113.

Section 7: Creating the Fourth Feature - Extruded Cut Feature

1. Invoke the Sketching environment by selecting the top planar face of the third feature as the sketching plane.

2. Press CTRL + 8 to change the orientation of the model as normal to the viewing direction.

3. Create the sketch of the fourth feature (a circle of diameter 28 mm), see Figure 7.114. Do not exit the Sketching environment.

4. Click on the **Features** tab and then click on the **Extruded Cut** tool in the **Features CommandManager**. The **Cut-Extrude PropertyManager** and the preview of the extruded cut feature appear. Next, change the orientation of the model to isometric.

5. Invoke the **End Condition** drop-down list of the **Direction 1** rollout, see Figure 7.115.

6.   Click on the **Up To Surface** option in the **End Condition** drop-down list. The **Face/Plane** field is enabled in the **Direction 1** rollout and is activated by default.

7.   Rotate the model such that the inner circular face of the base feature can be viewed, see Figure 7.116.

8.   Click on the inner circular face of the base feature as the face to terminate the creation of extruded cut feature, see Figure 7.116. The preview of the extruded cut feature appears in the graphics area.

9.   Click on the green tick-mark ✔ in the PropertyManager. The extruded cut feature is created, see Figure 7.117.

Note: In Figure 7.117, the display style of the model has been changed to the 'hidden lines visible' display style by clicking on the **Hidden Lines Visible** tool in the **Display Style** flyout of the **View (Heads-Up)** toolbar. Also, the orientation of the model has been changed to the Front view for better understanding of the cut feature.

7.116

Inner circular face

7.117

Section 8: Creating the Fifth Feature - Extruded Cut Feature

1.   Invoke the Sketching environment by selecting the right planar face of the model as the sketching plane, see Figure 7.118.

7.118

Right planar face

2. Press CTRL + 8 to change the orientation of the model as normal to the viewing direction.

3. Create a circle of diameter 12 mm and apply the required dimensions, see Figure 7.119. Note that you need to apply a vertical relation between the origin and the center point of the circle to make it fully defined.

4. Click on the **Circular Sketch Pattern** tool in the **Pattern** flyout of the **Sketch CommandManager**, see Figure 7.120 and then create a circular pattern of the circle for creating remaining circles of the same diameter, see Figure 7.121. Make sure that the center point of the circular pattern is at the origin. Next, exit the tool.

Note: Similar to patterning sketch entities in the Sketching environment, you can pattern features in the Part modeling environment. You will learn how to pattern features in the Part modeling environment in later chapters.

5. Click on the **Extruded Cut** tool in the **Features CommandManager**. The **Cut-Extrude PropertyManager** and the preview of the extruded cut feature appear. Next, change the orientation of the model to isometric, see Figure 7.122.

6. Invoke the **End Condition** drop-down list of the **Direction 1** rollout and then click on the **Up To Next** option.

7. Click on the green tick-mark ✓ in the PropertyManager. The extruded cut feature is created, see Figure 7.123.

Section 9: Creating the Sixth Feature - Extruded Cut Feature

1. Similar to creating the extruded cut feature on the right planar face of the model, create the extruded cut feature on the left planar face of the model, see Figure 7.124. You can also mirror the extruded cut feature by selecting the Right plane as the mirroring plane to create the extruded cut feature on the left planar face. You will learn about mirroring features in later chapters.

Section 10: Creating the Seventh Feature - Extruded Cut Feature

1. Similar to creating the extruded cut feature on the right and left planar faces of the model, create the extruded cut feature on the top planar face of the model, see Figure 7.125.

Section 11: Assigning the Material

1. Right-click on the **Material <not specified>** option in the FeatureManager Design Tree. A shortcut menu appears, see Figure 7.126.

2. Click on the **Edit Material** option in the shortcut menu. The **Material** dialog box appears, see Figure 7.127.

3. Expand the **SOLIDWORKS Materials** node, if not expanded by default. The different material categories such as Steel, Iron, and Aluminium Alloys appear in the dialog box.

4. Expand the **Steel** material category and then click on the **Alloy Steel** material, see Figure 7.127. All material properties of the Alloy Steel material appear on the right side of the dialog box.

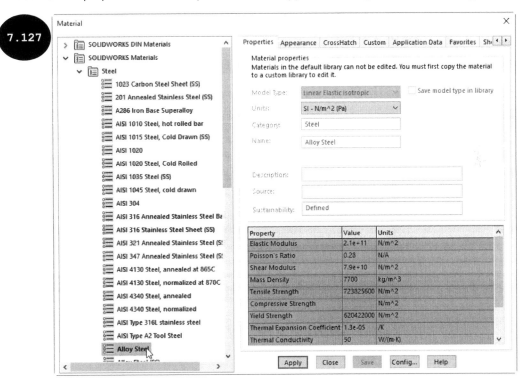

5. Click on the **Apply** button in the dialog box. The Alloy Steel material is applied to the model. Next, click on the **Close** button to exit the dialog box.

Section 12: Calculating Mass Properties

1. Click on the **Evaluate** tab in the CommandManager and then click on the **Mass Properties** tool in the **Evaluate CommandManager**, see Figure 7.128. The **Mass Properties** dialog box appears, which displays the mass properties of the model.

2. After reviewing the mass properties, exit the **Mass Properties** dialog box.

Section 13: Saving the Model

1. Click on the **Save** tool of the **Standard** toolbar. The **Save As** dialog box appears.

2. Browse to the Chapter 7 folder of the SOLIDWORKS folder and then save the file with the name Tutorial 2.

Tutorial 3

Create a model, as shown in Figure 7.129. After creating the model, assign the AISI 316 Stainless Steel Sheet (SS) material and calculate the mass properties of the model. All dimensions are in mm.

Section 1: Invoking the Part Modeling Environment
1. Start SOLIDWORKS and then invoke the Part modeling environment.

Section 2: Specifying Unit Settings
1. Invoke the **Unit System** flyout, see Figure 7.130.

2. Make sure that the **MMGS (millimeter, gram, second)** option is tick-marked in the flyout.

Section 3: Creating the Base/First Feature - Extruded Feature
1. Invoke the Sketching environment by selecting the Front plane as the sketching plane and then create the sketch of the base feature, see Figure 7.131. After creating the sketch, do not exit the Sketching environment.

Tip: To make the sketch of the base feature fully defined as shown in Figure 7.131, you need to apply the required relations such as tangent relations between connecting lines and arcs, equal relations between the entities having equal radius and diameter, and concentric relation between the arcs sharing the same center point.

---

2. Click on the **Features** tab in the CommandManager and then click on the **Extruded Boss/Base** tool. The **Boss-Extrude PropertyManager** and the preview of the extruded feature appear, see Figure 7.132.

3. Invoke the **End Condition** drop-down list in the **Direction 1** rollout, see Figure 7.133.

4. Click on the **Mid Plane** option in the **End Condition** drop-down list. The preview of the feature symmetric about the sketching plane appears in the graphics area.

5. Enter **90** in the **Depth** field in the **Direction 1** rollout of the PropertyManager.

6. Click on the green tick-mark ✓ in the PropertyManager. The extruded feature is created, see Figure 7.134.

Section 4: Creating the Second Feature - Extruded Cut Feature

1. Invoke the Sketching environment by selecting the top planar face of the base feature as the sketching plane. Next, change the orientation of the model as normal to the viewing direction.

2. Create a sketch of the second feature, see Figure 7.135. Do not exit the Sketching environment.

Tip: To create the sketch as shown in Figure 7.135, you can first create one side of the entities and then offset them at an offset distance of 15 mm with closed cap by using the **Offset Entities** tool.

3. Click on the **Extruded Cut** tool in the **Features CommandManager**. The **Cut-Extrude PropertyManager** and the preview of the extruded cut feature appear. Next, change the orientation of the model to isometric, see Figure 7.136.

4. Invoke the **End Condition** drop-down list in the **Direction 1** rollout, see Figure 7.137.

5. Click on the **Through All** option in the **End Condition** drop-down list.

6. Click on the **Flip side to cut** check box in the **Direction 1** rollout of the PropertyManager. The side of cut material gets flipped.

7. Click on the green tick-mark ☑ in the PropertyManager. An extruded cut feature is created, see Figure 7.138.

Section 5: Creating the Third Feature - Extruded Feature

To create the third feature of the model, you first need to create a reference plane at an offset distance of 205 mm from the Right plane.

1. Invoke the **Reference Geometry** flyout of the **Features CommandManager**, see Figure 7.139.

2. Click on the **Plane** tool in the **Reference Geometry** flyout. The **Plane PropertyManager** appears.

3. Expand the FeatureManager Design Tree, which is now available on the top left corner of the graphics area, by clicking on the arrow in its front.

4. Click on the **Right Plane** as the first reference. The preview of an offset reference plane appears in the graphics area.

5. Enter **205** in the **Distance** field of the **First Reference** rollout in the PropertyManager.

6. Click on the green tick-mark ✔ in the PropertyManager. The reference plane is created, see Figure 7.140.

   After creating the reference plane, you need to create the third feature of the model.

7. Invoke the Sketching environment by selecting the newly created reference plane as the sketching plane.

8. Press CTRL + 8 to change the orientation of the model as normal to the viewing direction.

9. Create the closed sketch of the third feature, see Figure 7.141. After creating the sketch, do not exit the Sketching environment.

Tip: To make the sketch of the third feature fully defined as shown in Figure 7.141, you need to apply the required relations such as tangent relations between connecting lines and arcs and concentric relation between the arcs sharing the same center point.

---

10. Click on the **Features** tab in the CommandManager to display the tools of the **Features** CommandManager.

11. Click on the **Extruded Boss/Base** tool in the **Features CommandManager**. The **Boss-Extrude PropertyManager** and the preview of the extruded feature appear. Next, change the orientation of the model to isometric, see Figure 7.142.

Extruded Boss/Base

12. Enter **55** in the **Depth** field in the **Direction 1** rollout of the PropertyManager. Next, press ENTER.

13. Click on the green tick-mark ☑ in the PropertyManager. The extruded feature is created, see Figure 7.143. Next, hide the reference plane.

Section 6: Assigning the Material

1. Right-click on the **Material <not specified>** option in the FeatureManager Design Tree. A shortcut menu appears, see Figure 7.144.

2. Click on the **Edit Material** option in the shortcut menu. The **Material** dialog box appears.

3. Expand the **SOLIDWORKS Materials** node, if not expanded by default. The different material categories such as Steel, Iron, and Aluminium Alloys appear in the dialog box.

4.   Expand the **Steel** category. The materials in the **Steel** category appear, see Figure 7.145.

5.   Click on the **AISI 316 Stainless Steel Sheet (SS)** material in the list of available materials, see Figure 7.145. The material properties of the selected material appear on the right panel of the dialog box.

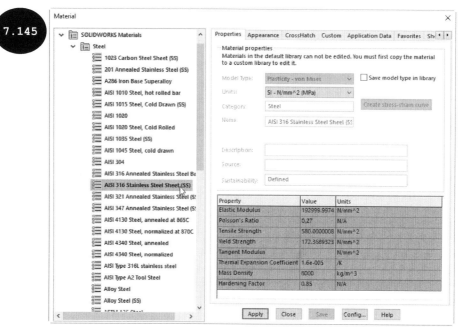

6.   Click on the **Apply** button of the dialog box. The material is applied to the model. Next, click on the **Close** button to exit the dialog box.

Section 7: Calculating Mass Properties

1.   Click on the **Evaluate** tab to display the tools of the **Evaluate CommandManager**.

2.   Click on the **Mass Properties** tool in the **Evaluate CommandManager**. The **Mass Properties** dialog box appears and displays the mass properties of the model.

3.   After reviewing the mass properties, exit the **Mass Properties** dialog box.

Section 8: Saving the Model

1.   Click on the **Save** tool of the **Standard** toolbar. The **Save As** dialog box appears.

2.   Browse to the Chapter 7 folder of the SOLIDWORKS folder and then save the model with the name Tutorial 3.

Hands-on Test Drive 1

Create a model, as shown in Figure 7.146. After creating the model, apply the Cast Alloy Steel material to the model and calculate its mass properties. All dimensions are in mm.

Hands-on Test Drive 2

Create a model, as shown in Figure 7.147. After creating the model, apply the Alloy Steel (SS) material to the model and calculate its mass properties. All dimensions are in mm.

Summary

This chapter discusses the advanced options for creating extruded and revolved features, creating cut features by using the **Extruded Cut** and **Revolved Cut** tools as well as how to work with different types of sketches such as closed sketches, open sketches, and nested sketches. The chapter also describes methods for creating multiple features by using a single sketch having multiple contours/regions, projecting the edges of existing features onto the current sketching plane by using the **Convert Entities** tool, and editing an existing feature and the sketch of a feature as per the design change.

Methods have been described for measuring distance and angle between lines, points, faces, planes, and so on by using the **Measure** tool, assigning an appearance/texture to a model, features, and faces, assigning material properties and calculating the mass properties of a model.

Questions

- The options in the _____ drop-down list are used for defining the start condition of extrusion.

- The _____ option is used for selecting a surface, a face, or a plane as the start condition of extrusion.

- The _____ option is used for defining the end condition or termination of extrusion by selecting a vertex.

- You can create extruded cut features by using the _____ tool.

- The _____ sketches have all the entities connected end to end with each other without any gaps.

- You can project the edges of existing features as sketch entities onto the current sketching plane by using the _____ tool.

- The _____ tool is used for calculating mass properties such as the mass and volume of a model.

- A revolved cut feature is created by removing material from the model by revolving a sketch around a centerline or an axis. (True/False)

- You can edit individual features and their sketches as per your requirement. (True/False)

- In SOLIDWORKS, you cannot customize material properties. (True/False)

Advanced Modeling - II

This chapter discusses the following topics:

*   Creating a Sweep Feature
*   Creating a Sweep Cut Feature
*   Creating a Lofted feature
*   Creating a Lofted Cut Feature
*   Creating a Boundary Feature
*   Creating a Boundary Cut Feature
*   Creating Curves
*   Splitting Faces of a Model
*   Creating 3D Sketches

In the previous chapters, you have learned about the primary modeling tools that are used for creating 3D parametric models. You have also learned about the basic workflow of creating models, which is to first create the base feature of a model and then create the remaining features of the model one after the other.

In this chapter, you will explore some of the advanced tools such as **Swept Boss/Base**, **Lofted Boss/Base**, and **Boundary Boss/Base**. You will also learn how to split faces of a model and create different types of 3D curves and sketches.

Creating a Sweep Feature

A sweep feature is created by adding material by sweeping a profile along a path. Figure 8.1 shows a profile and a path. Figure 8.2 shows the resultant sweep feature created by sweeping the profile along the path.

It is evident from the above figures that for creating a sweep feature, you first need to create a path and a profile where the profile follows the path and creates a sweep feature. To create a profile, you need to identify the cross-section of the feature to be created. To create a path, you need to identify the route/path taken by the profile for creating the feature. In SOLIDWORKS, you can create a sweep feature by using the **Swept Boss/Base** tool of the **Features CommandManager**. Note that for creating a sweep feature, you need to take care of the following points:

1. The profile must be a closed sketch. You can also select a face of a model as a profile. Besides, you can also select an edge or a group of edges of a model that form a closed loop as a profile.
2. The path can be an open or a closed sketch, which is made up of a set of end to end connected sketched entities, a curve, or a set of model edges.
3. The starting point of the path must intersect the plane of the profile.
4. The profile and path as well as the resultant sweep feature must not self-intersect.

After creating the path and the profile, click on the **Swept Boss/Base** tool in the **Features CommandManager**. The **Sweep PropertyManager** appears, see Figure 8.3. The options in the PropertyManager are discussed next.

Profile and Path
The options in the **Profile and Path** rollout of the PropertyManager are used for selecting a profile and a path. The options are discussed next.

Sketch Profile

The **Sketch Profile** radio button of the **Profile and Path** rollout is selected, by default. As a result, the **Profile** and the **Path** fields are available in the PropertyManager, refer to Figure 8.3. The **Profile** field is used for selecting a profile of the sweep feature. You can select a closed sketch, a face, or an edge/group of edges that form a closed loop as a profile, see Figure 8.4. The **Path** field is used for selecting a path of the sweep feature, see Figure 8.4. You can select an open or a closed sketch, an edge, or a curve as a path of the sweep feature.

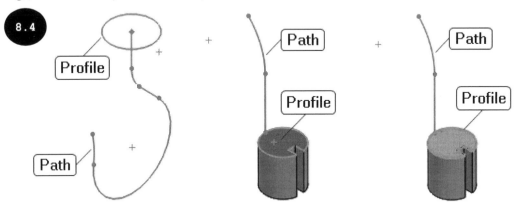

As soon as you select a profile and a path, a preview of the resultant sweep feature appears in the graphics area, see Figure 8.5.

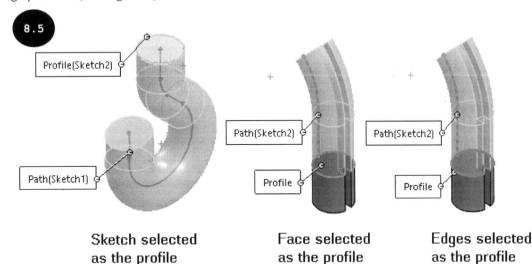

| Sketch selected | Face selected | Edges selected |
| as the profile | as the profile | as the profile |

Note: If the profile is created between the endpoints of the path, see Figure 8.6, then the preview of the sweep feature appears on either side of the profile, see Figure 8.7. Also, three buttons: **Direction 1**, **Bidirectional**, and **Direction 2** become available in the **Profile and Path** rollout, see Figure 8.8. The **Direction 1** and **Direction 2** buttons are used for sweeping the profile to either side, whereas the **Bidirectional** button is used for sweeping the profile to both its sides.

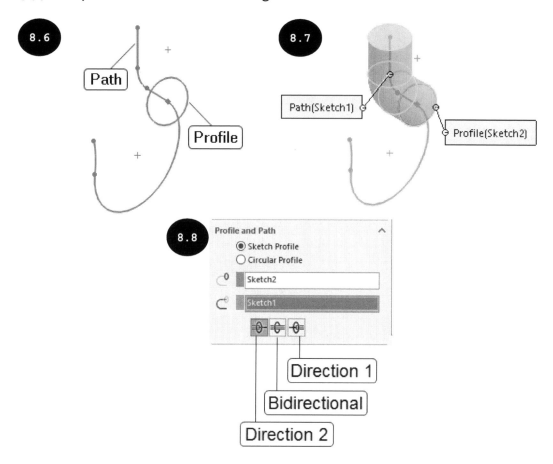

To accept the preview of the sweep feature, click on the green tick-mark ✓ in the PropertyManager. The sweep feature is created. The remaining options of the **Sweep PropertyManager** are discussed next.

Circular Profile

The **Circular Profile** radio button of the **Profile and Path** rollout is used for creating a sweep feature that has a circular cross section such as solid rod or hollow tube by specifying the diameter value. To create a sweep feature by using this radio button, you do not need to select a profile. When you select the **Circular Profile** radio button, the **Path** and **Diameter** fields become available in the rollout, see Figure 8.9.

The **Path** field is used for selecting a path of the sweep feature. By default, this field is active. As a result, you can select an open or a closed sketch, an edge, or a curve as the path of the sweep feature. The **Diameter** field of the rollout is used for specifying the diameter value of the circular profile. After selecting the path, a preview of the sweep feature having circular profile of specified diameter appears in the graphics area, see Figure 8.10. In this figure, an edge is selected as the path of the sweep feature.

The options in the other rollouts of the **Sweep PropertyManager** are used for controlling the parameters of the sweep feature. These options are discussed next.

Options

By default, the **Options** rollout of the PropertyManager is collapsed. To expand this rollout, click on the arrow available on its right, see Figure 8.11. Note that some of the options of the **Options** rollout are not available while creating a base/first feature. Also, the availability of options in this rollout depends upon the selection of **Sketch Profile** or **Circular Profile** radio button in the **Profile and Path** rollout of the PropertyManager. The options of the **Options** rollout are discussed next.

Profile orientation drop-down list

The options in the **Profile orientation** drop-down list are used for controlling the orientation of the profile along the path, see Figure 8.12. The options are discussed next.

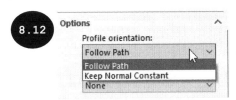

Follow Path

By default, the **Follow Path** option is selected in the drop-down list. As a result, the profile follows the path by maintaining the same angle of orientation from start to end by aligning itself normal to the path, see Figures 8.13 and 8.14.

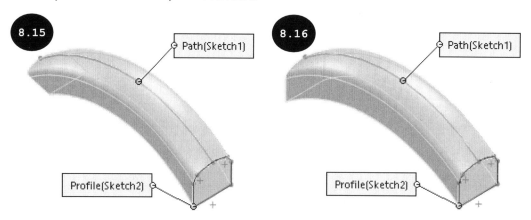

Keep Normal Constant

On selecting the **Keep Normal Constant** option, the profile follows a path such that it remains parallel throughout the path. In other words, the start and end sections of the resultant sweep feature are parallel to each other. Figure 8.15 shows the preview of a sweep feature when the **Follow Path** option is selected and Figure 8.16 shows the preview of the sweep feature when the **Keep Normal Constant** option is selected.

Profile Twist drop-down list

The options in the **Profile Twist** drop-down list are used for controlling the twisting or alignment of the profile along the path, see Figure 8.17. The options are discussed next.

None

By default, the **None** option is selected in the **Profile Twist** drop-down list. As a result, the profile follows a path such that it maintains normal alignment.

Specify Twist Value

By selecting the **Specify Twist Value** option, you can twist the profile along the path, see Figures 8.18 through 8.21. Figures 8.18 and 8.20 show the path and profile, respectively and Figures 8.19 and 8.21 show the preview of the resultant twisted sweep feature.

After selecting the **Specify Twist Value** option, the **Twist control** drop-down list and **Direction 1** field become available in the **Options** rollout, see Figure 8.22. The options in the **Twist control** drop-down list are used for controlling the twisting of the profile along the path. The options are discussed next.

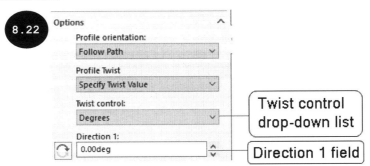

Degrees: By default, the **Degrees** option is selected in the **Twist control** drop-down list. As a result, you need to specify the twist angle in degrees in the **Direction 1** field of the rollout.

Radians: The **Radians** option is used for specifying the twist angle in radians in the **Direction 1** field of the **Options** rollout.

Revolutions: By selecting the **Revolutions** option, you can specify the number of revolutions for the profile along the path in the **Direction 1** field. Figures 8.23 and 8.24 show the preview of a sweep feature after entering 3 in the **Direction 1** field as the number of revolutions.

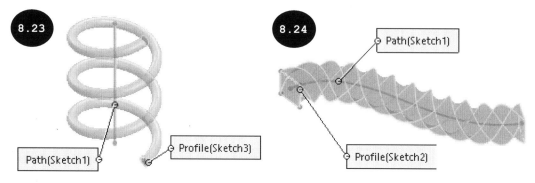

Note: If the profile is created between the endpoints of the path, refer to Figure 8.25, and you are creating a bidirectional sweep feature, see Figure 8.26, then on selecting the **Specify Twist Value** option in the **Profile Twist** drop-down list, the **Direction 2** field also becomes available in the rollout along with the **Twist control** drop-down list and the **Direction 1** field. The **Direction 2** field specifies the twist angle in the second direction of the sweep feature, see Figure 8.27.

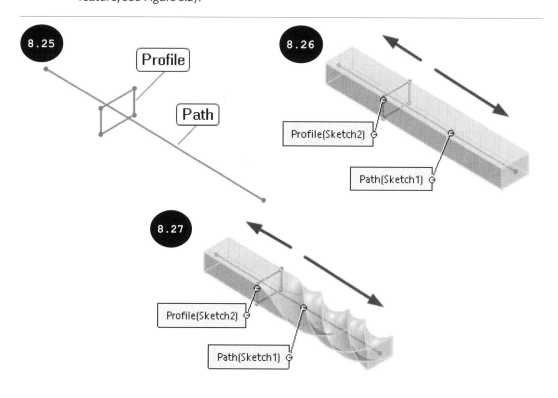

Specify Direction Vector

On selecting the **Specify Direction Vector** option in the **Profile Twist** drop-down list, the **Direction Vector** field becomes available. The **Direction Vector** field is used for selecting a direction vector for aligning the profile. You can select a plane, a planar face, a line, or a linear edge as the direction vector. Figure 8.28 shows a path, a profile, and a direction vector. Figure 8.29 shows the preview of the resultant sweep feature by selecting the Top plane as the direction vector.

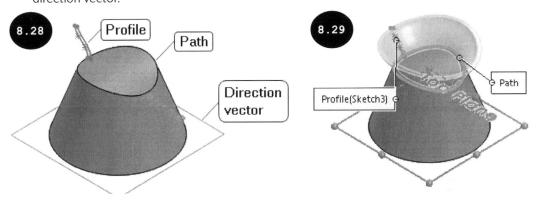

Tip: The path shown in the Figure 8.28 is a 3D closed edge of the model. You can select an open or a closed edge of a model as a path for creating the sweep feature.

Minimum Twist

On selecting the **Minimum Twist** option in the **Profile Twist** drop-down list, a minimum twist is applied to the profile while following the path in order to avoid self-intersection, see Figure 8.30. Note that this option works better with a 3D path and is available in the drop-down list only if a 3D sketch or a 3D edge is selected as the path of the sweep feature. You will learn more about creating 3D sketches later in this chapter. Figure 8.30 shows the preview of a sweep feature when the **Minimum Twist** option is selected.

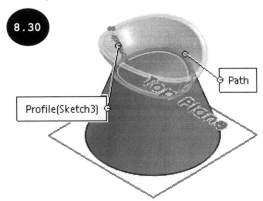

Tangent to Adjacent Faces

On selecting the **Tangent to Adjacent Faces** option, the profile maintains tangency with the adjacent face of the path, see Figure 8.31. This option works only if the path has an adjacent face.

Natural

On selecting the **Natural** option in the **Profile Twist** drop-down list, the profile follows a path such that it maintains natural twist, see Figure 8.32. Note that this option works better with a 3D path and is available in the drop-down list only if a 3D sketch or a 3D edge is selected as the path of the sweep feature. You will learn more about creating 3D sketches later in this chapter.

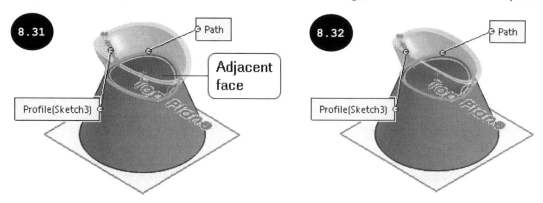

Follow Path and First Guide Curve

On selecting the **Follow Path and First Guide Curve** option, the profile follows the path as well as the first guide curve, see Figures 8.33 and 8.34. A guide curve is used for guiding the profile (section) of the sweep feature. Note that this option is available in the drop-down list only after selecting a guide curve by using the **Guide Curves** rollout of the PropertyManager. To select a guide curve, expand the **Guide Curves** rollout by clicking on the arrow available on its front, see Figure 8.35. The field in this rollout is activated by default and is used for selecting guide curves from the graphics area. Make sure that the guide curve you select has a pierce relation with the profile of the sweep feature. Figure 8.33 shows a path, a profile, and a guide curve. Figure 8.34 shows the preview of the resultant sweep feature.

> **Note:** In Figure 8.33, the path and the guide curve are created on the Front plane as individual sketches, and the profile is created on the Top plane. Also, the start point of the guide curve has a pierce relation with the profile of the sweep feature.

Follow First and Second Guide Curve

On selecting the **Follow First and Second Guide Curve** option, the profile follows the path, and the first and second guide curves, see Figures 8.36 and 8.37. By using this option, you can guide the profile (section) of a sweep feature by using two guide curves. Note that this option is available in the drop-down list only after selecting two guide curves by using the **Guide Curves** rollout of the PropertyManager. To select guide curves, expand the **Guide Curves** rollout, refer to Figure 8.35. Next, select two guide curves one by one in the graphics area. Figure 8.36 shows a path, a profile, and two guide curves. Figure 8.37 shows the preview of the resultant sweep feature.

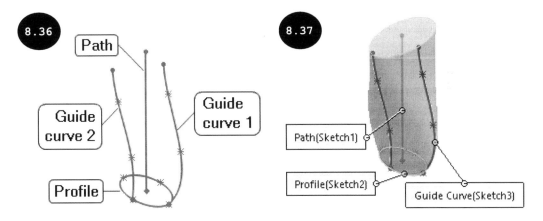

> **Note:** In Figure 8.36, the path and the guide curve 1 are created on the Front plane as individual sketches, and the guide curve 2 is created on the Right plane. Also, a profile is created on the Top plane.

> **Tip:** If the profile fails to follow both the guide curves, then you need to make sure that the resultant sweep feature does not self intersect. Also, the guide curves must have a pierce relation with the profile of the sweep feature.

Merge tangent faces

On selecting the **Merge tangent faces** check box in the **Options** rollout, the tangent faces of the resultant sweep feature get merged and appear as a single face. Figure 8.38 shows a sweep feature that is created by selecting the **Merge tangent faces** check box, whereas Figure 8.39 shows a sweep feature that is created by clearing the **Merge tangent faces** check box.

Merge result

By default, the **Merge result** check box is selected in the **Options** rollout, see Figure 8.40. As a result, the resultant sweep feature merges with the existing features of the model and forms a single body. On clearing this check box, the sweep feature will not merge with the existing features of the model and make a separate body. Note that this check box is not available while creating the base/first feature of a model.

Align with end faces

On selecting the **Align with end faces** check box, the end section of the sweep feature gets aligned with the face of an existing feature, which is encountered by the path. Note that this check box is not available if the sweep feature being created is the base feature of a model. Figure 8.41 shows the preview of a sweep feature when the **Align with end faces** check box is selected and Figure 8.42 shows the preview of a sweep feature when the **Align with end faces** check box is cleared.

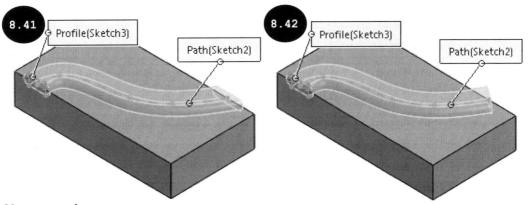

Show preview

By default, the **Show preview** check box is selected. As a result, while creating a sweep feature, its preview appears in the graphics area.

Guide Curves

The **Guide Curves** rollout of the **Sweep PropertyManager** is used for selecting guide curves for creating the sweep feature, see Figure 8.43. The options in the **Guide Curves** rollout are discussed next.

Guide Curves field

The **Guide Curves** field is used for selecting guide curves in the graphics area. Guide curves are used for guiding the profile of the sweep feature along the path. On selecting guide curves, their names appear in this field in a sequence in which they are selected. You can select one or two guide curves for creating a sweep feature, as discussed earlier. Note that the guide curves should have a pierce relation with the profile of the sweep feature.

Move Up and Move Down

The **Move Up** and **Move Down** buttons are used for changing the order or sequence of guide curves in the **Guide Curves** field. These buttons are available to the left of the **Guide Curves** field.

Merge smooth faces

By default, the **Merge smooth faces** check box is selected. As a result, the smooth or tangent segments of the sweep feature get merged together. Figure 8.44 shows a sweep feature that is created by selecting the **Merge smooth faces** check box. Figure 8.45 shows a sweep feature that is created by clearing the **Merge smooth faces** check box.

Show Sections

The **Show Sections** button of the rollout is used for viewing the intermediate sections of the sweep feature being created by using guide curves. By default, the **Show Sections** button is not activated. To activate this button, click on it. The **Section Number** field gets enabled in the rollout. On entering a section number in this field, the preview of the respective section appears in the graphics area, see Figure 8.46.

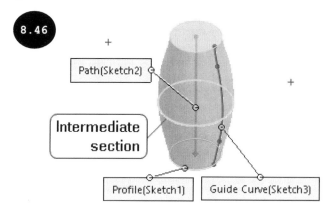

Start and End Tangency

The options in the **Start and End Tangency** rollout of the PropertyManager are used for specifying the start and end tangency of the sweep feature. This rollout has two drop-down lists: **Start tangency type** and **End tangency type**, see Figure 8.47. The options in the drop-down lists are discussed next.

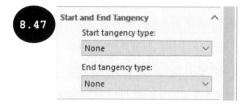

Start tangency type

The options in the **Start tangency type** drop-down list are used for specifying the start tangency for a sweep feature. By default, the **None** option is selected in this drop-down list. As a result, tangency is not maintained at the start of the sweep feature. On selecting the **Path Tangent** option, the sweep feature maintains tangency with the path at its start. Figure 8.48 shows the preview of a sweep feature when the **None** option is selected and Figure 8.49 shows the preview of a sweep feature when the **Path Tangent** option is selected as the start tangency type.

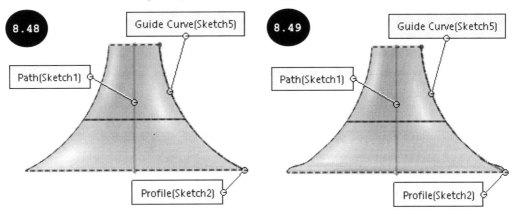

End tangency type

The options in the **End tangency type** drop-down list are used for specifying the end tangency type for a sweep feature. By default, the **None** option is selected in this drop-down list. As a result, the tangency is not maintained at the end of the sweep feature. On selecting the **Path Tangent** option, the sweep feature maintains tangency with the path at its end.

Thin Feature

The **Thin Feature** rollout of the PropertyManager is used for creating a thin sweep feature, see Figure 8.50. To create a thin sweep feature, expand this rollout by clicking on the check box on its title bar, see Figure 8.51. The options for creating the thin sweep feature are the same as those discussed earlier while creating the thin extruded and thin revolved features.

Curvature Display

The options in the **Curvature Display** rollout are used for controlling the display style of the preview that appears in the graphics area, see Figure 8.52. The options are discussed next.

8.52

Curvature Display

☐ Mesh preview

☐ Zebra stripes

☐ Curvature combs

Mesh preview

This check box is used for displaying a mesh preview in the graphics area, see Figure 8.53. You can control the mesh density by using the **Mesh density** slider that appears below this check box.

8.53   Path(Sketch1)

Profile(Sketch2)

Zebra stripes

This check box is used for turning on the appearance of zebra stripes in the preview of the feature, see Figure 8.54. The zebra strips help you find small changes made in the feature by making them visible, which are hard to see in the standard display style.

Curvature combs

This check box is used for turning on the appearance of curvature combs in the preview of the feature, see Figure 8.55. You can control the scale and density of the displayed curvature combs by using the **Scale** and the **Density** sliders of the rollout.

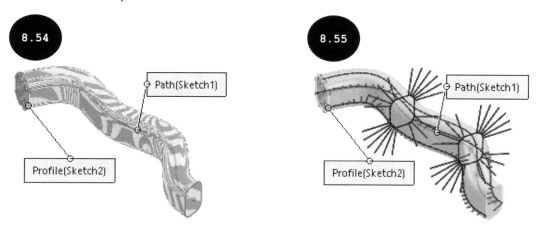

8.54   Path(Sketch1)

Profile(Sketch2)

8.55   Path(Sketch1)

Profile(Sketch2)

Procedure for Creating a Sweep Feature with Sketch Profile

1. Click on the **Swept Boss/Base** tool. The **Sweep PropertyManager** appears.
2. Make sure that the **Sketch Profile** radio button is selected in the **Profile and Path** rollout.

3. Select a closed sketch, a face, or an edge/edges that form a closed loop as the profile.
4. Select an open or a closed sketch, an edge, or a curve as the path of the sweep feature. The preview of the sweep feature appears.
5. Click on the green tick-mark ☑ in the PropertyManager. The sweep feature is created.

Procedure for Creating a Sweep Feature with Circular Profile

1. Click on the **Swept Boss/Base** tool. The **Sweep PropertyManager** appears.
2. Click on the **Circular Profile** radio button in the **Profile and Path** rollout.
3. Select an open or a closed sketch, an edge, or a curve as the path of the sweep feature in the graphics area. The preview of the sweep feature appears with a default diameter of the profile.
4. Enter the diameter value for the circular profile in the **Diameter** field of the rollout.
5. Click on the green tick-mark ☑ in the PropertyManager. The sweep feature is created.

Procedure for Creating a Sweep Feature with One Guide Curve

1. Create a path, a profile, and a guide curve as individual sketches.
2. Click on the **Swept Boss/Base** tool. The **Sweep PropertyManager** appears.
3. Make sure that the **Sketch Profile** radio button is selected in the **Profile and Path** rollout.
4. Select the profile of the sweep feature in the graphics area.
5. Select the path of the sweep feature. A preview of the sweep feature appears.
6. Expand the **Guide Curves** rollout of the PropertyManager.
7. Select the guide curve in the graphics area. A preview of the sweep feature appears such that the profile follows the path and its outer shape is maintained by the guide curve.
8. Click on the green tick-mark ☑ in the PropertyManager. The sweep feature is created.

Procedure for Creating a Sweep Feature with Two Guide Curves

1. Create a path, a profile, and two guide curves as individual sketches.
2. Invoke the **Sweep PropertyManager**.
3. Make sure that the **Sketch Profile** radio button is selected in the **Profile and Path** rollout.
4. Select the profile and then select the path of the sweep feature in the graphics area.
5. Expand the **Guide Curves** rollout of the PropertyManager.
6. Select the first guide curve and then select the second guide curve. A preview of the sweep feature appears such that the profile follows the path and its outer shape is maintained by the guide curves.
7. Click on the green tick-mark ☑ in the PropertyManager. The sweep feature is created.

Procedure for Creating a Sweep Feature with Twist

1. Invoke the **Sweep PropertyManager**.
2. Make sure that the **Sketch Profile** radio button is selected in the **Profile and Path** rollout.
3. Select a closed sketch, a face, or an edge/edges that form a closed loop as the profile.
4. Select an open or a closed sketch, an edge, or a curve as the path of the sweep feature. The preview of the sweep feature appears.
5. Expand the **Options** rollout of the PropertyManager.
6. Select the **Specify Twist Value** option in the **Profile Twist** drop-down list of the **Option** rollout.
7. Select the **Degrees, Radians,** or **Revolutions** option in the **Twist control** drop-down list.
8. Enter the twist value in the **Direction 1** field. A preview of the twist sweep feature appears.
9. Click on the green tick-mark ☑ in the PropertyManager. The twisted sweep feature is created.

Creating a Sweep Cut Feature

The method for creating a sweep cut feature is the same as creating a sweep feature with the only difference that a sweep cut feature is created by removing material from the model, see Figures 8.56 through 8.59. You can create sweep cut features by using the **Swept Cut** tool. Figures 8.56 and 8.58 show the profile and the path, respectively. Figures 8.57 and 8.59 show the resultant sweep cut feature created such that the material is removed from the model by sweeping the profile along the path.

Note: In Figure 8.56, a helical curve has been created as the path and a circle has been created as the profile. You will learn about creating helical curves later in this chapter.

To create a sweep cut feature, click on the **Swept Cut** tool in the **Features CommandManager**. The **Cut-Sweep PropertyManager** appears, see Figure 8.60. In this PropertyManager, the **Sketch Profile** radio button is selected, by default. As a result, the **Profile** and **Path** fields are enabled in the PropertyManager. Select a profile of the sweep cut feature in the graphics area. You can select a closed sketch, a face, or an edge/a group of edges that form a closed loop as a profile. Next, select a path of the sweep cut feature. You can select an open or a closed sketch, an edge, or a curve as the path of the sweep cut feature. After selecting the profile and path, a preview of the sweep cut feature appears in the graphics area.

On selecting the **Circular Profile** radio button of the PropertyManager, you can create a circular sweep cut feature similar to creating a circular sweep feature without creating the sketch of the profile.

On selecting the **Solid Profile** radio button, the **Tool body** and **Path** fields get enabled in the PropertyManager, see Figure 8.61. The **Tool body** field is activated, by default and is used for selecting a tool body that follows the path in order to create a sweep cut feature. Figure 8.62 shows a tool body and a helical path, and Figure 8.63 shows the resultant sweep cut feature. Also, refer to Figures 8.64 and 8.65 for a tool body, a path, and the resultant sweep cut feature. Note that the options for creating a sweep cut feature are the same as those discussed earlier while creating the sweep feature.

Note: In Figures 8.62 and 8.64, a solid body has been used as a tool body to follow the path. The tool body should be created as a separate body. To create a separate body, you need to clear the **Merge result** check box in the respective PropertyManager, while creating it. On clearing the **Merge result** check box, the resultant feature is treated as a separate body. Also, in Figure 8.62, a helical curve has been used as the path. You will learn about creating a helical curve later in this chapter.

Creating a Lofted feature

A lofted feature is created by lofting two or more than two profiles (sections) such that the cross-sectional shape of the lofted feature transits from one profile to another. Figure 8.66 shows two dissimilar profiles/sections that are created on different planes having an offset distance between each other. Figure 8.67 shows the resultant lofted feature created.

It is evident from the above figures that for creating a lofted feature, you first need to create all its sections that define the shape of the lofted feature. In SOLIDWORKS, you can create a lofted feature by using the **Lofted Boss/Base** tool of the **Features CommandManager**. Note that for creating a lofted feature, you need to take care of the following points:

1.   Two or more than two profiles/sections (similar or dissimilar) must be available in the graphics area before invoking the **Lofted Boss/Base** tool.

2. Profiles must be closed. You can select closed sketches, faces, or edges as profiles.
3. All profiles must be created as different sketches.
4. The profiles and the resultant lofted feature must not self intersect.

To create a lofted feature, click on the **Lofted Boss/Base** tool in the **Features CommandManager**. The **Loft PropertyManager** appears, see Figure 8.68. The options in this PropertyManager are discussed next.

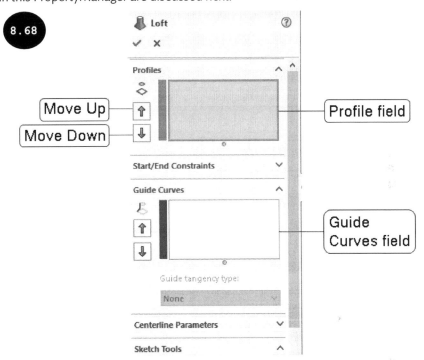

Profiles

The **Profiles** rollout of the PropertyManager is used for selecting profiles of the lofted feature. You can select two or more than two similar or dissimilar closed profiles for creating a lofted feature. After selecting the profiles, a preview of the lofted feature appears in the graphics area with connectors, that connect the profiles, see Figure 8.69. Also, the names of the selected profiles appear in the **Profile** field of the rollout in an order in which they are selected. You can change the order of selection by using the **Move Up** and **Move Down** buttons of the **Profile** rollout, refer to Figure 8.68.

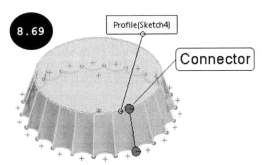

Note: You can drag the connectors that appear in the preview of a lofted feature to create a twist in the feature. By default, in the preview of a lofted feature, only one handle appears with its connectors, refer to Figure 8.69. You can turn on the display of all handles in the preview of the lofted feature. For doing so, right-click in the graphics area and then select the **Show All Connectors** option in the shortcut menu that appears.

Start/End Constraints

The options in the **Start/End Constraint** rollout are used for defining normal, tangent, or curvature continuity as the start and end constraints of a lofted feature. By default, this rollout is collapsed. To expand the rollout, click on the arrow in its title bar, see Figure 8.70. The options in this rollout are discussed next.

Start constraint

The options in the **Start constraint** drop-down list are used for defining the start constraint for a lofted feature, see Figure 8.71. The options in this drop-down list are discussed next.

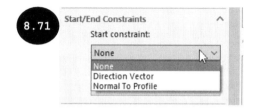

None

By default, the **None** option is selected in the **Start constraint** drop-down list. As a result, no constraint is applied and the cross-sectional shape transits from one profile to another, linearly, see Figures 8.72 and 8.73. Figure 8.72 shows profiles and Figure 8.73 shows the preview of the resultant lofted feature.

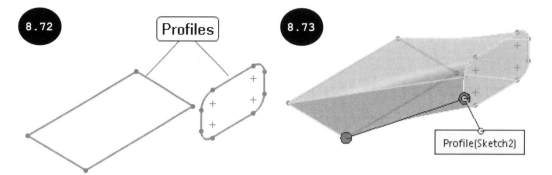

Direction Vector

On selecting the **Direction Vector** option, the **Direction Vector**, **Draft angle**, and **Start Tangent Length** fields become available in the rollout, see Figure 8.74.

The **Direction Vector** field is used for selecting a direction vector that defines the start constraint for a lofted feature. You can select a plane, a linear edge, a linear sketch entity, or an axis as direction vector. Figure 8.75 shows a preview of the lofted feature after selecting the Top plane as the direction vector.

The **Draft angle** field is used for defining the draft angle for start constraint. By default, the draft angle is set to 0 degree. You can specify the draft angle, as required. Figure 8.76 shows the front view of the preview of a lofted feature having the draft angle set to 0 degree and Figure 8.77 shows the front view of the preview of a lofted feature having the draft angle set to 20 degrees.

The **Start Tangent Length** field is used for defining the start tangent length for start constraint. By default, the start tangent length is specified as 1. Figure 8.78 shows a preview of the lofted feature with the draft angle set to 0-degree and the start tangent length is set to 2.

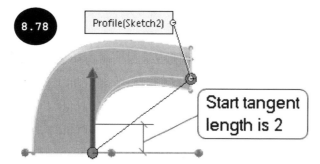

Normal To Profile

On selecting the **Normal To Profile** option in the **Start constraint** drop-down list, the tangency constraint is applied normal to the start section of the lofted feature. Also, the **Draft angle** and **Start Tangent Length** fields are enabled. The methods for specifying draft angle and start tangent length are the same as those discussed earlier.

Tangency To Face

On selecting the **Tangency To Face** option in the **Start constraint** drop-down list, the start section of the lofted feature maintains tangency with the adjacent face of existing geometry, see Figure 8.79. You can define the start tangent length of the feature in the **Start Tangent Length** field of the rollout.

> **Note:** The **Tangency To Face** option becomes available only when an adjacent face of an existing geometry is available in the graphics area. If the loft feature being created is the base/first feature, then this option will not be available in the drop-down list.

Curvature To Face

On selecting the **Curvature To Face** option, the start profile of a lofted feature maintains curvature continuity with the adjacent faces of the existing geometry.

> **Note:** If the loft feature being created is the base/first feature, then the **Curvature To Face** option will not be available in the drop-down list.

Reverse Direction and Reverse Tangent Direction

The **Reverse Direction** and **Reverse Tangent Direction** buttons of the **Start/End Constraint** rollout are used for reversing the direction of the applied constraints, see Figure 8.80. Note that the **Reverse Direction** button is available in the rollout after selecting the **Direction Vector** or **Normal To Profile** option in the **Start constraint** drop-down list. On the other hand, the **Reverse Tangent Direction** button is available in the rollout if the **Direction Vector, Normal To Profile, Tangency To Face,** or **Curvature To Face** option is selected.

Apply to all

The **Apply to all** check box is selected in the rollout, by default. As a result, only one handle appears in the preview of a lofted feature, see Figure 8.81 and it is used for controlling constraints of the entire profile. If you clear the **Apply to all** check box, multiple handles appear in the preview of the lofted feature, see Figure 8.82. These handles are used for controlling the constraints of individual segments for the profile. You can modify the constraints of a lofted feature by dragging the handles that appear in the preview of the lofted feature.

End constraint

The **End constraint** drop-down list is used for defining the end constraint of a lofted feature. The options in this drop-down list are same as those discussed earlier with the only difference that these options are used for defining the end constraint. Figure 8.83 shows the preview of a lofted feature when the start and end constraints are not defined, whereas Figure 8.84 shows the preview of a lofted feature when the end constraint is defined as normal to the profile.

Guide Curves

Guide curves are used for guiding the cross-sectional shape of a lofted feature. You can create multiple guide curves for controlling the cross-sectional shape of a lofted feature. The **Guide Curves** rollout of the PropertyManager is used for selecting guide curves of the lofted feature. Figure 8.85 shows two profiles and two guide curves, and Figure 8.86 shows the resultant lofted feature. Note that guide curves must have pierce relations with the profiles of the feature.

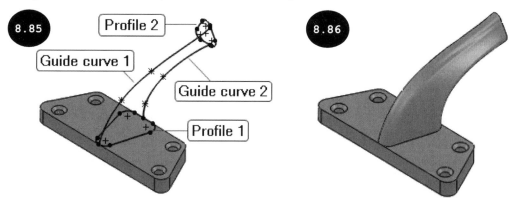

To select guide curves, click on the **Guide Curves** field in the **Guide Curves** rollout and then select the guide curves. The preview of the lofted feature appears such that its cross-sectional shape has been controlled by the guide curves. Also, the **Guide curves influence type** drop-down list appears, see Figure 8.87. The options in this drop-down list are used for controlling the influence of guide curves. The options are discussed next.

To Next Guide

The **To Next Guide** option in the **Guide curves influence type** drop-down list is used for extending the influence of the guide curve to the next guide curve only. Figure 8.88 shows two profiles and a guide curve. Figure 8.89 shows the preview of the resultant lofted feature when the **To Next Guide** option is selected.

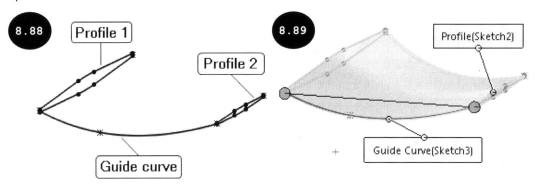

To Next Sharp

The **To Next Sharp** option is used for extending the influence of the guide curve to the next sharp, see Figure 8.90. A sharp is a hard corner of the profile.

To Next Edge

The **To Next Edge** option is used for extending the influence of the guide curve to the next edge.

Global

The **Global** option is used for extending the influence of the guide curve to the entire lofted feature, see Figure 8.91.

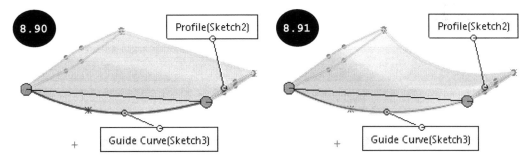

Centerline Parameters

The **Centerline Parameters** rollout of the PropertyManager is used for selecting a centerline for creating a lofted feature. Centerline is used for maintaining the neutral axis of the lofted feature. To select a centerline, expand the **Centerline Parameters** rollout after selecting all profiles of the lofted feature. Next, select a centerline for the lofted feature. A preview of the resultant lofted feature appears in the graphics area such that its intermediate sections become normal to the centerline. Figure 8.92 shows different profiles and a centerline, and Figure 8.93 shows the preview of the resultant lofted feature after selecting the centerline.

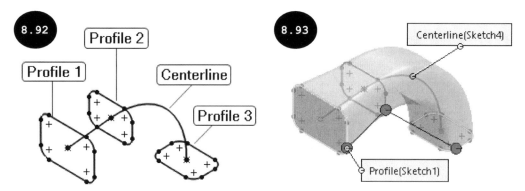

The **Show Sections** button of the **Centerline Parameters** rollout is used for showing different sections of the lofted feature in the graphics area. On activating this button, the display of different sections is turned on. Also, the **Section Number** field is enabled. In this field, you can enter the section number to be displayed in the graphics area.

Sketch Tools

The **Sketch Tools** rollout is used for editing the 3D sketch sections/profiles of a lofted feature, see Figure 8.94. You can edit the 3D profiles of a lofted feature by dragging them in the graphics area by using the **Drag Sketch** button of this rollout. Note that the **Drag Sketch** button is enabled only when the profiles of the lofted feature being edited are drawn as 3D sketches. You will learn about drawing 3D sketches later in this chapter.

Options

The options in the **Options** rollout of the PropertyManager are used for merging tangent faces of the feature, create close lofted features, show preview, and merge result, see Figure 8.95. The options of this rollout are discussed next.

Merge tangent faces

On selecting the **Merge tangent faces** check box, the tangent faces of the feature merge with each other. Figure 8.96 shows a lofted feature that is created when the **Merge tangent faces** check box is selected and Figure 8.97 shows a lofted feature that is created when the **Merge tangent faces** check box is cleared.

Close Loft

The **Close loft** check box is used for creating a lofted feature such that the start and end profiles of the lofted feature join automatically with each other and create a closed lofted feature. Figure 8.98 shows the preview of an open lofted feature when the **Close loft** check box is cleared and Figure 8.99 shows the preview of a closed lofted feature when the **Close loft** check box is selected.

Note: To create a closed lofted feature, minimum three sections are required. Also, the total angle between the start and end sections should be more than 120 degrees.

Show preview

The **Show preview** check box is used for showing the preview of the lofted feature in the graphics area. By default, this check box is selected. As a result, a preview of the lofted feature appears in the graphics area.

Thin Feature

The **Thin Feature** rollout is used for creating a thin lofted feature, see Figure 8.100. The options in this rollout are same as those discussed earlier while creating the thin extruded and revolved features.

Curvature Display

The options in the **Curvature Display** rollout are used for controlling the display style of the preview that appears in the graphics area and are the same as discussed earlier.

Procedure for Creating a Lofted Feature

1.   Click on the **Lofted Boss/Base** tool. The **Loft PropertyManager** appears.
2.   Select all profiles of the lofted feature one by one in the graphics area. You can select a closed sketch, a face, or an edge that forms a closed loop as a profile A preview of the lofted feature with connectors appears in the graphics area.
3.   Make sure that the connectors are in one direction to avoid twisting in the feature. To twist a lofted feature, you can change the position of the connectors by dragging them.
4.   Click on the green tick-mark ✓ in the PropertyManager. The lofted feature is created.

Procedure for Creating a Lofted Feature using Guide Curves

1.   Create all the profiles and guide curves of the lofted feature as individual sketches.
2.   Click on the **Lofted Boss/Base** tool. The **Loft PropertyManager** appears.
3.   Select all profiles one by one in the graphics area. The preview of the lofted feature with connectors appears in the graphics area.
4.   Make sure that the connectors are in one direction to avoid twisting in the feature.
5.   Expand the **Guide Curves** rollout and then click on the **Guide Curves** field to activate it.
6.   Select a guide curve in the graphics area. A preview of the lofted feature appears such that its shape is controlled by the guide curve. You can select one or more than one guide curves.
7.   Click on the green tick-mark ✓ in the PropertyManager. The lofted feature is created.

Procedure for Creating a Lofted Feature using Centerline

1.   Create all profiles and a centerline of the lofted feature.
2.   Invoke the **Loft PropertyManager**.
3.   Select all profiles of the lofted feature one by one in the graphics area.
4.   Expand the **Centerline Parameters** rollout and then select the centerline in the graphics area. A preview of the lofted feature appears with respect to the centerline selected.
5.   Click on the green tick-mark ✓ in the PropertyManager. The lofted feature is created.

Creating a Lofted Cut Feature

The method for creating a lofted cut feature is the same as of creating a lofted feature with the only difference that a lofted cut feature is created by removing material from the model. You can create a lofted cut feature by using the **Lofted Cut** tool in the **Features CommandManager**. Figure 8.101 shows profiles of a lofted cut feature. Figure 8.102 shows a preview of the resultant lofted cut feature and Figure 8.103 shows the resultant lofted cut feature created.

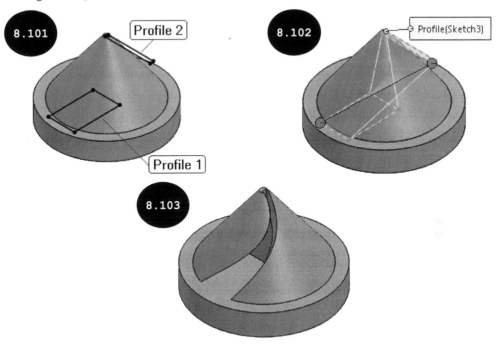

Creating a Boundary Feature

Boundary features are high quality, complex shaped, and accurate features. These are used for maintaining high curvature continuity as well as for creating complex shape features. You can create boundary features by using the **Boundary Boss/Base** tool, which is a powerful tool in the Part modeling environment. To create a boundary feature, you need to create all sections of a boundary feature as direction 1 guides and all curves as direction 2 guides. Figure 8.104 shows two sections as direction 1 guides and two curves as direction 2 guides of a boundary feature. Figure 8.105 shows the resultant boundary feature.

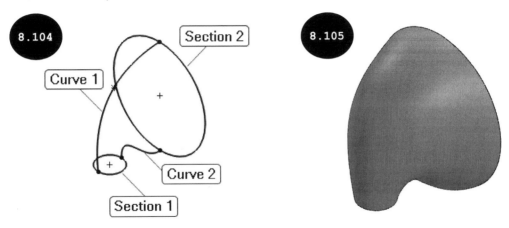

Figure 8.106 shows one section as direction 1 guide and three curves as direction 2 guides. Figure 8.107 shows the resultant boundary feature.

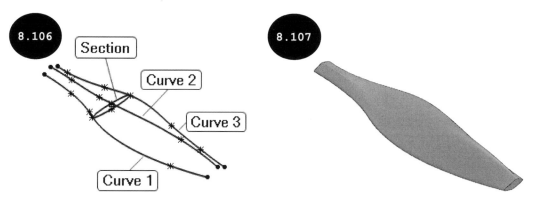

To create a boundary feature, create all sections and curves as direction 1 and direction 2 guides of the boundary feature, respectively, and then click on the Boundary Boss/Base tool in the **Features CommandManager**. The **Boundary PropertyManager** appears, see Figure 8.108. The options in this PropertyManager are discussed next.

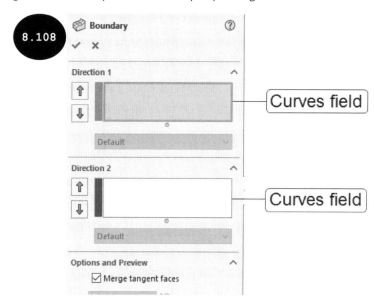

Direction 1

The **Curves** field in the **Direction 1** rollout is used for selecting sections as direction 1 guides. By default, this field is activated. As a result, you are prompted to select sections. Select the sections as direction 1 guides in the graphics area one by one, see Figure 8.109. A preview of the boundary feature appears in the graphics area, see Figure 8.110. Also, the **Tangent Type** drop-down list and the **Draft angle** field get enabled in the **Direction 1** rollout, see Figure 8.111. You can select multiple sections or a single section as direction 1 guide curve. The options in the **Tangent Type** drop-down list are the same as those discussed earlier, while creating the lofted feature.

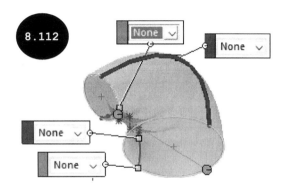

Tip: In the preview of the boundary feature, you can drag the connectors, which are connecting the sections in order to create twist in the boundary feature, as required.

Direction 2

The **Curves** field in the **Direction 2** rollout is used for selecting the curves as direction 2 guides. Click on this field and then select curves in the graphics area. The preview of the boundary feature is modified with respect to the curves selected, see Figure 8.112. You can select multiple curves as direction 2 guide curves to control the shape of the boundary feature. Besides, you can specify the type of tangent continuity by using the options in the **Tangent Type** drop-down list of the **Direction 2** rollout. You can also control the influence of curves by using the options in the **Curve Influence Type** drop-down list of this rollout.

Tip: You can also flip the connectors in order to achieve the required shape. To flip the direction of connectors, select the curve/section whose connectors are to be flipped in the **Curves** field of the **Direction 1** or **Direction 2** rollout. Next, right-click to display a shortcut menu. In this shortcut menu, click on the **Flip Connectors** option. The direction of connectors gets flipped.

Options and Preview

The options in the **Options and Preview** rollout are the same as those discussed earlier, while creating the lofted feature except the **Trim by direction 1** check box, which is discussed next.

Trim by direction 1

The **Trim by direction 1** check box is used for trimming an extended portion of a feature, which is beyond the direction 1 guides. To trim the extended portion of the feature by direction 1 curves, select this check box. Figure 8.113 shows two sections as direction 1 guides and one curve as a direction 2 guide. Figure 8.114 shows a preview of the resultant boundary feature when the **Trim by direction 1** check box is cleared and Figure 8.115 shows a preview of the resultant boundary feature when the **Trim by direction 1** check box is selected.

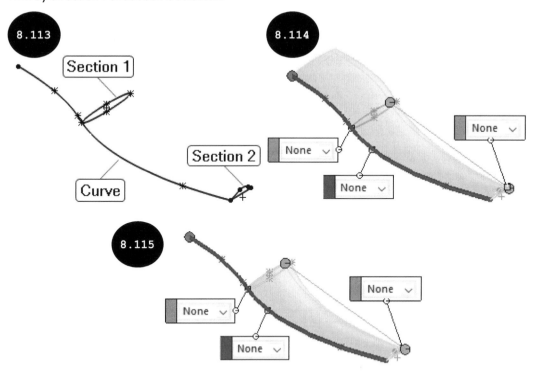

Thin Feature

The **Thin Feature** rollout is used for creating a thin boundary feature, see Figure 8.116. The options in this rollout are the same as those discussed earlier while creating the thin extruded and revolved features.

Curvature Display

The options in the **Curvature Display** rollout are the same as discussed earlier.

Procedure for Creating a Boundary Feature

1. Create profiles and curves of the boundary feature as direction 1 and direction 2 guide curves.
2. Click on the **Boundary Boss/Base** tool. The **Boundary PropertyManager** appears.
3. Select all profiles one by one in the graphics area as the direction 1 guides.
4. Click on the **Curves** field in the **Direction 2** rollout and then select curves as direction 2 guides.
5. Click on the green tick-mark ✓ in the PropertyManager. The boundary feature is created.

Creating a Boundary Cut Feature

The method for creating a boundary cut feature is the same as creating a boundary feature with the only difference that the boundary cut feature is created by removing material from the model. You can create a boundary cut feature by using the **Boundary Cut** tool in the **Features CommandManager**.

Creating Curves

In SOLIDWORKS, you can create different types of curves. Curves are mainly used as the path, guide curves, and so on for creating features such as sweep, lofted, and boundary. The tools for creating different types of curves are grouped together in the **Curves** flyout, see Figure 8.117. The methods for creating different types of curves are discussed next.

Creating Projected Curves

In SOLIDWORKS, you can create projected curves by using the **Project Curve** tool. The **Project Curve** tool is used for creating projected curves by using two methods: Sketch on Faces and Sketch on Sketch. In Sketch on Faces method, the projected curve is created by projecting a sketch on to an existing face of a model, see Figure 8.118. You can select planar faces or curved faces to project a sketch.

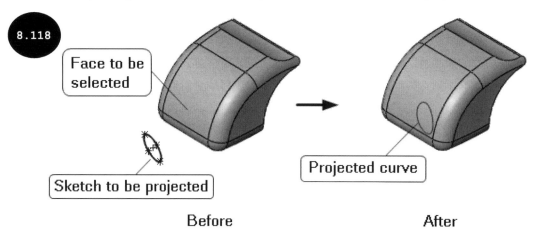

Before   After

In the Sketch on Sketch method, the projected curve is created by projecting one sketch on to the other sketch such that the resultant projected curve represents the intersection of sketches, see Figure 8.119.

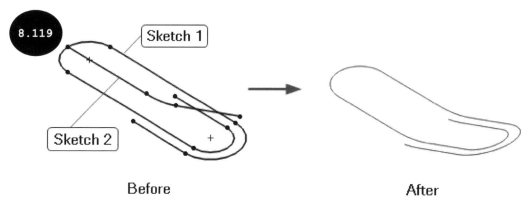

Before   After

Tip: In Figure 8.119, Sketch 1 is created on the Top plane and Sketch 2 is created on the Front plane.

To create a projected curve, invoke the **Curves** flyout by clicking on the arrow at its bottom in the **Features CommandManager**, refer to Figure 8.117. Next, click on the **Project Curve** tool in the flyout. The **Projected Curve PropertyManager** appears, see Figure 8.120. The options in this PropertyManager are discussed next.

Selections

The options in the **Selections** rollout of the PropertyManager are used for selecting the projection method. Also, depending upon the projection method selected, the options of this rollout are used for selecting reference objects to create a projected curve. The options are discussed next.

Sketch on faces

The **Sketch on faces** radio button is used for creating projected curves by projecting a sketch on to an existing face of a model. On selecting this radio button, the **Sketch to Project** and the **Projection Faces** fields are enabled in the rollout, see Figure 8.120. By default, the **Sketch to Project** field is activated. As a result, you can select a sketch to be projected. In SOLIDWORKS, you can select a sketch that has multiple closed or open contours. Additionally, you can also select a 3D sketch. Click on the sketch to be projected in the graphics area, see Figure 8.121. The name of the sketch selected appears in the **Sketch to Project** field. Also, the **Projection Faces** field gets activated and you are prompted to select projection faces. Click on one or more faces in the graphics area, see Figure 8.121. The preview of the projected curve appears on the selected faces in the graphics area, see Figure 8.122. Make sure that the direction of projection is toward the selected projection face. You can reverse the direction of projection by using the **Reverse projection** check box. In SOLIDWORKS, you can also project the sketch on both sides of the sketching plane by selecting the **Bi-directional** check box in the PropertyManager, see Figure 8.123. You can also define the direction of projection by activating the **Direction of Projection** field and selecting a plane, an edge, a sketch entity, or a face as the direction of the projected curve. Next, click on the green tick-mark [✓] in the PropertyManager. The projected curve is created.

By default, the direction of projection is normal to the sketching plane, refer to Figures 8.122 and 8.123. In SOLIDWORKS, you can also define the direction of projection by selecting an axis, a linear sketch entity, a linear edge, a plane, or a planar face. For doing so, click on the **Direction of Projection** field in the PropertyManager and then select an entity as the direction of projection in the graphics area.

Sketch on sketch

The **Sketch on sketch** radio button is used for projecting one sketch onto another sketch such that the resultant projected curve represents the intersection of sketches. On selecting this radio button, the **Sketches to Project** field is enabled in the rollout. By default, this field is activated. As a result, you can select sketches to be projected. Select the sketches to be projected in the graphics area one by one by clicking the left mouse button, see Figure 8.124. A preview of the projected curve appears in the graphics area. Next, click on the green tick-mark ✓ in the PropertyManager. The projected curve is created, see Figure 8.125.

Tip: In Figure 8.124, Sketch 1 is created on the Top plane and Sketch 2 is created on the Front plane.

Creating Helical and Spiral Curves

You can create helical and spiral curves by using the **Helix and Spiral** tool of the **Curves** flyout. You can use helical and spiral curves as paths, guide curves, and so on, for creating sweep and lofted features. Figure 8.126 shows a helical curve and a circular profile, as well as the resultant sweep feature that is created by using them. To create a helical curve or a spiral curve in SOLIDWORKS, you first need to create a circle which defines the start diameter of the helical or the spiral curve.

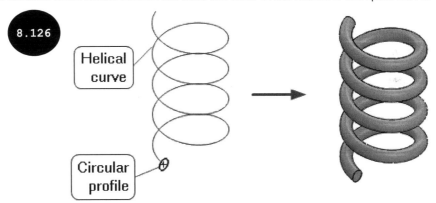

To create a helical or a spiral curve, create a circle and then invoke the **Curves** flyout. Next, click on the **Helix and Spiral** tool. The **Helix/Spiral PropertyManager** appears, see Figure 8.127. Also, you are prompted to select a circle or a sketching plane for creating a circle. Click on the circle in the graphics area that defines the start diameter of the curve. The **Helix/Spiral PropertyManager** gets modified, see Figure 8.128. Also, the preview of the curve appears in the graphics area with default parameters, see Figure 8.129.

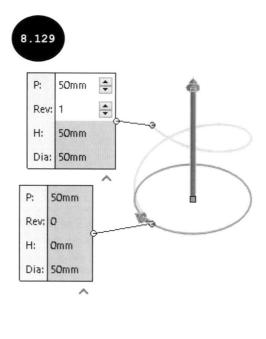

Note: You can select a circle before or after invoking the **Helix and Spiral** tool. If the circle is selected before invoking the tool, then the modified **Helix/Spiral PropertyManager** and the preview of the curve appear directly in the graphics area.

The options in the **Helix/Spiral PropertyManager** are used for creating constant pitch helical curves, variable pitch helical curves, and spiral curves. The options are discussed next.

Defined By

The **Defined By** rollout is used for defining the type of curve (helical or spiral) to be created and the method to be adopted for creating it. The options in this rollout are available in a drop-down list, see Figure 8.130. The options are discussed next.

Pitch and Revolution

The **Pitch and Revolution** option is used for creating a helical curve by defining its pitch and number of revolutions. On selecting this option, the options for creating a helical curve by defining its pitch and revolutions get enabled in the **Parameters** rollout of the PropertyManager.

Height and Revolution

The **Height and Revolution** option is used for creating a helical curve by defining its total height and number of revolutions. On selecting this option, the options for creating a helical curve by defining its height and revolutions are enabled in the **Parameters** rollout of the PropertyManager.

Height and Pitch

The **Height and Pitch** option is used for creating a helical curve by defining its total height and pitch. On selecting this option, the options for creating a helical curve by defining its height and pitch are enabled in the **Parameters** rollout of the PropertyManager.

Spiral

The **Spiral** option is used for creating a spiral curve by defining its pitch and number of revolutions. On selecting this option, the options for creating a spiral curve by defining its pitch and revolutions are enabled in the **Parameters** rollout. Figure 8.131 shows a spiral curve.

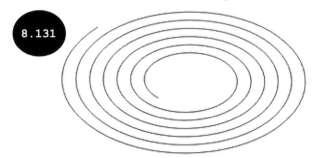

8.131

Parameters

The **Parameters** rollout of the PropertyManager is used for specifying the parameters for creating a curve. The availability of most of the options in this rollout depends upon the option selected in the **Defined By** rollout. The options of this rollout are discussed next.

Constant pitch

The **Constant pitch** radio button is used for creating a helical curve with constant pitch throughout the helix height, see Figure 8.132.

8.132

Pitch, Revolutions, Height, and Start angle

The **Pitch, Revolutions, Height**, and **Start angle** fields are used for specifying pitch, revolutions, height, and start angle for the curve, respectively.

Reverse direction

The **Reverse direction** check box is used for reversing the direction of curve creation.

Clockwise and Counterclockwise

The **Clockwise** and **Counterclockwise** radio buttons are used for specifying the direction of revolution as clockwise or counterclockwise, respectively.

Variable pitch

The **Variable pitch** radio button is used for creating a helical curve with variable pitch and variable diameter, see Figures 8.133 and 8.134. On selecting this radio button, the **Region parameters** table appears in the rollout, see Figure 8.135. In the **Region parameters** table, you can enter a variable pitch and diameter in the respective fields for creating a helical curve, see Figure 8.135. Note that the availability of options in this table depends upon the option selected in the **Defined By** rollout of the PropertyManager.

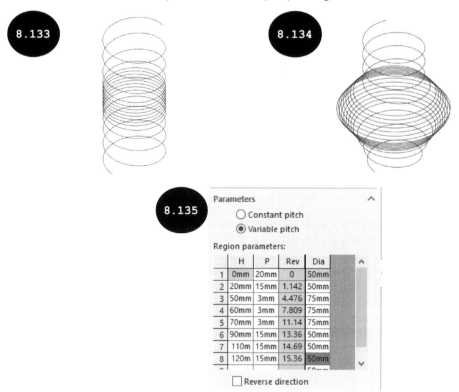

8.133

8.134

8.135

Parameters

○ Constant pitch
◉ Variable pitch

Region parameters:

	H	P	Rev	Dia
1	0mm	20mm	0	50mm
2	20mm	15mm	1.142	50mm
3	50mm	3mm	4.476	75mm
4	60mm	3mm	7.809	75mm
5	70mm	3mm	11.14	75mm
6	90mm	15mm	13.36	50mm
7	110m	15mm	14.69	50mm
8	120m	15mm	15.36	50mm

☐ Reverse direction

Note: If the **Height and Pitch** option is selected in the **Defined By** rollout then in the **Region parameters** table, you can enter a variable pitch at different heights as well as variable diameter at different heights, see Figure 8.135. If you select the **Height and Revolution** option, then the **Region parameters** table allows you to specify revolutions and variable diameter at different height. Also, a variable pitch of the curve will automatically be calculated based on the number of revolutions at different heights. To enter values in the table, click on the respective fields of the table.

Taper Helix

The **Taper Helix** rollout of the PropertyManager is used for creating a tapered helical curve, see Figure 8.136. This rollout is available when the **Constant pitch** radio button is selected in the **Parameters** rollout. By default, the options of the **Taper Helix** rollout are not activated. To activate the options of this rollout, select the check box in its title bar. The **Taper Angle** field of this rollout is used for specifying the taper angle of the helical curve. Note that if the **Taper outward** check box is cleared in this rollout, then the helical

8.136

curve tapers inward to the sketch. If you select the **Taper outward** check box, then the helical curve tapers outward to the sketch.

Creating Curves by Specifying XYZ Points

You can create a curve by specifying coordinates (X, Y, Z), which define the shape of the curve. For doing so, invoke the **Curves** flyout and then click on the **Curve Through XYZ Points** tool. The **Curve File** dialog box appears, see Figure 8.137.

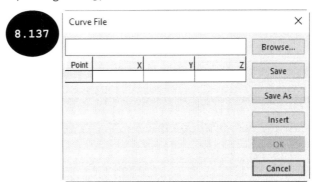

8.137

In the **Curve File** dialog box, you can specify the coordinates (X, Y, Z) of multiple points with respect to the origin (0, 0, 0) for creating a curve. Besides specifying coordinates of points, you can import .sldcrv or .txt (notepad) files containing the coordinates of a curve.

To specify coordinates in the dialog box, double-click on the field corresponding to the first row and the **X** column to activate it. Once this field has been activated, you can enter the X coordinate of the first point with respect to the origin. Similarly, you can activate the **Y** and **Z** fields and then enter the Y and Z coordinates of the first point. Note that, by default, only one row is available in this dialog box. However, the moment you activate a field of the first row, the second or next row gets added automatically in the dialog box. Specify the coordinates of the second point in the second row of the dialog box. Similarly, you can specify the coordinates of the other points in the dialog box. Note that as you specify the coordinate in the dialog box, a preview of the curve appears in the graphics area. Figure 8.138 shows the **Curve File** dialog box with coordinates of multiple points specified and Figure 8.139 shows the resultant curve.

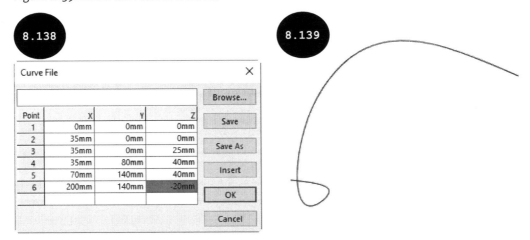

8.138   8.139

You can also save all coordinates of the points specified in the dialog box as *.sldcrv* file in the local drive of your computer for further use. To save the coordinates of the points as *.sldcrv* file, click on the **Save** button in the dialog box. The **Save As** dialog box appears. In this dialog box, browse to the location where you want to save the file and then specify a name for the file in the **File name** edit box. Next, click on the **Save** button in the **Save As** dialog box. The file is saved as *.sldcrv* file. Once you have specified the coordinates of the points in the dialog box, click on the **OK** button. The curve is created.

If you have *.sldcrv* or *.txt* (notepad) file containing information about the coordinates of the points for creating a curve, click on the **Browse** button in the **Curve File** dialog box. The **Open** dialog box appears. In this dialog box, browse to the location where the *.sldcrv* or *.txt* (notepad) file is saved. Note that by default, the **Curves (*.sldcrv)** option is selected in the **File Type** drop-down list of the dialog box. As a result, you can only import *.sldcrv* file. To import a *.txt* (notepad) file, you need to select the **Text Files (*.txt)** option in the **File Type** drop-down list. After selecting the required file type in the drop-down list, select the file and then click on the **Open** button. The coordinate points of the selected file get filled in the dialog box. Also, a preview of the curve appears in the graphics area.

Tip: In *.txt* (notepad) file, the coordinates of all points should be written in separate lines. Also, the coordinates (X, Y, Z) of a point should be separated by a comma and a space (X, Y, Z).

Creating Curves by Selecting Reference Points

In SOLIDWORKS, you can create 3D curves by selecting reference points in the graphics area. The reference points can be located in the same or different planes. You can also select vertices of the model or sketch points as reference points for creating a curve. To create a curve by selecting reference points, invoke the **Curves** flyout and then click on the **Curve Through Reference Points** tool. The **Curve Through Reference Points PropertyManager** appears, see Figure 8.140. Next, select sketch points or vertices in the graphics area one by one by clicking the left mouse button. A preview of the respective curve appears, see Figure 8.141. Also, the name of the selected points/vertices get listed in the **Thought Points** field of the PropertyManager.

8.140

8.141

Reference curve

Sketch points

Note: On selecting the **Closed curve** check box in the PropertyManager, a closed curve is created by connecting the specified start point and end point of the curve.

Procedure for Creating a Curve by Selecting Reference Points

1. Click on the **Curve Through XYZ Points** tool in the **Curves** flyout.
2. Select reference points (sketch points and vertices) one by one from the graphics area.
3. Click on the green tick-mark ☑ in the PropertyManager. The curve is created.

Creating a Composite Curve

A composite curve is created by joining two or more than two curves together. You can join multiple curves or sketches together and create a single composite curve by using the **Composite Curve** tool of the **Curves** flyout.

To create a composite curve, click on the **Composite Curve** tool in the **Curves** flyout. The **Composite Curve PropertyManager** appears, see Figure 8.142. Next, select curves one by one in the graphics area by clicking the left mouse button and then click on the green tick-mark ☑ in the PropertyManager. A composite curve is created. You can select sketch entities, curves, and edges for creating a composite curve. Note that the curves to be joined must be connected end to end and have a pierce relation with each other. Figure 8.143 shows individual curves (five curves) and Figure 8.144 shows the resultant composite curve. Figure 8.145 shows a sweep feature created by sweeping a profile (circle) along the composite curve shown in Figure 8.144.

Procedure for Creating a Composite Curve

1. Invoke the **Curves** flyout.
2. Click on the **Composite Curve** tool in the **Curves** flyout. The **Composite Curve PropertyManager** appears.
3. Select curves one by one in the graphics area by clicking the left mouse button.
4. Click on the green tick-mark ✔ in the PropertyManager. The composite curve is created.

Note: In SOLIDWORKS, when you create a feature by using reference curves such as projected curves, composite curves, helical curves, and spiral curves; the used reference curves are not absorbed by the feature and appear separately in the FeatureManager Design Tree so that they can be used further for creating other features.

Splitting Faces of a Model

You can split faces of a model by creating split lines. In SOLIDWORKS, you can create split lines by using the **Split Line** tool. For doing so, click on the **Split Line** tool in the **Curves** flyout. The **Split Line PropertyManager** appears, see Figure 8.146. The options in this PropertyManager are discussed next.

Type of Split

The options in the **Type of Split** rollout are used for selecting the type of split method to be used for splitting the faces of a model. The options are discussed next.

Projection

The **Projection** radio button is used for splitting faces by projecting a sketch. Figure 8.147 shows a sketch to be projected and a face of a model to be split. Figure 8.148 shows the resultant model after splitting the face by creating split lines. Note that split lines divide a face into different faces with respect to the projected sketch. After splitting a face into multiple faces, you can apply different textures or appearances to them.

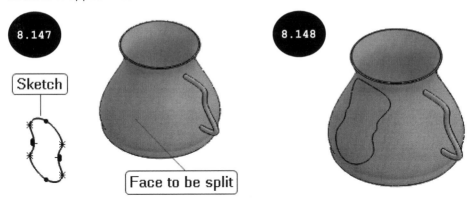

On selecting the **Projection** radio button, the **Sketch to Project** and **Faces to Split** fields are enabled in the **Selections** rollout of the PropertyManager, see Figure 8.149. By default, the **Sketch to Project** field is activated. As a result, you can select the sketch to be projected. After selecting the sketch to be projected, the **Faces to Split** field gets activated in the PropertyManager. Now, select the faces to be split. You can select curve faces or planar faces as the faces to be split. To project the split line in one direction, select the **Single direction** check box and to reverse the direction of projection, click on the **Reverse direction** check box in the PropertyManager. Next, click on the green tick-mark ✓ in the PropertyManager. The selected faces are split.

Intersection

The **Intersection** radio button is used for splitting faces by creating split lines at the intersection of two objects. The objects can be solid bodies, surfaces, faces, or in combination with a plane. Figure 8.150 shows the face of a model and a plane. Figure 8.151 shows the resultant model after splitting the face at the intersection with the plane.

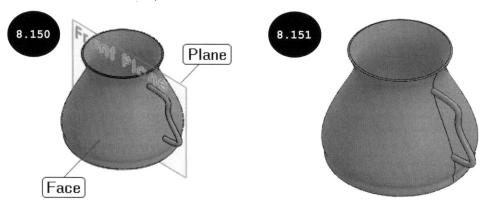

On selecting the **Intersection** radio button, the **Splitting Bodies/Faces/Planes** and **Faces/Bodies to Split** fields are enabled in the **Selections** rollout of the PropertyManager. By default, the **Splitting Bodies/Faces/Planes** field is activated. As a result, you can select bodies, faces, or planes as the splitting objects, see Figure 8.152. After selecting the splitting objects, click on the **Faces/Bodies to Split** field and then select faces or bodies to be split, see Figure 8.152. The preview of split lines appears in the graphics area, see Figure 8.153. Next, click on the green tick-mark ☑ in the PropertyManager. The selected face gets split, see Figure 8.154. Note that in Figure 8.154, the visibility of the splitting object is turned off.

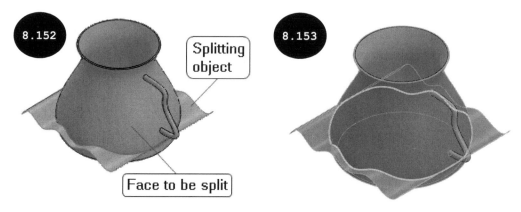

Note: The splitting object shown in Figure 8.152 is an extruded surface. An extruded surface is created by using the **Extruded Surface** tool in the **Surfaces CommandManager**. The options for creating an extruded surface are same as those discussed earlier, while creating an extruded solid feature with the only difference that the extruded surface has zero thickness.

Silhouette

The **Silhouette** radio button is used for splitting faces at the intersection between a direction of projection and a curved face. Figure 8.155 shows a direction of projection and a curved face to be split. Figure 8.156 shows the split line created at the intersection of projection direction and the curve face selected.

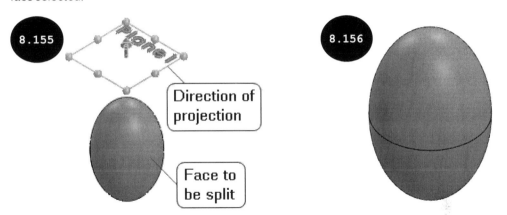

On selecting the **Silhouette** radio button, the **Direction of Pull** and **Faces to Split** fields are enabled in the **Selections** rollout of the PropertyManager. By default, the **Direction of Pull** field is activated. As a result, you can select a plane or a planar face as the direction of projection or pull. After selecting a plane or a planar face as the direction of projection, see Figure 8.155, the **Faces to Split** field gets activated. Now, you can select the curved faces to be split. Note that in case of creating the silhouette split line, you can only select curved faces as the faces to be split. After selecting the curved faces, specify the draft angle value in the **Angle** field of the PropertyManager. Next, click on the green tick-mark ✓ in the PropertyManager. The split line is created.

Figure 8.156 shows the split line created with the draft angle value set to 0 degree in the **Angle** field. Figure 8.157 shows the split line created with the draft angle value set to 40 degrees.

Creating 3D Sketches

In SOLIDWORKS, in addition to creating 2D sketches and 3D curves, you can also create 3D sketches in the 3D Sketching environment. Most of the time, 3D sketches are used as a 3D path and a guide curve for creating sweep, lofted, and boundary features. To create 3D sketches, you need to invoke the 3D Sketching environment of SOLIDWORKS. For doing so, click on the arrow at the bottom of the **Sketch** tool in the **Sketch CommandManager**, see Figure 8.158. The **Sketch** flyout appears. In this flyout, click on the **3D Sketch** tool, see Figure 8.158. The 3D Sketching environment is invoked, see Figure 8.159. Now, you can create 3D sketches by using the tools of the **Sketch CommandManager**. Note that in the 3D Sketching environment, some of the tools such as **Polygon**, **Ellipse**, **Offset Entities**, and **Move Entities** are not enabled. This is because these tools cannot be used for creating 3D sketches. Some of the tools of the 3D Sketching environment are discussed next.

Using the Line Tool in the 3D Sketching Environment

1.   Invoke the 3D Sketching environment by clicking on the **3D Sketch** tool in the **Sketch** flyout that appears on clicking the arrow at the bottom of the **Sketch** tool in the **Sketch CommandManager**, refer to Figure 8.158.

2.   Click on the **Line** tool in the **Sketch CommandManager**. The cursor changes to line cursor with the display of **XY** at its bottom, see Figure 8.160. The display of XY indicates that the XY plane (Front plane) is activated as the current sketching plane. You can press the **TAB** key to switch from one sketching plane to another for creating a 3D sketch.

3. Press the **TAB** key until the required sketching plane is activated.
4. Specify the start point of the line by clicking the left mouse button in the graphics area.
5. Move the cursor to a distance from the start point. A rubber band line appears whose one end is fixed at the specified start point and the other end is attached to the cursor, see Figure 8.161.

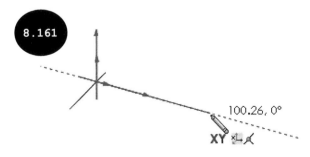

Tip: You can toggle the sketching plane even after specifying the start point of the line by using the **TAB** key.

---

6. Move the cursor to the required location in the drawing area and then click to specify the endpoint of the first line when the length of the line appears close to the required one, near the cursor. Next, move the cursor to a distance. A preview of the rubber band line appears.
7. Press the **TAB** key to switch the sketching plane, if required.
8. Move the cursor to the required location and then click to specify the endpoint of the next line, see Figure 8.162. In Figure 8.162, the sketching plane has been changed to YZ.
9. Similarly, create other line entities of the 3D sketch in different sketching planes, as required, see Figure 8.163.

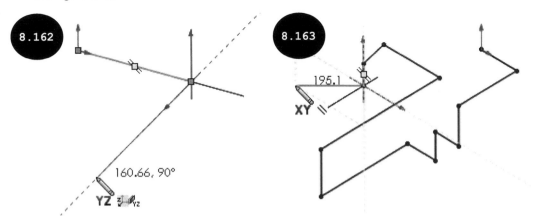

10. After creating all sketch entities of the 3D sketch, right-click in the graphics area, and then click on the **Select** option in the shortcut menu that appears to exit the **Line** tool.

Note: The procedure for applying dimensions to a 3D sketch in the 3D Sketching environment is same as applying dimensions to a 2D sketch by using the dimension tools.

11.   Click on the 3D **Sketch** tool in the **Sketch CommandManager** to exit the 3D Sketching environment. Alternatively, click on the **Exit Sketch** icon in the Confirmation corner.

Figure 8.164 shows a 3D Sketch and Figure 8.165 shows a sweep feature created by sweeping a circular profile along the 3D sketch.

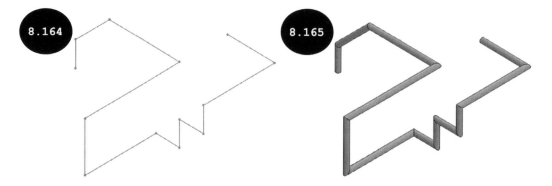

Using the Spline Tool in the 3D Sketching Environment

1.   Invoke the 3D Sketching environment by clicking on the 3D **Sketch** tool in the **Sketch** flyout that appears on clicking the arrow at the bottom of the **Sketch** tool in the **Sketch CommandManager**.
2.   Press CTRL + 7 to change the current orientation of the sketch to isometric.
3.   Click on the **Spline** tool in the **Sketch CommandManager**. The display of cursor changes such that **XY** appears at its bottom, see Figure 8.166. The display of XY indicates that the XY plane (Front plane) is activated as the current sketching plane. You can press the **TAB** key to switch from one sketching plane to another for creating a 3D sketch.

4.   Press the **TAB** key until the required sketching plane has been activated and its name appears below the cursor.
5.   Click to specify the first control point of the spline in the graphics area. Next, move the cursor to a distance from the specified control point. A rubber band spline appears whose one end is fixed at the first control point and the other end is attached to the cursor, see Figure 8.167.
6.   Press the **TAB** key to switch the sketching plane, as required.
7.   Move the cursor to the required location and then click to specify the second control point of the spline, see Figure 8.168. Next, move the cursor to a distance. The preview of another rubber band spline appears such that it passes through the specified control points.

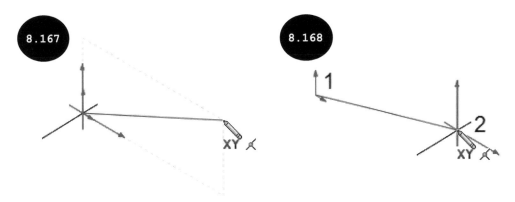

Tip: In Figure 8.168, the second control point of the spline is specified on XY plane.

8. Press the **TAB** key to switch the sketching plane, if required. Next, move the cursor to the required location and then click to specify the third control point of the spline, see Figure 8.169.

Tip: In Figure 8.169, the third control point of the spline is specified on XY plane.

9. Press the **TAB** key to switch the sketching plane, as required. Next, move the cursor to the required location and then click to specify the fourth control point of the spline, see Figure 8.170. In Figure 8.170, the fourth control point of the spline is specified on YZ plane.

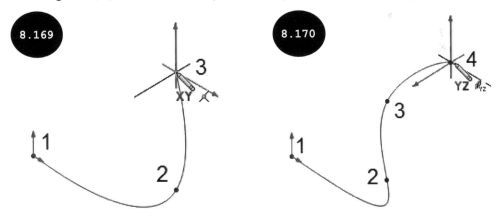

10. Similarly, specify remaining control points of the spline on different planes, as required. Once you have specified all control points of the spline, press the ESC key to exit the **Spline** tool. Figure 8.171 shows a spline created by specifying control points on different planes.

Tip: After creating the 3D spline, you can further control the shape of the spline by dragging its control points, as discussed while creating 2D spline. Once the 3D spline is created and the required modification has been made, exit the 3D Sketching environment. Figure 8.172 shows a 3D spline and Figure 8.173 shows the resultant sweep feature created by sweeping a rectangular profile along the 3D spline.

The use of the rectangle, arc, circle, point, and centerline tools in the 3D sketching environment is the same as discussed earlier while creating 2D sketches.

Tutorial 1

Create a model, as shown in Figure 8.174. The different views and dimensions are given in the same figure. All dimensions are in mm.

Section 1: Starting SOLIDWORKS

1. Start SOLIDWORKS by double-clicking on the SOLIDWORKS icon on your desktop. The startup user interface of SOLIDWORKS appears along with the **Welcome** dialog box.

> **Note:** If SOLIDWORKS is already open and the **Welcome** dialog box does not appear on the screen, then you can invoke the same by clicking on the **Welcome to SOLIDWORKS** tool 🏠 in the **Standard** toolbar or by pressing the CTRL + F2 keys.

Section 2: Invoking the Part Modeling Environment

1. Click on the **Part** button in the **Welcome** dialog box. The Part modeling environment is invoked.

> **Tip:** You can also invoke the Part modeling environment by using the **New SOLIDWORKS Document** dialog box. For doing so, click on the **New** tool in the **Standard** toolbar. The **New SOLIDWORKS Document** dialog box appears. In this dialog box, make sure that the **Part** button is selected and then click on the **OK** button.

Once the Part modeling environment has been invoked, you can set the unit system and create the base/first feature of the model.

Section 3: Specifying Unit Settings

1. Move the cursor toward the lower right corner of the screen over the Status Bar and then click on the **Unit System** area in the Status Bar. The **Unit System** flyout appears, see Figure 8.175.

2. Make sure that the **MMGS (millimeter, gram, second)** option is tick-marked in this flyout.

Section 4: Creating the Base/First Feature - Sweep Feature

1. Invoke the Sketching environment by selecting the Front plane as the sketching plane and then create a path of the sweep feature and apply dimensions, see Figure 8.176.

2. Exit the Sketching environment by clicking on the **Exit Sketch** tool in the **Sketch CommandManager**. Next, click anywhere in the graphics area to exit the current selection.

After creating the path of the sweep feature, you need to create a sweep feature having a circular profile.

3. Click on the **Swept Boss/Base** tool in the **Features CommandManager**. The **Sweep PropertyManager** appears.

4. Click on the **Circular Profile** radio button in the **Profile and Path** rollout of the PropertyManager.

5. Click on the path of the sweep feature in the graphics area. The preview of the sweep feature appears with the default diameter of a circular profile.

6. Enter **60** in the **Diameter** field of the **Profile and Path** rollout and then press ENTER. The preview of the sweep feature appears, see Figure 8.177. Change the orientation of the model to isometric.

7. Expand the **Thin Feature** rollout of the PropertyManager by selecting the check box in its title bar, see Figure 8.178.

8. Enter **8** in the **Thickness** field of the **Thin Feature** rollout.

9. Click on the **Reverse Direction** button in the **Thin Feature** rollout to reverse the direction of material addition such that the material is added inward to the profile, see Figure 8.179.

10. Click on the green tick-mark in the PropertyManager. The thin sweep feature is created, see Figure 8.180.

Section 5: Creating Second Feature - Extruded Feature

1. Rotate the model such that the bottom face of the base feature (sweep) can be viewed, see Figure 8.181. To rotate a model, right-click in the graphics area and then click on the **Rotate View** option in the shortcut menu that appears. Next, press and hold the left mouse button and

then drag the cursor. Alternatively, press and hold the middle mouse button and then drag the cursor in the graphics area.

2. Invoke the Sketching environment by selecting the bottom face of the base feature (sweep) as the sketching plane.

3. Press CTRL + 8 to change the orientation of the model as normal to the viewing direction.

4. Create the sketch of the second feature, see Figure 8.182. After creating the sketch, do not exit the Sketching environment.

Tip: The sketch created in Figure 8.182 is symmetric about the vertical and horizontal centerlines. Also, the arcs of the sketch are of same radius and are created by using the **Fillet** tool.

5. Click on the **Features** tab in the CommandManager to display the tools of the **Features** CommandManager.

6. Click on the **Extruded Boss/Base** tool in the **Features CommandManager**. The **Boss-Extrude PropertyManager** and the preview of the extruded feature appear. Next, change the orientation of the model to isometric, see Figure 8.183.

7. Enter **12** in the **Distance** field of the **Direction 1** rollout in the PropertyManager.

8. Click on the green tick-mark ☑ in the PropertyManager. The extruded feature is created, see Figure 8.184.

Section 6: Creating the Third Feature - Extruded Cut Feature

1. Invoke the Sketching environment by selecting the top planar face of the second feature as the sketching plane.

2. Press CTRL + 8 to change the orientation of the model as normal to the viewing direction.

3. Create the sketch (four circles of diameter 10 mm) of the third feature, see Figure 8.185.

Tip: The sketch of the third feature shown in Figure 8.185 has four circles of the same diameter; therefore, an equal relation is applied among all the circles. Also, a concentric relation is applied between the center point of circles and the respective semi-circular edges of the second feature. You can also create one circle and then pattern it circularly to create remaining circles.

4. Click on the **Features** tab in the CommandManager and then click on the **Extruded Cut** tool. The **Cut-Extrude PropertyManager** and the preview of the cut feature appear. Next, change the orientation of the model to isometric, see Figure 8.186.

5. Invoke the **End Condition** drop-down list in the **Direction 1** rollout of the PropertyManager and then select the **Through All** option.

6. Click on the green tick-mark ✅ in the PropertyManager. The extruded cut feature is created, see Figure 8.187.

Section 7: Creating the Fourth Feature - Extruded Feature

1. Invoke the Sketching environment by selecting the top planar face of the sweep feature (first feature) as the sketching plane, see Figure 8.188.

2. Press CTRL + 8 to change the orientation of the model as normal to the viewing direction.

3. Create the sketch (two circles of diameter 90 mm and 44 mm) of the fourth feature, see Figure 8.189.

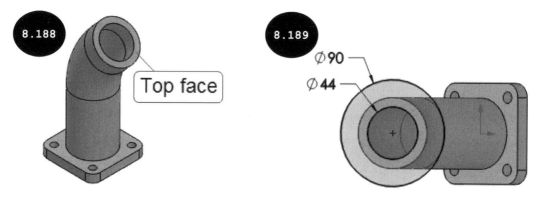

Tip: The sketch of the fourth feature shown in Figure 8.189 has two circles, which are concentric to the top circular edge of the sweep feature. You need to take the reference of the top circular edges of the sweep feature for specifying the center point of the circles.

4. Click on the **Features** tab in the CommandManager and then click on the **Extruded Boss/Base** tool. The **Boss-Extrude PropertyManager** and the preview of the extruded feature appear. Next, change the orientation of the model to isometric, see Figure 8.190.

5. Enter **12** in the **Distance** field of the **Direction 1** rollout in the PropertyManager.

6. Click on the green tick-mark ✓ in the PropertyManager. The extruded feature is created, see Figure 8.191.

Section 8: Creating the Fifth Feature - Extruded Cut Feature

1. Invoke the Sketching environment by selecting the top planar face of the fourth feature as the sketching plane.

2. Press CTRL + 8 to change the orientation of the model as normal to the viewing direction.

3. Create a circle of diameter 10 mm, see Figure 8.192. Next, create a circular pattern of it to create the remaining circles of the same diameter by using the **Circular Sketch Pattern** tool, see Figure 8.193. Note that you need to change the position of the center point of the pattern to the center point of the circular edge of the fourth feature by dragging the dot that appears at the tip of the arrow in the pattern preview.

Tip: In Figure 8.192, the center point of the circle has coincident relation with the vertical centerline. Also, the start point of the vertical centerline is coincident with the center point of the circular edge of the fourth feature.

While specifying the start point of the vertical centerline shown in Figure 8.192, move the cursor over the outer circular edge of the fourth feature. The center point of the circular edge gets highlighted. Next, move the cursor to the highlighted center point and then click to specify the start point of the vertical centerline when the cursor snaps to it.

4.   Click on the **Extruded Cut** tool in the **Features CommandManager**. The **Cut-Extrude** **PropertyManager** and the preview of the extruded cut feature appear. Next, change the orientation of the model to isometric, see Figure 8.194. Extruded Cut

5.   Invoke the **End Condition** drop-down list in the **Direction 1** rollout of the PropertyManager and then click on the **Up to Next** option.

6.   Click on the green tick-mark ✓ in the PropertyManager. The extruded cut feature is created, see Figure 8.195.

Section 9: Saving the Model

1.   Click on the **Save** tool of the **Standard** toolbar. The **Save As** window appears.

2.   Browse to the SOLIDWORKS folder and then create a folder with the name **Chapter 8** in the SOLIDWORKS folder.

3.   Enter **Tutorial 1** in the **File name** field of the dialog box as the name of the file and then click on the **Save** button. The model is saved with the name Tutorial 1 in the Chapter 8 folder.

Tutorial 2

Create a model, as shown in Figure 8.196. The different views and dimensions are given in the same figure. All dimensions are in mm.

Section 1: Invoking the Part Modeling Environment

1. Start SOLIDWORKS and then invoke the Part modeling environment.

   Once the Part modeling environment has been invoked, you can set the unit system and create the base/first feature of the model.

Section 2: Specifying Unit Settings

1. Make sure that the **MMGS (millimeter, gram, second)** unit system is selected as the current unit system for the document, see Figure 8.197.

Section 3: Creating the Base/First Feature - Sweep Feature

1. Invoke the Sketching environment by selecting the Right plane as the sketching plane and then create the path of the sweep feature, see Figure 8.198.

2. Exit the Sketching environment by clicking on the **Exit Sketch** tool in the **Sketch** CommandManager.

   After creating the path of the sweep feature, you need to create the profile for the sweep feature.

3. Invoke the Sketching environment by selecting the Front plane as the sketching plane and then press CTRL + 8 to change the orientation as normal to the viewing direction.

4. Create the sketch of the profile (two circles of diameter 45 mm and 35 mm), see Figure 8.199.

5. Exit the Sketching environment by clicking on the **Exit Sketch** tool in the **Sketch** CommandManager.

6. Change the orientation of the model to isometric, see Figure 8.200.

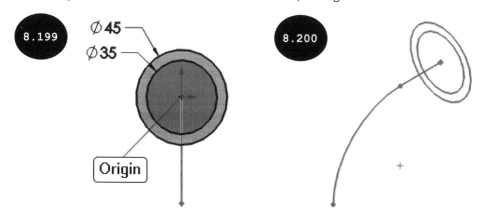

After creating the path and the profile, you need to create the sweep feature.

7. Click on the **Swept Boss/Base** tool. The **Sweep PropertyManager** appears.

8. Make sure that the **Sketch Profile** radio button is selected in the **Profile and Path** rollout of the PropertyManager.

9. Click on the profile (two circles) of the sweep feature in the graphics area. The **Path** field in the **Sweep PropertyManager** gets activated.

10. Click on the path of the sweep feature in the graphics area. The preview of the sweep feature appears in the graphics area, see Figure 8.201.

Tip: Instead of creating a sketch of the profile (two circles) for creating the sweep feature, you can also select the **Circular Profile** radio button in the **Sweep PropertyManager** and then specify the diameter of circular profile in the **Diameter** field of the PropertyManager. This is because the profile of the sweep feature is a circular profile.

---

11. Click on the green tick-mark ✓ in the PropertyManager. The sweep feature is created, see Figure 8.202.

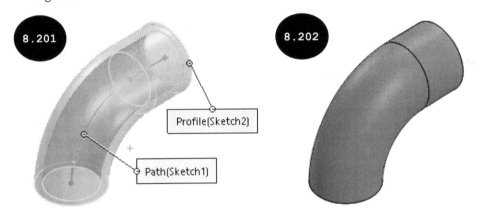

Section 4: Creating the Second Feature - Sweep Feature

To create the second feature of the model, you first need to create a reference plane at an offset distance of 80 mm from the Front plane.

1. Invoke the **Reference Geometry** flyout in the **Features CommandManager**, see Figure 8.203.

2. Click on the **Plane** tool in the flyout. The **Plane PropertyManager** appears.

3. Expand the FeatureManager Design Tree, which is now available on the top left corner of the graphics area by clicking on the arrow in front of it and then click on the **Front Plane** as the first reference. The preview of an offset reference plane appears in the graphics area.

4. Enter **80** in the **Distance** field of the **First Reference** rollout. Make sure that the direction of the plane creation is same as shown in the Figure 8.204.

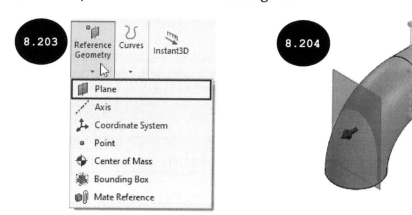

5. Click on the green tick-mark ✓ in the PropertyManager. The offset reference plane is created.

6. Invoke the Sketching environment by selecting the newly created reference plane as the sketching plane. Next, press CTRL + 8 to change the orientation of the model as normal to the viewing direction.

7. Create the path of the second sweep feature, see Figure 8.205. Note that in this figure, an equal relation has been applied between both the arcs of the sketch having the same radius.

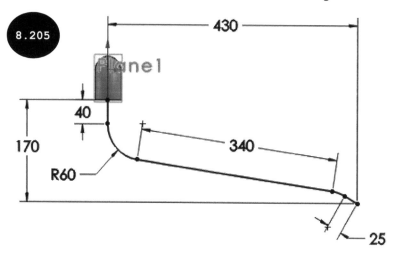

8. Exit the Sketching environment by clicking on the **Exit Sketch** tool in the **Sketch CommandManager**. Next, press CTRL + 7 to change the orientation to isometric.

    After creating the path of the sweep feature, you need to create the sweep feature.

9. Click on the **Swept Boss/Base** tool in the **Features CommandManager**. The **Sweep PropertyManager** appears.

10. Make sure that the **Sketch Profile** radio button is selected in the **Profile and Path** rollout.

11. Rotate the model such that the bottom face of the first feature (sweep) can be viewed, see Figure 8.206. To rotate the model, right-click in the graphics area and then click on the **Rotate View** tool in the shortcut menu that appears. Next, press and hold the left mouse button and then drag the cursor. Once the required orientation of the model has been achieved, press the ESC key to exit the **Rotate View** tool.

12. Select the bottom face of the first feature (sweep) as the profile of the second sweep feature, see Figure 8.206.

13. Click on the path of the sweep feature in the graphics area. The preview of the sweep feature appears, see Figure 8.207. Next, press CTRL + 7 to change the orientation of the model to isometric.

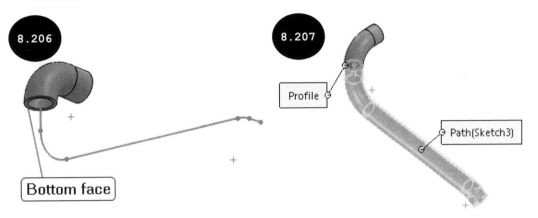

14. Click on the green tick-mark ✓ in the PropertyManager. The sweep feature is created, see Figure 8.208. Next, hide the reference plane.

Section 5: Creating the Third Feature - Extruded Feature

To create the third feature of the model, you first need to create a reference plane at an offset distance of 50 mm from the Top plane.

1. Invoke the **Reference Geometry** flyout in the **Features CommandManager** and then click on the **Plane** tool to invoke the **Plane PropertyManager**.

2. Expand the FeatureManager Design Tree, which is now available on the top left corner of the graphics area, by clicking on the arrow in front of it.

3. Click on the **Top Plane** in the FeatureManager Design Tree as the first reference. The preview of an offset reference plane appears in the graphics area.

4. Enter **50** in the **Distance** field of the **First Reference** rollout of the PropertyManager.

5. Select the **Flip offset** check box in the **First Reference** rollout to reverse the direction of the plane to downward.

6. Click on the green tick-mark ☑ in the PropertyManager. The offset reference plane is created, see Figure 8.209.

7. Invoke the Sketching environment by selecting the newly created reference plane as the sketching plane.

8. Press CTRL + 8 to change the orientation of the model as normal to the viewing direction.

9. Create the sketch of the third feature (three circles of same diameter), see Figure 8.210.

10. Click on the **Features** tab in the CommandManager to display the tools of the **Features** CommandManager.

11. Click on the **Extruded Boss/Base** tool in the **Features** CommandManager. The **Boss-Extrude** PropertyManager and the preview of the extruded feature appear. Next, change the orientation of the model to isometric, see Figure 8.211.

12. Click on the **Reverse Direction** button in the **Direction 1** rollout to reverse the direction of extrusion to downward.

13. Invoke the **End Condition** drop-down list of the **Direction 1** rollout and then select the **Up To Next** option in the drop-down list. The preview of the extruded feature appears in the graphics area such that it has been terminated at its next intersection.

14. Click on the green tick-mark ✓ in the PropertyManager. The extruded feature is created, see Figure 8.212.

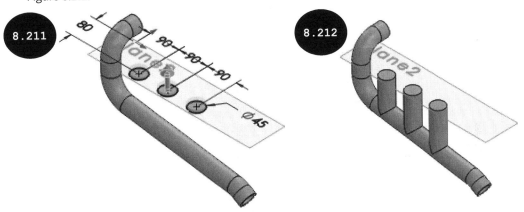

15. Hide the reference plane by clicking on the **Hide** option in the Pop-up toolbar that appears as soon as you select the plane to be hidden in the graphics area.

Section 6: Creating the Fourth Feature - Extruded Cut Feature

1. Invoke the Sketching environment by selecting the top planar face of the third feature as the sketching plane, see Figure 8.213.

Top planar face

2. Press CTRL + 8 to change the orientation of the model as normal to the viewing direction.

3. Create the sketch of the fourth feature (three circles of same diameter), see Figure 8.214.

> **Tip:** The sketch of the fourth feature shown in Figure 8.214 has three circles, which are concentric to the circular edges of the extruded feature. Also, an equal relation has been applied between all the circles.

4. Click on the **Extruded Cut** tool in the **Features CommandManager**. The **Cut-Extrude PropertyManager** and the preview of the extruded cut feature appear. Next, change the orientation of the model to isometric.

5. Invoke the **End Condition** drop-down list in the **Direction 1** rollout of the PropertyManager.

6. Click on the **Up To Next** option in the **End Condition** drop-down list. The preview of the extruded cut feature appears in the graphics area such that it has been terminated at its next intersection.

7. Click on the green tick-mark ✓ in the PropertyManager. The extruded cut feature is created, see Figure 8.215.

Section 7: Creating the Fifth Feature - Sweep Feature

To create the fifth feature of the model, you first need to create a reference plane at an offset distance of 90 mm from the Right plane.

1. Invoke the **Reference Geometry** flyout in the **Features CommandManager**, see Figure 8.216.

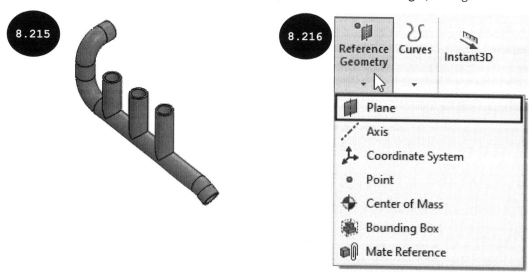

2. Click on the **Plane** tool in the flyout. The **Plane PropertyManager** appears.

3. Expand the FeatureManager Design Tree by clicking on the arrow in its front, which is now available on the top left corner of the graphics area.

4. Click on the **Right Plane** in the FeatureManager Design Tree as the first reference. The preview of an offset reference plane appears in the graphics area.

5. Enter **90** in the **Distance** field of the **First Reference** rollout of the **Plane PropertyManager**.

6. Click on the green tick-mark ✓ in the PropertyManager. The offset reference plane is created, see Figure 8.217.

7. Invoke the Sketching environment by selecting the newly created reference plane as the sketching plane. Next, press CTRL + 8 to change the orientation of the model as normal to the viewing direction.

8. Create the path of the sweep feature, see Figure 8.218.

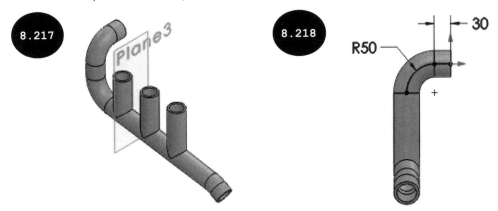

9. Exit the Sketching environment by clicking on the **Exit Sketch** tool in the **Sketch CommandManager**.

10. Change the current orientation of the model to isometric, see Figure 8.219. Next, hide the reference plane.

   After creating the path, you need to create the sweep feature.

11. Click on the **Swept Boss/Base** tool. The **Sweep PropertyManager** appears.

12. Make sure that the **Sketch Profile** radio button is selected in the **Profile and Path** rollout of the PropertyManager.

13. Select the top planar face of the extruded feature as the profile of the sweep feature, see Figure 8.220.

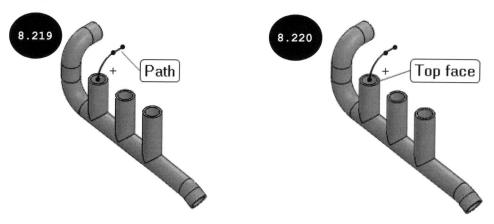

14. Select the path of the sweep feature in the graphics area. The preview of the sweep feature appears, see Figure 8.221.

15. Click on the green tick-mark ✔ in the PropertyManager. The sweep feature is created, see Figure 8.222.

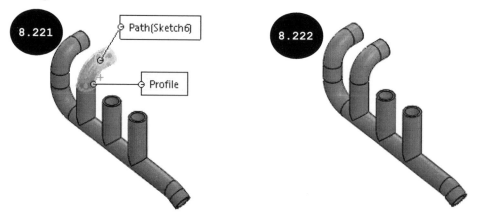

Section 8: Creating the Sixth and Seventh Features - Sweep Features

To create the sixth and seventh features (sweep), you can use the sketch of the fifth feature (sweep) of the model as the path.

1. Expand the node of the fifth feature (previously created sweep feature) in the FeatureManager Design Tree, see Figure 8.223.

2. Select the sketch (path) of the fifth feature (sweep feature) in the FeatureManager Design Tree, see Figure 8.223.

3. Click on the **Swept Boss/Base** tool in the **Features CommandManager**. The **Sweep PropertyManager** appears. Also, the selected sketch of the fifth feature is selected as the path of the sixth feature (sweep), see Figure 8.224.

4. Select the top planar face of the extruded feature as the profile of the sweep feature, see Figure 8.224. A preview of the sweep feature appears in the graphics area, see Figure 8.225.

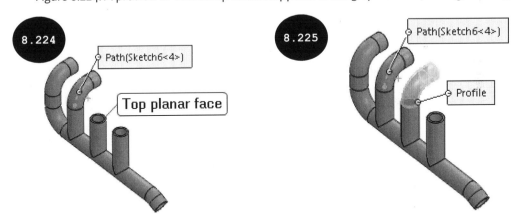

5. Click on the green tick-mark ✓ in the PropertyManager. The sweep feature is created, see Figure 8.226.

6. Similarly, create the seventh feature, which is a sweep feature, by using the sketch of the fifth feature as the path. Figure 8.227 shows the final model.

Section 9: Saving the Model

1.   Click on the **Save** tool in the **Standard** toolbar. The **Save As** window appears.

2.   Browse to the Chapter 8 folder of the SOLIDWORKS folder and then save the model with the name Tutorial 2.

Tutorial 3

Create a model, as shown in Figure 8.228. All dimensions are in mm.

Section 1: Invoking the Part Modeling Environment

1.   Start SOLIDWORKS and then invoke the Part modeling environment.

Once the Part modeling environment is invoked, you need to set the unit system and create the base/first feature of the model.

Section 2: Specifying Unit Settings

1. Make sure that the **MMGS (millimeter, gram, second)** unit system is set as the current unit system for the opened part document.

Section 3: Creating the Base/First Feature - Lofted Feature

To create the base/first feature (lofted feature) of the model, you first need to create all its sections (profiles) on different planes.

1. Invoke the Sketching environment by selecting the Right plane as the sketching plane.

2. Create the first section (profile) of the lofted feature, which is a circle of diameter 85 mm, see Figure 8.229.

3. Exit the Sketching environment and then press CTRL + 7 to change the orientation of the model to isometric.

   After creating the first section (profile) of the lofted feature, you need to create the second section at an offset distance of 40 mm from the Right plane.

4. Create a reference plane at an offset distance of 40 mm from the Right plane by using the **Plane** tool of the **Reference Geometry** flyout, see Figure 8.230.

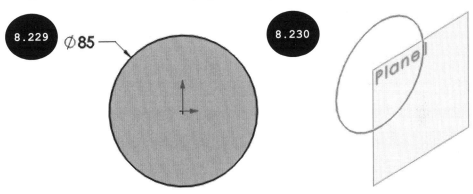

5. Invoke the Sketching environment by selecting the newly created reference plane as the sketching plane.

6. Press CTRL + 8 to change the orientation of the model as normal to the viewing direction.

7. Create the second section (a circle of diameter 80 mm) of the lofted feature, see Figure 8.231. Next, exit the Sketching environment.

8. Press CTRL + 7 to change the orientation of the model to isometric.

   After creating the second section (profile) of the lofted feature, you need to create the third section of the feature.

9. Create a reference plane at an offset distance of 65 mm from the Right plane by using the **Plane** tool in the **Reference Geometry** flyout, see Figure 8.232.

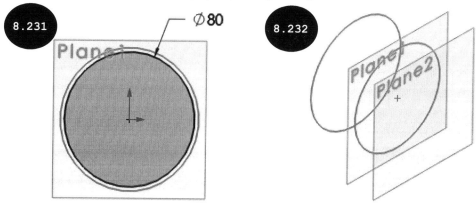

10. Invoke the Sketching environment by selecting the newly created reference plane as the sketching plane. Next, press CTRL + 8 to change the orientation of the model as normal to the viewing direction.

11. Create the third section (a circle of diameter 50 mm) of the lofted feature, see Figure 8.233. Next, exit the Sketching environment.

12. Press CTRL + 7 to change the current orientation of the model to isometric.

   After creating the third section (profile), you need to create the fourth section of the feature.

13. Create a reference plane at an offset distance of 90 mm from the Right plane by using the **Plane** tool, see Figure 8.234.

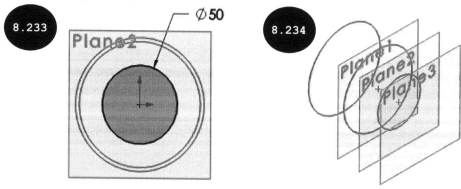

14. Invoke the Sketching environment by selecting the newly created reference plane as the sketching plane.

15. Press CTRL + 8 to change the orientation of the model as normal to the viewing direction.

16. Create the fourth section (rectangle of 65 X 60) of the lofted feature, see Figure 8.235.

17. Exit the Sketching environment and then press CTRL + 7 to change the current orientation to isometric, see Figure 8.236.

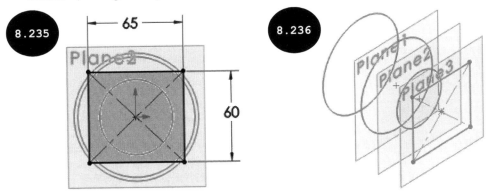

After creating all sections of the lofted feature, you can create the lofted feature.

18. Click on the **Lofted Boss/Base** tool in the **Features CommandManager**. The **Loft PropertyManager** appears.

19. Select all the sections (profiles) of the lofted feature in the graphics area one by one by clicking the left mouse button. The preview of the lofted feature appears in the graphics area, see Figure 8.237. Make sure that the connectors appear in one direction in the preview to avoid twisting in the feature, see Figure 8.237.

20. Click on the green tick-mark ☑ in the PropertyManager. The lofted feature is created, see Figure 8.238. In Figure 8.238, the reference planes have been hidden.

21. Hide the reference planes by clicking on the **Hide** tool in the Pop-up toolbar, which appears as soon as you select a plane to be hidden.

Section 4: Creating the Second Feature - Lofted Feature

Now, you need to create the second feature of the model, which is a lofted feature.

1. Create a reference plane at an offset distance of 210 mm from the right planar face of the base feature by using the **Plane** tool, see Figure 8.239.

2.   Invoke the Sketching environment by selecting the newly created reference plane as the sketching plane. Next, change the orientation of the model as normal to the viewing direction.

3.   Create the section (rectangle of 150 X 5) of the lofted feature, see Figure 8.240.

4.   Exit the Sketching environment and then change the current orientation to isometric.

Now, you need to create a guide curve for the lofted feature on the Front plane.

5.   Invoke the Sketching environment by selecting the Front plane as the sketching plane.

6.   Press CTRL + 8 to change the orientation of the model as normal to the viewing direction.

7.   Create the guide curve (an arc of radius 220 mm) of the lofted feature, see Figure 8.241.

Note: The endpoints of the guide curve (arc) shown in the Figure 8.241 have Pierce relation with the rectangular section of the lofted feature and the top edge of the right planar face of the base feature, respectively.

8.   Exit the Sketching environment and then change the current orientation to isometric.

Now, you need to create the lofted feature.

9.   Click on the **Lofted Boss/Base** tool in the **Features CommandManager**.
The **Loft PropertyManager** appears.

10.   Select the right planar face of the base feature as the first section of the lofted feature and then select the rectangular section (rectangle of 150 X 5) as the second section of the lofted feature. The preview of the lofted feature appears in the graphics area, see Figure 8.242.

11.   Make sure that the connectors appear in one direction, in the preview to avoid twisting in the feature, see Figure 8.242. If needed, you can change the position of the connectors by dragging them.

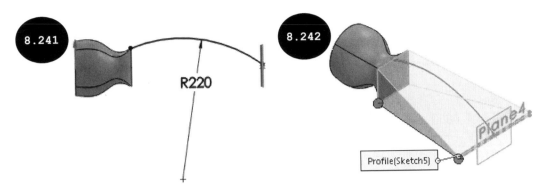

12. Click on the **Guide Curves** field in the **Guide Curves** rollout of the PropertyManager. The **Guide Curves** field is activated.

13. Click on the guide curve (arc of radius 220 mm) in the graphics area. A preview of the lofted feature appears such that it is guided by the guide curve, see Figure 8.243.

14. Click on the green tick-mark ☑ in the PropertyManager. The lofted feature is created, see Figure 8.244.

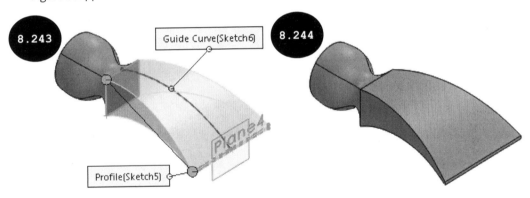

Section 5: Saving the Model

1. Click on the **Save** tool of the **Standard** toolbar. The **Save As** window appears.

2. Browse to the Chapter 8 folder of the SOLIDWORKS folder and then save the model with the name Tutorial 3.

Tutorial 4

Create a model, as shown in Figure 8.245. All dimensions are in mm.

Helical spring
Height = 15 mm
Revolutions = 2.4
Start angle = 270°

Section 1: Invoking the Part Modeling Environment
1.   Start SOLIDWORKS and then invoke the Part modeling environment.

Once the Part modeling environment is invoked, you can set the unit system and create the base/first feature of the model.

Section 2: Specifying Unit Settings
1.   Make sure that the MMGS (millimeter, gram, second) unit system is set for the currently opened part document.

Section 3: Creating the First Curve - Helical Curve
1.   Invoke the Sketching environment by selecting the Right plane as the sketching plane and then create a circle of diameter 60 mm, which will define the diameter of the helical curve, see Figure 8.246.

2. Exit the Sketching environment by clicking on the **Exit Sketch** button.

3. Invoke the **Curves** flyout in the **Features CommandManager** and then click on the **Helix and Spiral** tool. The **Helix/Spiral PropertyManager** appears.

Note: If the circle has been selected before invoking the **Helix and Spiral** tool, then the Helix/Spiral **PropertyManager** as well as the preview of the helical curve appear. You can select the circle to define the diameter of the helical curve before or after invoking the **Helix and Spiral** tool.

---

4. Click on the circle in the graphics area. The preview of the helical curve appears, see Figure 8.247. Change the orientation to isometric.

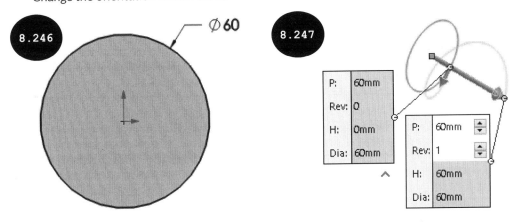

5. Invoke the **Type** drop-down list in the **Defined By** rollout of the PropertyManager, see Figure 8.248.

6. Select the **Height and Revolution** option in the **Type** drop-down list.

7. Enter **15** in the **Height** field, **2.4** in the **Revolutions** field, and **270** in the **Start angle** field of the **Parameters** rollout in the PropertyManager.

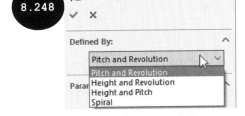

8. Select the **Reverse direction** check box in the **Parameters** rollout. The direction of the curve creation gets reversed, see Figure 8.249.

9. Make sure that the **Counterclockwise** radio button is selected in the rollout.

10. Click on the green tick-mark ✔ in the PropertyManager. The helical curve is created, see Figure 8.250.

Section 4: Creating the Second Curve - Helical Curve

After creating the first helical curve, you need to create the second helical curve at an offset distance of 45 mm from the Right Plane.

1. Create a reference plane at an offset distance of 45 mm from the Right plane by using the **Plane** tool, see Figure 8.251.

2. Invoke the Sketching environment by selecting the newly created reference plane as the sketching plane.

3. Press CTRL + 8 to change the orientation of the model as normal to the viewing direction.

4. Create a circle of diameter 60 mm to define the diameter of the second helical curve, see Figure 8.252.

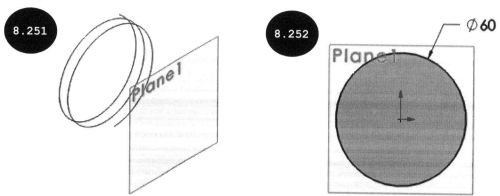

5. Invoke the **Curves** flyout in the **Features CommandManager** and then click on the **Helix and Spiral** tool. A preview of the helical curve as well as the **Helix/Spiral PropertyManager** appear.

6. Press CTRL + 7 to change the current orientation of the model to isometric.

7. Select the **Height and Revolution** option in the **Type** drop-down list of the **Defined By** rollout.

8. Enter 15 in the **Height** field, 2.4 in the **Revolutions** field, and 270 in the **Start angle** field of the **Parameters** rollout of the PropertyManager.

9. Make sure that the **Reverse direction** check box is cleared in the rollout.

10. Make sure that the **Counterclockwise** radio button is selected in the rollout.

11. Click on the green tick-mark ✓ in the PropertyManager. The second helical curve is created, see Figure 8.253.

12. Hide the reference plane by selecting the **Hide** option in the Pop-up toolbar that appears on selecting the plane.

Section 5: Creating the Third Curve - Sketch

After creating the helical curves, you need to create a sketch on a reference plane, which is parallel to the Top Plane and passing through the start point of the first helical curve.

1. Create a reference plane parallel to the Top Plane and passing through the start point of the first helical curve, see Figures 8.254 and 8.255. Figure 8.254 shows the preview of the plane.

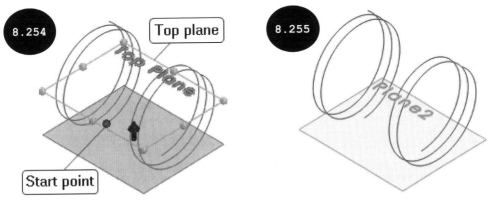

Note: To create a reference plane parallel to the Top plane and passing through the start point of the first helical curve, you need to select the Top plane as the first reference and the start point of the first helical curve as the second reference.

2. Invoke the Sketching environment by selecting the newly created reference plane as the sketching plane.

3. Press CTRL + 8 to change the orientation of the model as normal to the viewing direction.

4. Create a sketch as the third curve in the drawing area, see Figure 8.256. Note that both the endpoints of the sketch shown in Figure 8.256 have a pierce relation with the respective helical curves.

5. Exit the Sketching environment by clicking on the **Exit Sketch** tool.

6. Press CTRL + 7 to change the orientation of the model to isometric, see Figure 8.257.

Section 6: Creating the Fourth Curve - Sketch

You need to create the fourth curve on a reference plane, which is parallel to the Right plane and passing through the endpoint of the first helical curve.

1. Create a reference plane parallel to the Right plane and passing through the endpoint of the first helical curve, see Figures 8.258 and 8.259. Figure 8.258 shows a preview of the reference plane.

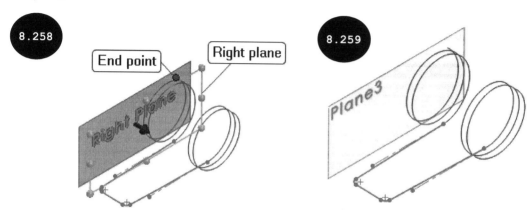

Note: To create a reference plane parallel to the Right plane and passing through the endpoint of the first helical curve, you need to select the Right plane as the first reference and the endpoint of the first helical curve as the second reference for creating the plane.

2. Invoke the Sketching environment by selecting the newly created reference plane as the sketching plane.

3. Press CTRL + 8 to change the orientation of the model as normal to the viewing direction.

4. Create the fourth sketch (an inclined line of length 60 mm), see Figure 8.260.

Note: The start point of the inclined line shown in Figure 8.260 has a pierce relation with the first helical curve. To apply the Pierce relation, select the start point of the line and then select the first helical curve. A Pop-up toolbar appears. In this Pop-up toolbar, click on the **Pierce** tool. You may need to rotate the model to select the first helical curve.

5. Exit the Sketching environment by clicking on the **Exit Sketch** button and then hide the reference plane.

6. Press CTRL + 7 to change the current orientation of the model to isometric, see Figure 8.261.

Section 7: Creating the Fifth Curve - Sketch

You need to create the fifth curve on a reference plane, which is parallel to the Right plane and passing through the endpoint of the second helical curve.

1. Create a reference plane parallel to the Right plane and passing through the endpoint of the second helical curve, see Figures 8.262 and 8.263. Figure 8.262 shows a preview of the reference plane.

2.   Invoke the Sketching environment by selecting the newly created reference plane as the sketching plane.

3.   Press CTRL + 8 to change the orientation of the model as normal to the viewing direction.

4.   Create the sketch (an inclined line of length 60 mm), see Figure 8.264. Note that the inclined line shown in Figure 8.264 has been created by specifying its start point and endpoint on the start point and endpoint of the existing inclined line, respectively.

5.   Exit the Sketching environment by clicking on the **Exit Sketch** tool and then hide the reference plane.

6.   Press CTRL + 7 to change the current orientation of the model to isometric, see Figure 8.265.

Section 8: Creating the Composite Curve - Sweep Path

After creating all curves (helical curve and sketches), you need to create a composite curve as the path of the sweep feature by combining all the curves together.

1.   Invoke the **Curves** flyout in the **Features CommandManager** and then click on the **Composite Curve** tool. The **Composite Curve PropertyManager** appears.

2. Select all the curves (two helical curves and three sketches), one by one in the graphics area by clicking the left mouse button.

3. Click on the green tick-mark ☑ in the PropertyManager. The composite curve is created, see Figure 8.266.

Section 9: Creating the Sweep Feature

After creating the path, you need to create a sweep feature with circular profile.

1. Click on the **Swept Boss/Base** tool in the **Features CommandManager**. The **Sweep PropertyManager** appears.

2. Click on the **Circular Profile** radio button in the **Profile and Path** rollout of the PropertyManager.

3. Click on the path (composite curve) of the sweep feature in the graphics area. The preview of the sweep feature appears with default diameter of the circular profile.

4. Enter **6** in the **Diameter** field of the **Profile and Path** rollout and then press ENTER. The preview of the sweep feature appears, see Figure 8.267.

5. Click on the green tick-mark ☑ in the PropertyManager. The sweep feature is created, see Figure 8.268.

Note: In Figure 8.268, the composite curve (path) has been hidden. To hide the composite curve, click on the composite curve in the FeatureManager Design Tree and then click on the **Hide** tool in the Pop-up toolbar that appears.

Section 10: Saving the Model

1. Click on the **Save** tool of the **Standard** toolbar. The **Save As** window appears.

2. Browse to the Chapter 8 folder of the SOLIDWORKS folder and then save the model with the name Tutorial 4.

Hands-on Test Drive 1

Create a model, as shown in Figure 8.269. After creating the model, apply the Cast Alloy Steel material and then calculate its mass properties. All dimensions are in mm.

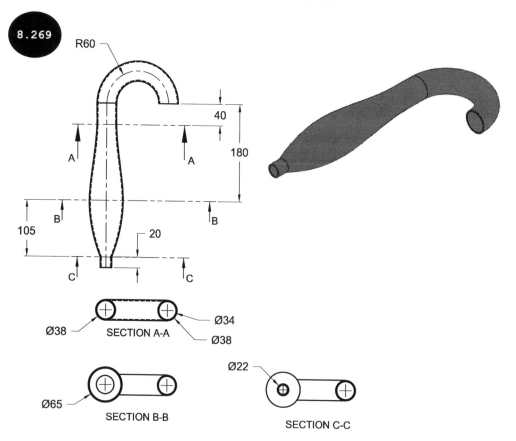

8.269

Hands-on Test Drive 2

Create a model, as shown in Figure 8.270 and then apply the Alloy Steel material. Also, calculate the mass properties of the model. All dimensions are in mm and start angle is 90-degrees.

8.270

Variable Helical Spring		
Pitch	Revolution	Diameter
2	0	7
2	4	7
1.25	5	4.50
1.25	7.50	4.50

Start Angle = 90°

12

Ø7

Ø1

Summary

This chapter discusses how to create sweep features, sweep cut features, lofted features, lofted cut features, boundary features, boundary cut features, curves, split face, and 3D Sketches.

A sweep feature is created by sweeping a profile along a path. The profile of the sweep feature can be a closed sketch, whereas a path can be an open or a closed sketch. You can also use guide curves to guide the profile (section) of the sweep feature. Additionally, you can twist the profile along the path or create a thin sweep feature. While creating the sweep cut feature, you can use a closed sketch and a solid body as the profile to sweep along the path.

A lofted feature is created by lofting two or more than two profiles (sections) such that its cross-sectional shape transits from one profile to another. You can also use guide curves to control the cross-sectional shape of the lofted feature. You can create closed lofted feature, and similar to creating lofted features, you can also create boundary features, which are high quality and complex shaped features.

The chapter also describes methods for creating projected curves, helical and spiral curves, curves by specifying XYZ points, curves by selecting reference points, and composite curves, and splitting the faces of a model and create 3D sketches.

Questions

- The _____ tool is used for creating sweep features.

- While creating a sweep feature, the _____ option is selected by default. As a result, the profile follows the path.

- Selecting the _____ option creates a sweep feature such that the profile twists along a path.

- By selecting the _____ option, you can select a tool body following the path to create a sweep cut feature.

- You can create projected curves by using two methods: _____ and _____.

- The _____ radio button is used for creating helical curve with a variable pitch.

- By selecting the _____ option, you can create a helical curve by defining its pitch and number of revolutions.

- The _____ tool is used for creating a curve by specifying coordinate points.

- The profiles/sections of a lofted feature must be closed. (True/False)

- In SOLIDWORKS, you cannot create tapered helical curves. (True/False)

- For creating a sweep feature, the start point of the path must lie on the plane of the profile created. (True/False)

Patterning and Mirroring

This chapter discusses the following topics:

- Patterning Features/Faces/Bodies
- Creating a Linear Pattern
- Creating a Circular Pattern
- Creating a Curve Driven Pattern
- Creating a Sketch Driven Pattern
- Creating a Table Driven Pattern
- Creating a Fill Pattern
- Creating a Variable Pattern
- Mirroring Features/Faces/Bodies

Patterning and mirroring tools are very powerful tools that help designers to speed up the creation process of a design, increase efficiency, and save time. For example, if a plate has 1000 holes of the same diameter, instead of creating all the holes one by one, you can create one hole and then pattern it to create all the remaining holes. Similarly, if the geometry is symmetric, you can create one of its sides and mirror it to create the other sides. The various methods used for patterning and mirroring features, faces, or bodies are discussed next.

Patterning Features/Faces/Bodies

In SOLIDWORKS, you can create different types of patterns, such as linear pattern, circular pattern, curve driven pattern, sketch driven pattern, table driven pattern, fill pattern, and variable pattern. The tools used for creating different types of patterns are grouped together in the **Pattern** flyout of the **Features CommandManager**, see Figure 9.1.

Different types of patterns that can be created by using the pattern tools are listed below and discussed next.

Creating a Linear Pattern

Creating multiple instances of features, faces, or bodies in one or two linear directions is known as a linear pattern, see Figure 9.2.

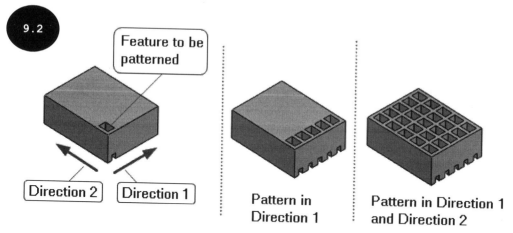

To create a linear pattern, click on the **Linear Pattern** tool in the **Features CommandManager**. The **Linear Pattern PropertyManager** appears, see Figure 9.3. The options in this PropertyManager are discussed next.

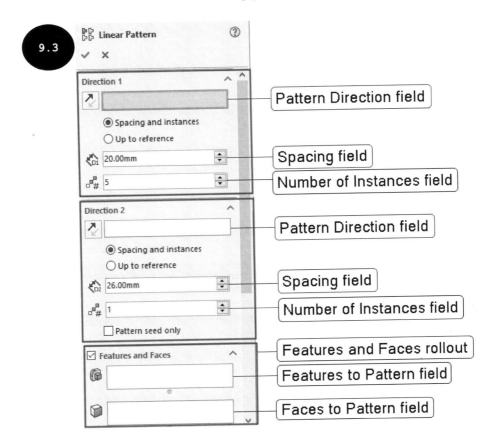

Features and Faces

The **Features and Faces** rollout of the PropertyManager is used for selecting features and faces to be patterned, see Figure 9.4. To select features to be patterned, click on the **Features to Pattern** field in this rollout and then select features from the graphics area or from the FeatureManager Design Tree. On selecting the features to be patterned, the names of the selected features appear in the **Features to Pattern** field. The features selected to be patterned are known as seed or parent features.

You can also pattern faces of a model that form a closed volume. For doing so, click on the **Faces to Pattern** field in the rollout and then select faces to be patterned in the graphics area. Note that faces to be patterned should form a closed volume and make up a feature.

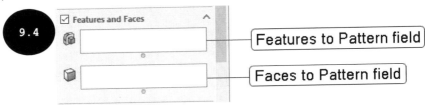

Bodies

The **Bodies** rollout is used for selecting bodies to be patterned. To select bodies, you need to expand the **Bodies** rollout by clicking on the check box in the title bar of this rollout and then select the bodies to be patterned from the graphics area or from the FeatureManager Design Tree.

> **Tip:** You can select features, faces, or bodies to be patterned before and after invoking the **Linear Pattern** PropertyManager.

After selecting features, faces, or bodies to be patterned, you need to define the directions of pattern by using the **Direction 1** and **Direction 2** rollouts of the PropertyManager, which are discussed next.

Direction 1

The options in the **Direction 1** rollout of the PropertyManager are used to create multiple instances or copies of selected features, faces, or bodies in Direction 1, see Figure 9.5. The options are discussed next.

Pattern Direction

The **Pattern Direction** field is used for specifying the direction of the pattern. For doing so, click on the **Pattern Direction** field and then specify the direction of the pattern. You can select a linear edge, a linear sketch entity, an axis, a planar face, a conical/circular face, a circular edge, a reference plane, or a dimension as the direction of the pattern. After specifying the direction of the pattern, a preview of the linear pattern appears in the graphics area with a callout attached to the specified direction and an arrow appears pointing toward the direction of pattern, see Figures 9.6 and 9.7. In Figure 9.6, a linear edge is selected as the pattern direction and in Figure 9.7, a circular face is selected as the pattern direction.

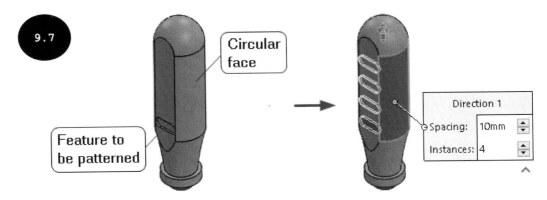

Spacing and instances

The **Spacing and instances** radio button is selected, by default. As a result, the **Spacing** and **Number of Instances** fields become available in the rollout. These fields are discussed next.

Spacing: The **Spacing** field is used for specifying spacing between two pattern instances. You can also specify the spacing between pattern instances by using the callout, which appears in the preview of the linear pattern in the graphics area. For doing so, click on the **Spacing** field in the callout and then enter the required value as the spacing between the pattern instances in it.

Number of Instances: The **Number of Instances** field is used for specifying the number of instances to be created in the direction of the pattern. Note that the number of instances specified in the **Number of Instances** field also includes the parent feature. You can also specify the number of instances in the callout, which appears in the preview of the linear pattern in the graphics area.

Reverse Direction

The **Reverse Direction** button is used for reversing the direction of pattern.

Up to reference

On selecting the **Up to reference** radio button, the options of the **Direction 1** rollout appear, as shown in Figure 9.8. These options are used for creating a linear pattern by specifying a reference geometry up to which the linear pattern is to be created based on the number of instances or spacing between the instances that are specified in the respective fields. The options are discussed next.

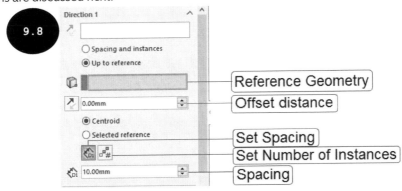

Reference Geometry: The **Reference Geometry** field is used for selecting a reference geometry, which controls the pattern based on the number of pattern instances or spacing specified. Note that on modifying the reference geometry, the respective pattern also gets modified automatically by adjusting the number of instances or spacing between instances. Figure 9.9 shows a preview as well as the resultant linear pattern with a vertex selected as the reference geometry where the spacing between pattern instances is defined as 15 mm. Figure 9.10 shows the linear pattern after increasing the length of the model. Note that on modifying the length of the model, the linear pattern also gets modified by adjusting the number of pattern instances such that the specified spacing between the pattern instances remains same.

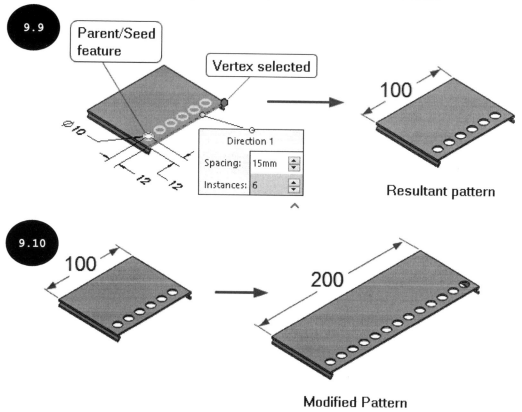

Offset distance: The **Offset distance** field is used for specifying the offset distance between the last pattern instance and the reference geometry.

Centroid: On selecting the **Centroid** radio button, the offset distance specified in the **Offset distance** field is measured from the center of the last pattern instance to the reference geometry.

Selected reference: On selecting the **Selected reference** radio button, the **Seed Reference** field becomes available in the rollout. By using this field, you can select a reference of the parent feature to measure the offset distance from the reference geometry.

Set Spacing: The **Set Spacing** button 🔧 is used for specifying the spacing between the pattern instances in the **Spacing** field, which is enabled below this button in the rollout.

Set Number of Instances: The **Set Number of Instances** button 🔧 is used for specifying the number of pattern instances in the **Number of Instances** field, which is enabled below this button.

Direction 2

The options in the **Direction 2** rollout are used for creating multiple instances of the selected feature in Direction 2. Figure 9.11 shows the preview of a linear pattern with 9 instances in Direction 1 and 4 instances in Direction 2.

The options in the **Direction 2** rollout are the same as the **Direction 1** rollout, except the **Pattern seed only** check box, which is discussed next.

Pattern seed only

On selecting the **Pattern seed only** check box, the pattern is created such that only the seed/parent feature gets patterned and the pattern instances of Direction 1 are not replicated in Direction 2, see Figure 9.12.

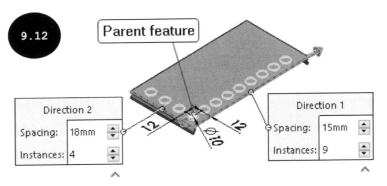

Instances to Skip

The **Instances to Skip** rollout is used for skipping some of the instances of the pattern. To skip pattern instances, expand the **Instances to Skip** rollout by clicking on the arrow in the title bar of this rollout, see Figure 9.13. On expanding the **Instances to Skip** rollout, pink dots are

displayed at the center of all pattern instances in the graphics area, see Figure 9.14. Move the cursor over the pink dot of a pattern instance to be skipped and then click the left mouse button when the appearance of the cursor changes to the hand cursor, see Figure 9.14. The selected pattern instance disappears or skips and the pink dot changes to white, see Figure 9.15. Also, the pattern instance number appears in the **Instances to Skip** field of the rollout. Similarly, you can skip multiple instances of the pattern, as required. You can also use Window selection and Lasso selection methods to skip pattern instances. To skip pattern instances by using the Window selection method, draw a window around the instances by dragging the cursor after pressing and holding the left mouse button. Similarly, to skip pattern instances by using the Lasso selection method, right-click in the graphics area and then click on the **Lasso Selection** option in the shortcut menu that appears. Next, drag the cursor by pressing and holding the left mouse button around the pattern instances to be skipped. You can also restore the skipped instances by clicking on the white dot of the instance to be restored in the graphics area or by using the Window and Lasso selection methods.

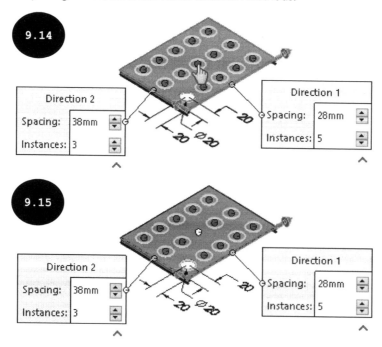

Options

The options in the **Options** rollout are discussed next.

Vary sketch

The **Vary sketch** check box is used for varying instances of a pattern with respect to a path. Figure 9.16 shows a feature to be patterned and Figure 9.17 shows the resultant variable linear pattern created by selecting the **Vary sketch** check box. Note that the **Vary sketch** check box is enabled only on selecting a dimension as the pattern direction, see Figure 9.16.

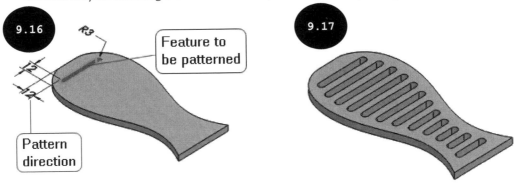

Note: The sketch of the feature to vary must contain a reference sketch/curve, which is used as the path to be followed by the feature, see Figure 9.18. Also, the varying length of the sketch must not be restricted by dimensions, see Figure 9.18. In this figure, the sketch of the cut feature to be varied has been fully defined by applying dimensions with respect to the reference curve (path) and the length of the feature has not been dimensioned.

Geometry pattern

By default, the **Geometry pattern** check box is cleared. As a result, all the pattern instances maintain the same geometrical relations as those of the parent feature. For example, Figure 9.19 shows the front view of a model in 'hidden lines visible' display style, in which the cut feature is created by defining the end condition as 4 mm offset from the bottom face of the model. Figure 9.20 shows the resultant pattern of the cut feature that is created by clearing the **Geometry pattern** check box, whereas Figure 9.21 shows the resultant pattern of the cut feature when the **Geometry pattern** check box is selected.

Propagate visual properties

By default, this check box is selected. As a result, all the visual properties such as colors, textures, and cosmetic thread of the parent feature are propagated to all the instances of the pattern.

Full preview and Partial preview

The **Full preview** and **Partial preview** radio buttons are used for displaying full and partial previews of the pattern in the graphics area, respectively.

Instances to Vary

The **Instances to Vary** rollout is used for creating a pattern with incremental spacing between pattern instances in Direction 1 and Direction 2. Besides creating a pattern with incremental spacing between instances, you can also vary the geometry of instances. Note that this rollout is enabled only after selecting a feature to be patterned and a direction of the pattern. Once this rollout is enabled, you need to expand it by selecting the check box in its title bar, see Figure 9.22. The options in this rollout are discussed next.

Direction 1 Increments

The **Direction 1 Increments** area of this rollout is used for specifying incremental values for the pattern instances in Direction 1. The options in this area are discussed below:

Direction 1 Spacing Increment: This field is used for specifying the incremental spacing between pattern instances. Figure 9.23 shows the preview of a pattern with an incremental spacing of 5 mm specified in this field.

9.23

Direction 1	
Spacing:	10mm
Instances:	6
Dimension:	Increment
Space Increment (10mm) :	5mm

Choose Feature dimensions to vary in Direction 1: This field is used for selecting the dimensions of the parent feature such as diameter and height to be varied in the pattern instances. Click on the dimensions in the graphics area to be varied. A table with dimension name, dimension value, and increment value columns appears in this field, see Figure 9.24. Now, you can double-click on the field corresponding to the increment value column to activate its editing mode and then enter the increment value for the selected dimension. Figure 9.25 shows a linear pattern created with an incremental spacing of 5 mm, incremental diameter of 2 mm, and incremental height of 4 mm.

9.24

☑ Instances to Vary

Direction 1 Increments

5.00mm

Dimension	Value	Increment
D2@Sketch	6mm	0mm
D1@Boss-E	20mm	0mm

9.25

Direction 2 Increments

The **Direction 2 Increments** area is used for specifying the incremental spacing between pattern instances and the incremental dimensions in Direction 2. The options in this area are the same as those discussed in the **Direction 1 Increments** area. Note that the options in this area are enabled only when you pattern features in Direction 2.

Creating a Circular Pattern

Creating multiple instances of features, faces, or bodies, circularly around an axis results in a circular pattern, see Figure 9.26. To create a circular pattern, click on the arrow at the bottom of the **Linear Pattern** tool. The **Pattern** flyout appears, see Figure 9.27. In this flyout, click on the **Circular Pattern** tool. The **CirPattern PropertyManager** appears, see Figure 9.28. The options in the **CirPattern PropertyManager** are discussed next.

Features and Faces

The **Features and Faces** rollout is used for selecting features or faces to be patterned, circularly around an axis. By default, the **Features to Pattern** field is activated in this rollout. As a result, you can select features to be patterned from the graphics area or from the FeatureManager Design Tree. After selecting the features to be patterned, the names of the selected features get listed in the

Features to Pattern field. You can select features to be patterned before and after invoking the PropertyManager.

To select the faces to be patterned, click on the **Faces to Pattern** field in the rollout and then select the faces of the model to be patterned. Note that the faces to be patterned should form a closed volume.

Direction 1

The options in the **Direction 1** rollout are used for specifying parameters for creating circular pattern in Direction 1 around a pattern axis. The options are discussed next.

Pattern Axis

The **Pattern Axis** field is used for selecting an axis around which you want to create a circular pattern. For doing so, click on the **Pattern Axis** field and then select an axis, a circular face, a circular edge, a linear edge, a linear sketch, or an angular dimension as the pattern axis, see Figure 9.29. This figure shows the preview of a circular pattern when a circular face is selected as the pattern axis. Note that in case of selecting a circular face, a circular edge, or an angular dimension as the pattern axis, the respective center axis gets automatically determined and is used as the axis of the circular pattern. After selecting a pattern axis, the preview of the circular feature appears in the graphics area with a callout attached to the pattern axis, see Figure 9.29.

Angle

The **Angle** field is used for specifying the angle value between pattern instances. You can also specify the angle between pattern instances by using the callout that appears in the graphics area. Note that if the **Equal spacing** radio button is selected in the rollout then the angle value specified in the **Angle** field is considered as the total angle of the pattern and all pattern instances are arranged within the specified angle value with equal angular spacing among all instances. If the **Instance spacing** radio button is selected in the rollout then the angle value specified in the **Angle** field is used as the angle between two pattern instances.

Number of Instances

The **Number of Instances** field is used for specifying the number of instances to be created in the pattern. Figure 9.30 shows the preview of a circular pattern with 5 pattern instances. Note that the number of instances specified in this field also includes the parent or seed feature. You can also specify the number of instances in the callout that appears in the graphics area.

Reverse Direction

The **Reverse Direction** button is used for reversing the angle of rotation.

Direction 2

The options in the **Direction 2** rollout are used for specifying parameters for creating a circular pattern in Direction 2 around the pattern axis, see Figure 9.31. This figure shows the preview of a circular pattern with 5 instances in Direction 1 and 2 instances in Direction 2.

The options in the **Direction 2** rollout are same as the options discussed in the **Direction 1** rollout of the PropertyManager except for the **Symmetric** check box, which is used for creating a circular pattern symmetrically, in both directions of the parent or seed feature.

The options in the remaining rollouts of the PropertyManager such as **Instances to Skip** and **Instances to Vary** are the same as those discussed while creating the linear pattern.

Creating a Curve Driven Pattern

Creating multiple instances of features, faces, or bodies along a curve is known as a curve driven pattern, see Figure 9.32. This figure shows a feature to be patterned, a closed sketch as the curve, and the resultant curve driven pattern. You can select a 2D/3D open or closed sketch, or an edge as the curve to drive the pattern instances.

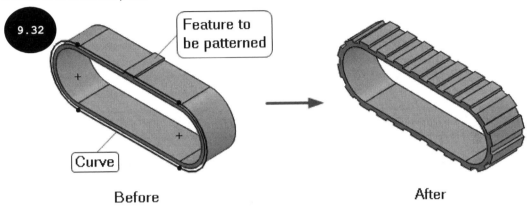

To create a curve driven pattern, click on the arrow at the bottom of the **Linear Pattern** tool. The **Pattern** flyout appears, see Figure 9.33. In this flyout, click on the **Curve Driven Pattern** tool. The **Curve Driven Pattern PropertyManager** appears, see Figure 9.34. The options in this PropertyManager are discussed next.

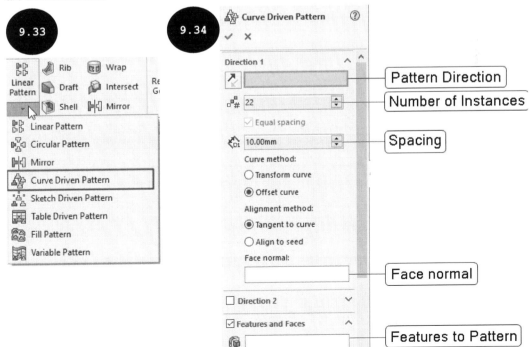

Features and Faces

The **Features and Faces** rollout of the PropertyManager is used for selecting features or faces to be patterned. To select the features to be patterned, click on the **Features to Pattern** field in this rollout and then select the features either from the graphics area or from the FeatureManager Design Tree. You can select features to be patterned before and after invoking the PropertyManager.

To select faces to be patterned, click on the **Faces to Pattern** field in the rollout and then select the faces in the graphics area. Note that faces to be patterned should form a closed volume.

Direction 1

The options in the **Direction 1** rollout are used for selecting a driving curve and for specifying parameters for creating a curve driven pattern in Direction 1. The options of this rollout are discussed below:

Pattern Direction

The **Pattern Direction** field is used for selecting a curve as the path for driving pattern instances. You can select a 2D/3D open or closed sketch, or an edge as the path for driving pattern instances. For doing so, click on the **Pattern Direction** field and then select a curve from the graphics area. After selecting a curve, the preview of the curve driven pattern appears in the graphics area with default parameters, see Figures 9.35 and 9.36. Figure 9.35 shows the preview of a curve driven pattern in which a closed sketch is selected as the path for driving pattern instances and in Figure 9.36, an open sketch is selected as the path for driving pattern instances.

Note: If the sketch to be selected as the curve to drive pattern instances has multiple entities/segments, then it is recommended to select the sketch from the FeatureManager Design Tree.

Number of Instances

The **Number of Instances** field is used for specifying the number of instances in a pattern.

Equal spacing

When the **Equal spacing** check box is selected, the spacing among all pattern instances is equally arranged in accordance with the total length of the curve selected. If you clear this check box, the **Spacing** field gets enabled, which is used to specify the spacing between two pattern instances.

Reverse Direction

The **Reverse Direction** button is used for reversing the direction of pattern.

Curve method

This area is used for selecting a method for transforming pattern instances along the curve, see Figure 9.37. The options in this area are discussed next.

9.37

Transform curve: When the **Transform curve** radio button is selected, the delta X and delta Y distances between the parent feature and the origin of the curve are maintained by pattern instances, see Figure 9.38.

Offset curve: When the **Offset curve** radio button is selected, the normal distance between the parent feature and the origin of the curve is maintained by pattern instances, see Figure 9.39.

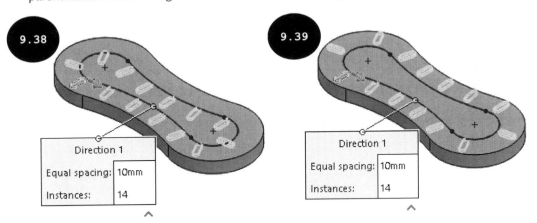

9.38   9.39

Note: The Transform curve method and the Offset curve method discussed above work in combination with the Alignment method (**Tangent to curve** or **Align to seed**), which is discussed next. In Figures 9.38 and 9.39, the **Tangent to curve** alignment method is selected.

Alignment method

This area is used for specifying an alignment method for aligning pattern instances along the curve, see Figure 9.40. The options in this area are discussed next.

Tangent to curve: On selecting the **Tangent to curve** radio button, each pattern instance is aligned tangentially to the selected curve, see Figures 9.38 and 9.39.

Note: Figure 9.38 shows the preview of a curve driven pattern when the **Transform curve** and **Tangent to curve** radio buttons are selected and in Figure 9.39, the **Offset curve** and **Tangent to curve** radio buttons are selected.

Align to seed: On selecting the **Align to seed** radio button, each pattern instance is aligned to match the parent feature, see Figures 9.41 and 9.42.

Note: Figure 9.41 shows the preview of a curve driven pattern when the **Transform curve** and **Align to seed** radio buttons are selected and in Figure 9.42, the **Offset curve** and **Align to seed** radio buttons are selected.

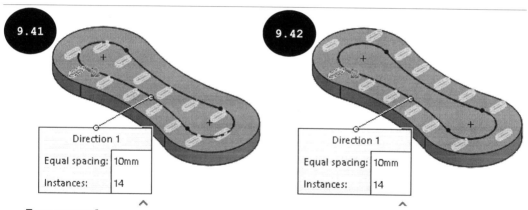

Face normal

The **Face normal** field of the **Direction 1** rollout is used for selecting a face, which is normal to the 3D curve selected as the path for driving instances, see Figure 9.43. Note that when you select a 3D curve as the path for driving pattern instances, you may need to select a face which is normal to the 3D curve. Figure 9.43 shows a feature to be patterned, a 3D curve (helix curve), a face normal, and the resultant curve driven pattern.

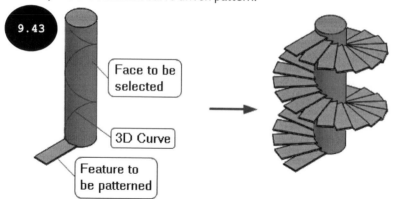

Direction 2

The options in the **Direction 2** rollout are used for creating pattern instances in Direction 2. The options in this rollout are the same as those in **Direction 1** rollout. Figure 9.44 shows the preview of a curve driven pattern in Direction 1 and Direction 2.

The options in the remaining rollouts such as **Bodies**, **Instances to Skip**, and **Options** of the PropertyManager are the same as those discussed earlier.

Creating a Sketch Driven Pattern

Creating multiple instances of features, faces, or bodies by using sketch points of a sketch is known as sketch driven pattern. In a sketch driven pattern, the parent/seed feature is propagated to each sketch point of the sketch, see Figure 9.45. Figure 9.45 shows a sketch having multiple points, a feature to be patterned, and the resultant sketch driven pattern.

To create a sketch driven pattern, invoke the **Pattern** flyout and then click on the **Sketch Driven Pattern** tool. The **Sketch Driven Pattern PropertyManager** appears, see Figure 9.46. The options in the PropertyManager are discussed next.

Features and Faces

The **Features and Faces** rollout of the PropertyManager is used for selecting the features or faces to be patterned. To select features to be patterned, click on the **Features to Pattern** field in this rollout and then the select features either from the graphics area or from the FeatureManager Design Tree. You can select the features to be patterned before or after invoking the PropertyManager. To select the faces to be patterned, click on the **Faces to Pattern** field in the rollout and then select faces of a model that form a closed volume.

Selections

The options in the **Selections** rollout are used for selecting sketch points. The options are discussed below:

Reference Sketch

The **Reference Sketch** field is used for selecting a sketch having multiple points for driving the pattern instances. For doing so, click on the **Reference Sketch** field to activate it and then select a sketch in the graphics area.

Centroid

By default, the **Centroid** radio button is selected. As a result, the centroid of the parent feature can be used as the base point for creating pattern instances and the center point of each pattern instance is coincident with the sketch point, see Figure 9.47.

Selected point

On selecting the **Selected point** radio button, the **Reference Vertex** field appears in the rollout, which allows you to select a reference point as the base point for the pattern, see Figure 9.48.

Vertex selected

The options in the remaining rollouts such as **Bodies** and **Options** of the PropertyManager are same as those discussed earlier.

Creating a Table Driven Pattern

A table driven pattern is created by specifying coordinates (X, Y) for each pattern instance with respect to a coordinate system. To create a table driven pattern, you need to have a coordinate system created in the graphics area. You can create a coordinate system by using the **Coordinate System** tool available in the **Reference Geometry** flyout, as discussed in Chapter 6. After creating a coordinate system, click on the **Table Driven Pattern** tool in the **Pattern** flyout. The **Table Driven Pattern** dialog box appears, see Figure 9.49. Most of the options in this dialog box are same as those discussed earlier and the remaining options are discussed next.

Features to copy

The **Features to copy** field is used for selecting features to be patterned. For doing so, click on this field in the dialog box and then select features either from the graphics area or from the FeatureManager Design Tree.

Coordinate system

The **Coordinate system** field of the dialog box is used for selecting a coordinate system from the graphics area. Note that the origin of the selected coordinate system is used as the origin for the table driven pattern. Figure 9.50 shows a feature to be patterned and a coordinate system.

Coordinate table

The **Coordinate table** is available at the bottom of the **Table Driven Pattern** dialog box and is used for specifying X and Y coordinates for each pattern instance with respect to the selected coordinate system, see Figure 9.51. To specify the X coordinate of point 1 (first pattern instance), double-click on the X field corresponding to the **Point 1** field in the table. Similarly, specify the Y coordinate of point 1 (first pattern instance). Note that each row of this table represents a pattern instance and its X and Y fields represent the coordinates of the pattern instance. You can add multiple rows in the table to specify coordinates of multiple pattern instances. Note that a new row is added automatically in the table as soon as you double-click on a field of the last row in the table. Figure 9.51 shows the **Coordinate table** of the dialog box, in which coordinates of 5 pattern instances, including the coordinates of the parent feature are specified.

Point	X	Y
0	10mm	35mm
1	30mm	40mm
2	60mm	45mm
3	90mm	40mm
4	120mm	35mm
5		

Note: To delete a row in the table, select the row to be deleted and then press DELETE.

Save/Save As

The **Save/Save As** button is used for saving the coordinates of the pattern instances specified in the table as external *Pattern Table* file (*.sldptab) for later use.

Read a file from

The **Read a file from** field is used for reading an existing *Pattern Table* (*.sldptab) or .txt (notepad) file containing coordinate points for creating the pattern. To create a pattern by using an existing file, click on the **Browse** button. The **Open** dialog box appears. Select the *Pattern Table* (*.sldptab) or .txt (notepad) file and then click on the **Open** button. The coordinate points specified in the imported file get filled automatically in the **Coordinate table** of the dialog box.

OK

After specifying parameters for creating the table driven pattern, click on the **OK** button in the dialog box. Figure 9.52 shows the table driven pattern created by specifying coordinates shown in Figure 9.51.

Creating a Fill Pattern

A fill pattern is created by populating an area with pattern instances. In the fill pattern, you can create multiple instances of features, faces, bodies, or a predefined cut shape by filling in a particular area of a model. To define an area to be filled in with pattern instances, you can select a face of a model or a closed sketch, see Figures 9.53 and 9.54. Figure 9.53 shows a feature to be patterned, a face to be filled, and the resultant fill pattern. Figure 9.54 shows the feature to be patterned, a closed sketch to be filled, and the resultant fill pattern.

To create a fill pattern, invoke the **Pattern** flyout and then click on the **Fill Pattern** tool. The **Fill Pattern PropertyManager** appears, see Figure 9.55. The options in the PropertyManager are discussed next.

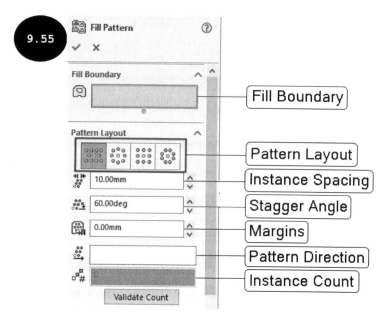

Fill Boundary
By default, the **Fill Boundary** field is activated in the **Fill Boundary** rollout of the PropertyManager. As a result, you are prompted to select a boundary to be filled in with pattern instances. You can select a face or a closed sketch as the boundary to be filled.

Features and Faces
The **Features and Faces** rollout of the PropertyManager is used for selecting features, faces, or a predefined cut shape to be patterned. By default, the **Selected features** radio button is selected in the rollout, see Figure 9.56. As a result, the **Features to Pattern** field is enabled. Click on this field to activate it and then select features to be patterned. After specifying a boundary to be filled and a feature to be patterned, the preview of the filled patterned appears in the graphics area, see Figure 9.57. In this figure, a face is selected as the boundary.

To select the faces to be patterned, click on the **Faces to Pattern** field of the rollout and then select faces to be patterned. Note that the faces to be patterned should form a closed volume.

On selecting the **Create seed cut** radio button in the **Features and Faces** rollout, different types of predefined cut shape buttons appear in the rollout, see Figure 9.58. By default, the **Circle** button is selected. As a result, the selected boundary is filled in with predefined circular cut features, see Figure 9.59. You can specify the required diameter for the predefined circular cut feature by using the **Diameter** field of the rollout. The **Vertex or Sketch Point** field is used for defining the center of the parent or seed feature. You can select a vertex or a sketch point to define the center of the parent feature. On doing so, the pattern starts from the defined center of the parent feature. Note that if you do not define the center of the parent feature, then the pattern will start from the center of the boundary face that is selected to be filled.

You can select circular, square, diamond, and polygon predefined cut shape by clicking on the respective button in the rollout, see Figures 9.59 through 9.62.

Pattern Layout
The options in the **Pattern Layout** rollout are used for selecting the type of layout for the fill pattern. You can select the **Perforation**, **Circular**, **Square**, or **Polygon** button for defining the type of layout to be used for the fill pattern, see Figures 9.63 through 9.66.

Perforation layout

Circular layout

Square layout

Polygon layout

You can use the remaining options of the **Pattern Layout** rollout to control the parameters of the pattern layout such as spacing between pattern instances, margin between the fill boundary and the outermost instance, and pattern direction.

Note: On selecting a face as the boundary of the fill pattern, the pattern direction is automatically selected and a preview of the pattern appears in the graphics area. However, on selecting a closed sketch as the boundary of the fill pattern, you may need to select a pattern direction. You can select a linear edge or a sketch entity as the pattern direction.

Creating a Variable Pattern

In SOLIDWORKS, you can create a variable pattern by using the **Variable Pattern** tool of the **Pattern** flyout. This tool is used for creating a variable pattern such that you can vary dimensions and reference geometries of a feature, see Figure 9.67. In this figure, a variable pattern has been created by varying the length and angle of the slot feature.

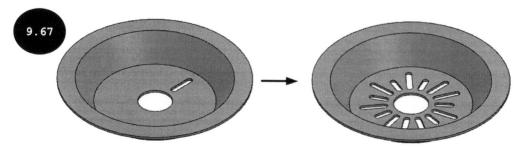

To create a variable pattern, invoke the **Pattern** flyout and then click on the **Variable Pattern** tool. The **Variable Pattern PropertyManager** appears, see Figure 9.68. The options in this PropertyManager are discussed next.

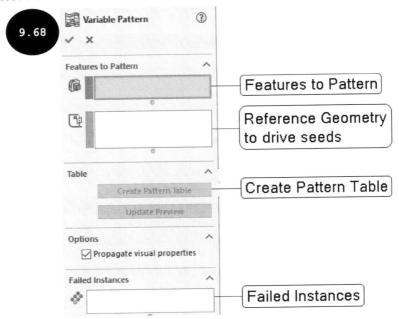

Figure 9.68

Features to Pattern

The **Features to Pattern** field is used for selecting features to be patterned. By default, this field is activated. As a result, you can select features to be patterned either from the graphics area or from the FeatureManager Design Tree. You can select extruded, cut extruded, revolved, cut revolved, sweep, cut sweep, lofted, cut lofted, fillet, chamfer, dome, and draft features as the features to be patterned for creating a variable pattern. Once you select a feature to be patterned, the respective dimensions appear in the graphics area so that you can select the dimensions to be varied in the pattern, see Figure 9.69.

Figure 9.69

Reference Geometry to drive seeds

The **Reference Geometry to drive seeds** field is used for selecting reference geometries on which the selected seed or parent feature is dependent. For doing so, click on the **Reference Geometry to drive seeds** field in the **Features to Pattern** rollout and then select the reference geometries. After selecting reference geometries, respective dimensions of the selected geometries appear in the graphics area so that you can select them as the dimensions to be varied. You can select the axis, plane, point, curve, 2D sketch, or 3D sketch as reference geometries. Figure 9.70 shows an extruded feature that is selected as the feature to be patterned as well as the respective reference geometries (a plane and a 3D point) selected on which the extruded feature is dependent. Note that the extruded feature shown in the figure has been created on a non-planar face of the model with the help of a reference plane and a 3D point.

9.70

Create Pattern Table

The **Create Pattern Table** button of the PropertyManager is used for invoking the **Pattern Table** dialog box. The **Pattern Table** dialog box is used for selecting the dimensions of the features and reference geometries to be varied. Once the **Pattern Table** dialog box has been invoked, you can select the dimensions to be varied. Once you select the dimensions to be varied, the selected dimensions get listed in the **Pattern Table** dialog box, see Figure 9.71. In this figure, the angle and length dimensions of the slot feature of the model shown in Figure 9.69 are selected as the dimensions to be varied.

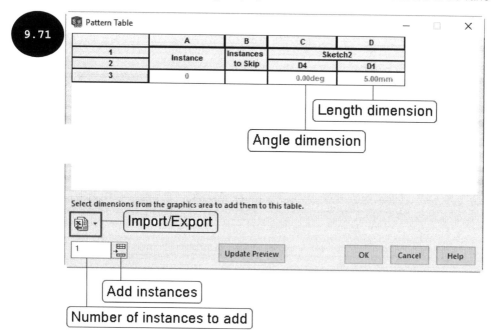

9.71

The **Number of instances to add** field of the **Pattern Table** dialog box is used for entering the number of instances to be created. After specifying the number of instances in this field, click on the **Add instances** button in the dialog box. The multiple rows equivalent to the number of instances specified are added in the **Pattern Table** dialog box, see Figure 9.72. Note that each row of this dialog box represents a pattern instance. You can modify the dimensions for each pattern instance by entering the required dimension values in the respective fields of the dialog box, see Figure 9.72. This dialog box works in the same way as that of the *Microsoft Office Excel*.

9.72

Pattern Table

Instance	Instances to Skip	Sketch2	
		D4	D1
0		0.00deg	5.00mm
1	☐	24.00deg	3.00mm
2	☐	48.00deg	5.00mm
3	☐	72.00deg	3.00mm
4	☐	96.00deg	5.00mm
5	☐	120.00deg	3.00mm
6	☐	144.00deg	5.00mm
7	☐	168.00deg	3.00mm
8	☐	192.00deg	5.00mm
9	☐	216.00deg	3.00mm
10	☐	240.00deg	5.00mm
11	☐	264.00deg	3.00mm
12	☐	288.00deg	5.00mm
13	☐	312.00deg	3.00mm
14	☐	336.00deg	5.00mm

Select dimensions from the graphics area to add them to this table.

| 1 | | Update Preview | OK | Cancel | Help |

After modifying the dimension values in the dialog box for each pattern instance, click on the **Update Preview** button. This button is used for updating the preview of pattern instances in the graphics area. You can also import an excel file (*.xlsx) containing variable dimensions of pattern instances by using the **Import from Excel** option of the dialog box. The **Export to Excel** option of the dialog box is used for saving the variable dimensions as an external excel file for later use. After specifying variable dimensions for all pattern instances, click on the **OK** button. A variable pattern is created, see Figure 9.73.

9.73

Mirroring Features/Faces/Bodies

In SOLIDWORKS, you can mirror features, faces, or bodies about a mirroring plane by using the Mirror tool. You can select a plane or a planar face of the model as the mirroring plane. Figure 9.74 shows features to be mirrored, mirroring plane, and the resultant mirror feature created.

9.74

Features to be mirrored

Plane

Mirroring plane

Before

Plane

After

Mirror   To create a mirror feature, click on the **Mirror** tool in the **Features CommandManager**. The **Mirror PropertyManager** appears, see Figure 9.75. You can also invoke the **Mirror** tool from the **Pattern** flyout. The options in the **Mirror PropertyManager** are discussed next.

Mirror Face/Plane

The Mirror Face/Plane field is used for selecting a mirroring plane. By default, this field is activated. As a result, you can select a mirroring plane from the graphics area. You can select a plane or a planar face of the model as the mirroring plane.

Features to Mirror

The **Features to Mirror** field is used for selecting features to be mirrored. For doing so, click on this field and then select features either from the graphics area or from the FeatureManager Design Tree. After selecting the mirroring plane and the features to be mirrored, the preview of the mirror feature appears in the graphics area.

Faces to Mirror and Bodies to Mirror

The **Faces to Mirror** and **Bodies to Mirror** rollouts of the PropertyManager are used for selecting faces and bodies to be mirrored, respectively. Note that faces to be mirrored should form a closed volume and make up a feature.

Options

The options in the **Options** rollout are same as those discussed earlier while creating patterns. By default the **Geometry Pattern** check box is cleared in this rollout. As a result, the resultant mirror feature maintains the same geometrical relations as the parent feature. Figure 9.76 shows the front view of a model having cut feature in the 'hidden lines visible' display style. This cut feature is created by defining its end condition as 4 mm offset from the bottom face of the model by using the **Offset from Surface** option. Figure 9.77 shows the resultant mirror feature created by clearing the **Geometry Pattern** check box and Figure 9.78 shows the resultant mirror feature created by selecting the **Geometry Pattern** check box.

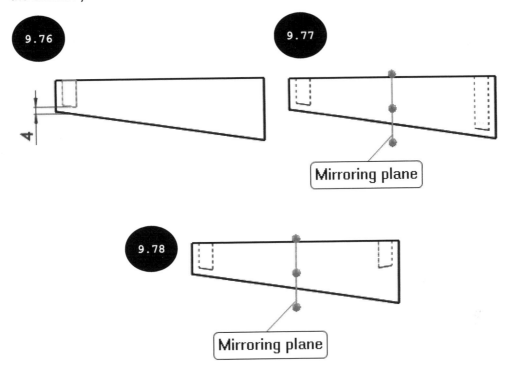

By default, the **Propagate visual properties** check box is selected in the **Options** rollout. As a result, all the visual properties such as colors, textures, and cosmetic thread of the parent feature are propagated to the resultant mirror feature.

Tutorial 1

Create a model, as shown in Figure 9.79. All dimensions are in mm.

DETAIL B

Section 1: Starting SOLIDWORKS

1. Start SOLIDWORKS by double-clicking on the SOLIDWORKS icon on your desktop. The startup user interface of SOLIDWORKS appears along with the **Welcome** dialog box.

Note: If SOLIDWORKS is already open and the **Welcome** dialog box does not appear on the screen, then you can invoke the same by clicking on the **Welcome to SOLIDWORKS** tool 🏠 in the **Standard** toolbar or by pressing the CTRL + F2 keys.

Section 2: Invoking the Part Modeling Environment

1. Click on the **Part** button in the **Welcome** dialog box. The Part modeling environment is invoked.

Tip: You can also invoke the Part modeling environment by using the **New SOLIDWORKS Document** dialog box. For doing so, click on the **New** tool in the **Standard** toolbar. The **New SOLIDWORKS Document** dialog box appears. In this dialog box, make sure that the **Part** button is selected and then click on the **OK** button.

Once the Part modeling environment has been invoked, you can set the unit system and create the base/first feature of the model.

Section 3: Specifying Unit Settings

1. Make sure that the **MMGS (millimeter, gram, second)** unit system is selected as the current unit system for the opened part document, see Figure 9.80.

Section 4: Creating the Base Feature - Extruded Feature

1. Invoke the Sketching environment by selecting the Top plane as the sketching plane.

2. Create the sketch of the base feature of the model, see Figure 9.81. After creating the sketch, do not exit the Sketching environment.

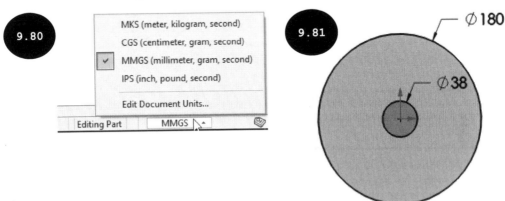

3. Click on the **Features** tab in the CommandManager to display the tools of the **Features** CommandManager.

4. Click on the **Extruded Boss/Base** tool. The **Boss-Extrude PropertyManager** and the preview of the extruded feature appear.

5. Enter **2** in the **Depth** field of the **Direction 1** rollout and then press ENTER.

6. Click on the green tick-mark ☑ in the PropertyManager. The extruded feature is created, see Figure 9.82.

Section 5: Creating the Second Feature - Extruded Cut Feature

1. Invoke the Sketching environment by selecting the top planar face of the base feature as the sketching plane.

2. Press CTRL + 8 to change the orientation of the model as normal to the viewing direction.

3. Create the sketch of the second feature, see Figure 9.83. After creating the sketch, do not exit the Sketching environment.

4. Click on the **Features** tab in the CommandManager to display the tools of the **Features** CommandManager.

5. Click on the **Extruded Cut** tool in the **Features CommandManager**. The **Cut-Extrude PropertyManager** and the preview of the extruded cut feature appear. Next, change the orientation of the model to isometric.

6. Invoke the **End Condition** drop-down list in the **Direction 1** rollout and then select the **Through All** option in it.

7. Click on the green tick-mark ✔ in the PropertyManager. The extruded cut feature is created, see Figure 9.84.

Section 6: Creating the Third Feature - Circular Pattern

1. Click on the arrow at the bottom of the **Linear Pattern** tool. The **Pattern** flyout appears, see Figure 9.85.

2. Click on the **Circular Pattern** tool in the **Pattern** flyout, see Figure 9.85. The **CirPattern PropertyManager** appears.

3. Expand the FeatureManager Design Tree, which is now available on the top left corner of the graphics area, by clicking on the arrow in front of it.

4. Click on the second feature (extruded cut) in the FeatureManager Design Tree as the feature to be patterned.

5. Click on the **Pattern Axis** field in the **Direction 1** rollout of the PropertyManager to activate it.

6. Click on the circular edge of the base feature to define the pattern axis, see Figure 9.86. The preview of the circular pattern appears, see Figure 9.86.

7. Make sure that the **Equal spacing** radio button is selected in the **Direction 1** rollout of the PropertyManager.

8. Enter **6** in the **Number of Instances** field of the **Direction 1** rollout.

9. Click on the green tick-mark ☑ in the PropertyManager. The circular pattern is created, see Figure 9.87.

Section 7: Creating the Fourth Feature - Extruded Cut Feature

1. Invoke the Sketching environment by selecting the top planar face of the base feature as the sketching plane.

2. Press CTRL + 8 to change the orientation of the model as normal to the viewing direction.

3. Create the sketch of the fourth feature of the model, see Figure 9.88. Do not exit the Sketching environment.

9.88

4. Click on the **Features** tab in the CommandManager and then click on the **Extruded Cut** tool. The **Cut-Extrude PropertyManager** and the preview of the extruded cut feature appear. Next, change the orientation of the model to isometric.

5. Invoke the **End Condition** drop-down list in the **Direction 1** rollout of the PropertyManager and then select the **Through All** option in it.

6. Click on the green tick-mark ☑ in the PropertyManager. The extruded cut feature is created, see Figure 9.89.

9.89

Section 8: Creating the Fifth Feature - Circular Pattern

1. Click on the arrow at the bottom of the **Linear Pattern** tool. The **Pattern** flyout appears, see Figure 9.90.

2. Click on the **Circular Pattern** tool in the **Pattern** flyout. The **CirPattern PropertyManager** appears.

3. Expand the FeatureManager Design Tree, which is now available on the top left corner of the graphics area, by clicking on the arrow in its front.

4. Click on the fourth feature (previously created extruded cut feature) in the FeatureManager Design Tree as the feature to be patterned.

5. Click on the **Pattern Axis** field in the **Direction 1** rollout of the PropertyManager to activate it.

6. Click on the circular edge of the base feature to define the pattern axis. A preview of the circular pattern appears, see Figure 9.91.

7. Make sure that the **Equal spacing** radio button is selected in the **Direction 1** rollout of the PropertyManager.

8. Enter **25** in the **Number of Instances** field of the **Direction 1** rollout.

9. Click on the green tick-mark ☑ in the PropertyManager. The circular pattern is created, see Figure 9.92.

Section 9: Creating the Sixth Feature - Extruded Cut Feature

1. Invoke the Sketching environment by selecting the top planar face of the base feature as the sketching plane.

2. Press CTRL + 8 to change the orientation of the model as normal to the viewing direction.

3. Create the sketch of the sixth feature (circle of diameter 5 mm), see Figure 9.93. Do not exit the Sketching environment.

9.93

4. Click on the **Features** tab in the CommandManager and then click on the **Extruded Cut** tool. The **Cut-Extrude PropertyManager** and the preview of the extruded cut feature appear. Next, change the orientation of the model to isometric.

Extruded Cut

5. Select the **Through All** option in the **End Condition** drop-down list of the **Direction 1** rollout.

6. Click on the green tick-mark ☑ in the PropertyManager. The extruded cut feature is created, see Figure 9.94.

9.94

Section 10: Creating the Seventh Feature - Circular Pattern

1. Invoke the **Pattern** flyout and then click on the **Circular Pattern** tool. The **CirPattern PropertyManager** appears.

2. Expand the FeatureManager Design Tree, which is now available on the top left corner of the graphics area, by clicking on the arrow in front of it.

3. Click on the sixth feature (previously created extruded cut feature) from the FeatureManager Design Tree as the feature to be patterned.

4. Click on the **Pattern Axis** field in the **Direction 1** rollout of the PropertyManager.

5. Click on the circular edge of the base feature to define the pattern axis. A preview of the circular pattern appears, see Figure 9.95.

6. Make sure that the **Equal spacing** radio button is selected in the **Direction 1** rollout.

7. Enter **6** in the **Number of Instances** field of the **Direction 1** rollout.

8. Click on the green tick-mark ☑ in the PropertyManager. A circular pattern is created, see Figure 9.96.

Section 11: Saving the Model

1. Click on the **Save** tool in the **Standard** toolbar. The **Save As** window appears.

2. Browse to the SOLIDWORKS folder and then create a folder with the name Chapter 9.

3. Enter **Tutorial 1** in the **File name** field of the dialog box and then click on the **Save** button. The model is saved with the name Tutorial 1 in the Chapter 9 folder.

Tutorial 2

Create a model, as shown in Figure 9.97. The different views and dimensions are given in the same figure. All dimensions are in mm.

Section 1: Invoking the Part Modeling Environment

1. Start SOLIDWORKS and then invoke the Part modeling environment.

    Once the Part modeling environment is invoked, you need to set the unit system and create the base/first feature of the model.

Section 2: Specifying Unit Settings

1. Make sure that the MMGS (millimeter, gram, second) unit system is set for the currently opened part document.

Section 3: Creating the Base Feature - Extruded Feature

1. Invoke the Sketching environment by selecting the Top plane as the sketching plane.

2. Create a sketch of the base feature of the model, see Figure 9.98. After creating the sketch, do not exit the Sketching environment.

3. Click on the **Features** tab in the CommandManager. The tools of the **Features** CommandManager are displayed.

4. Click on the **Extruded Boss/Base** tool. The **Boss-Extrude PropertyManager** and the preview of the extruded feature appear.

5. Invoke the **End Condition** drop-down list in the **Direction 1** rollout of the PropertyManager.

6. Select the **Mid Plane** option in the **End Condition** drop-down list.

7. Enter **50** in the **Depth** field of the **Direction 1** rollout and then press ENTER.

8. Click on the green tick-mark ☑ in the PropertyManager. The extruded feature is created, see Figure 9.99.

Section 4: Creating the Second Feature - Extruded Feature

1. Invoke the Sketching environment by selecting the top planar face of the base feature as the sketching plane.

2. Press CTRL + 8 to change the orientation of the model as normal to the viewing direction.

3. Create a sketch (two circles of diameter 145 mm and 40 mm) of the second feature, see Figure 9.100. After creating the sketch, do not exit the Sketching environment.

4. Click on the **Extruded Boss/Base** tool in the **Features CommandManager**. The **Boss-Extrude PropertyManager** and a preview of the extruded feature appear. Next, change the orientation of the model to isometric.

5. Invoke the **Start Condition** drop-down list in the **From** rollout of the PropertyManager, see Figure 9.101.

6. Select the **Offset** option in the **Start Condition** drop-down list of the **From** rollout.

7. Enter **12** in the **Enter Offset Value** field of the **From** rollout in the PropertyManager.

8. Click on the **Reverse Direction** button in the **From** rollout to reverse the direction of material addition downward.

9. Enter **5** in the **Depth** field of the **Direction 1** rollout in the PropertyManager.

10. Click on the green tick-mark ☑ in the PropertyManager. The extruded feature is created, see Figure 9.102.

Section 5: Creating the Third Feature - Extruded Cut Feature

1. Invoke the Sketching environment by selecting the top planar face of the second feature (previously created extruded feature) as the sketching plane.

2. Press CTRL + 8 to change the orientation of the model as normal to the viewing direction.

3. Create a circle of diameter 6 mm as the sketch of the third feature, see Figure 9.103. Do not exit the Sketching environment.

4. Click on the **Features** tab in the CommandManager and then click on the **Extruded Cut** tool. The **Cut-Extrude PropertyManager** and a preview of the extruded cut feature appear. Next, change the orientation of the model to isometric.

5. Invoke the **End Condition** drop-down list of the **Direction 1** rollout and then select the **Through All** option.

6. Click on the green tick-mark ☑ in the PropertyManager. The extruded cut feature is created, see Figure 9.104.

Section 6: Creating the Fourth Feature - Circular Pattern

1. Invoke the **Pattern** flyout by clicking on the arrow at the bottom of the **Linear Pattern** tool.

2. Click on the **Circular Pattern** tool in the **Pattern** flyout. The **CirPattern** PropertyManager appears.

3. Expand the FeatureManager Design Tree, which is now available on the top left corner of the graphics area, by clicking on the arrow in its front.

4. Click on the third feature (previously created extruded cut) in the FeatureManager Design Tree as the feature to be patterned.

5. Click on the **Pattern Axis** field in the **Direction 1** rollout of the PropertyManager to activate it.

6. Click on the outer circular face of the base feature in the graphics area to define the pattern axis, see Figure 9.105. A preview of the circular pattern appears, see Figure 9.105.

7. Make sure that the **Equal spacing** radio button is selected in the **Direction 1** rollout of the PropertyManager.

8. Enter **8** in the **Number of Instances** field of the **Direction 1** rollout.

9. Click on the green tick-mark ☑ in the PropertyManager. A circular pattern is created, see Figure 9.106.

Section 7: Creating the Fifth Feature - Extruded Feature

The fifth feature of the model is an extruded feature and its sketch is to be created on a reference plane, which is at an offset distance of 200 mm from the Right plane.

1. Invoke the **Plane PropertyManager** by clicking on the **Plane** tool in the **Reference Geometry** flyout and then create a reference plane at an offset distance of 200 mm from the Right plane, see Figure 9.107.

2. Invoke the Sketching environment by selecting the newly created reference plane as the sketching plane.

3. Press CTRL + 8 to change the orientation of the model as normal to the viewing direction.

4. Create the sketch of the extruded feature, see Figure 9.108. After creating the sketch, do not exit the Sketching environment.

9.108

Note: In Figure 9.108, a tangent relation has been applied between the connecting tangent arcs and lines of the sketch. Also, the center point of the arc having a radius of 25 mm is coincident with the origin.

5. Click on the **Features** tab in the CommandManager and then click on the **Extruded Boss/Base** tool. The **Boss-Extrude PropertyManager** and a preview of the extruded feature appear. Next, change the orientation of the model to isometric.

6. Invoke the **End Condition** drop-down list in the **Direction 1** rollout of the PropertyManager.

7. Select the **Up To Surface** option in the **End Condition** drop-down list. The **Face/Plane** field becomes available in the **Direction 1** rollout and is activated, by default.

8. Click on the outer circular face of the base feature. The preview of the extruded feature appears in the graphics area such that it is extruded up to the selected face, see Figure 9.109.

9. Click on the green tick-mark ✓ in the PropertyManager. The extruded feature is created, see Figure 9.110. Next, hide the reference plane.

9.109   **9.110**

Section 8: Creating the Sixth Feature - Circular Pattern

1. Invoke the **Pattern** flyout by clicking on the arrow at the bottom of the **Linear Pattern** tool.

2. Click on the **Circular Pattern** tool in the **Pattern** flyout. The **CirPattern**   Circular Pattern
    PropertyManager appears.

3. Select the fifth feature (previously created extruded feature) as the feature to be patterned
    from the graphics area.

4. Click on the **Pattern Axis** field in the **Direction 1** rollout of the PropertyManager.

5. Click on the outer circular face of the base feature in the graphics area to define the pattern
    axis. The preview of the circular pattern appears.

6. Make sure that the **Equal spacing** radio button is selected in the **Direction 1** rollout.

7. Enter **8** in the **Number of Instances** field of the **Direction 1** rollout.

8. Click on the green tick-mark ☑ in the PropertyManager. A circular pattern is created, see
    Figure 9.111.

9.111

Section 9: Saving the Model

1. Click on the **Save** tool in the **Standard** toolbar. The **Save As** dialog box appears.

2. Browse to the Chapter 9 folder of the SOLIDWORKS folder and then save the model with the
    name Tutorial 2. You need to create these folders, if not created earlier.

Hands-on Test Drive 1

Create a model, as shown in Figure 9.112. The different views and dimensions are given in the same figure for your reference. All dimensions are in mm.

SECTION A-A

Hands-on Test Drive 2

Create a model, as shown in Figure 9.113. The different views and dimensions are given in the same figure for your reference. All dimensions are in mm.

9.113

Hands-on Test Drive 3

Create a model, as shown in Figure 9.114. The different views and dimensions are given in the same figure for your reference. All dimensions are in mm.

9.114

Summary

The chapter discusses the use of various patterning and mirroring tools using which, you can create different types of patterns such as linear pattern, circular pattern, curve driven pattern, and sketch driven pattern.

The linear pattern is created by making multiple instances of features, faces, or bodies, linearly in Direction 1 and Direction 2. You can also skip pattern instances which are not required in the pattern. The circular pattern is created by making multiple instances of features, faces, or bodies in a circular manner about an axis. You can select an axis, a circular face, a circular edge, a linear edge, a linear sketch or an angular dimension to define the axis of circular pattern. The curve driven pattern is created by making multiple instances of features, faces, or bodies along a curve. You can select a 2D/3D sketch/curve or an edge as curve to drive pattern instances. The sketch driven pattern is created by using sketch points of a sketch. The table driven pattern is created by specifying coordinate points for each pattern instance with respect to a coordinate system. The fill pattern is created by filling an area with pattern instances of the selected feature. You can also use the predefined cut shapes to fill in the defined area or boundary in the fill pattern. The variable pattern is created by varying the dimensions and reference geometries of the features to be patterned. In addition to describing the different types of patterns, the chapter also discusses how to mirror features, faces, or bodies about a mirroring plane.

Questions

- The _____ tool is used for creating multiple instances of features, faces, or bodies in one or two linear directions.

- The _____ tool is used for creating multiple instances of features, faces, or bodies along a curve.

- You can create a variable pattern by using the _____ tool.

- In a variable pattern, you can vary _____ and _____ of the features to be patterned.

- When the _____ check box is unchecked, all the instances of the linear pattern maintain same geometrical relations as the original or parent feature.

- The _____ pattern is created by specifying coordinate points for each pattern instance with respect to a coordinate system.

- While creating a linear pattern, you cannot vary pattern instances with respect to a path. (True/False)

- In SOLIDWORKS, you can mirror features as well as faces of a model. (True/False)

Advanced Modeling - III

This chapter discusses the following topics:

- Working with the Hole Wizard
- Creating Advanced Holes
- Adding Cosmetic Threads
- Creating Threads
- Creating Fillets
- Creating Chamfers
- Creating Rib Features
- Creating Shell Features
- Creating Wrap Features

In this chapter, you will learn about creating standard or customized holes such as counterbore, countersink, straight tap, and tapered tap as per the standard specifications by using the **Hole Wizard** tool and the **Advanced Hole** tool. Besides, you will learn about other advanced modeling tools such as **Cosmetic Thread**, **Thread**, **Rib**, **Shell**, **Wrap**, **Fillet**, and **Chamfer**.

Working with the Hole Wizard `Updated`

The **Hole Wizard** tool is used for creating standard holes such as counterbore, countersink, and straight tap as per standard specifications. To create standard holes by using the **Hole Wizard** tool, click on the **Hole Wizard** tool in the **Features CommandManager**. The **Hole Specification PropertyManager** appears, see Figure 10.1. The options in this PropertyManager are discussed next.

Type Tab

The **Hole Specification PropertyManager** has two tabs: **Type** and **Positions**. By default, the **Type** tab is activated. As a result, the options for specifying the type of hole and hole specifications are displayed in different rollouts of the PropertyManager. The options are discussed next.

Hole Type

The **Hole Type** rollout of the PropertyManager is used for selecting the type of hole such as counterbore, countersink, or straight tap. Depending upon the type of hole to be created, you can click on the **Counterbore**, **Countersink**, **Hole**, **Straight Tap**, **Tapered Tap**, or **Legacy Hole** button in this rollout. Figure 10.2 shows counterbore holes and Figure 10.3 shows countersink holes created on the top face of the model.

Using this rollout, you can not only create standard holes, but also slot holes by selecting the **Counterbore Slot**, **Countersink Slot**, and **Slot** buttons. Figure 10.4 shows counterbore slots and Figure 10.5 shows countersink slots created on the top face of the model. The remaining options of this rollout are discussed next.

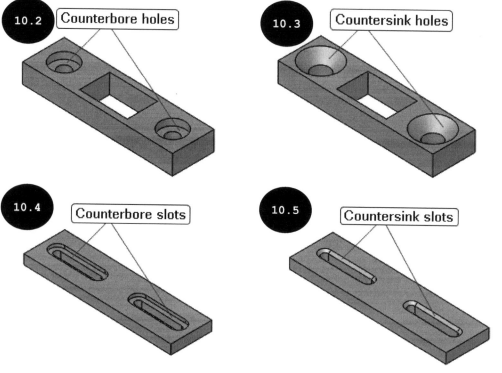

Counterbore holes

Countersink holes

Counterbore slots

Countersink slots

Standard

The **Standard** drop-down list is used for selecting the type of standard such as ANSI Metric, ANSI Inch, BSI, IS, JIS, or ISO for creating the hole, see Figure 10.6.

Type

The **Type** drop-down list is used for specifying the type of fastener to be inserted into the hole. The availability of options in this drop-down list depends upon the type of hole and standard selected. Figure 10.7 shows the **Type** drop-down list when the **Counterbore** hole and the **ANSI Metric** standard are selected.

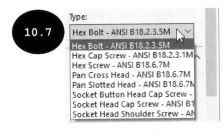

Hole Specifications

The **Hole Specifications** rollout of the PropertyManager is used for defining specifications for the fastener to be inserted into the hole. The options of this rollout are discussed next.

Size

The **Size** drop-down list is used for selecting the size of the fastener to be inserted. The availability of options in this drop-down list depends upon the type of hole and standard selected.

Fit

The **Fit** drop-down list is used for selecting the type of fit between the fastener and hole. You can specify close, normal, or loose fastener fit.

Note: The size of the hole depends upon the size of the fastener and the type of fit. In SOLIDWORKS, the size of the hole is automatically adjusted depending upon the specification of the fastener and the type of fit selected.

Show custom sizing

The **Show custom sizing** check box is used for displaying and customizing the standard size of the hole. On selecting the **Show custom sizing** check box, the standard size of the hole as per the specified specifications appears in the respective fields of the rollout, see Figure 10.8.

You can modify the standard specifications of the hole by entering the required values in the respective fields. Note that the background color of the fields, whose values are edited or customized, are changed to yellow color. After editing the specifications, if you want to restore the default standard specifications, click on the **Restore Default Values** button in this rollout.

End Condition

The options in the **End Condition** rollout are used for defining the end condition or termination method for a hole, see Figure 10.9. Some of the options for defining the end condition of the hole are the same as those discussed earlier while creating the extruded feature. The remaining options are discussed next.

Depth up to Shoulder ⬛

On selecting the **Depth up to Shoulder** button, the specified depth of the hole is measured upto the shoulder of the hole, see Figure 10.10. Note that this button is not available if the **Through All** or **Up to Next** option is selected in the **End Condition** drop-down list of the **End Condition** rollout.

Depth up to Tip ⬛

On selecting the **Depth up to Tip** button, the specified depth of the hole is measured upto the tip of the hole, see Figure 10.11. Note that this button is not available if the **Through All** or **Up to Next** option is selected in the **End Condition** drop-down list of the **End Condition** rollout.

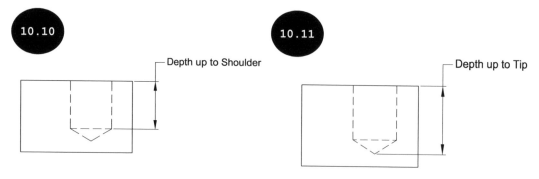

Options

The availability of the options in the **Options** rollout depends upon the type of hole selected. Figure 10.12 shows the **Options** rollout when the **Counterbore** hole type is selected. The options are discussed next.

10.12

Head clearance

On selecting the **Head clearance** check box, the **Head Clearance** field appears below it. In this field, you can specify the head clearance value for the counterbore or countersink hole. In other words, the value entered in the **Head Clearance** field is used for defining the clearance between the top face of the fastener head and the hole.

Near side countersink

The **Near side countersink** check box is used for creating the countersink shape at the near side of the placement face of the hole, see Figure 10.13. On selecting the **Near side countersink** check box, the **Near Side Countersink Diameter** and **Near Side Countersink Angle** fields appear in the rollout. These fields are used for specifying the diameter and angle of the countersink shape to be created at the near side of the placement face of the hole. Figure 10.13 shows a counterbore hole with countersink shape created at its near side of the placement face.

10.13

Far side countersink

The **Far side countersink** check box is used for creating the countersink shape at the far side of the placement face of the hole, see Figure 10.14. On selecting the **Far side countersink** check box, the **Far Side Countersink Diameter** and **Far Side Countersink Angle** fields appear in the rollout. These fields are used for specifying countersink diameter and angle for the countersink shape to be created at the far side of the placement face of the hole. Figure 10.14 shows a counterbore hole with countersink shape created at the far side of the placement face.

10.14

Under head countersink

The **Under head countersink** check box is used for creating the countersink shape under the hole head, see Figure 10.15. On selecting the **Under head countersink** check box, the **Under Head Countersink Diameter** and **Under Head Countersink Angle** fields appear. These fields are used for specifying the countersink diameter and angle for the countersink shape to be created under the hole head diameter. Figure 10.15 shows a counterbore hole with countersink shape created under the head diameter.

Note that if the **Straight Tap** hole type is selected in the **Hole Type** rollout, the options in the **Options** rollout appear as shown in Figure 10.16. These options are discussed next.

10.15

10.16

Tap drill diameter

Cosmetic thread

Remove thread

Tap drill diameter, Cosmetic thread, and Remove thread

The **Tap drill diameter** button is used for creating a Straight tap hole having the same diameter as the tapped diameter of the hole with no thread representation, see Figure 10.17. The

Cosmetic thread button is used for creating a Straight tap hole having the same diameter as the tapped hole with the cosmetic representation of thread, see Figure 10.18. The **Remove thread** button is used for creating a Straight tap hole having a diameter equal to the thread diameter of the tapped hole, see Figure 10.19.

Thread class

On selecting the **Thread class** check box, the **Thread class** drop-down list becomes available in front of it. By using this drop-down list, you can select a class for the threaded or tapped holes.

Tolerance/Precision

In SOLIDWORKS, you can also specify tolerance and precision values for the hole parameters by using the **Tolerance/Precision** rollout of the PropertyManager, see Figure 10.20. Note that the availability of the options in this rollout depends upon the type of hole selected. The options are discussed next.

Callout value

The **Callout value** drop-down list is used for selecting an element of the hole such as **Thru Hole Diameter, CounterBore Diameter**, or **CounterBore Depth** to define the tolerance values for its parameter, see Figure 10.21. Note that the availability of the options in this drop-down list depends upon the type of hole selected. Figure 10.21 shows the **Callout value** drop-down list when the **Counterbore** hole type is selected.

Note: You can specify tolerance to the parameter of each element of the hole one by one by selecting them in the **Callout value** drop-down list.

Tolerance Type

The options in the **Tolerance Type** drop-down list are used for selecting the type of tolerance to be applied to the parameter of the selected hole element. By default, the **None** option is selected in this drop-down list. As a result, no tolerance is applied. Depending upon the type of tolerance selected in this drop-down list, the corresponding fields are enabled below this drop-down list in the **Tolerance/Precision** rollout in order to specify tolerance values. Figure 10.22 shows the **Tolerance/Precision** rollout when the **Bilateral** option is selected in the **Tolerance Type** drop-down list.

Unit Precision

The **Unit Precision** drop-down list is used for selecting the unit of precision or number of digits after the decimal point in a tolerance value.

> **Note:** The tolerance values specified in this rollout will automatically propagate to the hole callouts in the drawing. Also, if you make any change in the hole callout in the Drawing environment, the same change automatically gets updated in the part and vice-versa. You will learn about creating drawings in the Drawing environment in Chapter 14.

After specifying all specifications in the **Type** tab of the PropertyManager, you need to define the placement point for the hole in the model by using the **Position** tab of the PropertyManager.

Positions Tab

The **Positions** tab of the PropertyManager is used for defining the position of the hole. After specifying all specifications for the hole in the **Type** tab, click on the **Positions** tab in the PropertyManager. The name of the PropertyManager changes to **Hole Position PropertyManager**, see Figure 10.23. Also, you are prompted to specify the placement face for the hole. You can select a planar face, a plane, or a curved face as the placement face of the hole. Click on a face of the model as the placement face of the hole. The placement face is defined and the preview of the hole appears, which follows the cursor as you move it over the placement face. Now, you need to define the placement point of the hole. Click the left mouse button arbitrarily to specify the placement point of the hole. The center point of the hole is placed at the defined placement point. Similarly, you can specify multiple placement points for creating multiple holes of similar parameters. After specifying the placement points arbitrarily, you can use the dimension tools of the **Sketch CommandManager** to position the placement point of the hole, as required, see Figure 10.24. You can also apply horizontal and vertical relations to position the placement point of the hole. Once the position of the hole is defined by applying dimensions, click on the green tick-mark ☑ in the PropertyManager. The hole is created.

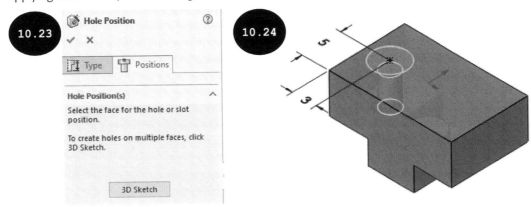

Note: On selecting the planar face as the placement face of the hole, the 2D sketch environment gets invoked. As a result, you can only create multiple holes on the selected placement face. However, on selecting a curved face as the placement face, the 3D sketch environment gets invoked. As a result, you can create multiple holes on different placement faces. You can also invoke the 3D sketch environment by clicking on the **3D Sketch** button in the PropertyManager for creating holes on different faces.

Procedure for Creating a Hole by using the Hole Wizard Tool

1. Click on the **Hole Wizard** tool. The **Hole Specification PropertyManager** appears.
2. Specify the type of hole and other hole specifications, as required.
3. Specify the tolerance and precision values for each element of the hole by using the options of the **Tolerance/Precision** rollout, if needed.
4. After specifying the hole specifications, click on the **Position** tab in the PropertyManager.
5. Click on a planar face, a plane, or a curved face as the placement face of the hole.
6. Click to specify the placement point of the hole on the placement face.
7. Apply dimensions and relations to position the hole, as required.
8. Click on the green tick-mark ☑ in the PropertyManager. The hole is created.

Tip: In SOLIDWORKS, the settings specified in the **Hole Specification PropertyManager** are retained and appear while editing the hole.

Creating Advanced Holes

In SOLIDWORKS, you can also create advanced holes such as manifolds and multi-stepped holes by using the **Advanced Hole** tool. You can also define customized hole types with the combinations of different standard holes such as counterbore, countersink, straight tap, and tapered by using this tool. This is a very powerful tool for creating complex multi-stepped holes in a single command. To invoke the **Advanced Hole** tool, click on the arrow at the bottom of the **Hole Wizard** tool. A flyout appears, see Figure 10.25. In this flyout, click on the **Advanced Hole** tool. The **Advanced Hole PropertyManager** and the **Near Side** flyout appear, see Figure 10.26. The options in the PropertyManager and the flyout are discussed next.

Near And Far Side Faces

The **Near And Far Side Faces** rollout of the PropertyManager is used for selecting the near and far side faces of a hole. By default, the **Near Side Faces** field is available in this rollout. As a result, you can select one or more faces as the near side faces of the hole. Select a face of the model as the near side face of the hole, see Figure 10.27. A preview of the hole with default specifications appears on the selected face, see Figure 10.27.

After selecting the near side face of the hole, you can define the near side hole elements by using the **Near Side** flyout. By default, Counterbore is selected as the first near side element in this flyout. Invoke the **Near Side** flyout by clicking on the arrow facing downward, see Figure 10.28. In this flyout, you can click on the required button: **Near Side Counterbore, Near Side Countersink, Near Side Tapered Tap, Hole,** or **Straight Tap** as the near side element. Once you have defined the first near side hole element by using the **Near Side** flyout, you need to define the hole element specifications such as type of hole, standard, and size by using the options of the **Element Specification** rollout in the PropertyManager. The options in this rollout of the PropertyManager are same as discussed earlier. After defining the first near side hole element and its specifications, you can add the second near side hole element. For doing so, click on the **Insert Element Below Active Element** button in the flyout, see Figure 10.28. The default second hole element is added below the first hole element in the flyout, see Figure 10.29. Also, the preview of the hole in the graphics area is modified such that the second hole element with its default specifications is added. Now, you need to define the required type of the second hole element such as Counterbore, Countersink, or Straight Tap by using the **Near Side** flyout and then specify its specifications by using the **Element Specification** rollout of the PropertyManager. Similarly, you can add multiple near side hole elements by using the **Near Side** flyout. Note that you can also add a hole element above an active hole element by using the **Insert Element Above Active Element** button of the flyout. To delete a hole element, click on the element to activate it and then click on the **Delete Active Element** button of the flyout. You can also reverse the direction of a hole by using the **Reverse Stack Direction** button of the flyout.

To define the far side face of the hole, select the **Far Side** check box in the **Near And Far Side Faces** rollout of the PropertyManager, see Figure 10.30. The **Far Side Face** field and the **Far Side** flyout appears, see Figure 10.30. By default, the **Far Side Face** field is activated in the rollout. As a result, you can select a face of the model as the far side face of the hole, see Figure 10.31. After selecting a far side face, the preview of the hole is modified in the graphics area such that the default far side hole element is added, see Figure 10.31.

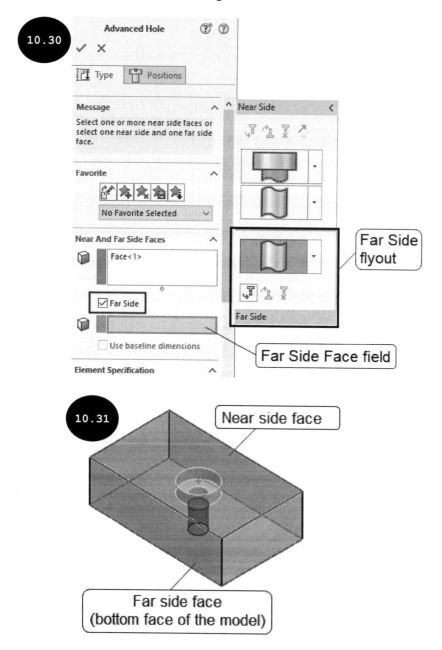

You can select a required far side hole element by using the **Far Side** flyout. To select a far side hole element, click on the arrow next to the far side hole element in the **Far Side** flyout, see Figure 10.32 and then click on the **Far Side Counterbore**, **Far Side Countersink**, **Far Side Tapered Tap**, **Hole**, or **Straight Tap** button, as required.

After selecting the required first far side hole element, you need to define its specifications by using the options of the **Element Specification** rollout in the PropertyManager. You can also add multiple far side elements by using the **Insert Element Below Active Element** and **Insert Element Above Active Element** buttons of the **Far Side** flyout. Figure 10.33 shows the preview of a multi-stepped hole having multiple near and far side elements.

Note: The transparency of the model shown in Figure 10.33 has been changed so as to view the preview of the advance hole clearly. For doing so, right-click on the model and then click on the **Change Transparency** option in the shortcut menu that appears.

In SOLIDWORKS, you can customize the hole callout for the advanced hole as per the order and variables required for the manufacturing processes and apply it in the drawing. For doing so, expand the **Hole Callout** rollout of the PropertyManager, see Figure 10.34 and then select the **Customize callout** radio button. Now, you can change the order of the callout strings by using the **Move Up** and **Move Down** buttons of the rollout, as needed in the drawing. Note that these buttons are enabled on selecting a callout string to be reordered in the hole callout. You can also edit the variables of a callout string. For doing so, double-click on a callout string. The **Callout Variables** button and symbol buttons appear in the rollout. Click on the **Callout Variables** button to invoke the **Callout Variables** dialog box. By using this dialog box, you can select the required variable and then click on the **OK** button. Besides, you can also add symbols to a callout string by clicking on the respective symbol buttons in the rollout. Note that the changes made in the **Hole Callout** rollout of the PropertyManager, are reflected in the hole callout of the advanced hole in the Drawing environment. You will learn about adding the hole callout in the Drawing environment in Chapter 14.

After defining the required near and far side elements of the hole with the required specifications, you need to define the placement point of the hole. For doing so, click on the **Positions** tab in the PropertyManager. The name of PropertyManager changes to **Hole Position PropertyManager**, see Figure 10.35. Also, you are promoted to specify the placement point for the hole. Click the left mouse button arbitrarily on the near side face of the hole to specify its placement point. The center point of the hole is placed at the defined placement point. Similarly, you can create multiple instances of the hole by specifying the placement points. After specifying the placement points arbitrarily, you can use the dimension tools of the **Sketch CommandManager** to position the

placement point of the hole, as required. You can also skip the instances of the hole by using the **Instances To Skip** rollout of the PropertyManager. Once the position of the hole is defined by applying dimensions, click on the green tick-mark in the PropertyManager. The hole is created.

Adding Cosmetic Threads   Updated

A Cosmetic thread represents the real thread of a feature without removing the material. It is recommended to add cosmetic threads to holes, fasteners, or cylindrical features of a model, because adding cosmetic threads helps in reducing the complexity of the model and improves the overall performance of the system. Figure 10.36 shows a cosmetic thread added to a cylindrical feature and Figure 10.37 shows cosmetic threads added to hole/cut extruded features.

To add a cosmetic thread, click on the **Insert > Annotations > Cosmetic Thread** in the SOLIDWORKS Menus. The **Cosmetic Thread PropertyManager** appears, see Figure 10.38. The options in this PropertyManager are discussed next.

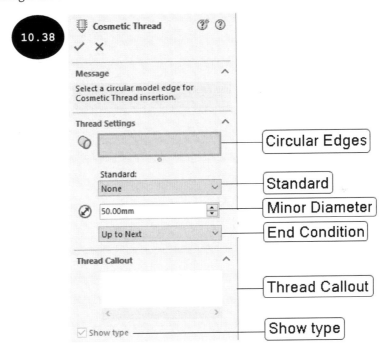

Thread Settings
The options in the Thread Settings rollout of the PropertyManager are used for defining the thread settings and are discussed next.

Circular Edges
The **Circular Edges** field of the **Thread Settings** rollout is activated by default. As a result, you can select a circular edge of a feature for adding the cosmetic thread. Click on a circular edge of a feature for adding a cosmetic thread. A dotted circle appears in the graphics area, which represents the minor or major diameter of the thread, see Figures 10.39 and 10.40. Also, the name of the selected circular edge appears in the **Circular Edges** field.

> **Note:** On selecting the circular edge of a cylindrical feature, the dotted circle represents the minor (inner) diameter of the thread, see Figure 10.39, whereas on selecting the circular edge of a cut/hole feature, the dotted circle represents the major (outer) diameter of the thread, see Figure 10.40.

Standard

The Standard drop-down list is used for selecting the type of standard such as ANSI Inch, ANSI Metric, or ISO to be followed for creating the cosmetic thread.

Type

The Type drop-down list is used for selecting the type of thread to be added. Note that this drop-down list will not be available if the None option is selected in the Standard drop-down list.

Size

The Size drop-down list is used for selecting the standard size of the thread. Note that this drop-down list will not be available if the None option is selected in the Standard drop-down list.

Minor Diameter or Major Diameter

The Minor Diameter or Major Diameter field is used for specifying the minor or major diameter of the thread, respectively. Note that this field (Minor Diameter or Major Diameter) is enabled only if the None option is selected in the Standard drop-down list. Also, the field (Minor Diameter or Major Diameter) appears, depending upon the circular edge selected for applying the thread. If the circular edge of a cylindrical feature is selected, the Minor Diameter field appears and if the circular edge of a hole feature is selected, the Major Diameter field appears.

End Condition

The End Condition drop-down list is used for specifying the end condition or termination for the cosmetic thread. Note that the circular edge that is selected for adding the cosmetic thread is the start condition of the cosmetic thread.

Thread class

In SOLIDWORKS, when you select the **Thread class** check box in the PropertyManager, the **Thread class** drop-down list becomes available in front of it. By using this drop-down list, you can select a thread class for the cosmetic thread.

Thread Callout

The **Thread Callout** field is used for entering text or comment for a thread, that appears in the thread callout of the drawing view. You can create drawing views in the Drawing environment of SOLIDWORKS. You will learn about creating drawing views in later chapters.

Note: The **Thread Callout** field of the **Thread Callout** rollout is activated only if the **None** option is selected in the **Standard** drop-down list. If you select a standard such as ANSI Inch or ANSI Metric then this field is not activated. However, the default standard text appears in this field, depending upon the type of standard and thread selected.

In SOLIDWORKS 2020, you can include or exclude the display of thread type from the default standard text that appears in the **Thread Callout** field by selecting or clearing the **Show type** check box in the **Thread Callout** rollout respectively. Note that this check box is not activated if the **None** option is selected in the **Standard** drop-down list.

After specifying all parameters for adding cosmetic thread in the PropertyManager, click on the green tick-mark ✓ in the PropertyManager. The cosmetic thread is added and appears in the graphics area, see Figure 10.41. Also, a cosmetic thread feature is added under the node of the feature in the FeatureManager Design Tree, see Figure 10.42.

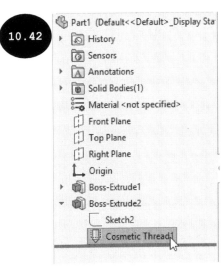

Note: In Figure 10.41, the shaded display style of the cosmetic thread is turned off. As a result, only the dotted circle representing the thread diameter appears in the graphics area. To turn on the shaded display style, right-click on the **Annotations** node in the FeatureManager Design Tree and then click on the **Details** option in the shortcut menu that appears, see Figure 10.43. The **Annotation Properties** dialog box appears. In this dialog box, select the **Shaded cosmetic threads** check box to turn on the shaded display style of the cosmetic thread. Figure 10.44 shows a cosmetic thread in the shaded display style.

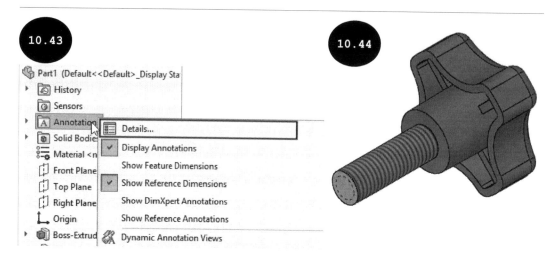

Procedure for Adding a Cosmetic Thread

1. Click on **Insert > Annotations > Cosmetic Thread** in the SOLIDWORKS Menus.
2. Select a circular edge of a model to add the cosmetic thread.
3. Specify parameters such as standard, size, and end condition for the cosmetic thread.
4. Click on the green tick-mark ✓ in the PropertyManager. The cosmetic thread is added.

Creating Threads

In SOLIDWORKS, in addition to adding cosmetic threads, you can create real threads on cylindrical or circular features by removing material from the model, see Figure 10.45. For doing so, click on the arrow at the bottom of the **Hole Wizard** tool in the **Features CommandManager**. A flyout appears, see Figure 10.46. In this flyout, click on the **Thread** tool. The **SOLIDWORKS** message window appears. Click on the **OK** button in this window. The **Thread PropertyManager** appears, see Figure 10.47. The options in this PropertyManager are discussed next.

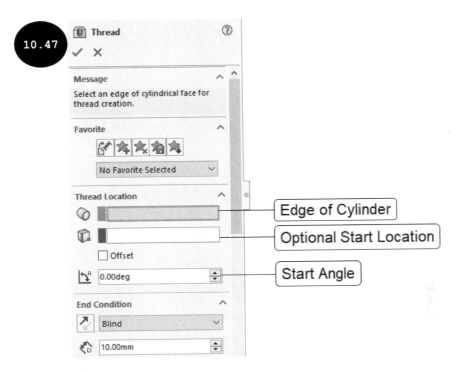

10.47

Thread Location

By default, the **Edge of Cylinder** field in the **Thread Location** rollout is activated. As a result, you can select a circular edge of a cylindrical feature or a hole feature for creating the thread. Click on a circular edge of a cylindrical feature or a hole feature. A preview of the thread appears with default parameters in the graphics area, see Figure 10.48. Note that by default, the selected circular edge is used as the start location of the thread. You can define the start location of the thread other than the selected circular edge. For doing so, click on the **Optional Start Location** field in the **Thread Location** rollout and then select a vertex, an edge, a plane, or a planar face as the start location of the thread.

The **Offset** check box is used for creating the thread at an offset distance from the start location, see Figure 10.49. To create the thread at an offset distance from the start location, select the **Offset** check box. The **Offset Distance** field becomes available below the check box. In this field, enter the offset distance. The **Start Angle** field of the **Thread Location** rollout is used for defining the start angle for the helix of the thread. Note that the start angle must be positive.

10.48 **10.49** Offset distance

End Condition

The **End Condition** rollout of the PropertyManager is used for specifying the end condition for the thread. On selecting the **Blind** option in the **End condition** drop-down list, you can enter the depth value for the thread in the **Depth** field. On selecting the **Revolutions** option in the **End Condition** drop-down list, you can specify the number of revolutions for the thread in the **Revolutions** field. On selecting the **Up To Selection** option, the **End Location** field becomes available in the rollout. As a result, you can select a vertex, an edge, a plane, or a planar face as the end condition for the thread.

The **Maintain thread length** check box is used for maintaining a constant length for the thread from its starting location. Note that this check box is available only if the offset distance from the start location is defined by selecting the **Offset** check box in the **Thread Location** rollout and the **Blind** or the **Revolutions** option is selected in the **End Condition** drop-down list of the PropertyManager.

Specification

The **Specification** rollout is used for defining specifications for the thread such as type and size. The **Type** drop-down list of this rollout is used for selecting the type of the thread and the **Size** drop-down list is used for selecting the standard size of the thread.

The **Diameter** field of the **Specification** rollout is used for displaying the helix diameter of the thread, which depends on the cylindrical edge selected for creating the thread, see Figure 10.50. You can override the helix diameter of the thread by using the **Override Diameter** button. On clicking the **Override Diameter** button, the **Diameter** field gets enabled. In this field, you can enter the override value for the helical diameter of the thread. Similarly, on clicking the **Override Pitch** button, the **Pitch** field gets enabled for entering the override value for the helix pitch of the thread.

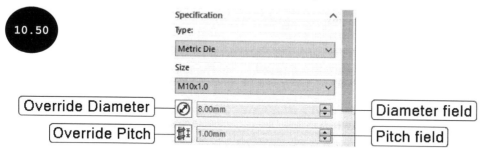

By default, the **Cut Thread** radio button is selected as the thread method in the **Specification** rollout. As a result, the thread is created by removing material from the model, see Figure 10.51. On selecting the **Extrude Thread** radio button, you can create a thread by adding the material in the feature, see Figure 10.52.

> **Note:** While creating a thread on a cylindrical feature by adding material using the **Extrude Thread** radio button, you need to flip the thread profile by selecting the **Mirror Profile** check box. Similarly, while creating a thread on a hole feature by removing the material using the **Cut Thread** radio button, you need to flip the thread profile by selecting the **Mirror Profile** check box.

The **Mirror Profile** check box is used for flipping the thread profile about its horizontal or vertical axis by using the **Mirror horizontally** or **Mirror vertically** radio button, respectively. Note that these radio buttons become available after selecting the **Mirror Profile** check box. The **Rotation Angle** field is used for specifying the rotation angle for the thread helix. On clicking the **Locate Profile** button in the rollout, the profile of the thread is zoomed such that you can change the sketch points or vertices of the thread profile.

Thread Options

By default, the **Right-hand thread** radio button is selected in the **Thread Options** rollout, see Figure 10.53. As a result, the resultant thread is created as right hand thread (clockwise direction). On selecting the **Left-hand thread** radio button, the resultant thread is created as left hand thread (counter clockwise direction).

In SOLIDWORKS, you can align the thread to the start and end faces of the feature by using the **Trim with start face** and **Trim with end face** check boxes of the **Thread Options** rollout, respectively. Figure 10.54 shows the start edge and the end face of the cylindrical feature to be selected for creating the thread by adding the material using the **Extrude Thread** radio button. Figure 10.55 shows the resultant thread feature created when the **Trim with end face** check box is cleared and Figure 10.56 shows the resultant thread feature created when the **Trim with end face** check box is selected.

Note: To define the end face of a thread, you need to select the **Up To Selection** option in the **End Condition** drop-down list of the **End Condition** rollout and then select a face as the end face of the thread.

In SOLIDWORKS, you can also specify multiple starts for a thread by selecting the **Multiple Start** check box. On selecting this check box, the **Number of Starts** field becomes available in the rollout, which allows you to specify the number of starts for the thread. Note that the number of starts specified in this field define the number of times the thread is created in an equally spaced circular pattern around the feature, see Figure 10.57. In this figure, the thread has been created by specifying 5 as the number of starts for the thread. Note that the pitch of the thread must allow multiple starts for the thread. If the pitch of the thread does not allow multiple starts then self-intersection between the threads occur which does not allow you to create the thread with multiple starts.

Preview Options
The options of the **Preview Options** rollout are used for specifying the type of preview to be displayed in the graphics area.

Procedure for Creating a Thread
1. Click on the arrow at the bottom of the **Hole Wizard** tool. A flyout appears.
2. Click on the **Thread** tool in the flyout. The **Thread PropertyManager** appears.
3. Select a circular edge to create the thread.
4. Specify parameters such as end condition, type, and size of the thread.
5. Select the thread method: **Cut thread** or **Extrude thread** radio button in the **Specification** rollout.

6. Select the **Mirror Profile** check box to flip the direction of thread profile, if needed.
7. Click on the green tick-mark ☑ in the PropertyManager. The thread is created.

Creating Fillets

A fillet is a curved face of a constant or variable radius and is used for removing sharp edges of a model that may cause injury while handling the model. Figure 10.58 shows a model before and after creating a constant radius fillet on an edge.

Fillet

In SOLIDWORKS, you can create fillets by using two methods: Manual and FilletXpert. The Manual method is used for creating fillets manually. By using this method, you can create four types of fillets: constant radius fillet, variable radius fillet, face fillet, and full round fillet. On the other hand, the FilletXpert method is used for creating fillets automatically. By using this method, you can only create constant radius fillets in a model.

To create fillets by using the Manual method, click on the **Fillet** tool in the **Features CommandManager**. The **Fillet PropertyManager** appears, see Figure 10.59. If the **FilletXpert PropertyManager** appears on clicking the **Fillet** tool, then click on the **Manual** tab in the PropertyManager to invoke the **Fillet PropertyManager**. The methods for creating different types of fillets manually are discussed next.

Creating a Constant Radius Fillet

A constant radius fillet is a fillet that has a constant radius throughout the selected edge, see Figure 10.60. You can create a constant radius fillet by clicking on the **Constant Size Fillet** button in the **Fillet Type** rollout of the PropertyManager, see Figure 10.61. The options for creating a constant radius fillet that appear in the PropertyManager after selecting this button are discussed next.

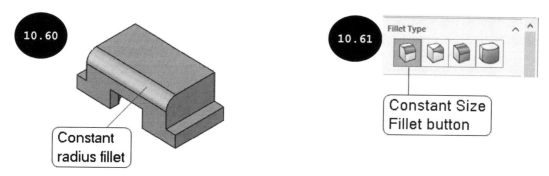

Items To Fillet

The options in the **Items To Fillet** rollout are used for selecting entities such as edges, faces, and features to create a fillet. The options are discussed next.

Edges, Faces, Features and Loops

The **Edges, Faces, Features and Loops** field of this rollout is activated by default. As a result, you can select edges, faces, features, or loops for creating a constant radius fillet. On selecting the edges, faces, features, or loops, a preview of the constant radius fillet appears in the graphics area with the default radius value.

Note: If you select a face to create a fillet, all the edges of the selected face get filleted, see Figure 10.62 and if you select a feature, all the edges of the selected feature get filleted, see Figure 10.63. Both these figures show the fillet preview.

Tangent propagation

The **Tangent propagation** check box is used for applying fillet to all the edges that are tangent to the selected edge. Figure 10.64 shows an edge to be selected for applying the fillet. Figures 10.65 and 10.66 show the preview of the resultant fillet when the **Tangent propagation** check box is cleared and selected, respectively.

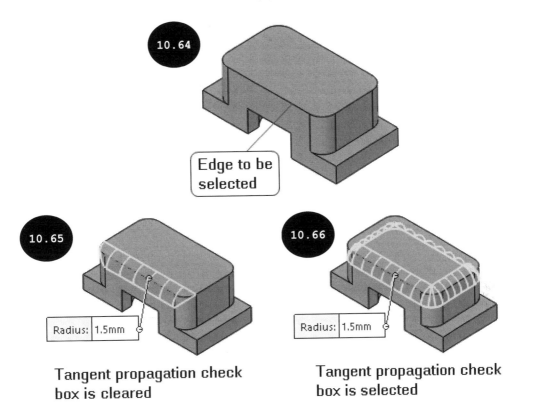

10.64

Edge to be selected

10.65

Radius: 1.5mm

Tangent propagation check
box is cleared

10.66

Radius: 1.5mm

Tangent propagation check
box is selected

Show selection toolbar

The **Show selection toolbar** check box of the **Items To Fillet** rollout is selected by default. As a result, the **Selection** toolbar appears on selecting an entity for creating a fillet, see Figure 10.67. The tools of the **Selection** toolbar help you in selecting multiple edges of the feature for creating the fillet.

10.67

Selection toolbar

Radius: 1.5mm

Full preview, Partial preview, and No preview

The **Full preview** radio button is used for displaying full preview of the fillet, which includes the preview of all fillet edges. On selecting the **Partial preview** radio button, the partial view of the fillet appears. Note that in case of partial preview, the preview appears only in one fillet edge. On selecting the **No preview** radio button, the display of preview is turned off.

Fillet Parameters

The options in the **Fillet Parameters** rollout are used for specifying fillet parameters, see Figure 10.68. The options are discussed next.

Fillet Method

The **Fillet Method** drop-down list is used for selecting the type of method to be used for creating the fillet. By selecting the **Symmetric** option, you can create a fillet, which is symmetric on both sides of the edge selected for creating the fillet, see Figure 10.69. When this option is selected, the **Radius** field becomes available in the rollout, which is used for entering symmetric radius of the fillet. On selecting the **Asymmetric** option, the **Distance 1** and **Distance 2** fields become available in the rollout, which are used for specifying two different radii for both the sides of the edge, see Figure 10.70.

Multiple radius fillet

By selecting the **Multiple radius fillet** check box, you can assign different radius values for the selected edges. For example, if you have selected two edges for applying fillet, then on selecting this check box, you can assign different radius values or control the radius of both the edges, individually. By default, this check box is cleared. As a result, all edges selected for applying the fillet have the same radius value.

Profile

The **Profile** drop-down list is used for selecting the type of fillet profile. Note that the fillet profile defines the cross sectional shape of the fillet. You can select the **Circular, Conic Rho, Conic Radius,** or **Curvature Continuous** option from this drop-down list to define the fillet profile. On selecting the **Circular** option, a fillet of circular shape is created, see Figure 10.71. If you select the **Conic Rho** option, the **Conic Rho** field becomes available below this drop-down list. In this field, you can specify the Rho value for the fillet. Note that you can define the Rho value in the range between 0 and 1, see Figures 10.72 through 10.74.

> **Tip:** If the Rho value is less than 0.5 then the fillet profile is of elliptical shape. If the Rho value is 0.5 then the fillet profile is of parabola shape. If the Rho value is greater than 0.5 then the fillet profile is of hyperbola shape.

By selecting the **Conic Radius** option, the **Conic Radius** field appears below the drop-down list, which is used for specifying the radius of curvature at the corner of the fillet. By selecting the **Curvature Continuous** option, a fillet is created such that it maintains a smooth curvature between the adjacent faces of the edge selected for creating the fillet.

Setback Parameters

The options in the **Setback Parameters** rollout are used for defining parameters for creating a setback fillet. A setback fillet is a fillet that has a smooth transition from fillet edges to a common intersecting vertex. You can create a setback fillet on three or more than three edges that are intersecting at a common vertex, see Figure 10.75. To create a setback fillet, expand the **Setback Parameters** rollout by clicking on the arrow that is available at its title bar, see Figure 10.76. The options in the **Setback Parameters** rollout are discussed next.

Setback Vertices
The **Setback Vertices** field is used for selecting a vertex where the fillet edges intersect each other.

Distance
The **Distance** field is used for specifying the fillet setback distance, which is calculated from the selected setback vertex.

Setback Distances
The **Setback Distances** field is used for specifying the setback distance for the individual edge of the fillet from the setback vertex. Note that as soon as you select the setback vertex, a list of corresponding edges appears in this field. To assign the setback distance to an edge, select an edge from this field and then enter the setback distance in the **Distance** field. Next, press ENTER. Similarly, you can assign the setback distance to other edges of the setback fillet. Figure 10.75 shows the preview of a setback fillet with different setback distances assigned.

Set All
The **Set All** button is used for assigning the current specified setback distance to all the edges that are listed in the **Setback Distance** field.

Partial Edge Parameters
In SOLIDWORKS, you can also create a partial fillet by specifying its start and end position along the edge of a model by using the **Partial Edge Parameters** rollout of the PropertyManager. For doing so, expand the **Partial Edge Parameters** rollout by selecting the check box that is available at its title bar, see Figure 10.77. The options in the **Partial Edge Parameters** are discussed next.

Start condition

The options in the **Start condition** drop-down list are used for defining the start condition of the partial fillet. By default, the **Distance Offset** option is selected in the **Start condition** drop-down list. As a result, you can specify the offset distance from the start point of the fillet in the **Offset distance from start point** field of the PropertyManager. Alternatively, you can also drag the start handle that appears in the graphics area to define the start position of the partial fillet along the edge, see Figure 10.78.

On selecting the **Percentage Offset** option in the **Start condition** drop-down list, you can define the start position of the fillet by specifying a percentage value in the **Percentage offset from start point** field that appears in the rollout. Note that the percentage value is calculated in terms of the total length of the selected edge. On selecting the **Reference Offset** option, you can select a sketch point, a reference point, or a planar face to define the start position of the fillet in the field that appears in the rollout.

End condition

The options in the **End condition** drop-down list are used for defining the end condition of the partial fillet. The options in this drop-down list are same as discussed earlier. You can also drag the end handle that appears in the preview of the fillet to define the end condition of the fillet. Figure 10.79 shows the preview of a partial fillet by defining its start and end conditions.

Note: The **Partial Edge Parameters** rollout is only available for constant radius fillets.

Fillet Options

The **Fillet Options** rollout is shown in Figure 10.80. The options in this rollout are discussed next.

Select through faces

By selecting the **Select through faces** check box, you can select the invisible edges of the model for applying fillets, see Figure 10.81. In this figure, three edges are visible and the fourth edge is not visible from the front. You can select the invisible edges of the model from the front when the **Select through faces** check box is selected.

Keep features

After selecting the **Keep features** check box, if you apply a fillet of large radius which covers the other feature (extruded boss or cut) of a model, then the fillet created is such that the covered feature remains available in the model. However, if you clear this check box, then the fillet created is such that the covered feature is no longer available in the model. Figure 10.82 shows the preview of a fillet with large radius, which covers a cylindrical feature of the model. Figures 10.83 and 10.84 show the resultant models after creating the fillets when the **Keep features** check box is selected and cleared, respectively.

Note: In SOLIDWORKS 2020, you can repair fillets that have missing edges. For example, while creating a model, if some of the filleted edges have been removed, or are no longer available in the model, then the respective fillet feature displays an error of missing edges, see Figure 10.85. To repair a fillet that has missing edges or errors, click on it in the FeatureManager Design Tree and then click on the **Edit Feature** tool in the Pop-up toolbar that appears, see Figure 10.85. The **Fillet PropertyManager** appears with a list of all the missing edges of the fillet, see Figure 10.86. Next, right-click on the missing edge to be repaired and then click on the **Repair All Missing References** option in the shortcut menu that appears, see Figure 10.86. SOLIDWORKS attempts to reattach or repair all the missing references of the fillet. You can also clear all the missing references of the fillet by using the **Clear All Missing References** option of the shortcut menu. You can also define new references for the missing edges, manually. After reparing the fillet, click on the green tick-mark button in the PropertyManager.

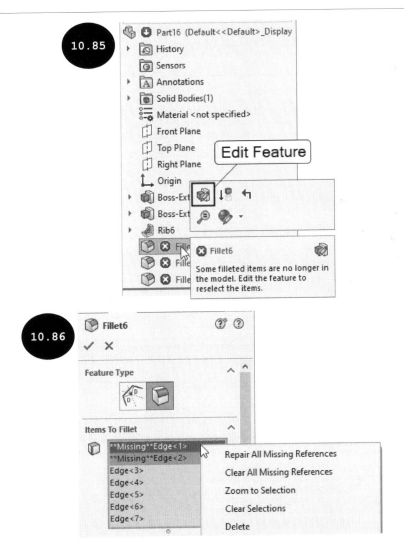

Procedure for Creating a Constant Radius Fillet

1. Click on the **Fillet** tool. The **Fillet PropertyManager** appears.
2. Make sure that the **Constant Size Fillet** button is selected in the **Fillet Type** rollout.
3. Select edges, faces, features, or loops to create a constant radius fillet.
4. Specify the radius value of the fillet in the **Radius** field of the **Fillet Parameters** rollout.
5. Click on the green tick-mark ✓ in the PropertyManager. The constant radius fillet is created.

> **Note:** In SOLIDWORKS, after creating a constant radius fillet, you can convert it into a chamfer and vice-versa. To convert a constant radius fillet into a chamfer, select the constant radius fillet in the FeatureManager Design Tree or in the graphics area. A Pop-up toolbar appears near the cursor. In this Pop-up toolbar, click on the **Edit Feature** tool 🖉. The **Fillet PropertyManager** appears. In this PropertyManager, click on the **Chamfer Type** 🖉 button to convert the selected fillet into the chamfer. Next, click on the green tick-mark button.

Creating a Variable Radius Fillet

A variable radius fillet is a fillet that has variable radii along an edge, see Figure 10.87. You can create a variable radius fillet by selecting the **Variable Size Fillet** button in the **Fillet Type** rollout, see Figure 10.88. The options to create a variable radius fillet that appear in the PropertyManager after selecting the **Variable Size Fillet** button are discussed next.

Items To Fillet

The **Edges to Fillet** field of the **Items To Fillet** rollout is activated, by default. As a result, you can select edges for creating variable radius fillet. The options in the **Items To Fillet** rollout are the same as those discussed earlier, while creating the constant radius fillet.

Variable Radius Parameters

The options in the **Variable Radius Parameters** rollout are used for defining parameters for creating the variable radius fillet, see Figure 10.89. The options are discussed next.

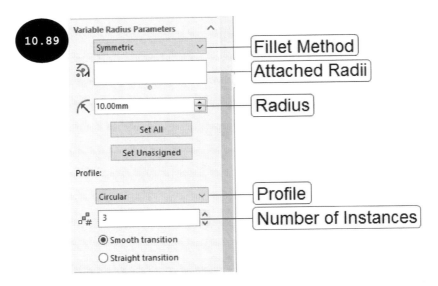

10.89

Attached Radii

The **Attached Radii** field displays a list of all vertices and control points of the selected edge or edges. Note that you can define a different radius value for each vertex and control point of the edge.

Number of Instances

The **Number of Instances** field is used for specifying the number of control points to be attached along the selected edge. You can specify different radius value for each control point. After specifying the number of control points, press ENTER. The pink dots representing control points appear along the edge selected for applying the fillet, see Figure 10.90.

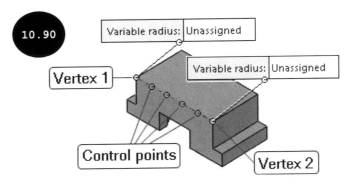

10.90

To specify a different radius value for each control point, click on the control points one by one that appear along the selected edge in the graphics area. The callouts having **R** and **P** fields appear attached to each selected control point in the graphics area, see Figure 10.91. By using the **R** field of a callout, you can specify the radius value for the control point and by using the **P** field, you can specify the location of the control point along the edge in terms of percentage value. Note that to edit the value in a callout, you need to click on its field to be edited.

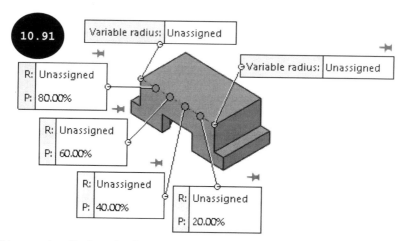

In addition to the display of callouts in the graphics area, the names of the selected control points appear in the **Attached Radii** field of the PropertyManager. You can also specify the radius value for a control point by selecting its name in the **Attached Radii** field and then entering the radius value in the **Radius** field of the PropertyManager.

Set All
The **Set All** button is used for assigning the radius value that is specified in the **Radius** field to all the control points and vertices of the edge.

Set Unassigned
The **Set Unassigned** button is used for assigning the specified radius value to all control points and vertices whose radius value is not assigned.

Smooth transition
The **Smooth transition** radio button is selected by default. As a result, the variable fillet created is such that a smooth transition is carried out from one radius value to another, see Figure 10.92.

Straight transition
On selecting the **Straight transition** radio button, a linear or straight transition is carried out from one radius value to another, see Figure 10.93.

The remaining options in the PropertyManager are same as those discussed earlier while creating the constant radius fillet.

Procedure for Creating a Variable Radius Fillet

1. Click on the **Fillet** tool. The **Fillet PropertyManager** appears.
2. Click on the **Variable Size Fillet** button in the **Fillet Type** rollout of the PropertyManager.
3. Select edges to create a variable radius fillet.
4. Specify the number of control points in the **Number of Instances** field of the **Variable Radius Parameters** rollout in the PropertyManager and then press ENTER.
5. Click on the control points that appear in the graphics area, one by one.
6. Specify the radius value and location for each control point by using the respective callouts.
7. Click on the green tick-mark ✔ in the PropertyManager. A variable radius fillet is created.

Creating a Face Fillet

A face fillet is created between two non-adjacent or non-continuous faces of a model, see Figure 10.94.

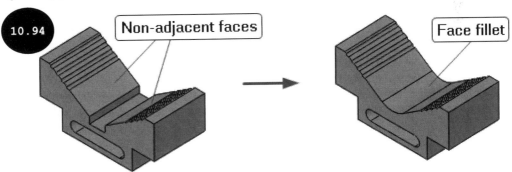

To create a face fillet, invoke the **Fillet PropertyManager** and then click on the **Face Fillet** button in the **Fillet Type** rollout of the PropertyManager, see Figure 10.95. The options for creating face fillet are discussed next.

Items To Fillet

The options in the **Items To Fillet** rollout are used for selecting non-adjacent faces and are discussed next.

Face Set 1

The **Face Set 1** field is used for selecting the first set of non-continuous faces, see Figure 10.96.

Face Set 2

The **Face Set 2** field is used for selecting the second set of non-continuous faces of the model, see Figure 10.96. On selecting two non-continuous faces, a preview of the face fillet appears, see Figure 10.97. In case the preview of the face fillet does not appear, you need to adjust its radius value.

The other options in the PropertyManager are same as those discussed earlier while creating the constant radius fillet. Once you have specified all the parameters for creating the face fillet, click on the green tick-mark ☑ in the PropertyManager. The face fillet is created.

> **Note:** In SOLIDWORKS, after creating a face fillet, you can convert it into a chamfer and vice-versa. To convert a face fillet into a chamfer, select the face fillet in the graphics area. A Pop-up toolbar appears. In this Pop-up toolbar, click on the **Edit Feature** tool ⚙. The **Fillet PropertyManager** appears. In this PropertyManager, click on the **Chamfer Type** 🔧 button to convert the fillet into the chamfer. Next, click on the green tick-mark button.

Procedure for Creating a Face Fillet

1. Click on the **Fillet** tool. The **Fillet PropertyManager** appears.
2. Click on the **Face Fillet** button in the **Fillet Type** rollout of the PropertyManager.
3. Select the first non-continuous face of a model.
4. Click on the **Face Set 2** field in the **Items To Fillet** rollout to activate it.
5. Select the second non-continuous face of the model.
6. Specify the fillet radius value in the **Radius** field of the **Fillet Parameters** rollout.
7. Click on the green tick-mark ☑ in the PropertyManager. A face fillet is created.

Creating a Full Round Fillet

A full round fillet is created tangent to three adjacent faces of a model, see Figure 10.98.

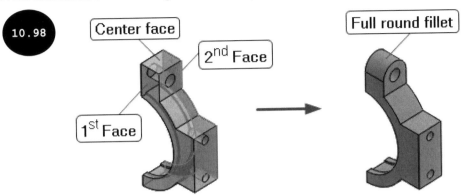

To create a full round fillet, invoke the **Fillet PropertyManager** and then click on the **Full Round Fillet** button in the **Fillet Type** rollout of the PropertyManager, see Figure 10.99. The options for creating a full round fillet are discussed next.

Items To Fillet

The options in the **Items To Fillet** rollout are used for selecting three adjacent faces for creating the full round fillet. The options are discussed next.

Face Set 1

The **Face Set 1** field is used for selecting the first or start adjacent face of the model for creating the full round fillet in the graphics area, see Figure 10.100.

Center Face Set

The **Center Face Set** field is used for selecting the center adjacent face of the model for creating the full round fillet, see Figure 10.100.

Face Set 2

The **Face Set 2** field is used for selecting the end adjacent face of the model for creating the full round fillet, see Figure 10.100.

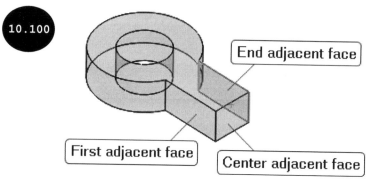

On selecting the three adjacent faces of the model, the preview of the full round fillet appears in the graphics area, see Figure 10.101.

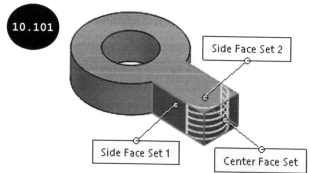

The other options in the PropertyManager are same as those discussed earlier while creating the constant radius fillet. Once you have specified all the parameters for creating the full round fillet, click on the green tick-mark ✔ in the PropertyManager. The full round fillet is created.

Procedure for Creating a Full Round Fillet

1. Click on the **Fillet** tool. The **Fillet PropertyManager** appears.
2. Click on the **Full Round Fillet** button in the **Fillet Type** rollout of the PropertyManager.
3. Select the first adjacent face of the model in the graphics area.
4. Click on the **Center Face Set** field in the **Items To Fillet** rollout to activate it.
5. Select the center adjacent face of the model.
6. Click on the **Face Set 2** field in the **Items To Fillet** rollout to activate it.
7. Select the end adjacent face of the model.
8. Click on the green tick-mark ✔ in the PropertyManager. A full round fillet is created.

Creating Chamfers Updated

A chamfer is a bevel face that is non perpendicular to its adjacent faces, see Figure 10.102. You can create different types of chamfers: Angle Distance chamfer, Distance Distance chamfer, Vertex chamfer, Offset Face chamfer, and Face Face chamfer by using the **Chamfer** tool.

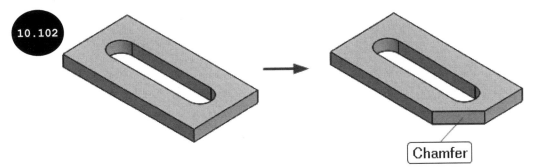

10.102

Chamfer

To create a chamfer, click on the arrow at the bottom of the **Fillet** tool in the CommandManager. A flyout appears, see Figure 10.103. Next, click on the **Chamfer** tool in the flyout. The **Chamfer PropertyManager** appears, see Figure 10.104. The options in this PropertyManager are discussed next.

10.103

10.104

Chamfer Type

The **Chamfer Type** rollout of the PropertyManager is used for selecting the type of chamfer to be created by clicking on the respective button in this rollout, see Figure 10.105. The different types of chamfers are discussed next.

10.105

Angle Distance Chamfer

The **Angle Distance** button of the **Chamfer Type** rollout is used for creating an Angle Distance chamfer by specifying its angle and distance values. For doing so, click on the **Angle Distance** button and then select edges, faces, or loops as entities to create a chamfer. After selecting one or more entities, a preview of the chamfer with the default values appears, see Figure 10.106. You can specify the required angle and distance values of the chamfer by using the **Angle** and **Distance** fields of the **Chamfer Parameters** rollout, see Figure 10.107. You can also specify the distance and angle values of the chamfer by using the callout that appears in the preview of the chamfer. Note that in the preview of a chamfer, an arrow appears that points toward the direction of the distance value. You can flip the direction of the distance value by selecting the **Flip direction** check box in the **Chamfer Parameters** rollout.

Note: On selecting a face as the entity to chamfer, all the edges of the selected face get selected to apply the chamfer.

Distance Distance Chamfer

The **Distance Distance** button of the **Chamfer Type** rollout is used for creating a Distance Distance chamfer by specifying symmetric or asymmetric distance values on both sides of the chamfer edge. For doing so, click on the **Distance Distance** button in the **Chamfer Type** rollout of the PropertyManager and then select edges, faces, or loops as the entities to create chamfer. After selecting one or more entities, a preview of the chamfer with default parameters appears, see Figure 10.108. Note that if the **Symmetric** option is selected in the **Chamfer Method** drop-down list of the **Chamfer Parameters** rollout then the **Distance** field is available in the rollout, see Figure 10.109. Also, a preview of the chamfer appears such that the value specified in the **Distance** field is symmetric on both sides of the selected entity.

On selecting the **Asymmetric** option in the **Chamfer Method** drop-down list, the **Distance 1** and **Distance 2** fields become available in the rollout, see Figure 10.110. In these fields, you can specify different distance values on both sides of the selected entity, see Figure 10.111. You can also specify the required distance values of the chamfer by using the callout that appears in the preview of the chamfer.

Vertex Chamfer

The **Vertex** button of the **Chamfer Type** rollout is used for creating a chamfer on a vertex of a model. For doing so, click on the **Vertex** button in the **Chamfer Type** rollout of the PropertyManager and then select a vertex of the model. A preview of the chamfer with default parameters appears in the graphics area, see Figure 10.112. Also, the **Distance 1**, **Distance 2**, and **Distance 3** fields appear in the **Chamfer Parameters** rollout, see Figure 10.113. These fields are used for specifying different distance values on all sides of the selected vertex. If you select the **Equal distance** check box in the rollout, only the **Distance** field becomes available and the distance specified in this field is equally applied on all sides of the vertex.

Offset Face Chamfer

The **Offset Face** button of the **Chamfer Type** rollout is used for creating an offset face chamfer by specifying symmetric or asymmetric offset distance values from the adjacent faces of the chamfer edge, see Figures 10.114 and 10.115.

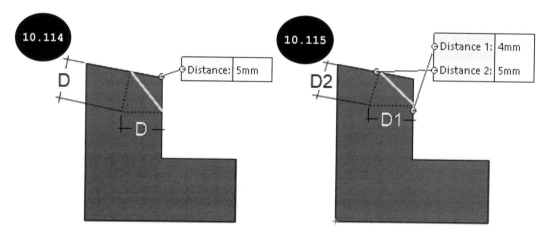

To create an offset face chamfer by specifying the offset distance values, click on the **Offset Face** button and then select one or more edges of a model. A preview of the chamfer with default offset distance values appears in the graphics area. Note that if the **Symmetric** option is selected in the **Chamfer Method** drop-down list of the **Chamfer Parameters** rollout then the **Offset Distance** field is available in the rollout. Also, the preview of the chamfer appears such that the offset distance value specified in this field is symmetric from both the adjacent faces of the chamfer edge, refer to Figure 10.114. On selecting the **Asymmetric** option in the **Chamfer Method** drop-down list, the **Offset Distance 1** and **Offset Distance 2** fields become available in the rollout. In these fields, you can specify different offset distance values from the adjacent faces of the chamfer edge, refer to Figure 10.115.

The **Multi Distance Chamfer** check box of the **Chamfer Parameters** rollout is used for creating multiple offset face chamfers of different sizes. On selecting this check box, a callout attached to each selected edge of the model appears in the preview, see Figure 10.116. By using these callouts, you can specify different offset distance values for each chamfer edge. To specify an offset distance value in a callout, click on the default value specified in the callout and then specify the new offset distance value. In addition to selecting edges for creating multiple offset face chamfers of different sizes, you can also select faces, features, or loops. Note that the **Multi Distance Chamfer** check box is available in the rollout only when the **Symmetric** option is selected in the **Chamfer Method** drop-down list.

In SOLIDWORKS, you can also create a partial offset face chamfer by specifying its start and end positions along the edge of a model by using the **Partial Edge Parameters** rollout of the PropertyManager, see Figure 10.117. The method for creating a partial chamfer is same as discussed earlier while creating a partial fillet. Note that the **Partial Edge Parameters** rollout is only available for offset face chamfers. The other options in the PropertyManager are same as those discussed earlier. Next, click on the green tick-mark in the PropertyManager. An offset face chamfer of specified parameters is created.

10.117

Note: The chamfer created by using the **Offset Face** button can be converted to a fillet and vice-versa. For doing so, select an offset face chamfer in the FeatureManager Design Tree or in the graphics area and then right-click to display the shortcut menu. In this shortcut menu, click on the **Convert Chamfer to Fillet** option, see Figure 10.118. The offset face chamfer gets converted to a fillet. Similarly, you can convert the fillet back to the chamfer.

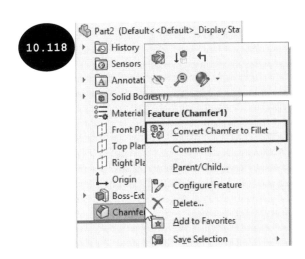

10.118

Face Face Chamfer

The **Face Face** button of the **Chamfer Type** rollout is used for creating a Face Face chamfer between non-adjacent or non-continuous faces of a model. For doing so, click on the **Face Face** button in the **Chamfer Type** rollout of the **Chamfer PropertyManager**. The **Face Set 1** and **Face Set 2** fields become available in the **Items To Chamfer** rollout, see Figure 10.119. The **Face Set 1** field is activated, by default. As a result, you can select the first set of non-adjacent faces. After selecting the first set of non-adjacent faces, click on the **Face Set 2** field to activate it. Next, select the second set of non-adjacent faces. A preview of the chamfer appears in the graphics area with default parameters, see Figure 10.120. In this figure, two non-adjacent faces are selected for creating the chamfer. In case, the preview of the chamfer does not appear, you need to adjust its distance value in the **Offset Distance** field of the **Chamfer Parameters** rollout.

The remaining options in the PropertyManager are same as those discussed earlier. Next, click on the green tick-mark button in the PropertyManager. The chamfer is created.

> **Note:** The chamfer created by using the **Face Face** button can be converted to a fillet and vice-versa. For doing so, select the chamfer in the FeatureManager Design Tree or in the graphics area and then right-click to display the shortcut menu. In this shortcut menu, click on the **Convert Chamfer to Fillet** option. The selected chamfer gets converted to a fillet. Similarly, you can convert the fillet back to the chamfer.

Procedure for Creating a Chamfer

1. Click on the **Chamfer** tool. The **Chamfer PropertyManager** appears.
2. Select the required type of chamfer to be created by clicking on the respective button in the **Chamfer Type** rollout of the PropertyManager.

3. Select one or more entities to be chamfered. A preview of the chamfer with default parameters appears.
4. Specify the required chamfer parameters in the **Chamfer Parameters** rollout of the PropertyManager. Note that the availability of chamfer parameters depends upon the type of chamfer selected.
5. Click on the green tick-mark ✔ in the PropertyManager. The chamfer is created.

Note: In SOLIDWORKS 2020, similar to repairing or clearing the missing edges of a fillet, you can also repair or clear all the missing edges of a chamfer that have been removed or are no longer available in the model, as discussed earlier.

Creating Rib Features

Rib features act as supporting features and are generally used for increasing the strength of a model. You can create a rib feature from an open or closed sketch by adding thickness in a specified direction. Figure 10.121 shows a model with an open sketch and the resultant rib feature created.

To create a rib feature, create an open sketch on a plane that intersects with the model, see Figure 10.122. Note that the projection of both the ends of the sketch should lie on the geometry of the model. After creating the sketch of the rib feature, click on the **Rib** tool in the **Features CommandManager**. The **Rib PropertyManager** appears and you are promoted to select either a sketching plane for creating the sketch of the rib feature or an existing sketch of the rib feature. If you have already created a sketch for the rib feature, then select it from the graphics area. The modified **Rib PropertyManager** appears as shown in Figure 10.123. Also, a preview of the rib feature appears in the graphics area, see Figure 10.124. The options in the PropertyManager are discussed next.

> **Note:** You can select the sketch of the rib feature before or after invoking the **Rib** tool.

Parameters

The options in the **Parameters** rollout of the PropertyManager are used for specifying parameters of the rib feature. The options are discussed next.

Thickness ≡▤≡

The **Thickness** area of the **Parameters** rollout has three buttons: **First Side**, **Both Sides**, and **Second Side**. On selecting the **First Side** button, thickness is added to one side of the rib sketch. On selecting the **Both Sides** button, thickness is equally added to both sides of the rib sketch. On selecting the **Second Side** button, thickness is added to the second or the other side of the sketch.

Rib Thickness

The **Rib Thickness** field is used for specifying the thickness value of the rib feature.

Extrusion direction ◈◈

The **Extrusion direction** area has two buttons: **Parallel to Sketch** and **Normal to Sketch**. On selecting the **Parallel to Sketch** button, the rib feature is created by adding material parallel to the sketch. On selecting the **Normal to Sketch** button, the rib feature is created by adding material normal to the sketch. Figure 10.125 shows a sketch of a rib feature. Figures 10.126 and 10.127 shows the resultant rib feature created by selecting the **Parallel to Sketch** and **Normal to Sketch** buttons, respectively.

Flip material side

The **Flip material side** check box is used for flipping the direction of extrusion of the rib feature.

Draft On/Off

The **Draft On/Off** button is used for adding draft to the rib feature. On activating this button, the **Draft Angle** field and the **Draft outward** check box become available in the PropertyManager. Also, the **At sketch plane** and **At wall interface** radio buttons become available below the **Rib Thickness** field. By default, the **At sketch plane** radio button is selected. As a result, the specified thickness value is defined as the rib thickness at the sketching plane. On selecting the **At wall interface** radio button, the specified thickness value is defined as the rib thickness at the interface of the model. By using the **Draft Angle** field, you can specify the draft angle value of the rib feature. Note that by default, the draft angle is added inward to the sketch of the rib feature. To add the draft angle outward to the sketch, select the **Draft outward** check box.

Selected Contours

The **Selected Contours** rollout is used for selecting the required contour of the sketch for creating the rib feature.

Procedure for Creating a Rib Feature

1. Click on the **Rib** tool in the **Features CommandManager**. The **Rib PropertyManager** appears.
2. Select the sketch of the rib feature in the graphics area.
3. Specify the thickness of the rib feature in the **Rib Thickness** field of the PropertyManager.
4. Specify the direction of extrusion of the rib feature by clicking on the **Parallel to Sketch** button or the **Normal to Sketch** button in the PropertyManager.
5. Select the **Flip material side** check box to flip the direction of material side, if required.
6. Click on the green tick-mark ☑ in the PropertyManager. A rib feature is created.

Creating Shell Features

A shell feature is a thin walled feature, which is created by making a model hollow from inside, see Figure 10.128. In this figure, the models are shown in 'hidden line visible' display style for clarity.

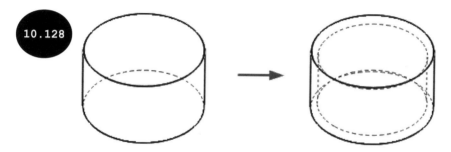

To create a shell feature, click on the **Shell** tool in the **Features CommandManager**. The
Shell PropertyManager appears, see Figure 10.129. The options in this PropertyManager
are discussed next.

Parameters

The options in the **Parameters** rollout are used for specifying parameters for creating the shell feature.
The options are discussed next.

Thickness

The **Thickness** field is used for specifying wall thickness for the shell feature. Note that the thickness
specified in this field is applied to all walls of the feature, such that a shell feature with uniform
thickness is created.

Faces to Remove

The **Faces to Remove** field is used for selecting faces of the model to be removed. Figure 10.130
shows a face of a model to be removed and Figure 10.131 shows the resultant model after creating
the shell feature. Note that if you do not select any face to be removed then a closed hollow model
is created.

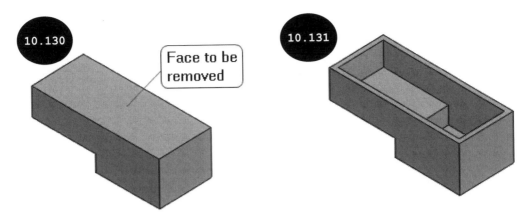

Shell outward

On selecting the **Shell outward** check box, thickness is added on the outer side of the model.

Show preview

On selecting the **Show preview** check box, a preview of the shell feature appears in the graphics area.

Multi-thickness Settings

The options in the **Multi-thickness Settings** rollout of the PropertyManager are used for creating multi-thickness shell features. The options are discussed next.

Multi-thickness Faces

The **Multi-thickness Faces** field is used for selecting faces of the model on which thickness is to be applied other than the one specified in the **Thickness** field of the **Parameters** rollout. After selecting a face, the **Multi-thickness(es)** field gets enabled, which allows you to specify thickness value for the selected face of the model. You can select multiple faces of the model and apply different thickness values to them. Figure 10.132 shows a shell model with multi-thickness walls.

Procedure for Creating a Shell Feature with Uniform Thickness

1. Click on the **Shell** tool in the **Features CommandManager**. The **Shell PropertyManager** appears.
2. Enter wall thickness for the shell feature in the **Thickness** field.
3. Select a face or faces to be removed from the model, if needed.
4. Click on the green tick-mark ✔ in the PropertyManager. A shell feature is created.

Procedure for Creating a Shell Feature with Multi-Thickness

1. Click on the **Shell** tool. The **Shell PropertyManager** appears.
2. Enter wall thickness for the shell feature in the **Thickness** field.
3. Select one or more faces to be removed from the model, if needed.
4. Click on the **Multi-thickness Faces** field in the **Multi-thickness Settings** rollout.
5. Select one or more faces of the model to apply different thickness values. The names of the selected faces appear in the **Multi-thickness Faces** field of the PropertyManager.
6. Specify a thickness value for each selected face in the **Multi-thickness(es)** field one by one. Note that the thickness value specified in the **Multi-thickness(es)** field is applied to the face currently selected in the **Multi-thickness Faces** field.
7. Click on the green tick-mark ✔ in the PropertyManager. The multi-thickness shell feature is created.

Creating Wrap Features

A Wrap feature is created by wrapping a sketch onto one or more faces of a model, see Figure 10.133. This figure shows a sketch to be wrapped, a face, and the resultant model after wrapping the sketch onto the face of the model.

To wrap a sketch onto a face, select a sketch to be wrapped either from the FeatureManager Design Tree or from the graphics area and then click on the **Wrap** tool in the **Features CommandManager**. The **Wrap PropertyManager** appears, see Figure 10.134. The options in the PropertyManager are discussed next.

Wrap Type

The options in the **Wrap Type** rollout of the PropertyManager are used for selecting the type of wrap: emboss, deboss, or scribe to be created. The options are discussed next.

Emboss

The **Emboss** button in the **Wrap Type** rollout is used for creating a wrap feature by adding material on the face, refer to Figure 10.133.

Deboss

The **Deboss** button is used for creating a wrap feature by removing material from the face of the model, see Figure 10.135.

Scribe

The **Scribe** button is used for creating a wrap feature by splitting the face of the model such that an imprint of the sketch is created on the face, see Figure 10.136.

Wrap Method

The options in the **Wrap Method** rollout of the PropertyManager are used for selecting a wrap method: Analytical or Spline Surface for creating the wrap feature. Both are discussed next.

Analytical

The **Analytical** button of the **Wrap Method** rollout is used for wrapping a sketch completely around a cylindrical or a conical face of a model. Note that by using this button, you can wrap a sketch only onto the planar or non-planar faces of cylindrical, conical, extruded, or revolved features of the model.

Spline Surface

The **Spline Surface** button of the **Wrap Method** rollout is used for creating a wrap feature by wrapping a sketch onto any face of a model. However, by using this method, you cannot wrap a sketch completely around a cylindrical or conical face of a model.

Wrap Parameters

The options in the **Wrap Parameters** rollout are used for specifying parameters for creating the wrap feature, see Figure 10.137. The options are discussed next.

Source Sketch

The **Source Sketch** field of the PropertyManager is used for selecting a sketch to be wrapped. Note that if you select a sketch before invoking the **Wrap** PropertyManager then the name of the selected sketch appears in this field, which indicates that the sketch is selected.

Face for Wrap Sketch

The **Face for Wrap Sketch** field is used for selecting one or more faces of the model for wrapping the sketch. Note that if the **Analytical** button is selected in the **Wrap Method** rollout then you can only select planar or non planar faces of cylindrical, conical, extruded, or revolved features of a model.

Thickness

The **Thickness** field is used for specifying thickness of the wrap feature. Note that this field becomes available only if the **Emboss** button is enabled in the **Wrap Type** rollout.

Depth

The **Depth** field is used for specifying the depth of the wrap feature. Note that this field becomes available only if the **Deboss** button is enabled in the **Wrap Type** rollout.

Reverse Direction

The **Reverse Direction** check box is used for reversing the direction of projection, see Figures 10.138 and 10.139.

Tutorial 1

Create a model, as shown in Figure 10.140. All dimensions are in mm.

Section 1: Invoking the Part Modeling Environment

1. Start SOLIDWORKS and then invoke the Part modeling environment.

   Once the Part modeling environment is invoked, you need to set the unit system and create the base/first feature of the model.

Section 2: Specifying Unit Settings

1. Make sure that the MMGS (millimeter, gram, second) unit system is set for the currently opened part document.

Section 3: Creating the 3D Path - Sweep Feature

The base feature of the model is a sweep feature. To create this sweep feature, you need to create a 3D sketch as the path of the sweep feature.

1. Click on the **Sketch** tab in the CommandManager to display the tools of the **Sketch** CommandManager.

2. Click on the arrow at the bottom of the **Sketch** tool in the **Sketch CommandManager**. The **Sketch** flyout appears, see Figure 10.141.

3.   Click on the **3D Sketch** tool in the **Sketch** flyout. The 3D Sketching environment is invoked.

4.   Click on the **Line** tool in the **Sketch CommandManager**. The **Line** tool is invoked and the
     display of **XY** appears near the cursor, see Figure 10.142.

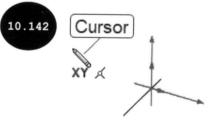

Note: The display of XY near the cursor indicates that the XY (Front) plane is the current
            sketching plane. You can press the TAB key to switch between the sketching planes for
            creating a 3D sketch.

5.   Move the cursor to the origin and then click to specify the start point of the line when the
     cursor snaps to the origin.

6.   Move the cursor vertically upward and click to specify the endpoint of the line when the length
     of the line appears close to 120 mm near the cursor, see Figure 10.143.

7.   Press the TAB key twice to activate the ZX plane (Top plane) as the sketching plane, see
     Figure 10.144.

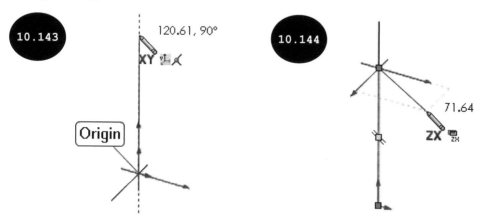

8.   Move the cursor toward right at an angle to the X axis, see Figure 10.145. Next, click to specify
     the endpoint of the second line when the length of the line appears close to 180 mm near the
     cursor, see Figure 10.145.

9.   Move the cursor to a distance and then move it back to the last specified point. A dot appears
     at the endpoint in the graphics area, see Figure 10.146.

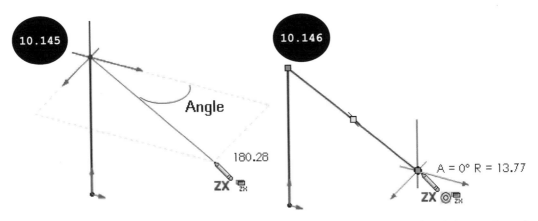

10. Move the cursor to a distance toward right. The arc mode gets activated and the preview of a tangent arc appears in the graphics area, see Figure 10.147.

11. Click to specify the endpoint of the arc when the radius of the arc appears close to 80 mm, see Figure 10.147.

12. Right-click in the graphics area. A shortcut menu appears. Next, click on the **Select** option in the shortcut menu to exit the **Line** tool.

13. Invoke the **Centerline** tool and then create a horizontal centerline along the X axis direction, of any length by specifying its start point at the endpoint of the first line entity, see Figure 10.148. Next, exit the **Centerline** tool.

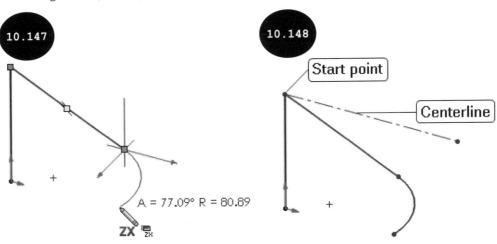

Section 4: Applying Dimensions

1. Click on the **Smart Dimension** tool and then click on the vertical line (first line entity) in the graphics area. The linear dimension is attached to the cursor.

2. Click in the graphics area to specify the placement point for the attached dimension. The **Modify** dialog box appears.

3. Enter **120** in the **Modify** dialog box and then click on the green tick-mark ☑ button. The length of the line changes to 120 mm and the dimension is applied to the line, see Figure 10.149.

4. Click on the inclined line (second line entity) in the graphics area to apply the dimension. The dimension is attached to the cursor.

5. Click in the graphics area to specify the placement point for the attached dimension. The **Modify** dialog box appears.

6. Enter **180** in the **Modify** dialog box and then click on the green tick-mark ☑ button. The length of the line changes to 180 mm and the dimension is applied to the line, see Figure 10.150.

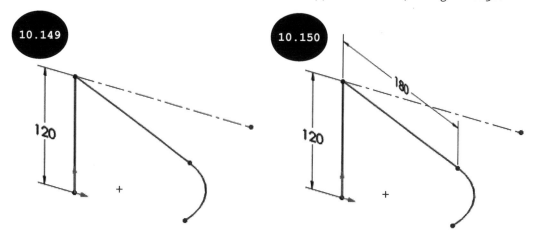

7. Click on the inclined line (second line entity) and then the horizontal centerline. An angular dimension is attached to the cursor.

8. Click in the graphics area to specify the placement point for the attached dimension. The **Modify** dialog box appears.

9. Enter **35** in the **Modify** dialog box and then click on the green tick-mark ☑. An angular dimension is applied between the inclined line entity and the centerline, see Figure 10.151.

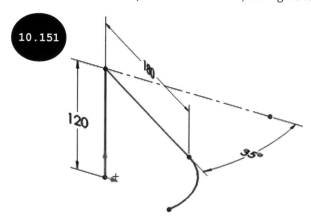

10. Click on the arc entity to apply radius dimension. The radius dimension is attached to the cursor.

11. Click in the graphics area to specify the placement point for the attached dimension. The **Modify** dialog box appears.

12. Enter **80** in the **Modify** dialog box and then click on the green tick-mark ✔. The radius of the arc changes to 80 mm and the dimension is applied to the arc, see Figure 10.152.

13. Change the current orientation of the sketch to the front view by clicking on the **Front** tool in the **View Orientation** flyout, see Figure 10.153. Alternatively, press CTRL + 1 to change the orientation of the sketch to the front view.

14. Click on the vertical line (first line entity) and then click on the second line entity in the graphics area. The angular dimension appears attached to the cursor.

15. Click in the graphics area to specify the placement point for the angular dimension. The **Modify** dialog box appears.

16. Enter **90** in the **Modify** dialog box and then click on the green tick-mark ✔ button. An angular dimension is applied, see Figure 10.154. Next, exit the **Smart Dimension** tool.

Section 5: Applying Relation

1. Press CTRL + 5 to change the current orientation of the sketch to the top view.

2. Press and hold the CTRL key and then select the center point of the arc as well as the endpoint of the arc in the graphics area, see Figure 10.155. Next, release the CTRL key. A Pop-up toolbar appears near the cursor, see Figure 10.155.

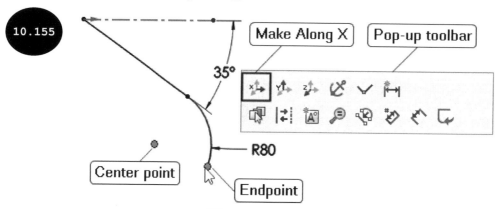

3. Click on the **Make Along X** tool in the Pop-up toolbar. The Along X relation is applied between the center point and the endpoint of the arc.

4. Similarly, apply the Along X relation to the horizontal centerline, if not applied by default.

5. Press CTRL + 7 to change the current orientation of the sketch to isometric.

Section 6: Creating Fillet

1. Click on the **Sketch Fillet** tool in the **Sketch CommandManager**. The **Sketch Fillet PropertyManager** appears.

2. Enter **60** in the **Fillet Radius** field of the **Fillet Parameters** rollout in the PropertyManager.

3. Click on the vertex of the sketch. A preview of the fillet appears, see Figure 10.156. Make sure that the **Keep constrained corners** check box is cleared.

4. Click on the green tick-mark ☑ in the PropertyManager. A fillet of radius 60 mm is created on the selected vertex of the sketch. Next, exit the PropertyManager.

5. Exit the 3D Sketching environment by clicking on the **Exit Sketch** icon ⌐↓ of the Confirmation Corner, which is available at the top right corner of the graphics area.

Section 7: Creating the Base Feature - Sweep Feature

After creating the path of the sweep feature, you need to create the sweep feature with circular profile.

1. Click on the **Swept Boss/Base** tool in the **Features CommandManager**. The **Sweep PropertyManager** appears.

2. Click on the **Circular Profile** radio button in the **Profile and Path** rollout.

3. Select the 3D sketch as the path of the sweep feature in the graphics area. A preview of the sweep feature appears with the default diameter of the circular profile.

4. Enter **80** in the **Diameter** field of the **Profile and Path** rollout and then press ENTER. A preview of the sweep feature appears as shown in Figure 10.157.

5. Click on the green tick-mark ☑ in the PropertyManager. A sweep feature is created, see Figure 10.158.

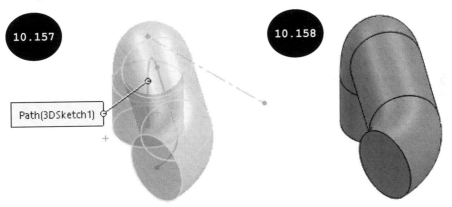

Section 8: Creating the Second Feature - Mirror Feature

The second feature of the model can be created by mirroring the first feature about a reference plane, which passes through the center of the end circular face of the first feature and is parallel to the Right plane. To create this reference plane, you need to first create a reference point at the center of the end circular face of the first feature.

1. Invoke the **Reference Geometry** flyout in the **Features CommandManager** and then click on the **Point** tool, see Figure 10.159. The **Point PropertyManager** appears.

2. Click on the end circular face of the first feature (sweep), see Figure 10.160. A preview of the reference point appears at the center of the circular face selected.

3. Click on the green tick-mark ☑ in the PropertyManager. The reference point is created.

   Now, you need to create a reference plane by using the **Plane** tool.

4. Invoke the **Reference Geometry** flyout, refer to Figure 10.159 and then click on the **Plane** tool. The **Plane PropertyManager** appears.

5. Expand the FeatureManager Design Tree, which is now available at the top left corner of the graphics area, by clicking on the arrow in front of it.

6. Click on the **Right Plane** in the FeatureManager Design Tree as the first reference. The preview of an offset reference plane appears in the graphics area.

7. Click on the reference point in the graphics area as the second reference. The preview of a reference plane, which is parallel to the Right plane and passes through the reference point appears in the graphics area, see Figure 10.161.

8. Click on the green tick-mark ☑ of the PropertyManager. The reference plane is created, see Figure 10.162.

After creating the reference plane, you need to mirror the first feature (sweep) about it.

9. Click on the **Mirror** tool in the **Features CommandManager**. The **Mirror** | ⊨⊣ Mirror | **PropertyManager** appears.

10. Click on the newly created reference plane as the mirroring plane.

11. Click on the base feature (sweep feature). The preview of the mirror feature appears.

12. Click on the green tick-mark ✔ in the PropertyManager. The mirror feature is created, see Figure 10.163. Next, hide the reference plane and the reference point in the graphics area.

10.163

Section 9: Creating the Third Feature - Shell Feature

1. Click on the **Shell** tool in the **Features CommandManager**. The **Shell PropertyManager** appears.

2. Enter **10** in the **Thickness** field of the **Parameters** rollout in the PropertyManager.

3. Select the three end faces of the model as the faces to be removed, see Figure 10.164.

4. Click on the green tick-mark ✔ button. The shell feature is created, see Figure 10.165.

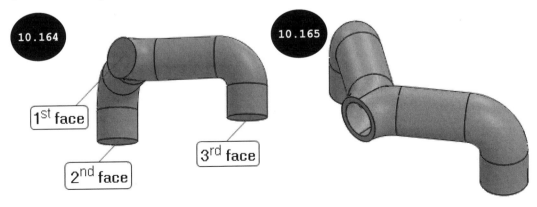

10.164

1st face

2nd face

3rd face

10.165

Section 10: Creating the Fourth Feature - Extruded Feature

1. Invoke the Sketching environment by selecting the Top plane as the sketching plane.

2. Press CTRL + 8 to change the orientation of the model as normal to the viewing direction.

3. Create the sketch of the fourth feature (extruded feature), see Figure 10.166. After creating the sketch, do not exit the Sketching environment.

Note: The sketch of the fourth feature shown in Figure 10.166 has been fully defined by applying the required dimensions and relations. You need to apply tangent relations between each set of connected line and arc entities of the sketch. You also need to apply a symmetric relation between the center points of the upper and lower arcs of the sketch to the horizontal centerline. Besides, you need to apply an equal relation between the upper and lower arcs of the sketch.

---

4. Click on the **Features** tab in the CommandManager to display the tools of the **Features CommandManager**.

5. Click on the **Extruded Boss/Base** tool in the **Features CommandManager**. The **Boss-Extrude PropertyManager** and a preview of the extruded feature appear. Next, change the orientation of the model to isometric.

6. Click on the **Reverse Direction** button in the **Direction 1** rollout of the PropertyManager to reverse the direction of extrusion downward.

7. Enter 15 in the **Depth** field of the **Direction 1** rollout in the PropertyManager.

8. Click on the green tick-mark ✔ of the PropertyManager. An extruded feature is created, see Figure 10.167.

Section 11: Creating the Fifth Feature - Mirror Feature

1. Click on the **Mirror** tool in the **Features CommandManager**. The Mirror PropertyManager appears.

2. Expand the FeatureManager Design Tree, which is now available at the top left corner of the graphics area, by clicking on the arrow in its front.

3. Click on the reference plane (Plane 1) in the FeatureManager Design Tree as the mirroring plane, see Figure 10.168.

4. Click on the fourth feature (previously created extruded feature) as the feature to be mirrored in the graphics area. The preview of the mirror feature appears, see Figure 10.168.

5. Click on the green tick-mark ✓ in the PropertyManager. The mirror feature is created.

Section 12: Creating the Sixth Feature - Extruded Feature

1. Invoke the Sketching environment by selecting the front planar face of the model as the sketching plane, see Figure 10.169.

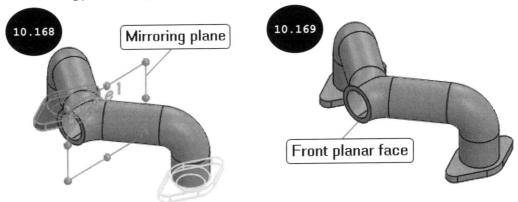

2. Press CTRL + 8 to change the orientation of the model as normal to the viewing direction.

3. Create the sketch of the sixth feature (extruded feature), see Figure 10.170. After creating the sketch, do not exit the Sketching environment.

10.170

R18

∅60

R50

140

4. Click on the **Features** tab in the CommandManager to display the tools of the **Features CommandManager**.

5. Click on the **Extruded Boss/Base** tool in the **Features CommandManager**. The **Boss-Extrude PropertyManager** and a preview of the extruded feature appear. Next, change the orientation of the model to isometric.

Extruded Boss/Base

6. Enter **15** in the **Depth** field of the **Direction 1** rollout.

7. Click on the green tick-mark ✔ in the PropertyManager. An extruded feature is created, see Figure 10.171.

10.171

Section 13: Creating the Seventh Feature - Hole Feature

In this section, you need to create holes by using the **Hole Wizard** tool.

1. Click on the **Hole Wizard** tool in the **Features CommandManager**. The **Hole Specification PropertyManager** appears, see Figure 10.172.

Hole Wizard

2. Click on the **Hole** button in the **Hole Type** rollout of the PropertyManager.

3. Select the **ANSI Metric** option in the **Standard** drop-down list of the **Hole Type** rollout.

4. Select the **Drill sizes** option in the **Type** drop-down list.

5. Select the **ø16.0** option in the **Size** drop-down list of the **Hole Specifications** rollout.

6. Select the **Up To Next** option in the **End Condition** drop-down list.

7. Make sure that the **Near side countersink** and the **Far side countersink** check boxes are cleared in the **Options** rollout of the PropertyManager.

After specifying the hole type and the hole specifications, you need to define the placement of the hole.

8. Click on the **Positions** tab in the **Hole Specification PropertyManager**. The name of the PropertyManager changes to the **Hole Position PropertyManager**.

9. Move the cursor over the top planar face of the right extruded feature, see Figure 10.173 and then click on it as the placement face.

10. Move the cursor over the front semi-circular edge of the right extruded feature, see Figure 10.174. The center point of the semi-circular edge gets highlighted.

11. Move the cursor over the highlighted center point of the semi-circular edge and then click to specify the center point of the hole when the cursor snaps to it. A preview of the hole appears at the specified location in the graphics area.

12. Similarly, move the cursor over the back semi-circular edge of the right extruded feature, see Figure 10.175. The center point of the semi-circular edge gets highlighted.

13. Move the cursor over the highlighted center point of the semi-circular edge and then click to specify the center point of the hole when the cursor snaps to it. A preview of the hole appears at the specified location in the graphics area.

14. Similarly, move the cursor over the semi-circular edges of the left extruded feature and then specify the center points of the holes on its top planar face, see Figure 10.176.

10.175

10.176

15. Click on the green tick-mark ✔ in the PropertyManager. The holes are created, see Figure 10.177. Also, the PropertyManager is closed.

16. Similarly, create holes on the front planar face of the middle extruded feature by using the **Hole Wizard** tool, see Figure 10.178.

10.177

10.178

Section 14: Saving the Model

1. Click on the **Save** tool in the **Standard** toolbar. The **Save As** dialog box appears.

2. Browse to the SOLIDWORKS folder and then create a folder with the name Chapter 10.

3. Enter **Tutorial 1** in the **File name** field of the dialog box and then click on the **Save** button. The model is saved with the name Tutorial 1 in the Chapter 10 folder.

Tutorial 2

Create a model, as shown in Figure 10.179. All dimensions are in mm.

Section 1: Invoking the Part Modeling Environment

1. Start SOLIDWORKS and then invoke the Part modeling environment.

    Once the Part modeling environment is invoked, you need to set the unit system and create the base/first feature of the model.

Section 2: Specifying Unit Settings

1. Make sure that the MMGS (millimeter, gram, second) unit system is set for the currently opened part document.

Section 3: Creating the Base Feature - Sweep Feature

The base feature of the model is a sweep feature having circular profile. To create a sweep feature having circular profile, you need to first create its path.

1. Invoke the Sketching environment by selecting the Front plane as the sketching plane.

2. Create the path of the sweep feature, see Figure 10.180.

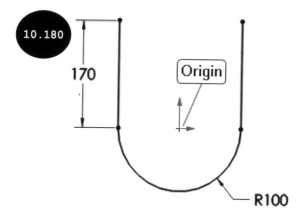

10.180

170

Origin

R100

Note: In Figure 10.180, the center point of the arc has coincident relation with the origin. Also, the connecting line and arc entities of the sketch have tangent relations with each other. In addition, an equal relation has been applied between the vertical lines of the sketch.

3. Exit the Sketching environment. Next, press CTRL + 7 to change the orientation of the sketch to isometric.

    After creating the path of the sweep feature, you need to create the sweep feature.

4. Click on the **Swept Boss/Base** tool in the **Features CommandManager**. The **Sweep PropertyManager** appears.

5. Click on the **Circular Profile** radio button in the **Profile and Path** rollout.

6. Select the path of the sweep feature. A preview of the sweep feature appears.

7. Enter **90** in the **Diameter** field of the **Profile and Path** rollout and then press ENTER. A preview of the sweep feature appears as shown in Figure 10.181.

8. Expand the **Thin Feature** rollout of the PropertyManager by clicking on the check box available in its title bar, see Figure 10.182.

10.181

Path(Sketch1)

10.182

9. Enter 10 in the **Thickness** field of the **Thin Feature** rollout.

10. Click on the **Reverse Direction** button in the **Thin Feature** rollout to reverse the direction of material inward.

11. Click on the green tick-mark ☑ in the PropertyManager. The sweep feature is created.

Section 4: Creating the Second Feature - Extruded Feature

1. Invoke the Sketching environment by selecting the top planar face of the base feature (sweep) as the sketching plane, see Figure 10.183.

2. Press CTRL + 8 to change the orientation of the model as normal to the viewing direction.

3. Create two circles as the sketch of the second feature, see Figure 10.184. After creating the sketch, do not exit the Sketching environment.

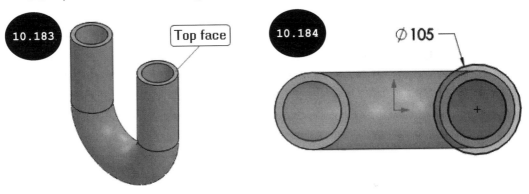

Note: The sketch of the second feature shown in the Figure 10.184 has two circles: the outer circle is of diameter 105 mm and the inner circle has a coradial relation with the inner circular edge of the sweep feature, since the inner circle of the sketch has the same diameter as the inner circular edge of the feature and shares the same center point.

4. Click on the **Features** tab in the CommandManager to display the tools of the **Features** CommandManager.

5. Click on the **Extruded Boss/Base** tool in the **Features CommandManager**. The Boss-Extrude PropertyManager and a preview of the extruded feature appear. Next, change the orientation of the model to isometric.

6. Enter **60** in the **Depth** field of the **Direction 1** rollout in the PropertyManager.

7. Click on the green tick-mark ☑ in the PropertyManager. The extruded feature is created, see Figure 10.185.

Section 5: Creating the Third Feature - Mirror Feature

1. Click on the **Mirror** tool in the **Features CommandManager**. The **Mirror** PropertyManager appears.

2. Expand the FeatureManager Design Tree, which is now available at the top left corner of the graphics area and then click on the **Right Plane** as the mirroring plane.

3. Click on the second feature (previously created extruded feature) as the feature to be mirrored in the graphics area. The preview of the mirror feature appears in the graphics area.

4. Click on the green tick-mark ✓ in the PropertyManager. The mirror feature is created, see Figure 10.186.

Section 6: Creating the Fourth Feature - Extruded Feature

To create the sketch of the fourth feature, you need to create a reference plane at an offset distance from the Top plane.

1. Click on the **Plane** tool in the **Reference Geometry** flyout. The **Plane PropertyManager** appears.

2. Click on the **Top Plane** in the FeatureManager Design Tree as the first reference. The preview of an offset reference plane appears.

3. Enter **190** in the **Distance** field of the **First Reference** rollout in the PropertyManager.

4. Click on the **Flip offset** check box in the rollout to reverse the direction of plane downward.

5. Click on the green tick-mark ✓ in the PropertyManager. A reference plane is created, see Figure 10.187.

6. Invoke the Sketching environment by selecting the newly created reference plane as the sketching plane.

7. Press CTRL + 8 to change the orientation of the model as normal to the viewing direction.

8. Create a circle of diameter 90 mm as the sketch of the fourth feature, see Figure 10.188. Note that the center point of the circle is at the origin.

9. Click on the **Features** tab in the CommandManager and then click on the **Extruded Boss/Base** tool. The **Boss-Extrude PropertyManager** and the preview of the extruded feature appear. Next, change the orientation of the model to isometric.

10. Select the **Up To Next** option in the **End Condition** drop-down list of the **Direction 1** rollout.

11. Click on the green tick-mark ✓ in the PropertyManager. The extruded feature is created, see Figure 10.189.

Section 7: Creating the Fifth Feature - Extruded Feature

1. Click on the **Extruded Boss/Base** tool in the **Features CommandManager**. The **Extrude PropertyManager** appears. Also, you are prompted to either select a sketch to be extruded or a sketching plane.

2. Click on the reference plane (Plane 1), which is created at an offset distance of 190 mm from the Top plane as the sketching plane. Next, press CTRL + 8 to change the orientation of the model as normal to the viewing direction.

3. Create a circle of diameter 250 mm as the sketch of the fifth feature, see Figure 10.190.

4.   Click on the **Exit Sketch** tool in the **Sketch CommandManager** to exit the Sketching environment. The **Boss-Extrude PropertyManager** and the preview of the extruded feature appear. Next, change the orientation of the model to isometric.

5.   Enter **30** in the **Depth** field of the **Direction 1** rollout in the PropertyManager.

6.   Click on the **Reverse Direction** button in the **Direction 1** rollout of the PropertyManager to reverse the direction of extrusion downward.

7.   Click on the green tick-mark ☑ in the PropertyManager. The extruded feature is created, see Figure 10.191.

8.   Click on the reference plane to hide it. A Pop-up toolbar appears. In this Pop-up toolbar, click on the **Hide** tool.

Section 8: Creating the Sixth Feature - Extruded Cut Feature

Extruded
Cut

1.   Click on the **Extruded Cut** tool in the **Features CommandManager**. The **Extrude PropertyManager** appears.

2.   Click on the top planar face of the fifth feature (previously created extruded feature) as the sketching plane.

3.   Press CTRL + 8 to change the orientation of the model as normal to the viewing direction.

4.   Create a circle of diameter 25 mm as the sketch of the sixth feature, see Figure 10.192.

10.191

10.192

98

Ø25

Note: In Figure 10.192, a vertical relation has been applied between the center point of the circle and the origin to make the sketch fully defined.

---

5.   Exit the Sketching environment. The **Cut-Extrude PropertyManager** appears. Next, change the orientation of the model to isometric.

6.   Select the **Through All** option in the **End Condition** drop-down list of the **Direction 1** rollout.

7. Click on the green tick-mark ☑ in the PropertyManager. The extruded cut feature is created, see Figure 10.193.

Section 9: Creating the Seventh Feature - Circular Pattern

1. Click on the arrow at the bottom of the **Linear Pattern** tool in the **Features CommandManager**. The **Pattern** flyout appears.

2. Click on the **Circular Pattern** tool. The **CirPattern PropertyManager** appears.

3. Select the sixth feature (previously created extruded cut feature) as the feature to be patterned in the FeatureManager Design Tree or in the graphics area.

4. Click on the **Pattern Axis** field in the **Direction 1** rollout of the PropertyManager.

5. Click on the outer circular face of the fifth feature to define the pattern axis, see Figure 10.194. A preview of the circular pattern appears with default parameters.

6. Make sure that the **Equal spacing** radio button is selected in the **Direction 1** rollout.

7. Enter **6** in the **Number of Instances** field of the **Direction 1** rollout.

8. Click on the green tick-mark ☑ in the PropertyManager. The circular pattern is created.

Section 10: Creating the Eighth Feature - Fillet

1. Click on the **Fillet** tool. The **Fillet PropertyManager** appears.

2. Make sure that the **Constant Size Fillet** button is activated in the **Fillet Type** rollout.

3. Click on the circular edge of the model to apply the fillet as shown in Figure 10.195.

4. Enter **15** in the **Radius** field of the **Fillet Parameters** rollout in the PropertyManager. Next, make sure that the **Symmetric** option is selected in the **Fillet Method** drop-down list.

5. Click on the green tick-mark ☑ in the PropertyManager. A fillet of radius 15 mm is created, see Figure 10.196.

Section 11: Creating the Ninth Feature - Rib Feature

1. Click on the **Rib** tool in the **Features CommandManager**. The **Rib PropertyManager** appears.

2. Select the **Front Plane** as the sketching plane in the FeatureManager Design Tree.

3. Press CTRL + 8 to change the orientation of the model as normal to the viewing direction.

4. Create an inclined line as the sketch of the rib feature, see Figure 10.197.

5. Click on the **Exit Sketch** tool in the **Sketch CommandManager**. The **Rib PropertyManager** appears. Next, press CTRL + 7 to change the orientation of the model to isometric.

6. Make sure that the **Both Sides** button is activated in the **Parameters** rollout.

7. Enter **16** in the **Rib Thickness** field of the **Parameters** rollout.

8. Make sure that the **Parallel to Sketch** button is activated in the **Parameters** rollout.

9. Select the **Flip material side** check box to flip the direction of extrusion inward, if needed.

10. Click on the green tick-mark ☑ in the PropertyManager. The rib feature is created, see Figure 10.198.

Section 12: Creating the Tenth Feature - Mirror Feature

1. Click on the **Mirror** tool. The **Mirror PropertyManager** appears.

2. Expand the FeatureManager Design Tree and then click on the **Right Plane** as the mirroring plane.

3. Click on the rib feature to be mirrored. The preview of the mirror feature appears.

4. Click on the green tick-mark ✓ in the PropertyManager. The mirror feature is created, see Figure 10.199.

Section 13: Creating the Eleventh Feature - Extruded Feature

1. Click on the **Extruded Boss/Base** tool. The **Extrude PropertyManager** appears.

2. Expand the FeatureManager Design Tree and then click on the **Right Plane** as the sketching plane. Next, press CTRL + 8 to change the orientation as normal to the viewing direction.

3. Create a rectangle as the sketch of the eleventh feature, see Figure 10.200.

4. Exit the Sketching environment. The **Boss-Extrude PropertyManager** and a preview of the extruded feature appear. Next, change the orientation of the model to isometric.

5. Select the **Up To Next** option in the **End Condition** drop-down list of the **Direction 1** rollout.

6. Expand the **Direction 2** rollout of the PropertyManager and then select the **Up To Next** option in the **End Condition** drop-down list of the **Direction 2** rollout.

7. Click on the green tick-mark ✓ in the PropertyManager. The extruded feature is created, see Figure 10.201.

Section 14: Creating the Twelfth Feature - Extruded Cut Feature

1.   Click on the **Extruded Cut** tool in the **Features** CommandManager. The **Extrude** PropertyManager appears.

2.   Click on the top planar face of the eleventh feature (previously created extruded feature) as the sketching plane.

3.   Press CTRL + 8 to change the orientation of the model as normal to the viewing direction.

4.   Create a circle of diameter 20 mm, whose center point is at the origin, see Figure 10.202.

5.   Exit the Sketching environment. The **Cut-Extrude PropertyManager** appears. Next, change the orientation of the model to isometric.

6.   Select the **Up To Next** option in the **End Condition** drop-down list of the **Direction 1** rollout.

7.   Click on the green tick-mark ☑ in the PropertyManager. The extruded cut feature is created, see Figure 10.203.

Section 15: Saving the Model

1.   Click on the **Save** tool of the **Standard** toolbar. The **Save As** dialog box appears.

2.   Browse to the Chapter 10 folder of the SOLIDWORKS folder and then save the model with the name Tutorial 2.

Hands-on Test Drive 1

Create a model, as shown in Figure 10.204. All dimensions are in mm.

10.204

DETAIL A

Hands-on Test Drive 2

Create a model, as shown in Figure 10.205. All dimensions are in mm.

10.205

Summary

The chapter discusses how to create standard or customized holes such as counterbore, countersink, straight tap, tapered tap, and multi-stepped holes as per standard specifications. Cosmetic threads can be used to represent real threads on the holes, fasteners, and cylindrical features to reduce the complexity of a model and improve the overall performance of the system. In addition to the cosmetic threads, the chapter discusses how to create realistic threads on a cylindrical feature or cut/hole feature of a model, adding constant and variable radius fillets to remove the sharp edges of a model, various methods of adding chamfer on the edges of a model, creating a rib feature by using the open or closed sketch, in addition to creating the shell and wrap features.

Questions

* The _____ tool is used for creating standard holes such as counterbore and countersink.

* The _____ tool is used for adding cosmetic threads to holes, fasteners, and cylindrical features.

* Using the **Fillet** tool, you can create _____ , _____ , _____ , and _____ fillets.

* If the Rho value is less than _____ then the resultant fillet profile becomes elliptical in shape.

* The _____ fillet is created tangent to three adjacent faces of a model.

* The _____ fillet is created between the two non-continuous faces of a model.

* You can create a rib feature by using the open or closed sketch. (True/False)

* You cannot create a rib feature with a draft angle. (True/False)

* While creating a hole by using the **Hole Wizard** tool, you cannot customize the size of the hole. (True/False)

* Using the **Hole Wizard** tool, you can create counterbore slot, countersink slot, or slot holes. (True/False)

Working with Configurations

This chapter discusses the following topics:

*   Creating Configurations by using the Manual Method
*   Creating Configurations by using the Design Table
*   Saving Configurations as a Separate File
*   Suppressing and Unsuppressing Features

Configurations is one of the most powerful features of SOLIDWORKS, which allows you to create multiple variations of a model within a single file. It helps you to quickly and easily manage multiple design alternates based on different dimensions, features, materials, and so on within a single file. For example, if you have to create ten hexagonal bolts with different diameters and heights then instead of creating ten hexagonal bolts as separate files, you can create one single bolt with ten different configurations. In SOLIDWORKS, you can create configurations by using the Manual method and Design Table method. Both these methods for creating configurations are discussed next.

Creating Configurations by using the Manual Method

In the Manual method, after creating the parent model in the Part modeling environment, you can create its configurations. You can create multiple configurations of a model and modify the model parameters for each configuration, as required. Consider the case of a plate as shown in Figure 11.1, in which you need to create three different designs. In the first design, you need to create four counterbore holes at each corner and one countersink hole at the center of the plate, see Figure 11.1. In the second design, you need to create only four counterbore holes at each corner, see Figure 11.2. In the third design, you need to create only one countersink hole at the center of the plate, see Figure 11.3.

Design 1

Design 2

Design 3

To create multiple configurations of a model, click on the **ConfigurationManager** tab, see Figure 11.4. The ConfigurationManager appears, which displays a list of all the available configurations of the current model. By default, the Default configuration of the current model is saved and is activated, see Figure 11.4. A green tick-mark in front of a configuration indicates that it is activated. Note that the model appears in the graphics area as per its active configuration.

After invoking the ConfigurationManager, right-click on the name of the model. A shortcut menu appears, see Figure 11.5. In this shortcut menu, click on the **Add Configuration** option. The **Add Configuration PropertyManager** appears to the left of the graphics area, see Figure 11.6. The options in the **Add Configuration PropertyManager** are discussed next.

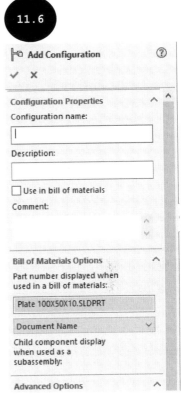

Configuration Properties

The **Configuration name** field of the **Configuration Properties** rollout in the PropertyManager is used for specifying the name of the configuration. It is recommended to specify some logical name for the configuration so that you can easily identify it in later use. The **Description** field of the **Configuration Properties** rollout is used for specifying a description for the configuration. On selecting the **Use in bill of materials** check box, the description specified in the **Description** field will be displayed in the BOM (Bill of Material). The **Comment** field of this rollout is used for specifying comments on the configuration.

Bill of Materials Options

The **Part number displayed when used in a bill of materials** drop-down list of the **Bill of Materials Options** rollout is used for selecting an option to display the name of the model in the Bill of Materials (BOM) when this configuration is used in the assembly. By default, the **Document Name** option is selected in this drop-down list. As a result, the name of the model is displayed in the BOM, when this configuration is used. On selecting the **Configuration Name** option in the drop-down list, the name of the configuration specified in the **Configuration name** field of the **Configuration Properties** rollout is displayed in the BOM, when this configuration is used. On selecting the **User Specified Name** option, you can specify a new name for the configuration, to be displayed in the BOM, in the field that appears above the drop-down list in the rollout.

Advanced Options

The **Suppress new features and mates** check box is selected by default in the **Advanced Options** rollout, see Figure 11.7. As a result, new features added to other configurations of the model are automatically suppressed in this configuration. If you clear this check box then the new features added in other configurations of the model are also included in this configuration. The **Use configuration specific color** check box is used for specifying a color for this configuration. To specify a color for this configuration, select this check box. The **Color** button gets enabled below the check box in this rollout. Click on the **Color** button to display the **Color** window. By using the **Color** window, you can specify a color for this configuration.

After specifying the configuration properties such as name and description, click on the green tick-mark in the **Add Configuration PropertyManager**. The configuration with specified properties is created and displayed in the ConfigurationManager, see Figure 11.8. In this figure, the **Design 1** configuration is added. Note that the newly created configuration becomes the active configuration of the model.

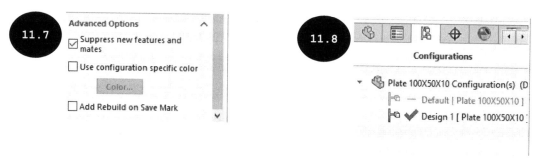

After creating a configuration, you can make the required modifications in the model such as suppressing or unsuppressing existing features, adding new features, and editing other properties. You will learn about suppressing and unsuppressing features later in this chapter. Note that the modifications made in the model are limited to the current active configuration only and will not affect the default or other configurations of the model. However, if you modify feature parameters such as extruded depth and dimensions of sketches then you need to specify whether the modification is for the current active configuration only or for all configurations of the model. For example, while modifying the depth of an extruded feature, you need to select the required radio button: **This configuration**, **All configurations**, or **Specify configurations** in the **Configurations** rollout of the respective PropertyManager, see Figure 11.9. If you select the **This configuration** radio button, then the modification is made in the current active configuration of the model only, whereas if you select the **All configuration** radio button, then the modification is made in all configurations of the model including the default configuration. Similarly, while modifying a dimension of a sketch, you need to specify whether the modification is for the current active configuration only or for all the configurations of the model by using the **Configuration** flyout of the **Modify** dialog box, which appears while modifying a dimension, see Figure 11.10.

To create the second configuration of a model, right-click on the name of the model in the ConfigurationManager to display a shortcut menu, see Figure 11.11. In this shortcut menu, click on the **Add Configuration** option. The **Add Configuration PropertyManager** appears. In this PropertyManager, specify the configuration properties such as name and description and then click on the green tick mark in the PropertyManager. A new configuration is created and its name appears in the ConfigurationManager, see Figure 11.12. In this figure, the **Design 1** and **Design 2** configurations are added. Note that the newly created configuration (**Design 2**) is the active configuration of the model. After creating the second configuration of a model, you can make the required modifications in the model. Similarly, you can create multiple configurations of a model. Figure 11.13 shows a model with three different configurations (Design 1, Design 2, and Design 3).

Design 1   Design 2   Design 3

Note: You can activate any existing configuration of a model by double-clicking on its name in the ConfigurationManager. Alternatively, right-click on the name of the configuration to be activated in the ConfigurationManager to display a shortcut menu and then click on the **Show Configuration** option. Once the required configuration is activated, you can make necessary modifications in the model for the active configuration.

Procedure for Creating Configurations by using the Manual Method

1. Invoke the ConfigurationManager by clicking on the **ConfigurationManager** tab.
2. Right-click on the name of the model in the ConfigurationManager. A shortcut menu appears.
3. In the shortcut menu, click on the **Add Configuration** option. The **Add Configuration PropertyManager** appears.
4. Specify configuration properties such as configuration name and description in the PropertyManager and then click on its green tick mark. The configuration with specified properties is created and its name is displayed in the ConfigurationManager. Also, the newly created configuration becomes the current active configuration of the model.
5. Modify the model such as suppressing or unsuppressing existing features or adding new features in the model. The modifications made in the model are part of the active configuration only and do not affect the Default or other configurations of the model. However, if you modify feature parameters such as extruded depth and dimensions, then you need to specify whether the modification is for the active configuration only or for all configurations.
6. Similarly, you can add multiple configurations and modify the model for each configuration.

Creating Configurations by using the Design Table

The Design Table method is a very easy and convenient way of creating multiple configurations of a model. It provides an embedded Microsoft excel worksheet, where you can easily create or manage multiple configurations by specifying parameters. For doing so, click on the **Insert > Tables > Design Table** in the SOLIDWORKS Menus, see Figure 11.14. The **Design Table PropertyManager** appears, see Figure 11.15. The options in the PropertyManager are discussed next.

11.14

Note: To create configurations by using the Design Table, you need to make sure that Microsoft Excel is installed on your computer.

Source

By default, the **Auto-create** radio button is selected in the **Source** rollout of the **Design Table PropertyManager**, see Figure 11.15. As a result, all parameters of the source model are automatically loaded in the design table. On selecting the **Blank** radio button, you are provided with a blank design table where you need to fill in the parameters for each configuration. On selecting the **From file** radio button, you can import an existing design table or a Microsoft excel file containing different configurations of the model with their parameters. When you select the **From file** radio button, the **Browse** button is enabled in the rollout. Click on the **Browse** button. The **Open** dialog box appears. In this dialog box, browse to the location where the existing design table or the Microsoft excel file is saved and then select it. Next, click on the **Open** button. The name and path of the selected design table or Microsoft excel file appears in the field below the **From file** radio button. If you select the **Link to file** check box in the rollout then the imported Microsoft excel file gets linked with the model. As a result, if you make any modifications in the excel file the same modifications are reflected in the model and vice-versa.

Edit Control

The **Allow model edits to update the design table** radio button is selected in the **Edit Control** rollout, by default, see Figure 11.15. As a result, if you make any modifications in the model, the same modifications are reflected in the design table as well. On selecting the **Block model edits that would update the design table** radio button, you are not allowed to make modifications in the model, which would update the parameters of the design table.

Options

The **New parameters** check box is selected in the **Options** rollout, by default. As a result, on adding a new parameter in the model, a new column for the parameter is added automatically in the design table. If the **New configurations** check box is selected in the rollout then on adding a new configuration in the model, a new row for the configuration is added automatically in the design table. If the **Warn when updating design table** check box is selected, then a warning message appears on updating the design table. If the **Enable cell drop-down lists** check box is selected, the cells of the design table contain drop-down lists for multiple entries.

In the **Design Table PropertyManager**, accept the default selected options and then click on the green tick-mark in it. The process of creating the design table starts. Also, the **Dimensions** window and an embedded Microsoft excel worksheet appear on the screen, see Figure 11.16. The **Dimensions** window displays a list of all dimensions of the model.

11.16

In the **Dimensions** window, select the dimensions of the model to be added in the design table by pressing and holding the CTRL key. After selecting the dimensions in the **Dimensions** window, click on the **OK** button. The design table appears as a Microsoft excel worksheet with the Default configuration of the model, see Figure 11.17. In the design table, the name of the selected dimensions of the model are added in separate columns and the Default configuration is added in a row. Also, the dimension values of the selected dimensions are added in cells, corresponding to the dimension name column and the Default configuration row, see Figure 11.17.

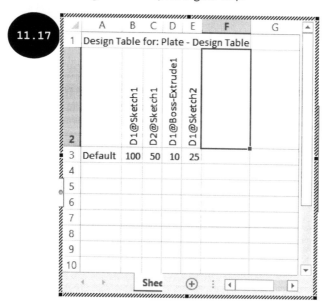

11.17

You can add multiple configurations of a model by entering their names in different rows of the table, see Figure 11.18. Note that for each configuration, you can specify different dimension values in the respective cells, see Figure 11.18. In this figure, in addition to the Default configuration, three more configurations (Plate 50X25X5, Plate 30X15X5, and Plate 200X100X10) of the model have been created with different dimension values.

In addition to specifying different dimension values for each configuration in the design table, you can specify the suppressed or unsuppressed state for the features of the model in each configuration. Consider a case of a plate having one circular cut feature at the center, see Figure 11.19. If you do not want the circular cut feature of the model to become a part of a configuration then you can specify its state as suppressed in the design table. To specify the suppressed or unsuppressed state of a feature in the design table, click on the column, next to the last dimension name in the design table, refer to Figure 11.18. Next, double-click on the name of the feature in the FeatureManager Design Tree. The name of the selected feature is added in the selected column of the design table, see Figure 11.20. Notice that, the unsuppressed state is specified for the Default configuration, by default. To specify suppressed state for a feature, enter S, 1, or SUPPRESSED in the cell corresponding to the feature and the configuration. Similarly, to specify unsuppressed state, enter U, 0, or UNSUPPRESSED. After creating different configurations and specifying parameters for each configuration, click anywhere in the graphics area. The SOLIDWORKS message window appears which informs you that the design table is generated with the specified configurations. Click on the OK button in the SOLIDWORKS message window. The configurations are created and are listed in the ConfigurationManager, see Figure 11.21.

	A	B	C	D	E	F	G
1	Design Table for: Plate - Design Table						
2		D1@Sketch1	D2@Sketch1	D1@Boss-Extrude1	D1@Sketch2	$STATE@Cut-Extrude1	
3	Default	100	50	10	25	UNSUPPRESSED	
4	Plate 50X25X5	50	25	5	12		
5	Plate 30X15X5	30	15	5	8		
6	Plate 200X100X10	200	100	10	50		
7							

Feature name

Configurations

Plate - Design Table Configuration(s

  Tables

  Default [Plate - Design Tab

  Plate 50X25X5

  Plate 30X15X5

  Plate 200X100X10

Note that in the ConfigurationManager, the Default configuration is activated. As a result, the model that appears in the graphics area is based on the parameters of the Default configuration. To activate a configuration, double-click on the name of the configuration to be activated in the ConfigurationManager. Alternatively, right-click on the name of the configuration and then click on the **Show Configuration** option in the shortcut menu that appears. The selected configuration gets activated and the model is updated in the graphics area, accordingly.

Note: After generating a design table with multiple configurations, you can further edit its parameters. For doing so, expand the **Tables** node in the ConfigurationManager and then right-click on the **Design Table** option in the expanded **Tables** node. A shortcut menu appears, see Figure 11.22. In this shortcut menu, click on the **Edit Table** option. The **Add Rows and Columns** window appears. Click on the **OK** button in this window. The design table as Microsoft excel worksheet appears. Now, you can make the necessary modifications in the parameters of the existing configurations and add new configurations as well. After editing the design table, click anywhere in the graphics area.

Configurations

Plate - Design Table Configuration(s

  Tables

    Design Table

  Default [Plat

  Plate 50X25X

  Plate 30X15X

  Plate 200X10(

Edit Feature

Edit Table

Edit Table in New Window

Save Table...

✕ Delete

Feature Properties

Procedure for Creating Configurations by using the Design Table

1. Click on the **Insert > Tables > Design Table** in the SOLIDWORKS Menus. The **Design Table PropertyManager** appears.

2. Accept the default selected options in the PropertyManager and then click on the green tick-mark in the PropertyManager. The **Dimensions** window appears in the graphics area.

3. Press and hold the CTRL key and then select the dimensions in the **Dimensions** window. Next, click on the **OK** button. The design table appears as a microsoft excel worksheet with a Default configuration.

4. Enter the names of the configurations to be created in different rows of the table and then specify the respective parameters for each configuration.

5. After creating different configurations and specifying parameters for each configuration, click anywhere in the graphics area. The **SOLIDWORKS** message window appears.

6. Click on the **OK** button in the window. The configurations are created and are listed in the ConfigurationManager. Now, you can double-click on a configuration to activate it.

Saving Configurations as a Separate File New

In SOLIDWORKS 2020, you can save a selected configuration of a part or an assembly as a separate file. To save a configuration or multiple configurations of a part as a separate part file, right-click on a configuration of the part in the ConfigurationManager and then click on the **Save Configurations** option in the shortcut menu that appears, see Figure 11.23. The **Save Configurations as a new Part** window appears, see Figure 11.24. In this window, you can select the required configurations to be saved as a separate part file. Note that the currently active configuration of the part is selected in this window, by default and cannot be removed from the selection set. Next, click on the **Save Selected** button. The **Save As** dialog box appears. In this dialog box, browse to the required location and then enter a new name for the file in the **File name** field of the dialog box. Next, click on the **Save** button. A new part file of specified name gets saved with the selected configurations. Similarly, you can save selected configurations of an assembly as a separate assembly file.

Suppressing and Unsuppressing Features

In SOLIDWORKS, you can suppress or unsuppress the features of a model. A suppressed feature is removed from the model and does not appear in the graphics area. Also, the name of the suppressed feature appears in gray color in the FeatureManager Design Tree. Note that a suppressed feature is not deleted from the model, it is only removed such that it does not load into the RAM (random access memory) while rebuilding the model. This helps you to speed up the overall performance of the system when you are working with complex models.

To suppress a feature of a model, select the feature to be suppressed either from the graphics area or from the FeatureManager Design Tree. A Pop-up toolbar appears, see Figure 11.25. In this Pop-up toolbar, click on the **Suppress** tool. The selected feature is suppressed.

To unsuppress a suppressed feature, select the suppressed feature from the FeatureManager Design Tree. A Pop-up toolbar appears. In this Pop-up toolbar, click on the **Unsuppress** tool. The feature is unsuppressed and appears in the model.

Tutorial 1

Create a model (Weld Neck Flange), as shown in Figure 11.26. After creating the model, create its three different configurations by using the Design Table method. The details of the configurations to be created are given in the table below. All dimensions are in mm.

TABLE								
	Bore Dia	Hub Dia	Overall Length	Flange Dia	Flange Thickness	Hole Dia	Hole PCD	No. of Holes
350 Bore Dia	350	400	300	550	35	35	470	12
400 Bore Dia	400	450	300	600	35	35	520	16
450 Bore Dia	450	500	300	650	35	35	570	20

Section 1: Starting SOLIDWORKS

1. Start SOLIDWORKS by double-clicking on the SOLIDWORKS icon on your desktop. The startup user interface of SOLIDWORKS appears along with the **Welcome** dialog box.

Section 2: Invoking the Part Modeling Environment

1. Click on the **Part** button in the **Welcome** dialog box. The Part modeling environment is invoked. Alternatively, click on the **New** tool in the **Standard** toolbar. The **New SOLIDWORKS Document** dialog box appears. In this dialog box, make sure that the **Part** button is selected and then click on the **OK** button.

Section 3: Specifying Unit Settings

1. Make sure that the MMGS (millimeter, gram, second) unit system is set for the currently opened part document.

Section 4: Creating the Base Feature - Extruded Feature

1. Invoke the Sketching environment by selecting the Top plane as the sketching plane.

2. Create a circle by specifying its center point at the origin, see Figure 11.27.

3. Click on the **Smart Dimension** tool in the **Sketch CommandManager**. Next, click on the circle in the drawing area. The diameter dimension of the circle gets attached to the cursor.

4. Click to specify the placement point for the diameter dimension in the drawing area. The **Modify** dialog box appears, see Figure 11.28.

5. Enter **350** as the diameter of the circle in the **Dimension** field of the **Modify** dialog box, see Figure 11.28.

6. Enter **Bore Dia** as the name of the dimension in the **Name** field, see Figure 11.28.

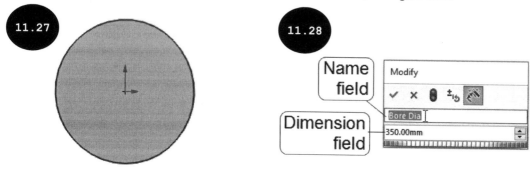

Tip: Specifying a name to each sketch dimension will help you in identifying them while specifying parameters for creating configurations in the design table.

7. Click on the green tick-mark button in the **Modify** dialog box. The diameter dimension with specified diameter value and name is applied to the circle.

8. Similarly, create another circle and specify its diameter value as **400 mm** and name as **Hub Dia**, see Figure 11.29.

9. Click on the **Extruded Boss/Base** tool in the **Features CommandManager**. The preview of the extruded feature appears. Also, the **Boss-Extrude PropertyManager** appears on the left of the graphics area.

10. Enter **300** in the **Depth** field of the PropertyManager and then click on its green tick-mark. The extruded feature is created, see Figure 11.30.

Section 5: Creating the Second Feature - Extruded Feature

1. Invoke the Sketching environment by selecting the top planar face of the base feature as the sketching plane.

2. Press CTRL + 8 to change the orientation of the model as normal to the viewing direction.

3. Create two circles by specifying their center points at the origin.

4. Apply a coradial ⃝ relation between a circle and the inner circular edge of the base feature.

5. Apply the diameter dimension to the second circle by specifying its diameter value as **550 mm** and name as **Flange Dia** in the **Modify** dialog box, see Figure 11.31.

6. Click on the **Extruded Boss/Base** tool in the Features CommandManager. The preview of the extruded feature appears. Next, change the orientation of the model to Isometric.

7. Enter 35 in the **Depth** field of the PropertyManager and then Press ENTER.

8. Click on the **Reverse Direction** button in the **Direction 1** rollout of the PropertyManager to reverse the direction of extrusion downward. Next, click on the green tick-mark in the PropertyManager. The extruded feature is created, see Figure 11.32.

Section 6: Creating the Third Feature - Cut Feature

1. Invoke the Sketching environment by selecting the top planar face of the model as the sketching plane.

2. Create the sketch of the third feature (cut feature) and then apply required dimensions and relations, see Figure 11.33. Note that you need to specify **Hole Dia** as the name of the diameter dimension 35 mm and **PCD** as the name of the diameter dimension 470 mm.

3. Click on the **Extruded Cut** tool in the **Features CommandManager**. The **Cut-Extrude PropertyManager** appears. Next, change the orientation of the model to isometric.

4. Select the **Up to Next** option in the **End Condition** drop-down list of the **Direction 1** rollout and then click on the green tick-mark. The cut feature is created, see Figure 11.34.

Section 7: Creating the Fourth Feature - Circular Pattern

1. Create the circular pattern of the previously created cut feature by specifying 12 as the number of instances, see Figure 11.35.

Section 8: Creating Configurations - Design Table

1. Click on the **Insert > Tables > Design Table** in the SOLIDWORKS Menus. The **Design Table PropertyManager** appears.

2. Accept the default selected options in the PropertyManager and click on the green tick-mark in the PropertyManager. The process of creating the design table gets started and the **Dimensions** window appears, see Figure 11.36.

3. Press and hold the CTRL key and then select all the dimensions listed in the **Dimensions** dialog box. Next, click on the **OK** button in the dialog box. The design table appears as a Microsoft excel worksheet with the Default configuration of the model, see Figure 11.37.

4. Enter three new configuration names: **350 Bore Dia, 400 Bore Dia,** and **450 Bore Dia** below the Default configuration in the design table and then specify their parameters, see Figure 11.38. Note that working with the design table is same as an excel file.

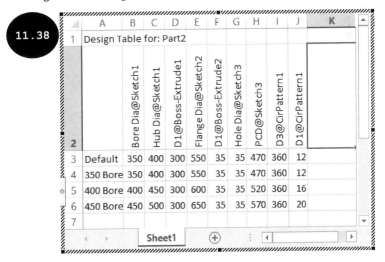

5. After specifying parameters for each configuration in the design table, click anywhere in the graphics area. The **SOLIDWORKS** message window appears, see Figure 11.39.

6. Click on the **OK** button in the **SOLIDWORKS** message window. Three new configurations are created in addition to the Default configuration. Notice that the names of all the configurations are listed in the ConfigurationManager, see Figure 11.40. In this figure, the Default configuration is activated.

7. Double-click on the name of each configuration in the ConfigurationManager one by one to review the respective design of the model. Note that the model appears in the graphics area as per the activated configuration.

Section 9: Saving the Model

1. Click on the **Save** tool in the **Standard** toolbar. The **Save As** dialog box appears.

2. Browse to the SOLIDWORKS folder and then create a folder with the name Chapter 11.

3. Enter **Tutorial 1** in the **File name** field of the dialog box as the name of the file and then click on the **Save** button. The model is saved with the name Tutorial 1 in the Chapter 11 folder.

Hands-on Test Drive 1

Create the model shown in Figure 11.41. After creating the model, create its two configurations: **With Slot Cut** and **Without Slot Cut** by using the Manual method. All dimensions are in mm.

11.41

Hands-on Test Drive 2

Create the model shown in Figure 11.42. After creating the model, create its three different configurations by using the Design Table method. The details of the configurations to be created are given in the table below. All dimensions are in mm.

Table		
	Bolt Diameter	Length
20 Bolt Dia	20	100
22 Bolt Dia	22	80
26 Bolt Dia	26	120

Summary

This chapter discusses how to create configurations of a model by using the Manual and Design Table methods and saving configurations as a separate file. Suppressing and unsuppressing features of a model have also been explained.

Questions

- You can create configurations of a model by using two methods: _____ and _____.

- By default, the _____ configuration is created for a model.

- You can suppress a feature by using the _____ tool.

- You cannot suppress features of a model by using the Design Table. (True/False)

Working with Assemblies - I

This chapter discusses the following topics:

- Working with Bottom-up Assembly Approach
- Working with Top-down Assembly Approach
- Creating an Assembly by using Bottom-up Approach
- Working with Degrees of Freedom
- Applying Relations or Mates
- Working with Standard Mates
- Working with Advanced Mates
- Working with Mechanical Mates
- Hiding Faces while Applying a Mate
- Moving and Rotating Individual Components
- Working with SmartMates

In the earlier chapters, you have learned about the basic and advanced techniques of creating real world mechanical components. In this chapter, you will learn about different techniques of creating mechanical assemblies. An assembly is made up of two or more than two components joined together by applying mates. You will learn about applying mates later in this chapter. Figure 12.1 shows an assembly, in which multiple components are assembled together by applying the required mates.

12.1

In SOLIDWORKS, you can create assemblies in the Assembly environment by using two approaches: Bottom-up Assembly Approach and Top-down Assembly Approach. Moreover, you can use a combination of both these approaches for creating an assembly. Both these approaches are discussed next.

Working with Bottom-up Assembly Approach

The Bottom-up Assembly Approach is the most widely used approach for assembling components. In this approach, first all the components of an assembly are created one by one in the Part modeling environment and then saved in a common location. Later, all the components are inserted one by one in the Assembly environment and then assembled with respect to each other by applying the required mates.

Tip: SOLIDWORKS has a bidirectional association between all its environments. As a result, if any change or modification is made into a component in the Part modeling environment, the same change automatically reflects in the Assembly environment as well as in the Drawing environment, and vice-versa.

Working with Top-down Assembly Approach

In the Top-down Assembly Approach, all the components of an assembly are created within the Assembly environment. It helps in creating a concept-based design, in which new components of an assembly are created by taking reference from the existing components of the assembly.

Creating an Assembly by using Bottom-up Approach

After creating all components of an assembly in the Part modeling environment and saving them in a common location, you need to invoke the Assembly environment of SOLIDWORKS for assembling them. To invoke the Assembly environment, click on the **New** tool in the **Standard** toolbar. The **New SOLIDWORKS Document** dialog box appears, see Figure 12.2. In this dialog box, click on the **Assembly** button and then click on the **OK** button. The Assembly environment is invoked with the **Begin Assembly PropertyManager** on its left. Also, the **Open** dialog box appears on the screen, see Figure 12.3. Note that along with the **Begin Assembly PropertyManager**, the **Open** dialog box appears every time on invoking the Assembly environment. This is because, in the **Options** rollout of the **Begin Assembly PropertyManager**, the **Automatic Browse when creating new assembly** check box is selected, by default. It is used for invoking the **Open** dialog box automatically, if no components are opened in the current session of SOLIDWORKS. By using the **Open** dialog box, you can insert a component in the Assembly environment. The methods for inserting components in the Assembly environment are discussed next.

Tip: You can also invoke the Assembly environment by clicking on the **Assembly** button in the **Welcome** dialog box, which appears every time you start SOLIDWORKS.

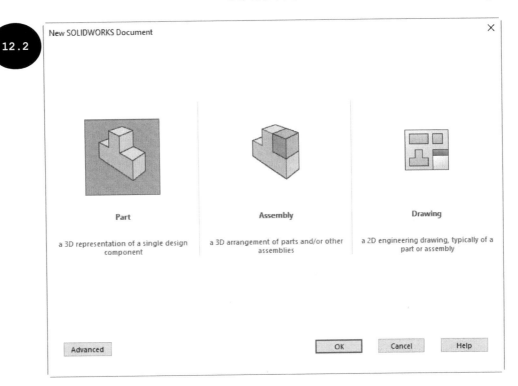

Note: The **Begin Assembly PropertyManager** appears every time on invoking the Assembly environment for inserting components in the Assembly environment. This is because, in the **Options** rollout of the **Begin Assembly PropertyManager**, the **Start command when creating new assembly** check box is selected, by default, refer to Figure 12.3. If you clear this check box, the **Begin Assembly PropertyManager** as well as the **Open** dialog box do not appear when you invoke the Assembly environment the next time. In such a case, you can insert components in the Assembly environment by using the **Insert Components** tool of the **Assembly CommandManager**. You will learn about inserting components by using the **Insert Components** tool later in this chapter.

Inserting Components in the Assembly Environment

As discussed, on invoking the Assembly environment, if no components are opened in the current session of SOLIDWORKS, the **Open** dialog box appears, automatically along with the **Begin Assembly PropertyManager**. If the **Open** dialog box does not appear then click on the **Browse** button in the **Begin Assembly PropertyManager** to invoke the **Open** dialog box. In the **Open** dialog box, browse to the location where all components of the assembly are saved and then select a component to be inserted. Next, click on the **Open** button in the dialog box. The selected component gets attached to the cursor and the **Rotate Context** toolbar appears in the graphics area, see Figure 12.4. If needed, you can change the orientation of the attached component by using the tools of the **Rotate Context** toolbar. By default, **90 degrees** is entered in the **Angle** field of the **Rotate Context** toolbar. As a result, when you click on the **X**, **Y**, or **Z** tool in this toolbar; the component rotates 90 degrees about the X, Y, or Z axis, respectively. You can enter the required angle of rotation value in the **Angle** field and rotate the component about the X, Y, or Z axis by using this toolbar.

Angle field

Rotate Context toolbar

12.4

Note: By default, the **Rotate Context** toolbar appears every time you insert a component in the Assembly environment, since the **Show Rotate context toolbar** check box is selected in the **Options** rollout of the **Begin Assembly PropertyManager**.

Once the orientation of the component has been set by using the **Rotate Context** toolbar, click anywhere in the graphics area. The component moves toward the origin of the assembly and becomes a fixed component with respect to the origin of the assembly. Notice that the name of the inserted component gets listed in the **FeatureManager Design Tree** with '(f)' sign in front of its name, see Figure 12.5. The '(f)' sign indicates that all degrees of freedom of the component are fixed and the component cannot move or rotate in any direction. In SOLIDWORKS, the first component you insert in the Assembly environment becomes the fixed component automatically and does not allow any translational or rotational movement. You can also change a fixed component to a floating component, whose all degrees of freedom are free. A floating component is free to move or rotate in the graphics area. To change a fixed component to a floating component, right-click on the name of the fixed component in the FeatureManager Design Tree and then click on the **Float** option in the shortcut menu that appears. In addition, notice that as soon as the first component is inserted in the Assembly environment, the **Begin Assembly PropertyManager** gets closed. Therefore, to insert the remaining components of the assembly in the Assembly environment, you need to use the **Insert Components** tool of the **Assembly CommandManager**. The method for inserting components by using the **Insert Components** tool is discussed next.

Note: If any component is opened in the current session of SOLIDWORKS then on invoking the Assembly environment; the **Open** dialog box will not be opened automatically and the names of the opened components are listed in the **Open documents** field of the **Begin Assembly PropertyManager**, see Figure 12.6. In this figure, five components are listed in the **Open documents** field. You can select a component to be inserted in the Assembly environment from the **Open documents** field or click on the **Browse** button to open the Open dialog box.

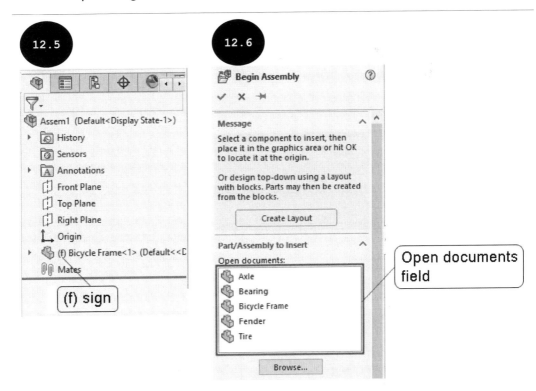

Tip: If you pin the **Begin Assembly PropertyManager** by clicking on the **Keep Visible** ⊀ icon available at the upper right corner of the PropertyManager then the display of the PropertyManager will not be closed after inserting the component and you can continue inserting the components by using the **Begin Assembly PropertyManager**.

Inserting Components by using the Insert Components Tool

To insert a component in the Assembly environment by using the **Insert Components** tool, click on the **Insert Components** tool in the **Assembly CommandManager**, see Figure 12.7. The **Insert Component PropertyManager** and the **Open** dialog box appear. Figure 12.8 shows the **Insert Component PropertyManager**.

Note that in the **Insert Component PropertyManager**, the **Automatic Browse when creating new assembly** check box is selected, by default. As a result, the **Open** dialog box appears, automatically if no components are opened in the current session of SOLIDWORKS. If the **Open** dialog box does not appear, then click on the **Browse** button in the **Insert Component PropertyManager** to invoke the **Open** dialog box. In the **Open** dialog box, browse to the location where all components of the assembly are saved and then select a component. Next, click on the **Open** button in the dialog box. The selected component is attached to the cursor. Also, the **Rotate Context** toolbar appears in the graphics area, see Figure 12.9.

12.9 90.00deg ⌃⌄ X Y Z

Note: The **Start command when creating new assembly** check box of the **Insert Component** PropertyManager is used for turning the display of the **Begin Assembly PropertyManager** on or off on invoking the Assembly environment.

Change the current orientation of the component by using the **Rotate Context** toolbar, as needed. Once the orientation of the component has been set as required, click the left mouse button anywhere in the graphics area to define the placement for the attached component. The attached component is placed on the defined location and the PropertyManager is closed. Also, the name of the inserted component is added in the FeatureManager Design Tree with '(-)' sign in front of its name, see Figure 12.10. The '(-)' sign indicates that all degrees of freedom of the component are not defined. This means that the component is free to move or rotate in the graphics area. You need to assemble the free component with the existing components of the assembly by applying the required relations or mates. You will learn about applying relations or mates later in this chapter. Similarly, you can insert multiple components in the Assembly environment one by one by using the **Insert Component PropertyManager**.

Tip: While defining the placement for a component in the graphics area, make sure that the component does not intersect with any existing component of the assembly.

Note: If you pin the **Insert Component PropertyManager** by clicking on the **Keep Visible** icon available at its upper right corner then the display of the PropertyManager will not be closed after inserting the component and the second instance of the inserted component is attached to the cursor. Click in the graphics area to insert the second instance of the same component. Similarly, you can insert multiple instances of a component in the Assembly environment by clicking the left mouse button.

After inserting the second component, it is recommended that you first assemble the second component with the first component by applying the required mates before inserting the third or next component in the Assembly environment. However, before you learn about applying mates between assembly components, it is important to first understand the concept of degrees of freedom, which is discussed next.

Working with Degrees of Freedom

A free component within the Assembly environment has six degrees of freedom: three translational and three rotational. This means that a free component in the Assembly environment can move as well as rotate along the X, Y, and Z axes. As discussed earlier, the first component inserted in the Assembly environment becomes the fixed component automatically and does not undergo any translational or rotational movement. This means that all its degrees of freedom are fixed. However, the second or further components inserted in the Assembly environment of SOLIDWORKS are free for all kind of movements, which means that the degrees of freedom of these components are not restricted. In such cases, a designer needs to fix the degrees of freedom of the components by applying mates. It is not just about fixing the degrees of freedom of the components, but also about maintaining actual relationships between them in exactly the same way as in the real world assembly. You need to allow movable components of an assembly to move freely in the respective directions. For example, the function of a shaft in an assembly is to rotate about its axis, therefore you need to retain its rotational degree of freedom so that it is free to rotate.

Note: To check the degrees of freedom of a component, you can move or rotate the component along or about its degrees of freedom by using the **Move Component** tool or **Rotate Component** tool, respectively. You can also move or rotate components along or about their free degrees of freedom by dragging them in the graphics area. You will learn about moving or rotating individual component of an assembly later in this chapter.

Applying Relations or Mates

In SOLIDWORKS, you can assemble components together by using three types of mates: Standard, Advanced, and Mechanical. All these types of mates can be applied by using the **Mate PropertyManager** that appears on clicking the **Mate** tool in the **Assembly CommandManager**.

To apply a mate between components, click on the **Mate** tool in the **Assembly CommandManager**. The **Mate PropertyManager** appears, see Figure 12.11. Note that the **Entities to Mate** field in the **Mate Selections** rollout of the PropertyManager is activated by default. As a result, you can select entities of two different components to mate. Select the required entities such as faces, edges, planes, or a combination of these to apply a mate. Note that the first selected component becomes transparent in the graphics area, see Figure 12.12. It helps you to easily select an entity of the second component, especially when it is not visible or it is behind the first component in the graphics area. This is so because the **Make first selection transparent** check box is selected in the **Options** rollout of the **Mate PropertyManager**. Notice that as soon as you select entities for applying a mate, the **Mate** Pop-up toolbar appears in the graphics area, see Figure 12.12. The availability of tools in the **Mate** Pop-up toolbar depends on the entities selected for applying the mate. Also, in the **Mate** Pop-up toolbar, the most suitable mate that can be applied between the selected entities is activated by default, and a preview of components appears after applying the most suitable mate, see Figure 12.12. In this figure, two cylindrical faces of the components are selected for applying a mate. As a result, the Concentric mate is activated by default and a preview of the selected entities appears concentric to each other. To accept the default selected mate, click on the green tick-mark ☑ in the **Mate** Pop-up toolbar. You can also apply a mate other than the mate selected by default. For doing so, click on the required mate tool to be applied between the selected entities in the **Mate** Pop-up toolbar. In addition to applying a mate by using the **Mate** Pop-up toolbar, you can also apply a mate between the entities by using the **Mate PropertyManager**. Different types of mates are discussed next.

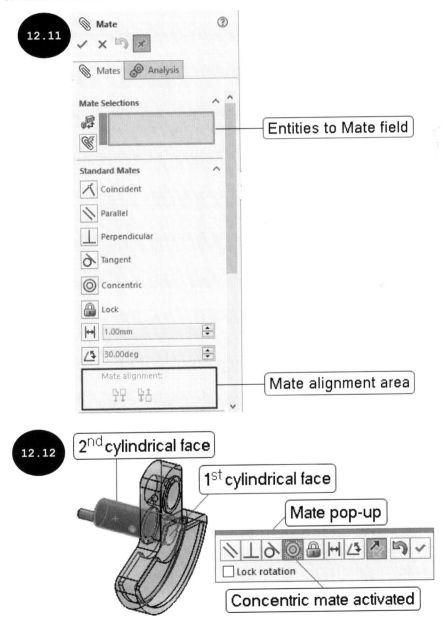

Note: The **Flip Mate Alignment** tool 📌 of the **Mate** Pop-up toolbar is used for flipping the mate alignment between the selected entities. You can also flip the mate alignment between the entities by using the **Aligned** and **Anti-Aligned** buttons of the **Mate alignment** area in the **Mate PropertyManager**, refer to Figure 12.11. Note that these buttons are enabled only after selecting the entities. You will learn more about mate alignment between the entities later in this chapter.

Working with Standard Mates

Standard mates are used for positioning components of an assembly by restricting or reducing the degrees of freedom of the components. You can apply standard mates such as coincident, parallel, perpendicular, concentric, and tangent between entities of the components to position them in the assembly. The standard mates are discussed next.

Coincident 🔨

Coincident mate is used for making the selected entities of two different components coincident to each other, see Figure 12.13. You can select faces, edges, planes, vertices, or a combination of these as entities for applying the coincident mate. On applying the coincident mate, the selected entities get aligned or share the same plane. Figure 12.13 shows two planar faces to be selected for applying the coincident mate and the resultant model after applying the coincident mate.

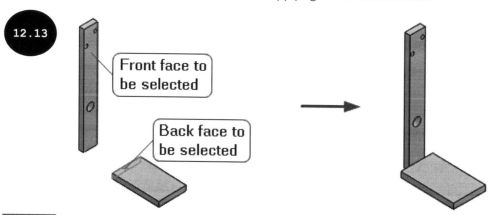

12.13

Front face to be selected

Back face to be selected

Note: If you click on the **Flip Mate Alignment** tool 📌 in the **Mate** Pop-up toolbar, the alignment of the selected entities changes from anti-aligned to aligned or vice versa, see Figure 12.14. You can also flip the alignment by using the **Aligned** and **Anti-Aligned** buttons of the **Mate alignment** area in the **Mate PropertyManager**.

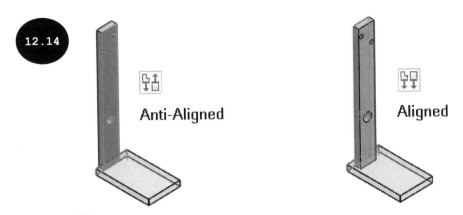

Anti-Aligned

Aligned

Parallel

The parallel mate is used for making the selected entities parallel to each other, see Figure 12.15. You can select planar faces, edges, planes, or a combination of these as entities for applying parallel mate. Figure 12.15 shows two planar faces and the resultant model after applying the parallel mate.

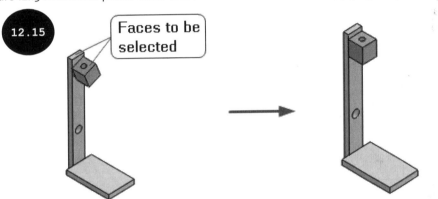

Faces to be selected

Perpendicular

The perpendicular mate is used for making the selected entities perpendicular to each other, see Figure 12.16. You can select planar faces, edges, planes, or a combination of these as entities for applying perpendicular mate. Figure 12.16 shows two planar faces and the resultant model after applying the perpendicular mate.

Faces to be selected

Note: In SOLIDWORKS, you can also apply a perpendicular mate between a non-analytic surface and a linear entity such as a line, an edge, an axis, or an axial entity.

Concentric

The concentric mate is used for making the selected circular entities concentric to each other, see Figure 12.17. You can apply concentric mate between two circular or semi-circular faces and edges. On applying concentric mate, both the selected circular entities share a common axis.

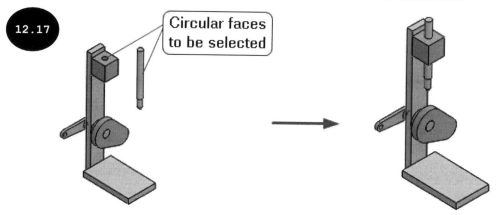

In SOLIDWORKS, you can also apply concentric mates between two pairs of misaligned holes having different center to center distance, see Figure 12.18. For doing so, after applying the concentric mate between the first pair of holes, apply the concentric mate between the second pair of holes. The Pop-up toolbar appears, see Figure 12.18. In this Pop-up toolbar, click on the **Concentric** tool and then click on the **Misaligned** button ⊕. Next, select an alignment option (**Align Linked mate, Align this mate,** or **Symmetric**) in the **Misalignment** drop-down list of the PropertyManager.

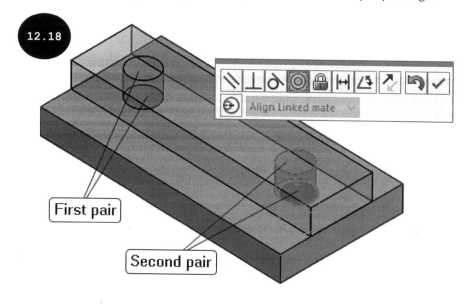

The **Align Linked mate** option is used for applying the perfect concentric mate to the first pair of holes and the misaligned concentric mate to the second pair of holes. The **Align this mate** option is used for applying the perfect concentric mate to the second pair of holes and the misaligned concentric mate to the first pair of holes. The **Symmetric** option is used for applying half misalignment to both the pairs of holes.

After applying concentric mates between two pairs of misaligned holes, click on the green tick-mark in the PropertyManager. Next, exit the PropertyManager. Notice that the applied concentric mates are listed separately in the **Misaligned** folder under the **Mates** folder in the FeatureManager Design Tree.

Note: You can enable or disable the creation of misalignment concentric mates. For doing so, click on **Options** tool in the **Standard** toolbar. The **System Options** dialog box appears. In this dialog box, click on the **Assemblies** option and then select or clear the **Allow creation of misaligned mates** check box. Next, click on the **OK** button in the dialog box.

Tangent

The tangent mate is used for making the selected entities tangent to each other. You can select a planar face, a curved face, an edge, or a plane as the first entity and a cylindrical, conical, or spherical face as the second entity for applying the tangent mate. Figure 12.19 shows two faces for applying tangent mate and the resultant model after applying the tangent mate.

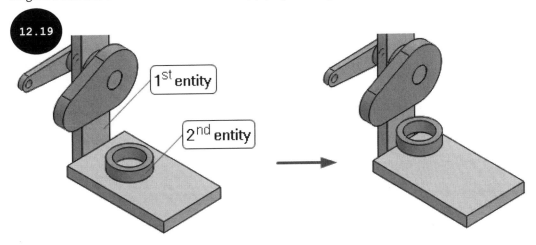

Distance

The distance mate is used for keeping distance between two entities. You can select planar faces, cylindrical faces, and planes as the entities to apply the distance mate. To apply the distance mate, after selecting the entities, click on the **Distance** button in the **Standard Mates** rollout of the PropertyManager or in the **Mate** Pop-up toolbar. Next, enter the required distance value in the **Distance** field. Figure 12.20 shows planar faces and the resultant model after applying the distance mate. In SOLIDWORKS, when you apply the distance mate between two cylindrical faces, the **Center to Center**, **Minimum Distance**, **Maximum Distance**, and **Custom Distance** buttons become available in the **Standard Mates** rollout of the PropertyManager, see Figure 12.21. By using these buttons, you can specify the type of distance measurement between the selected cylindrical faces, see Figure 12.22. In this figure, the distance mate is applied by measuring the center to center distance between the entities.

Angle

The angle mate is used for restricting entities of two components at a specified angular distance. Figure 12.23 shows faces to be selected and the resultant model after applying the angle mate.

Note: In case of the coincident, parallel, distance, and angle mates, you can flip the mate alignment between the selected entities from aligned to anti-aligned or vice versa.

Lock 🔒

The lock mate is used for locking the selected entities at a desired position in the graphics area. On applying the lock mate, all degrees of freedom of the selected entities get fixed.

Working with Advanced Mates

Advanced mates are special types of mates and work one step above the standard mates for restricting or reducing degrees of freedom of components. You can apply advanced mates such as profile center, symmetric, width, path mate, and linear/linear coupler between components of an assembly by using the **Mate** tool.

To apply advanced mates, click on the **Mate** tool in the **Assembly CommandManager**. The **Mate PropertyManager** appears. In this PropertyManager, expand the **Advanced Mates** rollout, see Figure 12.24. By using options such as **Profile Center**, **Symmetric**, **Width**, and **Path Mate** in the **Advanced Mates** rollout, you can apply the respective advanced mates between components. The different advanced mates are discussed next.

Profile Center Mate ⊕

The profile center mate is used for center-aligning two rectangular profiles, two circular profiles, or a rectangular and a circular profile of two different components with each other, see Figures 12.25 through 12.27.

Rectangular profiles

Circular profiles

Circular profile   Rectangular profile

To apply the profile center mate, click on the **Profile Center** button in the **Advanced Mates** rollout of the **Mate PropertyManager**. The **Offset Distance** field is enabled in the rollout, see Figure 12.28.

Offset Distance

Select entities for applying the profile center mate in the graphics area. After selecting the entities, a preview appears such that the selected entities get centrally aligned to each other. You can also specify the offset distance between the selected entities/profiles by using the **Offset Distance** field of the **Advanced Mates** rollout. By default, **o** (zero) is entered in this field. You can enter an offset distance between the selected profiles, as required. The **Flip dimension** check box of the **Advanced Mates** rollout is used for flipping the direction of the offset dimension between the entities. The **Lock rotation** check box is used for restricting the rotation movement of the circular profile. Note that the **Lock rotation** check box is enabled if any one of the selected entity is a circular profile.

Symmetric Mate

The symmetric mate is used for making two entities of different components symmetric about a plane or a planar face. You can select two vertices, two sketch points, two edges, two axes, two sketch lines, two planes, two planar faces, two curved faces of same radii, and so on as the entities to be made symmetric about a plane or a planar face.

To apply the symmetric mate, click on the **Symmetric** button in the **Advanced Mates** rollout. The **Entities to Mate** and **Symmetry Plane** fields are enabled in the **Mate Selections** rollout of the PropertyManager. By default, the **Symmetry Plane** field is activated. As a result, you can select a plane or a planar face as the symmetric plane. After selecting a plane or a planar face as the symmetric plane in the graphics area, the **Entities to Mate** field gets activated, automatically. Select two entities of different components to be made symmetric about the symmetric plane in the graphics area. Next, click on the green tick-mark in the PropertyManager. The symmetric mate is applied between the entities with respect to the symmetric plane. Figure 12.29 shows two planar faces as entities to be symmetric about a symmetric plane and the resultant model after applying the symmetric mate.

Width Mate

The width mate is used for making two planar faces, a cylindrical face, or an axis of a component centrally aligned between two planar faces of another component, see Figure 12.30. The width mate needs two pairs of selections: one pair of selection is known as width selection and the other pair of selection is known as tab selection, see Figure 12.30. After applying the width mate, the tab selection set is aligned centrally between the width selection set, by default. You can select two planar faces (parallel or non parallel), a cylindrical face, or an axis as the tab selection set. For a width selection set, you can select two parallel or non parallel faces. Figure 12.30 shows planar faces selected as the width and tab selection sets, and the resultant model after applying the width mate.

To apply the width mate, click on the **Width** button in the **Advanced Mates** rollout. The **Width selections** and **Tab selections** fields are enabled in the **Mate Selections** rollout of the PropertyManager. Also, the **Constraint** drop-down list becomes available in the **Advanced Mates** rollout, see Figure 12.31.

By default, the **Width selections** field is activated in the **Mate Selections** rollout. As a result, you can select width selection set in the graphics area. Select two entities (parallel or non parallel faces) as the width selection set. After selecting the width selection set, the **Tab selections** field gets activated, automatically. Select two planar faces or a cylindrical face as the tab selection set. A preview of the width mate appears. Figure 12.32 shows two planar faces as the width selection, a cylindrical face as the tab selection, and a preview of the resultant width mate.

Note that the **Centered** option is selected in the **Constraint** drop-down list of the **Advanced Mates** rollout, by default, refer to Figure 12.31. As a result, the tab selection set gets centered between the width selection set. You can also select the **Free**, **Dimension**, or **Percent** option in the **Constraint** drop-down list, as required. On selecting the **Free** option, the tab selection set can move freely within the limit of the width selection set. On selecting the **Dimension** option, you can control the position of the tab selection set by specifying a distance value in the **Distance from the End** field of the rollout. On selecting the **Percent** option, you can control the position of the tab selection set by specifying a percentage value in the **Percentage of Distance from the End** field of the rollout. You can also flip the mate alignment between the selection sets by using the **Aligned** and **Anti-Aligned** buttons of the **Mate alignment** area in the **Mate PropertyManager.** After selecting the required option in the **Constraint** drop-down list, click on the green tick-mark in the PropertyManager. The width mate is applied between the selected entities.

Path Mate

The path mate constraints a point or a vertex of a component with a path such that the component can move along the defined path, see Figure 12.33.

To apply the path mate, click on the **Path Mate** button in the **Advanced Mates** rollout. The **Component Vertex** and **Path Selection** fields are enabled in the **Mate Selections** rollout of the PropertyManager. By default, the **Component Vertex** field is activated. As a result, you can select a point or a vertex of a component for applying the path mate, refer to Figure 12.33. After selecting a point or a vertex, the **Path Selection** field gets activated. Select a sketch (open or close) or an edge as the path in the graphics area. You can use the **SelectionManager** button of the **Mate Selections** rollout to select a sketch having multiple segments as a path. On clicking this button, the **Selection** Pop-up toolbar appears, see Figure 12.34. By using the **Select Closed Loop** and the **Select Open Loop** tools of this Pop-up toolbar, you can select a closed loop or an open loop sketch as the path, respectively. After selecting the path by using the **Selection** Pop-up toolbar, click on the green tick-mark in the Pop-up toolbar.

Note that the **Free** option is selected in the **Path Constraint** drop-down list in the **Advanced Mates** rollout, see Figure 12.35. As a result, the component moves freely along the selected path. You can also select the **Distance Along Path** or **Percent Along Path** option from the **Path Constraint** drop-down list, as required. On selecting the **Distance Along Path** option, you can control the position of the component along the path by specifying a distance value in the **Distance from the**

End field of the rollout. On selecting the **Percent Along Path** option, you can control the position of the component along the path by specifying a percentage value in the **Percentage of Distance from the End** field of the rollout. Also, in the **Pitch/Yaw Control** and **Roll Control** drop-down lists of the rollout, the **Free** option is selected, by default. As a result, the pitch, yaw, and roll of the component are not constrained and the component can move freely along the path. On selecting the **Follow Path** option in the **Pitch/Yaw Control** drop-down list, you can make an axis (X, Y, or Z) of the component tangent to the path. On selecting the **Up Vector** option in the **Roll Control** drop-down list, you can align an axis (X, Y, or Z) of the component to a vector. You can select a linear edge or a planar face as the vector by using the field that appears on selecting the **Up Vector** option. After selecting the required option in the **Path Constraint, Pitch/Yaw Control,** and **Roll Control** drop-down lists, click on the green tick-mark in the PropertyManager. The path mate is applied.

Tip: To review the movement of the component along the path after applying the path mate, select the moveable component and then drag it such that it travels along the defined path.

Note: To achieve the correct path motion, you need to define the degrees of freedom of the component to be moved such that the component can only move along the desired path.

Linear/Linear Coupler Mate ⊿

The linear/linear coupler mate is used for translating the linear motion of components with respect to each other. After applying the linear/linear coupler mate between two components, when you move a component, the other component also moves accordingly, see Figure 12.36.

You can specify the translation ratio between the components by using the **Ratio** fields of the PropertyManager, see Figure 12.37. If the translation ratio is 1: 2 in mm unit, then on translating one component to a distance of 1 mm in a direction, the second component is translated automatically to a distance of 2 mm. You can reverse the translation direction of components by using the **Reverse** check box.

To apply the linear/linear coupler mate, click on the **Linear/Linear Coupler** button in the **Advanced Mates** rollout. Next, select linear edges of two components one by one as the direction to move the components with respect to each other. Next, specify the translation ratio in the **Ratio** fields of the PropertyManager and then click on the green tick-mark ✓ in the PropertyManager. The linear/linear coupler mate is applied.

Tip: To review the translation motion between two components after applying the linear/linear coupler mate, select a component and then drag it.

Distance Mate

The advanced distance mate of the **Advance Mates** rollout is used for specifying the minimum and maximum distance limit between two components. After applying this mate, the components can only move or translate within the specified distance limit, see Figure 12.38.

To apply the advanced distance mate, click on the **Limit Distance** button in the **Advanced Mates** rollout. The **Distance, Maximum Value,** and **Minimum Value** fields get enabled in the PropertyManager, see Figure 12.39. Specify the maximum distance value in the **Maximum Value** field. Next, specify the minimum distance value in the **Minimum Value** field. After specifying the maximum and minimum distance values, select two entities (faces, planes, edges, points, vertices, or a combination of these entities) of two different components and then click on the green tick-mark ✓ in the PropertyManager. The advanced distance mate is applied between the selected entities of the components such that the moveable component can move within the specified maximum and minimum distance limit, refer to Figure 12.38.

Tip: To review the distance motion between components, select the moveable component and then drag it.

Angle Mate

The advanced angle mate of the **Advance Mates** rollout is used for specifying the minimum and maximum angle limit between two components. After applying this mate, the components can only rotate within the specified angle limit, see Figure 12.40.

To apply the advanced angle mate, click on the **Limit Angle** button in the **Advanced Mates** rollout. The Angle, **Maximum Value**, and **Minimum Value** fields are enabled in the PropertyManager, see Figure 12.41. Specify the maximum angle value in the **Maximum Value** field. Next, specify the minimum angle value in the **Minimum Value** field of the rollout. After specifying the maximum and minimum angle values, select two faces of two different components and then click on the green tick-mark ✓ in the PropertyManager. The advanced angle mate is applied between the selected faces of the components such that the moveable component can rotate within the specified maximum and minimum angle limit, see Figure 12.40.

Tip: To review the angle motion between components, select the moveable component and then drag it.

Working with Mechanical Mates

Mechanical mates are used for creating a mechanism between components of an assembly. You can create cam and follower mechanism, gear mechanism, hinge mechanism, rack and pinion mechanism, screw mechanism, and universal joint mechanism between components of an assembly by using mechanical mates. Different types of mechanical mates are available in the **Mechanical Mates** rollout of the **Mate PropertyManager**.

Note: To create a mechanism between components of an assembly, it is necessary to have the required degrees of freedom of components such that the components can only be moved or rotated in the desired directions. For example, to create a gear mechanism between two components (gears), you need to first constraint the components such that they can only rotate about their axes using the standard and advanced mates.

To apply a mechanical mate, expand the **Mechanical Mates** rollout of the **Mate PropertyManager**, see Figure 12.42. Different types of mechanical mates are discussed next.

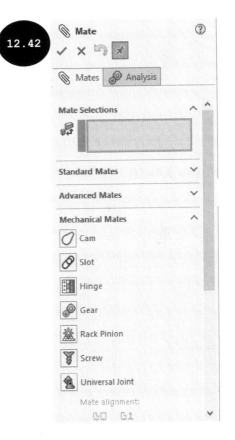

Cam Mate

The cam mate is used for creating cam and follower mechanism between two components of an assembly.

To apply the cam mate, click on the **Cam** button in the **Mechanical Mates** rollout. The **Cam Path** and **Cam Follower** fields appear in the **Mate Selections** rollout of the PropertyManager. By default, the **Cam Path** field is activated, therefore you can select a face of the cam component, which is tangent to the series of its other faces and forms a closed loop, see Figure 12.43. As soon as you select a face of the cam component, all faces that are tangent to the selected face get selected automatically and the cam component becomes transparent in the graphics area, see Figure 12.43. Also, the **Cam Follower** field gets activated in the **Mate Selections** rollout. As a result, you can select a face of the follower component. Select a cylindrical, a semi-cylindrical, or a planar face of the follower component, see Figure 12.44. The selected face of the follower component is placed over the cam component, see Figure 12.45. Next, click on the green tick-mark ✓ in the PropertyManager. The cam mate is applied between the cam and follower components. Now, on rotating the cam component, the follower component moves up and down with respect to the cam profile and forms a cam and follower mechanism.

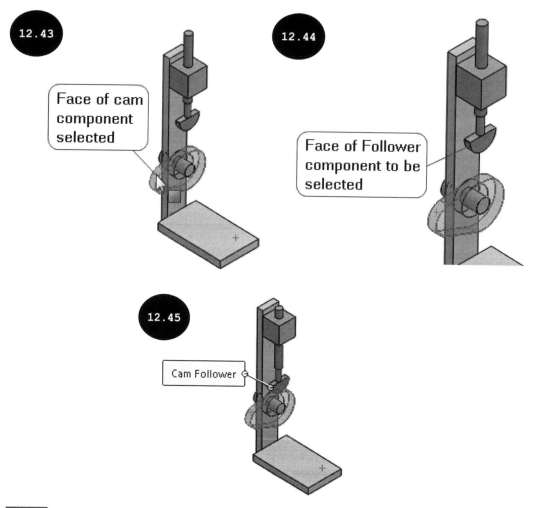

Tip: To review the cam and follower mechanism between the components, select the cam component and then drag it such that it rotates around its axis of rotation.

Note: To select faces of components for applying mates, you may need to move or rotate the assembly or its individual components. To rotate an assembly, drag the cursor by pressing and holding the middle mouse button. To pan the assembly, drag the cursor by pressing and holding the CTRL key plus middle mouse button. Alternatively, you can use the **Rotate** and **Pan** tools to rotate and pan the assembly, respectively. You will learn about moving or rotating individual components of an assembly later in this chapter.

Slot Mate

The slot mate is used for driving a bolt, a pin, or a cylindrical feature of a component along the slot feature of another component in an assembly, see Figure 12.46. You can also apply the slot mate mechanism between two slots of the components.

12.46

To apply the slot mate, click on the **Slot** button in the **Mechanical Mates** rollout. Next, select a face of the slot feature of a component, see Figure 12.47. All the remaining tangent faces of the slot feature get selected automatically, and the component becomes transparent in the graphics area, see Figure 12.47. Next, select a cylindrical face of another component (a bolt, a pin, or a cylindrical feature), see Figure 12.48. The cylindrical face is placed between the slot. Next, click on the green tick-mark ✓ in the PropertyManager. The slot mate is applied between the components and now you can review the slot mechanism by dragging the components.

12.47

Cylindrical face

Slot face selected

12.48

Note: When you click on the **Slot** button, the **Constraint** drop-down list appears in the rollout, see Figure 12.49. By default, the **Free** option is selected in this drop-down list. As a result, the component having the bolt, pin, or cylindrical feature can move freely within the slot feature of the other component. You can constraint the movement of components by using the **Center in Slot**, **Distance Along Slot**, or **Percentage Along Slot** option of the **Constraint** drop-down list.

12.49

Slot

Constraint:

Free

Hinge Mate

The hinge mate is used for creating a hinge mechanism between two components by fixing all degrees of freedom of the components except the rotational degree of freedom, see Figure 12.50. You can also limit the rotational degree of freedom by specifying the minimum and maximum angle of rotation.

To apply the hinge mate, click on the **Hinge** button, the **Concentric Selections** and **Coincident Selections** fields get enabled in the **Mate Selections** rollout of the PropertyManager. Select two circular faces or circular edges of two different components to be concentric with each other, see Figure 12.51. Next, select two planar faces of the components to be coincident with each other, see Figure 12.52. The concentric and coincident mates are applied between the selected faces of the components, see Figure 12.53. Next, click on the green tick-mark ☑ in the PropertyManager. The hinge mate is applied and now you can review the hinge mechanism by dragging the components.

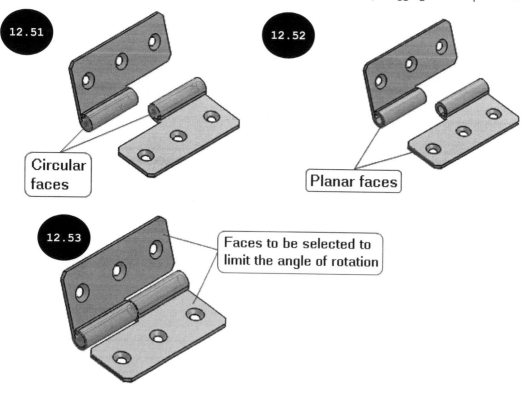

Note: By default, the angle of rotation for the hinge mechanism is 360 degrees. To limit the angle of rotation for the hinge mechanism, click on the **Specify angle limits** check box in the **Mate Selections** rollout of the PropertyManager. The **Angle Selections, Angle, Maximum Value,** and **Minimum Value** fields get enabled in the rollout. By default, the **Angle Selections** field is activated. As a result, you can select faces of the components to limit the angle of rotation between them. Select two planar faces of components, refer to Figure 12.53. Next, specify the maximum and minimum angle values in the **Maximum Value** and **Minimum Value** fields, respectively and then click on the green tick-mark ✓ in the PropertyManager.

Gear Mate

The gear mate is used for creating a gear mechanism between components such that the components can rotate relative to each other, see Figure 12.54.

12.54

To apply the gear mate, click on the **Gear** button in the **Mechanical Mates** rollout. Next, select a circular face of a gear teeth of the first gear component and the second gear component one by one, see Figure 12.55. On selecting the circular faces of the gear components, the axis of rotations of the gears are defined automatically. You can select circular faces, conical faces, axes, or linear edges of the gear components to define the axes of rotation. Next, specify the gear ratio in the **Ratio** fields of the **Mechanical Mates** rollout. Notice that based on the relative size of the faces selected for defining the axis of rotation, the gear ratio is automatically calculated. After defining the gear ratio, click on the green tick-mark ✓ in the PropertyManager. The gear mate is applied and now you can review the gear mechanism by dragging the gears.

12.55

Teeth/Diameter: 156

Faces selected

Teeth/Diameter: 53

Rack Pinion Mate

The rack pinion mate is used for translating linear motion of one component to rotational motion of another component and vice versa. This mate creates the rack and pinion mechanism, see Figure 12.56, where the linear motion of the rack component creates rotatory motion in the pinion component and vice versa.

12.56

To apply the rack pinion mate, click on the **Rack Pinion** button, the **Rack** and **Pinion/Gear** fields get enabled in the **Mate Selections** rollout of the PropertyManager. Select a linear edge of the rack component, which defines the direction of movement of the rack component, see Figure 12.57. After selecting a linear edge of the rack component, the **Pinion/Gear** field gets activated. Select a circular face of the pinion/gear component, which defines the axis of rotation of the pinion component, see Figure 12.57. Next, click on the green tick-mark ✓ in the PropertyManager. The rack pinion mate is applied between the components and now you can review the rack and pinion mechanism by dragging the components.

12.57

Linear edge

Pinion pitch diameter: 63

Rack

Circular face

Screw Mate

The screw mate applies the pitch relationship between the rotation of one component and the translation of the other component such that it forms a screw mechanism, see Figure 12.58. On applying the screw mate, the translational motion of one component causes rotational motion in the other component based on the specified pitch relationship. You can specify the pitch relationship between two components either by defining the number of revolutions of one component with respect to the per millimeter translation of another component or by defining the distance travelled by one component with respect to a revolution of the other component.

To apply the screw mate, click on the **Screw** button in the **Mechanical Mates** rollout. Next, select a circular face of the first component and then select a circular face of the second component to define their axes of rotation, see Figure 12.59. On selecting the circular faces of both the components, an arrow appears in the graphics area which indicates the direction of revolution, see Figure 12.59. You can reverse the direction of revolution by using the **Reverse** check box of the **Mechanical Mates** rollout. By default, the **Revolutions/mm** radio button is selected in the **Mechanical Mates** rollout, see Figure 12.60. As a result, you can specify the number of revolutions of one component with respect to the per millimeter translation of the other component in the **Revolutions/Distance** field. If you select the **Distance/revolution** radio button then you can specify the distance travelled by one component with respect to a revolution of the other component in the **Revolutions/Distance** field. Next, click on the green tick-mark ✓ in the PropertyManager. The screw mate is applied between the components and now you can review the screw mechanism by dragging the components.

Universal Joint

The universal joint mate is used for translating the rotational movement of one component to the rotational movement of another component about their axes of rotations, see Figure 12.61.

To apply the universal joint mate, click on the **Universal Joint** button in the **Mechanical Mates** rollout. Next, select two cylindrical faces of different components in the graphics area one by one, see Figure 12.61. After selecting the cylindrical faces, click on the green tick-mark ✓ in the PropertyManager. The universal joint mate is applied between the components and now you can review the universal joint mechanism by dragging the components.

Cylindrical faces

Hiding Faces while Applying a Mate

In SOLIDWORKS, while applying a mate, you can temporarily hide a face to select an obscured face of the assembly by pressing the ALT key. For doing so, click on the **Mate** tool and then hover the cursor over the face to be hidden and then press the ALT key. The face is temporarily hidden and the obscured face becomes visible in the graphics area. You can temporarily hide multiple faces by pressing the ALT key. To show the temporarily hidden face, hover the cursor over the face and then press the SHIFT + ALT keys. You can also show the temporarily hidden faces in a semi-transparent state by pressing the CTRL + SHIFT + ALT keys.

Tip: After selecting a face to apply a mate, the temporarily hidden faces become visible, automatically. You can also press the ESC key to restore the visibility of all the temporarily hidden faces.

Moving and Rotating Individual Components

In SOLIDWORKS, you can move and rotate individual components of an assembly about their free degrees of freedom by using the **Move Component** and **Rotate Component** tools of the **Assembly CommandManager** respectively, see Figure 12.62. Both the tools are discussed next.

Moving a Component by using the Move Component Tool

In SOLIDWORKS, you can move individual components of an assembly along their free degrees of freedoms by using the **Move Component** tool. For doing so, click on the **Move Component** tool in the **Assembly CommandManager**. The **Move Component PropertyManager** appears, see Figure 12.63. By default, the **Free Drag** option is selected in the **Move** drop-down list of the **Move** rollout in the PropertyManager. As a result, you can move the component freely along its free degrees of freedom. Select the component to be moved and then drag the cursor by pressing and holding the left mouse button. The selected component starts moving along with the cursor. To stop the movement of the component, release the left mouse button. The other options in the **Move** drop-down list are **Along Assembly XYZ**, **Along Entity**, **By Delta XYZ**, and **To XYZ Position**, see Figure 12.64. All these options are discussed next.

Note: A component cannot move along its fixed or restricted degrees of freedom. For example, if the translational degree of freedom along the X axis of the component is fixed by applying mates then you cannot move the component along the X axis.

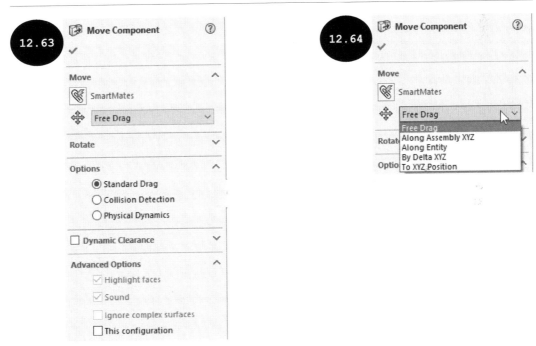

Along Assembly XYZ

On selecting the **Along Assembly XYZ** option, you can move a component along the X, Y, or Z axis of the assembly coordinate system.

Along Entity

On selecting the **Along Entity** option, the **Selected item** field appears in the **Move** rollout, see Figure 12.65. This field is used for selecting an entity as the direction along which the selected component has to be moved. You can select a linear edge, a sketch line, or an axis as the entity to define the direction along which the component has to be moved. After selecting the entity, select the component to be moved and then drag the cursor. The selected component starts moving along the direction of the entity selected.

By Delta XYZ

On selecting the **By Delta XYZ** option, the **Delta X**, **Delta Y**, and **Delta Z** fields appear, see Figure 12.66. In these fields, you can specify the X, Y, and Z distance values for moving the component with respect to the current location of the component. After specifying the X, Y, and Z distance values in the respective fields, select the component to be moved and then click on the **Apply** button. The selected component moves with respect to the specified distance values.

To XYZ Position

On selecting the **To XYZ Position** option, the **X Coordinate**, **Y Coordinate**, and **Z Coordinate** fields get enabled in the PropertyManager, see Figure 12.67. These fields are used for specifying the X, Y, and Z coordinate values of the location where you want to move the selected component. After specifying the coordinate values, click on the **Apply** button. The origin of the selected component is moved to the specified coordinate. Note that if you select a vertex or a point of the component to move then after clicking on the **Apply** button, the selected vertex or point of the component is moved to the specified coordinate location.

Note that, by default the movement of a component is not prevented from any interference or a collision occurring with other components of the assembly. This means that the component moves continuously even if any other component comes across its way, since the **Standard Drag** radio button is selected in the **Options** rollout of the **Move Component PropertyManager**, see Figure 12.68. By selecting the **Collision Detection** or **Physical Dynamics** radio button, you can detect collisions or analyze the motion between components of an assembly. The methods for detecting a collision and analyzing motion between components by using the **Collision Detection** and **Physical Dynamics** radio buttons are discussed next.

Detecting Collision between Components

You can detect a collision between components of an assembly while moving a component by using the **Collision Detection** radio button. For doing so, select the **Collision Detection** radio button in the **Options** rollout of the PropertyManager. The **All components** and **These components** radio buttons as well as the **Stop at collision** and **Dragged part only** check boxes appear in the **Options** rollout of the PropertyManager, see Figure 12.69.

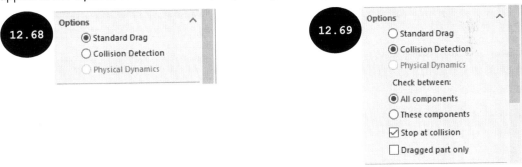

By default, the **All components** radio button is selected. As a result, a collision is detected when the moveable component collides with any component of the assembly. Note that as soon as a collision is detected between the components, the components get highlighted in the graphics area, see Figure 12.70. If the **Stop at collision** check box is selected in the rollout then the movement of the component is stopped as soon as it collides with the other component of the assembly.

On selecting the **These components** radio button, the **Components for Collision Check** field appears in the PropertyManager. This field is used for selecting components for the detection of collision. After selecting the components, click on the **Resume Drag** button and then drag the component to be moved. Note that the collision is detected only when the component being moved touches any of the selected components of the assembly. Note that the components which are not listed in the **Components for Collision Check** field are ignored by the moveable component.

When the **Dragged part only** check box is selected in the **Options** rollout, collision is checked only for the component which is selected to be moved. If this check box is cleared then the collision is checked even for the components that move along with the moveable component because of the mates with the moveable component.

Detecting Collision and Analyzing Motion between Components

Similar to the **Collision Detection** radio button, the **Physical Dynamics** radio button is also used for detecting a collision, with the only difference that it forces the components to move along with the moveable component, when a collision is detected between them. Note that components can only move or rotate within their free degrees of freedom.

Note: In addition to moving individual components and detecting collision, you can also rotate components by using the **Rotate Component PropertyManager**. You can invoke the **Rotate Component PropertyManager** by expanding the **Rotate** rollout of the **Move Component PropertyManager** or by clicking on the **Rotate Component** tool in the CommandManager. The method for rotating a component is discussed next.

Rotating a Component by using the Rotate Component Tool

Similar to moving individual components, you can rotate individual components of an assembly about their free degrees of freedom by using the **Rotate Component** tool. For doing so, click on the **Rotate Component** tool in the **Assembly CommandManager**, see Figure 12.71. The **Rotate Component PropertyManager** appears, see Figure 12.72.

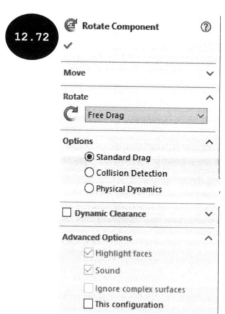

By default, the **Free Drag** option is selected in the **Rotate** drop-down list of the **Rotate** rollout in the PropertyManager. As a result, you can rotate a component freely about an axis by dragging the component. Select the component to be rotated in the graphics area and then drag the cursor about its free degrees of freedom by pressing and holding the left mouse button. The selected component starts rotating about the axis of rotation. Once you have rotated the component, release the left mouse button. All the options in the **Rotate Component PropertyManager** are same as those discussed earlier while moving the component by using the **Move Component PropertyManager**.

Working with SmartMates

SmartMates is a smart method for applying standard mates such as coincident, parallel, and perpendicular between the components of an assembly. By using this method, the designing process becomes faster and more efficient. The SmartMates method for applying mates can be invoked by clicking on the **SmartMates** button in the **Move Component PropertyManager**. Note that as soon as you click on the **SmartMates** button, the SmartMates PropertyManager appears, see Figure 12.73. As discussed, you can invoke the **Move Component PropertyManager** by clicking on the **Move Components** tool in the **Assembly CommandManager**.

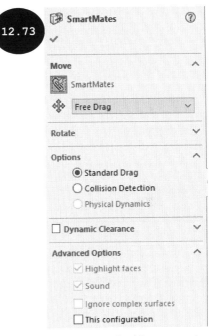

Once the **SmartMates PropertyManager** has been invoked, double-click on an entity of the component for applying a mate. The selected entity is highlighted and the component becomes transparent in the graphics area, see Figure 12.74. Next, click on an entity of another component of the assembly for applying the mate. The Mate Pop-up toolbar appears with the most suitable mate activated in it. Also, a preview appears such that the most suitable mate is applied between the selected entities of the components, see Figure 12.75. You can apply a mate by clicking the respective tool in the Pop-up toolbar. Next, click on the green tick-mark ☑ in the toolbar. The selected mate is applied between the entities of the components.

Note: You can also press the ALT key and then drag a component toward another component for applying a standard mate without invoking the **SmartMates PropertyManager**.

Tutorial 1

Create the assembly shown in Figure 12.76. Different views and dimensions of individual components of the assembly are shown in Figures 12.77 through 12.80. All dimensions are in mm.

12.76

12.77

DETAIL A

DETAIL B

Crank Case

12.78

40

R30
Ø40

30

20   30

Ø30

R25

Crank Shaft

12.79

2
5
3 TYP
4 TYP

DETAIL B

Ø40   R135
Ø30   A   5
B

16

100
45
20

A

Ø75
Ø86
Ø100

40

SECTION A-A

Piston

Connecting Rod

Section 1: Starting SOLIDWORKS and Creating Assembly Components

In this section, you will create all the components of the assembly in the Part modeling environment one by one.

1. Start SOLIDWORKS by double-clicking on the SOLIDWORKS icon on your desktop.

2. Create all components of the assembly one by one in the Part modeling environment. Refer to Figures 12.77 through 12.80 for the dimensions of each component. After creating the components, save them in the Tutorial 1 folder of the Chapter 12 folder. You need to create these folders in the SOLIDWORKS folder.

> **Note:** You can also download all the components of the assembly from *www.cadartifex.com*. If you are a first time user, you need to register yourself to access the online resources.

Section 2: Invoking the Assembly Environment

After creating all the components, you need to assemble them in the Assembly environment.

1. Click on the **New** tool in the **Standard** toolbar. The **New SOLIDWORKS Document** dialog box appears.

2. Click on the **Assembly** button and then click on the **OK** button in the dialog box. The Assembly environment is invoked and the **Open** dialog box appears along with the **Begin Assembly PropertyManager**, see Figure 12.81.

Note: On invoking the Assembly environment, the **Open** dialog box appears, automatically along with the **Begin Assembly PropertyManager**, if none of the components are opened in the current session of SOLIDWORKS. If the **Open** dialog box does not appear, then click on the **Browse** button in the **Begin Assembly PropertyManager** to open it.

Section 3: Inserting the First Component

1. Browse to the location where all the components of the assembly are saved (\SOLIDWORKS\ Chapter 12\Tutorial 1) by using the **Open** dialog box.

2. Select the *Crank Case* component and then click on the **Open** button in the dialog box. The selected component is attached to the cursor, see Figure 12.82. Also, the **Rotate Context** toolbar appears in the graphics area.

3.   Click anywhere in the graphics area, the attached component moves toward the origin of the assembly and becomes the fixed component.

Section 4: Inserting the Second Component

1.   Click on the **Insert Components** tool in the **Assembly CommandManager**. The **Open** dialog box appears, automatically along with the **Insert Component PropertyManager**.

Note: The **Open** dialog box appears only if none of the components are opened in the current session of SOLIDWORKS. If the **Open** dialog box does not appear, automatically then click on the **Browse** button in the **Insert Component PropertyManager** to open the **Open** dialog box.

2.   Browse to the location where all the components of the assembly are saved and then select the *Crank Shaft* component. Next, click on the **Open** button in the dialog box. The selected component is attached to the cursor, see Figure 12.83.

3.   Click anywhere in the graphics area to specify the placement point for the second component (*Crank Shaft*). The component (*Crank Shaft*) is placed in the specified location, see Figure 12.84. Make sure that you specify the placement point such that the inserted component does not intersect the first component of the assembly.

Note: By default, all degrees of freedom of the second component are free, which means that the second component is free to translate and rotate along and about its axes. You need to apply the required mates to fix its required degrees of freedom with respect to the first component of the assembly.

Section 5: Assembling the Second Component

Before you insert the third component in the Assembly environment, it is recommended to first assemble the second component with the first component of the assembly.

1.   Click on the **Mate** tool in the **Assembly CommandManager**. The **Mate PropertyManager** appears.

2. Select the circular face of the second component (*Crank Shaft*) as the first entity to apply a mate, see Figure 12.85. The circular face gets selected and the component (*Crank Shaft*) becomes transparent in the graphics area, see Figure 12.86.

3. Select the circular face of the first component (*Crank Case*) as the second entity to apply the mate, see Figure 12.87. A Pop-up toolbar appears with the **Concentric** tool activated in it, by default. Also, the selected faces of the components become concentric to each other, see Figure 12.88.

4. Click on the green tick-mark button in the Pop-up toolbar. The concentric mate is applied between the selected faces of the components.

5. Expand the FeatureManager Design Tree, which is now available on the top left corner of the graphics area, by clicking on the arrow in front of it.

6. Expand the **Crank Shaft** node in the FeatureManager Design Tree and then select its **Right Plane** as the first entity to apply the mate. The Right Plane gets selected and the component (*Crank Shaft*) becomes transparent in the graphics area, see Figure 12.89.

7. Expand the **Crank Case** node in the FeatureManager Design Tree and then select its **Right Plane** as the second entity to apply the mate. A Pop-up toolbar appears with the **Coincident** tool activated in it, by default. Accordingly, the selected planes of the components become coincident to each other, see Figure 12.90.

8. Click on the green tick-mark button in the Pop-up toolbar. The coincident mate is applied between the selected planes of the components. Next, exit the **Mate PropertyManager** by clicking on its green tick-mark.

Note: After applying the concentric and coincident mates, the second component (*Crank Shaft*) cannot translate in any direction. However, it can rotate about its axis. This is because the rotational degree of freedom of the component has not been restricted.

Section 6: Inserting the Third Component

1. Click on the **Insert Components** tool in the **Assembly CommandManager**. The **Open** dialog box appears along with the **Insert Component PropertyManager**. If the **Open** dialog box does not appear, automatically then click on the **Browse** button in the **Insert Component PropertyManager** to open the **Open** dialog box.

2. Select the third component (*Connecting Rod*) and then click on the **Open** button in the dialog box. The third component (*Connecting Rod*) is attached to the cursor, see Figure 12.91.

3. Click anywhere in the graphics area to specify the placement point for the third component (*Connecting Rod*). The component is placed in the specified location. Make sure that you specify the placement point such that the inserted component does not intersect the other components of the assembly.

Section 7: Assembling the Third Component

1. Click on the **Mate** tool in the **Assembly CommandManager**. The **Mate PropertyManager** appears.

2. Select the circular face of the third component (*Connecting Rod*) as the first entity to apply the mate, see Figure 12.92. The circular face gets selected and the component becomes transparent in the graphics area.

3. Select the circular face of the second component (*Crank Shaft*) as the second entity to apply the mate, see Figure 12.93. A Pop-up toolbar appears with the **Concentric** tool activated in it, by default. Accordingly, the selected faces of the components become concentric to each other, see Figure 12.94.

4. Click on the green tick-mark button in the Pop-up toolbar. The concentric mate is applied between the selected faces of the components.

5.   Expand the FeatureManager Design Tree, which is now available on the top left corner of the graphics area, by clicking on the arrow in front of it.

6.   Expand the **Connecting Rod** node in the FeatureManager Design Tree and then select its **Right Plane** as the first entity to apply the mate. The Right Plane gets selected and the component (*Connecting Rod*) becomes transparent in the graphics area, see Figure 12.95.

7.   Expand the **Crank Shaft** node in the FeatureManager Design Tree and then select its **Right Plane** as the second entity to apply the mate. A Pop-up toolbar appears with the **Coincident** tool activated in it, by default. Accordingly, the selected planes of the components become coincident to each other, see Figure 12.96.

8.   Click on the green tick-mark button in the Pop-up toolbar. The coincident mate is applied between the selected faces of the components. Next, exit the **Mate PropertyManager**.

Section 8: Inserting the Fourth Component

1.   Click on the **Insert Components** tool in the **Assembly CommandManager**. The **Open** dialog box appears along with the **Insert Component PropertyManager**. If the **Open** dialog box does not appear automatically, then click on the **Browse** button in the **Insert Component PropertyManager** to open the **Open** dialog box.

2.   Select the fourth component (*Piston*) and then click on the **Open** button in the dialog box. The fourth component (*Piston*) is attached to the cursor.

3.   Click anywhere in the graphics area to specify the placement point for the fourth component (*Piston*). The component (*Piston*) is placed in the specified location, see Figure 12.97.

Section 9: Assembling the Fourth Component

1. Click on the **Mate** tool in the **Assembly CommandManager**. The **Mate PropertyManager** appears.

2. Select the circular face of the hole of the fourth component (*Piston*) as the first entity to apply the mate, see Figure 12.98. The circular face gets selected and the component becomes transparent in the graphics area.

3. Select the inner circular face of the third component (*Connecting Rod*) as the second entity to apply the mate, see Figure 12.99. A Pop-up toolbar appears with the **Concentric** tool activated in it. Accordingly, the selected faces of the components become concentric to each other, see Figure 12.100.

4. Click on the green tick-mark ✓ in the Pop-up toolbar. The concentric mate is applied between the selected faces of the components.

5. Select the outer circular face of the fourth component (*Piston*) and the inner circular face of the first component (*Crank Case*) as the entities to apply the mate, see Figure 12.101. A Pop-up toolbar appears with the **Concentric** tool activated in it. Accordingly, the selected faces of the components become concentric to each other, see Figure 12.102.

6.   Click on the green tick-mark ☑ in the Pop-up toolbar. The concentric mate is applied between the selected faces of the components. Next, exit the **Mate PropertyManager**.

Tip: After creating the assembly, you can review its motion. For doing so, drag the *Crank Shaft* component of the assembly by pressing and holding the left mouse button.

Section 10: Saving the Assembly

1.   Click on the **Save** tool of the **Standard** toolbar. The **Save As** dialog box appears.

2.   Browse to the Tutorial 1 folder of the Chapter 12 folder and then save the assembly with the name Tutorial 1.

Tutorial 2

Create the assembly, as shown in Figure 12.103. An exploded view of the assembly is shown in Figure 12.104 for your reference only. Different views and dimensions of individual components of the assembly are shown in Figures 12.105 through 12.113. All dimensions are in mm.

12.104

12.105

Ø36

VIEW C

24 X Ø 5 THRU
M6X1.0 - 6H THRU

Ø90
Ø106

Ø28
Ø14

A

A

Ø36

25

6 X Ø 5 THRU
M6X1.0 - 6H THRU

25

Ø36

8

45
58

Crank Case

SECTION A-A

12.106

Crankshaft Counterweight

12.107

Connecting Rod Hub

12.108

Crankshaft Valve Crank

12.109

Crankshaft

12.110

Connecting Rod

12.111

Piston   SECTION A-A

12.112

Piston Ring

Crankshaft Pin

Section 1: Starting SOLIDWORKS and Creating Assembly Components

In this section, you will create all components of the assembly.

1. Start SOLIDWORKS by double-clicking on the SOLIDWORKS icon on your desktop.

2. Create all the components of the assembly one by one in the Part modeling environment. Refer to Figures 12.105 through 12.113 for the dimensions of each component. After creating all the components of the assembly, save them in the Tutorial 2 folder of the Chapter 12 folder. You need to create these folders in the SOLIDWORKS folder.

Note: You can also download all the components of the assembly from *www.cadartifex.com*. If you are a first time user, you need to register yourself to access the online resources.

Section 2: Invoking the Assembly Environment

1. Click on the **New** tool in the **Standard** toolbar. The **New SOLIDWORKS Document** dialog box appears.

2. Double-click on the **Assembly** button in the dialog box. The Assembly environment is invoked and the **Open** dialog box appears along with the **Begin Assembly PropertyManager**, see Figure 12.114.

Note: On invoking the Assembly environment, the **Open** dialog box appears, automatically along with the **Begin Assembly PropertyManager**, if none of the components are opened in the current session of SOLIDWORKS. If the **Open** dialog box does not appear, then click on the **Browse** button in the **Begin Assembly PropertyManager** to open it.

Section 3: Creating the Piston Sub-Assembly

In this section, you will create the Piston sub-assembly.

1. Browse to the Tutorial 2 folder of the Chapter 12 folder in the **Open** dialog box, where all the components of the assembly have been saved.

2. Select the first component (*Piston*) and then click on the **Open** button in the dialog box. The first component (*Piston*) is attached to the cursor. Also, the **Rotate Context** toolbar appears in the graphics area.

3. Click anywhere in the graphics area. The first component (*Piston*) moves toward the origin of the assembly and becomes the fixed component automatically, see Figure 12.115.

Now, you need to insert the second component of the Piston sub-assembly.

4. Click on the **Insert Components** tool in the **Assembly CommandManager**. The **Open** dialog box appears along with the **Insert Component PropertyManager**. If the **Open** dialog box does not appear automatically, then click on the **Browse** button in the **Insert Component PropertyManager** to open the **Open** dialog box.

Insert Components

5. Browse to the location where all components of the assembly have been saved and then select the second component (*Piston Ring*). Next, click on the **Open** button in the dialog box. The second component (*Piston Ring*) gets attached to the cursor.

6. Click anywhere in the graphics area to specify the placement point of the second component (*Piston Ring*). The component (*Piston Ring*) is placed in the graphics area, see Figure 12.116. Make sure that you specify the placement point such that the component does not intersect with the first component of the assembly.

Note: By default, all degrees of freedom of the second component are free, which means that the second component is free to translate and rotate along and about its axis. You need to apply the mates to fix its required degrees of freedom with respect to the first component of the assembly.

Now, you need to assemble the second component (*Piston Ring*) with the first component (*Piston*) by applying the required mates between them.

7. Click on the **Mate** tool in the **Assembly CommandManager**. The **Mate PropertyManager** appears.

8. Select the bottom planar face of the second component (*Piston Ring*) as the first entity to apply the mate, see Figure 12.117. The bottom face of the component (Piston Ring) is selected and the component becomes transparent in the graphics area. Note that to select the bottom face of the second component (*Piston Ring*), you need to rotate the assembly. After selecting the face, you can change the orientation of the assembly back to isometric.

Tip: To select the bottom face of the second component (*Piston Ring*) for applying the mate, you can also hover the cursor over the top planar face of the second component (*Piston Ring*) and then press the ALT key to hide it temporarily.

9. Select the planar face of the first component (*Piston*), see Figure 12.118 as the second entity to apply the mate. A Pop-up toolbar appears with the **Coincident** tool activated in it, by default. Accordingly, the selected faces of the components become coincident to each other.

10. Click on the green tick-mark ✔ in the Pop-up toolbar. The coincident mate is applied between the selected faces of the components.

11. Select the inner circular face of the second component (*Piston Ring*) as the first entity to apply the mate, see Figure 12.119.

12. Select the outer cylindrical face of the first component (Piston) as the second entity to apply the mate, see Figure 12.120. A Pop-up toolbar appears with the **Concentric** tool activated in it. Accordingly, the selected faces of the components become concentric to each other.

13. Click on the green tick-mark ☑ in the Pop-up toolbar. The concentric mate is applied between the selected faces of the components. Next, exit the **Mate PropertyManager**.

Now, you need to insert the second instance of the *Piston Ring* component.

14. Move the cursor over the name of the second component (*Piston Ring*) in the FeatureManager Design Tree and then press and hold the left mouse button and the CTRL key. Next, drag the cursor toward the graphics area. The second instance of the *Piston Ring* component appears attached to the cursor in the graphics area, see Figure 12.121.

15. Release the left mouse button and then the CTRL key. The second instance of the *Piston Ring* component is inserted in the Assembly environment.

16. Invoke the **Mate PropertyManager** and then assemble the second instance of the *Piston Ring* component with the first component (*Piston*) by applying the coincident and concentric mates between them, see Figure 12.122. After assembling the second instance of the *Piston Ring* component, exit the **Mate PropertyManager**.

Note: You can also insert the second instance of a component by using the **Insert Components** tool of the **Assembly CommandManager**.

Section 4: Saving the Piston Sub-Assembly

1. Click on the **Save** tool in the **Standard** toolbar. The **Save As** dialog box appears.

2. Browse to the Tutorial 2 folder of the Chapter 12 folder and then save the assembly with the name Piston Sub-Assembly.

3. Click on the **File** > **Close** in the SOLIDWORKS Menus to close the Piston Sub-Assembly.

Section 5: Creating the Main Assembly - Radial Engine

In this section, you need to create the main assembly (*Radial Engine*).

1. Click on the **New** tool in the **Standard** toolbar. The **New SOLIDWORKS Document** dialog box appears.

2. Double-click on the **Assembly** button in the dialog box. The Assembly environment is invoked and the **Open** dialog box appears along with the **Begin Assembly PropertyManager**. If the **Open** dialog box does not appear, automatically then click on the **Browse** button in the **Begin Assembly PropertyManager** to open the **Open** dialog box.

3. Select the first component (*Crank Case*) of the main assembly (*Radial Engine*) and then click on the **Open** button in the dialog box. The first component (*Crank Case*) gets attached to the cursor. Also, the **Rotate Context** toolbar appears in the graphics area.

4. Click anywhere in the graphics area. The first component (*Crank Case*) moves toward the origin of the assembly and becomes the fixed component, see Figure 12.123.

Section 6: Inserting and Assembling the Second Component

Now, you need to insert the second component (*Crankshaft Valve Crank*) of the main assembly (*Radial Engine*) in the Assembly environment.

1. Click on the **Insert Components** tool in the **Assembly CommandManager**. The **Open** dialog box appears along with the **Insert Component PropertyManager**. If the **Open** dialog box does not appear automatically, then click on the **Browse** button in the PropertyManager to open the **Open** dialog box.

2. Select the second component (*Crankshaft Valve Crank*) and then click on the **Open** button. The second component (*Crankshaft Valve Crank*) gets attached to the cursor, see Figure 12.124. Also, the **Rotate Context** toolbar appears in the graphics area.

3. Enter **180** in the **Angle** field in the **Rotate Context** toolbar and then click on the **Y** tool in the **Rotate Context** toolbar. The orientation of the component is changed similar to the one shown in Figure 12.125.

4. Click anywhere in the graphics area. The second component (*Crankshaft Valve Crank*) is placed in the specified location.

    Now, you need to assemble the second component (*Crankshaft Valve Crank*) with the first component of the assembly.

5. Invoke the **Mate PropertyManager**. Next, select the circular face of the second component (*Crankshaft Valve Crank*) and the circular face of the hole of the first component (*Crank Case*), see Figure 12.126 to apply the concentric mate. A Pop-up toolbar appears with the **Concentric** tool activated in it. Note that to select the faces of the components, you need to rotate the assembly such that the faces can be viewed.

6. Click on the green tick-mark ☑ in the Pop-up toolbar. The concentric mate is applied between the selected faces of the components.

7. Select the planar face of the second component (*Crankshaft Valve Crank*) and the planar face of the first component (*Crank Case*), see Figure 12.127. A Pop-up toolbar appears with the **Coincident** tool activated in it.

12.127

Planar faces to be selected

8. Click on the green tick-mark ✓ in the Pop-up toolbar. The coincident mate is applied between the selected faces of the components.

9. Exit the **Mate PropertyManager** and then change the orientation of the assembly to isometric.

Section 7: Inserting and Assembling the Third Component

1. Insert the third component (*Crankshaft Counterweight*) in the Assembly environment by using the **Insert Components** tool, see Figure 12.128.

2. Hide the first component (*Crank Case*) so that you can easily select the faces of the other components for applying mates, see Figure 12.129. To hide the first component (*Crank Case*), click on it in the graphics area. A Pop-up toolbar appears. In this Pop-up toolbar, click on the **Hide Components** tool ◥.

12.128

12.129

Now, you need to assemble the third component (*Crankshaft Counterweight*).

3. Invoke the **Mate PropertyManager** and then select the outer circular face of the second component (*Crankshaft Valve Crank*) and the inner circular face of the third component (*Crankshaft Counterweight*) as the entities to apply the mate, see Figure 12.130. A Pop-up toolbar appears with the **Concentric** tool activated in it, by default. Accordingly, the selected faces of the components become concentric to each other in the graphics area, see Figure 12.131.

4. Click on the **Flip Mate Alignment** tool in the Pop-up toolbar, if the alignment of the third component (*Crankshaft Counterweight*) does not appear similar to the one shown in Figure 12.131.

5. Click on the green tick-mark in the Pop-up toolbar. The concentric mate is applied between the selected faces of the components.

6. Select the circular face of the hole of the third component (*Crankshaft Counterweight*) and the circular face of the hole of the second component (*Crankshaft Valve Crank*), see Figure 12.132. A Pop-up toolbar appears with the **Concentric** tool activated in it.

7. Click on the green tick-mark ☑ in the Pop-up toolbar. The concentric mate is applied between the selected faces of the components, see Figure 12.133. Next, exit the **Mate PropertyManager**.

Section 8: Inserting and Assembling the Fourth Component

1. Insert the fourth component (*Crankshaft Pin*) in the Assembly environment by using the **Insert Components** tool, see Figure 12.134.

2. Select the inner circular face of the third component (*Crankshaft Counterweight*) and the circular face of the fourth component (*Crankshaft Pin*) by pressing the CTRL key, see Figure 12.135. Next, release the CTRL key. A Pop-up toolbar appears, see Figure 12.135.

3. Click on the **Concentric** tool in the Pop-up toolbar, see Figure 12.135. The selected faces of the components become concentric to each other.

4. Similarly, select the circular face of the hole of the third component (*Crankshaft Counterweight*) and the circular face of the hole of the fourth component (*Crankshaft Pin*) by pressing the CTRL key, see Figure 12.136. Next, release the CTRL key. A Pop-up toolbar appears.

Circular face selected

Tip: You can press the ALT key to temporarily hide faces of the assembly components to select an obscured face of a component to apply a mate.

Besides, you may need to move components to select their faces for applying mates. To move a component, press and hold the left mouse button over the component to be moved and then drag the cursor.

5. Click on the **Concentric** tool in the Pop-up toolbar. The selected faces of the components become concentric to each other.

Section 9: Inserting and Assembling the Fifth Component

1. Insert the fifth component (*Crankshaft Counterweight*) in the Assembly environment by using the **Insert Components** tool, see Figure 12.137.

2. Invoke the **Mate PropertyManager** and then assemble the fifth component (*Crankshaft Counterweight*) with the fourth component (*Crankshaft Pin*) by applying two concentric mates, see Figure 12.138. After applying the mates, exit the **Mate PropertyManager**.

Section 10: **Inserting and Assembling the Sixth Component**

1. Insert the sixth component (*Crankshaft*) in the Assembly environment, see Figure 12.139. You need to change the orientation of the component (*Crankshaft*) similar to the one shown in Figure 12.139 by using the **Rotate Context** toolbar.

2. Invoke the **Mate PropertyManager**. Next, select the circular face of the sixth component (*Crankshaft*) and the inner circular face of the bottom hole of the fifth component (*Crankshaft Counterweight*) as the entities to apply the mate, refer to Figure 12.140. A Pop-up toolbar appears with the **Concentric** tool activated in it and the selected faces of the components become concentric to each other, see Figure 12.140.

3. Click on the green tick-mark ✓ in the Pop-up toolbar. The concentric mate is applied between the selected faces of the components.

4. Similarly, apply the concentric mate between the circular face of the hole of the fifth component (*Crankshaft Counterweight*) and the circular face of the hole of the sixth component (*Crankshaft*), see Figure 12.141. After applying the mate, exit the **Mate PropertyManager**.

Circular faces

Section 11: Inserting and Assembling the Seventh Component

1.   Insert the seventh component (*Connecting Rod Hub*) in the Assembly environment by using the **Insert Components** tool, see Figure 12.142.

2.   Invoke the **Mate PropertyManager**. Next, select the inner circular face of the seventh component (*Connecting Rod Hub*) and the circular face of the fourth component (*Crankshaft Pin*), see Figure 12.143. A Pop-up toolbar appears with the **Concentric** tool activated in it.

3.   Click on the green tick-mark ☑ in the Pop-up toolbar. The concentric mate is applied between the selected faces of the components.

4.   Select the back planar face of the seventh component (*Connecting Rod Hub*) and the front planar face of the third component (*Crankshaft Counterweight*) as the entities to apply the mate, see Figure 12.144. A Pop-up toolbar appears with the **Coincident** tool activated in it.

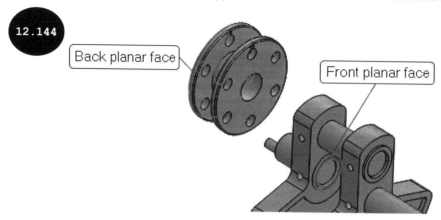

5.   Click on the green tick-mark ☑ in the Pop-up toolbar. The coincident mate is applied between the selected faces of the components. Next, exit the **Mate PropertyManager**.

Section 12: Inserting and Assembling the Eighth Component

1. Insert the eighth component (*Connecting Rod*) in the Assembly environment, see Figure 12.145. Note that you need to change the orientation of the eighth component (*Connecting Rod*) similar to the one shown in Figure 12.145 by using the **Rotate Context** toolbar.

2. Invoke the **Mate PropertyManager**. Next, select the circular face of the bottom hole of the eighth component (*Connecting Rod*) and the circular face of a hole of the seventh component (*Connecting Rod Hub*) as the entities to apply the mate, see Figure 12.146. The Pop-up toolbar appears with the **Concentric** tool activated in it.

3. Click on the green tick-mark ✔ in the Pop-up toolbar. The concentric mate is applied between the selected faces of the components.

4. Select the back planar face of the eighth component (*Connecting Rod*) and the inner planar face of the seventh component (*Connecting Rod Hub*), see Figure 12.147. A Pop-up toolbar appears with the **Coincident** tool activated in it.

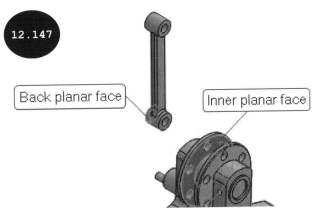

5. Click on the green tick-mark ✔ in the Pop-up toolbar. The coincident mate is applied between the selected faces of the components, see Figure 12.148. Next, exit the PropertyManager.

Section 13: Inserting and Assembling the Remaining Connecting Rods

1. Insert and assemble the five more instances of the *Connecting Rod* component with the remaining holes of the seventh component (*Connecting Rod Hub*) as discussed earlier, see Figure 12.149.

Note: To arrange the *Connecting Rod* components similar to the one shown in Figure 12.149, you need to fix the seventh component (*Connecting Rod Hub*). For doing so, right-click on the seventh component (*Connecting Rod Hub*) in the graphics area. A shortcut menu appears. Next, click on the **Fix** option in the shortcut menu. Once the seventh component (*Connecting Rod Hub*) has been fixed, you can arrange the *Connecting Rod* components one by one by dragging them. After arranging the *Connecting Rod* components, you need to make the seventh component (*Connecting Rod Hub*) a floating component again. For doing so, right-click on the seventh component (*Connecting Rod Hub*) in the graphics area and then click on the **Float** option in the shortcut menu that appears.

Section 14: Inserting and Assembling Piston Sub-Assembly

1. Insert the *Piston Sub-Assembly* in the Assembly environment by using the **Insert Components** tool, see Figure 12.150.

Tip: When you insert a sub-assembly in the Assembly environment, the sub-assembly becomes rigid and acts as a single component in the Assembly environment. You can change a rigid sub-assembly to a flexible sub-assembly, whose all components are free to move individually in their free degrees of freedom. For doing so, click on a rigid sub-assembly in the FeatureManager Design Tree. A Pop-up toolbar appears. In this Pop-up toolbar, click on the **Component Properties** ▣ tool. The **Component Properties** dialog box appears. In this dialog box, select the **Flexible** radio button in the **Solve as** area of the dialog box. Next, click the **OK** button.

2. Invoke the **Mate PropertyManager**. Next, select the inner circular face of the hole of the *Piston Sub-Assembly* and the inner circular face of the upper hole of a *Connecting Rod* component as the entities to apply the mate, see Figure 12.151. A Pop-up toolbar appears with the **Concentric** tool activated in it.

Circular faces selected

3. Click on the green tick-mark ✔ in the Pop-up toolbar. The concentric mate is applied between the selected faces of the components.

4. Expand the **Advanced Mates** rollout of the **Mate PropertyManager** and then click on the **Width** button. The **Width selections** and the **Tab selections** fields are enabled in the **Mate Selections** rollout of the PropertyManager.

5. Select the front and back planar faces of the *Connecting Rod* component as the width selection set, see Figure 12.152. Next, select the outer circular face of the *Piston Sub-Assembly* as the tab selection, see Figure 12.152. The axis of the tab selection is centered to the width selection set in the graphics area.

6. Click on the green tick-mark ✔ in the PropertyManager. The width mate is applied between the selected faces of the components. Next, exit the **Mate PropertyManager**.

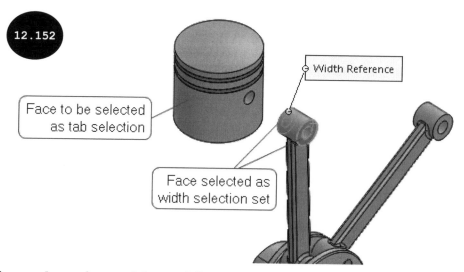

12.152

Width Reference

Face to be selected as tab selection

Face selected as width selection set

Section 15: Inserting and Assembling the Remaining Piston Sub-Assemblies

1. Insert and assemble the five more instances of the *Piston Sub-Assembly* with the remaining *Connecting Rod* components as discussed earlier, see Figure 12.153.

2. Turn on the visibility of the first component (*Crank Case*), see Figure 12.154. To turn on the visibility or display of the first component (*Crank Case*) in the graphics area, click on its name (*Crank Case*) in the FeatureManager Design Tree. A Pop-up toolbar appears. Next, click on the **Show Components** tool ⊙ in the Pop-up toolbar.

12.153

12.154

Now, you need to apply the concentric mate between each *Piston Sub-Assembly* and the first component (*Crank Case*).

3. Invoke the **Mate PropertyManager**. Next, select the outer circular face of a *Piston Sub Assembly* and the inner circular face of the respective hole of the first component (*Crank Case*), see Figure 12.155. A Pop-up toolbar appears with the **Concentric** tool activated in it.

4. Click on the green tick-mark ✓ in the Pop-up toolbar. The concentric mate is applied between the selected faces of the components.

5. Similarly, apply the concentric mate between the remaining instances of the *Piston Sub-Assembly* and the respective holes of the first component (*Crank Case*), see Figure 12.156.

Now, you need to apply the parallel mate between a face of the rectangular cut in the seventh component (*Connecting Rod Hub*) and an outer planar face of the first component (*Crank Case*).

6. Click on the **Parallel** button in the **Mate PropertyManager**. Next, select a planar face of the rectangular cut in the seventh component (*Connecting Rod Hub*), see Figure 12.157 and then select the parallel outer planar face of the first component (*Crank Case*), see Figure 12.158. A Pop-up toolbar appears with the **Parallel** tool activated in it.

7. Click on the green tick-mark ✔ in the Pop-up toolbar. The parallel mate is applied between the selected faces of the components. Next, exit the **Mate PropertyManager**. Figure 12.159 shows the final assembly after assembling all its components.

Tip: You can review the motion of the assembly. For doing so, drag the *Crankshaft* component of the assembly by pressing and holding the left mouse button.

12.159

Section 16: Saving the Model

1.   Click on the **Save** tool in the **Standard** toolbar. The **Save As** dialog box appears.

2.   Browse to the Tutorial 2 folder of the Chapter 12 folder and then save the assembly with the name Tutorial 2.

Hands-on Test Drive 1

Create the assembly, as shown in Figure 12.160. An exploded view of the assembly is shown in Figure 12.161 for your reference only. Different views and dimensions of individual components of the assembly are shown in Figures 12.162 through 12.169. You can also download all components of the assembly by logging in to the CADArtifex website (www.cadartifex.com). All dimensions are in mm.

12.160

ITEM NO.	PART NUMBER	DESCRIPTION	QTY.
1	BASE		1
2	FIXED JAW		1
3	SLIDING JAW		1
4	JAW PLATE		1
5	JAW SCREW		1
6	HANDLE BAR		1
7	NUT		2
8	VICE NUT		1

12.161

12.162

3X R10
3X Ø10
R50
R40
2X Ø12
2X R8
35
30°
R40
30
5
20 40
2X Ø9
6X R5
93
62

2X M8x1.0 Machine
Threads 1A

18 13
10
10
15
10

Base

12.163

2X Ø12
2X R15
R50
5
70
50
34
5

R10
3
R5
2
15
1

Detail A

R10
120°
45
A
28
40
150°
64
3
7
55
100

60
36
6
R7
2X Ø3 ⊽5
5
25°
2X R10
Ø34
2X R3
30
5
45
2X Ø5 ⊽5
50
10

Fixed Jaw

12.164

Detail A

Sliding Jaw

12.165

2X Ø5

Ø58

Ø16

Ø26

45

4 X 45°
CHAM

80

Ø29

10

48

Vice Nut

12.166

34

Ø16

155°

2X Ø5

57

23

5

30

50

Jaw Plate

12.167

2 X 45°

Ø12

Ø8

80

90

Handle Bar

12.168

Ø22
Ø16
3 X 45°
M14x2.0 Machine Threads
12
Ø8
140
24
189

Jaw Screw

12.169

Ø9
Ø18

R4

10

Nut

Hands-on Test Drive 2

Create an assembly, as shown in Figure 12.170. The exploded view of the assembly is shown in Figure 12.171 for your reference only. Different views and dimensions of individual components of the assembly are shown in Figures 12.172 through 12.181. You can also download all components of the assembly by logging in to the CADArtifex website (www.cadartifex.com). All dimensions are in mm.

12.172

688
344
4X Ø8
8
168
145°
280
A
A
20
70

28
4
26
34

DETAIL B

110
4
110°
4
126
35
201

SECTION A-A

12

Base Frame

12.173

R2 TYP
10
15
98
20
2X Ø14
2X Ø22

Connecting Rob

12.174

Lower Housing

12.175

SECTION A-A

Piston

12.176

Blower

12.177

132

5 TYP

185

202

5 TYP

R32 TYP

284

52 TYP

23

18

8X Ø10

Upper Housing

A

A

150

220

160

R220

R120

10

R40

R90

R14 TYP

SECTION A-A

146

105

Crank Shaft

12.179

SECTION A-A

Engine Block

Ø110
Ø102
R8
Ø60
3°
96
110
210
80
100
20
Ø46
Ø60
Ø10
50°
□88
□80

64
5
A
R16 TYP
7
55
70
96
13
R12 TYP
R10 TYP
4X Ø8
4X Ø12
A

A

4
16
75
65
45°
120
172
C
B

Ø45
R8 TYP
□60

DETAIL B
2
9 TYP
2 TYP

45°
DETAIL C
R5
Ø5

Engine Head

Engine Cover

Summary

This chapter discusses how to create assemblies by using the bottom-up assembly approach. In the bottom-up assembly approach, first all components are created in the Part modeling environment one by one and then assembled by applying mates/relations in the Assembly environment. In SOLIDWORKS, you can apply standard, advanced, and mechanical mates to assemble components with respect to each other. Note that a free component within the Assembly environment has six degrees of freedom: three translational and three rotational. Therefore, to assemble a component, you need to fix its degrees of freedom by applying the required mates. This chapter also explains how to move and rotate the individual components within the Assembly environment, detecting collisions between the components of an assembly, and applying standard mates by using the SmartMates method.

Questions

- In SOLIDWORKS, you can create assemblies by using the _____ and _____ approaches.

- If you make any change in a component in the Part modeling environment, the same change is automatically reflected in the assembly environment and vice-versa. This is because of the _____ property of SOLIDWORKS.

- The _____ toolbar allows you to change the orientation of a component before defining its placement point in the Assembly environment.

- A free component within the Assembly environment has _____ degrees of freedom.

- The _____ mate is used for center aligning two rectangular profiles, two circular profiles, or a rectangular profile and a circular profile with each other.

- The _____ mate allows two components to rotate relative to each other and form a gear mechanism.

- The _____ mate is used for translating linear motion into rotational motion from one component to another and vice versa.

- The _____ mate allows a component to move along a defined path.

- You can move the individual components of an assembly along its degrees of freedom. (True/False)

- You can apply the mechanical mates by using the SmartMates method. (True/False)

- In SOLIDWORKS, you can detect collisions between the components of an assembly. (True/False)

Working with Assemblies - II

This chapter discusses the following topics:

- Creating an Assembly by using the Top-down Approach
- Creating Flexible Components
- Editing Assembly Components
- Editing Mates
- Patterning Assembly Components
- Mirroring Components of an Assembly
- Creating Assembly Features
- Suppressing or Unsuppressing Components
- Inserting Parts having Multiple Configurations
- Creating and Dissolving Sub-Assemblies
- Publishing Envelopes
- Creating an Exploded View
- Collapsing an Exploded View
- Animating an Exploded View
- Editing an Exploded View
- Adding Explode Lines
- Detecting Interference in an Assembly
- Creating Bill of Material (BOM) of an Assembly

In the previous chapter, you have learned about creating assemblies by using the Bottom-up Assembly Approach, the different types of mates and how to move or rotate individual components of an assembly. In this chapter, you will learn about creating assemblies by using the Top-down Assembly Approach, editing assembly components, patterning and mirroring assembly components, creating assembly features, exploding assemblies, and so on.

Creating an Assembly by using the Top-down Approach

In the Top-down Assembly Approach, all components of an assembly are created within the Assembly environment itself. By using this approach, you can create a concept-based design, where new components of an assembly can be created by taking reference from the existing components and maintain relationships between them. The procedure for creating an assembly by using the Top-down Assembly Approach is discussed below:

1. Invoke the Assembly environment by using the **New** tool of the **Standard** toolbar, see Figure 13.1. Note that the **Open** dialog box appears along with the **Begin Assembly PropertyManager** in the startup user interface of the Assembly environment, by default.

2. Close the **Open** dialog box by clicking on the **Close** button and then close the **Begin Assembly PropertyManager** by clicking on the red cross-mark ⊠ available at its top. The reason behind closing the **Open** dialog box and the PropertyManager is to create components in the Assembly environment itself instead of importing them.

3. Click on the arrow at the bottom of the **Insert Components** tool in the **Assembly CommandManager**. A flyout appears, see Figure 13.2.

4. Click on the **New Part** tool in the flyout. A new empty part is inserted in the Assembly environment and its default name appears in the FeatureManager Design Tree, see Figure 13.3. Also, a green colored tick-mark appears attached to the cursor ⊾✓ in the graphics area.

5. Click on a plane in the FeatureManager Design Tree as the sketching plane for creating the sketch of the base feature of the inserted part. The Sketching environment is invoked within the Assembly environment for creating the base feature of the part, see Figure 13.4.

Note: You can click anywhere in the graphics area to define the position of the part instead of selecting a plane. By doing so, the position of the part gets defined such that the origin of the part becomes coincident to the origin of the assembly. However, the Sketching environment for creating the base feature does not get invoked. In this case, to invoke the Sketching environment, click on the name of the part in the FeatureManager Design Tree and then click on the **Edit Component** tool in the **Assembly CommandManager**. Next, click on the **Sketch** tool in the **Sketch CommandManager** and then select a plane or a planar face as the sketching plane for creating the sketch of the base feature.

6.   Press CTRL + 8 to change the orientation of the model as normal to the viewing direction. Alternatively, click on the **Normal To** tool in the **View Orientation** flyout, see Figure 13.5.

13.5

Normal To

Normal To   (Ctrl+8)
Rotates and zooms the model to the view orientation normal to the selected plane, planar face, or feature.

7.   Draw the sketch of the base feature by using the sketching tools, refer to Figure 13.6.

After creating the sketch, you need to convert it into a solid feature by using the solid modeling tools.

8.   Click on the **Features** tab in the CommandManager. The tools of the **Features CommandManager** appear. Now, by using the tools such as **Extruded Boss/Base** or **Revolved Boss/Base**, you can convert the sketch into a solid feature, refer to Figure 13.7. In this figure, the sketch is extruded to a depth of 15 mm by using the **Extruded Boss/Base** tool.

You need to create the second feature of the component.

9.   Invoke the Sketching environment again by selecting a planar face or a plane as the sketching plane for creating the second feature of the component.

10.   Create the sketch of the second feature, refer to Figure 13.8 and then convert it into a feature by using the solid modeling tools of the **Features CommandManager**, refer to Figure 13.9. In Figure 13.9, the sketch is extruded to a depth of 75 mm by using the **Extruded Boss/Base** tool. Similarly, you can create the remaining features of the part one by one.

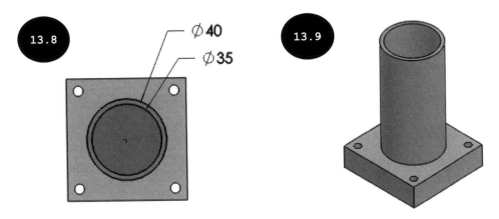

11. After creating all the features of the component, click on the **Edit Component** tool in the Features CommandManager. The first component is created and the Assembly environment is invoked.

Note: By default, the components created in the Assembly environment are fixed components and their degrees of freedom are restricted. This is because the Inplace mate is applied automatically between the plane of the component and the plane of the assembly. You can convert a fixed component into a floating component by deleting the Inplace mate. To delete the Inplace mate, expand the **Mates** node in the FeatureManager Design Tree and then select the InPlace mate to be deleted. Next, press the DELETE key.

If you have defined the placement of a component in the Assembly environment by clicking in the graphics area instead of selecting a plane then the component becomes fixed in the Assembly environment without applying the Inplace mate. In such cases, to convert a fixed component into a floating component, select the component in the FeatureManager Design Tree and then right-click to display a shortcut menu. Next, click on the **Float** option in the shortcut menu.

After creating the first component, you can create the second component of the assembly.

12. Click on the arrow at the bottom of the **Insert Components** tool, see Figure 13.10. Next, click on the **New Part** tool in the flyout that appears. A new empty part is inserted in the Assembly environment and its default name appears in the FeatureManager Design Tree.

13. Click anywhere in the graphics area. The position of the part gets defined such that the origin of the part becomes coincident to the origin of the assembly.

14. Click on the name of the newly inserted component in the FeatureManager Design Tree. A Pop-up toolbar appears, see Figure 13.11.

15. Click on the **Edit Part** tool in the Pop-up toolbar, see Figure 13.11. The Part modeling environment is invoked within the Assembly environment for creating the features of the second component. Also, the first component becomes transparent so that you can easily create the second component and take reference from the first component while creating it, refer to Figure 13.12.

16. Invoke the Sketching environment for creating the base feature of the second component by selecting a plane or a planar face of the first component as the sketching plane.

Note: While creating a component, if you take reference of a plane or a planar face of another component, that reference acts as external reference for the component being created.

17. Create the sketch of the base feature of the second component by taking reference from the first component, refer to Figure 13.13. In this figure, a rectangle and four circles have been created by projecting the edges of the first component onto the sketching plane.

18. Convert the sketch into a feature by using the tools of the **Features CommandManager**, refer to Figure 13.14. In this figure, the sketch is extruded to a depth of 15 mm by using the **Extruded Boss/Base** tool. Similarly, you can create the remaining features of the second component.

19. After creating all the features of the second component, click on the **Edit Component** tool in the **Features CommandManager**. The second component is created and the Assembly environment is invoked. Also, all components of the assembly appear in the shaded display style, refer to Figure 13.15.

20. Similarly, create the remaining components of the assembly one after another. Figure 13.16 shows an assembly in which all components are created one by one in the Assembly environment by using the Top-down Assembly Approach.

Note: As discussed, the components created by using the Top-down Assembly Approach become fixed in the Assembly environment. You can make these components floating components by deleting their respective Inplace mates or by selecting the **Float** option in the shortcut menu that appears on right-clicking on the component. A floated component can translate and rotate in all directions, which means all its degrees of freedom are free. You can restrict the required degrees of freedom of a floated component and assemble it with the other components of the assembly by applying the required mates. The method for applying mates between the components is the same as discussed in the previous chapter.

After creating all the components of the assembly, you can save the assembly file and its components externally or internally in the assembly file.

21. Click on the **Save** button in the **Standard** toolbar. The **Save Modified Documents** dialog box appears, see Figure 13.17.

By default, the **Save internally (inside the assembly)** radio button is selected in the **Save As** dialog box, see Figure 13.18. As a result, all the components of the assembly will be saved internally in the assembly file. On selecting the **Save externally (specify paths)** radio button, all the components of the assembly will be saved externally as individual components in the same folder, where the assembly file is saved.

22. Click on the **Save All** button in the dialog box. The **Save As** dialog box appears. Next, browse to the location where you want to save the assembly.

23. Enter the name of the assembly in the **File name** field of the dialog box and then click on the **Save** button. Another **Save As** dialog box appears, see Figure 13.18.

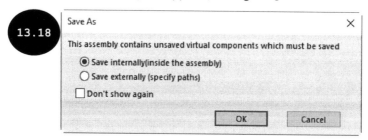

24. Select the **Save externally (specify paths)** radio button and then click on the **OK** button. All the components of the assembly and the assembly file are saved in the specified folder, individually.

Creating Flexible Components New

In SOLIDWORKS 2020, you can make a part flexible by using the **Make Part Flexible** tool. The **Make Part Flexible** tool is a very useful tool when you have inserted a component of an assembly into an another assembly and it gives an error of out-of-context references. In such cases, you can use the **Make Part Flexible** tool for re-attaching or defining the out-of-context references of the inserted component with the components of the new assembly.

To make a component flexible, click on a component of an assembly in the FeatureManager Design Tree and then click on the **Make Part Flexible** tool in the Pop-up toolbar that appears, see Figure 13.19. The **Activate Flexible Component PropertyManager** appears with a list of all external references of the selected component, see Figure 13.20. Note that the **Make Part Flexible** tool is available in the Pop-up toolbar only when the selected component is created by taking references from other components of an assembly file. Once the **Activate Flexible Component PropertyManager** is invoked, you can select an external reference in the PropertyManager and then re-attach or define its new reference with a geometry of an assembly component. A green tick-mark appears in front of the selected reference in the PropertyManager indicating that a new reference is defined correctly. Similarly, you can define new references for each of the external references one by one. Next, exit the PropertyManager. The external references of the component have been re-defined and the component becomes a flexible component. Now, if the position of any of the redefined references of the flexible component changes, the flexible component adjusts itself accordingly.

Tip: To change the state of a component from flexible to rigid, click on the flexible component in the FeatureManager Design Tree and click on the **Make Part Rigid** tool in the Pop-up toolbar that appears.

Editing Assembly Components

In the process of creating an assembly, you may need to edit its components depending upon the changes in the design, revisions, or so on. SOLIDWORKS allows you to edit each component of an assembly within the Assembly environment as well as in the Part modeling environment. Different methods for editing assembly components are discussed next.

Editing Assembly Components within the Assembly Environment

To edit a component of an assembly within the Assembly environment, select it either from the graphics area or from the FeatureManager Design Tree. A Pop-up toolbar appears, see Figure 13.21.

In this Pop-up toolbar, click on the **Edit Part** tool. The editing mode to edit the selected component is invoked within the Assembly environment itself, see Figure 13.22. Also, the other components of the assembly become transparent and the name of the selected component appears in blue in the FeatureManager Design Tree, see Figure 13.22.

Expand the node of the component being edited in the FeatureManager Design Tree to list all its features, see Figure 13.23. Next, select the feature to be edited in the expanded node of the FeatureManager Design Tree. A Pop-up toolbar appears, see Figure 13.23. Next, click on the **Edit Feature** tool in the Pop-up toolbar for editing the feature parameters such as extrusion depth and end condition. If you want to edit the sketch of the feature then click on the **Edit Sketch** tool in the Pop-up toolbar, see Figure 13.23. Depending upon the tool selected (**Edit Feature** or **Edit Sketch**), the respective environment gets invoked for editing the selected feature or sketch of the component. In addition to editing the existing feature of a component, you can also create new features of the component by using the tools of the **Features CommandManager**. Once all the required editing operations have been performed on the component, click on the **Edit Component** tool in the **Features CommandManager** to exit the editing mode and switch back to the Assembly environment. Alternatively, to exit the editing mode, click on the confirmation corner 🐾, which is available at the upper right corner of the graphics area.

Editing Assembly Components in the Part Modeling Environment

In addition to editing the components of an assembly in the Assembly environment, you can open a component of an assembly in the Part modeling environment and then perform the editing operations. For doing so, click on the component to be edited either in the FeatureManager Design Tree or in the graphics area. A Pop-up toolbar appears, see Figure 13.24. Next, click on the **Open Part** tool in the Pop-up toolbar, see Figure 13.24. The selected component is opened the Part modeling environment. Now, you can edit the component by editing its features and sketch. To edit a feature, click on the feature to be edited in the FeatureManager Design Tree and then click on the **Edit Feature** tool in the Pop-up toolbar that appears. To edit the sketch of a feature, click on the **Edit Sketch** tool in the Pop-up toolbar. Depending upon the tool selected (**Edit Feature** or **Edit Sketch**), the respective environment gets invoked, which allows you to edit the selected feature. You can also create new features in the component by using the tools of the **Features CommandManager**.

Once you have edited the component by using the tools of the Part modeling environment, click on the **Save** tool in the **Standard** toolbar to save the modified component. Next, click on **Window** > *name of the assembly* in the SOLIDWORKS Menus to switch to the Assembly environment. The **SOLIDWORKS** message window appears. Click on the **Yes** button in this window. The process of updating the assembly starts and once the assembly has been updated, the updated assembly with the modified component appears in the Assembly environment. The modifications made in the component are also reflected in the Assembly environment.

Note: SOLIDWORKS has bi-directional associative properties, which means that the modifications made in a component in any environment are also reflected in other environments of SOLIDWORKS.

Editing Mates

In SOLIDWORKS, you can edit existing mates of an assembly, which are applied between the components. To edit existing mates, expand the **Mates** node available at the bottom of the FeatureManager Design Tree, see Figure 13.25. The **Mates** node consists of a list of all mates that are applied between components of an assembly. Next, click on the mate to be edited in the expanded **Mates** node of the FeatureManager Design Tree. A Pop-up toolbar appears, see Figure 13.26. Also, the entities between which the selected mate is applied get highlighted in the graphics area. Next, click on the **Edit Feature** tool in the Pop-up toolbar, see Figure 13.26. The PropertyManager appears depending upon the type of mate selected. By using the options of the PropertyManager, you can select new entities for the mate, change the type of mate, type of mate alignment, and so on. Once the editing has been done, click on the green tick-mark ☑ in the PropertyManager to accept the changes and to exit the PropertyManager.

Patterning Assembly Components

Similar to patterning a feature of a component in the Part modeling environment, you can also pattern a component or components of an assembly in the Assembly environment, see Figure 13.27. In this figure, two components of the assembly are patterned to create other instances.

In the Assembly environment, you can create different types of patterns such as linear component pattern, circular component pattern, sketch driven component pattern, curve driven component pattern, pattern driven component pattern, and chain component pattern, by using the respective tools available in the **Pattern** flyout of the **Assembly CommandManager**, see Figure 13.28. The methods for creating linear component pattern, circular component pattern, sketch driven component pattern, and curve driven component pattern are same as discussed earlier while creating patterns in the Part modeling environment. The only difference is that in the Part modeling environment, you pattern features to create multiple instances, however, in the Assembly environment, you pattern components to create multiple instances. The methods for creating some of the pattern types are discussed next.

Creating a Linear Component Pattern Updated

A linear component pattern is created by patterning a component or components in an assembly, linearly in one or two linear directions, refer to Figure 13.27. Besides, you can also create a linear component pattern by rotating the pattern instances of a component along the pattern direction, see Figure 13.29.

Before   After

To create a linear component pattern, click on the **Linear Component Pattern** tool in the **Assembly CommandManager**. The **Linear Pattern PropertyManager** appears, see Figure 13.30. The options in this PropertyManager are same as discussed earlier while creating a linear pattern of features in the Part modeling environment except the **Rotate instances** check box. This check box is used for rotating the pattern instances along the pattern direction.

To rotate the pattern instances along the pattern direction, select the **Rotate instances** check box in the **Direction 1** rollout of the PropertyManager. The **Axis of Rotation** field, **Angle** field, and **Fixed axis of rotation** check box appear in the rollout, see Figure 13.31. The **Axis of Rotation** field is used for defining the axis of rotation for the pattern instances. You can select an axis, a line, or an edge as the axis of rotation. The **Angle** field is used for specifying the angular increment value for each pattern instance. On selecting the **Fixed axis of rotation** check box, the pattern instances rotate around a common axis that is selected in the **Axis of Rotation** field of the PropertyManager, see Figure 13.32. When the **Fixed axis of rotation** check box is cleared, each pattern instance rotates around their respective axis of rotation along direction 1, see Figure 13.33.

On selecting the **Align to seed** check box, each pattern instance is aligned to match the alignment of the parent component. Note that this check box is available only when the **Fixed axis of rotation** check box is selected in the PropertyManager. Figure 13.34 shows the preview of a linear component pattern with rotating pattern instances along the axis of rotation when the **Align to seed** check box is cleared. Figure 13.35 shows the preview of a linear component pattern when the **Align to seed** check box is selected.

You can also define the alignment type for the pattern instances by using the **Bounding box center** and the **Component origin** radio buttons. Note that these radio buttons become available when the **Align to seed** check box is selected. Figure 13.35 shows the alignment of pattern instances when the **Bounding box center** radio button is selected and Figure 13.36 shows the alignment of pattern instances when the **Component origin** radio button is selected.

In SOLIDWORKS 2020, you can also vary the linear spacing for individual instances, without disturbing other instances of the pattern. For doing so, click in the **Modified instances** field of the **Instances to Override** rollout in the PropertyManager. The pink dots are displayed at the center of all pattern instances in the graphics area, see Figure 13.37. Move the cursor over the pink dot of a pattern instance to be modified and then click the left mouse button when the appearance of the cursor changes to a hand cursor. Next, select the **Modify Instance** option in the shortcut menu that appears, see Figure 13.37. A callout gets attached to the selected instance with **Dir 1 distance from seed** and **Dir 1 offset from nominal** fields, see Figure 13.38. The **Dir 1 distance from seed** field displays the current distance of the selected instance from the parent instance while the **Dir 1 offset from nominal** field displays the current distance of the selected instance from its current position. You can specify the required distance value in these fields. The position of the selected instance gets changed, as specified.

The remaining options of the PropertyManager are the same as discussed earlier in the Part modeling environment. After specifying the parameters for creating the linear component pattern, click on the green tick-mark in the PropertyManager.

Creating a Circular Component Pattern   Updated

A circular component pattern is created by patterning a component or components of an assembly, circularly around an axis, see Figure 13.39. In the Assembly environment, you can create a circular component pattern by using the **Circular Component Pattern** tool. The method for creating a circular component pattern is same as discussed earlier while creating a circular pattern in the Part modeling environment.

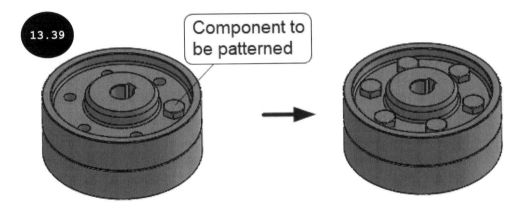

In SOLIDWORKS 2020, you can also vary the angle spacing for individual instances, without disturbing other instances of the pattern. For doing so, click in the **Modified instances** field of the **Instances to Override** rollout in the PropertyManager. The pink dots are displayed at the center of all pattern instances in the graphics area. Move the cursor over the pink dot of a pattern instance to be modified and then click the left mouse button when the appearance of the cursor changes to a hand cursor. Next, select the **Modify Instance** option in the shortcut menu that appears. A callout gets attached to the selected instance with **Angle from seed** and **Offset from nominal** fields, see Figure 13.40. The **Angle from seed** field displays the angle value of the selected instance from the parent instance while the **Offset from nominal** field displays the angle value of the selected instance from its current position. You can specify the required angle value in these fields. The position of the selected instance gets changed, as specified. Note that all other options in the PropertyManager are same as discussed earlier.

Creating a Pattern Driven Component Pattern Updated

A pattern driven component pattern is created by patterning a component in an assembly with respect to a pattern feature of another component. In this type of pattern, the component to be patterned is driven by a pattern feature of another component. Consider the case of an assembly shown in Figure 13.41, which has three components: Component 1, Component 2, and Component 3. Component 3 is to be patterned with respect to the circular pattern feature of Component 2. Figure 13.42 shows the resultant assembly, in which a pattern driven component pattern is created by patterning Component 3 with respect to the circular pattern feature of Component 2. Note that on modifying the number of instances of the pattern feature, the number of instances of the pattern driven component pattern are also automatically modified. This is because, the instances of the pattern driven component pattern are driven by the instances of the pattern feature.

To create a pattern driven component pattern, click on the arrow at the bottom of the **Linear Component Pattern** tool and then click on the **Pattern Driven Component Pattern** tool in the **Pattern** flyout that appears. The **Pattern Driven PropertyManager** appears, see Figure 13.43. The options of the PropertyManager are discussed next.

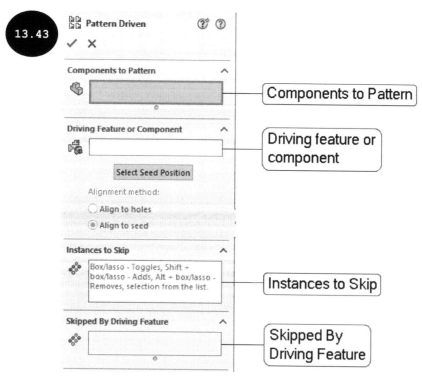

Components to Pattern

The **Components to Pattern** field is used for selecting components to be patterned. By default, this field is activated. As a result, you can select components to be patterned either from the graphics area or from the FeatureManager Design Tree.

Driving feature or component

The **Driving feature or component** field is used for selecting an instance of a pattern feature of a component as the driving feature, see Figure 13.44. To select a pattern instance (driving feature), click on this field in the PropertyManager and then select a pattern instance of a pattern. After selecting the component to be patterned and a pattern instance (driving feature), a preview of the pattern driven component pattern appears in the graphics area, see Figure 13.45.

13.44 Pattern instance / Component

13.45 Seed Feature

Note: By default, the position of the seed/parent instance of a pattern is taken as the position of the component being patterned. You can change the default position of the seed pattern instance by using the **Select Seed Position** button of the **Driving Feature or Component** rollout. On clicking the **Select Seed Position** button, a blue dot appears in the preview of each pattern instance in the graphics area. You can click on the blue dot of the pattern instance to select it as the seed feature of the pattern.

The **Alignment method** area becomes available in the PropertyManager, if a hole feature is created using the **Hole Wizard** or **Advanced Hole** tool and is selected as a driving feature for creating the pattern, see Figures 13.46 and 13.47. In the **Alignment method** area, the **Align to holes** radio button is selected, by default. As a result, all the pattern instances get aligned parallel to the respective hole axes, see Figure 13.48. On selecting the **Align to seed** radio button, all the pattern instances get aligned as per the alignment of the seed component, see Figure 13.49.

Instances to Skip

The **Instances to Skip** field is used for skipping pattern instances of the pattern. To skip pattern instances, click on the **Instances to Skip** field in the rollout. A pink dot appears on each pattern instance in the graphics area, see Figure 13.50. Move the cursor over the instance to be skipped and then click on it.

Skipped By Driving Feature

The **Skipped By Driving Feature** field is used for displaying the list of pattern instances, which are skipped in the pattern feature (driving) of the component.

Procedure for Creating a Pattern Driven Component Pattern

1. Invoke the **Pattern** flyout in the **Assembly CommandManager**.
2. Click on the **Pattern Driven Component Pattern** tool in the **Pattern** flyout.
3. Click on the component to be patterned in the graphics area.
4. Click on the **Driving feature or component** field and then click on an instance of a pattern feature of the component as the driving feature.
5. If needed, you can skip the pattern instances by using the **Instances to Skip** rollout.
6. Click on the green tick-mark ☑ in the PropertyManager. The pattern driven component pattern is created.

Creating a Chain Component Pattern

A chain component pattern is created by patterning a component along an open or a closed path to simulate the chain drive or cable carrier mechanism dynamically in an assembly, see Figure 13.51. In SOLIDWORKS, you can create a chain component pattern by using the **Chain Component Pattern** tool.

In a chain component pattern, the component drives along an open or closed path such that you can simulate its motion dynamically by dragging the pattern instances. To create a chain component pattern, invoke the **Pattern** flyout, see Figure 13.52 and then click on the **Chain Component Pattern** tool. The **Chain Pattern PropertyManager** appears, see Figure 13.53.

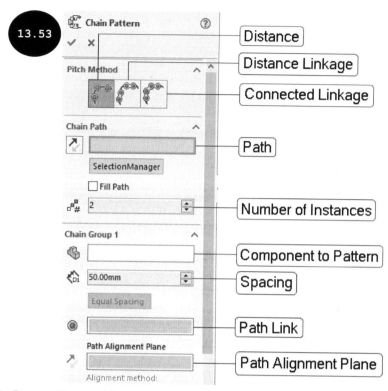

13.53

The **Chain Pattern PropertyManager** is used for creating three types of chain patterns: Distance, Distance Linkage, and Connected Linkage. The Distance chain pattern is used for patterning a component along a path with a single link among the pattern instances. The Distance Linkage chain pattern is used for patterning a component along a path with two non-connected links among the pattern instances. The Connected Linkage chain pattern is used for patterning a component along a path with connected links among the pattern instances. The procedures for creating different types of chain patterns are discussed next.

Procedure for Creating a Distance Chain Pattern

1. Click on the **Chain Component Pattern** tool in the **Pattern** flyout. The **Chain Pattern PropertyManager** appears.
2. Make sure that the **Distance** button is selected in the **Pitch Method** rollout of the PropertyManager.
3. Click on the **SelectionManager** button in the **Chain Path** rollout. The **Selection** toolbar appears, see Figure 13.54.

13.54

4. Click on the **Select Closed Loop** or **Select Open Loop** button in the **Selection** toolbar, depending upon the type of path (closed or open) to be selected.

5. Click on the path to be selected in the graphics area, see Figure 13.55. Next, click on the green tick-mark ☑ in the **Selection** toolbar. The path is selected.

6. Either select the **Fill Path** check box in the **Chain Path** rollout to fill in the path with pattern instances or specify the number of instances to be created in the **Number of Instances** field.

7. Click on the **Component to Pattern** field in the **Chain Group 1** rollout to activate it.

8. Click on the component to be patterned in the graphics area, see Figure 13.55.

9. Click on the **Path Link** field in the **Chain Group 1** rollout to activate it.

10. Click on a cylindrical face, a circular edge, a linear edge, or a reference axis as the link among the pattern instances in the graphics area, see Figure 13.55.

11. Select a plane or a planar face as the alignment plane for aligning the pattern instances along the path, see Figure 13.55. A preview of the chain pattern appears, see Figure 13.56.

12. Specify the spacing between the pattern instances in the **Spacing** field.

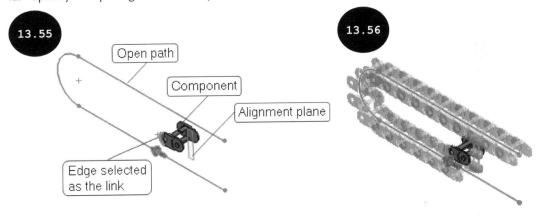

13. Click on the green tick-mark ☑ in the PropertyManager. The chain component pattern is created, see Figure 13.57.

Procedure for Creating a Distance Linkage Chain Pattern

1. Click on the **Chain Component Pattern** tool in the **Pattern** flyout. The **Chain Pattern** PropertyManager appears.

2. Click on the **Distance Linkage** button in the **Pitch Method** rollout of the PropertyManager.

3. Click on the **SelectionManager** button in the **Chain Path** rollout. The **Selection** toolbar appears.

4. Click on the **Select Closed Loop** or **Select Open Loop** button in the **Selection** toolbar, depending upon the type of path (closed or open) to be selected.

5. Click on the path to be selected in the graphics area, see Figure 13.58. Next, click on the green tick-mark ☑ in the **Selection** toolbar. The path is selected.

6. Either specify the number of pattern instances to be created along the path in the **Number of Instances** field or select the **Fill Path** check box to fill in the path with pattern instances.

7. Click on the **Component to Pattern** field in the **Chain Group 1** rollout to activate it.

8. Click on the component to be patterned in the graphics area.

9. Click on the **Path Link 1** field in the **Chain Group 1** rollout to activate it.

10. Click on a cylindrical face, a circular edge, a linear edge, or a reference axis as the link 1 among the pattern instances in the graphics area, see Figure 13.58.

11. Click on a cylindrical face, a circular edge, a linear edge, or a reference axis as the link 2 among the pattern instances, see Figure 13.58.

12. Click on a plane or a planar face as the alignment plane, see Figure 13.58. The preview of pattern appears, see Figure 13.59.

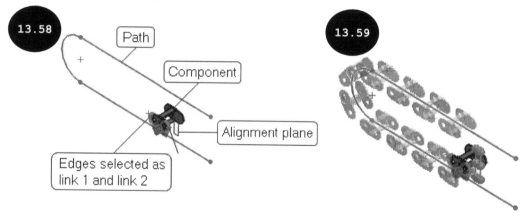

13. Specify the spacing between the pattern instances in the **Spacing** field.

14. Click on the green tick-mark ☑ in the PropertyManager. The distance linkage chain pattern is created, see Figure 13.60.

Note: In the **Options** rollout of the **Chain Pattern PropertyManager**, the **Dynamic** radio button is selected by default, see Figure 13.61. As a result, you can drag any pattern instance to move the chain. On selecting the **Static** radio button, you can move the chain only by dragging the parent or seed component of the pattern. The **Static** radio button helps in improving the overall performance of the system for large assemblies.

Procedure for Creating a Connected Linkage Chain Pattern

1. Click on the **Chain Component Pattern** tool in the **Pattern** flyout to invoke the **Chain Pattern PropertyManager**.
2. Click on the **Connected Linkage** button in the **Pitch Method** rollout of the PropertyManager.
3. Select an open or a closed path from the graphics area by using the **SelectionManager** button of the **Chain Path** rollout, see Figure 13.62.
4. Either specify the number of pattern instances to be created along the path in the **Number of Instances** field or select the **Fill Path** check box to fill in the path with pattern instances.
5. Click on the **Component to Pattern** field in the **Chain Group 1** rollout to activate it.
6. Click on the component to be patterned in the graphics area.
7. Click on the **Path Link 1** field in the **Chain Group 1** rollout to activate it.
8. Click on a cylindrical face, a circular edge, a linear edge, or a reference axis as the link 1 between the pattern instances in the graphics area, see Figure 13.62.
9. Click on a cylindrical face, a circular edge, a linear edge, or a reference axis as the link 2 between the pattern instances, see Figure 13.62.
10. Click on a plane or a planar face as the alignment plane, see Figure 13.62. A preview of the pattern appears, see Figure 13.63. If the pattern preview does not appear in the graphics area, you need to reverse the direction of the pattern by clicking on the arrow that appears along the path in the graphics area.

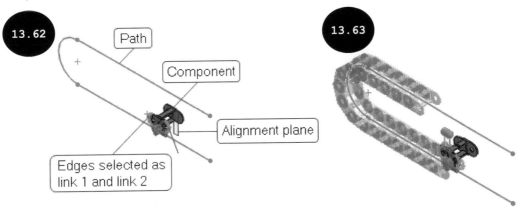

11. Click on the green tick-mark ☑ of the PropertyManager. The connected linkage chain pattern is created, see Figure 13.64.

Mirroring Components of an Assembly Updated

Similar to mirroring features in the Part modeling environment, you can also mirror components in the Assembly environment by using the **Mirror Components** tool of the **Pattern** flyout, see Figure 13.65.

To mirror components of an assembly, invoke the **Pattern** flyout and then click on the **Mirror Components** tool, see Figure 13.65. The **Mirror Components PropertyManager** appears, see Figure 13.66. The options of the PropertyManager are discussed next.

Mirror plane

The **Mirror plane** field is used for selecting a mirroring plane to mirror the selected components of an assembly. By default, this field is activated. As a result, you can select a plane or a planar face as the mirroring plane, see Figure 13.67.

Components to Mirror

The **Components to Mirror** field is used for selecting components to be mirrored about the mirroring plane. This field gets activated as soon as you select the mirroring plane. Select a component or components to be mirrored, see Figure 13.67.

After selecting the mirroring plane and the component to be mirrored, click on the green tick-mark ☑ in the PropertyManager. The selected component is mirrored about the mirroring plane, see Figure 13.68.

Note: You can also change the orientation of the mirrored component. To change the orientation of the mirrored component, click on the **Next** ⊚ button in the **Mirror Components PropertyManager** to display the **Step 2: Set Orientation** page of the PropertyManager. Select the required radio button (**Center of bounding box, Center of mass,** or **Component origin**) as the mirror type. Next, choose an orientation for the mirrored component by selecting the required button in the **Orient Components** rollout.

If you have selected a flexible sub-assembly as the component to be mirrored then you can synchronize the movement of the components of the mirrored sub-assembly with respect to the movement of the parent sub-assembly (flexible) by selecting the **Synchronize movement of flexible subassembly components** check box of the PropertyManager. After selecting this check box, if you move the components of the flexible sub-assembly (parent), the respective components of the mirrored sub-assembly also move, respectively and vice versa. Note that this check box is enabled only if the selected sub-assembly to be mirrored is a flexible sub-assembly. When the **Create opposite hand version** button 🔀 is activated in the **Orient Components** rollout of the PropertyManager, you can click on the **Next** ⊚ button in the **Mirror Components PropertyManager** to display the **Step 3: Opposite Hand** page of the PropertyManager. The options in the **Step 3: Opposite Hand** page of the PropertyManager are used for defining whether to create the mirrored component as a new derived configuration in the existing file or create a new file. You can also display the **Step 4: Import Features** page of the PropertyManager by again clicking on the **Next** ⊚ button in the **Mirror Components PropertyManager**. The options in the **Step 4: Import Features** page are used for defining the properties to be imported or transferred from the parent component to the mirrored component. You can also include custom properties in the mirrored component by selecting the **Custom Properties** check box in the **Step 4: Import Features** page of the PropertyManager. Also, on selecting the **Break link to original part** check box in the **Step 4: Import Features** page, the changes made in the parent component will not be reflected in the mirrored component.

Procedure for Mirroring Components of an Assembly

1. Invoke the **Pattern** flyout in the **Assembly CommandManager**.
2. Click on the **Mirror Components** tool in the **Pattern** flyout.
3. Select a plane or a planar face as the mirroring plane.
4. Select a component or components to be mirrored about the mirroring plane.
5. Click on the green tick-mark ✓ in the PropertyManager. The selected components are mirrored.

Creating Assembly Features

In a manufacturing unit or a shop floor, after assembling all components of an assembly, several cut operations may be carried out in the components in order to give a final touch-up and align the components perfectly with respect to each other. For this, SOLIDWORKS has tools to create cut features in the Assembly environment. Cut features created in the Assembly environment are known as assembly features and do not affect the original geometry of the components. For example, if you create an assembly feature (cut feature) on a component of an assembly in the Assembly environment; the assembly feature created will exist only in the assembly and if you open the same component in the Part modeling environment, you will not find the existence of the assembly feature. This means that the assembly features exist in the assembly only and will not affect the original geometry of the component.

In SOLIDWORKS, you can create assembly features such as holes, extruded cut, revolved cut, swept cut, and fillets. The tools for creating assembly features are provided in the **Assembly Features** flyout, see Figure 13.69. The procedure for creating assembly features is the same as creating features in the Part modeling environment. For example, to create an extruded cut feature, click on the **Extruded Cut** tool in the **Assembly Features** flyout. The **Extrude PropertyManager** appears. Select a plane or a planar face as the sketching plane. The Sketching environment is invoked. Create the sketch of the extruded cut feature and then exit the Sketching environment. As soon as you exit the Sketching environment, the preview of the cut feature appears in the graphics area. Specify the required parameters for the extrusion in the PropertyManager and then click on the green tick-mark. The extruded cut feature is created in the Assembly environment.

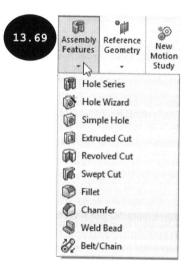

Note: You can also invoke the tools for creating the assembly features by clicking on **Insert > Assembly Feature** in the SOLIDWORKS Menus. In addition to creating the assembly features (cut features), you can mirror the assembly features about a mirroring plane by using the **Mirror** tool of the **Assembly Features** flyout. You can also create a linear pattern, circular pattern, table driven pattern, sketch driven pattern, and so on of the assembly features by using the respective tools available in the **Assembly Features** flyout. The tools for creating mirror and pattern features become available in the **Assembly Features** flyout only after creating an assembly feature in the Assembly environment.

Suppressing or Unsuppressing Components

In SOLIDWORKS, you can suppress or unsuppress components of an assembly. A suppressed component is removed from the assembly and does not appear in the graphics area. Also, the name of the suppressed component appears in gray color in the FeatureManager Design Tree. Note that a suppressed component is not deleted from the assembly, it is only removed such that it is not loaded into the RAM (random access memory) while rebuilding the assembly. It helps you to speed up the overall performance of the system when you are working with larger assemblies.

To suppress a component of an assembly, select the component to be suppressed either from the graphics area or from the FeatureManager Design Tree. A Pop-up toolbar appears, see Figure 13.70. In this Pop-up toolbar, click on the **Suppress** tool. The selected component is suppressed.

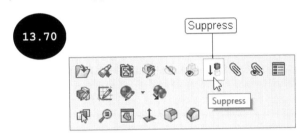

To unsuppress a suppressed component, select the suppressed component from the FeatureManager Design Tree. A Pop-up toolbar appears. Next, click on the **Unsuppress** tool in the Pop-up toolbar. The component is now unsuppressed and appears in the assembly.

Inserting Parts having Multiple Configurations

In SOLIDWORKS, you can choose a configuration of a component to be inserted in the Assembly environment. To choose the configuration of a component while inserting it in the Assembly environment, click on the **Insert Components** tool in the **Assembly CommandManager**. The **Open** dialog box appears automatically along with the **Insert Component PropertyManager**. Note that if the **Open** dialog box does not appear then click on the **Browse** button in the **Part/Assembly to Insert** rollout of the PropertyManager to open the **Open** dialog box. In the **Open** dialog box, browse to the location where the component to be inserted has been saved. Next, select the component that has multiple configurations and then invoke the **Configuration** drop-down list in the **Open** dialog box, see Figure 13.71. Now, select the required configuration of the component from this drop-down list that is to be inserted in the Assembly environment. Next, click on the **Open** button in the dialog box. The selected configuration of the component is attached to the cursor. Now, click in the graphics area to specify the position of the component.

Note: In SOLIDWORKS, you can create multiple configurations of a component in the Part modeling environment. For example, if a bolt of same geometry has to be used in an assembly several times with a different diameter, then you can create a single bolt with multiple configurations having different diameters. The different methods for creating multiple configurations are discussed in Chapter 11.

You can also choose the configuration of a component to be inserted in the Assembly environment by using the **Configuration** drop-down list of the **Insert Component PropertyManager** or the **Begin Assembly PropertyManager**. Additionally, you can change the configuration of a component even after inserting it in the Assembly environment. To change the configuration of an already inserted component, click on the component whose configuration has to be changed. A Pop-up toolbar appears with the **Configuration** drop-down list, see Figure 13.72. Next, invoke the **Configuration** drop-down list by clicking on the arrow and then select the required configuration of the component. Next, click on the green-tick mark that appears in front of the drop-down list to confirm the selection of the configuration. The configuration of the component changes to the selected configuration in the Assembly environment.

Creating and Dissolving Sub-Assemblies

SOLIDWORKS allows you to create sub-assemblies from the components of an assembly within the Assembly environment. To create a sub-assembly, select components to be included in the sub-assembly from the FeatureManager Design Tree by pressing the CTRL key and then right-click. A shortcut menu appears. In this shortcut menu, click on the **Form New Subassembly** option, see Figure 13.73. After selecting this option, a sub-assembly is created with a default name and the selected components become a part of the sub-assembly. In case, the **Assembly Structure Editing** window appears after selecting the **Form New Subassembly** option, click on the **Move** button. You can also include patterned and mirrored components in the sub-assembly. To rename the sub-assembly, select the sub-assembly in the FeatureManager Design Tree and then right-click. Next, click on the

Rename Assembly option in the shortcut menu that appears. The name of the sub-assembly appears in an edit field. Now, you can enter a new name for the sub-assembly.

You can also dissolve the created sub-assembly in the Assembly environment. To dissolve a sub-assembly, select the sub-assembly to be dissolved in the FeatureManager Design Tree and then right-click to display a shortcut menu. Next, click on the **Dissolve Subassembly** option in the shortcut menu. The selected sub-assembly is dissolved and its components become the individual components of the main assembly.

Publishing Envelopes

In SOLIDWORKS 2020, you can include components from a top level assembly (main assembly) as envelopes in a sub-assembly by using the **Envelope Publisher** tool. It helps to work in the sub-assembly with the included enveloped components, together in isolation from the main assembly. Figure 13.74 shows a component of an assembly to be included as envelope in a sub-assembly. Figure 13.75 shows a resultant sub-assembly and the enveloped component in isolation from the top level assembly. It helps to work easily and collaboratively in large assemblies.

To include components of a top level assembly as envelopes in a sub-assembly, click on **Tools > Envelope Publisher** in the SOLIDWORKS Menus. The **Envelope Publisher PropertyManager** appears and you are prompted to select components to be published as envelopes in a destination sub-assembly, see Figure 13.76. Note that the **Envelope Publisher** tool is available only when the main assembly contains a sub-assembly. The options in the PropertyManager are discussed next.

> **Note:** If the **Envelope Publisher** tool is not available in the **Tools** menu of the SOLIDWORKS Menus, then click on the **Options** tool in the **Standard** toolbar. Next, click on the **External References** option in the **System Options** tab of the dialog box that appears. Next, make sure that the **Allow creation of references external to the model** check box is selected in the **Assemblies** area of the right panel in the dialog box. Also, make sure that the **Any component** radio button is selected as the **Reference component type** and the **Top level assembly** radio button is selected as the **In the context of** in the **Assemblies** area of the dialog box.

Envelope Group name

The **Envelope Group name** field of the **Add a Group** rollout displays a default name for the envelope group being created. You can use the default name or edit it, as required.

Components to use as envelopes

By default, the **Components to use as envelopes** field is activated in the PropertyManager. As a result, you can select the components of a top level assembly to be published as envelopes in a destination sub-assembly. You can select components one by one either in the graphics area or in the FeatureManager Design Tree.

Destination subassemblies

The **Destination subassemblies** field is used for selecting a sub-assembly as a destination for the enveloped components that are selected in the **Components to use as envelopes** field of the PropertyManager. It is recommended to select a destination sub-assembly from the FeatureManager Design Tree.

After selecting the enveloped components and a destination sub-assembly, click on the **Add group** button in the PropertyManager. The envelope group gets created and its name appears in the **Envelope Groups** field of the PropertyManager. Similarly, you can create multiple envelope groups. Next, click on the green tick-mark in the PropertyManager. The selected components get published as envelopes in the selected destination sub-assembly and the **Published Envelopes** folder gets added under the sub-assembly folder in the FeatureManager Design Tree, see Figure 13.77. Now, when you open the sub-assembly by using the **Open Subassembly** or **Open Subassembly in Position** tool of the Pop-up toolbar that appears when you click on the sub-assembly in the FeatureManager Design Tree, the sub-assembly gets opened in a new window with its envelope components as external reference. Now, you can work with the sub-assembly and the included enveloped components together, in isolation from the main assembly.

Figure 13.77

Creating an Exploded View `Updated`

Creating an exploded view of an assembly is important from the presentation point of view. It helps you in easily identifying the position of each component of an assembly and in making technical documentation. It also helps technical and non-technical clients easily understand the inner components of an assembly. Figure 13.78 shows an assembly and Figure 13.79 shows its exploded view.

To create an exploded view of an assembly, click on the **Exploded View** tool in the **Assembly CommandManager**, see Figure 13.80. The **Explode PropertyManager** appears, see Figure 13.81. The options of the PropertyManager are discussed next.

Add a Step

The options in the **Add a Step** rollout are used for creating explode steps. Note that the availability of options in this rollout depends on the button (**Regular step** ⬛ or **Radial step** ⬛) selected in the rollout. By activating the **Regular step** button ⬛, you can explode the components of an assembly by translating and rotating them along and about an axis, see Figure 13.82. By activating the **Radial step** button ⬛, you can explode the components of an assembly by aligning them radially or cylindrically about an axis, see Figure 13.83.

Figure 13.84 shows the **Add a Step** rollout of the PropertyManager when the **Regular step** button is activated. The options of the **Add a Step** rollout are discussed next.

Explode Step Name

The **Explode Step Name** field of the **Add a Step** rollout displays a default name of the explode step. You can also specify a new name for an explode step in this field.

Explode Step Components

The **Explode Step Components** field is used for selecting components of the assembly to be exploded in the explode step. You can select one or more than one components to be exploded in an explode step from the graphics area. As soon as you select the components to be exploded, three rotation handles and three translation handles appear in the graphics area, see Figure 13.85. Note that these handles (three rotation and three translations) appear in the case of creating regular explode step by activating the **Regular step** button. In the case of creating the radial explode step by activating the **Radial step** button, one rotation handle and one translation handle appears in the graphics area, see Figure 13.86.

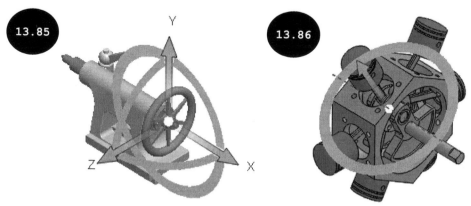

You can drag the required rotation handle or translation handle for creating the explode step. A translation handle is used for translating the selected components along its respective direction, whereas a rotation handle is used for rotating the components about its respective axis.

> **Tip:** For translation movement, move the cursor over the required translation handle and then drag it by pressing and holding the left mouse button. The selected component starts translating along the direction of translation handle. Once the desired location has been achieved, release the left mouse button. An explode step is created and appears in the **Explode Steps** rollout. Next, click on the **Done** button in the rollout.
>
> For rotational movement, move the cursor over the required rotation handle and then drag it by pressing and holding the left mouse button. The selected component starts rotating about the axis of the rotational handle. Next, release the left mouse button. An explode step is created. Next, click on the **Done** button in the rollout.

Explode Direction

The **Explode Direction** field displays the translation direction along which the selected components can translate. Note that the display of explode direction depends upon the translation handle selected.

Explode Distance

The **Explode Distance** field is used for specifying translation distance value for translating the selected components along the translation direction. After specifying translation distance value in this field, click on the **Add Step** button in the rollout of the PropertyManager. Note that if you translate the components by dragging the translation handle, then the translation distance value gets updated automatically in this field.

Rotation Axis
The **Rotation Axis** field displays the rotation axis about which the selected components are to be rotated. The display of the rotational axis depends upon the selection of rotation handle.

Rotation Angle
The **Rotation Angle** field is used for specifying a rotation angle value for rotating the selected components. After entering a rotation angle value in this field, click on the **Add Step** button. Note that if you rotate the components by dragging the rotation handle, then the rotational angle value gets updated automatically in this field.

Rotate about each component origin
On selecting the **Rotate about each component origin** check box, the selected components rotate about the origin of the component. This check box is available only when the **Regular Step** button is activated in the rollout.

Diverge from axis
On selecting the **Diverge from axis** check box, the selected components explode away from an axis. This check box is available only when the **Radial Step** button is activated in the rollout.

Reset
The **Reset** button is used for resetting the specified settings in the rollout to the default state.

Add Step
The **Add Step** button is used for creating the explode step as per the specified settings in the rollout.

Done
The **Done** button is used for accepting the preview and creating the explode step. This button is available in the rollout when you create an explode step by dragging an handle that appears in the graphics area.

Explode Steps
The **Explode Steps** rollout displays the list of all explode steps created for an exploded assembly, see Figure 13.87. Note that to create an exploded assembly, you may need to create multiple explode steps (regular and radial steps). In each explode step, one or more than one component can be exploded. You can also roll back or roll forward through the explode steps to display the results of each explode step by using the **Roll Back** ⊕ and **Roll Forward** ⊕ buttons of the **Explode Steps** rollout, respectively. You can also drag the Rollback Bar that appears at the end of the last explode step in the **Explode Steps** rollout to roll back through the explode steps.

Tip: To delete an explode step, right-click on it in the **Explode Steps** rollout and then click on the **Delete** option in the shortcut menu that appears. You can also suppress or unsuppress an explode step. For doing so, right-click on an explode step in the **Explode Steps** rollout and then click on the **Suppress** or **Unsuppress** option in the shortcut menu that appears, respectively.

Options

The options in the **Options** rollout are used for controlling the explode step, see Figure 13.88. Note that the availability of the options in this rollout depends upon the button (**Regular step** or **Radial step**) selected in the **Add a Step** rollout of the PropertyManager. Figure 13.88 shows the **Options** rollout when the **Regular step** button is selected. The options of the **Options** rollout are discussed next.

Auto-space components

The **Auto-space components** check box is used for translating or rotating a set of selected components with equal spacing automatically, on exploding the components along or about the selected direction. Note that the equal spacing value for exploding a set of selected components with equal spacing can be increased or decreased by using the **Spacing** slider that appears below this check box.

Note: In SOLIDWORKS 2020, you can change the order of auto-spacing of the selected components by selecting the required button (**Bounding box center**, **Bounding box rear**, or **Bounding box front**) available below the **Spacing** slider. You can also change the order of explosion by dragging the arrows that appear on individual exploded components in the graphics area.

Spacing

The **Spacing** slider is used to adjust the spacing between a set of selected components for exploding them, equally.

Show rotation rings

By default, the **Show rotation rings** check box is selected. As a result, the rotation handles/rings appear in the graphics area after selecting the components to be exploded. If you clear this check box, the display of rotation handles/rings is disabled.

Select subassembly parts

By selecting the **Select subassembly parts** check box, you can select individual components of a sub-assembly for explosion.

From Subassembly and From Part

The **From Subassembly** and **From Part** buttons are used for exploding components by using the previously defined explode steps for a sub-assembly or a multibody part, respectively. Note that the **From Subassembly** button is enabled when a sub-assembly has an exploded view and the **From Part** button is enabled when a multibody part has an exploded view.

Note: By default, the selected components can explode along the X, Y, and Z axes by using the handles appearing in the graphics area. To translate the component along an axis other than X, Y, and Z axes, move the cursor over a translation handle that appears in the graphics area and then right-click. A shortcut menu appears, see Figure 13.89. In this shortcut menu, click on the **Align with selection** or **Move to selection** option. Next, select a linear edge of a component. The selected handle gets aligned along the direction of the selected linear edge. Now, you can drag the aligned handle to translate the components along the direction of the aligned handle.

Procedure for Creating a Regular Exploded View

1. Click on the **Exploded View** tool. The **Explode PropertyManager** appears.
2. Make sure that the **Regular step** button is selected in the **Add a Step** rollout.
3. Select a set of components to be exploded as the first regular explode step.
4. Drag a translation handle or a rotation handle that appears in the graphics area by pressing and holding the left mouse button and then click on the **Done** button to create the first explode step. Alternatively, enter the translation distance or rotational angle value in the respective fields of the **Add a Step** rollout and then click on the **Add Step** button.
5. Similarly, create the other explode steps for the assembly.
6. Click on the green tick-mark ☑ button in the PropertyManager. The exploded view of the assembly is created.

Procedure for Creating a Radial Exploded View

1. Click on the **Exploded View** tool. The **Explode PropertyManager** appears.
2. Make sure that the **Radial step** button is selected in the **Add a Step** rollout.
3. Select a set of components to be exploded as the first explode step.
4. Drag the translation handle or the rotation handle to the required distance by pressing and holding the left mouse button and then click on the **Done** button to create the first explode step. Alternatively, enter the translation distance or rotation angle value in the respective fields of the rollout and then click on the **Add Step** button.
5. Similarly, create the other explode steps for the assembly.
6. Click on the green tick-mark ☑ in the PropertyManager. The exploded view of the assembly is created.

Note: You can create the exploded view of an assembly with a combination of the regular and radial explode steps.

Collapsing an Exploded View

After creating an exploded view of an assembly, you can restore the components of the assembly back to their original positions by collapsing the exploded view. To collapse the exploded view of an assembly, select the name of the assembly in the FeatureManager Design Tree and then right-click. A shortcut menu appears, see Figure 13.90. In this shortcut menu, click on the **Collapse** option.

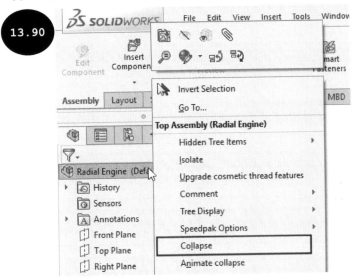

After the collapsed view of an assembly has been displayed, you can display the exploded view again. To display the exploded view of the assembly again, right-click on the name of the assembly in the FeatureManager Design Tree and then click on the **Explode** option in the shortcut menu that appears. The exploded view of the assembly is displayed.

Animating an Exploded View

After creating an exploded view of an assembly, you can animate the components of the assembly to display its collapsed and exploded states. For doing so, right-click on the name of the assembly in the FeatureManager Design Tree and then click on the **Animate collapse** or **Animate explode** option in the shortcut menu that appears. The components start animating and the **Animation Controller** toolbar appears, see Figure 13.91. By using the **Animation Controller** toolbar, you can control the animation of the components. You can also record the animation and save it as a *.avi*, *.bmp*, and *.tga* file.

Note: The availability of the **Animate collapse** or **Animate explode** option in the shortcut menu depends upon the current state of the assembly. If the assembly appears in its exploded state in the graphics area, then the **Animate collapse** option appears in the shortcut menu. If the assembly appears in its collapsed state, then the **Animate explode** option is available in the shortcut menu.

Editing an Exploded View

You can edit an existing exploded view of an assembly to make necessary changes in its explode steps and to create new explode steps. To edit an exploded view of an assembly, invoke the ConfigurationManager by clicking on the **ConfigurationManager** tab, see Figure 13.92. The ConfigurationManager displays a list of all configurations of the assembly. Figure 13.92 shows the default configuration of the assembly (**Default** [*name of the assembly*]). Expand the configuration of the assembly by clicking on the arrow that appears in front of it, see Figure 13.93.

Figure 13.93 shows the two exploded views: **Exploded View1** and **Exploded View2**, created for the assembly, out of which the **Exploded View1** is activated by default. You can activate the required exploded view by double-clicking on its name. To edit an exploded view, select the exploded view to be edited and then right-click to display a shortcut menu, see Figure 13.94. Next, click on the **Edit Feature** option in the shortcut menu. The **Exploded View PropertyManager** appears. Now, by using the options of this PropertyManager, you can edit the exploded view, as required.

Adding Explode Lines

After creating an exploded view of an assembly, you can add explode lines in it. Figure 13.95 shows an assembly and Figure 13.96 shows an exploded view of the assembly with explode lines.

Explode lines are used for showing relationships between components in an exploded view. You can create explode lines in an exploded view by using the **Explode Line Sketch** and the **Insert/Edit Smart Explode Lines** tools of the **Explode** flyout, see Figure 13.97. To invoke this flyout, click on the arrow at the bottom of the **Exploded View** tool in the **Assembly CommandManager**, see Figure 13.97. Both these tools are discussed next.

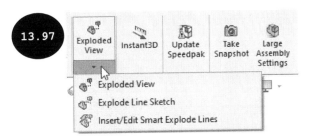

Creating Explode lines by using Explode Line Sketch

The **Explode Line Sketch** tool is used for creating the explode lines manually by selecting the faces or edges of the components in an exploded view. The steps for creating the explode lines by using this tool are discussed next.

1. Invoke the **Explode** flyout, refer to Figure 13.97 and then click on the **Explode Line Sketch** tool. The **Route Line PropertyManager** appears, see Figure 13.98.

2. Select faces, circular edges, straight edges, or planar faces of the components having same assembly line, one after another to connect them with a single route line.

3.   Select the **Reverse** check box to reverse the direction of route line, if needed. Also, you can select the **Alternate Path** check box to view the alternate route option between the selected components.

4.   Click on the green tick-mark ☑ in the PropertyManager. A route line is created among the selected components, which represents the assembly line of the components.

5.   Similarly, create route lines for remaining sets of components having the same assembly line.

6.   After creating all the explode lines, click on the green tick-mark in the PropertyManager.

Creating Explode lines by using Insert/Edit Smart Explode Lines

The **Insert/Edit Smart Explode Lines** tool is used for creating the explode lines automatically in an exploded view. The steps for creating the explode lines by using this tool are discussed next.

1.   Click on the **Insert/Edit Smart Explode Lines** tool in the **Explode** flyout of the **Assembly CommandManager**. The **Smart Explode Lines PropertyManager** appears, see Figure 13.99. Also, the preview of the explode lines appears automatically in the graphics area, see Figure 13.100. By default, all the exploded components of the assembly are selected in the **Components** rollout of the PropertyManager and the respective explode lines appear in the graphics area.

2.   Click on the green-tick mark in the PropertyManager. The explode lines are created.

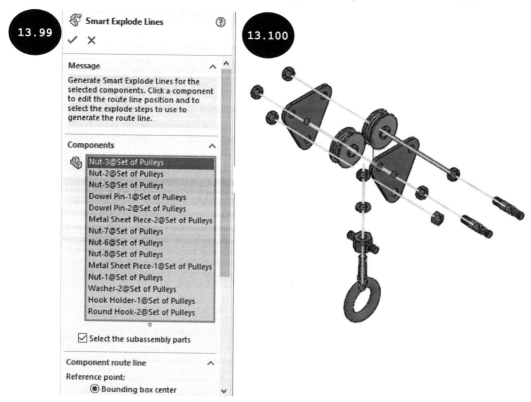

Note: The options in the **Component route line** rollout are used for locating the route line of the component which is selected in the **Components** rollout of the PropertyManager. By default, the **Bounding box center** radio button is selected in the **Component route line** rollout. As a result, the explode line gets located relative to the bounding box center of the selected component. On selecting the **Component origin** radio button, the explode line gets located relative to the origin of the selected component. On selecting the **Selected point** radio button, you can select a point, a vertex, a sketch arc, an edge arc, a sketch line, or an edge line as the point to locate the explode line of the selected component relative to it. On selecting the **Select the subassembly parts** check box in the **Components** rollout, the selection of the individual components of a sub-assembly is enabled.

Tip: To edit the explode lines created by using the **Insert/Edit Smart Explode Lines** tool, click on the **ConfigurationManager** tab and then expand the active configuration. Next, right-click on the **Exploded View** option and then click on the **Edit Smart Explode Lines** tool in the shortcut menu that appears. Now, you can edit the settings of the explode lines in the **Smart Explode Lines PropertyManager** that appears. Next, click on the green tick-mark.

Detecting Interference in an Assembly Updated

In complex assemblies, sometimes it becomes difficult to visually point out interference between components. The **Interference Detection** tool helps in determining any interference between the components of an assembly. To detect interference, click on the **Interference Detection** tool in the **Evaluate CommandManager**, see Figure 13.101. The **Interference Detection PropertyManager** appears, see Figure 13.102. The options in this PropertyManager are discussed next.

Selected Components

The name of the assembly appears in the **Selected Components** field, by default. Hence, you can calculate interference between all the components of the assembly. You can also check interference between required components instead of the entire assembly. For doing so, you first need to clear the current selection set by right-clicking on the **Selected Components** field and then clicking on the **Clear Selections** option in the shortcut menu that appears, see Figure 13.103. Next, select the required components in the graphics area or in the FeatureManager Design Tree. The names of the selected components appear in the **Selected Components** field. Next, click on the **Calculate** button. The interference results get calculated between the selected components and are displayed in the **Results** field of the PropertyManager.

Results

The **Results** field displays a list of all interferences that are determined between the selected components. On selecting an interference from the list, the selected interference gets highlighted in red in the graphics area, see Figure 13.104. You can also ignore the selected interference using the **Ignore** button such that it is no longer considered as an interference. On right-clicking an interference, you can choose to sort interferences according to size, ignore an interference, ignore certain interferences below a value, or isolate them in the graphics area to properly review them. Note that the **Results** field displays a list of interferences if the **Component view** check box is cleared. On selecting this check box, the **Results** field displays a list of all the components causing interference.

Excluded Components

The **Excluded Components** rollout of the PropertyManager is used for excluding components from interference calculation. To activate this rollout, select the check box in front of it.

Options

The options in the **Options** rollout of the PropertyManager are used to define whether to treat coincidence as interference, show ignored interferences, treat sub-assemblies as components, make interfering parts transparent, and so on by using the respective check boxes.

Non-interfering Components

The **Non-interfering Components** rollout of the PropertyManager is used to select a display style for the non-interfering components. You can choose wireframe, hidden, transparent, or the current used display style of the assembly as the display style for the non-interfering components of the assembly by selecting the required radio button.

Creating Bill of Material (BOM) of an Assembly

A Bill of Material (BOM) is one of the most important features of any drawing. It contains information related to the number of components, material, quantity, and so on. In addition to creating Bill of Material (BOM) in a drawing, SOLIDWORKS also allows you to create BOM in the Assembly environment. You will learn about creating Bill of Material (BOM) in a drawing later in Chapter 14. To create BOM in the Assembly environment, click on the **Bill of Materials** tool in the **Assembly CommandManager**. The **Bill of Materials PropertyManager** appears, see Figure 13.105. Accept the default parameters specified in the PropertyManager for creating the BOM and click on the green tick-mark ☑. The Bill of Material (BOM) gets attached to the cursor. Now, click in the graphics area to specify the location of the BOM. The BOM is placed on the specified location, see Figure 13.106.

ITEM NO.	PART NUMBER	DESCRIPTION	QTY.
1	Metal Sheet Piece		2
2	Dowel Pin		2
3	Pulley		2
4	Hook Holder		1
5	Round Hook		1
6	Nut		7
7	Washer		1

Tutorial 1

Create an assembly, as shown in Figure 13.107 by using the Top-down Assembly approach. Different views and dimensions of each assembly component are shown in Figures 13.108 through 13.110. All dimensions are in mm.

First Component

Second Component

Third Component

Section 1: Starting SOLIDWORKS

1. Start SOLIDWORKS by double-clicking on the SOLIDWORKS icon on your desktop. The startup user interface of SOLIDWORKS appears along with the **Welcome** dialog box.

Note: If SOLIDWORKS is already open and the **Welcome** dialog box does not appear on the screen, then you can invoke the **Welcome** dialog box by clicking on the **Welcome to SOLIDWORKS** tool ⌂ in the **Standard** toolbar or by pressing the CTRL + F2 keys.

Section 2: Invoking the Assembly Environment

1. Click on the **Assembly** button in the **Welcome** dialog box. The assembly environment is invoked with the display of the **Open** dialog box along with the **Begin Assembly PropertyManager**, by default.

Tip: You can also invoke the Assembly environment by using the **New SOLIDWORKS Document** dialog box. For doing so, click on the **New** tool in the **Standard** toolbar. The **New SOLIDWORKS Document** dialog box appears. In this dialog box, double-click on the **Assembly** button.

Section 3: Creating the First Component

1. Close the **Open** dialog box by clicking on the **Close** button and then close the **Begin Assembly PropertyManager** by clicking on the red cross mark ⊠ available at its top. This is because, in this tutorial, you need to create all components of the assembly within the Assembly environment itself.

2. Click on the arrow at the bottom of the **Insert Components** tool. A flyout appears, see Figure 13.111.

3. Click on the **New Part** tool in the flyout. A new empty part is added in the Assembly environment and appears in the FeatureManager Design Tree with its default name, see Figure 13.112. Also, a green color tick-mark appears attached to the cursor in the graphics area and you are prompted to define the placement for the newly added component in the graphics area.

4. Click anywhere in the graphics area to define the position of the first component with respect to the origin of the assembly.

Note: If you select a plane or a planar face to define the position of the first component, then the Sketching environment is invoked such that the selected plane or the planar face becomes the sketching plane for creating the base feature of the component. Also, the Inplace mate is applied between the selected plane and the plane of the component.

5. Click on the newly added component in the FeatureManager Design Tree. A Pop-up toolbar appears, see Figure 13.113.

6. Click on the **Edit Part** tool in the Pop-up toolbar, see Figure 13.113. The Part modeling environment is invoked within the Assembly environment.

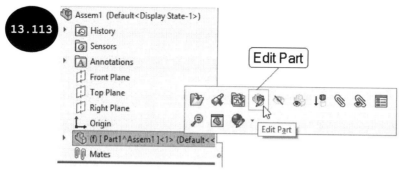

7. Click on the **Extruded Boss/Base** tool in the **Features CommandManager**. The **Extrude PropertyManager** appears.

8. Expand the FeatureManager Design Tree, which is now available at the top left corner of the graphics area and then expand the **Part1** node in it, which appears in blue color.

9. Click on the **Front Plane** available under the expanded **Part1** node in the FeatureManager Design Tree as the sketching plane, see Figure 13.114. The Sketching environment is invoked.

10. Press CTRL + 8 to change the orientation of the model as normal to the viewing direction.

11. Click on the **Sketch** tab in the CommandManager to display the tools of the **Sketch CommandManager**.

12. Create the sketch of the base feature of the component by using the sketching tools, see Figure 13.115.

13. After creating the sketch of the base feature, click on the **Exit Sketch** tool in the **Sketch CommandManager** to exit the Sketching environment. The **Boss-Extrude PropertyManager** and the preview of the extruded feature appear.

14. Change the orientation of the model to isometric.

15. Invoke the **End Condition** drop-down list of the **Direction 1** rollout in the **Boss-Extrude PropertyManager** and then click on the **Mid Plane** option in it.

16. Enter **100** in the **Depth** field of the **Direction 1** rollout of the PropertyManager.

17. Click on the green tick-mark in the PropertyManager. The component is created, see Figure 13.116.

18. Click on the **Edit Component** tool in the CommandManager to exit the Part modeling environment and switch to the Assembly environment.

Section 4: Creating the Second Component

1. Click on the arrow at the bottom of the **Insert Components** tool. A flyout appears, see Figure 13.117.

2. Click on the **New Part** tool in the flyout. A new empty part is added in the Assembly environment and appears in the FeatureManager Design Tree with its default name.

3. Click anywhere in the graphics area to define the position of the second component with respect to the origin of the assembly.

4. Click on the name of the newly added component (*Part2*) in the FeatureManager Design Tree. A Pop-up toolbar appears, see Figure 13.118.

5. Click on the **Edit Part** tool in the Pop-up toolbar, see Figure 13.118. The Part modeling environment is invoked and the first component of the assembly becomes transparent in the graphics area.

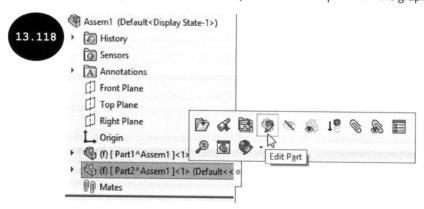

6. Click on the **Extruded Boss/Base** tool in the **Features CommandManager**. The **Extrude PropertyManager** appears.

7. Expand the FeatureManager Design Tree, which is now at the top left corner of the graphics area. Next, expand the **Part 2** node of the FeatureManager Design Tree, which appears in blue color.

8. Click on the **Front Plane** of the second component as the sketching plane in the FeatureManager Design Tree. The Sketching environment is invoked.

9. Click on the **Sketch** tab in the CommandManager to display the tools of the **Sketch** **CommandManager**.

10. Press CTRL + 8 to change the orientation of the model as normal to the viewing direction.

11. Create the sketch of the first feature of the second component, see Figure 13.119.

Note: To create the sketch of the base feature of the second component as shown in Figure 13.119, you can take the reference of the edges of the first component.

12. After creating the sketch of the base feature of the second component, click on the **Exit** **Sketch** tool in the **Sketch CommandManager** to exit the Sketching environment. The **Boss-Extrude PropertyManager** and the preview of the extruded feature appear.

13. Change the orientation of the model to isometric.

14. Invoke the **End Condition** drop-down list of the **Direction 1** rollout in the **Boss-Extrude** **PropertyManager** and then click on the **Mid Plane** option in it.

15. Enter **20** in the **Depth** field of the **Direction 1** rollout of the PropertyManager and then press ENTER.

16. Click on the green tick-mark ✓ in the PropertyManager. The base feature of the second component is created, see Figure 13.120.

Now, you need to create the second feature of the second component.

17. Click on the **Extruded Cut** tool in the **Features CommandManager** and then click on the top face of the base feature of the second component as the sketching plane.

18. Press CTRL + 8 to change the orientation of the model as normal to the viewing direction.

19. Create a circle of diameter 12 mm as the sketch of the second feature, see Figure 13.121.

20. After creating the sketch of the second feature, click on the **Exit Sketch** tool in the **Sketch CommandManager** to exit the Sketching environment. The **Cut-Extrude PropertyManager** and the preview of the cut feature appear.

21. Change the orientation of the model to isometric.

22. Invoke the **End Condition** drop-down list and then click on the **Up To Next** option in it.

23. Click on the green tick-mark in the PropertyManager. The second feature of the second component is created, see Figure 13.122.

⌀12

Now, you need to create the third feature of the second component.

24. Click on the **Fillet** tool in the **Features CommandManager**. The **Fillet PropertyManager** appears.

25. Make sure that the **Constant Size Fillet** button is selected in the **Fillet Type** rollout.

26. Enter **4** in the **Radius** field of the **Fillet Parameters** rollout in the PropertyManager.

27. Click on the required edges (4 edges) of the second component one by one as the edges to create the fillet. The preview of the fillet appears, see Figure 13.123.

28. Click on the green tick-mark ☑ in the PropertyManager. The third feature of the second component is created.

29. After creating all features of the second component, click on the **Edit Component** tool in the CommandManager to exit the Part modeling environment and switch to the Assembly environment. Figure 13.124 shows the assembly after creating its two components.

Section 5: Creating the Third Component

1. Click on the arrow at the bottom of the **Insert Components** tool. A flyout appears.

2. Click on the **New Part** tool in the flyout. A new empty part is added in the assembly and its default name gets added in the FeatureManager Design Tree.

3. Click on the top planar face of the second component as the sketching plane for creating the base feature of the third component. The Sketching environment is invoked and the top planar face of the second component becomes the sketching plane.

4. Press CTRL + 8 to change the orientation of the model as normal to the viewing direction.

5. Create a circle of diameter 12 mm as the sketch of the base feature of the third component, see Figure 13.125.

Note: To create a circle of diameter 12 mm as shown in Figure 13.125, you can take the reference of the circular edge of the second component and apply the coradial relation between them. Alternatively, you can use the **Convert Entities** tool to project the circular edge of the second component for creating the circle of diameter 12 mm.

6. Click on the **Extruded Boss/Base** tool in the **Features CommandManager**. The **Boss-Extrude PropertyManager** appears. Next, change the orientation of the model to isometric.

7. Invoke the **End Condition** drop-down list of the **Direction 1** rollout and then click on the **Mid Plane** option in it.

8. Enter **80** in the **Depth** field of the **Direction 1** rollout.

9. Click on the green tick-mark ✓ in the PropertyManager. The base feature of the third component is created, see Figure 13.126.

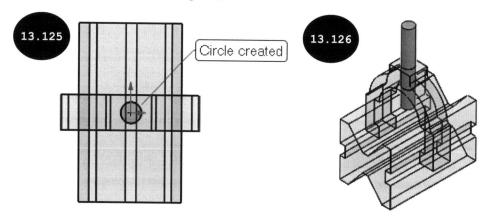

Now, you need to create the second feature of the third component.

10. Click on the **Extruded Boss/Base** tool in the **Features CommandManager** and then click on the top planar face of the base feature of the third component as the sketching plane.

11. Press CTRL + 8 to change the orientation of the model as normal to the viewing direction.

12. Create a circle of diameter 20 mm as the sketch of the second feature, see Figure 13.127.

13. Click on the **Exit Sketch** tool in the **Sketch CommandManager** to exit the Sketching environment. The **Boss-Extrude PropertyManager** and the preview of the extruded feature appear.

14. Change the orientation of the model to isometric.

15. Enter **20** in the **Depth** field of the **Direction 1** rollout in the PropertyManager.

16. Click on the green tick-mark ✓ in the PropertyManager. The second feature of the third component is created, see Figure 13.128.

Now, you need to create the third feature of the third component.

17. Click on the **Extruded Cut** tool in the **Features CommandManager.** The **Extrude PropertyManager** appears.

18. Expand the FeatureManager Design Tree, which is now at the top left corner of the graphics area. Next, expand the **Part 3** node, which appears in blue color in the FeatureManager Design Tree.

19. Click on the **Right Plane** in the **Part 3** node of the FeatureManager Design Tree as the sketching plane. The Sketching environment is invoked. Next, press CTRL + 8 to change the orientation of the model as normal to the viewing direction.

20. Create a circle of diameter 5 mm as the sketch of the third feature, see Figure 13.129.

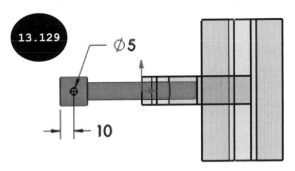

21. Click on the **Exit Sketch** tool in the **Sketch CommandManager** to exit the Sketching environment. The **Cut-Extrude PropertyManager** and the preview of the cut feature appear. Next, change the orientation of the model to isometric.

22. Invoke the **End Condition** drop-down list of the **Direction 1** rollout and then click on the **Through All - Both** option in it.

23. Click on the green tick-mark ☑ in the PropertyManager. The third feature of the third component is created, see Figure 13.130.

24. After creating all the features of the third component, click on the **Edit Component** tool in the CommandManager to exit the Part modeling environment and switch back to the Assembly environment. Figure 13.131 shows the final assembly after creating all the components.

Note: By default, the components created by using the Top-down approach become fixed components in the Assembly environment and applying mates between the components is not required. However, you can make the components float and then apply required mates between the components of the assembly.

Section 6: Saving Assembly and its Component

1. Click on the **Save** button. The **Save Modified Documents** dialog box appears.

2. Click on the **Save All** button in the dialog box. The **Save As** dialog box appears. Browse to the Tutorial folder of the Chapter 13 folder to save the assembly file. You need to create these folders in the SOLIDWORKS folder.

3. Enter **Tutorial 1** in the **File name** field of the dialog box as the name of the assembly and then click on the **Save** button in the dialog box. Another **Save As** dialog box appears, see Figure 13.132.

4. Select the **Save externally (specify paths)** radio button and then click on the **OK** button in the dialog box. All the components and the assembly file are saved in the specified location, individually.

Hands-on Test Drive 1

Open the assembly, created in Tutorial 2 of Chapter 12, see Figure 13.133 and then create its exploded view similar to the one shown in Figure 13.134. You also need to create explode lines in the exploded view of the assembly.

Hands-on Test Drive 2

Create an assembly, as shown in Figure 13.135 by using the Top-down approach. Different views and dimensions of the individual components of the assembly are shown in Figures 13.136 through 13.139. All dimensions are in mm.

13.136

DETAIL A

Base

13.137

Moving Jaw

13.138

Fixed Jaw

13.139

Washer

Screw Bar

Jaw Screw

Summary

In this chapter, you have learned about creating assemblies by using the Top-down assembly approach. In the Top-down assembly approach, you can create all the components of an assembly in the Assembly environment itself. Once the assembly has been created, you can edit its components within the Assembly environment or by opening the component to be edited in the Part modeling environment. You can also edit the existing mates applied between the components of an assembly as well as create different types of patterns such as a linear component pattern, pattern driven component pattern, and chain component pattern in the Assembly environment. Similar to mirroring features in the Part modeling environment, you can also mirror components in the Assembly environment by using the **Mirror Components** tool. In addition, you can also create assembly features, suppress or unsuppress the components of an assembly, and insert components having multiple configurations in the Assembly environment.

Moreover, you can create sub-assemblies of the components of an assembly within the Assembly environment, dissolve the already created sub-assemblies into the individual components of an assembly, check interference among assembly components. You can also create, edit, or collapse the exploded view of an assembly, animate the exploded/collapse view of an assembly, add explode lines in an exploded view, and create the Bill of Material (BOM) of an assembly.

Questions

- In the _____ approach, you can create all the components of an assembly in the Assembly environment.

- In the _____ pattern, the pattern components are driven by the pattern instances of the other components of an assembly.

- The _____ pattern allows you to dynamically simulate a chain drive or a cable carrier in an assembly.

- In SOLIDWORKS, you can create three types of chain patterns: _____, _____, and _____ .

- The _____ tool is used for creating an exploded view of an assembly.

- In SOLIDWORKS, you can create _____ and _____ types of exploded views.

- The _____ tool is used for creating explode lines in an exploded view.

- You can edit the components of an assembly within the Assembly environment. (True/False)

- In SOLIDWORKS, you can create cut features in the Assembly environment. (True/False)

- In SOLIDWORKS, you cannot create sub-assemblies from the components of an assembly. (True/False)

Working with Drawings

This chapter discusses the following topics:

- Invoking the Drawing Environment
- Creating the Base View of a Model
- Invoking Drawing Environment from the Part or the Assembly Environment
- Creating a Model View
- Creating Projected Views
- Creating 3 Standard Views
- Working with Angle of Projection
- Defining the Angle of Projection
- Editing the Sheet Format
- Creating other Drawing Views
- Creating a Section View
- Creating an Auxiliary View
- Creating a Detail View
- Creating a Removed Section View
- Creating a Broken-out Section View
- Creating a Break view
- Creating a Crop View
- Creating an Alternate Position View
- Applying Dimensions
- Modifying the Driving Dimension
- Modifying Dimension Properties
- Controlling the Default Dimension/Arrow Style
- Adding Notes
- Adding a Surface Finish Symbol
- Adding a Weld Symbol
- Adding a Hole Callout
- Adding Center Marks
- Adding Centerlines
- Creating the Bill of Material (BOM)
- Adding Balloons
- Detailing Mode

After creating parts and assemblies, you need to generate 2D drawings. 2D drawings are the technical drawings, which are used to fully and clearly communicate the information about the end product to be manufactured. 2D drawing is not only a drawing, but also a language used by engineers to communicate ideas and information about engineered products. By using 2D drawings, a designer can communicate the information about the component to be manufactured to the engineers on the shop floor. Underscoring the importance of 2D drawings, the role of designers becomes very important in generating accurate and error-free drawings for production. Inaccurate or missing information about a component in drawings can lead to faulty production. Keeping this in mind, SOLIDWORKS provides you with an environment that allows you to generate error-free 2D drawings. This environment is known as the Drawing environment.

You can invoke the Drawing environment for generating 2D drawings by clicking on the **Drawing** button in the **Welcome** dialog box. Alternatively, you can invoke the Drawing environment by using the **New** tool available in the **Standard** toolbar as well as in the **File** menu of the SOLIDWORKS Menus. You can also invoke the Drawing environment by using the **Make Drawing from Part/Assembly** tool, which is available within the Part and Assembly environments. Methods for invoking the Drawing environment are discussed next.

Invoking the Drawing Environment

To invoke the Drawing environment, click on the **New** tool in the **Standard** toolbar. The **New SOLIDWORKS Document** dialog box appears, see Figure 14.1. Next, click on the **Drawing** button in this dialog box and then click on the **OK** button. The **Sheet Format/Size** dialog box appears, see Figure 14.2. The options in this dialog box are used for selecting the sheet size/format to be used for creating drawings. You can also invoke the **Sheet Format/Size** dialog box by clicking on the **Drawing** button in the **Welcome** dialog box. The options in the **Sheet Format/Size** dialog box are discussed next.

14.1

New SOLIDWORKS Document

Part
a 3D representation of a single design component

Assembly
a 3D arrangement of parts and/or other assemblies

Drawing
a 2D engineering drawing, typically of a part or assembly

Advanced   OK   Cancel   Help

Standard sheet size

By default, the **Standard sheet size** radio button is selected in the **Sheet Format/Size** dialog box. As a result, a list of standard sheet sizes appears in the **Selection** area of the dialog box, see Figure 14.2. You can select a required standard sheet size in this area for creating drawing views. Note that if the **Only show standard formats** check box is selected in the dialog box, then the list of standard sheet sizes appears as per the current drawing standard only, see Figure 14.2. If this check box is cleared, all the standard sheet sizes are listed in this area.

Display sheet format

By default, the **Display sheet format** check box is selected in the dialog box. As a result, a drawing sheet will be displayed with the default standard sheet format. You can also select a sheet format other than the default one by clicking on the **Browse** button in the dialog box. When you click on the **Browse** button, the **Open** dialog box appears. In this dialog box, select the required sheet format and then click on the **Open** button. A preview of the sheet format appears in the **Preview** area of the dialog box. If you clear the **Display sheet format** check box, a blank drawing sheet will be displayed for creating drawings. Note that the **Display sheet format** check box is enabled only if the **Standard sheet size** radio button is selected in the dialog box.

Custom sheet size

On selecting the **Custom sheet size** radio button in the dialog box, the **Width** and **Height** fields are enabled and the other options in the dialog box get disabled, see Figure 14.3. In the **Width** and **Height** fields, you can specify the custom width and height values for the drawing sheet.

After selecting the required sheet size by using the options of the **Sheet Format/Size** dialog box, click on the **OK** button. The Drawing environment is invoked with the drawing sheet of specified size/format. Also, the **Model View PropertyManager** appears on its left, see Figure 14.4.

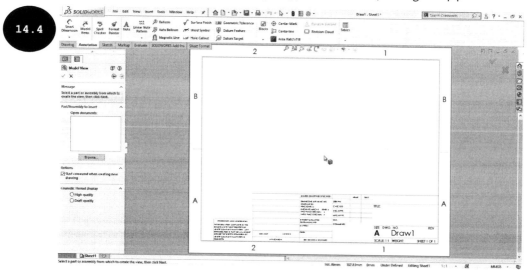

The options of the **Model View PropertyManager** are used for creating the base/model view of a component or an assembly. The method for creating the base/model view of a component or an assembly by using this PropertyManager is discussed next.

Note: The **Model View PropertyManager** appears each time on invoking the Drawing environment. This is because, in the **Options** rollout of the **Model View PropertyManager**, the **Start command when creating new drawing** check box is selected by default, see Figure 14.4. If you clear this check box, the **Model View PropertyManager** will not appear the next time you invoke the Drawing environment. In such a case, you can invoke the **Model View PropertyManager** by clicking on the **Model View** tool.

Creating the Base View of a Model Updated

To create the base view of a model, click on the **Browse** button in the **Part/Assembly to Insert** rollout of the **Model View PropertyManager**. The **Open** dialog box appears. In this dialog box, browse to the location where the model, whose drawing view is to be created, has been saved and then select it. Next, click on the **Open** button in the dialog box. A rectangular box representing the base view of the model is attached to the cursor, see Figure 14.5. Also, the options of the PropertyManager are modified. The options are discussed next.

14.5

Tip: You can also select a component or an assembly, for which drawing views are to be created from the **Open documents** field of the **Part/Assembly to Insert** rollout in the PropertyManager. Note that the models that are opened in the current session of SOLIDWORKS are displayed in the **Open documents** field of the PropertyManager. To select a model from the **Open documents** field, double-click on the name of the model in this field.

Reference Configuration

The drop-down list in the **Reference Configuration** rollout of the PropertyManager contains a list of all the configurations of the selected model. You can select the required configuration of the model for creating its drawing views. Note that if the selected model does not have any configuration created, then only the **Default** option is available in this drop-down list, see Figure 14.6.

Orientation

The options in the **Standard views** area of the **Orientation** rollout are used for selecting a standard view of the model to be created. By default, the **Front** button is activated in the **Standard views** area, see Figure 14.6. You can click on the required button in this area to create the respective front, top, right, left, back, bottom, or isometric drawing view.

You can also create dimetric or trimetric drawing views of the model by selecting the respective check box in the **More views** field of the rollout, see Figure 14.6.

By default, the **Preview** check box of the **Orientation** rollout is cleared, see Figure 14.6. As a result, an empty rectangular box appears attached to the cursor, which represents the selected view of the model. On selecting this check box, the preview of the selected standard view appears in the rectangular box. You can also create multiple drawing views of the selected component or the assembly by selecting the **Create multiple views** check box of this rollout, see Figure 14.6.

Import Options

The options in the **Import options** rollout are used for importing annotations of the model into the drawing view, see Figure 14.7. On selecting the **Import annotations** check box, the **Design annotations**, **DimXpert annotations**, **Include items from hidden features**, and **3D view annotations** check boxes are enabled in the rollout. Depending upon the check boxes selected in this rollout, the annotations of the model are imported into the drawing view. Note that the **DimXpert annotations** check box is enabled only if the model contains any dimxpert annotations.

Options

By default, the **Auto-start projected view** check box is selected in the **Options** rollout, see Figure 14.7. As a result, soon after creating the base/model view, the **Projected View PropertyManager** appears automatically. Also, a projected view of the model is attached to the cursor. The **Projected View PropertyManager** is used for creating the projected views of the model. You will learn more about projected views later in this chapter.

Display Style

The options in the **Display Style** rollout are used for selecting the type of display for the drawing view, see Figure 14.7. On selecting the **Wireframe** button, all the visible and hidden edges of the model appear as continuous lines in the drawing view, see Figure 14.8 (a).

If you select the **Hidden Lines Visible** button, the visible edges appear as continuous lines and the hidden edges appear as dotted lines in the drawing view, see Figure 14.8 (b). On selecting the **Hidden Lines Removed** button, only the visible edges of the model appear in the drawing view as continuous lines, see Figure 14.8 (c). On selecting the **Shaded With Edges** button, the drawing view is displayed in the shaded display style with the appearance of visible edges, see Figure 14.8 (d). If you select the **Shaded** button, the drawing view is displayed in the shaded model with the visible and hidden edges turned off, see Figure 14.8 (e).

Different display styles of a model

14.8

a)   b)   c)   d)   e)

Mirror

The **Mirror** rollout of the PropertyManager is used for creating a horizontal or vertical mirror view of the model relative to the selected standard view. To create the horizontal or vertical mirror view of the model, expand the **Mirror** rollout of the PropertyManager and then select the **Mirror view** check box, see Figure 14.9. Next, select the **Horizontal** or **Vertical** radio button to create the respective mirror view of the model relative to the selected standard view.

14.9

Scale

By default, the **Use sheet scale** radio button is selected in the **Scale** rollout, see Figure 14.10. As a result, the scale of the drawing view is the same as the scale of the drawing sheet. On selecting the **Use custom scale** radio button, the **Scale** field gets enabled. You can enter the required scale value in this field or choose a pre-defined scale value from the drop-down list which can be accessed by clicking on the down arrow ⌄ available in this field.

14.10

Dimension Type

The **Dimension Type** rollout is used for specifying the type of dimensions: True or Projected, for the drawing view. The Projected dimensions appear as 2D dimensions in a drawing view. They are mainly used in orthogonal views such as front, top, and right, see Figure 14.11. The True dimensions appear as accurate model dimensions in isometric, dimetric, and trimetric drawing views, see Figure 14.12.

Cosmetic Thread Display

The **High quality** and **Draft quality** radio buttons of the **Cosmetic Thread Display** rollout are used for controlling the display of cosmetic threads in the drawing view. On selecting the **High quality** radio button, the cosmetic threads appear in precise line fonts. On selecting the **Draft quality** radio button, the cosmetic threads appear with less detail in the drawing views.

After specifying the required settings for creating the base view such as type of view, display style, and scale factor, click on the drawing sheet to position the drawing view. The drawing view is created and is placed in the specified position on the drawing sheet. Also, the **Projected View PropertyManager** appears automatically. Notice, that on moving the cursor, a projected view appears attached to the cursor. You can create projection views by specifying the placement points in the drawing sheet. Most of the options of the **Projected View PropertyManager** are the same as those discussed earlier and are used for specifying the settings for the projected views. Figure 14.13 shows different projected views that can be created from the base view. Once you have created the required projected views, press the ESC key to exit the creation of projection views.

> **Note:** You can also control or modify the settings such as display style and scale factor for a drawing view that has been already placed in the drawing sheet. To modify the settings of a drawing view, click on the drawing view in the drawing sheet. The **Drawing View PropertyManager** appears. By using the options of this PropertyManager, you can control the settings of the selected drawing view. All options of this PropertyManager are same as those discussed earlier.

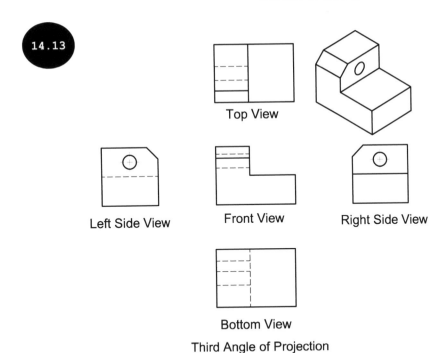

Top View

Left Side View   Front View   Right Side View

Bottom View

Third Angle of Projection

Invoking Drawing Environment from the Part or the Assembly Environment

Similar to invoking the Drawing environment by using the **New** tool and creating different drawing views of a model, you can also invoke the Drawing environment from the Part modeling environment or the Assembly environment. If you are in the Part modeling environment or in the Assembly environment, you can directly invoke the Drawing environment from there and start creating drawing views of a model that is currently available in the respective environment. To invoke the Drawing environment from the Part modeling environment or the Assembly environment, click on the down arrow available next to the **New** tool in the **Standard** toolbar. A flyout appears, see Figure 14.14.

Click on the **Make Drawing from Part/Assembly** tool in this flyout. The **Sheet Format/Size** dialog box appears. The options in this dialog box are used for specifying the required format/size of the drawing sheet and are same as those discussed earlier. After defining the format/size of the drawing sheet, click on the **OK** button. The Drawing environment is invoked with the display of the **View Palette Task Pane** to the right of the drawing sheet, see Figure 14.15.

Note that the bottom half area of the **View Palette Task Pane** displays drawing views of the model that were opened in the Part modeling environment or the Assembly environment. By using this task pane, you can drag and drop the required drawing view of the model onto the drawing sheet. The first placed view in the drawing sheet is known as a model, base, or parent view. As soon as you place the model/base view in the drawing sheet, the **Projected View PropertyManager** appears to the left of the drawing sheet. This is because the **Auto-start projected view** check box is selected in the upper half of the **View Palette Task Pane**, see Figure 14.15. Now, on moving the cursor in the drawing sheet, a projected view appears and attaches with the cursor, automatically. You can click on the drawing sheet to specify the position of the projected view. You can create multiple projected views one after another by clicking the left mouse button. Once you have created the required projected views, press the ESC key to exit the creation of projection views.

Creating a Model View

A model view is an independent view of a model. It is also known as base, first, or parent view. You can create a model view of a model by using the **Model View PropertyManager** and the **View Palette Task Pane**, which appears automatically on invoking the Drawing environment, as discussed earlier. Besides, you can also invoke the **Model View PropertyManager** by clicking on the **Model View** tool in the **Drawing CommandManager** for creating the model/base view of a model, see Figure 14.16.

Procedure for Creating a Model/Base View

1. Invoke the **Model View PropertyManager** by clicking on the **Model View** tool, if not invoked by default.
2. Click on the **Browse** button in the **Part/Assembly to Insert** rollout of the PropertyManager.

Tip: If the component or the assembly whose drawing view is to be created appears in the **Open documents** field of the **Part/Assembly to Insert** rollout in the PropertyManager, then you can directly select it from this field by double-clicking on it for creating its model view. The **Open documents** field displays a list of models, which are opened in the current session of SOLIDWORKS.

---

3. Select a part or an assembly, whose drawing views are to be created and then click on the **Open** button in the dialog box. A rectangular box appears attached to the cursor, which represents the model/base view of the selected part or assembly.
4. Specify the required settings such as standard view, display style, and scale factor for the drawing view by using the options in the PropertyManager.
5. Click on the drawing sheet to specify the position for the model/base view in the drawing sheet. The model view is created. Also, the **Projected View PropertyManager** appears. By using the **Projected View PropertyManager**, you can create the projected views of the model.
6. After creating the required views, press the ESC key to exit the creation of drawing views.

Creating Projected Views

Projected views are orthogonal views of an object, which are created by viewing an object from its different projection sides such as top, front, and side. Figure 14.17 and Figure 14.18 shows different projected views of an object.

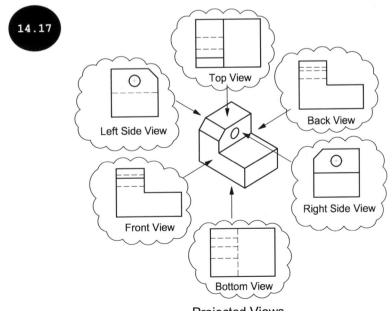

14.17

Left Side View • Top View • Back View • Right Side View • Front View • Bottom View

Projected Views

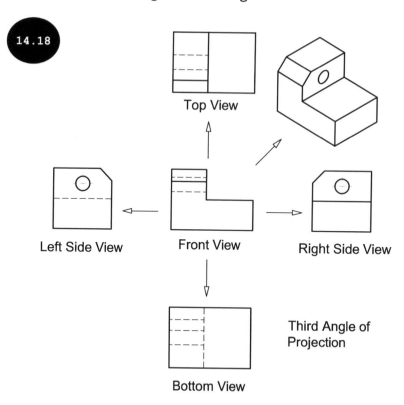

14.18

Top View

Left Side View   Front View   Right Side View

Third Angle of
Projection

Bottom View

You can create projected views by using the **Projected View PropertyManager**. As discussed earlier, the **Projected View PropertyManager** is invoked automatically as soon as you create the model/base view of a model by using the **Model View PropertyManager**. You can also invoke this PropertyManager by clicking on the **Projected View** tool in the **Drawing CommandManager**. The options in the **Projected View PropertyManager** are the same as those discussed earlier and are used for creating the projected views of a selected model/base view.

Procedure for Creating Projected Views

1. Invoke the **Projected View PropertyManager** by clicking on the **Projected View** tool.
2. Select a view as the model/base view whose projected views are to be created.

> **Note:** If only one drawing view is available in the drawing sheet then it is automatically selected for creating its projected views. Also, the preview of the projected view is attached to the cursor. However, if two or more than two views are available in the drawing sheet, then you need to select a view whose projected views are to be created.

3. Move the cursor to the required location in the drawing sheet and then click to specify the placement point for the projected view attached. You can continue creating other projected views by clicking the left mouse button in the drawing sheet.
4. Once you have created the projected views, press the ESC key.

Creating 3 Standard Views

In addition to creating drawing views by using the **Model View PropertyManager** and the **Projected View PropertyManager**, you can create three standard orthogonal views: front, top, and side by using the **Standard 3 View** tool of the **Drawing CommandManager**. On clicking this tool, the **Standard 3 View PropertyManager** appears. If the part or assembly, whose drawing views are to be created is displayed in the **Open documents** field of the PropertyManager then double-click on it. The three standard views are created automatically in the drawing sheet, see Figure 14.19. If the model is not displayed in the **Open documents** field, then click on the **Browse** button. The **Open** dialog box appears. In this dialog box, browse to a location where the required part or assembly has been saved and then select it. Next, click on the **Open** button in the dialog box.

14.19

Note: The creation of standard views depends upon the angle of projection defined for the drawing sheet. You can define the first angle of projection or the third angle of projection for creating the standard drawing views. The concept of angle of projection and the procedure to define the angle of projection for a drawing sheet are discussed next.

Working with Angle of Projection

Engineering drawings follow two types of angles of projection: first angle of projection and the third angle of projection. In the first angle of projection, the object is assumed to be kept in the first quadrant and the viewer views the object from the direction as shown in Figure 14.20. As the object has been kept in the first quadrant, its projections of views are on the respective planes as shown in Figure 14.20. Now on unfolding the planes of projections, the front view appears on the upper side and the top view appears on the bottom side. Also, the right side view appears on the left and the left side view appears on the right side of the front view, see Figure 14.21. Similarly, in the third angle of projection, the object is assumed to be kept in the third quadrant, see Figure 14.20. In this angle of projection, the projection of the front view appears on the bottom and the projection of the top view appears on the top side in the drawing. Also, the right side view appears on the right and the left side view appears on the left of the front view, see Figure 14.22.

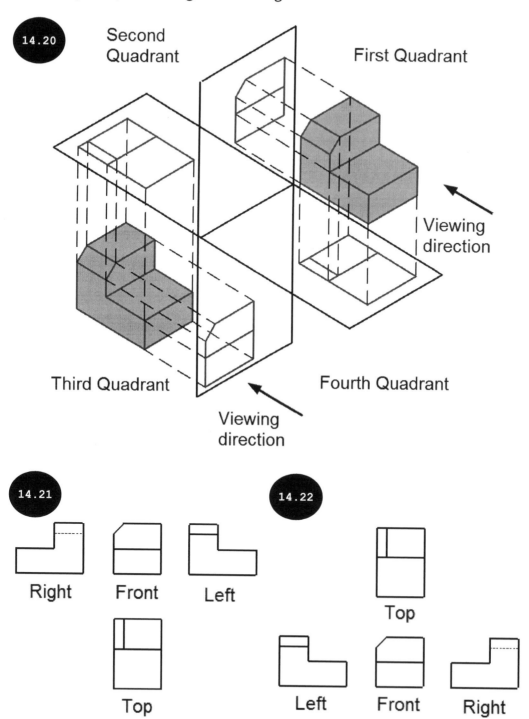

14.20

Second Quadrant

First Quadrant

Viewing direction

Third Quadrant

Fourth Quadrant

Viewing direction

14.21

Right   Front   Left

Top

14.22

Top

Left   Front   Right

Defining the Angle of Projection

In SOLIDWORKS, to define the required angle of projection for creating drawing views, select the **Sheet** node in the FeatureManager Design Tree and then right-click. A shortcut menu appears, see Figure 14.23. Next, click on the **Properties** option in the shortcut menu. The **Sheet Properties** dialog box appears, see Figure 14.24. In this dialog box, you can select the type of projection to be followed for creating drawing views by selecting the respective radio button in the **Type of projection** area of the dialog box. Next, click on the **Apply Changes** button to accept the change and to exit the dialog box.

Tip: In the **Sheet Properties** dialog box, you can also define the scale of the drawing sheet by using the **Scale** fields, refer to Figure 14.24. Alternatively, you can also define the sheet scale by selecting a pre-defined scale value in the **Scale** drop-down list available at the bottom right of the Status Bar, see Figure 14.25. In SOLIDWORKS 2020, on selecting the **User Defined** option in the **Scale** drop-down list, you can also define a custom scale for the drawing sheet. When you select this option, the **User Defined Scale** dialog box appears, see Figure 14.26. In the dialog box, enter the required sheet scale in x:x or x/x format and then click on the **OK** button.

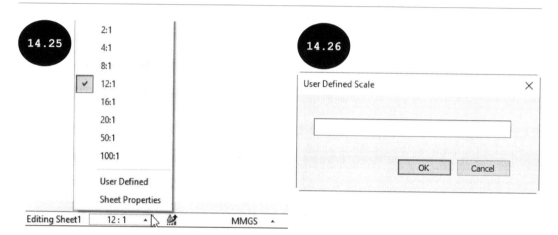

Editing the Sheet Format Updated

While invoking the Drawing environment, you can select the required sheet size and sheet format. Note that the sheet format contains title block, which has drawing information such as project name, drawn by, checked by, approved by, date, sheet number, and so on. You can create or edit the sheet format such that it matches the standard format of your company. To edit the sheet format of a sheet, select the **Sheet** node in the FeatureManager Design Tree and then right-click to display a shortcut menu, refer to Figure 14.23. Next, click on the **Edit Sheet Format** option in the shortcut menu. The editing mode for editing sheet format is invoked, see Figure 14.27. Now, you can edit or modify the existing text and lines of the title block. Also, you can add new lines and text in the title block by using the sketching tools of the **Sketch CommandManager**. To delete existing lines and text, select the lines and text of the title block to be deleted and then press the DELETE key. To edit the existing text, double-click on the text to be edited. The editing mode is invoked such that the text appears in the edit field. Now, you can write new text in the edit field. Once you have edited the sheet format, click on the Confirmation corner on the upper right corner of the drawing area to exit the editing mode and switch back to the drawing sheet.

Tip: In SOLIDWORKS 2020, you can also add surface finish and geometric tolerance annotations on the sheet format by using the respective tools available in the **Annotation CommandManager**. The method of adding surface finish annotations on the sheet format is same as adding them on a face of a model which is discussed later in this chapter with the only difference that the annotations on the sheet format do not include leaders.

After modifying the sheet format or creating a new sheet format, as per the requirement, you can also save it for future use in other drawings. To save the sheet format, click on **File > Save Sheet Format** in the SOLIDWORKS Menus. The **Save Sheet Format** dialog box appears. In this dialog box, specify the name and location for the sheet format and then click on the **Save** button.

Creating other Drawing Views

In SOLIDWORKS, in addition to creating orthogonal views such as front, top, and right of an object, you can also create the following types of drawing views:

- Section View
- Aligned Section View
- Auxiliary View
- Detail View
- Removed Section View
- Broken View
- Crop View
- Alternate Position View
- Broken-out Section View

Creating a Section View

A section view is created by cutting an object by using an imaginary cutting plane or a section line and then viewing the object from the direction normal to the cutting plane. Figure 14.28 shows a section view created by cutting an object using a cutting plane. A section view is used for illustrating internal features of the object clearly. It also reduces the number of hidden-detail lines, facilitates the dimensioning of internal features, shows cross-section, and so on. In SOLIDWORKS, you can create a full section view and a half section view by using the **Section View** tool of the **Drawing CommandManager**.

14.28

A

A   Viewing direction

Cutting Plane/Section line

Section View

SECTION A-A

Creating a Full Section View

Full section views are the most widely used section views in engineering drawings. In a full section view, an object is assumed to be cut through all its length by an imaginary cutting plane or a section line, refer to Figure 14.28. In SOLIDWORKS, you can create four types of full section views: horizontal, vertical, auxiliary, and aligned, by using the **Section View** tool.

To create a full section view, click on the **Section View** tool in the **Drawing CommandManager**. The **Section View Assist PropertyManager** appears, see Figure 14.29.

Section View

Note: In the Section View Assist PropertyManager, two tabs are available on its top: **Section** and **Half Section**. Out of which the **Section** tab is activated by default. As a result, the options to create a full section view appear in the PropertyManager. On activating the **Half Section** tab, the options to create a half section view appear. You can learn about creating half section views later in this chapter.

The **Cutting Line** rollout of the PropertyManager is used for selecting the type of cutting line for creating the respective full section view. You can create a vertical section view, horizontal section view, auxiliary section view, and aligned section view by using the respective buttons of the **Cutting Line** rollout. Different types of full section views are discussed next.

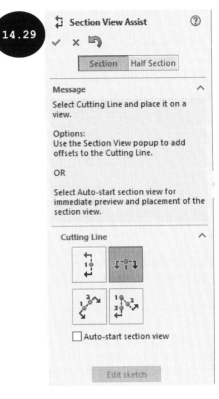

Creating a Horizontal/Vertical Section View

To create a horizontal section view, click on the **Horizontal** button in the **Cutting Line** rollout of the PropertyManager. A horizontal cutting line attached to the cursor appears. Next, select the **Auto-start section view** check box in the **Cutting Line** rollout. Now, move the cursor toward an existing drawing view and then click to specify the placement point for the horizontal cutting line. The preview of the horizontal section view appears attached to the cursor. Also, the **Section View PropertyManager** appears with additional options. Note that the direction of the arrows of the cutting section line represents the viewing direction. You can reverse the viewing direction by clicking on the **Flip Direction** button in the PropertyManager. In SOLIDWORKS, you can emphasize the outlines of the cutting faces such that they appear thicker than the object lines in the section view by selecting the **Emphasize outline** check box in the **Section View** rollout of the PropertyManager. Also, if needed, you can scale the hatch pattern of the section view by selecting the **Scale Hatch Pattern** check box of the **Section View** rollout in the PropertyManager. Next, click to specify the placement point for the horizontal section view at the required location on the drawing sheet. The horizontal section view is created, refer to Figure 14.28.

Note: If the **Auto-start section view** check box in the **Cutting Line** rollout is cleared, the **Section View** Pop-up toolbar appears soon after defining the placement point for the section line in a drawing view, see Figure 14.30. By using the tools of this Pop-up toolbar, you can modify or edit the section line, as required. Once you have edited or modified the section line, click on the green tick-mark in the Pop-up toolbar. The preview of the section view appears attached to the cursor based on the modified section line. Now, you can specify the placement point for the section view in the drawing sheet.

Similar to creating a horizontal section view, you can create a vertical section view by using the **Vertical** button of the **Cutting Line** rollout. Figure 14.31 shows a vertical section view created.

SECTION B-B

Note that if you are creating a section view of an assembly or a component having rib features, then soon after specifying the placement point for the section line, the **Section View** dialog box appears, see Figure 14.32.

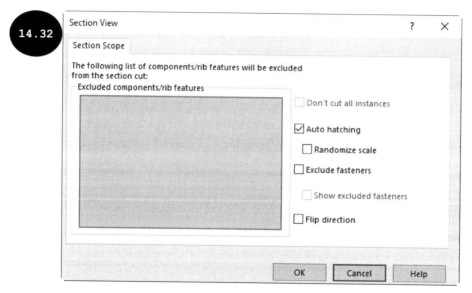

Note: The availability of the options in the **Section View** dialog box depends upon whether you are creating a section view of an assembly or a component having rib features. Figure 14.32 shows the **Section View** dialog box, which appears on creating the section view of an assembly.

By default, the **Excluded components/rib features** field is activated in the **Section View** dialog box. As a result, you can select components like fasteners and features like ribs to be excluded from the section cut. On selecting the **Auto hatching** check box, the alternate crosshatch patterns will be created between components of an assembly in the section view. In SOLIDWORKS, you can also randomize the hatch scale for the components having same material in the section view by selecting the **Randomize scale** check box. If this check box is cleared, the section view will be created by keeping the hatch scale identical for all the hatches of the components having same material. Once you have selected the components/features to be excluded, click on the **OK** button in the dialog box. A preview of the section view appears attached to the cursor, without cutting the selected components or features. Next, click to specify the placement point for placing the section view in the drawing sheet.

Tip: You can set the line font for the emphasized outlines of the cutting faces in the section view. For doing so, click on the **Options** tool in the **Standard** toolbar to invoke the **System Options** dialog box. Next, click on the **Document Properties** tab in the dialog box and then click on the **Line Font** option. Next, select the **Emphasized Section Outline** option in the **Type of edge** area of the dialog box and then set the font/style for the emphasized outlines using the options that appear in the dialog box.

Creating an Auxiliary Section View

An auxiliary section view is created by cutting an object using a sight line which is not parallel to any of the principal projection planes: frontal, horizontal, or profile and then viewing the object from the direction normal to the sight line, see Figure 14.33.

To create an auxiliary section view, click on the **Section View** tool to invoke the **Section View Assist PropertyManager**. Next, click on the **Auxiliary** button in the **Cutting Line** rollout. A section line is attached to the cursor. Move the cursor to an existing drawing view. Next, click to specify the center point of the section line and a placement point to define the angle of the section line. A preview of the auxiliary section view is attached to the cursor. If the **Section View** Pop-up toolbar appears soon after specifying the placement point then click on its green tick-mark to display the preview of the auxiliary section view. You can reverse the default viewing direction by clicking on the **Flip Direction** button in the PropertyManager. Next, click to specify the placement point for the auxiliary section view at the required location in the drawing sheet. The auxiliary section view is created, see Figure 14.33.

Creating an Aligned Section View

An aligned section view is created by cutting an object using the cutting section line, which comprises of two non-parallel lines and then straightening the cross-section by revolving it around the center point of the section line, see Figure 14.34.

Procedure for Creating an Aligned Section View

1. Invoke the **Section View Assist PropertyManager** by clicking on the **Section View** tool.
2. Click on the **Aligned** button in the **Cutting Line** rollout. A cutting section line, which comprises of two non-parallel lines gets attached to the cursor.
3. Move the cursor toward an existing drawing view as the parent view for creating the aligned section view.
4. Click to specify the center point for the cutting section line, see Figure 14.34.
5. Move the cursor to a distance and then click to specify the position for the first cutting line, see Figure 14.34.
6. Move the cursor to a distance and then click to specify the position for the second cutting line, see Figure 14.34. The preview of the aligned section view gets attached to the cursor.
7. Move the cursor to the required location and then click to specify the placement point for the aligned section view in the drawing sheet, see Figure 14.34.
8. Press ESC to exit.

SECTION A-A

Creating a Half Section View

A half section view is created by cutting an object using an imaginary cutting plane or section line that passes halfway through the object, see Figure 14.35. In SOLIDWORKS, you can create a half section view by using the **Section View** tool.

14.35

SECTION A-A

Procedure for Creating a Half Section View

1. Click on the **Section View** tool. The **Section View Assist PropertyManager** appears.

2. Click on the **Half Section** tab available at the top of the PropertyManager, see Figure 14.36. The options for creating pre-defined shape of half section views appear in the PropertyManager.

3. Click on the required button in the **Half Section** rollout of the PropertyManager. The respective half section cutting line gets attached to the cursor.

4. Move the cursor over an existing view in the drawing sheet and then click to specify the placement point for the half section cutting line at the required location. A preview of the half section view gets attached to the cursor.

5. If you want to flip the viewing direction, click on the **Flip Direction** button in the **Cutting Line** rollout of the PropertyManager or else skip this step.

6. Click to specify the position for the half section view at the required location in the drawing sheet. The half section view is created. Next, press the ESC key.

14.36

↹ **Section View Assist** ?

✓ ✗ ↰

| Section | **Half Section** |

Message ⌃

Select a Half Section Cutting Line and place it on a view.

Half Section ⌃

Edit sketch

Creating an Auxiliary View

An auxiliary view is a projected view, which is created by projecting the edges of an object normal to the edge of an existing drawing view, see Figure 14.37. You can create an auxiliary view by using the **Auxiliary View** tool in the **Drawing CommandManager**.

Procedure for Creating an Auxiliary View

1. Click on the **Auxiliary View** tool in the **Drawing CommandManager**.
2. Select an edge of an existing drawing view, see Figure 14.37. A preview of the auxiliary view gets attached to the cursor.
3. Click to specify the position of the auxiliary view in the drawing sheet, see Figure 14.37.
4. Press ESC to exit.

Creating a Detail View

A detail view is used for showing a portion of an existing drawing view in an enlarged scale, see Figure 14.38. You can define the portion of an existing drawing view to be enlarged by creating a circle or a closed sketch. You can create the detail view of a portion of an existing view by using the **Detail View** tool.

14.38

DETAIL B
SCALE 2 : 5

Procedure for Creating a Detail View

1. Click on the **Detail View** tool in the **Drawing CommandManager**. The **Detail View PropertyManager** appears. Also, you are prompted to draw a circle to define the portion of an existing drawing view to be enlarged.

2. Draw a circle around the portion of an existing view to be enlarged. The enlarged view of the portion of the existing view gets attached to the cursor. Also, the **Detail View PropertyManager** appears with additional options.

3. You can increase or decrease the default scale factor for the attached detail view by using the options of the **Scale** rollout in the PropertyManager, as required.

Note: In SOLIDWORKS, you can display the detail view with full outline around it by selecting the **Full outline** check box in the **Detail View** rollout of the PropertyManager, see Figure 14.39. Also, you can display the detail view without outline by selecting the **No outline** check box in the **Detail View** rollout of the PropertyManager, see Figure 14.39. Moreover, you can also display the detail view with a jagged outline by selecting the **Jagged outline** check box in the **Detail View** rollout, see Figure 14.39.

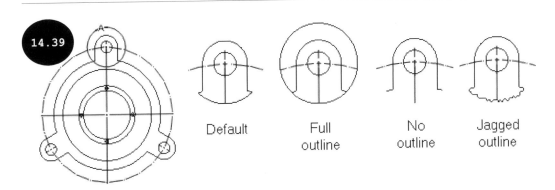

14.39

Default   Full   No   Jagged
                 outline   outline   outline

4.   After specifying the required settings for the detail view, move the cursor to the required location in the drawing sheet and then click to specify the placement point in the drawing sheet. The detail view is created.

5.   Press the ESC key to exit.

Note: In addition to defining the portion of a view to be enlarged by drawing a circle, you can also use a closed sketch, which defines the portion of a view to be enlarged. For doing so, before invoking the **Detail View** tool, first select an existing view and then draw a closed sketch by using the sketching tools of the **Sketch CommandManager**. Once the closed sketch is drawn, select it and then click on the **Detail View** tool. Figure 14.40 shows a detail view created by a closed sketch, which is drawn by using the **Spline** tool.

14.40

Creating a Removed Section View

A removed section view is used for showing a cross-sectional slice of an object at a specified location, see Figure 14.41. In this figure, the two cross-sectional slices of an object are shown at different locations.

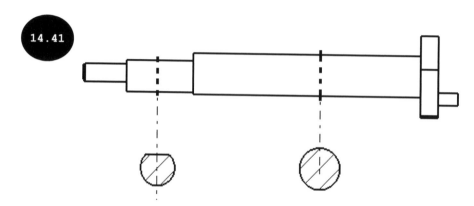

14.41

Procedure for Creating a Removed Section View

1. Click on the **Removed Section** tool in the **Drawing CommandManager**. The **Removed Section PropertyManager** appears.

2. Select two opposite or partially opposite edges of a drawing view one by one between which an object is to be sectioned, see Figure 14.42. A cutting line appears attached to the cursor. Also, the names of the selected edges appear in the **Edge** and **Opposed Edge** fields of the PropertyManager, respectively.

3. Make sure that the **Automatic** radio button is selected in the **Cutting Line Placement** rollout of the PropertyManager to define the position of the cutting line automatically between the selected edges.

> **Note:** On selecting the **Manual** radio button, you need to manually define the position of the cutting line between the selected edges by specifying two points.

4. Click to specify the placement point for the cutting line in the drawing view. A preview of the removed section view (slice) appears attached to the cursor, see Figure 14.42.

5. Click to specify the placement point for the removed section view in the drawing sheet. The removed section view is created.

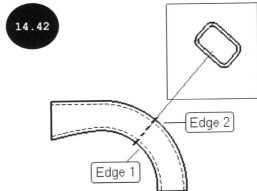

Creating a Broken-out Section View

A broken-out section view is created by removing the portion of an existing view up to a specified depth in order to view the inner details of an object, see Figure 14.43. You can define the portion of an existing view to be removed by drawing a closed sketch.

Before · After

Procedure for Creating a Broken-out Section

1. Click on the **Broken-out Section** tool in the **Drawing CommandManager**. The **Spline** tool is invoked to create a closed sketch for defining the portion to be removed.
2. Move the cursor over the existing drawing view whose portion is to be removed up to a specified depth.
3. Draw a closed profile around the portion of the existing drawing view to be removed. As soon as you draw a closed profile, the **Broken-out Section PropertyManager** appears.

Note: In SOLIDWORKS, you can also create broken-out section view on a section view, a detail view, and an alternate position view. You will learn about creating alternate position view later in this chapter.

---

4. Enter the depth value in the **Depth** field of the PropertyManager up to which the material is to be removed. Alternatively, you can select an edge or an axis of the view to define the depth by using the **Depth Reference** field of the PropertyManager.
5. Select the **Preview** check box to display the preview of the broken-out section view in the drawing sheet.
6. Click on the green tick-mark ✓ in the PropertyManager to accept the defined settings and to exit the PropertyManager. The broken-out section view is created, refer to Figure 14.43.

Creating a Break View

A break view is created by breaking an existing view using a pair of break lines such that the portion existing between the breaking lines is removed, see Figure 14.42. A break view is used for displaying a large scaled view on a small scale sheet by removing a portion of the view that has the same cross-section, see Figure 14.44.

14.44

Note: The dimension applied to a break view represents its actual dimension, see Figure 14.44. It is evident from this figure that even on breaking the view, the dimension value associated with it remains the same. You will learn more about applying dimensions later in this chapter.

Procedure for Creating a Break View

1. Click on the **Break View** tool. The **Break View PropertyManager** appears.
2. Move the cursor over an existing drawing view to be broken and then click on it. The first vertical or horizontal break line is attached to the cursor.

Note: The display of break line (vertical or horizontal) depends upon whether the **Add vertical break line** or the **Add horizontal break line** button is activated in the PropertyManager. If the **Add vertical break line** button is activated, a vertical break line appears and if the **Add horizontal break line** button is selected, a horizontal break line appears.

3. Make sure that the required button: **Add vertical break line** or **Add horizontal break line** is activated in the **Break View PropertyManager**.
4. Specify the placement point for the first break line by clicking the left mouse button on the required location of the drawing view. The second break line gets attached to the cursor.
5. Specify the placement point for the second break line in the view. The view is broken and the portion inside the break lines is removed, refer to Figure 14.44.

Note: You can also control the gap between the break lines by using the **Gap size** field of the PropertyManager. You can also select a required style or type for break lines by selecting the required button in the **Break line style** area of the PropertyManager. In SOLIDWORKS, you can also use the jagged break lines for breaking the view by selecting the **Jagged Cut** button in the **Break line style** area of the PropertyManager.

In SOLIDWORKS, you also can clip the sketch block in the break view by selecting the **Break sketch blocks** check box of the PropertyManager. If this check box is cleared, the sketch block will not be clipped in the break view. The method for creating sketch blocks are not covered in this textbook.

6. Click on the green tick-mark ☑ in the PropertyManager to confirm the creation of break view and to exit the PropertyManager.

Creating a Crop View

A crop view is created by cropping an existing view by using a closed sketch in such a way that only the portion that is lying inside the closed sketch is retained in the view, see Figure 14.45. You can create a crop view by using the **Crop View** tool. Note that to create a crop view, first you need to create a closed sketch by using the sketching tools of the **Sketch CommandManager**.

Before   After

Procedure for Creating a Crop View

1.   Select the view to be cropped.
2.   Draw a closed sketch around the portion of the view to be cropped, refer to Figure 14.45.
3.   Make sure that the sketch created is selected.
4.   Click on the **Crop View** tool. The crop view is created by retaining only the portion that lies inside the closed sketch. Next, press the ESC key.

Note: In SOLIDWORKS, after creating a crop view, you can display it with no outline or with a jagged outline. For doing so, select the crop view in the drawing sheet. The **Drawing View PropertyManager** appears. In this PropertyManager, expand the **Crop View** rollout and then select the required check box: **No outline** or **Jagged outline**.

Creating an Alternate Position View

In SOLIDWORKS, you can show or create an alternate position of an assembly in a drawing view by using the **Alternate Position View** tool, see Figure 14.46. You can also create multiple positions of an assembly in a drawing view by using this tool.

Procedure for Creating the Alternate Position View

1. Click on the **Alternate Position View** tool in the **Drawing CommandManager**. The **Alternate Position PropertyManager** appears.
2. Select a drawing view of an assembly. The **Alternate Position PropertyManager** is modified.

> **Note:** In the **Configuration** rollout of the PropertyManager, the **New configuration** radio button is selected by default. As a result, you can create a new alternative position for the assembly. Also, a default name for the alternate position appears in the **New Configuration Name** field. You can accept the default name or enter a new name in this field. The **Existing configuration** radio button is used for selecting the existing configuration of an assembly as the alternative view.

3. Make sure that the **New configuration** radio button is selected in the **Configuration** rollout.
4. Accept the default settings and then click on the green tick-mark ✔ in the PropertyManager. The Assembly environment is invoked with the display of the **Move Component PropertyManager** to the left of the graphics area.

> **Note:** In the **Move Component PropertyManager**, the **Free Drag** option is selected by default. As a result, you can freely drag the components of the assembly to the desired position.

5. Drag to rotate or move the components of the assembly whose alternate position is to be created to the desired position.
6. Once the desired position of the assembly components has been achieved, click on the green tick-mark ✔ in the **Move Component PropertyManager**. The Drawing environment is invoked again and the alternate position of the assembly components is created in the drawing view, refer to Figure 14.46. Note that the alternate position of the components is displayed in dotted lines.

Applying Dimensions

After creating various drawing views of a part or an assembly, you need to apply dimensions to them. In SOLIDWORKS, you can apply two types of dimensions: reference dimensions and driving dimensions. Reference dimensions are applied manually by using the dimension tools such as **Smart Dimension**, **Horizontal Dimension**, and **Vertical Dimension** whereas driving dimensions are generated automatically by retrieving the model dimensions. You can apply driving dimensions by using the **Model Items** tool of the **Annotation CommandManager**. The methods for applying both types of dimensions are discussed next.

Applying Reference Dimensions

You can apply reference dimensions by using the dimension tools such as **Smart Dimension**, **Horizontal Dimension**, and **Vertical Dimension** available in the **Dimension** flyout of the **Annotation CommandManager**, see Figure 14.47.

Applying reference dimension is the manual method of applying dimensions to drawing views and is the same as discussed in the Sketching environment while dimensioning sketch entities. For example, for applying dimension to a linear edge in a view, click on the **Smart Dimension** tool and then select the edge. The dimension value of the selected edge is attached to the cursor. Next, place the dimension to the required location in the drawing sheet.

Applying Driving Dimensions

Driving dimensions are applied automatically in drawing views by retrieving the model dimensions, which are applied in the sketches and features of the model. Note that on modifying a driving dimension, the respective sketch or feature of the model is also modified and vice-versa.

To apply driving dimensions, click on the **Model Items** tool in the **Annotation CommandManager**. The **Model Items PropertyManager** appears, see Figure 14.48. By using the options in the PropertyManager, you can retrieve dimensions, symbols, annotations, and other elements of the model in the drawing views. Some of the options of this PropertyManager are discussed next.

Source/Destination

The options in the **Source/Destination** rollout of the PropertyManager are used for selecting features or the entire model as the source and destination for retrieving and applying dimensions, symbols, annotations. By default, the **Selected feature** option is selected in the **Source** drop-down list. As a result, you can select a feature of the model in a drawing view as the source and destination for retrieving and applying dimensions, respectively. As soon as you select a feature in a drawing view, the dimensions of the selected feature are retrieved and applied to the drawing views. In Figure 14.49, the driving dimensions are applied to a hole feature by selecting it as the source and destination feature in the drawing view.

On selecting the **Entire model** option in the **Source** drop-down list, all dimensions, symbols, and annotations, which are applied in the model get retrieved and are applied in the drawing views. By default, the **Import items into all views** check box is selected in the **Source/Destination** rollout. As a result, items such as dimensions and annotations are applied to all views present in the drawing sheet.

Dimensions

The buttons in the **Dimensions** rollout of the PropertyManager are used for selecting the type of dimensions to be retrieved from the model and to be applied to the drawing views. On selecting the **Eliminate duplicates** check box in this rollout, duplicate dimensions in the drawing views will not be applied.

Annotations

The buttons in the **Annotations** rollout are used for selecting the type of annotations to be retrieved from the model and applied to the drawing views. You can click on the buttons to activate them in order to retrieve respective annotations in the drawing views. If you select the **Select all** check box, all the buttons of this rollout get activated, automatically.

Reference Geometry

The buttons in the **Reference Geometry** rollout are used for selecting the type of reference geometries such as planes, axis, and origin to be retrieved from the model and applied to the drawing views.

After selecting the required options in the **Model Items PropertyManager**, click on the green tick-mark in the PropertyManager. The respective dimensions, annotations, and reference geometries are retrieved and applied in the drawing views, see Figure 14.50.

> **Note:** Sometimes the driving dimensions applied in the drawing views neither appear in the required positions, nor do they maintain uniform spacing in the drawing views. You can drag the dimensions and place them in the required positions for maintaining proper spacing between them.

Modifying the Driving Dimension

On modifying a driving dimension in the Drawing environment, the same modification is reflected in the model as well. To modify a driving dimension, double-click on it in the drawing view. The **Modify** dialog box appears, see Figure 14.51. Enter the new dimension value in the field of this dialog box and then click on the green tick mark. The respective dimension and the feature of the model are modified accordingly.

14.51

Modify
✓ ✕ 🔋 ➚ ±₁₀
D2@Sketch Distance
140.00mm

Modifying Dimension Properties   Updated

In SOLIDWORKS, when you apply a dimension, it is applied with default properties. You can modify default dimension properties such as dimension style, tolerance, precision, and so on by using the **Dimension PropertyManager** that appears when a dimension is selected in the drawing sheet. To modify the dimension properties of a dimension, select it in the drawing sheet. The **Dimension PropertyManager** appears to the left of the drawing area, see Figure 14.52. The options in the **Dimension PropertyManager** are discussed next.

Value Tab

By default, the **Value** tab is activated in the **Dimension PropertyManager**. The options of this tab are used for modifying the properties related to the dimension value. The options are discussed next.

Style

The **Style** rollout of the **Value** tab is used for restoring default attributes such as dimension height, fonts, and arrow type. You can also add a new style, update existing style, delete style, save style, and load existing style in the current document by using the options of this rollout. The options of this rollout are discussed next.

14.52

Apply the default attributes to selected dimensions

This button of the **Style** rollout is used for applying the default dimension attributes such as dimension height, font, arrow type to the selected dimension. If you have modified dimension attributes, then on clicking this button, the dimension attributes will be restored back to the default.

Add or Update a Style

This button is used for adding a new dimension style or updating the existing dimension style. To add a new dimension style, specify different attributes such as dimension height, font, and arrow type, that you want in the new dimension style and click on the **Add or Update a Style** button. The **Add or Update a Style** dialog box appears, see Figure 14.53. Enter the name of the style to be added in the **Enter a new name or choose an existing name** field of this dialog box and then click the **OK** button. The new style is added and set as the current style for the document. Also, its name appears in the **Set a current Style** drop-down list of the **Style** rollout. You will learn more about specifying dimension attributes later in this section.

14.53

To update the existing dimension style, specify the required dimension attributes and click on the **Add or Update a Style** button of the **Style** rollout to display the **Add or Update a Style** dialog box. In this dialog box, click on the arrow on the right of the **Enter a new name or choose an existing name** field. A drop-down list appears. Select the dimension style to be updated. The **Update all annotations linked to this style** and **Break all links to this style** radio buttons are enabled in this dialog box. By default, the **Update all annotations linked to this style** radio button is selected. As a result, the modifications made in the attributes of the selected style reflect in all dimensions that are associated with it.

Note: If the modifications are not reflected in all dimensions of the style after choosing the **OK** button in the dialog box, then you need to click on the dimensions in the drawing sheet to update them.

On selecting the **Break all links to this style** radio button, the link between the selected dimension and the other dimensions assigned to the same style will be broken. In other words, the other dimensions associated with the selected dimension style will no longer be associated with it and modifications will only be reflected in the selected dimension.

Delete a Style

The **Delete a Style** button of the **Style** rollout is used for deleting an existing style, which is no longer required. To delete an existing style, select the style from the **Set a current Style** drop-down list of the **Style** rollout and then click on the **Delete a Style** button. The selected style is deleted from the current document.

Save a Style

The **Save a Style** button is used for saving a style as an external file so that the same style can be loaded in other documents as well. To save a style, select the style from the **Set a current Style** drop-down list and then click on the **Save a Style** button. The **Save As** window appears. Browse the location where the style is to be saved and then click on the **Save** button. The selected style is saved in the specified location with the *.sldstl* file extension.

Load Style

The **Load Style** button is used for loading the existing saved style in the current document. To load a style, click on the **Load Style** button. The **Open** window appears. Browse to a location where the style has been saved and then select it. Next, click on the **Open** button of the dialog box. The selected style is loaded in the current document and set as the current style.

Set a current Style

The **Set a current Style** drop-down list displays a list of all the styles that are added in the current document. By default, the **None** option is selected in this drop-down list. As a result, the default dimension style is used. You can select any dimension style from this drop-down list as the current dimension style for the document.

Tolerance/Precision

The options in the **Tolerance/Precision** rollout are used for specifying the tolerance and precision values for the selected dimension style. The options in this rollout are discussed next.

Tolerance Type

The **Tolerance Type** drop-down list is used for selecting the type of tolerance for the selected dimension style and dimension value. By default, the **None** option is selected in this drop-down list. As a result, no tolerance has been applied. Depending upon the type of tolerance selected in this drop-down list, the corresponding fields are enabled below this drop-down list in the **Tolerance/Precision** rollout in order to specify tolerance values. Figure 14.54 shows a dimension with a symmetric tolerance value of 0.05 mm applied.

Unit Precision

The **Unit Precision** drop-down list is used for selecting the unit of precision or number of digits after the decimal point in the dimension value.

Tolerance Precision

The **Tolerance Precision** drop-down list is used for selecting the precision or number of digits after the decimal point in the tolerance value.

Tolerance modifier

The options in the **Tolerance modifier** rollout are used for adding geometric symbols and text to the selected dimension and its tolerance limits, see Figure 14.55. Note that this rollout is not available if the **None** or **Basic** tolerance type is selected in the **Tolerance Type** drop-down list of the **Tolerance/Precision** rollout. The options in the **Tolerance modifier** rollout are discussed next.

General

On selecting the **General** radio button in the **Tolerance modifier** rollout, you can add symbols and text to the entire dimension, see Figure 14.55.

Specified limits

On selecting the **Specified limits** radio button, you can add symbols and text to the upper and lower tolerance limits of the dimension, see Figure 14.56. Note that the **Specified limits** radio button is enabled only when the **Bilateral, Limit, Fit, Fit with tolerance,** or **Fit (tolerance only)** option is selected in the **Tolerance Type** drop-down list of the **Tolerance/Precision** rollout.

Primary Value

The **Primary Value** rollout is used for controlling the information of the primary dimension value. The primary dimension value is the original dimension value of entities. The options in this rollout are discussed next.

Name

The **Name** field of the **Primary Value** rollout is used for displaying the name of the dimension selected. By default, the default names are assigned to the dimensions. You can enter a new name for the selected dimension in this field. Note that the name entered in this field is automatically followed by a suffix such as *@Sketch1* depending upon the dimension.

Dimension value

The **Dimension Value** field of the **Primary Value** rollout is used for modifying the dimension value of the selected dimension. You can enter a new dimension value in this field. The value entered in this field drives the entity.

> **Note:** The **Name** and **Dimension value** fields of the **Primary Value** rollout are enabled only when the selected dimension is a driving dimension that is applied by using the **Model Items** tool of the **Annotation CommandManager**.

Override value

On selecting the **Override value** check box in the **Primary Value** rollout, you can override the original dimension value by entering a new dimension value in the **Primary** field that appears below this check box. Note that the override dimension value is not the actual dimension of the entity.

Dimension Text

The **Dimension Text** rollout is used for adding text and geometric symbols for the selected dimension style and dimension text. The options in this rollout are discussed next.

Add Parenthesis

The **Add Parenthesis** button of the **Dimension Text** rollout is used for displaying dimension as a driven or reference dimension with parentheses, see Figure 14.57 (a).

Inspection Dimension

The **Inspection Dimension** button is used for displaying dimension with inspection, see Figure 14.57 (b).

Center Dimension

The **Center Dimension** button is used for displaying dimension text at the center of the extension lines of the dimension. Note that when you drag dimension text, the text snaps to the center of the extension line, see Figure 14.57 (c).

Offset Text

The **Offset Text** button is used for displaying dimension text at an offset distance from the dimension line by using a leader, see Figure 14.57 (d).

14.57

| Add Parenthesis (a) | Inspection Dimension (b) | Center Dimension (C) | Offset Text (d) |

Text Field

The **Text** field displays < DIM >, where DIM represents the dimension value. You can add text, prefixes, and suffixes before or after < DIM > in the field. Figure 14.58 shows a dimension value after adding 'L –' in front of < DIM > in the **Text** field.

14.58

L-50

Note: If you delete < DIM > from the **Text** field, the dimension value will also be deleted or removed from the drawing area. Also, the **Add Value** button ⌗ gets enabled in the **Dimension Text** rollout. On choosing the **Add Value** button ⌗, the dimension value gets restored in the drawing area. Also, < DIM > is displayed again in the **Text** field.

Left Justify/Center Justify/Right Justify

The **Left Justify**, **Center Justify**, and **Right Justify** buttons are used for defining the dimension text justifications to left, center, and right, respectively.

Top Justify/Middle Justify/Bottom Justify

The **Top Justify**, **Middle Justify**, and **Bottom Justify** buttons are used for defining the dimension text justifications to top, middle, and bottom, respectively.

Symbols

The **Symbols** area of the rollout is used for adding different types of symbols to the selected dimensions, see Figure 14.59. To add a symbol, click to place the cursor where you want to insert or add symbol in the **Text** field and then click on the respective symbol button. The selected symbol is added in the field as well as displayed in the drawing area. On clicking on the **More Symbols** button of this area, a flyout appears with the display of additional symbols. You can click on the required symbol to be added in the dimension. If you click on the **More Symbols** option in this flyout, the **Symbol Library** dialog box appears, see Figure 14.60.

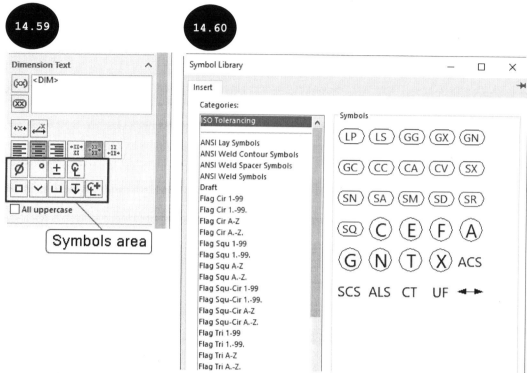

All uppercase

In SOLIDWORKS 2020, you can choose to display all dimension text in uppercase by selecting the **All uppercase** check box in the **Dimension Text** rollout.

Dual Dimension

The **Dual Dimension** rollout is used for displaying dual or alternative dimension measurement for entities. By default, this rollout is collapsed. As a result, the dimension values of entities are displayed only in the current document's unit system. To display dimensions in dual dimension unit, enable the **Dual Dimension** rollout by selecting the check box in its title bar. Next, expand the **Dual Dimension** rollout by clicking on the arrow in the **Dual Dimension** rollout. The options of the **Dual Dimension** rollout get enabled. Also, the default dual dimension unit along with the current document unit are displayed in the selected dimension, see Figure 14.61. You can specify a precision value and tolerance as required for the dual dimension by using the **Unit Precision** and **Tolerance Precision** drop-down lists of the expanded **Dual Dimension** rollout.

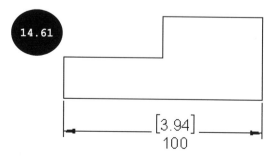

Note: You can also specify a required unit system for dual dimensions by using the **Document Properties - Units** dialog box. For doing so, click on the **Options** tool in the **Standard** toolbar. The **System Options - General** dialog box appears. In this dialog box, click on the **Document Properties** tab and then select the **Units** option. The **Document Properties - Units** dialog **box** appears. Next, specify the dual dimension unit in the field corresponding to the **Unit** column and **Dual Dimension Length** field in the dialog box.

Leaders Tab

The options in the **Leaders** tab of the **Dimension PropertyManager** are used for controlling the properties of dimension leader. Figure 14.62 shows the PropertyManager with the **Leaders** tab activated. The options in this tab are discussed next.

14.62

Witness/Leader Display

The **Witness/Leader Display** rollout is used for specifying parameters for dimension arrows. The options in this rollout are discussed next.

Outside

The **Outside** button is used for placing dimension arrows outside the extension lines of the dimension, see Figure 14.63 (a).

Inside

The **Inside** button is used for placing dimension arrows inside the extension lines of the dimension, see Figure 14.63 (b).

Smart

By default, the **Smart** button is activated in this rollout. As a result, the placement of the arrows is either inside or outside the extension lines depending on the availability of space between the extension lines of dimensions. For example, if the space available between the extension lines of a dimension is not adequate to place arrows inside, then the arrows are automatically placed outside the extension lines.

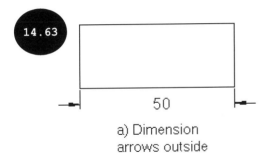

14.63

a) Dimension
arrows outside

b) Dimension
arrows inside

Directed Leader

The **Directed Leader** button is used for changing the orientation of a leader at an angle with respect to the surface on which it is applied in the Part modeling environment, see Figure 14.64. Note that this button is enabled only when the selected leader is applied on a cylindrical surface by using the tools available in the **MBD Dimensions CommandManager**.

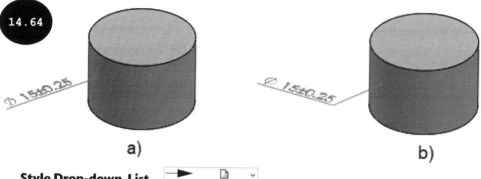

a) b)

Style Drop-down List

The **Style** drop-down list of the rollout is used for selecting the type of arrow style to be used for the selected dimension.

Radius

The **Radius** button is used for converting a diameter dimension to a radius dimension. Note that this button is enabled only if the selected dimension is either a diameter dimension or a radius dimension. On selecting the **Radius** button, the selected diameter dimension changes to radius dimension. Also, three buttons: **Foreshorten**, **Solid Leader**, and **Open Leader** get enabled below this button in the rollout, see Figure 14.65. By using these buttons, you can specify the type of leader for the radius dimension, see Figure 14.66.

Diameter

The **Diameter** button is used for converting a radius dimension to a diameter dimension. Note that this button is enabled only if the selected dimension is either a diameter dimension or a radius dimension. On selecting the **Diameter** button, the selected radius dimension changes to diameter dimension. Also, four buttons: **Two Arrows / Solid Leader**, **Two Arrows / Open Leader**, **One Arrow / Solid Leader**, and **One Arrow / Open Leader** appear below the **Diameter** button, see Figure 14.67. These buttons are used for specifying the type of leader, see Figure 14.68.

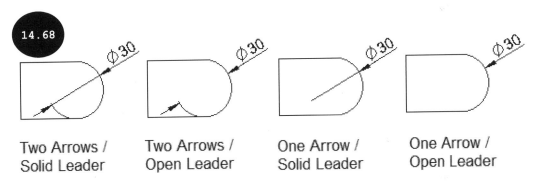

> **Note:** The **Two Arrows / Solid Leader** and **Two Arrows / Open Leader** buttons are enabled only when the **Use document second arrow** check box is cleared in the rollout. Besides, the availability of the buttons in the rollout depends upon the type of drafting standard selected in the **Document Properties - Drafting Standard** dialog box. To set the drafting standard, click on the **Options** tool in the **Standard** toolbar and then click on the **Document Properties** tab in the **System Options - General** dialog box that appears. Next, select the required drafting standard in the **Overall drafting standard** drop-down list of the dialog box.

Linear

The **Linear** button is used for displaying the diameter dimension as a linear diameter dimension. On selecting the **Linear** button, the selected diameter dimension changes to linear diameter dimension in the drawing. Also, two buttons: **Perpendicular To Axis** and **Parallel To Axis** get enabled. By using these buttons you can define whether the linear diameter dimension is perpendicular or parallel to the axis of the object.

Use document second arrow

The **Use document second arrow** check box is used for specifying the second arrow style for diameter dimension. By default, this check box is selected. As a result, the second arrow of the diameter dimension is specified as per the default document settings. Note that this check box is available only when the selected dimension is a diameter dimension or a radius dimension.

Note: To specify the default document settings for the second arrow of the diameter dimension, click on the **Options** tool in the **Standard** toolbar. The **System Options - General** dialog box appears. Next, click on the **Document Properties** tab and then expand the **Dimensions** node by clicking on the plus (+) sign available in front of it. Next, select the **Diameter** option from the expanded **Dimensions** node. The name of the dialog box is changed to **Document Properties - Diameter**. Now, you can specify the document settings for the second arrow of diameter dimensions by using the **Display second outside arrow** and **Display with solid leader** check boxes of the dialog box. On selecting the **Display second outside arrow** check box, the second arrow of the diameter dimension appears outside. If you select the **Display with solid leader** check box, then the second arrow for diameter dimension appears with solid leader.

Use document bend length

The **Use document bend length** check box is used for specifying the dimension leader length after the bend. If this check box is selected, then the default bend length, which is specified in the **Document Properties - Dimensions** dialog box is used for dimensions. However, if you clear this check box, you can specify the bend length for the selected dimension leader in the field available below this check box.

Note: To specify the default bend settings for leaders, click on the **Options** tool in the **Standard** toolbar. The **System Options - General** dialog box appears. In this dialog box, click on the **Document Properties** tab and then select the **Dimensions** node. The options related to dimension styles appear to the right of the dialog box. Also, the name of the dialog box changes to **Document Properties - Dimensions**. In this dialog box, specify the default bend length for dimension leaders in the **Leader length** field of the **Bent leaders** area.

Leader/Dimension Line Style

The options in the **Leader/Dimension Line Style** rollout are used for specifying style and thickness properties for the dimension leader. By default, the **Use document display** check box is selected in this rollout. As a result, the default properties of the leader style specified in the **Document Properties** dialog box are used. When you clear this check box, the **Leader Style** and **Leader Thickness** drop-down lists get enabled in this rollout. By using these drop-down lists, you can specify the style and the thickness for the selected dimension leader.

You can also specify default leader style and thickness for angle dimensions, arc length, chamfer, hole, linear, ordinate, and radius dimensions. To specify the default leader style and thickness for angle dimension, click on the **Options** tool in the **Standard** toolbar. The **System Options - General** dialog box appears. In this dialog box, click on the **Document Properties** tab and then expand the **Dimensions** node by clicking on the plus (+) sign available in front of it. Next, select the **Angle** option in the expanded **Dimensions** node. The name of the dialog box changes to **Document Properties - Angle**. In this dialog box, you can specify default leader style and thickness for angular dimensions by using the **Leader Style** and **Leader Thickness** drop-down lists of the **Leader Style** area. Similarly, you can specify the default leader style and thickness for arc length, chamfer, hole, linear, ordinate, and radius dimensions.

Custom Text Position

The options of the **Custom Text Position** rollout are used for customizing the position of dimension text with respect to the dimension leader. By default, this rollout is collapsed. As a result, the dimension text and leader are placed as per the default settings. Expand the **Custom Text Position** rollout by selecting the check box available in front of its title bar. If you click on the **Solid Leader, Aligned Text** button in the expanded rollout, the selected dimension will have the solid dimension leader with aligned dimension text, see Figure 14.69. On clicking the **Broken Leader, Horizontal Text** button, the selected dimension will have the broken dimension leader with horizontal dimension text, see Figure 14.69. On the other hand, if you click on the **Broken Leader, Aligned Text** button, the selected dimension will have the broken dimension leader with aligned dimension text, see Figure 14.69.

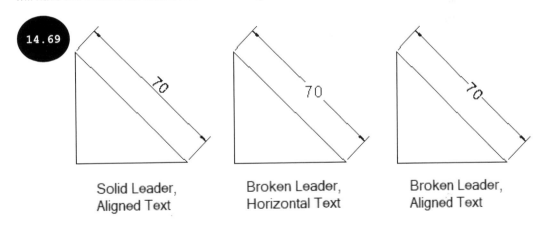

Solid Leader,
Aligned Text

Broken Leader,
Horizontal Text

Broken Leader,
Aligned Text

Other Tab

The options in the **Other** tab of the **Dimension PropertyManager** are discussed next.

Override Units

The **Override Units** rollout is used for overriding the default unit specified in the **Document Properties - Units** dialog box. For doing so, expand the **Override Units** rollout by selecting the check box in front of its title bar, see Figure 14.70. Next, select the unit type as the override unit for the selected dimension in the **Length Units** drop-down list of the rollout.

Note: The availability of other options in the **Override Units** rollout depends upon the type of unit selected in the **Length Units** drop-down list. For example, if **Inches** is selected in the **Length Units** drop-down list, then the **Decimal** and **Fractions** radio buttons become available in the **Override Units** rollout of the PropertyManager. You can select the required radio button in the rollout to display the override unit either in decimal or fractions.

Text Fonts

The **Text Fonts** rollout is used for specifying the font for the selected dimension. By default, the **Use document font** check box is selected in the rollout. As a result, the default dimension font is used for all dimensions. However, if you clear the **Use document font** check box, then the **Font** button gets enabled below this check box. Click on the **Font** button. The **Choose Font** dialog box appears, see Figure 14.71. By using this dialog box, you can specify the required font, font style, and dimension text height for the selected dimension.

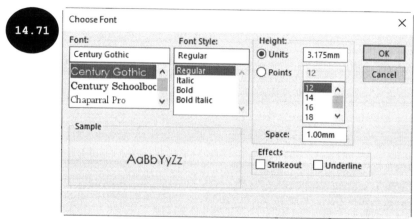

To specify the default dimension font for dimensions, click on the **Options** tool in the **Standard** toolbar. The **System Options - General** dialog box appears. In this dialog box, click on the **Document Properties** tab and then select the **Dimensions** option. Next, click on the **Font** button in the **Text** area of the dialog box. The **Choose Font** dialog box appears. Now, you can specify default font, font style, and text height for dimensions by using this **dialog** box. Once the default dimension font for dimensions has been set, click on the **OK** button in the dialog box.

Options

The **Options** rollout is provided with the **Read only** and **Driven** check boxes. On selecting the **Read only** check box, the selected dimension becomes read only and cannot be modified. Similarly, on selecting the **Driven** check box, the selected dimension becomes driven or reference dimension which cannot drive the entity.

Note: Similarly, you can modify the properties of dimensions in the Sketching environment by using the **Dimension PropertyManager**. The options for modifying dimension properties of a dimension in the Sketching environment are same as discussed above.

Controlling the Default Dimension/Arrow Style

In SOLIDWORKS, you can control dimension and arrow styles such as dimension font, dimension height, and arrow height by using the options in the **Document Properties - Dimensions** dialog box. To invoke this dialog box, click on the **Options** tool in the **Standard** toolbar. The **System Options - General** dialog box appears. Next, click on the **Document Properties** tab in the dialog box and then click on the **Dimensions** option. The name of the dialog box changes to **Document Properties - Dimensions**, see Figure 14.72. In this dialog box, click on the **Font** button in the **Text** area. The **Choose Font** dialog box appears. By using this dialog box, you can specify the required font, style, and height for dimension text. Next, click on the **OK** button in the **Choose Font** dialog box.

You can also control the dimension arrow height by using the options in the **Arrows** area of the **Document Properties - Dimensions** dialog box, see Figure 14.72. After specifying the settings for the dimension and arrow styles, click on the **OK** button.

14.72

Adding Notes

In SOLIDWORKS, you can add notes on a drawing sheet by using the **Note** tool. Generally, adding notes in drawings is used for conveying or providing additional information that is not available in the drawing views.

To add a note, click on the **Note** tool in the **Annotation CommandManager**. The **Note PropertyManager** appears, see Figure 14.73. Also, a rectangular box gets attached to the cursor. Now, specify the required settings such as text style, text format, type of leader, and leader style for the note by using the options in the PropertyManager. Next, move the cursor over an entity of a drawing view to add the note. The preview of the note with the leader attached to the entity of the drawing view appears. Next, click on the entity for adding the note. The leader arrow is

14.73

attached to the selected entity. Now, move the cursor to the required location and then click to place the note. An edit box and the **Formatting** toolbar appear. Now, you can type text in the edit box. You can use the **Formatting** toolbar to control the formatting of the text such as font, style, height, and alignment. Next, click anywhere on the drawing sheet. The note is added to the selected entity, see Figure 14.74. You can also add a note anywhere in the drawing sheet without selecting any entity.

14.74

Adding a Surface Finish Symbol

In SOLIDWORKS, you can add a surface finish symbol to specify the surface texture/finish for a face of a model. A surface finish symbol has three components: surface roughness, waviness, and lay, see Figure 14.75. Specifications for the surface finish given in a surface finish symbol are used to machine the respective surface of the object. You can add surface finish symbol to an edge of a surface in a drawing view by using the **Surface Finish** tool.

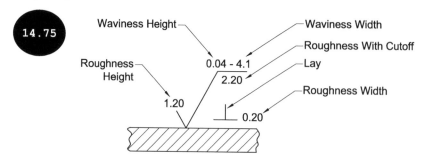

14.75

To add a surface finish symbol, click on the **Surface Finish** tool in the **Annotation CommandManager**. The **Surface Finish PropertyManager** appears, see Figure 14.76. Also, the default selected surface finish symbol gets attached to the cursor. Select the required type of surface finish symbol to be added from the **Symbol** rollout of the PropertyManager. Next, in the **Symbol Layout** rollout, specify the required specification for the surface finish (roughness, waviness, and lay) in the respective fields.

If needed, you can rotate the surface finish symbol at an angle by using the options in the **Angle** rollout of the PropertyManager. By using the options of the **Leader** rollout, you can select the type of leader to be attached to the surface finish symbol. Once you have specified the surface finish specification, move the cursor over the required edge in the drawing view and then click on it when it gets highlighted. The surface finish symbol is applied and attached to the selected edge, see Figure 14.77.

Adding a Weld Symbol

A weld symbol is added in a drawing view in order to represent the welding specification used while welding two parts. To add a weld symbol, click on an edge of a model in the drawing view, and then click on the **Weld Symbol** tool in the **Annotation CommandManager**. The **Properties** dialog box appears, see Figure 14.78. Also, the **Weld Symbol PropertyManager** appears to the left of the drawing sheet. By using the **Properties** dialog box, you can specify the welding properties to be included in the weld symbol. Note that the availability of options in the **Properties** dialog box depends upon the type of drafting standard selected in the **Document Properties - Drafting Standard** dialog box. Once you have specified the welding properties, click on the **OK** button in the dialog box. The weld symbol is added in the selected edge of the model, see Figure 14.79.

Tip: To invoke the **Document Properties - Drafting Standard** dialog box for specifying the drafting standard, click on the **Options** button in the **Standard** toolbar. The **System Options - General** dialog box appears. In this dialog box, click on the **Document Properties** tab. The **Document Properties - Drafting Standard** dialog box appears. Now, select the required type of drafting standard to be followed in the drawing by using the **Overall drafting standard** drop-down list of the dialog box. Next, close the dialog box.

Adding a Hole Callout   Updated

In SOLIDWORKS, you can add a hole callout to a hole in a drawing view. A hole callout contains hole specifications such as diameter and type of hole, see Figure 14.80. Note that on modifying the hole parameters of a model in the Part modeling environment, the respective hole callout gets updated accordingly in the Drawing environment.

To add a hole callout to a hole in a drawing view, click on the **Hole Callout** tool in the **Annotation CommandManager**. The symbol of the hole callout gets attached to the cursor. Move the cursor over the hole for adding the hole callout in a drawing view and then click the left mouse button on the hole when it gets highlighted. The preview of the hole callout gets attached to the cursor. Now, move the cursor to the required location and then click to specify the placement point for the hole callout, see Figure 14.80. Note that a hole callout also includes the mirrored holes in the count.

Note: In SOLIDWORKS 2020, you can also add hole callouts to cross-sectioned holes in section views, broken-out section views, and detail views. For doing so, click on the **Hole Callout** tool in the **Annotation CommandManager**. The symbol of the hole callout gets attached to the cursor. Move the cursor over an edge (side edge) of a hole cross-section in a section view, broken-out section view, or detailed view and then click the left mouse button when the hole edge gets highlighted. A preview of a hole callout gets attached to the cursor. Now, move the cursor to the required location and then click to specify the placement point for the hole callout. Note that to select the top or the bottom hole edge for adding a hole callout, you need to press SHIFT key.

In SOLIDWORKS, you can also add hole callouts to the advanced holes which are created by using the **Advanced Hole** tool in the Part modeling environment. You can also reverse the callout order of the advanced hole when you place it on the far side of the face by selecting the **Reverse callout order** check box of the **Dimension PropertyManager**, which appears to the left of the drawing sheet. Besides, you can add additional text, above or below the hole callout by using the **Text Above** and **Text Below** fields of the PropertyManager.

> **Note:** In SOLIDWORKS 2020, you can also add cosmetic thread callouts by using the **Smart Dimension** tool. For doing so, invoke the **Smart Dimension** tool and then select a circular edge of a cosmetic thread in a view. A preview of a thread callout gets attached to the cursor. Now, move the cursor to the required location and then click to specify the placement point for the thread callout. Note that to add cosmetic thread callout in a side view or section view, you need to select two linear thread edges one by one.

Adding Center Marks

Center marks are used as references for dimensioning circular edges, slot edges, or circular sketch entities in drawing views. To add center marks, click on the **Center Mark** tool in the **Annotation CommandManager**. The **Center Mark PropertyManager** appears, see Figure 14.81. By using this PropertyManager, you can add center marks automatically as well as manually.

To add center marks automatically to all holes, fillets, slots, or to all of them in a drawing view, select the respective check boxes such as **For all holes** and **For all fillets** in the **Auto Insert** rollout of the PropertyManager. Next, select a drawing view for adding center marks. The center marks are added automatically in the drawing view, depending upon the check boxes selected. In the automatic method of adding center marks, you can further control the connection among the center marks by using the check boxes: **Connection lines**, **Circular lines**, **Radial lines**, and **Base center mark** in the **Options** area of the **Auto Insert** rollout, see Figures 14.82 through 14.85. Note that the **Options** area appears after selecting a check box in the **Auto Insert** rollout, see Figure 14.86.

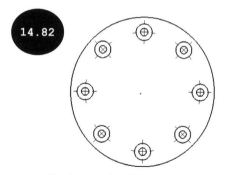

Center mark with connection lines

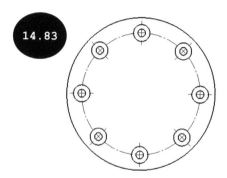

Center mark with circular lines

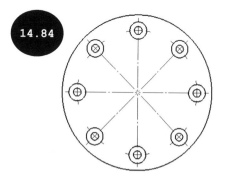

Center mark with radial lines

Center mark with base center mark

To add center marks manually, invoke the **Center Mark PropertyManager** and then move the cursor over a circular edge, a slot edge, or a circular sketch entity in a drawing view. Next, click on the entity when it gets highlighted. The center mark is added. Similarly, you can add center marks to the other entities of drawing views manually. In the manual method of adding center marks, you can select the type of center marks to be added by activating the respective button in the **Manual Insert Options** rollout of the PropertyManager, see Figure 14.87.

Once you have added center marks either by manual or automatic method, click on the green tick-mark ✓ in the PropertyManager.

Adding Centerlines

Centerlines are used as references for dimensioning circular cut features and hole features in drawing views, see Figure 14.88. In SOLIDWORKS, you can add a centerline between two linear edges that represent the edges of a circular cut or hole feature in a drawing view by using the **Centerline** tool, see Figure 14.88.

To add a centerline, click on the **Centerline** tool in the **Annotation CommandManager**. The **Centerline PropertyManager** appears. Next, select two linear edges one by one by clicking the left mouse button. The centerline is added at the center of the two selected edges, see Figure 14.88. You can also select two sketch segments, or a single cylindrical, conical, toroidal, or swept feature for adding a centerline.

Creating the Bill of Material (BOM)

After creating all the required drawing views of an assembly in the Drawing environment, you need to create the Bill of Material. The Bill of Material (BOM) contains all the required information such as the number of parts used in an assembly, part number, quantity of each part, and material. Since the Bill of Material (BOM) contains all the information, it serves as a primary source of communication between the manufacturer and the vendors as well as the suppliers.

To create the Bill of Material (BOM), click on the down arrow below the **Tables** tool in the **Annotation CommandManager**. A flyout appears, see Figure 14.89. In this flyout, click on the **Bill of Materials** tool. The **Bill of Materials PropertyManager** appears. Next, click on a drawing view of the assembly whose Bill of Material has to be created. The **Bill of Materials PropertyManager** gets modified and appears, as shown in Figure 14.90. The options of this PropertyManager are used to set the parameters for creating the Bill of Material. Some of the options of this PropertyManager are discussed next.

Tip: If a drawing view of an assembly is selected before invoking the **Bill of Materials** tool, then the modified **Bill of Material PropertyManager** appears directly as shown in Figure 14.90.

Table Template

The **Table Template** rollout is used for specifying a template for the Bill of Material (BOM). By default, **bom-standard** template is selected in this rollout. You can select the template other than the default one by clicking on the **Open table template for Bill of Materials** button of this rollout. As soon as you click on this button, the **Open** dialog box appears such that all the template files are displayed in it. You can select a required template in this dialog box and then click on the **Open** button.

Table Position

The **Table Position** rollout is used for specifying the position for the BOM table in the drawing sheet. By default, the **Attach to anchor point** check box is cleared in this rollout. As a result, on clicking the green tick-mark in the PropertyManager, the BOM gets attached to the cursor and you need to define its position in the drawing sheet by specifying the placement point. However, on selecting the **Attach to anchor point** check box, the BOM is placed directly in the drawing sheet such that the top left corner of the BOM is attached to the anchor point of the drawing sheet.

Note: You can define the position of the anchor point in the drawing sheet, as required. For doing so, select the **Sheet** node in the FeatureManager Design Tree and then right-click to display a shortcut menu. Next, click on the **Edit Sheet Format** option in the shortcut menu. The editing mode for defining the anchor point location is invoked, see Figure 14.91. Now, click on an existing vertex or a point of the drawing sheet, see Figure 14.91 and then right-click to display a shortcut menu. In this shortcut menu, select **Set as Anchor > Bill of Materials**, see Figure 14.92. The selected vertex/point is defined as the anchor point for the BOM. In addition to selecting an existing vertex or a point, you can create a new sketch point by using the **Point** tool of the **Sketch CommandManager** and then define it as the anchor point. After defining the anchor point, click on the Confirmation corner available at the upper right corner of the drawing sheet.

Item Numbers

The **Start at** field of the **Item Numbers** rollout in the PropertyManager is used for specifying the start number for the count of components, see Figure 14.93. By default, 1 is entered in this field. As a result, the counting of components starts from number 1 in the BOM. In the **Increment** field, you can specify the incremental value for the count of components. Note that on selecting the **Do not change item numbers** button of this rollout, the assigned components count/numbers are locked.

Border

The options of the **Border** rollout of the PropertyManager are used for defining the thickness of the Bill of Material (BOM) border, see Figure 14.94.

Accept the default parameters specified in the PropertyManager and then click on the green tick-mark ✔ in the PropertyManager. The Bill of Material (BOM) gets attached to the cursor. Next, click on the drawing sheet to specify the position of the Bill of Material (BOM). The Bill of Material (BOM) is placed at the specified position in the drawing sheet, see Figure 14.95.

14.95

ITEM NO.	PART NUMBER	DESCRIPTION	QTY.
1	Clamp Base		2
2	Clamp Spacer		1
3	Clamp foot		2
4	Clamp Left Elbow		1
5	Clamp Right Elbow		1
6	Clamp Tee		1
7	Clamp Rod		1
8	Clamp Hinge		1
9	Clamp Support		1
10	Clamp Lever		1
11	Clamp Screw		6
12	Clamp Waser		4

Adding Balloons

A Balloon is attached to a component with a leader line and displays the respective part number assigned in the Bill of Material (BOM), see Figure 14.96. In drawings, balloons are generally added to the individual components of an assembly in order to identify them easily with respect to the part number assigned in the Bill of Materials (BOM).

14.96

ITEM NO.	PART NUMBER	DESCRIPTION	QTY.
1	Clamp Base		2
2	Clamp Spacer		1
3	Clamp foot		2
4	Clamp Left Elbow		1
5	Clamp Right Elbow		1
6	Clamp Tee		1
7	Clamp Rod		1
8	Clamp Hinge		1
9	Clamp Support		1
10	Clamp Lever		1
11	Clamp Screw		6
12	Clamp Waser		4

In SOLIDWORKS, you can add balloons to the components of an assembly by using two methods: Automatic and Manual. In the Automatic method, balloons are added automatically to all the components of an assembly with respect to the part number assigned in the BOM whereas, in the Manual method, you need to add balloons manually to the components of an assembly one by one. Both these methods of adding balloons are discussed next.

Adding Balloons Automatically

To add balloons automatically to the components of an assembly, click on the **Auto Balloon** tool in the **Annotation CommandManager**. The **Auto Balloon PropertyManager** appears, see Figure 14.97. The options of this PropertyManager are used for setting parameters for balloons. Some of these options are discussed next.

Balloon Layout

The **Balloon Layout** rollout is used for defining the type of layout for balloons. The options of this rollout are discussed next.

Pattern type

The buttons in the **Pattern type** area of the **Balloon Layout** rollout are used for selecting the required type of layouts (Square, Circular, Top, Bottom, Left, or Right) for arranging balloons in the sheet.

Ignore multiple instances

By default, the **Ignore multiple instances** check box is selected in the **Balloon Layout** rollout. As a result, the duplicates are avoided by not adding balloons to all the instances of a component.

Insert magnetic line(s)

By default, the **Insert magnetic line(s)** check box is selected in the rollout. As a result, magnetic lines are inserted along with balloons such that balloons are aligned with each other. Note that this check box is not enabled if the **Layout Balloons to Circular** button is selected in the **Pattern type** area of the rollout.

Leader attachment

By default, the **Edges** radio button is selected in the **Leader attachment** area of the rollout. As a result, the leader lines of balloons are attached to the edges of components. On selecting the **Faces** radio button, balloons are attached to the faces of components through leader lines.

Balloon Settings

The **Balloon Settings** rollout is used for defining the settings for balloons such as balloon style, balloon size, and balloon text. The options of this rollout are discussed next.

Style

The **Style** drop-down list in the **Balloon Settings** rollout is used for selecting the required type of style for the border of balloons. By default, the **Circular** option is selected in this drop-down list. As a result, balloons appear with circular borders, refer to Figure 14.96. You can select a style such as triangle, hexagon, and diamond in this drop-down list. Note that on selecting the **None** option, balloons appear without borders, see Figure 14.98. If you select the **Circular Split Line** option, the border of balloons appears such that the circles are split into two areas, see Figure 14.99. By default, its upper area displays part number information and the lower area displays information about the quantity of component.

Size

The **Size** drop-down of the **Balloon Settings** rollout is used for selecting a pre-defined size for balloons. In addition to selecting a pre-defined size, you can also select the **User Defined** option in this drop-down list and specify the value for the required size of balloons in the **User defined** field of the rollout.

Balloon text

The **Balloon text** drop-down list is used for selecting a required text to be displayed in the balloons. By default, the **Item Number** option is selected. As a result, balloons appear with part numbers.

Lower text

The **Lower text** drop-down list is used for selecting a required text to be displayed in the lower area of the balloons. Note that this drop-down list is available only if the **Circular Split Line** option is selected in the **Style** drop-down list. By default, the **Quantity** option is selected in the **Lower text** drop-down list. As a result, the lower area of balloons displays the quantity information, refer to Figure 14.99.

After specifying the required parameters for balloons, click on the green tick-mark ☑ in the PropertyManager. The balloons are attached to the components of the assembly in the drawing view.

Adding Balloons Manually

To add balloons manually to the components of an assembly, click on the **Balloon** tool in the **Annotation CommandManager**. The **Balloon PropertyManager** appears, see Figure 14.100. The options in this PropertyManager are the same as those discussed earlier. By using this PropertyManager, you can add balloons to the components of an assembly one by one by selecting them in the drawing view. As soon as you click on a component in the drawing view, the leader line of the balloon gets attached to the component. Next, move the cursor to the required location and then click to specify the location for the balloon in the drawing sheet. Similarly, you can add balloons to all the components of the assembly one by one. Once you have added balloons to all the components, click on the green tick-mark ☑ in the PropertyManager.

Detailing Mode

In SOLIDWORKS 2020, you can open large drawings or drawings containing a large number of sheets or configurations, quickly using the detailing mode. This is useful in case you need to do minor editing to a large drawing. When you open a drawing in detailing mode, the model data is not loaded. Hence, only a limited number of features can be accessed. The following actions are permissible in detailing mode:

- Adding annotations such as notes, symbols, balloons, magnetic lines, and surface finish symbols.
- Print and Save As.
- Creating sketch entities.
- Adding and editing dimensions which do not require model information such as linear dimensions, radial dimensions, and diameter dimensions.

However, the features such as creating new drawing views, centerlines, center marks, hatching, adding and editing dimensions or annotations which require model information such as hole callouts, cosmetic threads, and so on are not available when you open a drawing in detailing mode.

To open a drawing in detailing mode, click on the **Open** tool available in the **Standard** toolbar as well as in the **File** menu of the SOLIDWORKS Menus. The **Open** dialog box appears. In this dialog box, select **SOLIDWORKS Drawing (*.drw;*.slddrw)** file extension in the **File Type** drop-down list. Browse to the location where the SOLIDWORKS document is saved and then click on the document to be opened. Select the **Detailing** option in the **Mode** area of the dialog box and click on the **Open** button. The **Detailing** window appears informing you about the permissible actions in the detailing mode. Next, click on the **OK** button. The selected document gets opened in detailing mode. Now, you can make the required changes and then save the file.

Note that the detailing mode symbol ▓ appears with the file name in the FeatureManager Design Tree when the drawing is opened in detailing mode. Also, **[Detailing]** appears along with the file name in the top bar. To shift from detailing mode to resolved mode, click on the **Resolve Drawing** tool available on the top left corner in the CommandManager.

Tutorial 1

Open the model created in Tutorial 2 of Chapter 7 and then create different drawing views: front, top, side, isometric, section, and detail, as shown in Figure 14.101 in the **A3 (ANSI) Landscape** sheet size. You also need to apply driving dimensions to the front, top, and right side drawing views of the model.

Section 1: Starting SOLIDWORKS

1.   Double-click on the **SOLIDWORKS** icon on your desktop to start SOLIDWORKS.

Section 2: Opening and Saving Model Created in Tutorial 2 of Chapter 7

1.   Open the model created in Tutorial 2 of Chapter 7 by using the **Open** button of the **Standard** toolbar, see Figure 14.102.

14.102

2. Click on **File > Save As** in the SOLIDWORKS Menus and then save the model with the name Tutorial 1 inside the Tutorial folder of the Chapter 14 folder. Note that you need to create these folders inside the SOLIDWORKS folder.

Section 3: Invoking Drawing Environment

1. Click on the arrow next to the **New** tool in the **Standard** toolbar. A flyout appears, see Figure 14.103.

14.103

2. Click on the **Make Drawing from Part/Assembly** tool in the flyout. The **Sheet Format/Size** dialog box appears, see Figure 14.104.

14.104

3. Make sure that the **Standard sheet size** radio button is selected in this dialog box, see Figure 14.104.

4. Select the **A3 (ANSI) Landscape** sheet size in the **Selection** area of the dialog box. If the **A3 (ANSI) Landscape** sheet size is not available in the **Selection** area of the dialog box, then you need to clear the **Only show standard formats** check box of the dialog box.

5. Make sure that the **Display sheet format** check box is selected in the dialog box.

6. Click on the **OK** button in the dialog box. The Drawing environment is invoked with the display of the **View Palette Task Pane** on the right of the drawing sheet, see Figure 14.105.

Section 4: Creating Front, Top, and Right Views

1. Drag and drop the front view of the model on the lower left corner of the drawing sheet from the **View Palette Task Pane** by pressing and holding the left mouse button, see Figure 14.106.

2. Move the cursor vertically upward. The projected view (top view) is attached to the cursor.

3. Click on the drawing sheet to specify the position for the top view, see Figure 14.107.

4. Move the cursor horizontally toward right. The projected view (right side view) of the model is attached to the cursor.

5. Click on the drawing sheet to specify the position for the right side view of the model, see Figure 14.107. Next, click on the green tick-mark ✔ in the PropertyManager or press ESC. The front, top, and right side views of the model are created.

14.107

Section 5: Creating the Vertical Section View

1. Click on the **Section View** tool in the **Drawing CommandManager**. The **Section View Assist PropertyManager** appears, see Figure 14.108.

2. Click on the **Vertical** button in the **Cutting Line** rollout of the PropertyManager to activate it. Note that on activating the **Vertical** button, the vertical section line appears attached to the cursor.

3. Move the cursor over the right side view of the model in the drawing sheet.

4. Click to specify the placement point for the vertical section line when the cursor snaps to the center point of the right side view of the model, see Figure 14.109. A preview of the section view appears

14.108

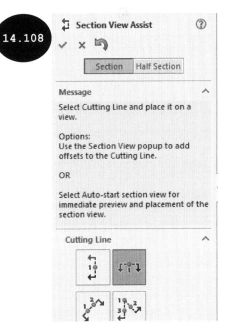

attached to the cursor. If the **Section View** toolbar appears, click on the green tick-mark ☑ in the **Section View** toolbar.

Tip: The **Section View** toolbar appears, if the **Auto-start section view** check box is cleared in the PropertyManager. By using the tools of the **Section View** toolbar, you can modify or edit the section line, as required.

14.109

5.   Move the cursor horizontally toward right and then click on the drawing sheet to specify the placement point for the section view, see Figure 14.110.

14.110

Section 6: Creating the Detail View

1.   Click on the **Detail View** tool in the **Drawing CommandManager**. The **Detail View** PropertyManager appears. Also, you are prompted to specify the center point of the circle.

2. Move the cursor over the right vertical edge of the model in the front view, see Figure 14.111 and then click to specify the center point of the circle.

3. Move the cursor to a distance and then click to define the radius of the circle, see Figure 14.112. The preview of the detail view gets attached to the cursor.

4. Select the **Jagged outline** check box in the **Detail View** rollout of the PropertyManager.

5. Click on the drawing sheet to define the placement point for the detail view, see Figure 14.113. The detail view is placed in the drawing sheet on the defined position.

Section 7: Creating the Isometric View

1. Click on the **Model View** tool in the **Drawing CommandManager**. The **Model View PropertyManager** appears.

2. Double-click on the **Tutorial 1** model in the **Open documents** area of the **Part/Assembly to Insert** rollout in the PropertyManager. A rectangular box representing the model view gets attached to the cursor. Also, the options of the PropertyManager get modified.

3. Click on the **Isometric** button in the **Standard views** area of the **Orientation** rollout to create an isometric view of the model.

4. Move the cursor toward the upper right corner of the drawing sheet and then click to specify the placement point for the isometric view, see Figure 14.114. Next, click anywhere in the drawing sheet.

Section 8: Changing the Display Styles

1. Click on the front view of the model in the drawing sheet. The **Drawing View PropertyManager** appears.

2. Click on the **Hidden Lines Visible** button in the **Display Style** rollout of the PropertyManager to display the hidden lines of the model in the drawing views, see Figure 14.114.

14.114

DETAIL B
SCALE 1 : 1

SECTION A-A

Tutorial 1

Section 9: Applying Driving Dimensions

1. Click on the **Annotation** tab in the CommandManager. The tools of the **Annotation CommandManager** are displayed.

2. Click on the **Model Items** tool in the **Annotation CommandManager**. The **Model Items** PropertyManager appears.

3. Make sure that the **Entire model** option is selected in the **Source** drop-down list of the **Source/Destination** rollout, see Figure 14.115.

14.115

4. Clear the **Import items into all views** check box in the **Source/Destination** rollout. The **Destination view(s)** field appears in the rollout.

5. Click on the front, top, and right side views of the model one by one in the drawing sheet as the views to import driving dimensions.

6. Click on the green tick-mark ☑ in the PropertyManager. The driving dimensions are applied to the selected drawing views, refer to Figure 14.116. Note that the applied dimensions are not placed in the proper locations nor do they maintain uniform spacing. You will learn about arranging driving dimensions in the next section of this tutorial.

Section 10: Arranging Driving Dimensions

1. Select all driving dimensions by dragging the cursor over the front, top, and right side views after pressing and holding the left mouse button, see Figure 14.116. Next, release the left mouse button, the **Dimension Palette Rollover** button ☒ appears in the drawing sheet.

14.116

2. Move the cursor over the **Dimension Palette Rollover** button ☒ in the drawing sheet. The **Dimension Palette** appears, see Figure 14.117.

14.117

3. Click on the **Auto Arrange Dimensions** button in the **Dimension Palette**, see Figure 14.117. All the dimensions are arranged automatically in the drawing sheet, refer to Figure 14.118. You can further drag individual dimensions and place them on the required location, see Figure 14.118. Next, click anywhere in the drawing sheet.

14.118

Note: You can also control dimension parameters such as dimension font, dimension height, and arrow height. For doing so, click on the **Options** tool in the **Standard** toolbar. The **System Options - General** dialog box appears. Next, click on the **Document Properties** tab in the dialog box and then click on the **Dimensions** option. Next, click on the **Font** button in the **Text** area of the dialog box. The **Choose Font** dialog box appears. By using this dialog box, you can specify the required font, style, and height for dimensions text. Next, click on the **OK** button in the **Choose Font** dialog box. You can also control the dimension arrow height by using the options in the **Arrows** area of the **Document Properties - Dimensions** dialog box.

Section 11: Saving the Model

1. Click on the **Save** tool in the **Standard** toolbar. The **Save As** dialog box appears.

2. Browse to the Tutorial folder of Chapter 14 folder and then save the drawing with the name Tutorial 1.

Hands-on Test Drive 1

Open the assembly created in Hands-on Test Drive 1 of Chapter 12 and then create different drawing views as shown in Figure 14.119. Also, you need to add balloons in the isometric view of the assembly and create the Bill of Material (BOM). In addition to creating different views and BOM, you need to create an alternate position view of the assembly in the front view, see Figure 14.119.

Summary

In this chapter, you have learned about creating 2D drawings from parts and assemblies. The 2D drawings are extremely important in order to manufacture components. In SOLIDWORKS, you can create 2D drawings in the Drawing environment. You can create various drawing views such as model/base views, projected views, section views, auxiliary views, and detail views of a component or an assembly by using the respective tools. The concept of angle of projections, defining the angle of projection for a drawing, and editing the sheet format has been discussed. After creating the required drawing views of a component or an assembly, you can apply reference and driving dimensions. The chapter also explains how to add notes, surface finish symbol, weld symbol, and hole callout in a drawing sheet. Also, you can add center mark, centerlines in drawing views, Bill of Material (BOM), balloons to the components of an assembly, and open a drawing in detailing mode.

Questions

• By using the _____ environment of SOLIDWORKS, you can generate error-free 2D drawings of a component or an assembly.

• The _____ PropertyManager is invoked automatically on invoking the Drawing environment.

• A _____ view is an independent first drawing view.

• The **Standard 3 View** tool is used for creating three standard orthogonal views: _____, _____, and _____.

• Engineering drawings follow the _____ and the _____ angles of projections.

• A _____ view is created by cutting an object with an imaginary cutting plane and viewing the object from a direction normal to the cutting plane.

• A _____ view is created in order to show the portion of an existing view at an enlarged scale.

• A _____ view is created by removing the portion of an existing view up to a specified depth in order to view its inner details.

• In SOLIDWORKS, you can apply the _____ and _____ dimensions in a view.

• A surface finish symbol has three components: _____, _____, and _____.

• On modifying reference dimensions in a drawing view, respective modifications are also reflected in a model. (True/False)

• In SOLIDWORKS, you can select standard or custom sheet size for creating drawing views. (True/False)

INDEX

Symbols
3 Point Arc Slot Tool 78
3 Point Arc Tool 72
3 Point Center Rectangle Tool 67
3 Point Corner Rectangle Tool 66
3D Sketch Tool 390

A
Activate Flexible Component
      PropertyManager 669
Add Configuration PropertyManager 560
Add Construction Lines Check box 65
Add Horizontal Break Line Button 751
Add or Update a Style Dialog box 757
Add Relation Tool 160
Add Relations PropertyManager 160
Add Vertical Break Line Button 751
Advanced Hole PropertyManager 489
Advanced Hole Tool 489
Align Linked Mate Option 591
Align to Holes Radio button 679
Align to Seed Check box 675
Align to Seed Radio button 448
Align with End Faces Check box 352
Aligned Button 744
All Configuration Radio button 562
Allow Creation of Misaligned Mates
      Check box 591
Along Curve Distance or Multiple Reference
      Point Button 256
Along Sketch Normal Radio button 250

Alternate Position View Tool 752
Ambient Occlusion Tool 228
Angle Distance Chamfer 520
Angle Mate 592, 600
Angle of Projection 735
Angle-Distance Radio button 127
Animating an Exploded View 701
Animation Controller Toolbar 701
Annotation CommandManager 33
Appearances Tool 304
Appearances, Scenes, and Decals
      Task Pane 30, 302
Apply Y-up Views Option 225
Apply Z-up Views Option 225
Arc Center Button 254
Arrow Keys Field 226
Assembly CommandManager 31
Assembly Features 688
Assigning a Customized Appearance 304
Assigning a Predefined
      Appearance/Texture 302
Assigning an Appearance/Texture 302
At Angle Button 244
At Sketch Plane Radio button 527
At Wall Interface Radio button 527
Attach to Anchor Point Check box 776
Auto Balloon PropertyManager 779
Auto Balloon Tool 779
Auto Hatching Check box 742
Auto Insert Dimension Tool 174
Automatic Browse when Creating New
      Assembly Check box 584
Auto-space Components Check box 699
Auto-start Projected View Check box 728
Auto-start Section View Check box 741

Auxiliary Button 743
Auxiliary View Tool 746
Axis PropertyManager 250
Axis Tool 250

B

Balloon PropertyManager 781
Balloon Text Drop-down List 780
Balloon Tool 781
Baseline Dimension Tool 170
Begin Assembly PropertyManager 30, 580
Best Fit Radio button 257
Bill of Materials Options 561
Bill of Materials PropertyManager 707, 775
Bill of Materials Tool 707, 775
Boss-Extrude PropertyManager 207, 278
Bottom-up Assembly Approach 580
Boundary Boss/Base Tool 371
Boundary Cut Tool 375
Boundary PropertyManager 372
Bounding Box PropertyManager 257
Bounding Box Tool 257
Break View PropertyManager 751
Break View Tool 751
Broken-out Section PropertyManager 750
Broken-out Section Tool 750

C

Callout Value Drop-down List 487
Cam Mate 601
Cam Path Field 601
Cap Ends Check box 114, 214
Cartoon Tool 228
Center Mark PropertyManager 773
Center Mark Tool 773
Center of Face Button 254
Center of Rotation Field 131
Center Point Field 122
Center Rectangle Tool 66
Centerline PropertyManager 775
Centerline Tool 62, 775
Centerpoint Arc Slot Tool 79
Centerpoint Arc Tool 71
Centerpoint Straight Slot Tool 78
Chain Component Pattern tool 681
Chain Dimension Tool 171
Chain Pattern PropertyManager 681

Chamfer PropertyManager 519
Chamfer Tool 519
Change Transparency Option 493
Choose Font Dialog box 768
Circle Tool 69
Circular Component Pattern Tool 676
Circular Option 507
Circular Pattern PropertyManager 121
Circular Pattern Tool 442
Circular Profile Radio button 344
Circular Sketch Pattern 121
Circular Split Line Option 780
Circumscribed Circle Radio button 75
CirPattern PropertyManager 442
Clear All Missing References Option 511
Close Loft Check box 369
Closed Sketches 285
Closed Spline Check box 89
Coincident Mate 588
Coincident Relation 158
Collapsing an Exploded View 701
Collinear Relation 158
Collision Detection Radio button 611
Color PropertyManager 304
CommandManager 24
Composite Curve PropertyManager 385
Composite Curve Tool 385
Concentric Mate 590
Concentric Relation 159
Configuration Drop-down List 689
ConfigurationManager Tab 560
Conic Radius Option 507
Conic Rho Option 507
Conic Tool 83
Connected Linkage Chain Pattern 685
Constant Pitch Radio button 381
Constant Size Fillet Button 504
Construction Geometry Tool 70
Contour Select Tool 287
Convert Chamfer to Fillet Option 523
Convert Entities PropertyManager 292
Convert Entities Tool 292
Coordinate system Field 451
Coordinate System PropertyManager 253
Coordinate System Tool 252
Coordinate Table 452
Copy Entities Tool 130

Copy PropertyManager 130
Coradial Relation 159
Corner Rectangle Tool 64
Cosmetic Thread Button 487
Cosmetic Thread Display 730
Cosmetic Thread PropertyManager 495
Create Multiple Views Check box 728
Create Opposite Hand Version Button 687
Create Pattern Table Button 458
Create Plane Parallel to Screen Option 249
Create Seed Cut Radio button 455
Crop View Tool 752
Curvature Combs Check box 356
Curvature To Face Option 364
Curve Driven Pattern PropertyManager 445
Curve Driven Pattern Tool 445
Curve File Dialog box 383
Curve Through Reference Points
          PropertyManager 384
Curve Through Reference Points Tool 384
Curve Through XYZ Points Tool 383
Custom Sheet Size Radio button 725
Custom Text Position 767
Customize Callout Radio button 493
Customize Dialog box 35
Customizing the CommandManager 36
Customizing the Context Toolbar 34
Cut Thread Radio button 500
Cut-Extrude PropertyManager 282
Cut-Revolve PropertyManager 284
Cut-Sweep PropertyManager 358
Cylindrical/Conical Face Button 252

D

Deboss Button 531
Degrees of Freedom 586
Depth up to Shoulder Button 484
Depth up to Tip Button 484
Design Library Task Pane 30
Design Table PropertyManager 564
Destination Subassemblies Field 693
Detail View PropertyManager 747
Detail View Tool 746
Detailing Mode 781
Detecting Interference in an Assembly 705
Display Grid Check box 47
Display Sheet Format Check box 725

Display/Delete Relations Tool 160
Dissolve Subassembly Option 691
Distance Chain Pattern 682
Distance Distance Chamfer 520
Distance Linkage Chain Pattern 683
Distance Mate 591, 599
Distance/Revolution Radio button 607
Distance-distance Radio button 127
Draft Angle Field 363
Draft On/Off Button 527
Drag Sketch Button 368
Driving Dimensions 754
DXF/DWG Import Dialog box 297
Dynamic Mirror Tool 117

E

Edit Appearance Tool 304
Edit Component Tool 663
Edit Feature Tool 295
Edit Material Option 307
Edit Part Tool 670
Edit Sheet Format Option 738, 776
Edit Sketch PropertyManager 42
Edit Sketch Tool 296
Edit Table Option 568
Ellipse Tool 80
Emboss Button 531
Emphasize Outline Check box 741
Emphasized Section Outline Option 743
End Location Field 500
End Tangency Type drop-down List 355
Entities to Convert Field 293
Entities to Mate Field 586
Entities to Mirror Field 116
Entities to Pattern Field 120
Envelope Publisher Tool 691
Equal Curve Length Relation 159
Equal Relation 159
Equation Driven Curve Tool 85
Evaluate CommandManager 25
Exit Sketch Tool 208
Explode Line Sketch Tool 703
Explode Option 701
Explode PropertyManager 694
Exploded View PropertyManager 702
Exploded View Tool 694
Extend Entities Tool 111

Extending Sketch Entities 111
Extrude Thread Radio button 500
Extruded Boss/Base Tool 207, 278
Extruded Cut Tool 282
Extruded Surface Tool 388
Extrusion Direction 526

F

Face Face Chamfer 524
Face Fillet Button 515
Face for Wrap Sketch Field 532
Faces to Remove Field 528
Faces to Split Field 387
Far Side Check box 491
Far Side Countersink Check box 485
FeatureManager Design Tree 28
Features CommandManager 24
Fill Boundary Field 454
Fill Pattern PropertyManager 454
Fill Pattern Tool 454
Fillet PropertyManager 503
Fillet Tool 503
Fit Spline PropertyManager 89
Fit Spline Tool 89
Fix Relation 159
Flexible Components 669
Flip Mate Alignment Tool 588
Flip Material Side Check box 527
Flip Side to Cut Check box 282
Float Option 667
Free Drag Option 609
Full Outline Check box 747
Full Round Fillet Button 517
Fully Defined Sketch 175

G

Gear Mate 605
Geometry Pattern Check box 439, 461
Global Option 367
Go To System Snaps Button 47
Guide Curves Field 353, 366

H

Half Section View 745
Head Clearance Check box 485
Height and Pitch Option 381
Height and Revolution Option 380

Helix and Spiral Tool 379
Helix/Spiral PropertyManager 379
Hidden Lines Removed Tool 227
Hidden Lines Visible Tool 227
High quality Radio button 730
Hinge Mate 604
Hole Callout Tool 772
Hole Position PropertyManager 488
Hole Specifications Rollout 483
Hole Wizard Tool 481
Horizontal Dimension Tool 170
Horizontal Relation 158

I

Identifying SOLIDWORKS Documents 34
Ignore Multiple Instances Check box 779
Inscribed Circle Radio button 75
Insert Component PropertyManager 584
Insert Components Tool 584, 689
Insert Style Spline PropertyManager 88
Insert/Edit Smart Explode Lines Tool 704
Installing SOLIDWORKS 20
Instance Spacing Radio Button 444
Instances to Skip 120
Instant2D Tool 174
Interference Detection PropertyManager 705
Interference Detection Tool 705
Intersecting Sketches 287
Intersection Button 255
Intersection Curve Tool 295
Intersection Radio button 388

J

Jagged Outline Check box 747

K

Keep Constrained Corners check box 125
Keep Features Check box 510
Keep Normal Constant Option 346
Keep Trimmed Entities as Construction
    Geometry 111

L

Lasso Selection Option 438
Leave this Dimension Driving Radio button 176
Limit Angle Button 600

Limit Distance Button 599
Line Tool 48, 55
Linear Component Pattern Tool 674
Linear Pattern Tool 432
Linear Sketch Pattern Tool 117
Linear/Linear Coupler Mate 598
Locate Profile Button 501
Lock Mate 593
Loft PropertyManager 361
Lofted Boss/Base Tool 360
Lofted Cut Tool 371

M

Maintain Thread Length Check box 500
Major Diameter Field 496
Major Grid Spacing Field 47
Make Drawing from Part/Assembly Tool 731
Make Edit Sketch Option 297
Make Part Flexible Tool 669
Make Part Rigid Tool 669
Make this Dimension Driven Radio button 176
Mass Properties Dialog box 310
Mass Properties Tool 310
Mate PropertyManager 586
Mate Tool 586
Material Dialog box 307
Measure Tool 298
Measure Units/Precision Dialog box 301
Measuring the Distance between Entities 298
Merge Relation 159
Merge Smooth Faces Check box 353
Merge Tangent Faces Check box 352, 368
Mesh Preview Check box 356
Midpoint Line Tool 63
Midpoint Relation 159
Minimum Twist Option 349
Minor Diameter Field 496
Minor-lines per Major Field 47
Mirror Components PropertyManager 686
Mirror Components Tool 686
Mirror Entities Tool 115
Mirror PropertyManager 115, 460
Mirror Tool 460
Misaligned Button 590
Misalignment Drop-down List 590
Model Items PropertyManager 754
Model Items Tool 753

Model View PropertyManager 727, 732
Model View Tool 732
Modified Instances Field 676
Modify Dialog box 163, 756
Move Component PropertyManager 609
Move Component Tool 609
Move Entities Tool 129
Move PropertyManager 129
Multi Distance Chamfer Check box 522
Multiple Radius Fillet Check box 506
Multiple Start Check box 502
Multi-thickness Faces Field 529

N

Named View Dialog box 224
Near Side Countersink Check box 485
Near Side Faces Field 490
Nested Sketches 285
New Part Tool 663
New Polygon Button 75
New Tool 22
New View Tool 224
No Outline Check box 747
Normal To Profile Option 364
Normal To Tool 223
Note PropertyManager 769
Note Tool 769
Number of Instances Field 118, 435

O

Offset Curve Radio button 447
Offset Distance 113
Offset Entities PropertyManager 112
Offset Entities Tool 112
Offset Face Chamfer 521
Offset From Surface Option 280
On Point Button 255
Open Part Tool 671
Open Sketches 285
Open Tool 38
Optional Start Location Field 499
Options Tool 45, 47
Ordinate Dimension Tool 171
Orientation Dialog box 224
Over Defined Sketch 175
Override Diameter Button 500
Override Mass Properties Dialog box 312

Override Pitch Button 500
Override Value Check box 760

P

Pan Tool 221
Parabola Tool 82
Parallel Button 243
Parallel Mate 589
Parallel Relation 158
Parallelogram Tool 68
Parametric Radio Button 86
Partial Edge Parameters Rollout 509
Partial Ellipse Tool 81
Path Length Dimension Tool 173
Path Length PropertyManager 173
Path Mate 597
Pattern Direction Field 434, 446
Pattern Driven Component Pattern Tool 678
Pattern Driven PropertyManager 678
Pattern Seed Only Check box 437
Pattern Table Dialog box 458
Perimeter Circle Tool 70
Perpendicular Button 243
Perpendicular Mate 589
Perpendicular Relation 158
Perspective Tool 228
Physical Dynamics Radio button 612
Pierce Relation 159
Pin/Unpin the Dialog Tool 224
Pitch and Revolution Option 380
Pitch/Yaw Control Drop-down List 598
Plane PropertyManager 242
Plane Tool 242
Point and Face/Plane Button 252
Point PropertyManager 91, 254
Point Tool 254
Polygon Tool 74
Power Trim 108
Previous View Tool 224
Profile Center Mate 593
Profile Drop-down List 507
Profile Orientation Drop-down List 345
Profile Twist Drop-down List 346
Project Button 244
Project Curve Tool 376
Projected Curve PropertyManager 376
Projected View PropertyManager 734

Projected View Tool 734
Projection Radio button 386
Propagate Visual Properties
        Check box 440, 461

R

Rack Pinion Mate 606
Radial Step Button 695
Rectangle PropertyManager 64
Reference Geometry Field 436
Reference Sketch Field 450
Reference Vertex Field 450
Regular Step Button 695
Remove Thread Button 487
Removed Section View 748
Repair All Missing References Option 511
Reset Standard Views Tool 224
Resolve Drawing Tool 782
Reverse Callout Order Check box 773
Reverse Stack Direction Button 491
Revolutions/Distance Field 607
Revolve PropertyManager 216, 281
Revolved Boss/Base Tool 215, 281
Revolved Cut Tool 283
Rho Value 84
Rib PropertyManager 525
Rib Thickness Field 526
Rib Tool 525
Rotate Component PropertyManager 612
Rotate Component Tool 612
Rotate Context Toolbar 582
Rotate PropertyManager 131
Rotate Tool 221
Rotating an Entity 131
Route Line PropertyManager 703

S

Save Configurations as a New Part
        Window 569
Save Configurations Option 569
Save Externally (Specify Paths)
        Radio button 668
Save Internally (Inside the Assembly)
        Radio button 668
Save Tool 38
Scale Entities Tool 132
Scale Hatch Pattern Check box 741

Scale PropertyManager 132
Scaling Sketch Entities 132
Screw Mate 606
Scribe Button 531
Section View Assist PropertyManager 740
Section View Dialog box 742
Section View Tool 739
Select All Inner Loops Button 293
Select Through Faces Check box 510
Set Spacing Button 437
Set Unassigned Button 514
Setback Distances Field 508
Setback Vertices Field 508
Shaded Cosmetic Threads Check box 498
Shaded Sketch Contours Tool 292
Shaded Tool 226
Shaded With Edges Tool 226
Shadows In Shaded Mode Tool 228
Sheet Format/Size Dialog box 31, 724, 731
Sheet Metal CommandManager 27
Sheet Properties Dialog box 737
Shell PropertyManager 528
Shell Tool 528
Show Custom Sizing Check box 483
Show Tool 288
Show Type Check box 497
Silhouette Entities PropertyManager 294
Silhouette Entities Tool 294
Silhouette Radio Button 389
Sketch Chamfer PropertyManager 126
Sketch Chamfer Tool 126
Sketch CommandManager 25
Sketch Driven Pattern PropertyManager 449
Sketch Driven Pattern Tool 449
Sketch Fillet Tool 125
Sketch on Faces Radio button 377
Sketch on Sketch Radio button 378
Sketch Text PropertyManager 128
Sketch to Project Field 377
Sketch Tool 42
Sketches to Project Field 378
Slot Mate 603
Slot PropertyManager 76
Smart Dimension Tool 163
Smart Explode Lines PropertyManager 704
SmartMates Button 613
SmartMates PropertyManager 613

Smooth Transition Radio button 514
Snap Points Per Minor Field 47
SOLIDWORKS Menus 24
SOLIDWORKS Resources Task Pane 29
SOLIDWORKS Search 24
Spacing and Instances Radio button 435
Spacing Field 118, 435
Specify Direction Vector Option 349
Specify Twist Value Option 347
Spiral Option 381
Spline Tool 84
Split Line PropertyManager 386
Split Line Tool 386
Splitting Faces of a Model 386
Standard 3 View PropertyManager 735
Standard 3 View Tool 735
Standard Sheet Size Radio button 725
Standard Toolbar 23
Start Tangency Type Drop-down List 354
Start Tangent Length Field 364
Status Bar 29
Stop at Collision Check box 611
Straight Slot Tool 76
Straight Transition Radio button 514
Stretch Entities Tool 134
Stretch PropertyManager 134
Stretching an Entity 134
Style Drop-down List 764
Style Spline Tool 88
Suppress tool 570, 689
Surface Finish PropertyManager 770
Surface Finish tool 770
Surface/Face/Plane Option 278
Surfaces CommandManager 26
Sweep PropertyManager 342
Swept Boss/Base Tool 342
Swept Cut Tool 358
Symmetric Mate 595
Symmetric Relation 159
Synchronize Movement of Flexible
        Subassembly Components
        Check box 687
System Options Dialog box 45

T
Table Driven Pattern Dialog box 451
Table Driven Pattern Tool 451

Tangency to Face Option 364
Tangent Arc Tool 72
Tangent Mate 591
Tangent Propagation Check box 504
Tangent Relation 158
Tangent to Curve Radio button 448
Tap Drill Diameter Button 486
Task Pane 29
Text Tool 128
Thought Points Field 384
Thread Callout Field 497
Thread Class Check box 487, 497
Thread Location Rollout 499
Thread PropertyManager 498
Thread Tool 498
To Next Edge Option 367
To Next Guide Option 367
To Next Sharp Option 367
Tolerance Precision Drop-down List 759
Tolerance Type Drop-down List 488, 758
Tool Body Field 359
Top-down Assembly Approach 580, 662
Transform Curve Radio button 447
Trim Away Inside 110
Trim Away Outside 110
Trim by Direction 1 Check box 374
Trim Entities Tool 108
Trim PropertyManager 108
Trim to Closest 110
Trim with End Face Check box 501
Trimming Sketch Entities 108
Twist Control Drop-down List 347
Two Planes Button 251
Two Points/Vertices Button 251

U
Under Defined Sketch 175
Under Head Countersink Check box 486
Universal Joint 608
Unsuppress Tool 570, 689
Up Axis Flyout 225
Up To Body Option 280
Up to Reference Radio button 435
Up To Surface Option 280
Up To Vertex Option 279

Update Standard Views Tool 224
Use Configuration Specific Color
        Check box 562
Use Document Bend Length Check box 766
Use Document Second Arrow Check box 766
User Defined Option 738
User Defined Scale Dialog box 738

V
Variable Pattern PropertyManager 457
Variable Pattern Tool 456
Variable Pitch Radio button 381
Variable Radius Parameters Rollout 513
Variable Size Fillet Button 512
Vary Sketch Check box 438
Vertex Chamfer 521
Vertex Option 279
Vertex or Sketch Point Field 455
Vertical Relation 158
View (Heads-Up) Toolbar 29
View Orientation Tool 222
View Origins Tool 43
View Selector Cube 225
View Selector Tool 223
View Sketch Relations Tool 162, 185

W
Welcome Dialog box 21
Welcome to SOLIDWORKS Tool 30
Weld Symbol PropertyManager 771
Weld Symbol Tool 771
Weldments CommandManager 28
Width Mate 595
Wireframe Tool 227
Wrap PropertyManager 531
Wrap Tool 530

Z
Zebra stripes Check box 356
Zoom In/Out Tool 220
Zoom to Area Tool 221
Zoom To Fit Tool 221
Zoom to Selection Tool 221